Proceedings of the 29th Annual

IEEE/ACM International Symposium on Microarchitecture

MICRO-29

AF718831

Proceedings of the 29th Annual

IEEE/ACM International Symposium on Microarchitecture

MICRO-29

December 2 – 4, 1996 Paris, France

Sponsored by

IEEE Computer Society Technical Committee on Microprogramming and Microarchitecture

Association for Computing Machinery SIGMICRO

IEEE Computer Society Press
Los Alamitos, California

Washington • Brussels • Tokyo

IEEE Computer Society Press
10662 Los Vaqueros Circle
P.O.Box 3014
Los Alamitos, CA 90720-1314

Copyright © 1996 by The Institute of Electrical and Electronics Engineers, Inc.
All rights reserved.

Copyright and Reprint Permissions: Abstracting is permitted with credit to the source. Libraries may photocopy beyond the limits of US copyright law, for private use of patrons, those articles in this volume that carry a code at the bottom of the first page, provided that the per-copy fee indicated in the code is paid through the Copyright Clearance Center, 222 Rosewood Drive, Danvers, MA 01923.

Other copying, reprint, or republication requests should be addressed to: IEEE Copyrights Manager, IEEE Service Center, 445 Hoes Lane, P.O. Box 1331, Piscataway, NJ 08855-1331.

The papers in this book comprise the proceedings of the meeting mentioned on the cover and title page. They reflect the authors' opinions and, in the interests of timely dissemination, are published as presented and without change. Their inclusion in this publication does not necessarily constitute endorsement by the editors, the IEEE Computer Society Press, or the Institute of Electrical and Electronics Engineers, Inc.

IEEE Computer Society Press Order Number PR07641
IEEE Order Plan Catalog Number 96TB100075
ACM Order Number 520960
ISBN 0-8186-7641-8
Microfiche ISBN 0-8186-7643-4
ISSN 1072-4451

Additional copies may be ordered from:

IEEE Computer Society Press
Customer Service Center
10662 Los Vaqueros Circle
P.O. Box 3014
Los Alamitos, CA 90720-1314
Tel: +1-714-821-8380
Fax: +1-714-821-4641
Email: cs.books@computer.org

IEEE Service Center
445 Hoes Lane
P.O. Box 1331
Piscataway, NJ 08855-1331
Tel: +1-908-981-1393
Fax: +1-908-981-9667
misc.custserv@computer.org

IEEE Computer Society
13, Avenue de l'Aquilon
B-1200 Brussels
BELGIUM
Tel: +32-2-770-2198
Fax: +32-2-770-8505
euro.ofc@computr.org

IEEE Computer Society
Ooshima Building
2-19-1 Minami-Aoyama
Minato-ku, Tokyo 107
JAPAN
Tel: +81-3-3408-3118
Fax: +81-3-3408-3553
tokyo.ofc@computer.org

Additional copies may be ordered prepaid from:

ACM Order Department
P.O. Box 12114
Church Street Station
New York, NY 10257

Phone: 1-800-342-6626 (U.S. and Canada)
1-212-626-0500 (all other countries)
Fax: 1-212-944-1318
E-mail: ACMPUBS@ACM.ORG

Editorial production by Penny Storms
Cover graphic by Frederic Goutier / Janvier Designs
Cover layout by Joseph Daigle / Studio Productions
Printed in the United States of America by Sony Electronic Publishing

The Institute of Electrical and Electronics Engineers, Inc.

Table of Contents

Preface

Thanks for your interest in Micro-29! We hope that you find it enjoyable and informative. We have tried a number of things new this year. They include:

1) Blind reviewing. All authors were asked to submit their papers for review without any names on the title page. Papers were kept track of by number only. The only time the names and papers were matched up was after the reviewing cycle was completed and the reviewers were checked for any conflicts with the papers they reviewed.

2) Web-based paper distribution and review submission. All papers were submitted in PostScript form and distributed to the reviewers via the www.micro29.org web page. All reviews were submitted via a form on the same server. Both of these worked very well.

3) CD-ROM version of proceedings. This is the first time a Micro conference has had a CD-ROM version of the proceedings in conjunction with the printed version.

We commend all of these to those who follow.

This is also only the second time a Micro has been off the North American continent, adding credibility to the "International" part of our title.

As with any endeavor of this size, there are a lot of groups who have contributed a lot. We'd first like to thank all the authors who submitted papers for the review process: this is the very heart of any conference. We received 94 papers, a Micro record. Many were excellent papers, making it difficult on the reviewers.

Speaking of reviewers, we had 139 of them who submitted over 400 reviews. Each paper had at least 4 reviews. The reviewers provided 37 pages of comments to the chairs, and over 200 pages of comments to the authors. The chairs went over all the reviews very carefully in order to ensure a fair judgement of all papers. Statistical analyses were performed on the reviews, and any anomalies were addressed. Of the 94 papers submitted, 30 were accepted for publication.

We would like to thank the program committee for their help during this past year. They helped with finding qualified reviewers, promoting the conference, and creating the program as you see it here. The steering committee helped with direction and continuity for this, and all Micro conferences. That Micro has become a premiere venue for ILP research is due in a large part to them. Finally we'd like to thank the Ecole Nationale Supérieure des Télécommunications (ENST) for allowing us to hold the conference at their facility in Paris and the valuable assistance of Ulrich Finger and his staff, without whose help we could have not put this on.

Steve Beaty **Steve Melvin**
Co-Chairs, Micro-29

Program and Steering Committees

General Co-Chairs

Stephen Melvin
Zytek Communications Corporation, USA
melvin@zytek.com

Steve Beaty
Hewlett-Packard Corporation, USA
beaty@fc.hp.com

Local Arrangements Chair

Ulrich Finger
Ecole Nationale Supérieure des Télécommunications, France
Ulrich.Finger@inf.enst.fr

Steering Committee

Richard Belgard, *Consultant*
belgard@umunhum.stanford.edu

James Bondi, *Texas Instruments, Dallas*
bondi@ti.com

Matthew Farrens, *University of California, Davis*
farrens@cs.ucdavis.edu

Stan Habib, *City University of New York*
habib@csp.gc.cuny.edu

Wen-mei Hwu, *University of Illinois, Urbana-Champaign*
hwu@crhc.uiuc.edu

Gearold Johnson, *National Technology University, Fort Collins*
gerry@lance.colostate.edu

Yale Patt, *University of Michigan, Ann Arbor*
patt@eecs.umich.edu

Andrew Wolfe, *Princeton University*
awolfe@princeton.edu

Program Committee

Vicki Allan, *Utah State*
Richard Belgard, *Consultant*
David Bernstein, *IBM Haifa*
Jim Bondi, *Texas Instruments*
Steve Carr, *Michigan Tech*
Tom Conte, *North Carolina State*
Henk Corporaal, *Delft University of Technology*
Edward Davidson, *University of Michigan*
Jim Dehnert, *Silicon Graphics*
Kemal Ebcioglu, *IBM Watson*
Christine Eisenbeis, *INRIA*
Daniel Etiemble, *LRI*
Matthew Farrens, *University of California, Davis*
Paolo Faraboschi, *Hewlett-Packard Laboratories*
Stephan Freudenberger, *Hewlett-Packard Laboratories*
Guang Gao, *McGill University*
Andy Glew, *Intel Corporation*
Stanley Habib, *City University of New York*
Wen-mei Hwu, *University of Illinois, Urbana-Champaign*
Gearold Johnson, *NTU*
Daniel Litaize, *IRIT*
Trevor Mudge, *University of Michigan*
Bill Mangione-Smith, *University of California, Los Angeles*
Yale Patt, *University of Michigan*
Bob Rau, *Hewlett-Packard Laboratories*
Uwe Schwiegelshohn, *University of Dortmund*
Andre Seznec, *IRISA*
Jim Smith, *University of Wisconson*
Mike Smith, *Harvard University*
Mark Smotherman, *Clemson University*
Guri Sohi, *University of Wisconson*
Phil Sweany, *Michigan Tech*
Gary Tyson, *University of California, Riverside*
Andrew Wolfe, *Princeton University*
Tse-Yu Yeh, *Intel Corporation*

Referee List

Alain Lichnewsky
Alexandre E. Eichenberger
Andre Seznec
Andreas Moshovos
Andrew Wolfe
Andy Glew
Antoine Sawaya
Artour Stoutchinin
B. Ramakrishna Rau
Ben-Chung Cheng
Benoit Dupont de Dinechin
Bill Havanki
Bill Mangione-Smith
Brad Calder
Brad Chen
Brian Deitrich
Brian Harvey
Cheng-Hsueh Hsieh
Chih-Chieh Lee
Christine Eisenbeis
Claude Timsit
Corinne Ancourt
Dan Connors
Dan Friendly
Dan Truong
Daniel Etiemble
Daniel Litaize
Daniel M. Lavery
Darko Kirovski
David August
David Bernstein
Donald Yeung
Dror Maydan
Ed Davidson
Ed Tam
Eddie Gornish
Eric Hao
Eric Rotenberg
Erik Altman
Francois Thomasset
Frank Vahid
Fred Chow
Gary Tyson
George Cai
Gerry Johnson
Gheith Abandah
Giuseppe Desoli
Glenn Ammons
Guei-Yuan Lueh
Guri Sohi
Haiying CAI
Henk Corporaal
Herbert H.J. Hum
I-Cheng Kevin Chen
J. Hordijk
James E. Smith
Jared Stark
Jason Fritts
Jian Wang
Jim Bondi
Jim Dehnert
Johan Janssen
John C. Gyllenhaal
John Matthews
Josh Fisher
Jude Rivers
Kalpana Ramakrishnan
Karen Tomko

Kelsey Lick
Kemal Ebcioglu
Kevin B. Theobald
Kevin Rich
Kishore Menezes
Lucile Cognard
Marco Fillo
Marius Evers
Mark Evers
Mark Smotherman
Mary Ann Hirsch
Matt Postiff
Matthew Farrens
Matthew Jennings
Michael D. Smith
Nathalie Drach
Olivier Temam
Paolo Faraboschi
Pascal Sainrat
Paul Racunas
Peter Markstein
Phil Sweany
Po-Yung Chang
R. Govindarajan
Ralph Kling
Raul Silvera
Rich Belgard
Richard Johnson
Robert Schreiber
Rohit Chandra
Roy Ju
Sadun Anik
Sanjay Patel
Santosh Abraham
Santosh Abraham
Scott Breach
Scott Mahlke
Sergei Larin
Shail Aditya Gupta
Shaohua Han
Shih-Hao Hung
Simonjit Dutta
Sreedhar
Stan Habib
Stefan Freudenberger
Stephan Jourdan
Stephen Melvin
Steve Beaty
Steve Carr
Steve Keckler
Steve Krueger
Sumedh Sathaye
T.N. Vijaykumar
Nam Dan Truong
Teresa L. Johnson
Tom Conte
Trevor Mudge
Tse-Yu Yeh
Uwe Schwiegelshohn
Vasanth Bala
Vicki Allan
Vincent Hummel
Vinod Kathail
Waleed Meleis
Wen-mei Hwu
Willie Glover
Yale Patt

Featured Speaker

Stamatis Vassiliadis,
Delft University of Technology

"Overcoming Superscalar Limitations"

Session 1

A Persistent Rescheduled-Page Cache for Low Overhead Object Code Compatibility in VLIW Architectures

Thomas M. Conte Sumedh W. Sathaye Sanjeev Banerjia
Department of Electrical and Computer Engineering
North Carolina State University
Raleigh, North Carolina 27695-7911
(919)-515-5067
e-mail: {conte, swsathay, sbanerj}@eos.ncsu.edu

Abstract

Object–code compatibility between processor generations is an open issue for VLIW architectures. A potential solution is a technique termed dynamic rescheduling, which performs run-time software rescheduling at the first-time page faults. The time required for rescheduling the pages constitutes a large portion of the overhead of this method. A disk caching scheme that uses a persistent rescheduled-page cache (PRC) *is presented. The scheme reduces the overhead associated with dynamic rescheduling by saving rescheduled pages on disk, across program executions. Operating system support is required for dynamic rescheduling and management of the PRC. The implementation details for the PRC are discussed. Results of simulations used to gauge the effectiveness of PRC indicate that (1) the PRC is effective in reducing the overhead of dynamic rescheduling, and (2) due to different overhead requirements of programs, a* split *PRC organization performs better than a* unified *PRC.*

The unified PRC was studied for two different page replacement policies: LRU and overhead-based *replacement. It was found that with LRU replacement, all the programs consistently perform better with increasing PRC sizes, but the* high-overhead *programs take a consistent performance hit compared to the* low-overhead programs. *With overhead-based replacement, the performance of* high-overhead *programs improves substantially, while the* low-overhead *programs perform only slightly worse than in the case of the LRU replacement.*

1 Introduction

Unlike contemporary superscalar processors [1] [2] [3] which employ dynamic scheduling, VLIW processors depend on a schedule of code generated by the compiler. The compiler has full knowledge of the machine model, described in terms of the hardware resources available, and the latencies related to execution on each resource. Correct execution of a program scheduled under one machine model assumptions is guaranteed only on processors that have exactly the same machine model or, its supersets where the assumptions are strictly held. Thus, a program scheduled for a particular generation in a VLIW family cannot be guaranteed to be binary compatible with other generations. This is known as the object–code compatibility problem in VLIW architectures [4]. Lack of object-code compatibility is a commonly cited reason why VLIWs may not become a general–purpose computing paradigm [5]. Solutions to the problem have been suggested and can be classified as hardware or software approaches. Hardware techniques typically employ scheduling hardware [6], [7], [4], [8], [9], which could substantially increase the hardware complexity of the machine. A common software approach is that of off–line recompilation of source programs, which yields excellent performance because the compiler has access to all the necessary information to expose the ILP in the program. The drawback of this technique is that it is cumbersome to use, because access to source code may not always be possible. A variant of this is off–line object-code translation, which is more practical when the source code is unavailable or a large set of programs for the older architecture exists [10]. Alternatively, an interpreter could be used to translate between the architectures at run–time [11] but this approach usually suffers from poor performance.

Another approach is *dynamic rescheduling* [12]. In this technique, a program binary scheduled for the target machine model of a VLIW generation is allowed to directly execute on any other generation of the VLIW. As the execution proceeds, each page-fault generated in the program instruction space results into a special action: the page being fetched is rescheduled for the machine model of the target generation. Per-page rescheduling is performed only at the first instance the page-fault occurs (i.e., only at *first-time*

1072-4451/96 $5.00 © 1996 IEEE

page faults). A page of code is considered as an atomic unit for rescheduling. Implementation of this technique requires support from the operating system, specifically in the page fault service routine. The extra time incurred for rescheduling constitutes the overhead of this technique.

This paper presents a scheme that reduces the overhead associated with dynamic rescheduling by caching on-disk rescheduled code on a per–page basis. It employs a structure called a *persistent rescheduled-page cache (PRC)* that holds rescheduled pages across multiple executions of a program. The organization of this paper is as follows. Section 2 reviews previous work on object–code compatibility and explains dynamic rescheduling and presents performance measurements of code subjected to dynamic rescheduling. Section 3 introduces the PRC as part of an operating system–managed disk caching scheme that reduces the overhead of dynamic rescheduling. The architecture and management of the PRC is detailed, and experimental results that measure its performance are presented. Section 4 presents the conclusions of the study and avenues for future work.

2 Object–Code Compatibility and Dynamic Rescheduling

Several hardware approaches have been reported previously to address the VLIW compatibility problem. Rau presented a technique called split-issue to perform superscalar-style dynamic scheduling of code in hardware [4]. The *fill-unit*, originally proposed by Melvin, Shebanow, and Patt [6], and later extended by Franklin and Smotherman [8] can be adapted to achieve a limited level of compatibility in VLIWs. These approaches are counter to the principle of hardware simplicity, one of the tenets of the VLIW philosophy. An obvious alternative is off–line recompilation and rescheduling. This technique has an advantage in terms of the performance but is extremely cumbersome to use, owing to its off-line nature. Similar to this is off–line binary translation, which was used to migrate VAX software to the Alpha platform [10]. Run–time software emulation can also be used, as implemented in Insignia Solution's SoftWindows product [13]. An approach employing both the emulation and translation techniques has been utilized in the FX!32 product from DEC [14]. May investigated using an interpreter to execute IBM System/370 binaries on an IBM RT PC [11]. These solutions attempt to achieve compatibility between widely varying architectures. Although such large differences will probably not exist between generations of a VLIW family, the techniques used are still of interest.

Interpreters can use caching of translated sections of code across executions as a means of reducing the amount of translation needed; disk storage is used as a cache for the translated code. Caching is an intuitive and effective technique for reducing run–time translation overhead. However, a majority of the literature on translation does not contain details on management of cached code segments.

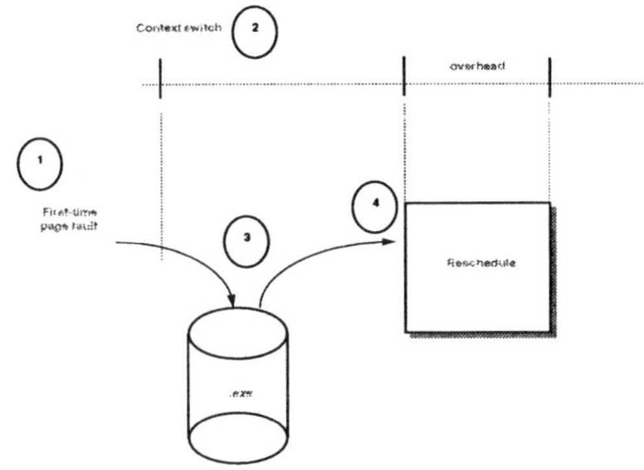

Figure 1. The sequence of events in Dynamic Rescheduling.

Events 1–3 are the detection of the page fault and generation mismatch, the context switch of the process, and the retrieval of the page from disk, respectively; these events are standard. The overhead of dynamic rescheduling is event 4, where the page is dynamically rescheduled.

Another technique for compatibility is *Dynamic Rescheduling (DR)* [12]. At all first–time page-faults, the OS invokes a module called the *dynamic rescheduler* to reschedule the page being accessed, for the host machine model. The sequence of events in dynamic rescheduling is illustrated in Figure 1. The detection of a first–time page fault is shown as Event 1. Events 1, 2, and 3 always take place at a page fault. In the case of dynamic rescheduling, however, this is treated as a special page fault; this is indicated as Event 4. The program binary contains a complete description of the machine for which it was originally compiled. If the page fault handler detects a generation mismatch between the host machine and the program, the rescheduler module is invoked. After the page is rescheduled, program execution resumes. If the rescheduled page is selected for replacement from physical memory before the program terminates, it is written to the text swap space [15], [16]; this eliminates the need to reschedule if the page is re–accessed. The net overhead of the dynamic rescheduling technique can be quantitatively expressed in terms of the following three factors: (1) the time spent in rescheduling pages at run-time, (2) the time to write rescheduled pages to text swap when pages are replaced, and (3) the amount of disk space used to save the rescheduled pages. The time for disk I/O during page replacement is negligible as writing to swap can be performed asynchronously [15]. The true overhead is reduced to the time for rescheduling and the disk space required to save rescheduled pages.

If dynamic rescheduling performed code motion, it would give rise to code size changes due to the compensation code it may have to insert and/or delete. Since it is not straightforward to handle any changes in code size dynamically, the DR framework avoids the size changes altogether, via a special binary encoding which eliminates explicit use of NOPs from the code. More discussion of the issues involved therein can be found in [12], and are beyond the scope of this paper. The PlayDoh [17] VLIW architecture from Hewlett-Packard Laboratories is used as a testbed in this paper. Also, it is assumed that no modifications other than the DR framework itself are made in the instruction space of the programs (such as those by self-modifying code).

2.1 Performance of Dynamic Rescheduling

The effectiveness of dynamic rescheduling was measured using programs from the SPECint92 suite[1] and several UNIX utility programs in [12], and is expanded here. In order to construct an interactive load, the benchmarks were divided into two categories: tools (cccp, compress, gcc, grep, and tbl) and applications (espresso, eqntott, li, lex, sc, and yacc). It was assumed that tools would be invoked twice as often as applications, but that there would be no other pattern in the workload. Two sets of inputs were used for each benchmark, and were alternated between invocations of the benchmark. Using these assumptions, several workloads were created and used to measure the performance of the benchmarks with and without dynamic rescheduling. Three machine models were used for the evaluation of the performance of the benchmarks in situations that required dynamic rescheduling: Generations 1, 2, and 3 (their organizations are shown in Figure 2). The types of functional units are shown horizontally, while the execution latency assumptions are shown vertically. The unit `pred` is used to perform predicate computation in integer compare operations. Predicate computation in FP compare operations is done in the FPAdd unit. A three part method was used to evaluate the dynamic rescheduling technique. In the first part, intermediate code for a benchmark was scheduled for a given machine model, using a VLIW scheduler; hyperblock scheduling was used for the initial compilation [18]. The intermediate code was then profiled in order to find the worst–case estimate of execution time in terms of the number of cycles. The number of times each page of code is accessed is also recorded, which also indicates each unique code page that is accessed. This was called the *Native* mode experiment. In the second part, the code scheduled for *Native* mode execution was rescheduled for the other machine models. Execution time estimates for the rescheduled code were also generated as described before. This time estimate indicates the performance of the rescheduled code without taking into account the rescheduling overhead incurred by the rescheduler. Hence this part was termed the *no overhead* experiment.

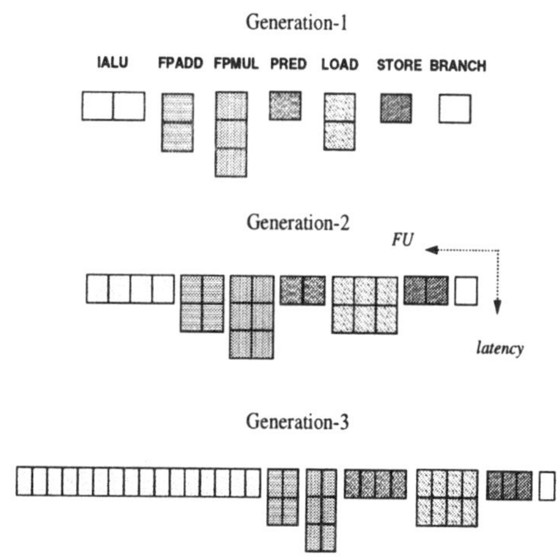

Figure 2. Simulated machine models.

In the third part, the rescheduler itself was compiled, scheduled for the machine model used in the first part, and then used as a benchmark. The input to the the rescheduler benchmark was pages taken from each of the other benchmarks. The performance of the rescheduler benchmark was used to find the average time to reschedule a single 4K page for each of the three machine models. This was found to be 54,272 cycles for Generation–1, 51,200 cycles for Generation–2, and 48,108 cycles for Generation–3. This was then combined with the number of unique page accesses from the first part of the experiment to estimate the total number of execution cycles for the rescheduling overhead. The rescheduling overhead was added to the execution times from the no–overhead experiment to derive execution times for the *w/overhead* experiment. Finally, to compare the performance achieved in the above three parts, the speedup with respect to a single-unit, single-issue processor model (the *base model*) was calculated. Speedup is: (*number of cycles of execution estimated in the experiment*)/(*number of cycles of execution estimated for the base model*). All three parts assumed a page size of 4K bytes, as is used in many contemporary operating systems [19] [20] and processors [21] [3]. Results from all three parts are shown in Figure 3. It can be observed that the no-overhead speedup of rescheduled benchmark code (marked $^{Gn-m}_{no\ ov}$) has comparable per-

[1] Performance characteristics of none of the FP programs in the presence of the PRC are presented because rescheduling of software pipelined loops has not yet been implemented in the current dynamic rescheduling framework.

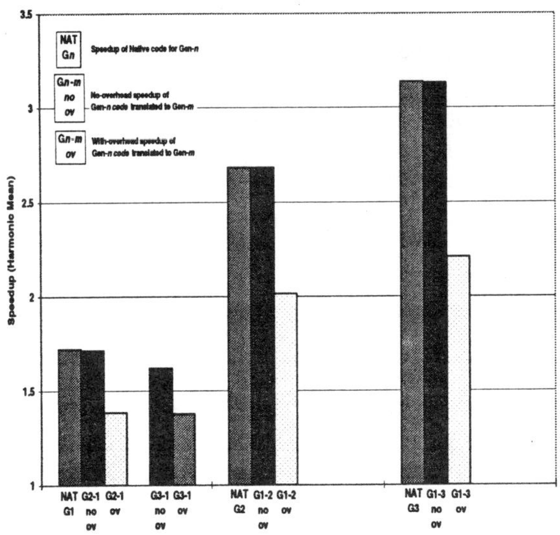

Figure 3. Speedups for programs under dynamic rescheduling framework.

Each bar is the harmonic mean of speedups of benchmarks for a specific generation–to–generation rescheduling. Each set of bars is identified on the x-axis by a Gn-m label, which indicates that code originally scheduled for Generation–n was rescheduled for Generation-m. The first bar in each set is native performance on Generation-m, the remaining bars show rescheduled performance, both with and without the overhead due to dynamic rescheduling.

formance as the native compiled code ($\overset{\text{NAT}}{Gn}$), but there is a prominent performance degradation when rescheduling overhead is taken into account ($\underset{ov}{Gn-m}$).

The dominant time in page fault handling is the time spent reading the page from disk if the executable is stored on the local machine. If the page is being accessed over a LAN, as is common in a client-server environment, the network latency is the most dominant factor, and is at least an order of magnitude more than the local disk access. The time spent rescheduling a page adds to this page access latency. To get an estimate of how much overhead DR would add to page fault handling in a local paging environment, an experiment was conducted to measure the page-fault service time when paging from a set of contiguous blocks on a local disk. The SAR performance analysis tool [22] was used to measure average page fault service time on two hardware platforms and was found to be about 2500 μs [2], when averaged over a total of 50 page-faults. Based on average execution times on a 100 MHz machine, dynamic rescheduling increases the page fault service time by about 20%, a significant increase (rescheduling a 4 kilobyte page, with 64-bit operations, from the Generation-2 code to Generation-1 code, for example, would take 54,272 cycles times 10 ns, which is approximately 543μs, more than 20% of the average page-fault service time measured here). It is apparent that in the case of paging over a LAN, the relative overhead of DR will be lower, but probably not small enough to completely neglect it.

There are two approaches that can be used to reduce overhead of DR: (1) improve the performance of the DR algorithm, or (2) reduce the number of pages that require rescheduling over multiple invocations of the program. The second component is the focus of the investigation in this paper. The OS saves rescheduled pages in the text swap if a program is swapped out during execution. These rescheduled pages are effectively *cached* on disk during a program's current execution. Extending this concept, the OS can aid in caching rescheduled pages not only during a single program execution but across multiple program executions as well. The following section introduces an OS–supported caching scheme that achieves this.

3 Disk caching and the Persistent Rescheduled-Page Cache

The significant overhead introduced by dynamic rescheduling can be largely alleviated through the use of a caching scheme that employs a *persistent rescheduled-page cache (PRC)*. A PRC is an OS–managed disk cache that holds binary images of rescheduled pages; if rescheduled pages are cached, they will not need to be rescheduled when re–accessed across program runs. A PRC is defined by its behavior during a program execution and at program termination. During execution, rescheduled pages are stored in text swap space. When a program terminates, its rescheduled pages are written to the PRC. Page placement and replacement policies are implemented within the OS.

The concept behind the persistent rescheduled-page cache originated from software–managed disk caching, a proven method for reducing I/O traffic [15], [16]. The idea is to cache the most recently accessed disk blocks in memory in the hope that they will be accessed again in the near future. Typical Unix systems implement a file system buffer cache to hold the most recently accessed disk blocks in memory using a LRU algorithm for replacement [15], [16]. The buffer cache effectively operates as a fragmented page cache also

[2]SAR was run on a 133 Mhz Pentium–based Data General computer running DG–UX, and a 99 MHz Hewlett–Packard 9000/715 computer running HP–UX.

and reduces the amount of I/O during page faults [3]. Variants of this have been used in distributed file systems such as Sprite [23] and Andrew [24], for the purposes of remote file caching. Disk caching has also been used to reduce translation overhead in architectural interpreters [11], and can be used effectively with dynamic rescheduling.

3.1 Persistent Rescheduled-Page Caches

A PRC can be organized as a system–wide cache: a portion of the file system that holds only rescheduled pages and managed by the OS. Pages from different programs can displace each other in this case. The primary configuration parameters for the PRC are the size, placement and replacement policies, and are discussed below.

During initial program execution on a non–native host, text pages are rescheduled at first–time page faults, as described in Section 2. If a rescheduled page is displaced from physical memory during program execution, it is written to the text swap space on disk; this prevents rescheduling a page multiple times during program execution. At the end of the initial execution, all of the rescheduled pages are written to the PRC (the page placement policy will be explained shortly). During subsequent executions, when a page fault occurs for a text page with a generation mismatch, the PRC is probed to check for the presence of a rescheduled version of the page. If a rescheduled version is present, it is retrieved and loaded into physical memory, and the overhead of rescheduling is not incurred. If a rescheduled version is not available, the page is retrieved from the binary image of the program, rescheduled, and then loaded into physical memory. If this page is replaced during program execution, it is written to the text swap space. At program termination, all rescheduled pages of a program are written to the PRC. A rescheduled page can be placed into any entry in the cache, which implies that the cache is effectively fully associative with a replacement policy such as LRU. An outline of the algorithm used for PRC management is shown in Figure 4.

Probing the PRC on disk for the presence of a page is an expensive operation. This can be eliminated by modifying a program's disk block pointers during execution and program exit. When a page is rescheduled and subsequently written to the PRC at program termination, a separate set of disk block pointers (*PRC pointers*) for the program are set to point to the rescheduled versions of pages in the cache. A PRC pointer is annotated to indicate which original page the rescheduled page replaces. This scheme implements a PRC probe as an examination of a program's disk block pointers in one central location rather than multiple locations in the PRC on disk. Disk block pointers can be cached by the OS, which can further reduce the number of disk probes. The

[3] The term "fragmented" is used because all of the disk blocks that comprise a page might not be in the buffer cache at the same time.

- Load program: if rescheduled pages exist, set page table entries to disk addresses in PRC.
- Run program.
- At program termination, write all rescheduled pages into PRC. If needed, displace LRU pages from PRC.
- Update program PRC disk block pointers to point to PRC. Update PRC pointers to point to program file data structure.

Figure 4. Persistent Rescheduled-Page Cache (PRC) management algorithm.

rescheduled version of a page is accessed without probing the PRC on disk and perhaps without any disk accesses at all, if the program's disk block pointers are in the in–memory cache. Rescheduled pages that are stored in swap during program execution are managed by the OS using known methods for managing text swap space [15].

The probing of multiple PRC pointers during page faults can also be eliminated. At program load time, the disk block and PRC pointers for the program are examined to determine if rescheduled versions of pages exist in the PRC. If a page has a rescheduled version, the loader modifies the page table entry (PTE) for that page to point to the rescheduled version. When a page fault occurs for a page that has a rescheduled version, the rescheduled version is accessed directly, using the updated PTE. No disk accesses or in–memory searches are required to implement a PRC probe: if the PTE for a page points into the PRC, a rescheduled version exists. The re-mapping of the PTE entries can be done at program load time [15], [16]. As rescheduled pages are displaced from the use of a PRC due to replacement, the PRC pointers to the displaced pages must be nullified. This can be accomplished with OS support. A table can be maintained by the PRC manager that lists the locations of the PRC pointers associated with each page in the cache. When a page is replaced, its PRC pointer is set to null.

3.2 PRC performance

Figure 5 presents the performance of PRCs of different sizes for rescheduling across four generation–to–generation combinations. The metric used is speedup over a single universal–unit, single–issue processor. Each set of bars shows the harmonic mean of speedups for a rescheduling

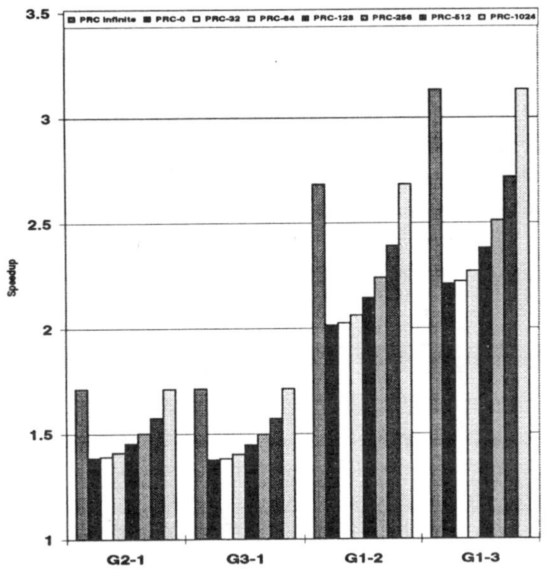

Figure 5. Speedups of benchmarks for PRC performance, unified PRC, LRU replacement

Each bar is a harmonic mean of speedups of the benchmarks for a particular generation–to–generation rescheduling and PRC size. Each set of bars is identified on the x-axis by a Gn-m label, which indicates that code originally scheduled for Generation–n was rescheduled for Generation–m. The first bar in each set of bars is the no–overhead performance, the second bar is the worst–case overhead (no PRC), and subsequent bars are performance with the indicated PRC size; PRC size is the maximum number of pages the cache holds.

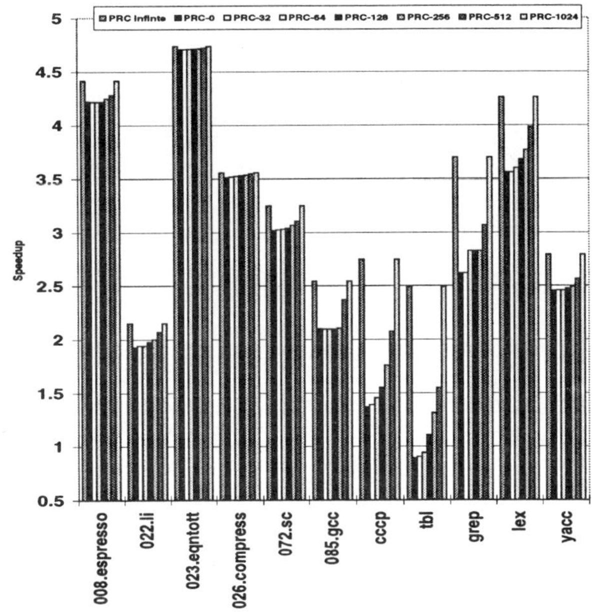

Figure 6. Generation–1 to Generation–3 rescheduling, unified PRC, LRU replacement

Each bar is the speedup for a Generation–1 to Generation–3 rescheduling for the specified PRC size. Each set of bars corresponds to an individual benchmark, as indicated by the labels on x-axis. The first bar in each set of bars is the no–overhead performance, the second bar is the worst–case overhead (no PRC), and subsequent bars are performance with the indicated PRC size; PRC size is the maximum number of pages the cache holds.

combination, for various PRC sizes. As indicated here, PRC-n means a PRC of size n pages. PRC-infinite indicates the performance when rescheduling of the unique page accesses was performed only at the initial invocations. This is essentially a PRC without an upper bound on its size. PRC-infinite speedups are the same as the no-overhead case speedups mentioned in Section 2.1. PRC-0 indicates the performance when no PRC is used, and all the pages uniquely accessed by the program are rescheduled at each invocation. This provides a measure of the worst-case overhead of rescheduling. A page can displace any other page in the PRC, based on the LRU replacement policy. This organization is called a *unified PRC*.

Performance of all of the rescheduling combinations benefits from the use of a PRC. The trend is that a larger PRC provides greater speedup. Note that for PRC-1024, perfect speedup (equal to the PRC-infinite) case is achieved. This happens because the total number of pages in the workload is less than the size of the PRC and all the programs completely reside in a PRC of that size without any requirement to reschedule once the PRC is populated.

All of the benchmarks do not benefit equally from the presence of a PRC. To illustrate this, Figure 6 presents speedups for individual benchmarks for Generation–1 to Generation–3 rescheduling. Some benchmarks – such as *008.espresso, 023.eqntott, 026.compress* – show only a small improvement with even a large PRC. Others, such as *cccp, tbl, grep* show substantial improvement with the increasing PRC size. Moderate improvement is shown by *022.li, 072.sc, 085.gcc, lex,* and *yacc*. The reason behind this behavior can be explained using the *overhead ratio* metric for a program. The overhead ratio is defined as:

$$O = R/(E + R)$$

where E is the execution time of the program, and R, the total rescheduling overhead = (*the Unique Page Count of*

Table 1. Unique page counts of the benchmarks.

BENCHMARK	UNIQUE PAGE COUNT
008.espresso	137
022.li	47
023.eqntott	25
026.compress	8
072.sc	60
085.gcc	323
cccp	34
tbl	50
grep	4
lex	45
yacc	56

Table 2. Overhead Ratio (O): Generation–1 to Generation–3 rescheduling.

BENCHMARK	OVERHEAD RATIO (percentage)	OVERHEAD CATEGORY
008.espresso	4.35	low
022.li	10.52	moderate
023.eqntott	0.64	low
026.compress	1.25	low
072.sc	6.29	moderate
085.gcc	17.50	moderate
cccp	50.09	high
tbl	64.15	high
grep	29.10	high
lex	16.51	moderate
yacc	12.19	moderate

the program $*$ avg. time required to reschedule a page). The *unique page count* of a program is defined as the number of first–time page faults that occur during the execution of the program. Values of the unique page counts are shown in Table 1. Table 2 shows the percentage values of the overhead ratio for Generation-1 to Generation-3 rescheduling. A high overhead ratio (20% and above in this case) indicates that the amount of time taken to reschedule is relatively high. Such programs benefit the most from the use of a PRC – *cccp, tbl,* and *grep* as shown here – and are termed *high-overhead* programs. For programs which showed the least performance improvement, the overhead ratio is relatively small (less than 5%). These programs are termed *low-overhead* programs (*008.espresso, 023.eqntott,* and *026.compress*). All the others (*022.li, 072.sc, 085.gcc, lex,* and *yacc* – they all have a value of O between 5% and 20%) are referred to as *moderate-overhead* programs.

In the unified PRC, the low- or moderate-overhead programs can evict the high-overhead programs completely if their unique page count is large. Thus, for example, even if the unique page count of a high-overhead program such as *cccp* is small (35 in this case), a moderate-overhead program such as *085.gcc* can replace all the pages allocated to *cccp* because it's unique page count is relatively high (323 in this case). If these two programs are run in an alternate fashion (which one would expect, because one is a C preprocessor, and the other is a C compiler), the number of pages for *cccp* that will have to be rescheduled could be sizable, thus increasing its overhead, especially for smaller PRC sizes. A better organization of the PRC which reduces this effect is presented next.

3.3 Split PRC

Because program behavior in the presence of a PRC varies directly with a program's overhead ratio, one approach is to *partition* the cache to hold pages for different classes of programs, based on the program overhead ratio. This should prevent *cache pollution*: a benchmark that benefits very little from a PRC displacing the pages of a program whose performance is substantially enhanced by a PRC. OS–gathered statistics can be dynamically used to compute the overhead ratios of the programs, and to determine which PRC partition a program should use. The OS needs to record the unique page counts, the program execution time, along with the average time take to reschedule a page, for this purpose.

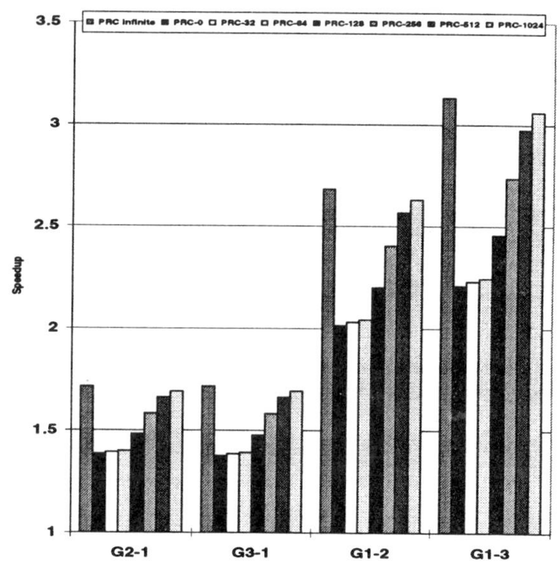

Figure 7. Speedups for PRC performance: 2-way split PRC, LRU replacement.

A PRC with two partitions can be labeled a *2-way split*

PRC: one partition to hold the low- and moderate-overhead programs, and the other for the exclusive use of the high-overhead programs. Figure 7 presents results for such a PRC across various generation–to–generation reschedulings and PRC sizes. (Here, both the partitions are of the same size, though this is not a requirement – the partition sizes can be varied depending on the program unique page counts.) Performance for practically all generation–to–generation rescheduling combinations improved using the 2-way split PRC over a unified PRC. In particular, for the Generation–1 to Generation–3 rescheduling using a PRC-512, the speedup was 91% of the speedup when using an infinite PRC (infinite PRC corresponds to the no–overhead experiment as described in Section 2.1). The Generation–1 to Generation–2 rescheduling also showed improvement with a split cache, particularly for PRC-256 and PRC-512. The general trend was that larger PRCs performed better, as was expected. The speedups of individual benchmarks with a 2-way split PRC, for Generation-1 to Generation-3 translation is shown in Figure 8. All of the high-overhead benchmarks fared well, compared to their performance under a unified PRC (Figure 6). Their low performance for the smaller PRC sizes is because they compete with each others in the same partition. It can also be observed that the cache pollution effect still persists, but is substantially reduced (for example, observe the improvement in performance for *cccp* and *tbl* as compared to the unified PRC, for all PRC sizes). Based on these experiments, an N-way split cache with M pages per partition would do better than a unified cache with $M * N$ entries. In an actual implementation, a PRC can be partitioned with as much granularity as the OS allows.

3.4 Unified PRC with overhead-based replacement

Another technique to reduce the cache pollution effect observed in the unified PRC is the use of an *overhead-based* PRC page replacement policy instead of LRU. This works as follows. With each page in the PRC is associated the overhead ratio for the program to which the page belongs. A page is not allowed to replace another page from the PRC unless its overhead ratio is higher than the overhead ratio of that page. This replacement policy ensures that more of the high-overhead programs stay PRC-resident, once placed in the PRC. The priority of use of the PRC is governed by the overhead ratio: the higher the overhead ratio, the higher the priority. Consequently, the low- and moderate- overhead programs incur higher rescheduling overhead, since a relatively less number of their pages get cached between invocations. Intuitively, this scheme is similar to the multiple dynamically resizable partitions within a PRC.

Figure 9 shows the performance of individual benchmarks for Generation–1 to Generation–3 translation for this scheme. It can be observed that the top three high-overhead programs – *cccp, tbl, grep* – perform much better for this replacement policy than for LRU (Figure 6). They show a perfect speedup for PRC sizes 128 and above. (The low speedups for small PRC sizes are due to a large number of capacity misses.) On the other hand, the rest of the programs show a decrease, albeit small, in the performance for smaller PRC sizes compared to LRU. For the larger PRCs, their performance has, however, improved [4]. This is based on the fact that for smaller PRC sizes, they too encounter a large number of capacity misses, effectively displacing each other from the PRC and incurring a larger rescheduling overhead.

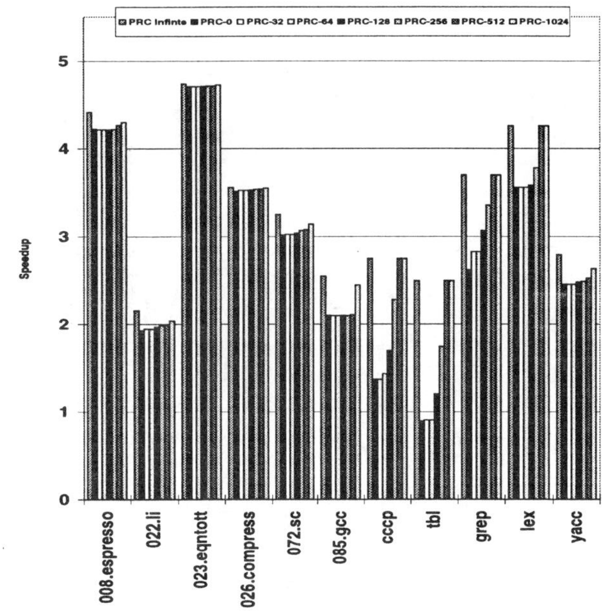

Figure 8. Generation–1 to Generation–3 rescheduling: 2-way split PRC, LRU replacement.

In the case of *008.espresso, 022.li, 023.eqntott, 026.compress, 072.sc*, and *lex*, however, there is little or no performance gain for any of the PRC sizes. This is explained by considering the case of *lex*. *Lex* has a relatively small unique page count of 45 (refer to Table 1), compared to the 323 of *085.gcc*. It's overhead ratio (16.51), however, is only slightly lower than that of *085.gcc* (17.50) (refer to Table 2). *Lex* gets displaced from the PRC after every invocation of *085.gcc*, and incurs the overhead of rescheduling all of it's pages at each subsequent invocation. It is speculated that

[4] As mentioned earlier, all the programs have a perfect speedup for PRC-1024 because it is large enough to hold the entire workload throughout the experiment.

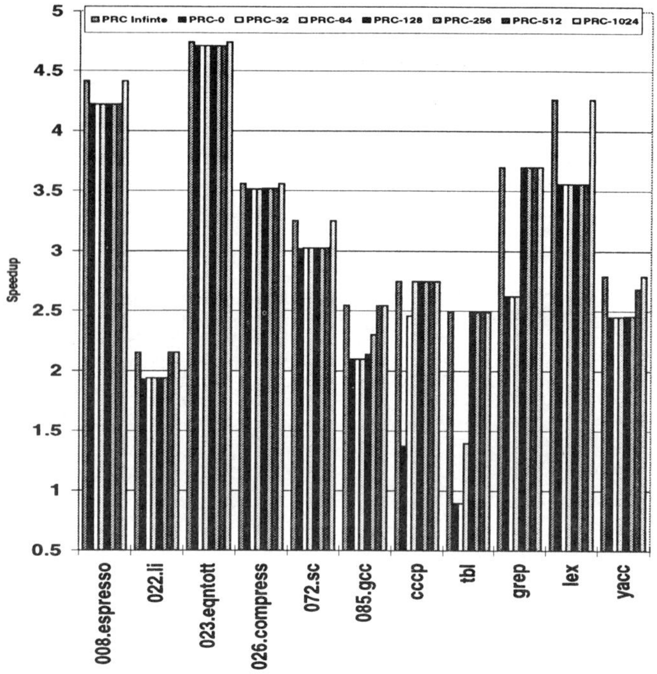

Figure 9. Generation–1 to Generation–3 rescheduling, Unified PRC, overhead-based replacement.

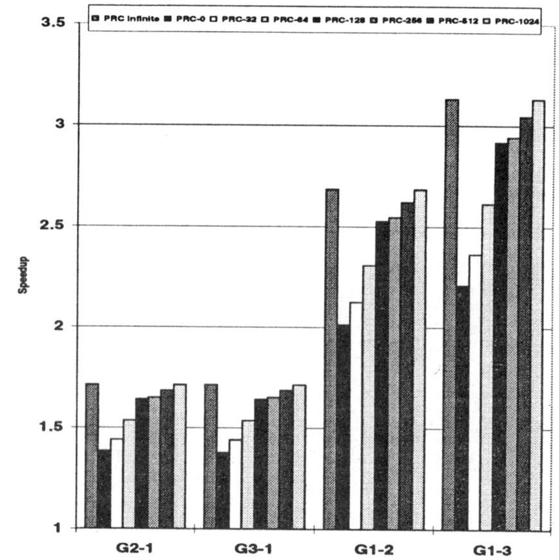

Figure 10. Speedups for PRC performance: Unified PRC, overhead-based replacement.

the impact of this phenomenon may be reduced if *085.gcc* was allowed to displace these programs only if they were invoked in the relatively remote past. A combination of the LRU and the overhead-based schemes may prove effective in such cases, and is a topic of future research.

Nonetheless, all of these programs (*008.espresso, 022.li, 023.eqntott, 026.compress, 072.sc*, and *lex*) being low- or moderate-overhead, the overall performance across all programs is better than the previous two schemes. This is apparent from Figure 10. When compared with the performance of the unified PRC with LRU replacement (Figure 5), and the 2-way split PRC with LRU replacement (Figure 7), the overhead-based replacement performs better across all the PRC sizes. The general performance trend observed for the overhead-based replacement policy confirms the intuition that the priority of use of the PRC is dictated by the overhead ratio.

4 Conclusion

The object–code compatibility problem for VLIWs can be approached by either software or hardware methods. A technique called dynamic rescheduling which uses operating system support to reschedule a program on a page–by–page basis during first–time page faults has been reviewed. The overhead of this technique is the time required to reschedule and the space required to save the rescheduled pages. The number of times a page has to be rescheduled can be reduced by saving the rescheduled version on disk, across program executions.

The persistent rescheduled-page cache was introduced as part of a scheme that saves rescheduled pages by using disk caching. The PRC reduces the number of times a page is rescheduled across multiple program executions. The architecture and management of the PRC was described. Specifically, the use and implementation of a system-wide, shared PRC was investigated. Unified caches were simulated to measure performance. The conclusion was drawn that PRCs in general are effective at reducing the overhead associated with dynamic rescheduling, but the effectiveness varies across programs and is dependent on the overhead ratio associated with a program. It was identified that the high-overhead programs are effectively displaced by the low overhead program from the PRC dependent on the invocation pattern in the workload. A partitioned cache organization was then introduced that classified programs based on their overhead ratios. A bi–partitioned scheme called a *Split* PRC was simulated and found to have improved performance over a unified PRC. In the third scheme, an overhead-based page replacement policy was implemented in a unified PRC, and it was found that the performance of the high-overhead programs improved substantially compared with the two previous schemes, while the low-overhead programs fared only slightly worse than the previous schemes.

Future research dealing with PRCs will investigate the use of other cache organizations. For example, determination of the number of partitions ideal for a split PRC and an investigation of a per–program PRC structure are underway. Also, a study of a combination algorithm for page replacement, based on the LRU and the overhead-based schemes is being conducted.

Acknowledgments

Discussions with Mary Ann Hirsch, Kishore Menezes, and the rest of the TINKER group have proved useful to the development of ideas in this paper. Mary Ann Hirsch also helped collect data from the Data General machines. This research was supported by the National Science Foundation under grants MIP-9696010 and MIP-9625007, in addition to research funding from Intel Corporation, Hewlett-Packard, and the International Business Machines Corporation. We especially thank the University of Illinois IMPACT group for use of the IMPACT compiler. The comments from the anonymous referees are also appreciated.

References

[1] D. B. Papworth, "Tuning the Pentium Pro microarchitecture," *IEEE Micro*, vol. 16, pp. 8–15, Apr. 1996.

[2] D. Alpert and D. Avnon, "Architecture of the Pentium microprocessor," *IEEE Micro*, vol. 13, pp. 11–21, June 1993.

[3] S. Weiss and J. E. Smith, *POWER and PowerPC*. San Francisco, CA: Morgan Kaufmann, 1994.

[4] B. R. Rau, "Dynamically scheduled VLIW processors," in *Proc. 26th Ann. International Symposium on Microarchitecture*, (Austin, TX), pp. 80–90, Dec. 1993.

[5] J. S. O'Donnell, "Superscalar vs. VLIW," *Computer Architecture News (ACM SIGARCH)*, pp. 26–28, Mar. 1995.

[6] S. Melvin, M. Shebanow, and Y. Patt, "Hardware support for large atomic units in dynamically scheduled machines," in *Proc. 21th Ann. International Symposium on Microarchitecture*, (San Diego, CA), pp. 60–66, Dec. 1988.

[7] G. Silberman and K. Ebcioğlu, "An architectural framework for supporting heteregeneous instruction–set architectures," *Computer*, vol. 26, pp. 39–56, June 1993.

[8] M. Franklin and M. Smotherman, "A fill-unit approach to multiple instruction issue," in *Proc. 27th Ann. International Symposium on Microarchitecture*, (San Jose, CA), pp. 162–171, Dec. 1994.

[9] G. Silberman and K. Ebcioğlu, "An architectural framework for migration from CISC to higher performance platforms," in *Proc. 1992 International Conference on Supercomputing*, pp. 198–215, 1992.

[10] R. L. Sites, A. Chernoff, M. B. Kirk, M. P. Marks, and S. G. Robinson, "Binary translation," *Comm. ACM*, vol. 36, pp. 69–81, Feb. 1993.

[11] C. May, "MIMIC: A Fast System/370 Simulator," in *Proc. ACM SIGPLAN '87 Symp. Interpreters and Interpretive Techniques*, pp. 1–13, June 1987.

[12] T. M. Conte and S. W. Sathaye, "Dynamic rescheduling: A technique for object code compatibility in VLIW architectures," in *Proc. 28th Ann. International Symposium on Microarchitecture*, (Ann Arbor, MI), Nov. 1995.

[13] Insignia Solutions, *SoftWindows for UNIX. Administrators's Guide, Version 2.0*. Mountain View, CA: Insignia Solutions, 1995.

[14] J. Turley, "Alpha runs x86 code with fx!32," *Microprocessor Report*, vol. 10, Mar. 1996.

[15] S. J. Leffler, M. K. McKusick, M. J. Karels, and J. S. Quarterman, *The Design and Implementation of the 4.3BSD Unix Operating System*. Addison-Wesley, 1989.

[16] M. J. Bach, *The design of the UNIX operating sustem*. Englewood Cliffs, NJ: Prentice–Hall, 1986.

[17] V. Kathail, M. Schlansker, and B. R. Rau, "HPL PlayDoh architecture specification: version 1.0," Tech. Rep. HPL-93-80, Hewlett-Packard Laboratories, Technical Publications Department, 1501 Page Mill Road, Palo Alto, CA 94304, Feb. 1994.

[18] S. A. Mahlke, D. C. Lin, W. Y. Chen, R. E. Hank, and R. A. Bringmann, "Effective compiler support for predicated execution using the Hyperblock," in *Proc. 25th Ann. Int'l. Symp. on Microarchitecture*, (Portland, OR), pp. 45–54, Dec. 1992.

[19] Hewlett Packard, *How HP–UX works: Concepts for the System Administrator (R9.0)*. Palo Alto, CA: Hewlett Packard, 1991.

[20] Data General, *Programming in the DG/UX Kernel Environment (R4.11)*. Westboro, MA: Data General, 1995.

[21] G. Kane, *MIPS RISC architecture*. Englewood Cliffs, NJ: Prentice-Hall, 1992.

[22] Data General, *Analyzing DG/UX System Performance (R4.11)*. Westboro, MA: Data General, 1995.

[23] M. Nelson, B. Welch, and J. K. Ousterhout, "Caching in the Sprite network file system," *ACM Trans. Comput. Sys.*, vol. 6, pp. 134–154, Feb. 1988.

[24] J. H. Morris, M. Satyanarayanan, M. H. Conner, J. H. Howard, D. S. H. Rosenthal, and F. D. Smith, "Andrew: a distributed personal computing environment," *Comm. ACM*, vol. 29, no. 3, pp. 184–201, 1986.

Integrating a Misprediction Recovery Cache (MRC) into a Superscalar Pipeline

James O. Bondi
Texas Instruments
Semiconductor Group
P.O. Box 660119, MS 8652
Dallas, TX 75266-0199

Ashwini K. Nanda[1]
IBM
T.J. Watson Research Center
P.O. Box 218
Yorktown Heights, NY 10958

Simonjit Dutta
Texas Instruments
Semiconductor Group
P.O. Box 660119, MS 8652
Dallas, TX 75266-0199

Abstract

In modern processors, deep pipelines couple with superscalar techniques to allow each pipe stage to process multiple instructions. When such a pipe must be flushed and refilled, as when predicted program flow beyond a branch is subsequently recognized as wrong, the temporary performance loss is significant. While modern branch target buffer (BTB) technology makes this flush/refill penalty fairly rare, the penalty that accrues from the remaining branch mispredictions is a serious impediment to even higher processor performance. Advanced mechanisms that can reduce this residual misprediction penalty can be of enormous value in future microprocessor designs. One promising new mechanism, the Misprediction Recovery Cache (MRC) is proposed in [1][2][3]. In this paper, we focus especially on MRC integration into existing pipelines.

1 Introduction

Modern microprocessors are employing ever deeper pipelines to enable ever higher clock rates. These deep pipelines, coupled with superscalar techniques allowing each pipe stage to process multiple instructions, result in increasingly severe performance penalties whenever the pipeline needs to be flushed and refilled.

Even with their many stages, modern microprocessor pipelines can be roughly viewed as just two groups of stages (Figure 1). These are the upper stages, involved with the fetch, decode, and preparation of instructions for execution, and the lower stages, involved with actual instruction execution and graduation. The instruction fetch unit, situated at the top of the upper stages, attempts to keep a supply of fetched instructions ready for the decode stages that follow. When a branch instruction is encountered, the fetch unit uses a branch flow prediction, typically from a branch prediction mechanism that we will call a Branch Target Buffer (BTB), to speculatively guide its fetching operation beyond this branch. The branch prediction cannot be verified until the branch is later "executed" in the lower pipe stages and the upper pipe has completely filled with speculatively fetched, decoded, and partially processed instructions. When branch "execution" occasionally proves the BTB's prediction wrong, all such partially processed instructions in the upper pipe must be discarded and the upper pipe completely refilled from the other (correct) branch path. If the upper pipe is "U" stages long, then this refill operation will penalize performance by consuming at least "U" wasted clocks before the first refill instruction can reach the lower pipe stages to begin execution [4][5].

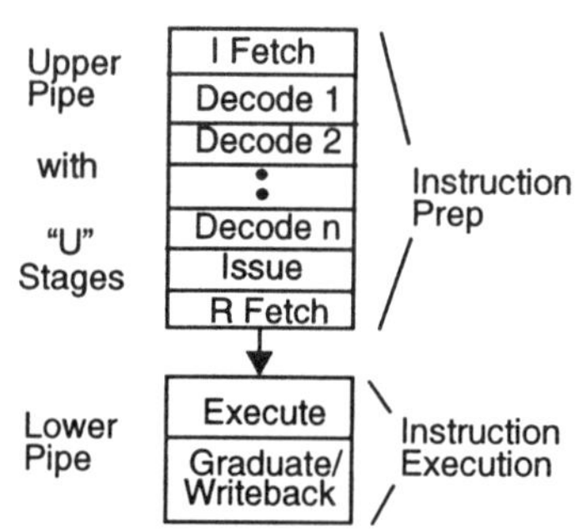

Figure 1: Basic (CISC) Pipeline w/o MRC

1. Author was with Texas Instruments when this work was undertaken.

1072-4451/96 $5.00 © 1996 IEEE

Note that "U" is, in fact, essentially just a lower bound on the number of penalty clocks wasted by the pipe of Figure 1 following branch misprediction. In some pipes, a small number of additional clocks are *always* needed to prepare and load the corrected target address into the fetch unit. If we call this consistent additional delay F_{reinit}, then the detailed recovery penalty after misprediction becomes

$$U + F_{reinit}$$

where F_{reinit} is typically very small relative to U. We will generally ignore other intermittent delay factors, such as instruction cache misses, that will just *sometimes* further add to the overall penalty experienced.

For a BTB with prediction accuracy of "B" (~0.9+),the average branch misprediction penalty that accumulates over program execution will be $(1-B)*(U+F_{reinit})$." As BTB technology has advanced recently from one-level to two-level history-based prediction algorithms [6] and even to correlation-based prediction algorithms [7], "B" has advanced nearer to 1 (~0.95) and helped hold average misprediction penalty in check. However, practical prediction algorithms with even better "B"s are no longer easily found, even though sophisticated tree-based algorithms are showing some promise [8].

Given these constraints on further increasing "B," we propose instead concentrating on means to effectively reduce "U." While "U" itself is an unchangeable architectural constant, perhaps portions of these "U" stages could often be avoided. Perhaps branch mispredictions could usually get a head start on pipe refill by allowing the lower-pipe to often draw temporarily from a special cache of already *fetched* and *decoded* instruction threads that each represent the beginning of an "other path." For an upper pipe in a modern CISC architecture, the full "U"+F_{reinit} can easily be 6+1=7 or higher. Thus, frequent reduction of "U" in this expression down to some perhaps fundamental residual minimum penalty, say just 1 or 2, can be very beneficial.

The Misprediction Recovery Cache (MRC) proposed in [1][2][3] is just such a special-purpose cache. Following most mispredictions, it will supply with very low latency the beginning of the program thread from the correct path. While this relatively short thread is drawn from the MRC, the fetch unit will be restarted at the program point just following the end of the thread. Then, when the thread ends, the source of material feeding the lower pipe will be switched back from the MRC to the regular upper pipe output.

Although the MRC uses a known architectural concept, the decoded instruction cache [9][10][11], to tackle a known architectural problem, branch misprediction penalty, it does so in a novel fashion. By selectively caching decoded instruction material, the MRC makes very efficient use of just a small decoded instruction cache. It need be large enough only to contain the beginning threads from the correct paths of a program's more commonly mispredicted branches. Branching statistics of x86 programs indicate that an MRC big enough to hold just 4-16 such thread starts can be extremely effective in reducing the average branch misprediction penalty.

The structure of the remainder of our paper is as follows. For a modern (CISC) microprocessor pipeline, Section 2 describes the addition/operation of the MRC. Section 3 discusses the x86 branch performance of the pipeline, first with BTB alone, then with an infinite-size MRC added, and finally with a finite-size MRC added. Section 4 compares the MRC with other schemes to cut branch misprediction penalty. Section 5 discusses our anticipated future MRC work. Section 6 presents our conclusions.

2 MRC Operation & Design

2.1 Modern CISC Pipeline w/o MRC

Examining Figure 1 in more detail, we see that the upper pipe begins with a look-ahead I Fetch stage. It keeps a buffer of prefetched instructions ready to decode. Then, up to n stages of decode steps follow where, for a CISC machine, n can easily be 3 or higher. The trend in modern CISC decoding is to break down each CISC operation into 1 or more "simple operations" that can each complete its specific execution work in 1 clock within simple but fast execution resources available in the lower pipe. After decode, the issue stage packs several simple ops together as a group that will subsequently execute in parallel in 1 clock on the set of execution resources. We will refer to this compacted grouping of simple ops as a "machine word" (MW). It is not uncommon for such a MW to need 50 or more bits per execution resource and for a complete machine word to be 256 bits or wider. Finally, to complete instruction preparation, a register fetch (R Fetch) stage retrieves needed register operands. (Read or write of any memory operand uses a separate load or store "simple op" that moves the operand to or from some register, respectively. The actual data memory hierarchy reference occurs in the execute phase of that "simple op" and can cause stage Execute to stall.)

Figure 1 makes it clear that modern microprocessors often spend as many or more steps preparing instructions as they spend actually executing them. Moreover, it seems likely that "U" will increase further with future pipeline sophistication. Without other architectural innovation, the average branch misprediction penalty will grow directly with "U." Thus, mechanisms like the MRC that reduce the average "U" experienced after branch misprediction will become increasingly attractive.

2.2 Pipeline with MRC Added

Figure 2 illustrates the basic coupling of a MRC with a modern, generic pipeline. The MRC's decoded instruction input comes from the output of the "issue" stage where "simple ops" have been packed appropriately to the machine's execution resources but data/operand fetching has not yet begun. The MRC can observe and record sequences of instruction stream activity, or program "threads," in decoded and compacted form. Although MRC entries contain just the beginnings of potentially infinite-length threads, we will call them simply "threads."

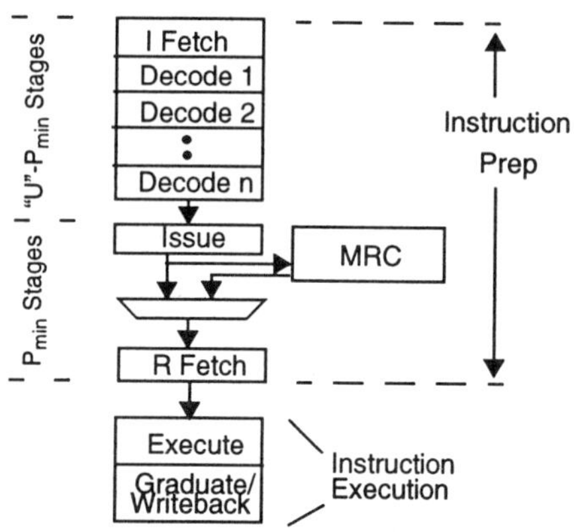

Figure 2: Basic MRC-to-Pipe Coupling

After the upper pipe has been flushed upon recognition of a branch as mispredicted, the multiplexor allows the MRC to replay a recorded thread. If the MRC holds the thread needed for recovery, the latency suffered until useful instruction material can again reach Execute will be just P_{min} stages, as implied in Figure 2.

Much discussion remaining in this Section 2.2, as well as in Section 2.3 and Section 2.5, involves tradeoffs revolving around the key MRC design issues of Table 1.

Table 1: Key MRC Design Issues

- MRC Interface
- Frequency Scalability
- MRC Entry Content
- Penalty Reduction per Thread
- MRC Addressing
- MRC Control
- Thread Length
- Thread Recording
- Thread Replay
- MRC Size
- Unique MRC Inefficiencies
- Adaptability to Existing Pipes
- Coherency
- Cost-Performance Variants

MRC Interface

Figure 3 illustrates more of the interconnection and interface detail needed to really integrate an MRC into a modern pipeline. Simplicity of MRC integration is highlighted by the fact that the surrounding components are virtually unchanged by its presence. Specifically, the "Branch Was Mispredicted" status signal and the "Corrected Target Address" coming from Execute are already needed by the conventional BTB and I Fetch unit. Similarly, the admittedly wide multiplexor above R Fetch and a simplified form of its selection control input are also typically present in CISC pipelines. Even without an MRC, the multiplexor supports use of microROM as an alternate source of control sequences for really complex CISC instructions. While the "Adjusted Target Address" produced by the MRC is a new input for I Fetch, it is treated by I Fetch just like its existing "Predicted Target Address" and "Corrected Target Address" inputs.

Frequency Scalability

We note here that assumption of *conservative, scalable design* principles would probably yield P_{min}=2. In Figure 3, a conservative design would assume that the "Corrected Target Address" produced in stage Execute is registered before use in accessing the MRC. Thus, two more clocks must next transpire, one to access the MRC and one to pass through stage R Fetch, before useful control material again reaches stage execute. By registering the corrected target address before use, we would achieve a design that easily tolerates today's roughly 200MHz frequencies and scales well to higher frequencies.

On the other hand, to realize a residual MRC penalty of just P_{min}=1, using this address before registration is not out of the question. Such an aggressive design would likely require customized circuitry in the MRC itself, in the illustrated multiplexor, and in stage Execute.

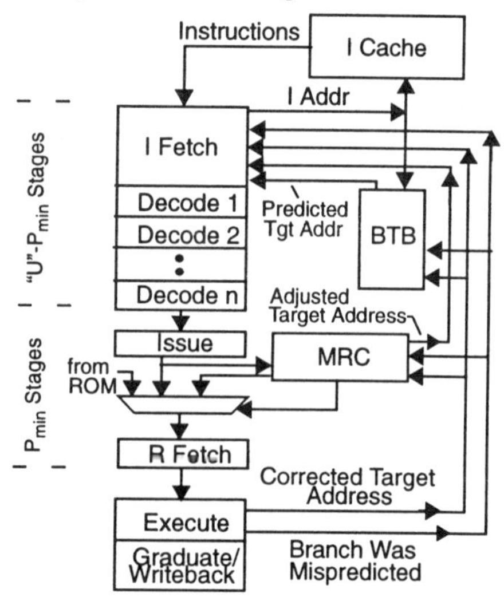

Figure 3: Pipe w MRC Integrated

In our accompanying experiments, we have generally calculated results based on assumed P_{min} values of both 1 and 2. This allows our work to be applicable to MRC implementations that range from conservative through aggressive.

2.3 MRC Operation and Structure

MRC Entry Content

Besides the program thread itself, each MRC entry will house other special fields (Figure 4). These fields will be used for functions such as redirecting/restarting the I Fetch unit (see "Adjusted Target Address" in Figure 3) and choosing which MRC entry to evict when replacement is necessary.

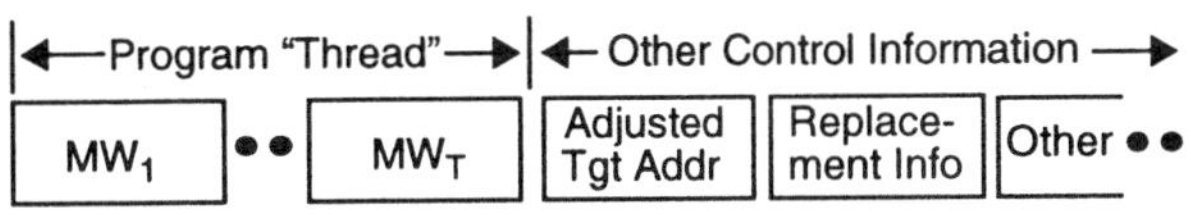

Figure 4: Structure of MRC Entry

Penalty Reduction per Thread

In an actual implementation, cached thread length may vary according to several design issues that we discuss later in more detail. However, one basic consideration is that branch misprediction penalty will be minimized whenever the "correct path" thread that the MRC provides is sufficiently long to keep the execute unit busy until stage Issue can start producing successor material to this cached thread. Thus, a conservative MRC design will cache threads that are long enough to accommodate all "U"-P_{min}+F_{reinit} clocks needed for the upper pipe stages above the MRC (Figure 3) to refill. Shorter threads would necessarily help less by alleviating just some of these "U" P_{min}+F_{reinit} clocks of penalty.

MRC Addressing

Hardware control of *where* to reference the MRC for a needed thread is straightforward. Unlike a BTB which typically locates entries based on the branch instruction address, threads stored in an MRC are best located according to the target address of the thread beginning. As stage Execute is producing the "Branch Was Mispredicted" indication, it is also computing the "Corrected Target Address" that is fed to the MRC to guide thread search.

MRC Control

Hardware control of *when* to reference the MRC for a needed thread is also very straightforward. The MRC will be referenced upon recognition of each and every branch misprediction by stage Execute. As Figure 3 implies, the "Branch Was Mispredicted" signal that already exists will be fed additionally to the MRC. While this signal is triggering the BTB to update the related misprediction entry and is triggering all "U" stages of the upper pipe to flush, it will also trigger a cache lookup within the MRC for the needed "other path" thread.

When MRC lookup yields a "hit," the mux of Figure 3 will be switched temporarily to provide MRC thread output to R Fetch. Also, the special "Adjusted Target Address" stored with this thread will be retrieved and fed to I Fetch to restart it just beyond the end of this thread. When the cached thread has been exhausted, the mux will be switched back to supply Issue output to R Fetch.

On the other hand, when MRC lookup yields a "miss," the mux of Figure 3 must remain unswitched so that Issue continues to supply R Fetch. When the first valid material again appears from Issue, the MRC will record the desired length thread for subsequent re-use. Recording will take place at the "Corrected Target Address" available from stage Execute. If, as statistics indicate is common, this same branch is later mispredicted again in the same fashion, this needed thread will likely still be in the MRC to provide a "hit" that reduces the penalty of each such subsequent misprediction to just P_{min} clocks.

2.4 MRC Operation Example

A simple example is now presented to help illustrate how the MRC achieves branch misprediction penalty reduction in support of real executing program code. Figure 5 illustrates C code utilizing a nested loop flow. Nested loops are a common structure for which MRC support can be tremendously beneficial.

```
outer_loop: for (i=1; i<=100; i++)
      { /* begin outer loop body */
                  .
      inner loop: for (j=1; j<=100; j++)
            { /* begin inner loop body */
                  .
            } /* end inner loop body */
                  .
      rare_path:  .
                  .
      } /* end outer loop body */
```

Figure 5: MRC Code Support Example

In Figure 5, for the backward conditional branch effecting the bottom of the inner loop, a typical modern BTB with a 2-bit history-based prediction algorithm would clearly settle into a "strongly taken" state as the loop executed through most of its 100 iterations. Then, as the 100th and final pass through the inner loop completes for the first time, this branch would be mispredicted still as "strongly taken." Subsequently, the pipe would be flushed, the history for this branch adjusted to (weakly) "taken," the MRC searched and "missed," and the upper pipe refilled from the beginning of "rare_path." The initial such refilling would suffer from a full "U"+F_{reinit} clocks of upper-pipe penalty *but the MRC would cache the first*

U-P_{min}+F_{reinit} clocks of this "other" thread that begins at "rare_path" as they come down the pipe.

When the inner loop is next re-entered, the BTB's prediction history state for the loop-bottom branch would correctly predict (weakly) "taken" on the first iteration, settle into "strongly taken" for the next 98 iterations, and then cause misprediction again, *just as before*, after the 100th and final iteration. However, *following this misprediction, the MRC search would yield "hit," the thread representing the beginning of rare_path would be replayed into the pipe, and would reach stage Execute after just P_{min} clocks of penalty.*

In fact, assuming that the thread representing the start of "rare_path" is not displaced from the MRC, *for all 99 exits of the inner loop following the first instance, the MRC would be "hit" and "U"-P_{min}+F_{reinit} clocks of upper-pipe refill penalty saved accordingly.* (Applied against this same code example, correlation-based predictors [7] tend to suffer the same misprediction pattern and, thus, experience the same MRC benefit.)

2.5 Other MRC Design Issues

Thread Length

As implied above, MRC threads of length T="U"-P_{min}+F_{reinit} clocks can always mask all possible penalty incurred in refilling the upper pipe stages above R Fetch. Threads longer than this will make the MRC bigger with no return benefit of further reducing/masking misprediction penalty. On the other hand, threads shorter than this will shrink the MRC but at the cost of allowing some of the otherwise maskable misprediction penalty to go unmasked.

Note that T="U"-P_{min}+F_{reinit} is a worst-case upper-bound on a fixed thread length that is long enough to mask all possible pipe penalty. If, as will sometimes happen, the lower execution-related pipe stalls temporarily during replay (from normal causes like a data cache miss), and if the upper pipe is capable of continuing during such a stall, as is common, then the upper pipe's production is given a chance to at least partially catch up with the lower pipe's consumption needs. In such instances, the replayed thread could be shortened by 1 MW for each clock of stall activity without permitting additional penalty to go unmasked. Advanced MRC designs can take advantage of this phenomenon by storing shorter threads that are *optimally sized* to mask only the typical, rather than worst-case, penalty.

Thread Recording

It will not be uncommon for one or more branch instructions to be encountered while recording. How should thread recording proceed after incorporation of a branch? Design alternatives include at least

1. building all threads to length T="U"-P_{min}+F_{reinit} by incorporating all encountered branches
1.a and, perhaps, cutting final word "U"-P_{min}+F_{reinit} after the last complete CISC instruction.
2. cutting all threads after the first branch.
3. cutting all threads after the nth branch.
4. cutting threads only after branches having very dynamic behavior, such as procedure returns.

Thread Replay

Recording approach 1, building all threads into Issue word "U"-P_{min}+F_{reinit}, will clearly form and cache threads that often contain 1 or more branches. If encountering these branches during "playback" meant suddenly calling upon the standard BTB, or maybe even some special extra BTB embedded within the MRC, to predict the flow of that branch, then playback using this approach would get complex. Indeed, it would tend to require extra prediction hardware, or complicate existing prediction hardware, or both. However, experimental results are showing that, for many/most branches, the original BTB-predicted flow that is statically snapshotted in the recorded MRC thread is *usually still the correct prediction for several subsequent encounters* of this same branch. Thus, a very viable replay approach is to play back each thread exactly as recorded, effectively reusing the original predictions for any embedded branches.

MRC Size

We are very encouraged that experimentation with recording approach 1 is indicating that a small MRC, containing on the order of just 4-16 threads, can be highly effective in reducing average branch misprediction penalty. This is true even though the simplistic approach 1 admittedly wastes some MRC space and replays some junk instruction material into the pipe.

How does silicon real estate consumed by an MRC compare to that of a BTB? Consider an MRC with 16 threads. Assume that a MW is 256 bits, or 32 bytes, and that each thread comprises 6 MWs, sized to mask worst-case penalty of an upper pipe with U=6, F_{reinit}=1, and P_{min}=1. Then, 16x6x32=3072 bytes are needed for basic thread MW content. To this, we must add, in each of the 16 threads, 4 bytes for the "Adjusted Target Address" and almost 4 bytes per tag, yielding nearly 3200 bytes altogether. Neglecting control circuitry, this makes a 16-entry MRC, worst-case, roughly equivalent to a 256-entry BTB in silicon area. Of course, if threads are sized to mask just the typical penalty, this MRC's size will drop accordingly. As we will see later in Figure 10, this 16-entry MRC can cancel about 46% of this BTB's residual penalty.

Unique MRC Inefficiencies

Regarding thread recording approaches, there are

definite tradeoffs to be considered between MRC design simplicity and MRC operation efficiency. Simplicity dictates a recording approach like 1 where threads are consistently recorded to "max length." However, with this approach, some embedded branches inevitably become "stale," thereafter guiding replay down no longer valid paths, and rendering the following subthreads junk. Additionally, embedding branches promotes some degree of wasteful "thread overlap," or partial inter-thread redundancy. With embedding, a small post-branch sequence of instructions can appear not only at the head of a recorded thread but also within the body of other threads, making some inter-thread redundancy generally unavoidable.

Adaptability to Existing Pipes

Like simplicity of thread recording and replay, ease of adaptation to existing pipelines is another design issue around which interesting potential tradeoffs revolve. When introducing Figure 3 earlier, we noted that an MRC can easily be adapted to an existing modern (CISC) pipeline. While this is generally true, the actual degree of ease does vary with the sophistication of the MRC implementation. For example, a simple MRC implementation that used approach 1.a for thread recording/replay and used standard LRU for thread replacement can be adapted with virtually no change to neighboring pipe components. However, if the thread recording/replay were changed instead to approach 1 for which threads may end in partially complete CISC instructions, then I Fetch would need to comprehend restarting at a specific "simple op" within a CISC instruction. This requirement would likely complicate design of 1 or more Decode stages. Similarly, if MRC replacement policy were refined to consider both a branch's prediction history and its BTB prediction state at replacement time, then the MRC would need visibility into BTB-internal state information. Providing this visibility to support sophisticated MRC replacement algorithms would necessarily complicate BTB design but might be justified for performance reasons.

Coherency

As a specialized form of an instruction cache, care must be taken to maintain MRC *coherency* with other stores of instruction material. Specifically, MRC coherency must be maintained with copies of instructions in main memory, with copies of instructions in the instruction cache, and with copies of the instructions already in the pipe but still not executed. The main threat to coherency among these many potential copies of instructions is *self-modifying code* which, at least in x86 legacy code, is common. Modern x86 processors essentially support snooping of both the instruction cache and the pre-execution instruction pipeline for possible address matches, or hits, with both externally generated and processor-internally-generated writes to memory. Checks over internally generated writes are employed to detect self-modifying code activity. Snoop hits within the instruction cache will generally cause selective invalidation of just the matching cache line while snoop hits within the pre-execution instruction pipe, for simplicity, will generally invalidate all still unexecuted instruction material within the pipe. While sophisticated, fine-grained snooping of the MRC could also be added, the MRC's generally small size makes such sophistication impractical. Instead, one simple yet still efficient enough scheme for most MRC sizes would be to simply invalidate the entire MRC whenever snoop of the regular instruction cache or the pre-execution instruction pipe detects a hit in either.

Cost-Performance Variants

In general, several *cost-performance variations* will be possible for an MRC implementation. Some designs may need to opt for the highest possible MRC performance (i.e., greatest possible reduction in average branch misprediction penalty) at the cost of extra hardware complexity in the forms we have been discussing. These more sophisticated MRC implementations will require both more complexity within the MRC itself and more invasiveness of existing pipeline hardware with which the MRC interacts. On the other hand, designs stressing low cost may need to settle for the simpler MRC implementations that sacrifice some performance to retain maximal hardware simplicity. Experimentation to date (with x86 code) is showing that even the simplest MRC implementation can yield significant performance benefit.

3 Baseline MRC Performance

3.1 X86 Simulation Experiments

We assessed MRC usefulness via a trace-based performance model [12] of a microprocessor design comprising a moderate-depth pipeline, 2-bit branch predictor, 4 integer execution resources, and on-chip instruction and data caches. We evaluated x86 traces on this performance model, both with and without MRC, and collected the necessary statistics.

MRC performance reported in this paper is based largely on the SPECint92 benchmarks but also on early work with Winstone96, particularly with Microsoft "Word" 6.0c. The SPECint92 traces were generated by running the subject programs on a PC under DOS after compilation with the gcc compiler from DJGPP.

3.2 Branch Performance w/o MRC

Let us first examine our pipeline's branch performance with no MRC present. Table 2 shows that our baseline 2-bit branch predictor performs about as expected, achieving misprediction rates ranging from 16.7% for gcc to 4.0% for sc, with an average misprediction rate of 9.1%.

Table 2: Branch Misprediction Rates

Program	Misprediction Rate
compress	9.1%
eqntott	5.9%
espresso	9.6%
gcc	16.7%
li	9.0%
sc	4.0%
Average	9.1%

However, even with less than 10% mispredictions occurring, the residual misprediction penalty which these programs incur still deteriorates processor performance significantly. In effect, branch misprediction penalty is a wasted fraction of the overall cpi expended in running these programs. For U=6, F_{reinit}=1, Figure 6 shows the total cpi for our model classified as *nor*mal processing, *br*anch misprediction penalty, and *mem*ory access wait cycles (imperfect cache). Of the total processing cycles expended, *nor* processing consumes about 70%, *br* consumes about 13%, and *mem* consumes about 17%. Together, *br* and *mem* waste about 30% of the overall processing effort while, alone, *br* wastes a quite significant 13%. In operation, an MRC can directly tackle and eliminate much of this last category of waste.

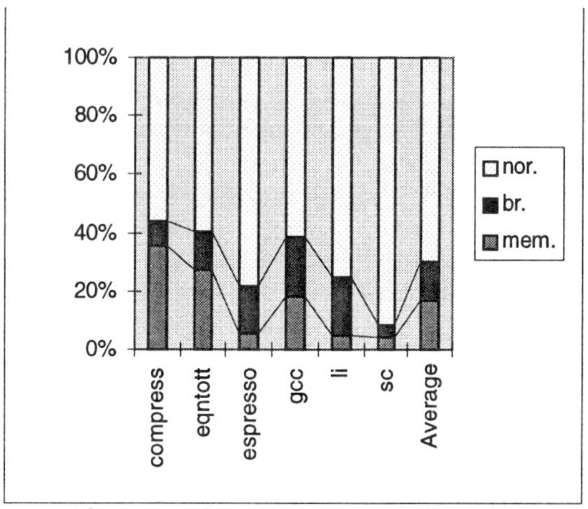

Figure 6: Components of Total CPI

Figure 7 breaks down the total set of mispredicted branch instructions into two categories: branches that are repeatedly mispredicted over program life and branches that are mispredicted just once over program life. Figure 7 clearly shows that *most mispredictions are caused by branches that have been mispredicted before*. This behavior suggests that an MRC which usually holds the needed recovery thread can support significant penalty reduction.

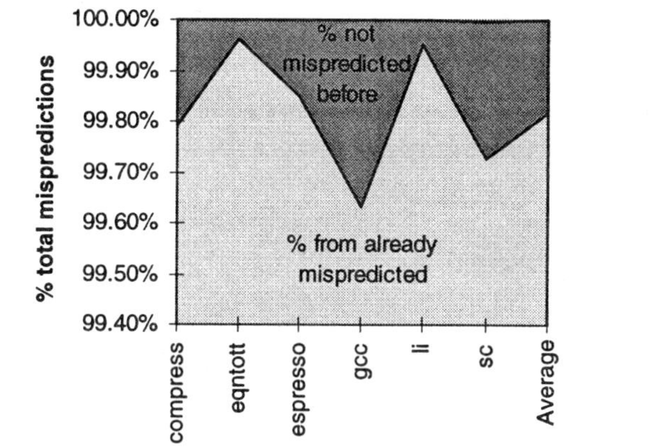

Figure 7: % Mispredictions Repeated

3.3 MRC Performance Parameters

3.3.1 Effective Thread Length

During thread replay, Execute cycles wasted equal

$$P_{min} + ((U-P_{min}+F_{reinit}) - \min(U-P_{min}+F_{reinit}, T_{eff}^{2}))$$

where the complex expression in parentheses represents the amount of pipe penalty, above P_{min}, that thread replay leaves still unmasked. T_{eff}, *effective thread length,* is the number of thread (machine) words that, during replay, actually succeed in masking penalty clocks. Even with threads recorded to maximal penalty masking length $T=U-P_{min}+F_{reinit}$, realized T_{eff} is often smaller because of thread-embedded branches that replay as mispredictions. Only the replay cycles prior to the first such misprediction can help mask and alleviate penalty cycles.

A conservative design response to this threat to thread effectiveness might be to cut all MRC threads, while recording, either after word $U-P_{min}+F_{reinit}$ or after the nth branch, whichever occurs first. Less conservative designs would allow larger n, while more conservative designs would cut at some small n. For U=6, P_{min}=1, Figure 8 shows how T_{eff} approaches $T=T_{eff\ max}$ as branches are included. Improvement to T_{eff} is strong for the first branch or two but then slows. MRC performance simulations show that conservative precutting of threads is generally not justified until, perhaps, U becomes quite large.

3.3.2 Hit Rate

Hit rate is the average percentage of MRC accesses, following misprediction, that succeed in finding the needed thread. This percentage determines how much of the MRC's penalty cancellation potential is realized.

2. This formula yields a minimum residual penalty of P_{min} when $T_{eff} >= U-P_{min}+F_{reinit}$. It yields a maximum penalty of $U+F_{reinit}$ when $T_{eff} = 0$.

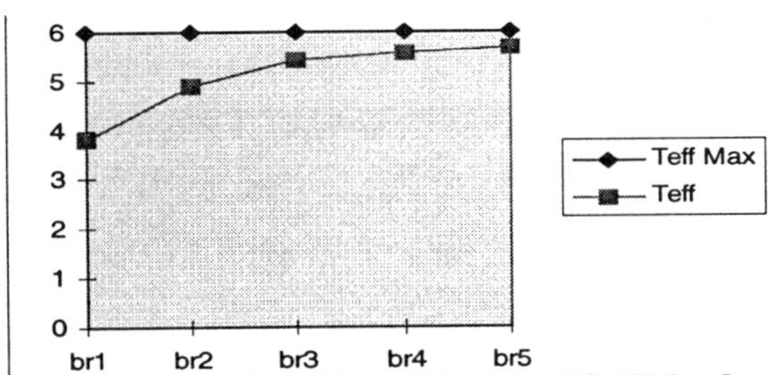

Figure 8: T_{eff}: Recording to Min[T, br_n]

3.3.3 Penalty Reduction Factor

Penalty reduction factor (PRF) is the ratio of misprediction penalty reduction achieved with a MRC to overall misprediction penalty without a MRC, or

$$PRF = \frac{Penalty_{w/o\ MRC} - Penalty_{w\ MRC}}{Penalty_{w/o\ MRC}}$$

We use PRF as a primary indicator of MRC performance. Intuitively, if the negative numerator term, $Penalty_{w\ MRC}$, can be driven to 0 by a superb MRC, then PRF -> 1, implying reduction of all possible penalty. Also intuitively, as $Penalty_{w\ MRC}$ gets larger and approaches $Penalty_{w/o\ MRC}$ for an inefficient MRC, then PRF -> 0. In truly pathological circumstances, $Penalty_{w\ MRC}$ can actually surpass $Penalty_{w/o\ MRC}$ in magnitude, thereby driving PRF below 0. We explain below.

3.3.4 Misprediction Inflation Factor

Bear in mind that observed MRC performance parameters naturally comprehend *all* MRC accesses. Because MRC-replayed branches will be at least slightly more inaccurate than BTB predictions, the total misprediction activity experienced by the pipe tends to inflate somewhat with the MRC operating.

We will use the term *misprediction inflation factor* (MIF) to refer to the ratio

$$MIF = \frac{Mispredictions_{w\ MRC}}{Mispredictions_{w/o\ MRC}}$$

MIF ranges upward from an ideal minimum of 1.

Intuitively, we expect misprediction inflation to contribute to some MRC inefficiency. To check our intuition, let's investigate how MIF affects MRC performance as measured by PRF. Substituting architectural detail into the PRF expression above and simplifying, we derive

$$PRF=1 - MIF * \{1 - Hit\ Rate_{w\ MRC} * \frac{T_{eff}}{U + F_{reinit}}\}$$

PRF is here expressed as its ideal value, 1, minus a complex expression representing real-world inefficiencies that deteriorate PRF. The magnitude of the overall deterioration tends to grow with increasing MIF, but typically leaves PRF at a net value between 0 and 1. For an MRC that is well tuned to its parent pipe and workload, MIF approaches 1 from above while both $T_{eff} / (U + F_{reinit})$ and $HitRate_{w\ MRC}$ approach 1 from below, making PRF approach 1 from below. However, in ill-suited operating environments with increasing degrees of replay misprediction, these terms trend the other way, making PRF trend downward toward 0. In pathological circumstances, PRF can even go negative, indicating that the MRC is actually hurting overall performance. However, our experiments show that, in most operating environments, proper MRC designs can deliver consistent performance improvement.

3.4 Branch Performance w MRC

3.4.1 Infinite MRC

We first investigate the performance possible with an infinite MRC, having unlimited thread storage. This helps us determine the performance limits which a highly optimized implementation of a finite-size MRC can approach.

For three mid-range pipe sizes of U=5, U=6, U=7, and assuming $P_{min=1}$, F_{reinit}=1, Table 3 presents the thread replay effectiveness, T_{eff}, realized for the SPECint92 programs and for "MS Word 6.0c." For correlation, Table 3 also shows the corresponding inter-branch distance of these programs. All threads were recorded to maximal penalty masking length

$T=U-P_{min}+F_{reinit}=T_{eff\ max}$.

Table 3: Infinite MRC: T_{eff}, P_{min}=1

Program	Avg MWs between branches	(T_{eff} = Penalty Saved per Replay)		
		U=5 F=1 T=5	U=6 F=1 T=6	U=7 F=1 T=7
compress	4.02	4.59	5.44	6.26
eqntott	3.26	4.47	5.23	5.93
espresso	4.26	4.97	5.94	6.90
gcc	3.93	4.88	5.80	6.70
li	3.59	4.84	5.68	6.51
sc	4.10	4.94	5.87	6.80
Average	3.86	4.79	5.66	6.52
MS Word	4.51	4.71	5.58	6.43

From Table 3, since T_{eff} for all three pipe sizes exceeds the average inter-branch distance, threads will often contain some embedded branches. Further, because T_{eff} is always near $T=T_{eff\ max}$, such branch embedding is generally beneficial. Specifically, Table 3 indicates that, for the three pipe sizes, thread replay respectively masks 4.79 of 5, 5.66 of 6, and 6.52 of 7 residual penalty clocks, on average for SPECint92, and 4.71 of 5, 5.58 of 6, and 6.43 of 7 clocks for MS "Word" 6.0c.

Table 4 continues with Hit Rate, PRF, and MIF for these same benchmarks. Hit Rates show that, as expected, an infinite MRC holds the needed thread for 98%-99% of the overall branch mispredictions. MIF shows the MRC slightly inflating its own activity to 1.15.

Table 4: Infinite MRC: PRF, P_{min}=1

Program	Hit Rate	PRF	MIF
compress	99.8%	0.73	1.19
eqntott	99.9%	0.67	1.30
espresso	99.8%	0.84	1.05
gcc	99.6%	0.80	1.12
li	99.9%	0.78	1.18
sc	99.7%	0.82	1.08
Average	99.8%	0.78	1.15
MS Word	98.2%	0.75	1.16

For an infinite MRC, Figure 9 displays PRF for both P_{min}=1 and P_{min}=2. The extremes of penalty reduction in Figure 9 range from about 52% for eqntott when P_{min}=2 to about 84% for espresso when P_{min}=1. Overall, for the SPECint92 "Average," penalty is reduced by 63%-78%. For MS "Word" 6.0c, penalty is reduced by 61%-75%.

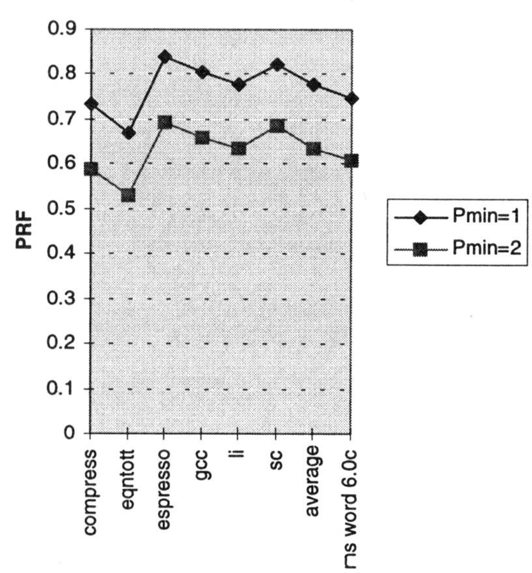

Figure 9: Infinite MRC: PRF

3.4.2 Finite-Size MRC

In finite MRCs, thread storage is limited. We repeated the same experiments as just described to compute PRF for both an aggressive P_{min}=1 and a conservative P_{min}=2, but now modeling the MRC at various fixed sizes. Figure 10 shows that, on "average" over SPEC, *even with just 16 threads, a conservative MRC eliminates 38% while an aggressive MRC eliminates 46% of the BTB-residual misprediction penalty.*

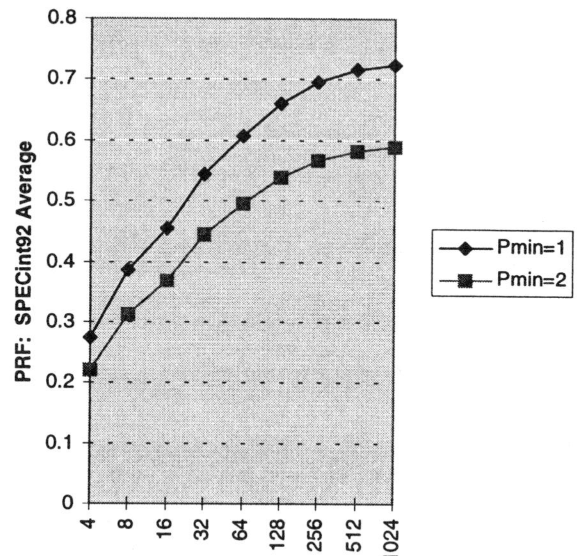

Figure 10: Finite MRC: PRF vs. Size

Preliminary results with MS Word 6.0c suggest that, to reach this same efficiency in some operating environments, slightly larger finite MRC sizes, or other MRC algorithmic refinements, may be needed. As more and more workloads are examined in future MRC work, we believe it likely that some refinements will be dictated to help maximize MRC efficiency across varied environments.

4 Related Work

The MRC supports reduction of branch misprediction penalty in a fashion that is, at worst, orthogonal to, and, at best, aided by other applicable branch misprediction penalty minimization techniques and other general performance enhancement techniques. For example, whether complementing a single-level BTB, two-level BTB, or even more advanced BTB, the MRC will work effectively to reduce the residual branch misprediction penalty. Likewise, the MRC can work with or without branch removal and "shadow" predication [13][14], and with or without earlier-than-Execute resolution of some branches [15]. Finally, we note that new compiler optimizations that eliminate many branches to form larger "super blocks"

[16] will yield executable code with increased average inter-branch distance, which then yields more efficient MRC threads with fewer embedded branches.

5 Future Work

Although results of our early MRC work are encouraging, much more remains to be done. We expect our future work to stress four areas: expansion of MRC analysis to cover *more branch predictor algorithms*, expansion of MRC analysis to cover *more workloads* (beyond SPEC and part of Winstone96), determination of *optimal thread length* at which threads efficiently mask only the typical penalty, and investigation of possible *smart algorithms* for various facets of MRC operation.

Because of the limited space in a small, finite-size MRC, smart algorithms seem potentially attractive in three areas. *Smart placement* will allow intelligent filtration of all candidate threads before permitting any to be cached, avoiding so-called "pollution"[17]. *Smart replacement* will allow intelligent selection of the thread to be evicted when placement of a new thread needs room. *Smart replay* will address replay policies beyond just unconditionally replaying threads exactly as recorded. For example, the BTB might observe all thread replay so that it can "check" replayed branches. "Disagreement" might then cause abortion of further replay and upper pipe restart/ continuation at the BTB's predicted target.

6 Conclusions

The Misprediction Recovery Cache (MRC) [1][2][3] is a promising new mechanism for reduction of branch misprediction penalty. In this paper, we have focused on integration of the MRC into modern pipelines. We have seen that the MRC can be implemented in many performance configurations. It can attack branch misprediction penalty stand-alone or in conjunction with other techniques such as branch removal. The MRC can have significant impact even at sizes as small as just 4-16 threads.

The MRC is best viewed, not as a substitute for good branch prediction, but as a complementary tool to apply where branch prediction stops. With efficient implementations of two-level branch prediction algorithms becoming common, it makes good sense to employ such algorithms in new designs. However, no matter how sophisticated the prediction algorithm, it also makes good sense to attack the residual penalty with a complementary MRC.

7 Acknowledgments

We gratefully acknowledge consultation from Texas Instruments colleague Don Steiss. Anonymous reviewer comments were also helpful.

8 References

[1] A.K. Nanda, J.O. Bondi, and S. Dutta, "Misprediction Recovery Cache (MRC): Concept, Analysis, and Design" TI-Internal Technical Paper, Jun. 1996, pp. 1-30.

[2] J.O. Bondi, S. Dutta, and A.K. Nanda, "Pipelined Microprocessor with Branch Misprediction Cache Circuits, Systems, and Methods," patent application TI-22458, Jun. 1996.

[3] A.K. Nanda, S. Dutta, and J.O. Bondi, "Misprediction Recovery Cache (MRC): A New Mechanism for Minimizing Branch Misprediction Penalty," submitted to *HPCA 3*.

[4] J.E. Smith, "A Study of Branch Prediction Strategies," *Proc. ISCA*, May 1981, pp. 135-148.

[5] J. Lee and A.J. Smith, "Branch Prediction Strategies and Branch Target Buffer Design," *Computer*,Jan.1984,pp.6-22.

[6] T-Y. Yeh and Y.N.Patt, "Two-Level Adaptive Training Branch Prediction," *Proc. Micro-24*, Nov. 1991, pp. 51-61.

[7] S.T. Pan, K. So, and J.T. Rahmeh, "Improving the Accuracy of Dynamic Branch Prediction Using Branch Correlation," *Proc. ASPLOS-V*, Oct. 1992, pp. 76-84.

[8] S. Dutta and M. Franklin, "Control Flow Prediction with Tree-Like Subgraphs for Superscalar Processors," *Proc. Micro-28*, Dec. 1995, pp. 258-263.

[9] W-M. Hwu and Y.N. Patt, "HPSm, A High Performance Restricted Data Flow Architecture Having Minimal Functionality," *Proc. ISCA*, Tokyo, 1986, pp. 297-306.

[10] S.W. Melvin, M.C. Shebanow, and Y.N. Patt, "Hardware Support for Large Atomic Units in Dynamically Scheduled Machines," *Proc.Micro-21*, San Diego, Dec.1988, pp.60-66

[11] M. Smotherman and M. Franklin, "Improving CISC Instruction Decoding Performance Using a Fill Unit," *Proc. Micro-28*, Dec. 1995, pp. 219-229.

[12] A.K. Nanda et al, "Improving the Accuracy of ... Performance Modeling Tools," TI-Internal Technical Paper, 1995.

[13] G.S. Tyson, "The Effects of Predicated Execution on Branch Prediction," *Micro-27*, Nov. 1994, pp. 196-206.

[14] S.A. Mahlke et al, "Characterizing the Impact of Predicated Execution on Branch Prediction," *Proc. Micro-27*, Nov. 1994, pp. 217-227.

[15] S. Song, M. Denman, and J. Chang, "The PowerPC 604 RISC Microprocessor," *IEEE Micro*, Oct. 1994, pp. 8-17.

[16] W.W.Hwu et al, "Compiler Technology for Future Microprocessors," *Proc. of the IEEE*, Dec. 1995, pp. 1625-1640.

[17] S.J. Walsh and J.A. Board, "Pollution Control Caching," *Proc. ICCD '95*, Oct. 1995, pp. 300-306.

Trace Cache: a Low Latency Approach to High Bandwidth Instruction Fetching

Eric Rotenberg
Computer Science Dept.
Univ. of Wisconsin - Madison
ericro@cs.wisc.edu

Steve Bennett
Intel Corporation
sbennett@ichips.intel.com

James E. Smith
Dept. of Elec. and Comp. Engr.
Univ. of Wisconsin - Madison
jes@ece.wisc.edu

Abstract

As the issue width of superscalar processors is increased, instruction fetch bandwidth requirements will also increase. It will become necessary to fetch multiple basic blocks per cycle. Conventional instruction caches hinder this effort because long instruction sequences are not always in contiguous cache locations.

We propose supplementing the conventional instruction cache with a trace cache. This structure caches traces of the dynamic instruction stream, so instructions that are otherwise noncontiguous appear contiguous. For the Instruction Benchmark Suite (IBS) and SPEC92 integer benchmarks, a 4 kilobyte trace cache improves performance on average by 28% over conventional sequential fetching. Further, it is shown that the trace cache's efficient, low latency approach enables it to outperform more complex mechanisms that work solely out of the instruction cache.

1. Introduction

High performance superscalar processor organizations divide naturally into an instruction fetch mechanism and an instruction execution mechanism (Figure 1). The fetch and execution mechanisms are separated by instruction issue buffer(s), for example queues, reservation stations, etc. Conceptually, the instruction fetch mechanism acts as a "producer" which fetches, decodes, and places instructions into the buffer. The instruction execution engine is the "consumer" which removes instructions from the buffer and executes them, subject to data dependence and resource constraints. Control dependences (branches and jumps) provide a feedback mechanism between the producer and consumer.

Processors having this organization employ aggressive techniques to exploit instruction-level parallelism. Wide dispatch and issue paths place an upper bound on peak instruction throughput. Large issue buffers are used to maintain a *window* of instructions necessary for detecting parallelism, and a large pool of physical registers provides destinations for all the in-flight instructions issued from the window.

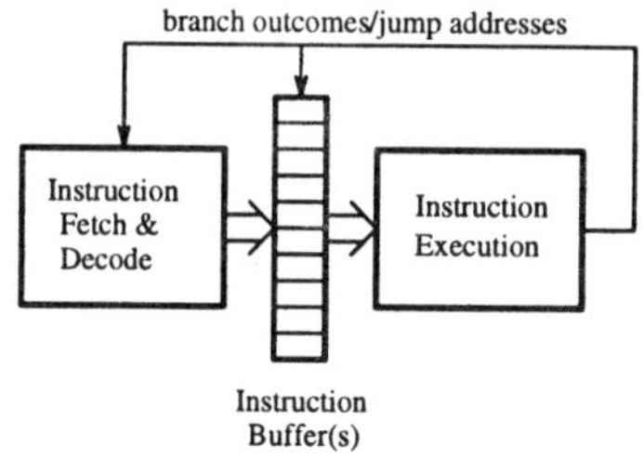

Figure 1. Decoupled fetch/execute engines.

To enable concurrent execution of instructions, the execution engine is composed of many parallel functional units. The fetch engine speculates past multiple branches in order to supply a continuous instruction stream to the window.

The trend in superscalar design is to increase the scale of these techniques: wider dispatch/issue, larger windows, more physical registers, more functional units, and deeper speculation. To maintain this trend, it is important to balance all parts of the processor – any bottlenecks diminish the benefit of aggressive ILP techniques.

In this paper, we are concerned with instruction fetch bandwidth becoming a performance bottleneck. Instruction fetch performance depends on a number of factors. Instruction cache hit rate and branch prediction accuracy have long been recognized as important problems in fetch performance and are well-researched areas. In this paper, we are interested in additional factors that are only now emerging as processor issue rates exceed four instructions per cycle:

- *branch throughput* – If only one conditional branch is predicted per cycle, then the window can grow at the rate of only one basic block per cycle. Predicting multiple branches per cycle allows the overall instruction throughput to be correspondingly higher.
- *noncontiguous instruction alignment* – Because of branches and jumps, instructions to be fetched during any given cycle may not be in contiguous cache locations. Hence, there must be adequate paths and logic available to fetch and align noncontiguous basic blocks and pass them up the pipeline. That is, it is not enough

1072-4451/96 $5.00 © 1996 IEEE

for the instructions to be present in the cache, it must also be possible to access them in parallel.

- *fetch unit latency* – Pipeline latency has a profound impact on processor performance. This is due to the cost of refilling the pipeline after incorrect control speculation. In the case of the fetch unit, we are concerned with the startup cost of redirecting fetching after resolving a branch misprediction, jump, or instruction cache miss. Inevitably, the need for higher branch throughput and noncontiguous instruction alignment will increase fetch unit latency; yet ways must be found to minimize the latency impact.

Current fetch units are limited to one branch prediction per cycle and can therefore fetch 1 basic block per cycle or up to the maximum instruction fetch width, whichever is smaller. The data in Table 1 shows that the average size of basic blocks is around 4 or 5 instructions for integer codes. While fetching a single basic block each cycle is sufficient for implementations that issue at most 4 instructions per cycle, it is not so for processors with higher peak issue rates. If we introduce multiple branch prediction [1][16], then the fetch unit can at least fetch multiple *contiguous* basic blocks in a cycle. Data for the number of instructions between taken branches shows that the upper bound on fetch bandwidth is still somewhat limited in this case, due to the frequency of taken branches. Therefore, if a taken branch is encountered, it is necessary to fetch instructions down the taken path in the same cycle that the branch is fetched.

Benchmark	taken %	avg basic block size	# instr between taken branches
eqntott	86.2%	4.20	4.87
espresso	63.8%	4.24	6.65
xlisp	64.7%	4.34	6.70
gcc	67.6%	4.65	6.88
sc	70.2%	4.71	6.71
compress	60.9%	5.39	8.85

Table 1. Branch and basic block statistics.

1.1. The trace cache

The job of the fetch unit is to feed the dynamic instruction stream to the decoder. A problem is that instructions are placed in the cache in their compiled order. Storing programs in static form favors fetching code that does not branch or code with large basic blocks. Neither of these cases is typical of integer code.

We propose a special instruction cache which captures dynamic instruction sequences. This structure is called a *trace cache* because each line stores a snapshot, or trace, of the dynamic instruction stream, as shown in Figure 2. A trace is a sequence of at most n instructions and at most m basic blocks starting at any point in the dynamic instruction stream. The limit n is the trace cache line size, and m is the branch predictor throughput. A trace is fully specified by a starting address and a sequence of up to $m-1$ branch outcomes which describe the path followed. The first time a trace is encountered, it is allocated a line in the trace cache. The line is filled as instructions are fetched from the instruction cache. If the same trace is encountered again in the course of executing the program, i.e. the same starting address and predicted branch outcomes, it will be available in the trace cache and is fed directly to the decoder. Otherwise, fetching proceeds normally from the instruction cache.

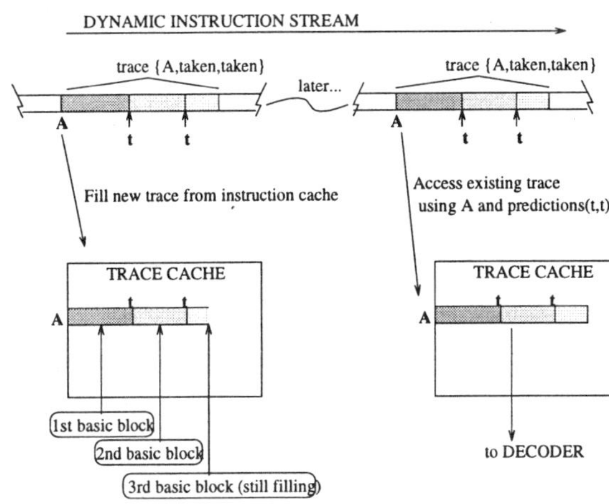

Figure 2. High level view of the trace cache.

The trace cache approach relies on dynamic sequences of code being reused. This may be the case for two reasons:

- *temporal locality* – like the primary instruction cache, the trace cache can count on instructions which have been recently used being used again in the near future.
- *branch behavior* – most branches tend to be biased towards one direction, which is why branch prediction accuracy is usually high. Thus, it is likely that certain paths through the control flow graph will be followed frequently.

1.2. Related prior work

Three recent studies have focused on high bandwidth instruction fetching and are closely related to the research reported here. All of these attempt to fetch multiple, possibly noncontiguous basic blocks each cycle from the instruction cache.

First, Yeh, Marr, and Patt [16] consider a fetch mechanism that provides high bandwidth by predicting multiple branch target addresses every cycle. The method features a *Branch Address Cache*, a natural extension of the branch target buffer [8]. With a branch target buffer, a single branch prediction and a BTB hit produces the starting address of the next basic block. Similarly, a hit in the branch address cache combined with multiple branch predictions produces the starting addresses of the next *several* basic blocks. These addresses are fed into a highly interleaved instruction cache to fetch multiple basic blocks in a single cycle.

A second study by Franklin and Dutta [2] uses a similar approach to the branch address cache (providing multiple branch targets), but with a new method for predicting multiple branches in a single cycle. Their approach hides multiple individual branch predictions within a single prediction; e.g. rather than make 2 branch predictions, make 1 prediction that selects from among 4 paths. This enables the use of more accurate two-level predictors.

Another hardware scheme proposed by Conte, Mills, Menezes, and Patel [1] uses two passes through an interleaved branch target buffer. Each pass through the branch target buffer produces a fetch address, allowing two non-adjacent cache lines to be fetched. In addition, the interleaved branch target buffer enables detection of any number of branches in a cache line. In particular, the design is able to detect short forward branches within a line and eliminate instructions between the branch and its target using a *collapsing buffer*. The work also proposes compiler techniques to reduce the frequency of taken branches.

Two previously proposed hardware structures are similar to the trace cache but exist in different applications. The fill unit, proposed by Melvin, Shebanow and Patt [10], caches RISC-like instructions which are derived from a CISC instruction stream. This predecoding eased the problem of supporting a complex instruction set such as VAX on the HPS restricted dataflow engine. Franklin and Smotherman [3] extended the fill unit's role to dynamically assemble VLIW-like instruction words from a RISC instruction stream, which are then stored in a *shadow cache*. The goal of this structure is to ease the issue complexity of a wide issue processor.

1.3. Problems with other fetch mechanisms

Recall that the job of the fetch unit is to feed the dynamic instruction stream to the decoder. Unlike the trace cache approach, previous designs have only the conventional instruction cache, containing a static form of the program, to work with. Every cycle, instructions from noncontiguous locations must be fetched from the instruction cache and assembled into the predicted dynamic sequence. There are problems with this approach:

- Pointers to all of the noncontiguous instruction blocks must be generated before fetching can begin. This implies a level of indirection, through some form of branch target table (e.g. branch target buffer), which translates into an additional pipeline stage before the instruction cache.
- The instruction cache must support simultaneous access to multiple, noncontiguous cache lines. This forces the cache to be multiported; if multiporting is done through interleaving, bank conflicts will occur.
- After fetching the noncontiguous instructions from the cache, they must be assembled into the dynamic sequence. Instructions must be shifted and aligned to make them appear contiguous to the decoder. This most likely translates into an additional pipeline stage after the instruction cache.

The trace cache approach avoids these problems by caching dynamic instruction sequences themselves, ready for the decoder. If the predicted dynamic sequence exists in the trace cache, it does not have to be recreated on the fly from the instruction cache's static representation. In particular, no additional stages before or after the instruction cache are needed for fetching noncontiguous instructions. The stages do exist, but not on the critical path of the fetch unit – rather, on the fill side of the trace cache. The cost of this approach is redundant instruction storage: the same instructions may reside in both the primary cache and the trace cache, and there might even be redundancy among lines in the trace cache.

1.4. Contributions

As with prior work in high bandwidth instruction fetching, this paper demonstrates the importance of fetching past multiple possibly-taken branches each cycle. Unlike other work in the area, we place equal emphasis on fetch unit latency. The end result is the trace cache as a means for low latency, high bandwidth instruction fetching.

Another contribution is a detailed simulation study comparing proposed high bandwidth fetch mechanisms including the trace cache. Previously, the approaches described in Section 1.2 could not be directly compared due to different experimental setups – different ISAs, processor execution models, branch predictors, caches, workloads, and metrics.

In the course of this work, many microarchitectural and logic design issues arose. We looked at issues for not only the trace cache, but other proposed mechanisms as well. The results of this detailed study are documented in [12].

1.5. Paper overview

In the next section the trace cache fetch unit is described in detail. Section 3 follows up with an analysis of other proposed high bandwidth fetch mechanisms. In Section 4 we describe the simulation methodology including the processor model, workload, and performance metric. Simulation results are presented in Section 5. As part of the study in Section 5, we compare the trace cache with previously proposed high performance fetch mechanisms.

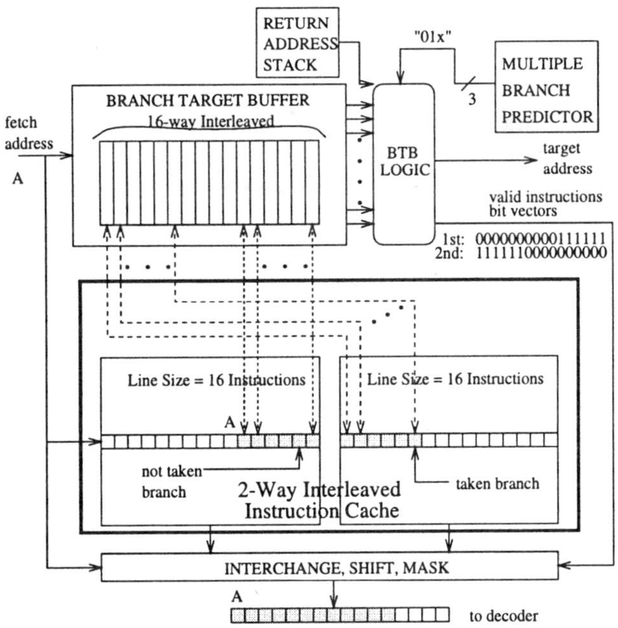

Figure 3. The core fetch unit.

2. Trace cache

In Section 1.1 we introduced the concept of the trace cache – an instruction cache which captures dynamic instruction sequences. We now present a trace cache implementation. Because the trace cache is not intended to replace the conventional instruction cache or the fetch hardware around it, we begin with a description of the core fetch mechanism. We then show how the core fetch unit is augmented with the trace cache.

2.1. Core fetch unit

The core fetch unit is implemented using established hardware schemes. It is called *interleaved sequential* in [1]. Fetching up to the first predicted taken branch each cycle can be done using the combination of an accurate multiple branch predictor [16], an interleaved branch target buffer (BTB) [1][8], a return address stack (RAS) [6], and a 2-way interleaved instruction cache [1][4]. Refer to Figure 3.

The core fetch unit is designed to fetch as many contiguous instructions possible, up to a maximum instruction limit and a maximum branch limit. The instruction constraint is imposed by the width of the datapath, and the branch constraint is imposed by the branch predictor throughput. For demonstration, a fetch limit of 16 instructions and 3 branches is used throughout.

The cache is interleaved so that 2 consecutive cache lines can be accessed; this allows fetching sequential code that spans a cache line boundary, always guaranteeing a full cache line or up to the first taken branch [4]. This scheme requires minimal complexity for aligning instructions: (1) logic to swap the order of the two cache lines (interchange switch), (2) a left-shifter to align the instructions into a 16-wide instruction latch, and (3) logic to mask off unused instructions.

All banks of the BTB are accessed in parallel with the instruction cache. They serve the role of (1) detecting branches in the instructions currently being fetched and (2) providing their target addresses, in time for the next fetch cycle. The BTB must be n-way interleaved, where n is the number of instructions in a cache line. This is so that all instructions within a cache line can be checked for branches in parallel [1]. The BTB can detect other types of control transfer instructions as well. If a jump is detected, the jump address may be predicted. (Jump target predictions are not considered in this paper, however.) Return addresses can almost always be obtained with no penalty by using a call/return stack. If the BTB detects a return in the instructions being fetched, it pops the address at the top of the RAS.

Notice in Figure 3 that the branch predictor is separate from the BTB. This is to allow for predictors that are more accurate than the 1-bit or 2-bit counters normally stored with each branch entry in the BTB. While storing counters with each branch achieves multiple branch prediction trivially, branch prediction accuracy is limited. Branch prediction is fundamental to ILP, and should have precedence over other factors. For high branch prediction accuracy, we use a 4kB GAg(14) correlated branch predictor [15]. The 14 bit global branch history register indexes into a single pattern history table. This predictor was chosen for its accuracy and because it is more easily extended to multiple branch predictions than other predictors which require address information [16][2]. Multiporting the pattern history table and changing its organization slightly extends the single correlated branch predictor to multiple predictions each cycle, as proposed in [16]. (Refer to [12] for an implementation.)

BTB logic combines the BTB hit information with the branch predictions to produce the next fetch address, and to generate trailing zeroes in the *valid instruction bit vectors* (if there is a predicted taken branch). The leading zeroes in the valid instruction bit vectors are determined by the low-order bits of the current fetch address. The masking logic is controlled by these bit vectors.

Both the interchange and shift logic are controlled by the low-order bits of the current fetch address. *This is a key point: the left-shift amount is known at the beginning of the fetch cycle, and has the entire cache access to fanout to the shifter datapath.* Further, if a transmission gate barrel shifter is used, instructions pass through only one transmission gate delay with a worst case capacitive loading of 15 other transmission gates on both input and output. In summary, control is not on the critical path, and datapath delay is minimal. Therefore, in our simulations we treat the core fetch unit as a single pipeline stage.

2.2. Adding the trace cache

The core fetch unit can only fetch contiguous sequences of instructions, i.e. it cannot fetch past a taken branch in the same cycle that the branch is fetched. The trace cache provides this additional capability. The trace cache together with the core fetch unit is shown in Figure 4.

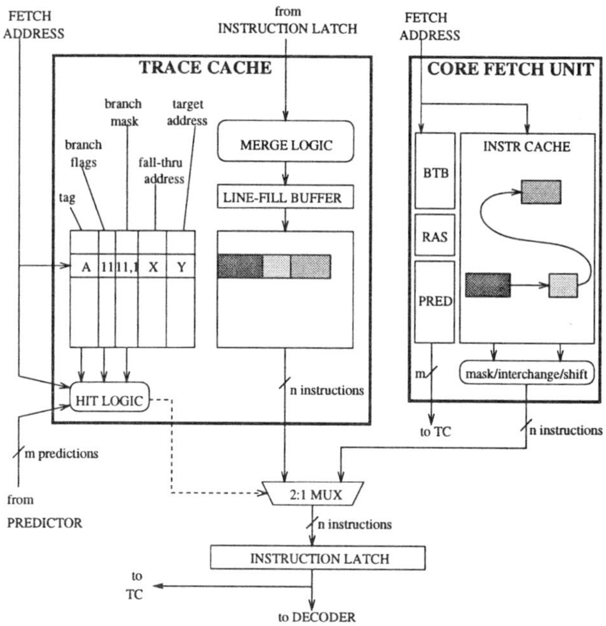

Figure 4. The trace cache fetch mechanism.

The trace cache is made up of instruction traces, control information, and line-fill buffer logic. The length of a trace is limited in two ways – by number of instructions n and by number of basic blocks m. The former limit n is chosen based on the peak dispatch rate. The latter limit m is chosen based on n and the average number of instructions in a basic block. m also determines, or is constrained by, the number of branch predictions made per cycle. In Figure 4, $n = 16$ and $m = 3$. The control information is similar to the tag array of standard caches but contains additional state information:

- *valid bit*: indicates this is a valid trace.
- *tag*: identifies the starting address of the trace.
- *branch flags*: there is a single bit for each branch within the trace to indicate the path followed after the branch (taken/not taken). The mth branch of the trace does not need a flag since no instructions follow it, hence there are only $m - 1$ bits instead of m bits.
- *branch mask*: state is needed to indicate (1) the number of branches in the trace and (2) whether or not the trace ends in a branch. This is needed for comparing the correct number of branch predictions against the same number of branch flags, when checking for a trace hit. This is also needed by the branch predictor to know how many predictions were used. The first $\lceil log_2(m + 1) \rceil$ bits encode the number of branches. One more bit indicates if the last instruction in the trace is a branch; if true, the branch's corresponding branch flag does not need to be checked since no instructions follow it.
- *trace fall-through address*: next fetch address if the last branch in the trace is predicted not taken.
- *trace target address*: next fetch address if the last branch in the trace is predicted taken.

The trace cache is accessed in parallel with the instruction cache and BTB using the current fetch address. The predictor generates multiple branch predictions while the caches are accessed. The fetch address is used together with the multiple branch predictions to determine if the trace read from the trace cache matches the predicted sequence of basic blocks. Specifically, a trace cache hit requires that (1) the fetch address match the tag and (2) the branch predictions match the branch flags. The branch mask ensures that the correct number of prediction bits are used in the comparison. On a trace cache hit, an entire trace of instructions is fed into the instruction latch, bypassing the instruction cache.

On a trace cache miss, fetching proceeds normally from the instruction cache, i.e. contiguous instruction fetching. The line-fill buffer logic services trace cache misses. In the example in Figure 4, three basic blocks are fetched one at a time from the instruction cache, since all branches are predicted taken. The basic blocks are latched one at a time into the line-fill buffer; the line-fill control logic serves to merge each incoming block of instructions with preceding instructions in the line-fill buffer. Filling is complete when either n instructions have been traced or m branches have been detected in the trace. At this point the contents of the line-fill buffer are written into the trace cache. The branch flags and branch mask are generated during the line-fill process, and the trace target and fall-through addresses are computed at the end of the line-fill. If the trace does not end in a branch, the target address is set equal to the fall-through address.

There are different classes of control transfer instructions – conditional branches, unconditional branches, calls or direct jumps, returns, indirect jumps, and traps – yet so far only conditional branches have been discussed. The complex alternative for handling all of these cases is to add additional bits to each branch flag to distinguish the type of control transfer instruction. Further, the line-fill buffer must stop filling a trace when a return, indirect jump, or trap is encountered, because these control transfer instructions have an indeterminite number of targets, whereas the predictor can only predict one of two targets. Lastly, the branch mask and the hit logic are made slightly more complex since unconditional branches and calls should not be involved in prediction (the outcome is known).

We simplify these complications in two ways. First, the trace cache does not store returns, indirect jumps, or traps at all; the line-fill buffer aborts a fill when it detects any of these instructions. Second, unconditional branches and calls can be viewed as conditional branches that are extremely predictable; from this point of view, they can be grouped into the conditional branch class and not be treated any differently. With these two simplifications, the trace cache has only to deal with conditional branches.

The size of a direct mapped trace cache with 64 lines, $n = 16$, and $m = 3$ is 712 bytes for tags/control and 4 kilobytes for instructions (comparable in area to the correlated branch predictor, 4kB). This configuration is used in the experiments which follow.

2.3. Trace cache design space

The trace cache depicted in Figure 4 is the simplest design among many alternatives. It is the implementation used in simulations of the trace cache. However, the design space deserves some attention:

1) associativity: The trace cache can be made more associative to reduce conflict misses.

2) multiple paths: A downside of the simple trace cache is that from a given starting address, only one trace can be stored. It might be advantageous to be able to store multiple paths eminating from a given address. This can be thought of as another form of associativity – *path associativity*. Adding path associativity could reduce thrashing between traces that start at the same address.

3) partial matches: An alternative to providing path associativity is to allow *partial hits*. If the fetch address matches the starting address of a trace and the first few branch predictions match the first few branch flags, provide only a prefix of the trace. This is in place of the simple "all or nothing" approach we use. The additional cost of this scheme is that intermediate basic block addresses must be stored for the same reason that trace target and fall-through addresses are stored. Also, there is the question of whether or not a partial hit be treated as a miss (i.e. to replace the line or not).

4) other indexing methods: The simple trace cache indexes with the fetch address and includes branch predictions in the tag match. Alternatively, the index into the trace cache could be derived by concatenating the fetch address with the branch prediction bits. This effectively achieves path associativity while keeping a direct mapped structure, because different paths starting at the same address now map to consecutive locations in the trace cache.

5) fill issues: While the line-fill buffer is collecting a new trace, the trace cache continues to be accessed by the fetch unit. This means a miss could occur in the midst of handling a previous miss. The design options in order of increasing complexity are: ignore any new misses, delay servicing new misses until the line-fill buffer is free, or provide multiple line-fill buffers to support concurrent misses. Another issue is whether to fill the trace cache with speculative traces or to wait for branch outcomes before committing a trace.

6) judicious trace selection: There are likely to be traces that are committed but never reused. These traces may displace useful traces, causing needless misses. To improve trace cache hit rates, the design could use a small buffer to store recent traces; a trace in this buffer is only committed to the trace cache after one or more hits to that trace.

7) victim trace cache: An alternative to judicious trace selection is to use a victim cache [5]. It may keep valuable traces from being permanently displaced by useless traces.

3. Other high bandwidth fetch mechanisms

In this section we analyze the organization of two previously proposed fetch mechanisms aimed at fetching and aligning multiple noncontiguous basic blocks each cycle. The analysis compares these mechanisms against the trace cache, with latency being a key point for comparison.

3.1. Branch address cache

The branch address cache fetch mechanism proposed by Yeh, Marr, and Patt [16] is shown in Figure 5. There are four primary components: (1) a branch address cache (BAC), (2) a multiple branch predictor, (3) an interleaved instruction cache, and (4) an interchange and alignment network. The BAC extends the BTB to multiple branches by storing a tree of target and fall-through addresses as depicted in Figure 6. The depth of the tree depends on the number of branches predicted per cycle.

In Figure 5, light grey boxes represent non-control transfer instructions and dark grey boxes represent branches; the fields in the BAC correspond to the tree in Figure 6, as indicated by the address labels A through O. The diagram depicts the two-stage nature of the design. In the first stage, an entry containing up to 14 basic block addresses is read from the BAC. From these addresses, up to 3 basic block addresses corresponding to the predicted path are selected. In this example, the next 3 branches are all predicted taken, corresponding to the sequence of basic blocks {C,G,O}. In the second stage, the cache reads the three basic blocks in parallel from its multiple banks. Since the basic blocks may be placed arbitrarily into the cache banks, they must pass through an alignment network to align them into dynamic program order and merge them into the instruction latch.

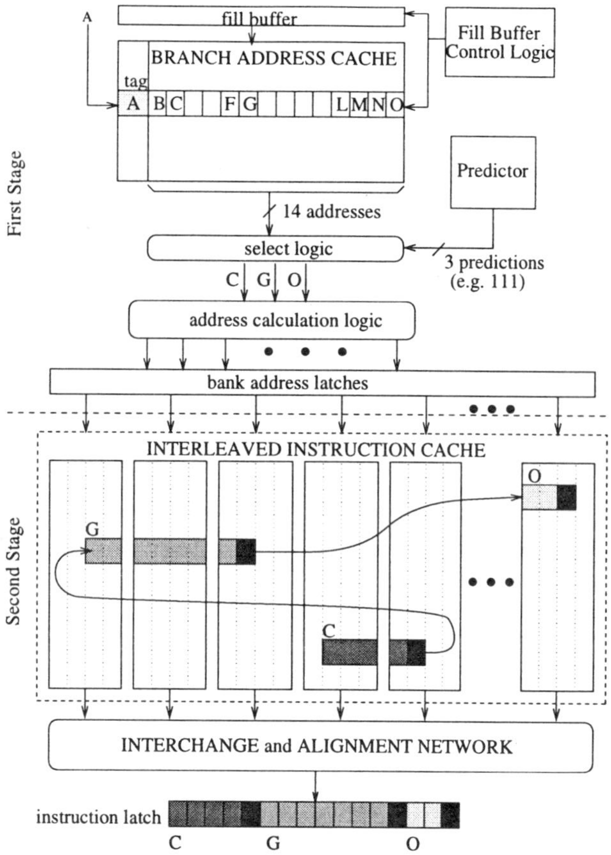

Figure 5. Branch address cache approach.

The two stages in this design are pipelined. During the second stage, while basic blocks {C,G,O} are being fetched from the instruction cache, the BAC begins a new cycle using address O as its index. In general, the last basic block address indexing into the instruction cache is also the index into the BAC.

If an address misses in the BAC, an entry is allocated for the portion of the control flow graph which begins at that address. Branch target and fall-through addresses are filled in the entry as paths through the tree are traversed; an entry may contain holes corresponding to branches which have not yet been encountered.

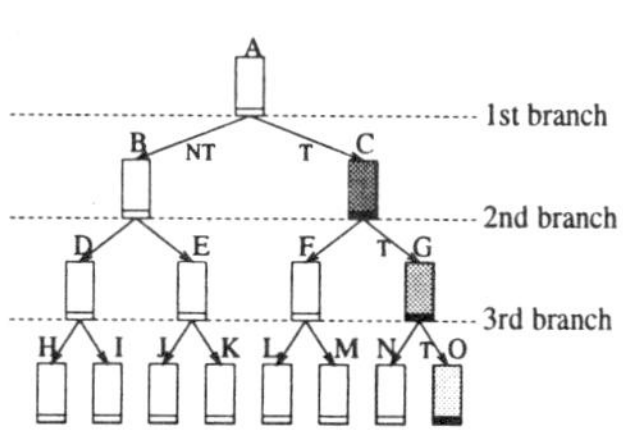

Figure 6. BAC stores subgraphs of the CFG.

Though conceptually the design has two pipeline stages, possibly one or more additional pipeline stages are implied by having the complicated alignment network. The alignment network must (1) interchange the cache lines from numerous banks (with more than two banks, the permutations grow quickly), and (2) collapse the basic blocks together, eliminating unused intervening instructions. Though not discussed in [16], logic like the collapsing buffer [1] discussed in the next section will be needed to do this.

3.2. Collapsing buffer

The instruction fetch mechanism proposed by Conte, Mills, Menezes, Patel [1] is illustrated in Figure 7. It is composed of (1) an interleaved instruction cache, (2) an interleaved branch target buffer (BTB), (3) a multiple branch predictor, (4) special logic after the BTB, and (5) an interchange and alignment network featuring a *collapsing buffer*.

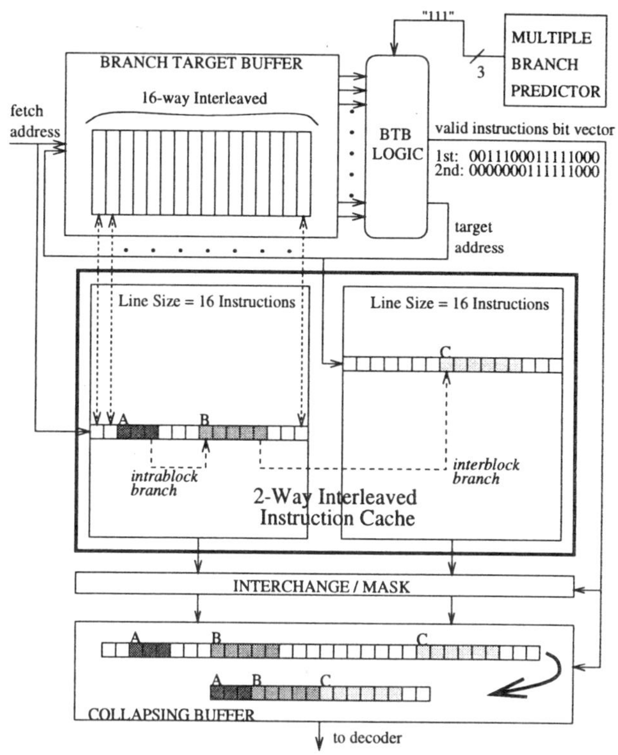

Figure 7. The collapsing buffer approach.

The hardware is similar to the core fetch unit of the trace cache (described in Section 3), but has two important distinctions. First, the BTB logic is capable of detecting *intrablock* branches – short hops within a cache line. Second, a single fetch goes through two BTB accesses. As will be described below, this allows fetching beyond one taken *interblock* branch – a branch out of the cache line. In both cases, the collapsing buffer uses control information generated by the BTB logic to merge noncontiguous basic blocks.

Figure 7 illustrates how three noncontiguous basic blocks labelled A, B, and C are fetched. The fetch address A accesses the interleaved BTB. The BTB indicates that there are two branches in the cache line, one at instruction 5 with target address B, the other at instruction 13 with target address C. Based on this branch information and branch predictions from the predictor, the BTB logic indicates which instructions in the fetched line are valid and produces the next basic block address, C.

The initial BTB lookup produces (1) a bit vector indicating the predicted valid instructions in the cache line (instructions from basic blocks A and B), and (2) the predicted target address C of basic block B. The fetch address A and target address C are then used to fetch two nonconsecutive cache lines from the interleaved instruction cache. This can be done only if the cache lines are in different banks. In parallel with this instruction cache access, the BTB is accessed again, using the target address C. This second, serialized lookup determines which instructions are valid in the second cache line and produces the next fetch address (the predicted successor of basic block C).

When the two cache lines have been read from the cache, they pass through masking and interchange logic and the collapsing buffer (which merges the instructions), all controlled by bit vectors produced by the two passes through the BTB. After this step, the properly ordered and merged instructions are captured in the instruction latches to be fed to the decoders.

This scheme has several disadvantages. First, the fetch line and successor line must reside in different cache banks. Bank conflicts can be reduced by adding more banks, but this requires a more complicated, higher latency interchange switch. Second, this scheme does not scale well for interblock branches; supporting additional interblock branches requires as many additional BTB accesses, all serialized. Third, the BTB logic requires a serial chain of n address comparators to detect intrablock branches, where n is the number of BTB banks. Most seriously, however, is that this fetch mechanism adds a significant amount of logic both before and after the instruction cache. The instruction fetch pipeline is likely to have three stages: (1) initial BTB lookup and BTB logic, (2) instruction cache access and second BTB lookup, and (3) interchange switch, masking, and collapsing buffer. The collapsing buffer takes only a single stage if implemented as a bus-based crossbar [1].

4. Simulation methodology

4.1. Processor model

Our simulation model follows the basic structure shown in Figure 1 – a fetch engine and an execute engine decoupled via instruction issue buffers. Various fetch engines – trace cache, branch address cache, and collapsing buffer – are modeled in detail. The processor execution part of the model is constrained only by true data dependences. *We assume unlimited hardware resources – any instructions in the instruction buffers that have their data available may issue.* This is done to place as much demand on the fetch unit as possible, making instruction fetch the performance bottleneck. In effect, unlimited register renaming and full dynamic instruction issue are assumed. Loads and stores are assumed to have oracle address disambiguation – loads and stores wait for previous stores only if there is a true address conflict. Also, the data cache always hits. The only hardware limitations imposed are the maximum size of the instruction buffer and the degree of superscalar dispatch. In all simulations, the size of the instruction buffer is 2048 useful instructions and the maximum fetch/dispatch bandwidth is 16 instructions per cycle. In summary, the amount of ILP exploited is limited by 5 factors:

- *maximum fetch/dispatch rate (16/cycle)*
- *maximum size of instruction window (2048)*
- *true data dependences in the program*
- *operation latencies*
- *performance of the fetch engine*

It is the last factor that we are interested in and which will vary between simulations.

The instruction pipeline is composed of 4 phases: fetch, dispatch, issue, and execution. The latency of the fetch phase is varied according to implementation, and the dispatch latency is fixed at 1 cycle. If all operands are available at or immediately after dispatch, instruction issue takes only 1 cycle; otherwise issue is delayed until operands arrive. Because of unlimited resources and unlimited register renaming, issue never stalls due to structural or register WAR/WAW hazards. After issue, execution takes a certain number of cycles based on the operation. Operation latencies are similar to those of the MIPS R10000 processor.

4.2. Workload

The six integer SPEC92 benchmarks and six benchmarks from the *Instruction Benchmark Suite* (IBS) [14] are used to evaluate the performance of the various fetch mechanisms. SPEC92 floating-point results can be found in [12].

The SPEC92 benchmarks were compiled on a Sun SPARCstation 10/30 using "gcc -O4 -static -fschedule-insns -fschedule-insns2". SPARC instruction traces were generated using *the Quick Profiler and Tracer* (QPT) [7] and then fed into the trace-driven SPARC processor simulator. The SPEC92 benchmarks were simulated to completion.

The IBS benchmarks are MIPS traces obtained via a logic analyzer connected to the CPU of a DECstation 3100. These benchmarks are a better test of instruction fetch performance than SPEC92 [14]. For one thing, a significant fraction of the traces are kernel and X-server references, increasing instruction path lengths. To simulate the IBS traces, we developed a trace-driven MIPS processor simulator similar to the SPARC one.

4.3. Performance metric

For measuring performance we use instructions completed per cycle (IPC), which is a direct measure of performance and is almost certainly the measure that counts most. The harmonic mean is used to average the performance of benchmarks.

5. Results

Table 2 summarizes the trace cache (TC), collapsing buffer (CB), and branch address cache (BAC) fetch unit parameters used in all experiments. In the sections which follow, results for the three high bandwidth implementations are compared.

As a base case for comparison, results are also presented for conventional instruction fetching. The core fetch unit of the trace cache (described in Section 2.1) is used as the base case. We will call the base case "sequential" (SEQ), since only sequential instructions can be fetched in a given cycle. To demonstrate the effect of branch throughput, two variations of SEQ are simulated: SEQ.1 is limited to one basic block per cycle, and SEQ.3 can fetch up to three contiguous basic blocks. Simulation parameters for SEQ are the same as those for TC in Table 2, but with the trace cache not present (and 1 or 3 branch predictions per cycle).

SIMULATION PARAMETER		INSTR SUPPLY MECHANISM TC	CB	BAC
instruction fetch limit		16 instructions per cycle		
Multiple Branch Predictor	BHR	14 bits		
	PHT	2^{14} 2-bit counters (4 KB storage)		
	# pred/cyc	up to 3 predictions each cycle		
Instr Cache	size	128 KB		
	assoc	direct mapped		
	interleave	2-way	2-way	8-way
	line size	16 instr	16 instr	4 instr
	prefetch	none	none	3 lines
	miss penalty	10 cycles		
Ret Stack	depth	unlimited		
Branch Target Buffer	size	1K entries	1K entries	n/a
	assoc	dir map	dir map	
	interleave	16-way	16-way	
Trace Cache	size	64 entries	n/a	
	assoc	dir map		
	line size	16 instr		
	# conc fills	1		
Branch Address Cache	size	n/a		1K entries
	assoc			dir map
	# conc fills			1

Table 2. Fetch unit configurations.

The results are split into two sets. The first set assumes all fetch units have a latency of 1 cycle, in order to demonstrate each mechanism's ability to deliver bandwidth performance. The second set shows what happens when the extra pipe stages implied by CB and BAC are actually simulated.

5.1. Single-cycle fetch latency

The first set of results, the two graphs in Figure 8, assumes a fetch unit latency of 1 cycle for all schemes. This is done to isolate the ability of the fetch mechanisms to supply instruction bandwidth.

The first observation is that SEQ.3 gives a substantial performance boost over SEQ.1. The graph in Figure 9 shows that fetching past multiple not-taken branches each cycle yields performance improvement above 7% for all of the SPEC benchmarks. Over half of the SPEC benchmarks show a 17% or better performance improvement. Four of the IBS benchmarks show a 7% or greater improvement.

The second observation is that for both SPEC and IBS workloads, fetching past taken branches is a big win. Adding the TC function to the SEQ.3 mechanism yields about as much performance improvement as extending SEQ.1 to multiple not-taken branches per cycle.

The graph in Figure 10 shows the performance improvement that BAC, CB, and TC yield over SEQ.3 (SEQ.3 is used as the base instead of SEQ.1 because it is aggressive, yet not much more complex than SEQ.1). One might expect that under the single-cycle fetch latency assumption, the three approaches would perform similarly. This is the case for much of the IBS workload, with TC always performing as well or better than the other two schemes.

For the SPEC workload, however, TC enjoys a noticeable lead over CB. This is most likely because the original collapsing buffer was not designed to handle backward taken intrablock branches [1], whereas the TC can handle any arbitrary trace.

For the majority of the benchmarks, BAC performs worst of the three, but this is particularly noticeable in the SPEC runs. There are two reasons for this. First, instruction cache bank conflicts are the primary performance loss for BAC. Data in [12] shows that BAC is comparable to TC if bank conflicts are ignored. Second, the BAC treats basic blocks as atomic units. As a result, a BAC entry will provide only as many basic block addresses as will fit within the 16 instruction fetch limit. Given hits in both the TC and BAC, the BAC can never supply more instructions than the TC.

To summarize the major results, TC performs on average 15% better than SEQ.3 for the SPEC workload and 9% better for the IBS workload – overall, a 12% performance gain. Compared to SEQ.1, TC improves performance by 37% for SPEC, 20% for IBS, and 28% for the combined workload.

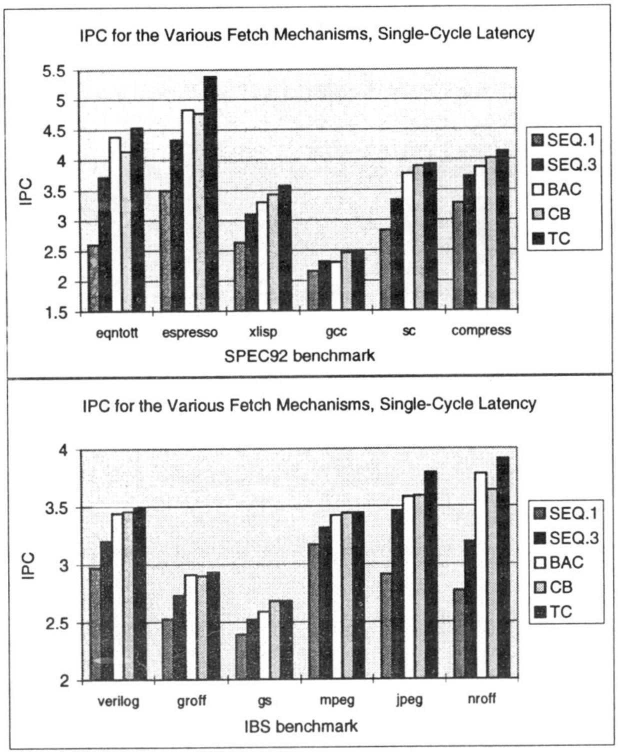

Figure 8. IPC results (fetch latency = 1 cycle).

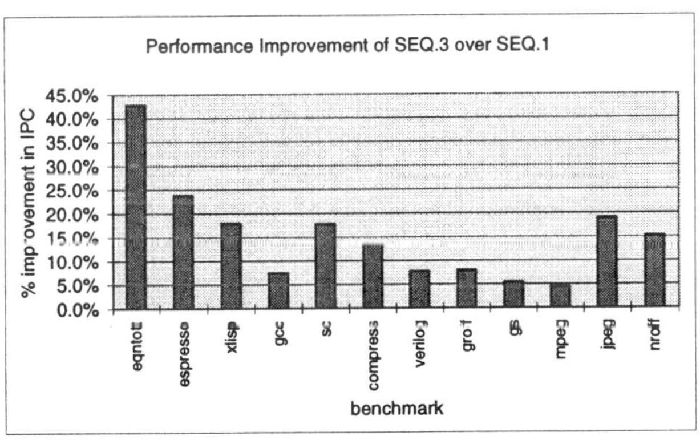

Figure 9. Improvement of SEQ.3 over SEQ.1.

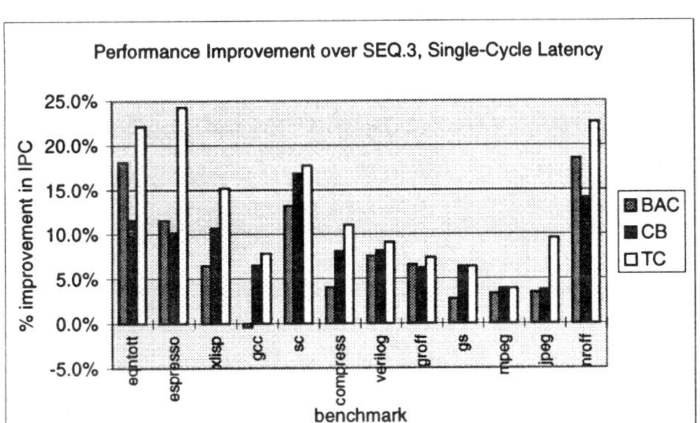

Figure 10. Improvement over SEQ.3.

5.2. The effect of latency

The effect of fetch unit latency is quantified by the graph in Figure 11. Since both CB and BAC add stages before and after the instruction cache, we give the performance of these schemes for fetch latencies of 2 and 3 cycles. CB and BAC fall well below the performance of TC. For all but 4 of the benchmarks, BAC with a latency of 2 cycles performs worse than SEQ.3. Likewise, for most of the benchmarks, CB with a latency of 3 cycles performs worse than SEQ.3.

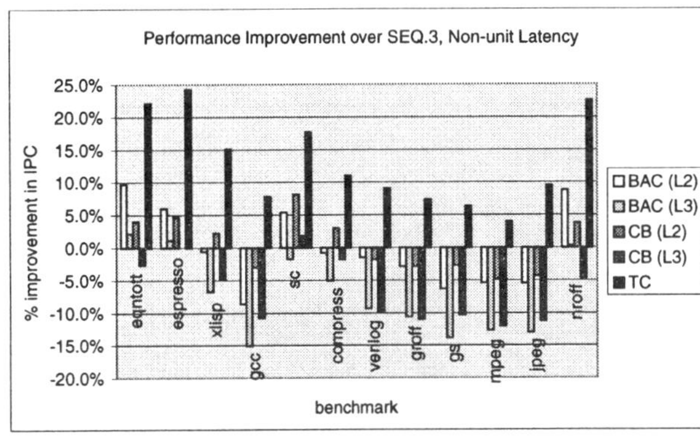

Figure 11. Improvement over SEQ.3 (*L2* and *L3* stand for 2 and 3 cycle latency.)

5.3. Trace cache effectiveness

To determine how effective the trace cache is, we establish an upper bound on its performance and measure how far short it falls from this bound. The bound is established by an "ideal" fetch model, defined as follows: as long as branch outcomes are predicted correctly and instructions hit in the instruction cache, up to 3 basic blocks or 16 instructions – whichever comes first – can be fetched every cycle.

Figure 12 shows that there is still performance to be gained by better instruction fetching. TC falls short of ideal performance due to trace cache and BTB misses. The trace cache used in the previous experiments has only 64 entries and is direct mapped; adding 2/4-way associativity or simply increasing the number of entries will narrow the performance gap between TC and ideal. Figure 12 provides incentive to explore the design space alternatives of Section 2.3 aimed at improving hit rate. To demonstrate the benefit of using a larger trace cache, we include IBS results for a 32 kilobyte, 4-way associative trace cache in the same graph.

Trace cache miss rate can be specified in two ways: in terms of traces (trace miss rate) and in terms of instructions (instruction miss rate). Trace miss rate is the fraction of accesses that do not find a trace present. Instruction miss rate is the fraction of instructions not supplied by the trace cache. Trace miss rate is a more direct measure of trace cache performance because it indicates the fraction of fetch cycles

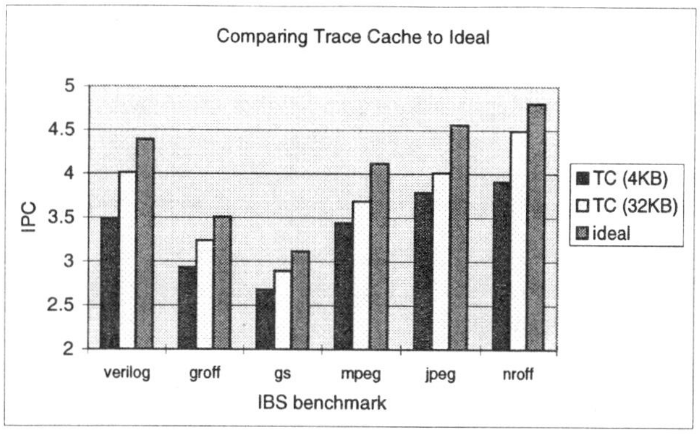

Figure 12. TC performance potential.

that benefit from higher bandwidth. However, instruction miss rate is also reported because it corresponds to cache miss rate in the traditional sense. Both trace miss rate (tmr) and instruction miss rate (imr) are shown in Table 3.

IBS	4 KB, 1-way		32 KB, 4-way		Spec	4 KB, 1-way	
	tmr	imr	tmr	imr		tmr	imr
veri	70%	48%	48%	25%	eqn	26%	8%
groff	76%	61%	60%	38%	esp	32%	14%
gs	76%	58%	60%	39%	xlisp	64%	40%
mpeg	70%	54%	51%	29%	gcc	71%	52%
jpeg	64%	43%	53%	25%	sc	50%	28%
nroff	62%	42%	45%	24%	comp	18%	6%

Table 3. Trace cache miss rates.

6. Conclusions

We have shown that it is important to design instruction fetch units capable of fetching past multiple, possibly taken branches each cycle. However, this additional bandwidth should not be achieved at the expense of longer fetch unit latency. The trace cache is successful in satisfying both of these requirements.

While a small trace cache performs well, comparison with the "ideal" noncontiguous instruction fetch model shows the potential for even higher performance. This experiment motivates investigation of larger and/or more complex trace cache designs, such as path associativity, partial matches, judicious trace selection, and victim trace caches.

7. Acknowledgements

This work was supported in part by NSF Grant MIP-9505853 and by the U.S. Army Intelligence Center and Fort Huachuca under Contract DABT63-95-C-0127 and ARPA order no. D346. The views and conclusions contained herein are those of the authors and should not be interpreted as necessarily representing the official policies or endorsements, either expressed or implied, of the U.S. Army Intelligence Center and Fort Huachuca, or the U.S. Government. Eric Rotenberg is funded by an IBM Graduate Fellowship.

References

[1] T. Conte, K. Menezes, P. Mills, and B. Patel. Optimization of instruction fetch mechanisms for high issue rates. *22nd Intl. Symp. on Computer Architecture*, pp. 333–344, June 1995.

[2] S. Dutta and M. Franklin. Control flow prediction with tree-like subgraphs for superscalar processors. *28th Intl. Symp. on Microarchitecture*, pp. 258–263, Nov 1995.

[3] M. Franklin and M. Smotherman. A fill-unit approach to multiple instruction issue. *27th Intl. Symp. on Microarchitecture*, pp. 162–171, Nov 1994.

[4] G. F. Grohoski. Machine organization of the ibm rs/6000 processor. *IBM Journal of R&D*, 34(1):37–58, Jan 1990.

[5] N. Jouppi. Improving direct-mapped cache performance by the addition of a small fully-associative cache and prefetch buffers. *17th Intl. Symp. on Computer Architecture*, pp. 364–373, May 1990.

[6] D. Kaeli and P. Emma. Branch history table prediction of moving target branches due to subroutine returns. *18th Intl. Symp. on Computer Architecture*, pp. 34–42, May 1991.

[7] J. Larus. Efficient program tracing. *IEEE Computer*, 26(5):52–61, May 1993.

[8] J. Lee and A. J. Smith. Branch prediction strategies and branch target buffer design. *IEEE Computer*, 21(7):6–22, Jan 1984.

[9] J. Losq. Generalized history table for branch prediction. *IBM Technical Disclosure Bulletin*, 25(1):99–101, June 1982.

[10] S. Melvin, M. Shebanow, and Y. Patt. Hardware support for large atomic units in dynamically scheduled machines. *21st Intl. Symp. on Microarchitecture*, pp. 60–66, Dec 1988.

[11] S.-T. Pan, K. So, and J. T. Rahmeh. Improving the accuracy of dynamic branch prediction using branch correlation. *5th Intl. Conf. on Architectural Support for Programming Languages and Operating Systems*, pp. 76–84, Oct 1992.

[12] E. Rotenberg, S. Bennett, and J. Smith. Trace cache: a low latency approach to high bandwidth instruction fetching. Tech Report 1310, CS Dept., Univ. of Wisc. - Madison, 1996.

[13] J. E. Smith. A study of branch prediction strategies. *8th Symp. on Computer Architecture*, pp. 135–148, May 1981.

[14] R. Uhlig, D. Nagle, T. Mudge, S. Sechrest, and J. Emer. Instruction fetching: Coping with code bloat. *22nd Intl. Symp. on Computer Architecture*, pp. 345–356, June 1995.

[15] T.-Y. Yeh. *Two-level Adaptive Branch Prediction and Instruction Fetch Mechanisms for High Performance Superscalar Processors.* PhD thesis, EECS Dept., University of Michigan - Ann Arbor, 1993.

[16] T.-Y. Yeh, D. T. Marr, and Y. N. Patt. Increasing the instruction fetch rate via multiple branch prediction and a branch address cache. *7th Intl. Conf. on Supercomputing*, pp. 67–76, July 1993.

[17] T.-Y. Yeh and Y. N. Patt. A comprehensive instruction fetch mechanism for a processor supporting speculative execution. *25th Intl. Symp. on Microarchitecture*, pp. 129–139, Dec 1992.

Session 2

Accurate and Practical Profile-Driven Compilation Using the Profile Buffer

Thomas M. Conte Kishore N. Menezes Mary Ann Hirsch
Department of Electrical and Computer Engineering
North Carolina State University
Raleigh, North Carolina 27695
{conte, knmeneze, mahirsch}@eos.ncsu.edu

Abstract

Profiling is a technique of gathering program statistics in order to aid program optimization. In particular, it is an essential component of compiler optimization for the extraction of instruction–level parallelism. Code instrumentation has been the most popular method of profiling. However, real-time, interactive, and transaction processing applications suffer from the high execution-time overhead imposed by software instrumentation. This paper suggests the use of hardware dedicated to the task of profiling. The hardware proposed consists of a set of counters, the profile buffer. A profile collection method that combines the use of hardware, the compiler and operating system support is described. Three methods for profile buffer indexing, address-mapping, selective indexing, and compiler indexing are presented that allow this approach to produce accurate profiling information with very little execution slowdown. The profile information obtained is applied to a prominent compiler optimization, namely superblock scheduling. The resulting instruction-level parallelism approaches that obtained through the use of perfect profile information.

1 Introduction

Profile information is steadily gaining importance in the optimization of program execution, especially in the areas of hand–tuning of programs [12], trace scheduling [11], superblock scheduling [6], data preloading [7], branch prediction [19], and improved instruction cache performance [6]. Issues in the exploitation of instruction–level parallelism inherent in programs, coupled with rapid developments in compiler research have generated interest in the role of profile information in smart compilation [4], [6], [13], [11], [18]. In one example, traditional optimizations when combined with profile-driven superblock formation enhance execution performance by an additional 15% [6]. However, profile collection has severe drawbacks that have limited its commercial use.

Traditionally, profiling is achieved through a long, tedious *instrument–run–recompile* sequence. During instrumentation, the compiler inserts additional instructions into the original program to collect accurate execution frequencies of basic blocks or the arcs that connect these basic blocks. Next, this instrumented code is executed with a variety of batch inputs. After these multiple executions, the program statistics are calculated based on the profiling information that has been collected. Finally, the original program is recompiled using profile-driven optimizations. Not only do these traditional techniques suffer from the need for multiple execution and compilation passes, they also suffer from slowdown of the program being profiled due to the added instructions. The MIPS basic block profiling tool, *pixie* [20], inserts about five instructions in every basic block [3]. Ball and Larus measured the slowdown of *pixie* required for arc–based profiling as between 1.11 to 5.24 times [3]. To offset this slowdown, modifications involving the reduction in the number of basic blocks or the arcs that need to be probed have been suggested in the literature [3], [4], [21], [17]. Ball and Larus investigated one such method which reduces the slowdown to a maximum of 2.05 times for the SPEC92 benchmarks. Unfortunately, this overhead is still too large for integrated software vendors to readily absorb. Commercial software vendors in general can tolerate a negligible amount of additional execution overhead (i.e., approximately $\leq$ 5%) [10]. Code instrumentation techniques, therefore, may not be appropriate for real–time, interactive, and transaction processing applications.

If profiling is to gain commercial acceptance, profiling must be smoothly integrated into the software development cycle. Unfortunately, this requires the reduction or elimination of the need for a sample input suite, as well as more efficient profiling methods. *Hardware based profiling* was introduced by Conte, *et al.* [8] as a way to address these problems. This technique uses existing branch prediction hardware to collect profile information at kernel entrances. It has

1072-4451/96 $5.00 © 1996 IEEE

a slowdown of 1.02 on average, and 1.05 as a worst case [8]. The use of hardware based profiling allows software vendors to supply instrumented versions of applications to alpha and beta testers. The profiled information based on actual day to day usage can be later retrieved, and final program optimization can be performed. The advantage to hardware based profiling is twofold: It eliminates the need for sample input suites (since actual usage can be captured), and the optimizations are based on actual program usage. Profiling in this manner is commercially appealing because vendors' alpha and beta testing processes are often very well defined, and the hardware based style of profiling leverages their existing investment to produce better optimized code [10].

Some profiling methods today utilize the hardware support for debugging to provide limited profiling capabilities. For example, the PA-RISC architecture provides for a performance monitoring coprocessor that may be employed for collecting profile data [14]. These techniques require frequent interrupts to be able to gather moderately accurate data. The information collected by such methods is inadequate for the requirements of a profile-driven optimizing compiler.

Although hardware-based profiling achieves very little slowdown, it provides less than ideal profiles [8],[9]. This is due to the small size of the branch prediction hardware [8] and the relatively coarse-grain nature of current branch prediction state machines. In this paper, the *profile buffer* is proposed for the collection of profile information that is similar in slowdown to branch predictor based profiling. However, it fulfills the profiling demands of an optimizing compiler by providing high accuracy. In order to evaluate its effectiveness, the profile information obtained from this method is applied to a prominent optimization, namely superblock scheduling [6]. The performance measurement data based on the execution of the optimized program indicates that a small buffer (16–64 entries) can obtain a high degree of accuracy for a relatively small amount of slowdown (1.02 times).

The design tradeoffs for the profile buffer are examined in this paper. The following section discusses Conte, *et al.*'s previous method of collecting profile information using the branch–handling hardware in a processor [8]. In addition, the *profile buffer* and its implications in terms of hardware, the instruction set architecture (ISA) and the operating system are discussed. Modified schemes of employing such a buffer are discussed in sections 2.2–2.4. In particular, three methods for profile buffer indexing, *address-mapping*, *selective indexing*, and *compiler indexing*, are presented. The *address mapping* scheme employs a hashing algorithm to map addresses into the profile buffer. The other techniques, *selective indexing* and *compiler indexing*, use minor extensions to the ISA. In the case of *selective indexing*, an additional bit is added to the branch instruction. However, the *compiler indexing* method uses an additional field for the encoding of the profile buffer index. Section 3 presents a summary of experimental results and discusses the tradeoffs between the various schemes. The paper concludes with comments and suggestions for future work.

2 Profiling in Hardware

The insertion of additional instructions required by dynamic profiling through software causes significant execution overhead. The use of efficient hardware schemes that utilize existing branch handling hardware with OS support to obtain profile information was proposed by Conte, *et al.* [8]. For example, the *two-level predictor* profiling scheme uses Yeh and Patt's PAs adaptive training branch predictor [23]. Briefly, one buffer in PAs, the *history register table* (HRT), contains histories for dynamically executing branch instructions. This buffer is referenced by the instruction address of each branch. The second buffer, *pattern table* (PT), contains a state machine for predicting the outcome of a branch [23]. When a branch access occurs, the HRT is referenced. The history obtained from the HRT is used to index into the PT to calculate a branch prediction. The actual outcome of the branch after execution is later used to update both the history and the state machine.

The profiling scheme for PAs periodically dumps the HRT to obtain the profile of the entire program. However, the limited size of each history register in the HRT (10 bits in [8]) results in sparse profile information being downloaded. Contentions due to the limited size of the HRT (1024 entries in [8]) also introduce error. The combined sampling error is reduced slightly by using a *marker* bit in each history register to mark the boundary between valid and invalid information [8],[9]. But the overall lower quality profile information collected when compared against traditional code instrumentation profiling is the main drawback of the scheme.

2.1 The profile buffer

In an effort to obtain near-accurate profile information and simultaneously maintain a low profiling overhead, a specialized buffer called the *profile buffer* is proposed. This buffer is illustrated in Figure 1. The profile buffer is composed of a set of counters, with each entry in the buffer consisting of two fields: the number of times the branch is taken (*num_taken*) and the number of times a branch is not-taken or falls-through (*num_not_taken*). The profile buffer works in close cooperation with a standard reorder buffer. On instruction completion, the reorder buffer entry for a branch contains the branch address and the information as to whether the branch was taken or not-taken. At write-back, when the branch retires, the profile buffer is referenced using the branch address or calculated index and one of the two fields of the corresponding *profile buffer* entry are updated based on whether the branch was taken.

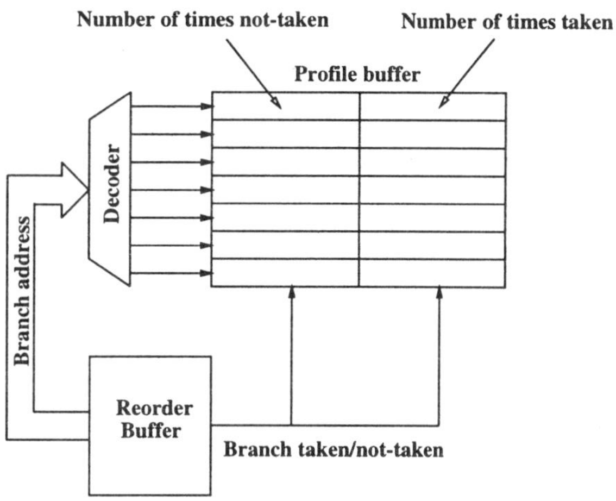

Figure 1. The profile buffer. (Entries in the buffer are counters).

The information in the *profile buffer* needs to be stored back to memory periodically. The storage of the buffer information may take place on a context-switch. Alternatively, the operating system may generate a timer interrupt and perform the required action. Because the updating of the information in the *profile buffer* is completely program-controlled and does not require intervention by the operating system, the storage back to memory constitutes the only slowdown possible. Branches that have been most recently accessed are likely to be accessed again in the near future (i.e., they have temporal locality). Therefore, the interrupts may be spaced well apart without degrading the information contained in the *profile buffer*, thereby minimally affecting the execution speed of the program. Experiments to measure slowdown using branch–handling hardware and dumping out its contents on a context–switch were conducted in [8]. The authors reported a maximum slowdown of 1.046 times for the SPECint92 benchmarks, with an average slowdown of 1.02 times on a Pentium-based AT&T server system when the size of the branch hardware employed in the experiments was a 512-entry buffer. A large buffer was required to provide for the many branches in each of the SPECint92 benchmarks studied [8]. The profile buffer is dumped out in a manner similar to branch handling hardware but this buffer is much smaller (e.g., 32 entries). Therefore, the schemes proposed in this paper have a slowdown comparable to or lower than the average of 1.02 times. Additionally, the hardware proposed does not impact the cycle time because the actions associated with the *profile buffer* constitute a write-only, post-completion phase, where the branch is allowed to update the counters in the buffer over a multiple number of cycles.

The profile buffer must be as small as possible to minimize the cost of additional hardware. As a consequence of this, a design space ranging from eight to 64 entries in the buffer is considered, where each entry is divided into two 16-bit counters. The profiling information obtained in this manner may not be accurate because the buffer size may be too small to handle the large number of branches that may exist in a program. Given a restricted design space such as in this paper, the reduction of contentions is highly relevant to the profile buffer indexing scheme. Contentions cause the inaccuracies in the profiling information obtained during program execution. The inaccuracy caused due to contentions is measured by using the *arc error* metric. Assume,

$$\Delta e_i = \mid e_{ij} - \hat{e}_{ij} \mid \qquad (1)$$

where, $\hat{e}_{ij}$ is the frequency of the edge from i to j in the measured profile, e_{ij} is the frequency in the *true* profile. Then, the distribution function is given by,

$$f(E) = \sum_{i_{s.t.} W_i = W} \Delta e_i \qquad (2)$$

where, W_i is the execution weight of block i, and W is an execution weight category (e.g. execution weight of 100–1000).

The SPECint92 benchmarks were used to evaluate performance. Each program was divided into a collection of blocks of instructions in which control may only enter at the top but may leave at one or more exit points (better known as *superblocks* [13]). The profile information collected using the profile buffer scheme was applied to a superblock formation algorithm implemented in the University of Illinois IMPACT compiler [5],[15]. The execution rate of useful instructions retired per cycle (IPC) of the profile-based scheduled code was used as the metric of comparison. All experiments were simulated on an eight–issue machine with uniform functional units. As a standard for all tables that contain IPC information, the *exact* column indicates the IPC obtained through the use of accurate profile information obtained through code instrumentation and superblock scheduling. The column *none* shows the IPC for the benchmarks compiled without any instrumentation for profiling (i.e., basic-block only scheduling).

The following three sections present the performance of the profile buffer of different sizes and indexing schemes. The three indexing schemes that were reviewed, address mapping, selective indexing, and compiler indexing, are described below.

Table 1. The performance (IPC) of code compiled using profiling results obtained from buffers that employ the *address mapping* scheme.

Benchmark	Instructions/cycle					
	exact	8	16	32	64	*none*
compress	2.71	1.66	1.64	1.64	1.63	1.38
espresso	2.36	1.36	1.36	1.35	1.36	1.20
eqntott	1.86	1.24	1.24	1.24	1.24	1.01
gcc	1.83	1.35	1.36	1.39	1.39	1.27
li	1.65	1.24	1.25	1.26	1.26	1.15
sc	2.29	1.33	1.39	1.35	1.37	1.25
harmonic mean	2.06	1.35	1.36	1.36	1.36	1.20

Table 2. Contentions as percentage of total accesses for *address mapping*.

Benchmark	Percent Contentions			
	8	16	32	64
compress	41.3%	26.0%	12.6%	7.9%
espresso	29.7%	19.1%	13.4%	5.2%
eqntott	6.1 %	3.7 %	1.8 %	0.5%
gcc	63.4%	55.4%	48.3%	40.9%
li	74.3%	68.1%	55.3%	41.6%
sc	66.4%	45.8%	28.0%	27.2%
mean	46.9%	36.3%	26.6%	20.6%

2.2 Address Mapping

The first approach to indexing the profile buffer is *address mapping*. This simple method uses the branch instruction address to directly reference the profile buffer. It is identical to indexing schemes used in branch prediction hardware, and its performance is comparable to that presented in [8],[9][1]. No complicated optimization of access schemes are necessary because every branch instruction is used in *address mapping*. The results for this scheme are presented in Table 1. A distinct performance increase is seen through the use of profile information collected using the profile buffer with *address mapping*. However, the performance levels achieved fall short of those possible with exact profile information (*exact* in Table 1). This performance degradation is due to an abundance of contentions when simple *address mapping* is employed. The contentions for entries in the profile buffer are shown in Table 2. It is evident that the number of contentions are large over all the benchmarks. In fact, the benchmark *li* has almost three contentions per every four profile buffer accesses for an eight-entry buffer. The effect of the contentions is seen in Figure 2. The *arc error* reduces as the size of the buffer is increased, but is still unacceptably high. These results indicate that reducing the number of contentions should be a priority for obtaining better profile information. Traditionally, branch target buffers (BTB) that have similar properties as the profile buffer have overcome the problem by employing larger buffers (512 or 1024 entry) [1], [22], but this implies added hardware cost. An alternative solution is to reduce the number of branches that access the buffer. This alternative is explored in the next two sections.

[1]The performance of address mapping is slightly higher than that of the PAs profiling of [8],[9] because the profiling buffer employs two, 16 bit counters instead of 10 bit history registers. However, because it is the lowest performance of the three indexing schemes presented here, it also serves to represent the upper bound of performance for PAs profiling from [9] for the purposes of this study.

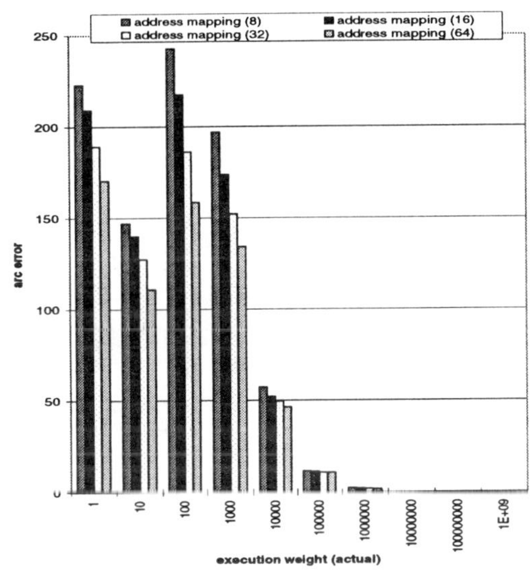

Figure 2. Arc error for the address mapping technique vs. the actual execution weights of the branches.

2.3 Selective indexing

A control flow graph (CFG) is a directed graph that uses basic blocks as nodes and control transfers as arcs. A CFG that will serve as a running example is given in Figure 3. The *arc-based profile* is a method of profiling where code is added to record the flow of execution along all block-to-block transitions (arcs) in the CFG [2]. This simple implementation of *arc-based profiling*, however, requires that the frequencies of all arcs be calculated. When using a profile buffer, this implies that every branch is tabulated in the profile buffer, thereby causing an excessive number of accesses to the buffer. Reducing the number of accesses to the buffer can be expected to greatly reduce the number of contentions, and consequently the error in the profile information. Several algorithms have been suggested to reduce overhead in the code instrumentation methods of profiling [3], [17], [21]. Knuth and Stevenson [17] describe a method for reduction in the number of nodes that need to be probed. Their algorithm is based on Kirchoff's first law, which states that the flow into a vertex equals the flow out of that vertex. Therefore, if there are n vertices and m arcs in a CFG, then only $m-n-1$ arc flow frequencies need to be measured in order to determine the frequencies of all the arcs in the original CFG. The Knuth-Stevenson algorithm is best illustrated by an example. A detailed example of this algorithm is given in Figures 3–6. The arcs represent possible flows of control as the algorithm is performed.

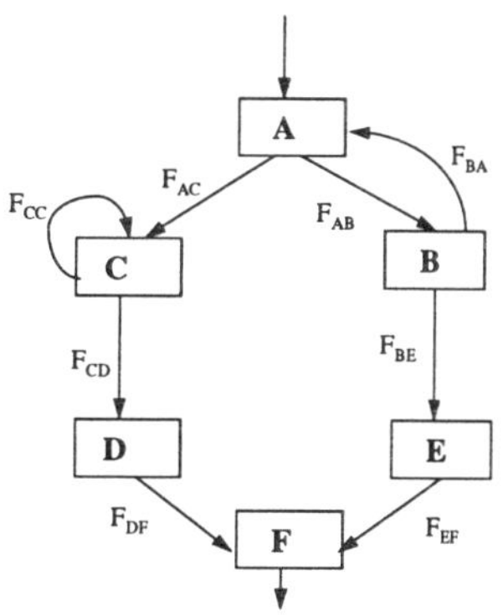

Figure 3. An example CFG.

The *selective indexing* profiling scheme uses the Knuth-Stevenson algorithm to determine the branches that should access the profile buffer. The profile buffer uses an arc-based profiling scheme because it endeavors to measure the frequencies of the arcs. However, the instrument of measurement, namely the branch instruction, exists in a node. Therefore, the Knuth-Stevenson algorithm can be directly applied to reduce the number of branches that need to be profiled, consequently reducing the number of accesses to the profile buffer and the number of contentions. In order to distinguish the branches that need to be profiled from those that should not be profiled, a minor modification is required in the instruction encoding of a branch. For this investigation, an additional bit is added to indicate whether or not the instruction needs to update information in the *profile buffer*.

There is an alternative to changing the existing ISA if the ISA provides for complements of every branch condition (for example, branch equal (BEQ) and branch not equal (BNE)). One half of these branch conditions can be intercepted by the *profile buffer* while the complements are

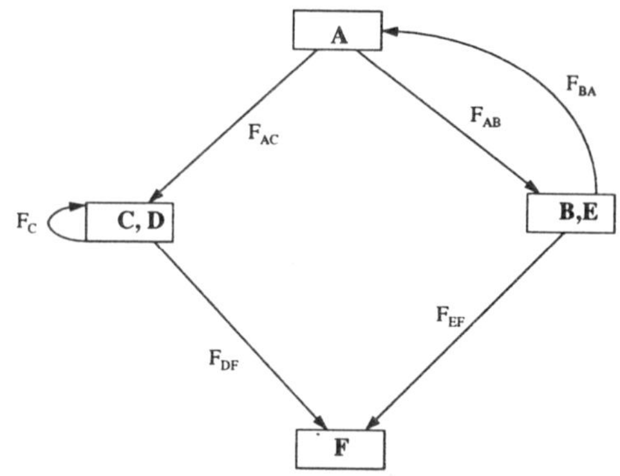

Figure 4. The first step in the Knuth-Stevenson reduction procedure. In this step, multiple vertices will be merged into a single combined vertex. For example, because $F_C = F_{CC} + F_{CD}$, we can make F_C by merging vertices, C and D.

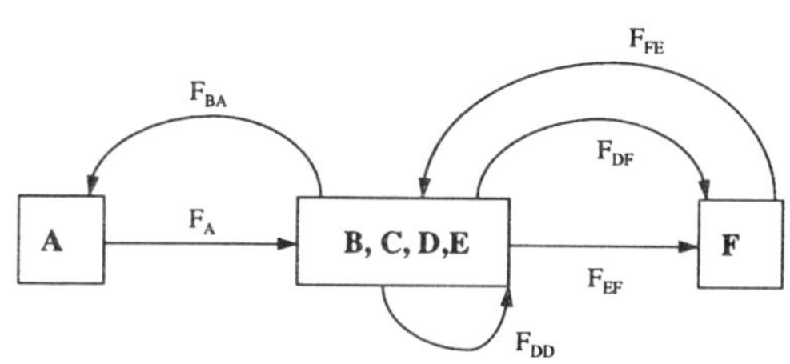

Figure 5. The second step in the Knuth-Stevenson reduction procedure. In this step, nodes are merged together so the number of vertices can be reduced further. For instance, F_{AC} and F_{AB} are merged into F_A.

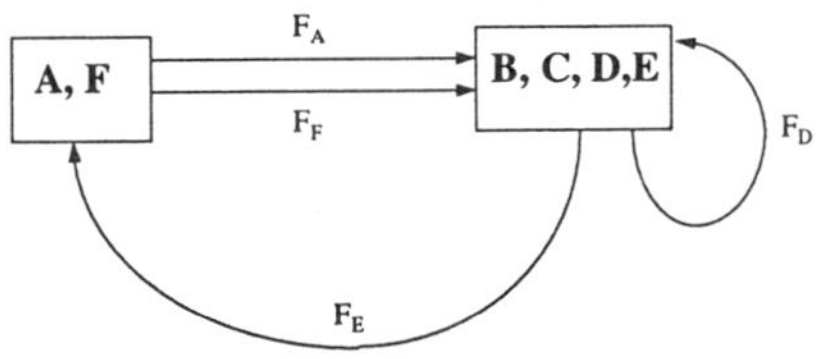

Figure 6. The Knuth-Stevenson reduced form of CFG. This CFG is produced by recursively applying step 2 until the CFG is in an optimal form. The nodes, A and E, are merged together so F_F is formed from F_{DF} and F_{EF}.

Table 3. Effect of reduction in profiling branches using *selective indexing*. (Contentions are shown as percentage of original accesses).

Benchmark	Change in accesses	Percent Contentions			
		8	16	32	64
compress	-46.2%	20.2%	12.1%	3.5%	0.5%
espresso	-30.5%	27.0%	10.4%	5.5%	2.1%
eqntott	-39.1%	34.1%	0.8%	0.1%	0.0%
gcc	-42.6%	28.1%	22.5%	17.2%	12.0%
li	-51.6%	30.6%	26.7%	20.1%	14.3%
sc	-43.1%	18.8%	6.7%	1.4%	0.3%
mean	-42.2%	26.5%	13.2%	8.0%	4.9%

ignored. For example, a BEQ operation could update the buffer while the BNE operation would not. If an operation is BNE and it's information needs to be recorded, this condition could be inverted and the recording operation could be changed to BEQ during code generation. Another alternative for architectures that use predicated branches (such as *HPL PlayDoh* [16]), is to profile every branch predicated on even-numbered predicates, but not profile branches predicated on odd-numbered ones. Thus, selective indexing can be retrofitted into an existing ISA without modification to the encoding.

The results for the *selective indexing* scheme using the suggested ISA change are presented in Table 3. The percent change in accesses is computed against the results produced by *address mapping*. The percent change in the number of accesses is considerable for all benchmarks. In particular, the number of accesses for four of the benchmarks are reduced by more than 40%. *Selective indexing* also affects the number of contentions across the buffer sizes. The percentage of contentions for *gcc* in an eight-entry buffer is 28.1% compared with 63.4% for *address mapping*. For 64 entries,

Table 4. The performance (IPC) of code compiled using profiling results obtained from buffers that employ the *selective indexing* scheme.

Benchmark	Instructions/cycle					
	exact	8	16	32	64	*none*
compress	2.71	2.32	2.78	2.45	2.50	1.38
espresso	2.36	2.05	1.93	2.18	2.29	1.20
eqntott	1.86	1.86	1.98	1.86	1.86	1.01
gcc	1.83	1.60	1.66	1.72	1.74	1.27
li	1.65	1.36	1.40	1.51	1.49	1.15
sc	2.29	1.71	2.00	2.20	2.10	1.25
harmonic mean	2.06	1.76	1.88	1.93	1.94	1.20

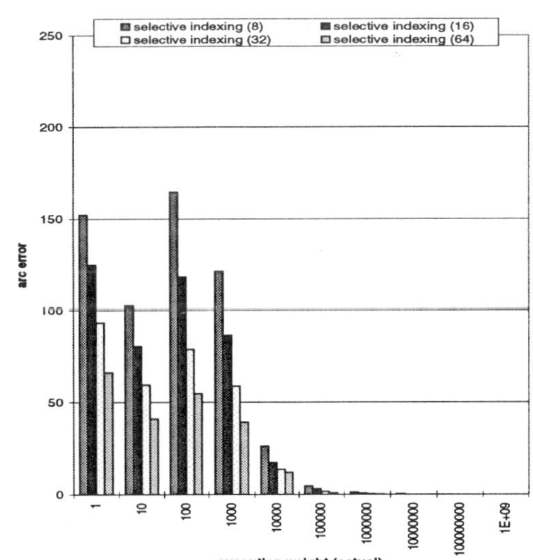

Figure 7. Arc error for the selective indexing technique.

the percentage of contentions for *gcc* is reduced to 12% from 40.9%. In addition, *li* also has a significant decrease in the percentage of contentions in an eight-entry buffer, 30.6% compared with 74.3% for *address mapping*. These reductions in contentions are due to the decrease in the number of branches competing for the same entries in the buffer.

Figure 7 shows the dramatic reduction in *arc error* resulting from the reduction in contentions. The error for branches that execute from a 100–1000 times is reduced by approximately 32% when compared to the address mapping technique for the eight–entry buffer. The reduction in error is seen across all buffer sizes. As seen in Table 4, the higher accuracy of the profile information assists in providing better performance (IPC). The results for superblock scheduling using the information obtained through the *selective indexing* approach in general are comparable to those obtained with *exact* profile information. However, in the case of *espresso*, a 16-entry buffer produces worse results than the eight-entry buffer. This is primarily due to erroneous profile information which causes the superblock formation algorithm to make incorrect decisions. Because the number of instructions in a basic block vary from one block to another, the addresses of the branch instructions do not follow any fixed pattern. This situation could lead to adjacent branches or branches in close proximity to access the same location in the buffer, thereby causing error in the profile information obtained. The error, however, can be reduced by controlling the buffer access pattern (shown in the section 2.4).

The performance for the benchmark *compress* in conjunction with *selective indexing* in some cases produces performance results that are better than their *exact* counterpart. This phenomenon was discussed in [9], where code scheduled for benchmarks such as *compress* were examined by hand. Two explanations were discovered: (*i*) erroneous profiles produce better performance because the error resulted in a larger superblock, which in turn produces a larger scope for the scheduler; and, (*ii*) there were benefits for scheduling down the less-likely path when the difference between arc counts was small. As an example of the latter, several cases were found where the error changed the superblock selection from the not-taken path of the branch to the taken path. Although the taken path was not executed as frequently as the not-taken path, the scheduler found many more opportunities for code motion along the less-likely path, resulting in higher overall performance. This evidence supports the fact that this phenomenon is due to a slight non-optimality caused by decoupling superblock formation from scheduling, rather than a shortcoming of hardware-based profiling [9].

2.4 Compiler indexing

A further refinement of the profile buffer indexing scheme is possible if the profiling process can be provided with extensive compiler support. In the *selective indexing* approach, one bit in the branch instruction was used to indicate that a branch instruction should be profiled. However, due to the limitations of mapping into the buffer with the address of the branch instruction, the results obtained are in some cases inaccurate. To improve the situation, the *compiler indexing* method encodes the profile buffer index into the branch instruction as an added field in the instruction set architecture. This index indicates the entry in the *profile buffer* that is to be updated by the branch instruction. The compiler initially selects branches for profiling as guided by the Knuth–Stevenson algorithm. It then assigns indexes to the selected branches in such a way as to guarantee that adjacent or near-by branches do not map into the same entry.

The efficiency of the *compiler indexing* scheme is illustrated in Table 5. The further reduction in contentions is indicative of the number of adjacent or near-by branches that caused the excessive contentions in the *address mapping* and *selective indexing* approaches. For example, the number of contentions for *gcc* is reduced to 26.8% (eight entries) as compared with 28.1% for *selective indexing*. Therefore the profile information obtained through this support from the compiler is expected to be more accurate and consistent.

The *arc error* for the *compiler indexing* scheme as shown

Table 5. Percent contentions of original accesses after reduction in profiling branches and using *compiler indexing*.

Benchmark	Percent Contentions			
	8	16	32	64
compress	15.5%	6.3%	0.0%	0.0%
espresso	11.8%	3.6%	0.9%	0.2%
eqntott	1.5%	0.2%	0.2%	0.2%
gcc	26.8%	22.3%	16.9%	11.1%
li	30.4%	25.5%	20.2%	15.6%
sc	10.2%	7.8%	0.5%	0.3%
mean	16.01%	10.96%	6.45%	4.56%

Table 6. The performance (IPC) of code compiled using profiling results obtained from buffers that employ the *compiler indexing* scheme.

Benchmark	Instructions/cycle					
	exact	8	16	32	64	*none*
compress	2.71	2.44	2.37	2.71	2.71	1.38
espresso	2.36	2.17	2.21	2.32	2.35	1.20
eqntott	1.86	1.86	1.67	1.86	1.86	1.01
gcc	1.83	1.49	1.59	1.68	1.71	1.27
li	1.65	1.37	1.41	1.46	1.52	1.15
sc	2.29	2.07	2.10	2.18	2.21	1.25
harmonic mean	2.06	1.82	1.83	1.95	1.98	1.20

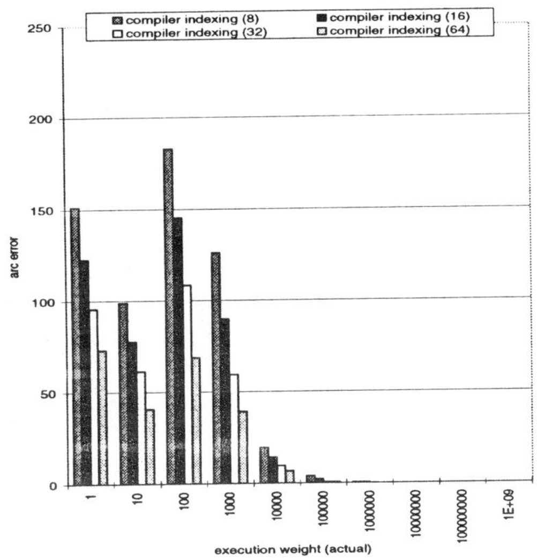

Figure 8. Arc error for the compiler indexing technique.

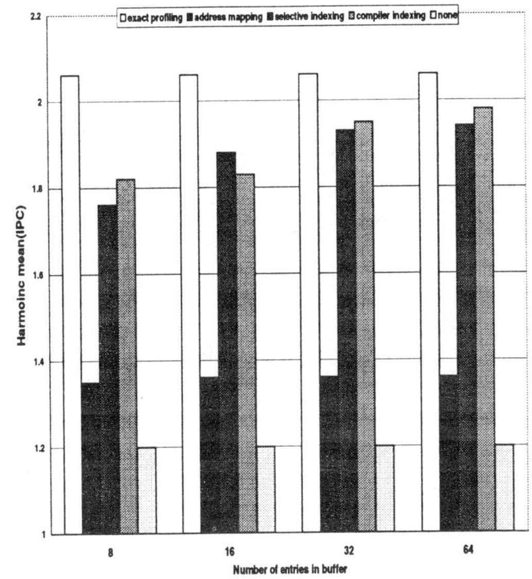

Figure 9. Comparison of the profile buffer schemes.

in Figure 8 is much lower that that for the *address mapping* technique and comparable to that for *selective indexing*. The technique yields lower errors than *selective indexing* for the most-frequently executed branches (i.e., execution weights 10^5–10^9). Table 6 shows the results of superblock formation obtained using the profile information from *compiler indexing*. The harmonic mean throughput is now seen to consistently increase as the size of the buffer is increased, demonstrating the increase in the accuracy of the profile information due to the reduction in contentions. The IPC achieved for a 32-entry and 64-entry buffer even approaches that obtained by using *exact* profile information. In the case of an eight-entry or 16-entry buffer, the IPC achieved is far better than without the use of any profile-information. However, the IPC prediction for the benchmark, *gcc*, is less accurate when *compiler indexing* is used. This is due to the fact that benchmarks such as *gcc* and *li* have a large number of function calls causing branches across functions to conflict. This could be remedied by inter–procedural index assignment or hardware *profile buffer* windows (discussed further below).

3 Analysis

The performance of the profile buffer is dependent on its size and its indexing scheme. This section presents some analysis of the results from the previous sections. The *harmonic mean* of the IPC is used in the performance analysis that follows, because the performance of the profile buffer schemes is expressed as a rate (IPC). The performance for all the profile buffer indexing schemes, *exact* profiling, and no profiling (*none*) are shown in Figure 9. It can be seen that the simple *address mapping* scheme provides a 13% execution performance increase when compared with the no profiling version. However, this scheme only provides about 78% of the possible peak performance. This failure to deliver peak performance is caused by the incompleteness of the information the *address mapping* scheme provides to the compiler due to the excessive number of contentions. In this scheme, there is almost one contention for every two access to the profile buffer (from Table 2).

The other two schemes, *selective indexing* and *compiler indexing*, show significant increases in performance when compared against no profiling and *address mapping*. *Selective indexing* achieves 85% – 94% of the performance of *exact* profiling, while *compiler indexing* provides a slightly higher 88% – 96% of the peak performance. The *selective indexing* approach performs almost as well as the *compiler indexing* method because *compiler indexing* only approximates *selective indexing* for workloads that use many function calls, such as *li* and *gcc*. This effect is more prominent when the buffer size is small (such as an eight or 16-entry buffer). Figure 10 shows a comparison in *arc error* between *selective indexing* and *compiler indexing* for the branches with high execution weights. In the case of such branches, *compiler indexing* yields lower error since the method of indexing limits the number of contentions when branches in close proximity are executed frequently, such as in tight inner loops. Figure 11 compares the arc error between the two techniques for lightly and medium executed branches. *Se-*

lective indexing provides comparable and sometimes more accurate information for such branches. This is a result of the naive implementation of compiler indexing which suffers when programs make frequent function calls as in *gcc* and *li*. The higher accuracy for medium-executed branches using *selective indexing* results in performance comparable to *compiler indexing* after superblock formation. At larger buffer sizes, the *compiler indexing* method can be expected to do better than *selective indexing* (see Figure 9). This suggests that integrating detailed inter-procedural analysis into the index allocation algorithm would improve *compiler indexing*, allowing for buffer sizes less than 32 entries.

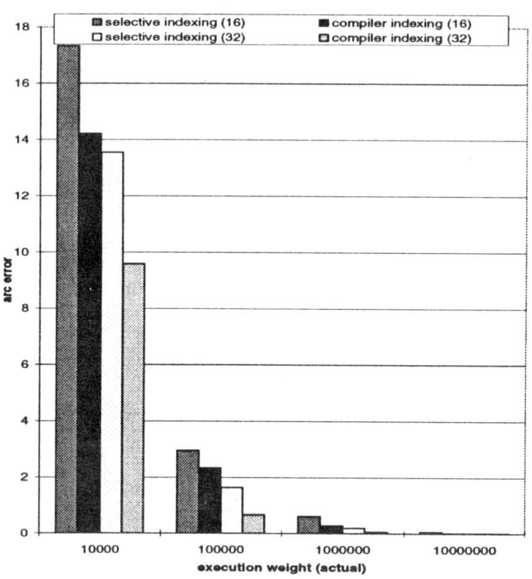

Figure 10. Comparison of indexing techniques for blocks with high execution weights.

4 Conclusion

A large amount of research in recent years has concentrated on the exploitation of instruction–level parallelism through automated compiler optimization using information obtained from previous runs of a program [11],[6],[7],[19],[6]. The techniques of gathering the required profile information, however, have depended upon traditional code instrumentation methods, which are not suitable for real–time, operating system, or interactive workloads, due primarily to the slowdown software profiling introduces. Fast and non-intrusive methods are required for effective, efficient profiling in order to gain commercial acceptance of profiling.

This paper further developed the ideas presented by

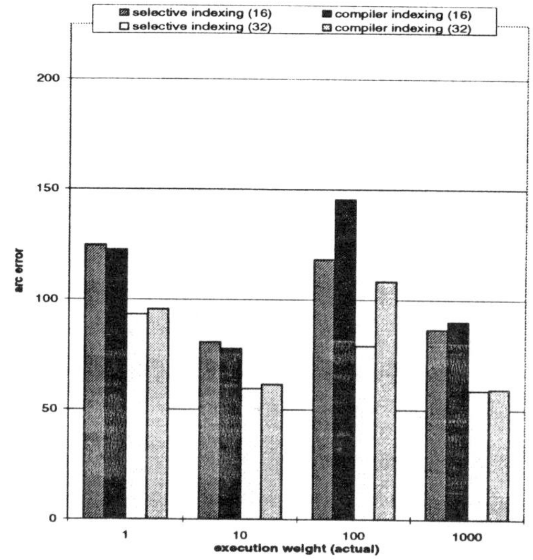

Figure 11. Comparison of indexing techniques for blocks with low execution weights.

Conte, *et al.* [8] for a hardware based profiling technique that does not significantly impact run–time. The goal of this paper was to improve accuracy of the information for compiler optimization. This was achieved by using a set of hardware based counters called the *profile buffer*. Three schemes for accessing the profile buffer were investigated. The first approach, *address mapping*, accessed the profile buffer for each and every dynamic branch, but suffered from excessive buffer contention for small buffers. The other two methods, *selective indexing*, and *compiler indexing*, limited the number of branches that could possibly access the *profile buffer*. The branches that access the buffer were determined using the Knuth-Stevenson algorithm. In the *selective indexing* scheme, one bit in the branch instruction was used to indicate a branch instruction to be profiled. In the *compiler indexing* scheme, however, a branch instruction contains an index into the *profile buffer* that is assigned at compile time.

The *address mapping* and *selective indexing* schemes are easily applicable to existing architectures without much overhead in cost. For *selective indexing*, one bit in the branch instruction is required to indicate the branch to be profiled. It is also possible to implement *selective indexing* without change in the ISA if the ISA provides for complements of every branch condition (for example, branch equal (BEQ) and branch not equal (BNE)). In the *compiler indexing* scheme, a few additional bits are required depending on the size of the *profile buffer*. The dumping of the buffer on a context–switch is the only demand placed on the operating system. One other advantage of the profile buffer is that it is not in the critical path, allowing for a lazy-increment implementation of its counters to further reduce its implementation cost.

All of the proposed indexing approaches provide high performance when used for superblock formation, even though the size of the profile buffer required to generate moderately accurate and complete profile information is small. In fact, even small profile buffers of 16-32 entries employing *selective indexing* or *compiler indexing* perform well. The experimental results further indicate that a buffer with 32 or more entries provides about 95% of the performance that is achieved with the use of the exact multiple pass profiling sequence. When coupled with alpha/beta testing software development processes that are already used by most commercial software vendors, the low impact of hardware based profiling using the profiling buffer becomes a viable and commercial technique to aid profile-driven optimization.

Acknowledgments

This work was supported by Intel Corporation and the National Science Foundation under grants MIP-9696010 and MIP-9625007.

We especially thank the University of Illinois IMPACT group for use of the IMPACT compiler.

References

[1] D. Alpert and D. Avnon. Architecture of the Pentium microprocessor. *IEEE Micro*, 13(3):11–21, June 1993.

[2] T. Ball and J. R. Larus. Optimally profiling and tracing programs. Technical Report 1031, Computer Sciences Dept., University of Wisconsin-Madison, 1991.

[3] T. Ball and J. R. Larus. Optimally profiling and tracing programs. In *Proceedings of the ACM SIGPLAN '92 Conference on Principles of Programming Languages*, pages 59–70, 1992.

[4] T. Ball and J. R. Larus. Branch prediction for free. In *Proceedings of the ACM SIGPLAN '93 Conference on Programming Language Design and Implementation*, pages 300–313, Albuquerque, NM, June 1993.

[5] P. P. Chang, S. A. Mahlke, W. Y. Chen, N. J. Warter, and W. W. Hwu. IMPACT: An architectural framework for multiple-instruction-issue processors. In *Proc. 18th Ann. International Symposium Computer Architecture*, pages 266–275, Toronto, Canada, May 1991.

[6] P. P. Chang, S. A. Mahlke, and W. W. Hwu. Using profile information to assist classic code optimizations. *Software–Practice and Experience*, 21(12):1301–1321, Dec. 1991.

[7] W. Y. Chen. *Data preload for superscalar and VLIW processors*. PhD thesis, Dept. of Electrical and Computer Engineering, University of Illinois, Urbana-Champaign, IL, 1993.

[8] T. M. Conte, B. A. Patel, and J. S. Cox. Using branch handling hardware to support profile-driven optimization. In *Proc. 27th Ann. International Symposium on Microarchitecture*, San Jose, CA, Nov. 1994.

[9] T. M. Conte, B. A. Patel, K. Menezes, and J. S. Cox. Hardware-based profiling: An effective technique for profile-driven optimization. *Internation Journal of Parallel Programming*, 24(2), Feb. 1996.

[10] J. S. Cox, D. P. Howell, and T. M. Conte. Commercializing profile-driven optimization. In *Proc. 28th Hawaii Int'l. Conf. on System Sciences*, volume 1, Maui, HI, Jan. 1995.

[11] J. A. Fisher. Trace scheduling: A technique for global microcode compaction. *IEEE Trans. Comput.*, C-30(7):478–490, July 1981.

[12] S. L. Graham, P. B. Kessler, and M. K. McKusick. gprof: A call graph execution profiler. In *Proc. 1982 SIGPLAN Symp. Compiler Construction*, pages 120–126, June 1982.

[13] R. E. Hank, S. A. Mahlke, J. C. Gyllenhaal, R. Bringmann, and W. W. Hwu. Superblock formation using static program analysis. In *Proc. 26th Ann. Int'l. Symp. on Microarchitecture*, pages 247–255, Austin, TX, Dec. 1993.

[14] Hewlett-Packard. *PA-RISC 1.1 Architecture and Instruction Set Reference Manual*. California, USA, 1994.

[15] W. W. Hwu, S. A. Mahlke, W. Y. Chen, P. P. Chang, N. J. Warter, R. A. Bringmann, R. G. Ouellette, R. E. Hank, T. Kiyohara, G. E. Haab, J. G. Holm, and D. M. Lavery. The superblock: An effective structure for VLIW and superscalar compilation. *The Journal of Supercomputing*, 7(1):229–248, Jan. 1993.

[16] V. Kathail, M. Schlansker, and B. R. Rau. HPL PlayDoh architecture specification: version 1.0. Technical Report HPL-93-80, Hewlett-Packard Laboratories, Technical Publications Department, 1501 Page Mill Road, Palo Alto, CA 94304, Feb. 1994.

[17] D. E. Knuth and F. R. Stevenson. Optimal measurement points for program frequency counts. *BIT*, 13:313–322, 1973.

[18] S. A. Mahlke, R. E. Hank, J. E. McCormick, D. I. August, and W. M. Hwu. A comparison of full and partial predicated execution support for ILP processors. In *Proc. 22nd Ann. International Symposium Computer Architecture*, pages 138–149, Santa Margherita Ligure, Italy, June 1995.

[19] S. McFarling and J. L. Hennessy. Reducing the cost of branches. In *Proc. 13th Ann. International Symposium Computer Architecture*, pages 396–403, Tokyo, Japan, June 1986.

[20] MIPS Computer Systems. *UMIPS-V Reference Manual*. Sunnyvale, CA, 1990.

[21] A. D. Samples. *Profile-Driven Compilation*. PhD thesis, Computer Science Division, University of California, Berkeley, California, Apr. 1991. Report No. UCB/CSD 91/627.

[22] S. Weiss and J. E. Smith. *POWER and PowerPC*. Morgan Kaufmann, San Francisco, CA, 1994.

[23] T. Yeh and Y. N. Patt. Two-level adaptive training branch prediction. In *Proc. 24th Ann. International Symposium on Microarchitecture*, pages 51–61, Albuquerque, NM, Nov. 1991.

Efficient Path Profiling

Thomas Ball
Bell Laboratories
Lucent Technologies
tball@research.bell-labs.com

James R. Larus*
Dept. of Computer Sciences
University of Wisconsin-Madison
larus@cs.wisc.edu

Abstract

A path profile *determines how many times each acyclic path in a routine executes. This type of profiling subsumes the more common basic block and edge profiling, which only approximate path frequencies. Path profiles have many potential uses in program performance tuning, profile-directed compilation, and software test coverage.*

This paper describes a new algorithm for path profiling. This simple, fast algorithm selects and places profile instrumentation to minimize run-time overhead. Instrumented programs run with overhead comparable to the best previous profiling techniques. On the SPEC95 benchmarks, path profiling overhead averaged 31%, as compared to 16% for efficient edge profiling. Path profiling also identifies longer paths than a previous technique, which predicted paths from edge profiles (average of 88, versus 34 instructions). Moreover, profiling shows that the SPEC95 train *input datasets covered most of the paths executed in the* ref *datasets.*

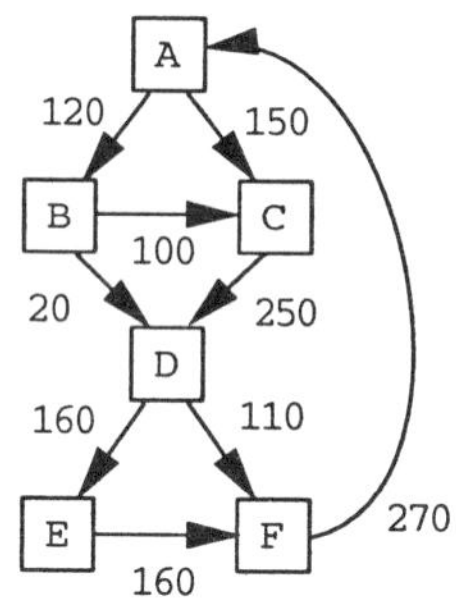

Path	Prof1	Prof2
ACDF	90	110
ACDEF	60	40
ABCDF	0	0
ABCDEF	100	100
ABDF	20	0
ABDEF	0	20

Figure 1. Example in which edge profiling does not identify the most frequently executed paths. The table contains two different path profiles. Both path profiles induce the same edge execution frequencies, shown by the edge frequencies in the control-flow graph. In path profile $Prof1$, path $ABCDEF$ is most frequently executed, although the heuristic of following edges with the highest frequency identifies path $ACDEF$ as the most frequent.

1 Introduction

Program profiling counts occurrences of an event during a program's execution. Typically, the measured event is the execution of a local portion of a program, such as a routine or line of code. Recently, fine-grain profiles—of basic blocks and control-flow edges—have become the basis for profile-driven compilation, which uses measured frequencies to guide compilation and optimization.

One use of profile information is to identify heavily executed paths (or traces) in a program [Fis81, Ell85, Cha88, YS94]. Unfortunately, basic block and edge profiles, although inexpensive and widely available, do not always correctly predict frequencies of overlapping paths. Consider, for example, the control-flow graph (CFG) in Figure 1. Each edge in the CFG is labeled with its frequency, which normally results from dynamic profiling, but in the figure is induced by *both* path profiles in the table. A commonly used heuristic to select a heavily executed path follows the most frequently executed edge out of a basic block [Cha88], which identifies path $ACDEF$. However, in path profile $Prof1$, this path executed only 60 times, as compared to 90 times for path $ACDF$ and 100 times for path $ABCDEF$. In profile $Prof2$, the disparity is even greater although the edge profile is exactly the same.

This inaccuracy is usually ignored, under the assumption that accurate path profiling must be far more expensive than basic block or edge profiling. Path profiling is the ultimate form of control-flow profiling, as it uniquely deter-

*This research supported by: Wright Laboratory Avionics Directorate, Air Force Material Command, USAF, under grant #F33615-94-1-1525 and ARPA order no. B550; NSF NYI Award CCR-9357779, with support from Hewlett Packard, Sun Microsystems, and PGI; NSF Grant MIP-9225097; and DOE Grant DE-FG02-93ER25176. The U.S. Government is authorized to reproduce and distribute reprints for Governmental purposes notwithstanding any copyright notation thereon. The views and conclusions contained herein are those of the authors and should not be interpreted as necessarily representing the official policies or endorsements, either expressed or implied, of the Wright Laboratory Avionics Directorate or the U. S. Government.

1072-4451/96 $5.00 © 1996 IEEE

mines both basic block and edge profiles, although the converse does not hold, as Figure 1 shows. Also, the number of blocks or edges in a program is finite and linear in the program's size, but a program with loops offers an unbounded number of potential paths. Considering only acyclic paths bounds this set, but, in the worst case, its size is still exponential in the program's size.

This paper shows that accurate profiling is neither complex nor expensive. It describes a new and efficient technique for *path profiling*. Our algorithm places instrumentation that accurately determines dynamic execution frequency of control-flow paths in a routine. The instrumentation is not only simple and low-cost, but it is placed in a way that minimizes its overhead. Remarkably, although path profiling collects far more information than block or edge profiling, its overhead can be lower and is usually comparable—on the SPEC95 benchmarks, path profiling's average overhead is 31%, while efficient edge profiling's overhead is 16%.

Efficient path profiling opens new possibilities for program optimization and performance tuning. Instead of relying on heuristics, which fully predict only 38% of the executed acyclic paths in the SPEC95 benchmarks, profile-driven compilers can base their decisions on accurate measurements.

Another potential application of path profiling is software test coverage, which quantifies the adequacy of a test data set by profiling a program and reporting unexecuted statements or control-flow. Few, if any, coverage tools measure path coverage. Instead, tools rely on weaker criteria, such as statement or control-flow edge coverage. Edge profiling is less complete than path profiling, as shown in Figure 1, where the two path profiles cover different sets of paths yet induce the same edge profile. Besides an efficient algorithm for path profiling, this paper also presents measurements that show that most *routines* in a small sample of programs have few (< 3000) potential paths, so that path coverage testing could be feasible for large portions of a program. On the other hand, the measurements also demonstrate the difficulty of developing test data sets, since the programs *as a whole* executed an average of 2696 paths (249–24414), as compared to the millions of potential paths identified by the path profiling algorithm.

1.1 Algorithm Overview

The essential idea behind the path profiling algorithm is to identify sets of potential paths with states, which are encoded as integers. Consider for a moment a routine without a loop. Upon entry to the routine, all paths are possible. Taking a conditional branch narrows the set of potential paths and corresponds to a transition to a new state. At the routine's exit, the final state represents the single path taken

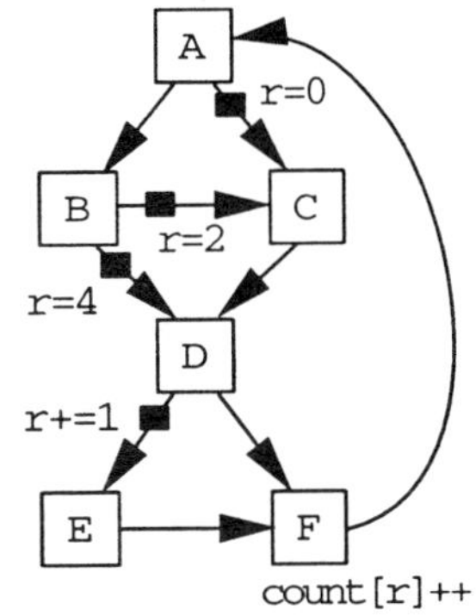

Path	Encoding
ACDF	0
ACDEF	1
ABCDF	2
ABCDEF	3
ABDF	4
ABDEF	5

Figure 2. Path profiling instrumentation. Each path from A to F produces a unique state in register r, which indexes an array of counters in F.

through the routine. This paper presents an efficient algorithm that:

- Numbers final states from $0 \ldots n-1$, where n is the number of potential paths in a routine. With this compact numbering, a final state can directly index an array of counters.
- Places instrumentation so that transitions need not occur at every conditional branch.
- Assigns states so that transitions can be computed by a simple arithmetic operation, without an explicit state transition table or memory reference.
- Transforms a control-flow graph containing loops or huge numbers of potential paths into an acyclic graph with a limited number of paths.

Figure 2 illustrates the technique. Edges labeled by small squares contain instrumentation, which updates the state in register r. The loop contains six unique paths, and each one computes a different value for r, as shown in the table. At the end of the loop body (block F), register r holds the index to increment an array of counters.

1.2 Extensions

The algorithm in this paper can be easily extended in several ways. First, instead of intraprocedural profiling, it could be applied to a program's call graph, to record call paths. An interesting complication is indirect calls, which require a dynamic data structure to record calls along edges that are not in the call graph.

Also, instead of just counting the number of times a path executes, the profiling algorithm can easily accumulate a metric for a path. Some processors provide accessible counters for metrics such as the number of processor cycles, stalls, cache misses, or page faults. A minor change to the path profiling code could increment a path's counter by the change in a counter over the path.

1.3 Paper Overview

The path profiling algorithm instruments a program to record paths with low run-time overhead. The algorithm uses previous results on efficient profiling and tracing [BL94] and efficient event counting [Bal94] to determine which edges to instrument. The contribution of this paper is combine these algorithms, apply them to a new problem, and develop a new algorithm to compute an update constant for each instrumented edge. The algorithm ensures that each distinct path generates a unique value. Furthermore, the path encoding is compact and minimal, so that the maximum value for any path is the number of unique paths through a CFG (minus one), as in Figure 2. A simple, linear-time algorithm achieves both goals (Section 3).

This paper only considers intra-procedural acyclic paths, which result from removing loop backedges before instrumentation (Section 4). This process produces a profile that does not capture paths that cross a backedge. However, acyclic path profiling counts the number of times that a loop iterates and records both paths into the first iteration and out of the last loop iteration. The same approach, of removing edges, can also limit the number of paths in complex routines, so that states can be represented as 32-bit integers. Even so, large routines can have too many states to use an array of counters. In this case, a hash table records paths that actually execute, so that the space overhead is proportional to the number of dynamic paths, rather than the number of potential static paths. The relatively high cost of hashing accounts for the higher overhead of path profiling, as compared to edge profiling.

We implemented the algorithms presented here in a profiling tool, *PP*, which uses the EEL library [LS95] to insert instrumentation into executable binaries (Section 5). This paper compares PP against QPT2, another profiling tool built with EEL, which uses an efficient edge profiling algorithm [BL94]. QPT2 usually incurred less overhead, but the two system were roughly comparable. Profiling the SPEC95 benchmarks, PP's overhead averaged 31% (6–97%) while QPT2's overhead averaged 16% (-2.6–53%) (Section 6). The measurements also compare profiled paths against paths predicted using edge profiles and show that for the SPEC95 benchmarks, which execute few unique paths, profiling identifies longer paths (an average of 7 CFG edges and 88 instructions, versus 5 edges and 34 instructions for predicted paths). Moreover, path profiling shows that the paths executed with the SPEC95 *train* dataset cover most of the dynamically executed instructions in the *ref* dataset, which suggests that path profiles could help improve SPEC95 peak numbers.

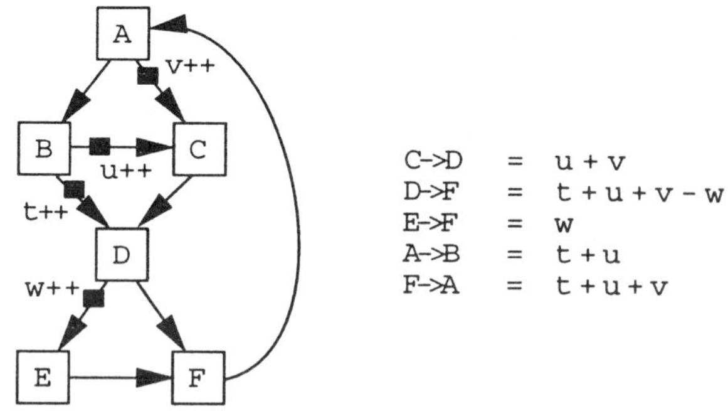

Figure 3. Instrumentation for edge profiling.

2 Related Work

The path profiling algorithm, like previous work on efficient profiling and tracing techniques [BL94, Gol91], uses a spanning tree to determine a minimal, low-cost set of edges to instrument. For example, Figure 3 shows the control-flow graph from Figure 2 instrumented for edge profiling (the uninstrumented edges form a spanning tree). The same set of edges are instrumented in both cases. However, for edge profiling, each instrumented edge has its own counter (held in memory), which is incremented each time the edge executes. Figure 3 also shows how uninstrumented edges' counts are derived from recorded counts.

Path profiling produces a more detailed profile, although it instruments the same set of edges. Moreover, most path profiling instrumentation consists of register instructions, while every edge profiling instrumentation increments memory. In general, a path that executes N memory increments for edge profiling will execute N register initializations/adds plus one memory increment for path profiling. In practice, there are many procedures for which the number of potential paths is small (so arrays may be used) and path profiling incurs less overhead than edge profiling. However, there are procedures that have so many potential paths that a hash table must be used to store the profile.

Young and Smith used a limited form of program tracing to record paths for their branch correlation studies [YS94]. In a FIFO buffer, they recorded the last n branches, each of which consists of a basic block number and branch outcome. This technique is both more expensive than path profiling and also requires another level of indirection to associate a counter with a path, which consists of a sequence of block numbers. Unlike path profiling, this technique need not distinguish cyclic from acyclic paths since it truncates both at the FIFO boundary.

Bit tracing is another approach to path profiling. Bit tracing associates a 1-bit value with the outcome of each two-

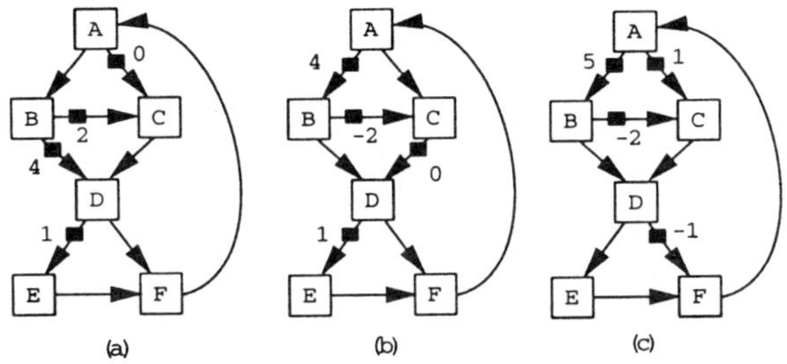

Figure 4. Three possible placements of instrumentation for the control-flow graph from Figure 1.

way branch [BL94, Bal96]. When a branch executes, instrumentation code appends a bit to a trace buffer that records branch outcomes. By recording multiple bits, the approach can be extended to multi-way branches. The contents of the buffer form an index into an array or as a hash value.

It is easy to see that bit tracing uses the minimal number of bits necessary to distinguish paths. For simple control-flow graphs, such as a chain of if-then-else statements, bit tracing, like our approach, produces a compact representations of paths. However, in general, bit tracing may not yield the most compact representations of paths possible. It is easy to construct examples for which the maximal path value under bit tracing is not minimal, no matter the choice of bit labellings. In the worst case, the number of entries in an array of counters may be twice our method.

In addition, bit tracing is likely to have higher run-time overhead than our approach. First, every predicate must be instrumented, whereas our approach allows flexibility in placing instrumentation to reduce overhead. Second, on most machines, the instrumentation to append to a bit string is more complex and slower than a register-to-register addition.

3 Path Profiling of DAGs

As described previously, path profiling tracks a path in a directed acyclic graph (DAG) by updating a register along certain edges of the DAG. This section shows how to compute the necessary updates, efficiently place instrumentation, and derive an executed path from the resulting profile.

The example in Figure 4 shows that many placements of instrumentation yield equivalent results. However, some placements incur less run-time overhead than others. For example, all three graphs in Figure 4 produce the same sum along any acyclic path from A to F. However, in graph (a), the largest number of instrumented edges on any path from A to F is two, while graphs (b) and (c) have up to four and three, respectively.

The path profiling algorithm first labels edges in a DAG with integer values, such that each path from the entry to the exit of the DAG produces a unique sum of the edge values along that path (the *path sum*). However, placements from this step may have sub-optimal run-time overhead, as above.

In the next step, another algorithm [Bal94] improves this computation, by finding an equivalent computation that uses a minimal number of additions along DAG edges that are not in the DAG's spanning tree. In each graph in Figure 4, the uninstrumented edges (those without squares along them) form a spanning tree. Since a DAG may have many spanning trees, the algorithm has the freedom to place instrumentation along edges less likely to be executed.[1]

After reviewing the basic graph terminology in Section 3.1, this section describes the four basic steps to path profile a DAG:

1. Assign integer values to edges such that no two paths compute the same path sum (Section 3.2). This encoding is minimal.
2. Use a spanning tree to select edges to instrument and compute the appropriate increment for each instrumented edge (Section 3.3).
3. Select appropriate instrumentation (Section 3.4).
4. After collecting the run-time profile, derive the executed paths (Section 3.5).

3.1 Terminology

For the remainder of this paper, unless otherwise noted, control-flow graphs (CFGs) have been converted into directed acyclic graphs (DAG) with a unique source vertex $ENTRY$ and sink vertex $EXIT$. Section 4 shows how to transform an arbitrary CFG into a DAG, which can be path profiled. For technical reasons, the increment computation (Section 3.3) requires a "dummy" edge $EXIT \rightarrow ENTRY$ (although this creates an unexecutable cycle, the graph can still be treated as a DAG by ignoring this backedge).

An execution of a DAG produces an acyclic, directed path starting at $ENTRY$ and ending at $EXIT$. The term *path* refers to an acyclic directed path, unless otherwise noted. Of course, a DAG may execute many times, as it may consist of a loop body or a procedure.

A spanning tree of a graph G is a subgraph that is a tree and contains all vertices of G. Edges in a spanning tree are bidirectional and need not follow the direction of graph

[1] This approach requires computing (or obtaining from a profile) a weight for each edge that statically approximates the edge's execution frequency. A maximum spanning tree of the graph, with respect to that weighting, maximizes the weight (execution frequency) of the uninstrumented edges. PP uses the same previously published, effective algorithm for statically computing a weighting as QPT [BL94].

```
foreach vertex v in reverse topological order {
  if v is a leaf vertex {
    NumPaths(v) = 1;
  } else {
    NumPaths(v) = 0;
    for each edge e = v->w {
      Val(e) = NumPaths(v);
      NumPaths(v) = NumPaths(v) + NumPaths(w);
    }
  }
}
```

Figure 5. Algorithm for assigning values to edges in a DAG.

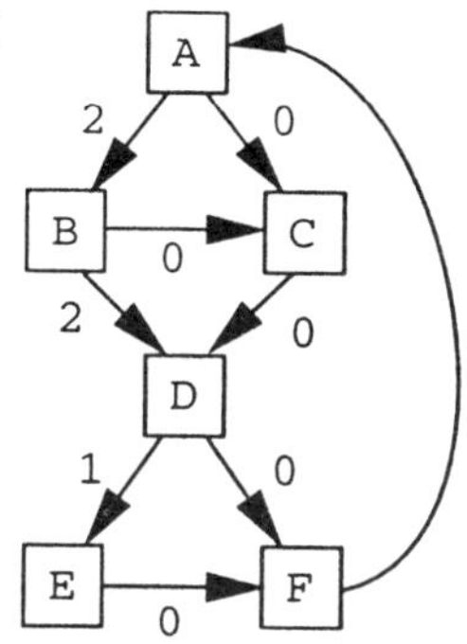

Vertex v	NumPaths(v)
A	6
B	4
C	2
D	2
E	1
F	1

Figure 6. Control-flow graph from Figure 1, with values computed by the algorithm in Figure 5.

edges. If T is the set of spanning tree edges, then any graph edge not in T is a *chord* of the spanning tree.

For example, in the graph of Figure 2, vertex A is the $ENTRY$ vertex and vertex F is the $EXIT$ vertex. The unadorned graph edges comprise a spanning tree. The edges labeled by squares are chords of the spanning tree.

3.2 Compactly Representing Paths with Sums

The first step in path profiling is to assign a non-negative constant value $Val(e)$ to each edge e in a DAG, such that the sum of values along any path from $ENTRY$ to $EXIT$ is unique. Furthermore, the path sums should lie in the range from 0 to the number of paths (minus one), so that the encoding is minimal.

The algorithm in Figure 5 computes such a Val relation by visiting vertices of the DAG in reverse topological order. This order ensures that all the successors of a vertex v are visited before v itself. Associated with each vertex v is a value $NumPaths(v)$, which records the number of paths from v to $EXIT$. The algorithm is simple. At vertex v, the algorithm visits all of v's outgoing edges $v \rightarrow w_i$, $1 \leq i \leq n$, and assigns the kth outgoing edge the value:

$$Val(v \rightarrow w_k) = \sum_{i=1}^{k-1} NumPaths(w_i)$$

The following theorem proves the algorithm correct:

Theorem 1 *Given a DAG, after the algorithm of Figure 5 visits vertex v, $NumPaths(v)$ is the number of paths from v to $EXIT$ and each path from v to $EXIT$ generates a unique value sum in the range $0 \ldots NumPaths(v) - 1$.*

Proof. By induction on the height of a vertex in the DAG (i.e., the max number of steps to the sink vertex $EXIT$).

Base Case: v has height equal to zero (that is, $v = EXIT$), so $NumPaths(v) = 1$. The theorem is trivially satisfied.

Induction Step: Show that the theorem holds for any vertex v of height H ($H > 0$). All successors $w_1 \ldots w_n$ of v must have height less than H (because the graph is a DAG), so the theorem holds for all w_i. It is trivial to see that the number of paths from v to $EXIT$ is $\sum_{i=1}^{n} NumPaths(w_i)$, which the algorithm computes. By the induction hypothesis, each path from w_k to $EXIT$ generates a unique value sum in the range $0 \ldots NumPaths(w_k) - 1$. Therefore, any path from v to $EXIT$ starting with edge $v \rightarrow w_k$ will generate a unique value in the range $\sum_{i=1}^{k-1} NumPaths(w_i) \ldots (\sum_{i=1}^{k} NumPaths(w_i)) - 1$. Since all $NumPaths(w_i)$ values are greater than 0, it follows that no two paths from v to $EXIT$ generate the same value sum. □

Figure 6 illustrates how the algorithm operates on the example control-flow graph. Note that vertices are labeled in topological ordering, so $FEDCBA$ is a reverse topological order. Any vertex with a single outgoing edge e, such as C and E, always has $Val(e) = 0$.

3.3 Efficiently Computing Sums

Given an edge value assignment, the second step of the algorithm finds a minimal cost set—with respect to a weighting (Section 3)—of edges along which to compute these values, while preserving the two properties of the value assignment.

This step of the algorithm finds a maximal cost spanning tree of the graph (to find a minimal cost set of chord edges), and applies an efficient event counting technique [Bal94] to determine the increment $Inc(c)$ for each chord c in a spanning tree. The event counting algorithm ensures that the sum of Inc values for any path P from $ENTRY$ to $EXIT$ is identical to the sum of Val values for P. Note that some of the Inc values may be negative, as in Figure 4. The edge $EXIT \rightarrow ENTRY$ is required for this step (if this edge is

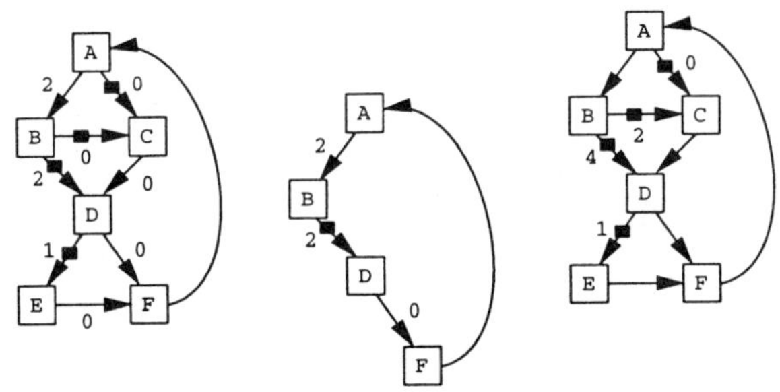


```
Inc(B->D)  = Val(A->B) + Val(B->D) + Val(D->F) + Val(F->A)
           = 2 + 2 + 0 + 0
           = 4
```

Figure 7. Application of event counting algorithm to determine chord increments.

selected as a chord, then its instrumentation can be placed in the $EXIT$ vertex).

Figure 7 shows how the event counting algorithm applies to the example control-flow graph. The graph on the left contains the value assignment and the chord edges (those with squares along them). The graph in the middle shows the unique cycle of spanning tree edges associated with chord $B \rightarrow D$. The values along edges in this cycle determine the increment for chord $B \rightarrow D$, which in this case is four. Informally, the algorithm propagates the value of two from edge $A \rightarrow B$ to the chord $B \rightarrow D$. The graph on the right contains increments for all chords. Each path from A to F in this graph yields the same path sum as in the graph on the left.

3.4 Instrumentation

After computing chord increments, the algorithm selects instrumentation. Of course, at the start of a program's execution, the array of counters must be allocated and initialized to 0. At program termination, this array is written to permanent storage.

Besides this prelude and postlude instrumentation, the remaining instrumentation has three tasks: initializing path register r [`r = 0`] in the $ENTRY$ vertex; updating r in chord c [`r += Inc(c)`]; and incrementing a path's memory counter in the $EXIT$ vertex [`count[r]++`]. However, in many cases, an optimization can combine updates with the other two operations, as shown in Figure 2.

The optimization for initialization is:

> (1) A chord c may initialize the path register [`r=Inc(c)`] if and only if c is the first chord in every path from $ENTRY$ to $EXIT$ containing c.

If there exists a path in which chord c is the first chord and another path in which c is not the first chord, then chord c must update rather than initialize r. However, in this case, moving the initialization [`r=0`] as close to c as possible avoids redundant initialization of r.

A similar optimization works for counter increments:

> (2) A chord c may increment the path register and memory counter [`count[r+Inc(c)]++`] if and only if c is the last chord in every path from $ENTRY$ to $EXIT$ containing c.

This optimization can fold an addition into a memory address calculation.

If a chord c contains initialization as well as a counter increment, the instrumentation simply becomes `count[Inc(c)]++`.

The algorithm in Figure 8 places instrumentation properly. The first **while** loop moves initialization code to chord edges when possible, and otherwise moves it far enough from the $ENTRY$ vertex so that no initialization is redundant. The second loop places the memory increment code. The invariant of the first loop is that for each vertex w added to the working set, there is only one path from $ENTRY$ to w in the DAG and this path contains no chords. Note that if there are two paths from $ENTRY$ to a vertex w, one of these paths must contain a chord, so any chord encountered from w onward cannot satisfy this condition. A similar invariant is maintained by the second **while** loop.

Figure 9 shows the instrumentation for the control-flow graph from Figure 1. Note that edges $A \rightarrow C$, $B \rightarrow C$ and $B \rightarrow D$ now initialize register r, eliminating the need to initialize r at vertex A. Furthermore, the update along edge $D \rightarrow E$ has been combined with the counter increment code. However, notice that a counter increment is required along edge $D \rightarrow E$ as well.

3.5 Regenerating a Path

To recreate a path profile from the path counters recorded at run time, it is necessary to map from the integer representing a path to the path itself. This is done using the value assignment computed previously (Section 3.2).

The regeneration algorithm is straight forward. Regeneration starts from a control flow graph's $ENTRY$ node and traverses the graph, using the path value to select which edge to follow out of a basic block. Let v be a vertex in the reconstructed path and let R be the path value. Initially, $v = ENTRY$ and R is the number of the path to regenerate. At each block, find $e = v \rightarrow w$, which is the outgoing edge of v with the largest $Val(e) \leq R$. As the path traverses edge e, let $v = w$ and $R = R - Val(e)$. Repeat this process until control reaches the $EXIT$ vertex.

For example, consider the control-flow graph in Figure 6. Suppose that the initial path value R is 3. At vertex A, the algorithm will choose edge $A \rightarrow B$ and decrement R by 2.

```
// Register initialization code
//
WS.add(ENTRY);
while not WS.empty() {
  vertex v = WS.remove();
  for each edge e = v->w
    if e is a chord edge
      instrument(e, 'r=Inc(e)');
    else if e is the only incoming edge of w
      WS.add(w);
    else instrument(e, 'r=0');
}

// Memory increment code
//
WS.add(EXIT)
while not WS.empty() {
  vertex w = WS.remove();
  for each edge e = v->w
    if e is a chord edge {
      if e's instrumentation is 'r=Inc(e)'
        instrument(e, 'count[Inc(e)]++');
      else
        instrument(e, 'count[r+Inc(e)]++');
    } else if e is the only outgoing edge of v
      WS.add(v);
    else instrument(e, 'count[r]++');
}

// Register increment code
//
for all uninstrumented chords c
  instrument(c,'r+=Inc(c)')
```

Figure 8. Algorithm for placing instrumentation.

At vertex B, $R = 1$, so the algorithm traverses edge $B \to C$ and then $C \to D$. At vertex D, R still has a value of 1, so the path traverses edge $D \to E$, followed by $E \to F$. The resulting regenerated path is $ABCDEF$, which is the path that generates the path sum 3.

3.6 Early Termination

Like other efficient profiling algorithms [BL94], path profiling requires extra information to derive correct profiles for routines that terminate unexpectedly because of exceptions, unrecognized non local gotos, or calls to exit. This information consists of the address of unterminated calls and can easily be obtained from a program's stack at an unexpected event. The event counting algorithm provides a way to correctly update the counters in these routines [Bal94].

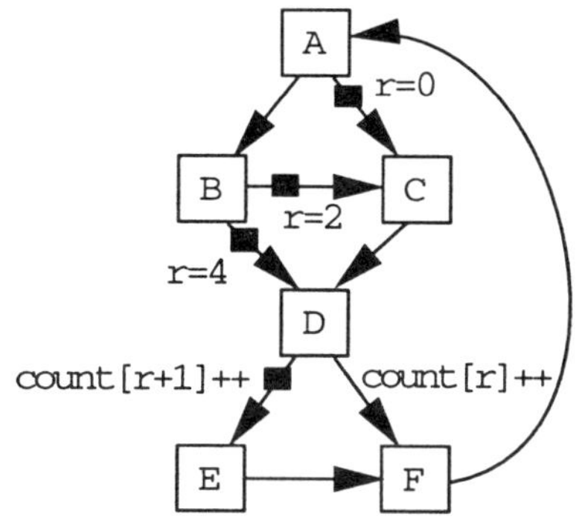

Figure 9. Optimization of instrumentation for the control-flow graph of Figure 1.

4 Path Profiling of Arbitrary Control-Flow

This section extends path profiling to arbitrary control-flow graphs that contain cycles (including irreducible loops). Any cycle in a control-flow graph must contain a backedge (as identified by a depth-first search of the graph). The algorithm in Section 3 only works for acyclic paths, which correspond to backedge-free paths.

Our approach to handling general CFGs instruments each backedge with a path counter increment and path register initialization [`count[r]++; r = 0`], which records the path up to the backedge and prepares to record the path after the backedge.

Suppose that $v \to w$ and $x \to y$ are backedges. A general CFG contains four possible types of acyclic (backedge-free) paths:

- A path from $ENTRY$ to $EXIT$.
- A path from $ENTRY$ to v, ending with execution of backedge $v \to w$.
- A path from w to x (after execution of backedge $v \to w$), ending with execution of backedge $x \to y$ (note: $v \to w$ and $x \to y$ may be the same edge).
- After executing backedge $v \to w$, a path from w to $EXIT$.

Removing all backedges from a control-flow graph produces a DAG (as defined in Section 3.1). However, simply applying the profiling algorithm from Section 3 to this DAG will not correctly distinguish the above four types of paths. Figure 10(a) contains a control-flow graph with a loop consisting of the vertices B, C, D, and E. Suppose the graph is instrumented by eliminating the backedge $E \to B$, thus yielding a DAG, and applying the path profiling algorithm for DAGs. The resulting assignment does not ensure that different paths yield different paths sums. For example, the

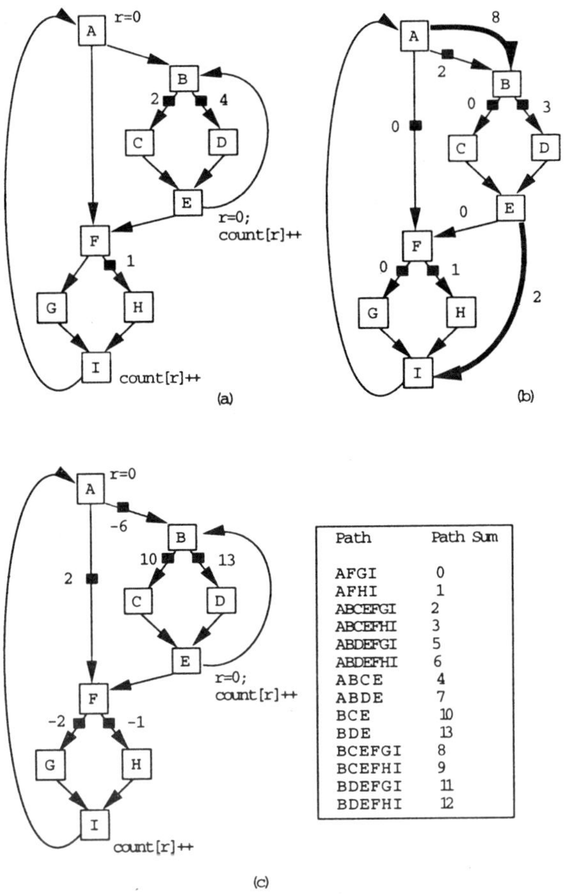

Path	Path Sum
AFGI	0
AFHI	1
ABCEFGI	2
ABCEFHI	3
ABDEFGI	5
ABDEFHI	6
ABCE	4
ABDE	7
BCE	10
BDE	13
BCEFGI	8
BCEFHI	9
BDEFGI	11
BDEFHI	12

Figure 10. Control-flow graph with a loop.

paths BCE, $ABCE$, $BCEFGI$ and $ABCEFGI$ all compute the identical path sum of 2. Not surprisingly, only paths that start at $ENTRY = A$ and end at $EXIT = I$ are correctly distinguished.

The solution to this problem consists of three steps:

- For each vertex v that is the target of one or more backedges, add a dummy edge $ENTRY \dashrightarrow v$. For each vertex w that is the source of one (or more) backedges, add a dummy edge $w \dashrightarrow EXIT$. If one of these edges is not in the spanning tree, it will be instrumented, which is efficient as the edge's increment can be combined with the code always added to a loop backedge to record a path.

- Eliminate backedges from the graph (except for the edge $EXIT \dashrightarrow ENTRY$, which was added for increment computation).

- Apply the first two steps of the path profiling algorithm (Section 3) to compute a value assignment and chord increments.

The dummy edges create extra paths from $ENTRY$ to $EXIT$, which the value assignment algorithm takes into account. The dummy edge from $ENTRY$ to a loop head corresponds to reinitializing the path register along the loop's backedge. The dummy edge from the loop's bottom to $EXIT$ corresponds to incrementing the path counter along the backedge.

Figure 10(b) shows the graph after this transformation and edge value assignment. Dummy edges are the thicker edges. As a result, the chord increments correctly distinguish the four classes of paths listed above. Figure 10(c), shows the chord increments computed and the path sum for each possible path through the graph.

Path regeneration must follow the first two steps (adding dummy edges and removing backedges) to compute the same value assignment, before using the regeneration algorithm from Section 3.5 on the resulting graph.

4.1 Self Loops

The approach described must be slightly modified to handle self-loop edges, which are backedges with the same source and target vertex. Removing this edge does not leave any edge in the loop to instrument. These edges can be handled specially, by adding a counter along them to record the number of times they execute, rather than instrumenting them with the code [`count[r]++; r = 0`].

5 Implementation

We implemented the algorithms described previously in a tool called PP, which instruments SPARC binary executables to extract path profiles. PP is built on EEL (Executable Editing Library), which is a C++ library that hides much of the complexity and system-specific detail of editing executables [LS95]. EEL provides abstractions that allow a tool to analyze and modify binary executables without being concerned with particular instruction sets, executable file formats, or the consequences of deleting existing code and adding foreign code (i.e., instrumentation).

5.1 Registers

Path profiling requires a local register throughout each routine's execution to hold the current path and a temporary register for some instrumentation code, such as the memory increment code. EEL scavenges free registers by using dataflow analysis to find the dead registers throughout a control-flow graph. If EEL cannot find an unused local register, it frees the least heavily used local register by spilling it to the routine's stack frame. In most routines, EEL found unused local registers, although many larger and computationally intensive routines require spill code. The SPARC's register windows ensure that all local registers are caller saved. Other architectures would need to save the path register before and after calls.

EEL also provides a facility to add procedure calls at arbitrary points in a routine. PP uses this feature, which relies on program analysis to save only live values, to call the hashing code (see Section 5.3).

5.2 Optimizations

A simple strength-reduction optimization saves two instructions per path by having the path register hold a counter's address, instead of its index. PP initializes a path register to the base of the counter array. Each increment adds its update, scaled by the size of a counter (4 bytes). This optimization saves three instructions in the code that increments a path's counter, at the cost of an additional instruction in the code that initializes the path register. Unfortunately, the optimization reduces the range of increments that fit in an instruction's immediate field. Since the SPARC's immediate field is 13 bits, this optimization is limited to routines in which the largest increment is 1023 (rather than 4095). However, most routines have fewer or far more paths.

Moreover, a simple change can reduce the range of increments in a routine. The algorithm in Figure 5 can visit a node's successors in any order. By visiting the successor with the largest number of paths (`NumPath`) last, the value (`Val`) assigned to the last edge is minimized, and hence so are the increments added at run time.

5.3 Routines with Many Paths

PP employs two techniques to handle routines with a large number of paths. The first, which PP applies to any routine in which an increment is larger than an instruction's immediate field, replaces the array of counters with a hash table. On the SPARC, this means that routines with more than 4000–6000 paths require hash tables. Hash tables have the advantage of requiring space proportional to the number of executed paths, but have the disadvantage of being an order of magnitude more costly than a simple memory increment and forcing a function call in awkward places. This technique limits counter space for a routine to roughly 16K bytes (most routines require far less space). PP uses two hash routines. The one called from loop backedges keeps a pointer to the last path and hash bucket, so that repeated lookups of the same path are very fast. This is very beneficial since procedures often spend their time in tight loops, repeating the same path over and over.

PP's other technique is necessary for very complex routines in which the number of possible paths exceeded the range of a 32 bit integer. In these routines, PP terminates the value computation (Section 3.2) when the number of paths reachable from a node exceeded a threshold (currently 100,000,000). At this point, PP removes all outgoing edges from the node—using the same approach to terminate these paths as for loop backedges (Section 4)—and reruns the value computation. The only information lost was the relation of the path before a cut edge with the path after the cut edge. Larger (64 bit) words would alleviate, though probably not eliminate, the need to truncate paths.

6 Experimental Results

This section uses the SPEC95 benchmarks to compare path profiling (PP) against edge profiling (QPT2), which has the lowest overhead of conventional profiling techniques [BL94]. The programs ran stand-alone on a Sun Ultraserver E5000–167Mhz UltraSPARC processors and 2GB of memory–running Solaris 2.5.1 with a local file system. Table 1 presents measurements of the SPEC95 benchmarks using the *ref* input data.[2] C benchmarks were compiled with gcc (version 2.7.1) and Fortran benchmarks were compiled with Sun's f77 (version 3.0.1). Both compilers used only the -O option.

PP's overhead (across all input files) averaged 30.9% (5.5–96.9%) and QPT2's overhead averaged 16.1% (-2.6–52.8%). PP's overhead averaged 2.8 times QPT2's overhead (0.7–14.5). PP's overhead is explained in part by the final two columns in Table 1, which report the fraction of path increments that required hashing and the average number of instructions between increments. However, the table does not report the cache interference caused by profiling code and data. In general, programs with little hashing (e.g., compress, li, ijpeg, turb3d) have PP overhead comparable or lower than QPT2. Programs with considerable hashing (e.g., tomcatv, fpppp, and wave5) can still have low overheads if blocks are large or paths are long and path increments execute infrequently.

Table 2 reports some characteristics of the program's acyclic paths. In all programs, the number of executed paths was small (fewer than 2300 in all except 099.go and 126.gcc) and is dwarfed by the potential paths–which number hundreds of millions to tens of billions, even after path truncation.

The table also reports the length of the longest and average acyclic paths. Not surprisingly, the weighted number of instructions in a path in the CFP95 benchmarks, 91.7 (43.1–636.0), is significantly longer than CINT95 benchmarks, 21.4 (15.1-33.2). More aggressive compiler optimizations would further increase these numbers by loop unrolling and procedure in-lining.

[2] Since PP measures a single process's execution, the tables report program behavior for each benchmark's last input file.

Benchmark	Base Time (sec)	PP Overhead %	QPT2 Overhead %	PP/ QPT	Path Inc (million)	Edge Inc (x Path)	Hashed Inc %	Inst/ Inc
099.go	885.0	53.4	24.1	2.2	1002.4	1.5	27.7	33.2
124.m88ksim	571.0	35.6	18.7	1.9	4824.9	1.2	3.9	16.2
126.gcc	322.0	96.9	52.8	1.8	9.4	1.7	16.8	15.1
129.compress	351.0	19.4	21.9	0.9	3015.7	1.5	0.0	16.6
130.li	480.0	25.4	26.7	1.0	3282.4	1.4	1.2	16.8
132.ijpeg	749.0	17.4	16.3	1.1	1164.9	1.1	1.2	31.0
134.perl	332.0	72.9	51.5	1.4	1133.0	1.9	23.4	22.2
147.vortex	684.0	37.7	34.1	1.1	3576.3	1.5	23.7	20.3
CINT95 Avg:		44.8	30.8	1.4	22251.1	1.5	12.2	21.4
101.tomcatv	503.0	19.9	2.8	7.1	574.6	1.1	95.8	93.0
102.swim	691.0	8.4	0.6	14.5	163.4	1.0	0.2	162.9
103.su2cor	465.0	10.1	5.8	1.7	558.1	1.2	21.5	92.8
104.hydro2d	811.0	37.7	5.8	6.5	1690.7	1.7	77.8	43.1
107.mgrid	872.0	6.3	3.2	2.0	1035.2	1.0	7.7	133.5
110.applu	715.0	71.0	12.0	5.9	2111.4	1.1	99.1	44.8
125.turb3d	1066.0	5.5	7.4	0.7	2952.8	1.1	0.0	56.5
141.apsi	492.0	7.7	1.8	4.2	599.3	1.1	3.5	84.0
145.fpppp	1927.0	14.6	-2.6	-5.6	395.0	1.8	42.5	636.0
146.wave5	620.0	16.9	6.1	2.8	737.3	1.3	65.0	74.1
CFP95 Avg:		19.8	4.3	4.0	1081.8	1.2	41.3	142.1
Average:		30.9	16.1	2.8	1601.5	1.3	28.4	88.4

Table 1. Comparison of path profiling (PP) against Ball-Larus edge profiling (QPT2). *Base Time* is elapsed time of uninstrumented program with the *ref* dataset. Overhead is the increase in execution time due to profiling. *PP/QPT2* is the ratio of the overheads. The remaining numbers report a program's behavior on its last input file. *Path Inc* is the number of increments of path counters. *Edge Inc* is the ratio of edge profiling increments to path increments. *Hash Inc* is the fraction of path increments that required hashing. *Inst/Inc* is the average number of instructions between increments.

Benchmark	Num	Path Profile				%	Edge Profile Paths				Routines		
		Longest		Avg			Longest		Avg		Exec	Max	Avg
	Path	Edge	Inst	Edge	Inst	Correct	Edge	Inst	Edge	Inst		Path	Path
099.go	24414	105	314	10.9	33.2	4.3	84	252	5.0	19.3	407	1574	60.0
124.m88ksim	1113	138	360	5.8	16.2	29.8	138	360	4.3	9.1	220	70	5.1
126.gcc	9319	711	1074	7.4	15.1	20.8	711	1074	4.6	10.5	1027	163	9.1
129.compress	249	80	146	6.5	16.7	43.0	80	146	4.6	8.8	69	34	3.6
130.li	770	153	252	9.0	16.8	38.1	62	109	7.0	14.6	216	64	3.6
132.ijpeg	1199	139	416	7.0	31.0	36.4	139	202	5.1	22.2	252	194	4.8
134.perl	1421	123	305	10.7	22.2	24.5	115	207	7.3	16.7	233	125	6.1
147.vortex	2223	584	841	8.9	20.3	39.5	584	841	8.5	13.6	627	65	3.5
CINT Avg:	5088	254	464	8.3	21.4	29.5	239	399	5.8	14.4	381	286	12.0
101.tomcatv	421	83	326	4.1	93.0	49.6	82	201	3.9	25.2	146	56	2.9
102.swim	378	106	310	2.3	162.9	57.1	106	310	2.2	57.6	143	25	2.6
103.su2cor	905	136	954	6.7	92.8	45.9	73	781	5.5	59.3	209	127	4.3
104.hydro2d	1456	344	488	6.5	43.1	33.2	344	436	5.8	36.2	227	434	6.4
107.mgrid	589	83	320	2.3	133.5	44.8	78	320	2.1	15.8	160	73	3.7
110.applu	619	240	3557	3.7	44.8	54.1	240	3557	2.4	26.6	144	82	4.3
125.turb3d	674	162	692	7.1	56.5	46.6	162	692	5.1	28.2	189	39	3.6
141.apsi	1064	712	1196	6.1	84.0	40.8	136	734	4.6	69.0	242	54	4.4
145.fpppp	821	85	11455	14.9	636.0	25.8	76	11455	9.0	122.6	143	322	5.7
146.wave5	896	90	1180	5.2	74.1	47.8	90	1180	4.8	49.5	212	69	4.2
CFP Avg:	782	204	2048	5.9	142.1	44.6	139	1967	4.5	49.0	182	128	4.2
Average:	2696	226	1344	6.9	88.4	37.9	183	1270	5.1	33.6	270	198	7.7

Table 2. Characteristics of executed acyclic paths. Paths are from the last input file in the *ref* dataset. *Num Paths* is the number of paths executed. *Longest* is the longest executed path. *Avg* is the average path length, weighted by execution frequency. *% Correct* is the fraction of paths predicted entirely correctly by edge profiling. Statistics on edge-predicted paths are up to the first misprediction. The final columns report the executed routines, and maximum and average number of paths per executed routine.

Benchmark	Common Paths			Common Instructions	
	Number	Static	Dynamic	Number	Dynamic
099.go	13670	52.8%	99.5%	32823357655	98.6%
124.m88ksim	800	71.1%	97.1%	68794935104	93.3%
126.gcc	9058	63.5%	94.6%	140747413	88.9%
129.compress	201	78.2%	99.2%	49206874856	98.0%
130.li	522	67.8%	87.4%	48285966561	87.7%
132.ijpeg	1099	85.3%	99.9%	36098785257	100.0%
134.perl	687	41.8%	71.9%	16041579783	63.8%
147.vortex	2160	96.0%	100.0%	72589443060	100.0%
101.tomcatv	418	90.9%	100.0%	53422202701	100.0%
102.swim	373	98.2%	100.0%	26607743709	100.0%
103.su2cor	880	95.5%	100.0%	51766673091	100.0%
104.hydro2d	1336	90.1%	100.0%	72892099182	100.0%
107.mgrid	577	97.3%	100.0%	138157253535	100.0%
110.applu	582	87.5%	100.0%	94622106074	100.0%
125.turb3d	651	94.5%	100.0%	166724577396	100.0%
141.apsi	992	91.0%	91.2%	37648860455	74.3%
145.fpppp	764	91.9%	99.9%	250229811735	99.6%
146.wave	5821	88.5%	98.8%	52996842799	96.9%

Table 3. Comparison of paths with the SPEC95 *ref* and *train* input datasets. *Common Paths* reports the number of paths executed for both input datasets. *Static* is the fraction of executed *ref* dataset paths executed by the *train* dataset. *Dynamic* is this fraction, weighted by execution frequency. *Common Instructions* reports the number and fraction of instructions along common paths.

The table also compares paths predicted using edge profiling against measured paths. For this experiment, PP followed each executed path, starting at a function entry or loop head, and used the most frequently executed edge out of a block to predict the next step in a path. If two edges had the same frequency, PP followed the not taken edge. This approach predicts, in their entirety, an average of 37.9% (4.3–57.1%) of the paths. PP also computed the length of a predicted path, up to their first mispredicted edge. Weighted by execution frequency, edge predicted paths were nearly as long as measured paths (5.1 versus 6.9 CFG edges), but contained significantly fewer (33.6 versus 88.4) instructions. In part, this result reflects the simple behavior of the SPEC95 benchmarks, which execute an average of 7.7 (2.6–60.0) paths in each routine. It is also consistent with previous work in dynamic and static branch prediction [FF92, BL93], which found that branches in a program typically follow one direction with very high probability, and this high-probability direction generally remains the same for different inputs.

Table 3 compares paths executed with the SPEC95 *train* and *ref* input datasets. In the CINT benchmarks, the *train* dataset identified 41.8–96.0% of the paths executed in the *ref* dataset. However, these common paths were the important ones that account for 71.9-100.0% of path executions and 63.8–100.0% of instruction executions. The CFP benchmarks were even more striking, as the *train* dataset identified a minimum of 87.5% of the executed paths, which in all except one case (147.apsi) account for 99+% of instructions. This result is again consistent with earlier work that found program behavior to be independent of program data [FF92, BL93]. These measurements suggest that path profiles could greatly improve peak SPEC95 performance by providing an inexpensive and accurate basis for profile-driven compilation.

7 Summary

This paper describes a new algorithm for path profiling. A path profile records the execution frequencies of acyclic paths in a routine. Although these profiles provide far more information than basic block or edge profiles, they can be obtained at a cost comparable to the best known profiling algorithms.

We also compared path profiles against paths predicted by a common heuristic that selects the highest frequency edge out of a basic block. Path profiles yielded slightly longer paths that contained significantly more instructions. If edge profiling was significantly cheaper or easier than path profiling, it might be a reasonable heuristic. However, since path profiling is similar in cost and complexity to edge profiling, there is little reason to forgo the benefits of measurement.

Moreover, path profiles obtained from short runs on short, training datasets covered most of the paths and instructions found in full runs. The profiles from these short runs form an inexpensive and accurate basis for profile-driven compilation.

Acknowledgements

Many thanks to Vasanth Bala for helpful discussions about path profiling. Chris Lukas and David Wood provided helpful comments on this paper.

References

[Bal94] Thomas Ball. Efficiently counting program events with support for on-line queries. *ACM Transactions on Programming Languages and Systems*, 16(5):1399–1410, September 1994.

[Bal96] Vasanth Bala. Low overhead path profiling. Technical report, Hewlett Packard Labs, 1996.

[BL93] Thomas Ball and James R. Larus. Branch prediction for free. In *Proceedings of the SIGPLAN '93 Conference on Programming Language Design and Implementation (PLDI)*, pages 300–313, June 1993.

[BL94] Thomas Ball and James R. Larus. Optimally profiling and tracing programs. *ACM Transactions on Programming Languages and Systems*, 16(4):1319–1360, July 1994.

[Cha88] Pohua P. Chang. Trace selection for compiling large C application programs to microcode. In *21th Annual Workshop on Microprogramming and Microarchitecture (MICRO 21)*, pages 21–29, November 1988.

[Ell85] John R. Ellis. Bulldog: A compiler for VLIW architectures. Technical Report YALEU/DCS/RR-364, Yale University, Department of Computer Science, February 1985.

[FF92] Joseph A. Fisher and Stefan M. Freudenberger. Predicting conditional branch directions from previous runs of a program. In *Proceedings of the Fifth International Conference on Architectural Support for Programming Languages and Operating Systems (ASPLOS V)*, pages 85–95, October 1992.

[Fis81] Joseph A. Fisher. Trace scheduling: A technique for global microcode compaction. *IEEE Transactions on Computers*, C-30(7):478–490, July 1981.

[Gol91] Aaron Goldberg. Reducing overhead in counter-based execution profiling. Technical Report CSL-TR-91-495, Computer System Laboratory, Stanford University, October 1991.

[LS95] James R. Larus and Eric Schnarr. EEL: Machine-independent executable editing. In *Proceedings of the SIGPLAN '95 Conference on Programming Language Design and Implementation (PLDI)*, pages 291–300, June 1995.

[YS94] Cliff Young and Michael D. Smith. Improving the accuracy of static branch prediction using branch correlation. In *Proceedings of the Sixth International Conference on Architectural Support for Programming Languages and Operating Systems (ASPLOS VI)*, pages 232–241, October 1994.

Profile-Driven Instruction Level Parallel Scheduling with Application to Super Blocks

C. Chekuri
Dept. of Comp. Sci.
Stanford Univ.
Stanford, CA 94305

R. Johnson
Hewlett Packard Labs
1501 Page Mill Rd
Palo Alto, CA 94304

R. Motwani
Dept. of Comp. Sci.
Stanford Univ.
Stanford, CA 94305

B. Natarajan[1], B.R. Rau, M.Schlansker
Hewlett Packard Labs
1501 Page Mill Rd
Palo Alto, CA 94304

Abstract

Code scheduling to exploit instruction level parallelism (ILP) is a critical problem in compiler optimization research, in light of the increased use of long-instruction-word machines. Unfortunately, optimum scheduling is computationally intractable, and one must resort to carefully crafted heuristics in practice. If the scope of application of a scheduling heuristic is limited to basic blocks, considerable performance loss may be incurred at block boundaries. To overcome this obstacle, basic blocks can be coalesced across branches to form larger regions such as super blocks. In the literature, these regions are typically scheduled using algorithms that are either oblivious to profile information (under the assumption that the process of forming the region has fully utilized the profile information), or use the profile information as an addendum to classical scheduling techniques. We believe that even for the simple case of linear code regions such as super blocks, additional performance improvement can be gained by utilizing the profile information in scheduling as well. We propose a general paradigm for converting any profile-insensitive list scheduler to a profile-sensitive scheduler. Our technique is developed via a theoretical analysis of a simplified abstract model of the general problem of profile-driven scheduling over any acyclic code region, yielding a scoring measure for ranking branch instructions. The ranking digests the profile information and has the useful property that scheduling with respect to rank is provably good for minimizing the expected completion time of the region, within the limits of the abstraction. While the ranking scheme is computationally intractable in the most general case, it is practicable for super blocks and suggests the heuristic that we present in this paper for profile-driven scheduling of super blocks. Experiments show that our heuristic offers substantial performance improvement over prior methods on a range of integer benchmarks and several machine models.

[1] Address all correspondence to this author

1. Introduction

The performance of a VLIW machine depends strongly on the ability of the compiler to exploit instruction level parallelism (ILP) in programs. Unfortunately, the task of the compiler is made difficult by the presence of a number of intractable optimization problems such as instruction scheduling and register allocation. In this paper, we study one such problem — scheduling with profile information. We believe that our results will serve as a good starting point for developing practical heuristics that are to be included in compilers for VLIW machines. As evidence, we present experimental results validating heuristics suggested by our analysis.

A basic block is a program fragment that may only be entered at the top and exited at the bottom. The precedence graph of a single basic block will be a directed acyclic graph (DAG) [2], and in practice, typically consists of fewer than 10 vertices. Scheduling small basic blocks consecutively and separately leads to underutilization of the functional units due to sequentialization effects at the block boundaries. To overcome this limitation two broad approaches have been proposed. One called if-conversion, eliminates the branches via hardware support for predicated execution, allowing instructions to be moved outside of their basic blocks, see [4] for instance. The other approach does not require hardware support, and involves the formation of larger code regions such as traces, [7], and super blocks, [14]. A super block consists of a sequence of basic blocks strung together, with conditional exits at the branch points that separate the basic blocks. Super blocks are typically formed as follows. Given is a code region with branch probabilities available at each branch in the region. These probabilities can be obtained by profiling — collecting usage statistics when the code is executed. Starting at the entry point to the code region, follow the dominant fork at each branch. If at a certain branch, the probability of reaching the branch from the start falls below a certain threshold level, terminate the path. Alternatively, if neither fork in the branch is predom-

1072-4451/96 $5.00 © 1996 IEEE

inant, terminate the path. The chain of basic blocks along the path traced in this manner is a super block. Delete the chain of basic blocks defining the super block from the code region and repeat the process on the modified portion. Since some of the basic blocks that are deleted might have entries into them from other blocks in the code region, these blocks must be duplicated in the modified region. This process is called "tail duplication." It is clear that the amount of tail duplication will affect the size of the overall code, thereby affecting performance in the face of fixed instruction cache sizes. In light of this, the threshold and the parameters defining the notion of predominance are empirically determined and are outside the scope of this paper.

Much of the literature on scheduling ignores profile information, under the assumption that the region formation algorithm has fully digested the profile information. For instance, super blocks are typically scheduled with heuristics that are oblivious to the profile information, although there are techniques that use profile information as an addendum to classical scheduling techniques, e.g., the speculative yield technique of [3], following [7]. (Example 1 examines several of these techniques.) As region formation algorithms become more sophisticated and produce non-linear code regions encompassing balanced branches, they will be less effective in digesting the profile information. As a result, it will be increasingly important that the code-region be annotated with profile information, and that the scheduling technique effectively utilize this profile information. We believe that our paper offers a first step in this direction.

One might argue that it would be better to tackle the problem of profile driven scheduling from first principles, by treating general code regions, rather than processed code regions such as super blocks. However, there are two good reasons for restricting our study to processed regions. (1) as we will see shortly, profile-driven scheduling of generic code regions is computationally intractable and is impractical unless the number of branches in the region is small, say fewer than 16; and, (2) tail duplication during the formation of simpler regions such as super blocks often exposes more instruction level parallelism than is extant in the generic code region. Thus, it is a legitimate goal to study good scheduling heuristics even for the limited case of super blocks.

We now make precise our abstraction of the general problem of scheduling with profile information. We are given a directed acyclic precedence graph derived from the source program as described above. Each vertex in the graph represents an operation τ_i with specified execution time t_i, which is the time required to execute τ_i. Each vertex also carries a weight w_i. The weight w_i is the probability that the program exits at vertex i. In other words, w_i is the probability that only the portion of the precedence graph rooted at vertex i needs to be computed, i.e., only those vertices upon which vertex i depends need to be computed. We assume that the target machine has m functional units. We are to schedule the vertices of the graph on the m functional units to achieve the lowest cost, i.e., shortest weighted execution time. Specifically, we are to find a schedule to minimize $\sum_i w_i f_i$, where $f_i = s_i + t_i$ is the finish time of operation τ_i and s_i is its start time.

The general problem in which every node has a weight has been shown to be NP-hard even for $m = 1$ provided we permit arbitrary precedence constraints on the operations [9, 15]. The problem is polynomially solvable when the precedence graph is a forest [12] or a generalized series-parallel graph [1, 15]. For $m \geq 1$, the problem is NP-hard even without precedence constraints, unless the weights are all identical in which case it is polynomially solvable; on the other hand, the problem is strongly NP-hard even when all weights are identical and the precedence graph is a collection of chains [5]. In light of the intractable nature of the problem, we adopt the standard approach of designing approximation algorithms with a bounded performance ratio. The performance ratio of an approximation algorithm is defined as the worst-case ratio of the cost of the approximate solution and the optimal solution.

We begin with a general lemma that shows how to construct an optimal sequential schedule for a general precedence graph with weights. The construction of the lemma can be efficiently exploited only for two restricted versions of the problem, the case where the precedence graph is a tree, i.e., each vertex has exactly one outgoing edge, and the S-graph case where the weights are non-zero only on a single path. The S-graph, to be defined formally in the next section, is the abstraction of the super block. We then show that using the optimal sequential schedule as a list to drive a list scheduling algorithm for multiple functional units guarantees a performance ratio of 2. Finally, in a heuristic extension to our basic lemma, we present a generic scheme for converting any list scheduling algorithm that is insensitive to profile information into a scheduling algorithm for super blocks that is sensitive to profile information. We cannot show tight performance guarantees on this heuristic, but we do present experimental results on a number of sample super blocks obtained by applying the Impact compiler on SPEC benchmark programs. We report that significant savings are possible as compared to prior methods.

Example 1 *Consider the precedence graph of Figure 1, which is the precedence graph of a super block with three branch vertices, vertices 3, 7, and 28 as marked in the figure. The probability that the program will exit via vertex 3, is 0.1. Similarly the probability that it will exit via vertices 7 and 28 are 0.3 and 0.6 respectively. We assume we are given a non-pipelined processor with two identical functional units with all operations having a latency of one cycle. We now schedule this graph on the processor in three ways. First, we carry out critical path scheduling. This is equivalent to*

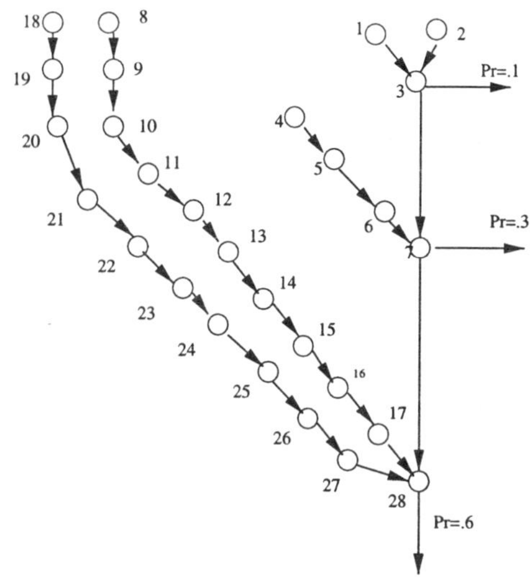

Figure 1. Precedence graph of a super block. Each vertex corresponds to unit latency operation. The probability labels on the branch exits of the graph are the probabilities that the exits will be taken.

list scheduling with the distance from the last exit (vertex 28) as the list priority. Table 1 shows the schedule we would obtain in this case, along with the expected finish time of the schedule.

Secondly, we schedule using speculative yield priorities, as in [3]. Here, the priority of a vertex is the weighted sum of its longest path length from each exit, where the weight is the probability of the exit being taken. The list of vertices sorted in descending order of priority is the list for scheduling. Table 2 shows the schedule we would obtain in this case, and it has a better expected finish time than scheduling by critical path from the last exit.

Lastly, we construct a list schedule that seeks to retire each exit in order at the earliest possible time, as described below. We will call this successive retirement *scheduling. Construct a priority list, based on the critical path priority, of all vertices preceding and inclusive of the earliest exit, (vertex 3 in the figure). Delete all vertices on this list from the graph. Iterate this procedure until the graph is consumed, appending in order the lists created at each iteration. List-schedule, using the list so created. Table 3 shows the schedule we would obtain in this case, along with the expected finish time of the schedule. Although the*

Cycle	1	2	3	4	5	6	7	8
FU1	8	9	10	11	12	13	14	4
FU2	18	19	20	21	22	23	24	25
Cycle	9	10	11	12	13	14	15	
FU1	1	15	3*	16	17	27	28*	
FU2	5	2	6	26	7*			

Table 1. List schedule for the super block of Figure 1 for a two functional unit machine, using the critical path from the last exit as the list. Exits are marked with a *. Expected completion time = 14.0 cycles.

Cycle	1	2	3	4	5	6	7	8
FU1	8	9	10	11	12	4	13	2
FU2	18	19	20	21	22	23	1	5
Cycle	9	10	11	12	13	14	15	
FU1	14	3*	15	16	7*	27	28*	
FU2	24	6	25	26	17			

Table 2. Speculative yield schedule for the super block of Figure 1 for a two functional unit machine. Exits are marked with a *. Expected completion time = 13.9 cycles.

Cycle	1	2	3	4	5	6	7	8
FU1	1	3*	5	6	7*	19	20	21
FU2	2	4	8	18	9	10	11	12
Cycle	9	10	11	12	13	14	15	
FU1	22	23	24	25	26	27	28*	
FU2	13	14	15	16	17			

Table 3. Successive retirement list schedule for the super block of Figure 1 for a two functional unit machine. Exits are marked with a *. Expected completion time = 10.7 cycles.

successive retirement schedule ignored the profile information completely, it has the lowest finish time of the three schedules.

2. Theoretical Results

Let $G = (V, E)$ denote the precedence graph. A sink in the graph is a vertex with no outgoing edges. We assume, without loss of generality, that the graph has exactly one sink, since we can easily ensure this by the addition of a dummy vertex with in-edges from the sinks of the given graph. Each vertex i is assigned a weight w_i. Let P be a path from a source to a sink in a precedence graph G. We now define the notion of an S-graph, the graph-theoretic abstraction of a super block. Recall that a super block consists of a chain of basic blocks with conditional exits at the branch points separating the basic blocks. The graph G is said to be an S-graph with respect to P if the weights w_i are zero everywhere except on the path P. Without loss of generality, we assume that the weight on the sink is non-zero. If not, we can delete the sink and break the graph into a number of components, retaining only the component containing P. The precedence graph of a super block will contain precedence edges between the branch vertices, since these cannot be executed out of order. Since the branch vertices are the only vertices with non-zero exit probabilities, the precedence graph of a super block is an S-graph.

We say that u immediately precedes v if and only if there is an edge from u to v in the graph. A vertex u precedes a vertex v if and only if there is a path from u to v. For any vertex $u \in V$, let G_u denote the subgraph of G induced by the set of vertices preceding u. A subgraph is said to be closed under precedence if for every vertex u in the subgraph, all vertices preceding u are also in the subgraph.

We define the rank of a vertex i to be the ratio $r_i = t_i/w_i$. Although a vertex can have infinite rank, as will become evident shortly, we will only be interested in those of finite rank. For any set of vertices $A \subseteq V$, we define its weight as $w(A) = \sum_{v_i \in A} w_i$, and its execution time as $t(A) = \sum_{v_i \in A} t_i$; based on this, the rank is $r(A) = t(A)/w(A)$. For instance, the rank of the set of vertices preceding vertex 7 in Figure 1 is 7/.4 = 17.5. The notion of the rank of a set of vertices is meant to capture their relative importance, comparing the sum of their weights to the cost of executing them. Intuitively, the sum of the weights is the contribution made by the set of vertices to the weighted finish time, while the sum of their execution times is the delay suffered by the rest of the graph as a result of scheduling the set of vertices first. As will become evident in our basic lemma, the notion of rank plays a key role in characterizing the optimal sequential schedule.

2.1. The Basic Lemma

In this section we develop a basic lemma characterizing optimal sequential schedules of weighted precedence graphs, i.e., schedules on a single functional unit. Efficient algorithms for the two cases where the precedence graph is a tree, and the precedence graph is an S-graph, can be obtained as special applications of the basic lemma. Previously, optimal sequential algorithms for weighted trees have been described in the literature [1, 8, 12]. Applying the basic lemma to general weighted graphs would cost time exponential in the number of vertices with non-zero weights, a cost that can be practical, if the number of such vertices, i.e., the number of branches is small. From a theoretical point of view, the best known approximation algorithm [11] for sequential scheduling of weighted DAGS has a performance guarantee of 2; however, this algorithm is based on rounding solutions of linear programs and is impractical for the compiler setting.

The following terms are defined with respect to a specific schedule S. We use the term *segment* to refer to a set of consecutive operations in a schedule. Two segments B_1 and B_2 in the schedule are *independent* if there are no operations $u \in B_1$ and $v \in B_2$ such that u precedes v or v precedes u.

Given a weighted precedence graph G, we define G^* to be the smallest precedence-closed *proper* subgraph of G of minimum rank.

We now prove our main lemma.

Lemma: For any graph G, there exists an optimal sequential schedule where the optimal schedule for G^* occurs as a segment which starts at time zero.

Proof: Let S be an optimal schedule for G in which G^* is decomposed into a minimum number of maximal segments. Suppose that G^* is decomposed into two or more segments in S. For $k > 1$, let $B_1, B_2, \ldots, B_k$ be the segments of G^* in S, in increasing order of starting times. Let the segment between B_{i-1} and B_i be denoted by C_i. Let α denote $r(G^*)$ and C^j denote the union of the blocks $C_1, C_2, \ldots, C_j$. From the definition of G^* it follows that $r(C^j) \geq \alpha$ since otherwise we could have included C^j in G^*. Let B^j similarly denote the union of the blocks $B_1, B_2, \ldots, B_j$. It follows that $r(B^k - B^j) < \alpha$ for otherwise $r(B^j) \leq \alpha$ and B^j is smaller than G^*.

Let S' be the schedule formed from S by moving all the B_i's ahead of C_i's while preserving their order within themselves. The schedule S' is legal since G^* is precedence closed. We will show that the cost of S' is no more than that of S which will finish the proof. While comparing the costs of the two schedules, we can ignore the contribution of the vertices that come after B_k since their status remains the same in S'. For the schedule S' we have

$$Cost(S') = \sum_{i \leq k} w(C_i)t(B^k) + \sum_{i \leq k} w(C_i)t(C^i) + \sum_{i \leq k} w(B_i)t(B^i) .$$

For the schedule S,

$$Cost(S) = \sum_{i \leq k} w(B_i)t(C^i) + \sum_{i \leq k} w(C_i)t(B^{i-1}) + \sum_{i \leq k} w(C_i)t(C^i) + \sum_{i \leq k} w(B_i)t(B^i) .$$

Taking their difference gives,

$$\begin{aligned} & Cost(S) - Cost(S') \\ &= \sum_{i \leq k} w(B_i)t(C^i) - \sum_{i \leq k} w(C_i)t(B^k - B^{i-1}) . \\ &\geq \sum_{i \leq k} w(B_i)\alpha w(C^i) - \sum_{i \leq k} w(C_i)\alpha w(B^k - B^{i-1}) \\ &\geq \alpha \sum_{i \leq k} w(B_i)w(C^i) - \alpha \sum_{i \leq k} w(B_i)w(C^i) \geq 0 . \end{aligned}$$

The second inequality above follows from our earlier observations about $r(C^i)$ and $r(B - B^j)$. The third step follows from a simple reordering of the order of summation.

2.2. Schedules

The main lemma essentially reduces the scheduling problem to the problem of finding G^*. Then, we can recursively schedule G^* and the graph formed by removing G^* and put their schedules together to obtain an optimal schedule for the entire graph. Unfortunately, the problem of finding G^* for an arbitrary precedence graph is NP-hard. However, if the number of vertices in the graph that have non-zero weight are small, then G^* can be feasibly determined by exhaustive enumeration. Next, we show that finding G^* and hence finding optimal sequential schedules is relatively straightforward if the precedence graph is an S-graph. Let G be an S-graph with respect to a path P. If G^* has a sink not on path P or a sink of zero weight, such a sink can be deleted and both the rank and the number of vertices in G^* reduced appropriately. Thus G^* must be a subgraph with a single sink, and the sink must be a vertex on P with non-zero weight–determining G^* is straightforward. The schedule so obtained is essentially the one obtained by greedily scheduling successive vertices on the path defining the S-graph as early as possible. In terms of the corresponding super block, this amounts to scheduling the basic blocks comprising the super block in control-flow order, exactly the successive retirement schedule given in Example 1.

We can also obtain good ILP schedules for super blocks from the sequential schedule. Specifically, we can show that list scheduling using the optimal sequential schedule as the list, gives good approximate solutions for S-graphs. We defer the proof to the full paper.

Theorem: For an S-graph where all operations have equal execution time, the list scheduling algorithm, using the optimal sequential schedule as the list, is an approximation algorithm with a performance ratio 2.

3. The Practical Heuristic

Notice that our theorem for profile-driven ILP scheduling above is quite limited since it requires that all operations have equal execution time. For the practical situation, we offer a quality heuristic, based on our theoretical analysis from the earlier sections.

3.1. The Modified Rank Function

In our basic lemma, we computed the rank of a set of vertices to be the sum of the latencies in the set divided by the sum of the exit probabilities. For the single unit case, the numerator is a good measure of the length of the time required to compute the set of vertices. Extending our notion of rank from the sequential setting to the ILP setting, we will replace the numerator by the length of the schedule to compute the set of vertices. We call this the modified rank or the *mrank* of a set of vertices, where

$$mrank(A) = \frac{\text{length of schedule for A}}{\text{sum of exit probabilities in A}} .$$

As in the basic lemma, G^* is defined to be the smallest precedence closed subgraph of G of minimum *modified* rank. The intuition behind the modified rank is that the numerator is the time required to retire A, while the denominator is the benefit in retiring A. Thus, the ratio reflects the amount of computatational time required per unit of exit probability. Minimizing this ratio in selecting G^* has the effect of maximizing the "return on investment" in the schedule. Given an S-graph, G^* can found by the following simple procedure.

Algorithm Finding G^* under modified rank

For each branch b of the S-graph,
  On the given processor,
  construct a list schedule for the
  subgraph G_b rooted at b,
  ignoring profile information
  Let T be the length of the schedule
  and let W be the sum of the exit
  probabilities of all exits in G_b.
  rank(G_b) = T/W
G^* is G_b for the earliest b in control
order that has the minimum modified rank.

In the algorithm for computing G^* under modified rank, there is considerable flexibility in selecting the list scheduler, including those that are oblivious to profile information.

3.2. The Heuristic

Now that we know how to compute G^* under modified rank, we can proceed to the scheduling heuristic, given below. In words, the heuristic converts any list scheduler for precedence graphs, to one that is sensitive to profile information for S-graphs. In this sense, the heuristic takes a profile-insensive list scheduling algorithm, and bootstraps it to be profile-sensitive. To start, the heuristic finds G^* under modified rank, using the insensitive list scheduler. It then makes the list for G^* the initial portion of the list for G. The heuristic deletes G^* from G, and iterates, appending the lists each time till all of G is consumed.

Algorithm Scheduler

1. Profile-list = empty.
2. Find G^* under modified rank
   using the insensitive scheduler
3. Append the schedule list of G^* to Profile-list.
4. Remove G^* from the DAG
5. If there are branches remaining, then goto Step 2.
6. List schedule using Profile-list.

Example 2 *We return to the graph of Figure 1, and apply our scheduling heuristic to it. We will use critical path scheduling as the insensitive list scheduler that is oblivious to profile information. Once again, we assume a processor with two identical functional units and equal latencies for all vertices. We have 3 candidates for G^* initially consisting of the subgraph rooted at vertex 3, denoted by G_3, the subgraph rooted at vertex 7, denoted by G_7 and the entire graph G. Computing their modified ranks, we get $rank(G_3) = 2/0.1 = 20, rank(G_7) = 4/0.4 = 10$ and $rank(G_{28}) = 15/1 = 15$, where the numerators are the length of the critical path schedules on the given processor. Since G_7 has the lowest rank, it is G^*. We therefore set Profile-list to be the critical path list for G_7, and remove G_7 from G. Since vertex 28 is the only exit remaining, we append its critical path list to Profile-list. List scheduling using Profile-list on the two functional unit processor yields the schedule of Table 4. Notice that the expected finish time of this schedule is lower than that of the critical path schedule of Table 1 the speculative yield schedule of Table 2 and the successive retirement schedule of Table 3.*

Cycle	1	2	3	4	5	6	7	8
FU1	4	5	6	7*	8	9	10	11
FU2	1	2	3*	18	19	20	21	22
Cycle	9	10	11	12	13	14	15	
FU1	12	13	14	15	16	17	28*	
FU2	23	24	25	26	27			

Table 4. The list schedule constructed by our heuristic for the super block of Figure 1 for a two functional unit machine, using a critical path scheduler as the insensitive scheduler. Exits are marked with a *. Expected completion time = 10.5 cycles.

4. Experimental Results

We now study the performance of the heuristic on a number of optimized super blocks generated by the Impact compiler from the SPEC benchmark programs. We restrict our attention to integer benchmarks, since broadly speaking the floating-point benchmarks yield super blocks with near-zero side-exit probabilities, [16]. We used the Impact compiler to compile these benchmarks, decomposing each program into super blocks and basic blocks only. We report our results on scheduling these blocks over two different classes of machine models, processors with uniform functional units, and processors with heterogenous functional units. All the models are non-pipelined with opcode execution times of as specified in Table 6. The assumption that the machines are not pipelined is only in the interest of simplicity, and is not an inherent limitation of our technique. The uniform processor models have 2, 4, and 8 identical functional units respectively, and are denoted u_2, u_4 and u_8. While uniform machine models are unrealistic in practice, they serves well to study the effect of scaling the number of functional units in a processor. The heterogenous models h_3, h_5 and h_8 are as shown in 5. Model h_3 has one IALU, one FALU and one

Model	#IALU	#FALU	#MEM
h_3	1	1	1
h_5	2	1	2
h_8	3	2	3

Table 5. Functional units of the three heterogenous processors.

Opcode	Time
IALU	1 cycle
FALU	4 cycles
FDIV	8 cycles
LOAD	2 cycles
STORE	1 cycle
BRANCH	1 cycle

Table 6. Opcodes and execution times.

load/store unit, model h_5 has two IALUs, one FALU and two load/store units, while model h_8 has three IALUs, two FALU and three MEM (load/store) units. We assume that BRANCH operations can be performed on the FALU.

First, we use the critical path scheduler as the profile-insensitive scheduling algorithm to drive our heuristic, and compare its performance against three algorithms: **(1)** critical path scheduling from the last exit; **(2)** speculative yield as in Example 1 and [3]; **(3)** successive retirement as in Example 1.

Table 7 shows the improvements achieved by our heuristic over critical-path scheduling for the benchmarks studied over the various machine models. For each benchmark and machine model, we show the improvement in the total schedule length of the benchmark. Formally, we define the *total schedule length* of a benchmark to be the weighted sum of the schedule lengths for all the basic blocks and super blocks for that benchmark, where the weights are the execution frequencies obtained via profiling. In our experience, this is a good measure of the run-time of the benchmark on a typical machine with a sufficient number of registers. Table 8 shows the improvements achieved by our heuristic over speculative yield scheduling, and Table 9 shows the improvements achieved by our heuristic over successive retirement scheduling. Referring to Table 9, notice that on narrow machines such as u_2 and h_3, little performance gain is evidenced. This is because successive retirement is optimal on the sequential processor as shown in our theoretical analysis, and is likely a good schedule on narrow machines.

To substantiate our claim that our heuristic is a general paradigm for converting a profile-insensitive scheduler to

Benchmark	Improvement %					
	u_2	u_4	u_8	h_3	h_5	h_8
espresso	12.8	9.2	5.4	11.3	10.5	8.9
li	6.0	1.4	1.2	3.6	2.1	0.9
compress	6.1	5.9	5.2	5.8	5.3	3.8
alvinn	0.6	0.8	0.9	0.6	0.6	0.8
ear	2.0	1.9	1.5	0.5	1.6	1.0
sc	4.7	4.8	5.1	5.4	6.2	5.1
cccp	4.3	4.7	4.1	3.1	4.6	3.8
cmp	1.2	2.2	2.5	1.1	1.8	2.0
eqn	2.4	2.3	2.1	2.0	1.9	2.0
grep	0.7	1.0	0.9	0.6	0.8	0.8
lex	1.9	0.8	0.9	1.6	1.3	1.0
qsort	10.9	11.3	5.7	6.2	6.2	9.9
tbl	1.4	1.3	1.4	0.9	1.1	1.2
wc	3.8	3.8	4.0	3.0	3.7	4.5
yacc	6.9	4.1	4.3	4.7	4.5	4.4
Average	4.1	3.5	2.8	3.1	3.3	3.1

Table 7. Comparison of heuristic against critical path scheduling. Critical path scheduling is the profile-insensitive scheduler. Shown is improvement in total schedule length of benchmarks.

Benchmark	Improvement %					
	u_2	u_4	u_8	h_3	h_5	h_8
espresso	5.4	3.7	4.7	3.5	3.8	4.8
li	1.3	0.4	0.5	0.3	0.5	0.4
compress	3.6	4.4	5.1	3.6	3.1	3.0
alvinn	0.8	0.4	0.9	0.6	0.6	0.9
ear	1.9	0.8	1.5	0.4	1.6	1.6
sc	2.8	4.2	5.5	3.0	3.7	4.6
cccp	2.8	3.8	4.0	2.3	3.4	4.0
cmp	1.2	2.2	2.5	1.1	1.8	2.0
eqn	1.4	2.0	2.1	1.5	2.0	2.1
grep	0.5	0.9	1.0	0.5	0.8	0.9
lex	1.1	0.7	0.8	1.0	0.9	0.9
qsort	8.9	10.1	6.4	2.9	3.8	7.6
tbl	0.6	1.5	1.3	0.7	1.0	0.7
wc	2.9	3.8	4.0	2.1	2.2	5.1
yacc	3.6	3.4	4.2	2.8	3.9	3.7
Average	2.4	2.7	2.8	1.6	2.1	2.6

Table 8. Comparison of heuristic against speculative yield scheduling. Critical path scheduling is the profile-insensitive scheduler. Shown is improvement in total schedule length of benchmarks.

Benchmark	Improvement %					
	u_2	u_4	u_8	h_3	h_5	h_8
espresso	-0.4	4.7	4.9	-0.4	5.2	6.7
li	-2.1	1.2	0.3	-0.1	3.0	3.8
compress	0.7	4.9	5.3	0.5	4.3	6.1
alvinn	1.1	1.5	1.2	0.5	-0.1	1.7
ear	0.8	-0.5	1.7	0.3	0.6	1.2
sc	0.4	4.9	6.2	2.3	4.0	4.3
cccp	1.8	6.9	3.7	2.5	7.7	5.2
cmp	0.1	3.5	2.5	1.1	3.4	0.2
eqn	2.8	-0.2	2.1	0.9	6.3	6.4
grep	-0.3	0.1	1.0	0.2	2.2	-0.3
lex	1.6	1.7	1.1	2.0	1.5	1.5
qsort	2.1	6.4	9.5	2.7	4.9	8.4
tbl	-3.5	-0.4	1.1	0.1	3.1	1.8
wc	2.9	5.8	4.5	2.1	7.1	3.2
yacc	2.6	5.1	5.4	3.1	5.0	5.3
Average	0.7	2.8	3.2	1.1	3.6	3.5

Table 9. Comparison of heuristic against successive retirement scheduling. Critical path scheduling is the profile-insensitive scheduler. Shown is improvement in total schedule length of benchmarks.

Benchmark	Improvement %					
	u_2	u_4	u_8	h_3	h_5	h_8
espresso	-0.4	4.7	4.9	-0.4	5.1	6.7
li	-2.1	1.5	0.3	0.1	2.9	4.1
compress	0.7	4.1	4.8	0.5	4.7	5.6
alvinn	1.1	1.5	1.2	0.5	-0.1	1.7
ear	0.7	-0.5	1.7	0.3	0.6	1.2
sc	0.4	4.9	6.0	2.3	4.0	4.2
cccp	1.7	6.9	3.7	2.5	7.8	5.1
cmp	0.1	3.5	2.5	1.1	3.4	0.2
eqn	2.8	-0.3	2.1	0.9	6.2	6.4
grep	-0.3	0.1	1.0	0.2	2.2	-0.3
lex	1.6	1.7	1.1	2.0	1.4	1.5
qsort	1.5	6.7	9.7	2.4	4.8	4.9
tbl	-3.5	-0.4	1.1	0.1	3.1	1.8
wc	2.6	5.8	4.5	2.1	7.1	3.2
yacc	2.6	5.3	5.4	3.1	5.0	5.0
Average	0.6	2.8	3.1	1.1	3.6	3.2

Table 10. Comparison of heuristic against successive retirement scheduling. Successive retirement scheduling is the profile-insensitive scheduler. Shown is improvement in total schedule length of benchmarks.

profile-sensitive one, we apply our heuristic using successive retirement as the profile insensitive scheduler, over the same set of benchmarks and machine models. The results are shown in Table 10.

4.1. Discussion

In our performance studies above, the total schedule length of a benchmark depends on the nature and mix of basic blocks and the super blocks produced during compilation. Our heuristic is designed to improve the performance of super blocks that have side exits with substantial exit frequency. If the compiler is not aggressive in creating such super blocks, or if side exits occur very infrequently, the opportunities for performance gains are limited. To examine this in detail, we introduce the notion of the critical path ratio of a super block, which aims to measure the relative importance of the side exits of a super block. To this end, we define the expected critical path length as the weighted sum of the lengths of the critical paths of all the exits, weighted by their exit probabilities. The critical path ratio is the ratio of the expected critical path length to the length of the critical path of the last exit. If the critical path ratio is small compared to unity, then the side exits are significant, and if the critical path ratio is close to unity, then the last exit is predominant. It is clear that every basic block will have a critical path ratio of unity.

Figure 2 shows the average improvement achieved by our heuristic over critical path scheduling, as a function of the critical path ratio. The plots represent averages over all the basic blocks and super blocks obtained from compiling the benchmarks studied. The plots marked u_2, u_4 and u_8 in the figure refer to the respective uniform processor models. As an example of how to read these plots, observe that blocks with critical path ratio of 0.2 enjoy a 30% improvement on average when scheduled by our heuristic, as compared to scheduling by critical path from the last exit, with respect to the two-functional unit machine u_2. As the critical path ratio nears unity, the achieved improvement falls off, as is to be expected since in this case the last exit is predominant, and our heuristic converges to critical path scheduling. Notice also that as the number of available functional units increases from u_2 to u_4 and u_8, the achieved improvement falls off. This is because critical path scheduling is increasingly good for wider processors, (optimal in the limiting case of infinitely wide processors), and there is reduced opportunity for performance gains by rearranging the schedule. Also shown in the figure is the distribution of the blocks, depicted as cumulative percentage against critical path ratio. As an example of how to read this plot, observe that roughly 30% of the blocks in the sample have a critical path ratio of 0.8 or less. At this value of critical path ratio, the performance improvement is down to a few percent. Hence, the remaining 70% of the blocks are not good candidates for improvement via our scheduling heuristic. This suggests that if super block formation heuristics could form super blocks with lower critical path ratios, our scheduling algorithm would have increased opportunity for performance gains.

Another factor that affects the performance gains realized by our scheduling heuristic is the amount of parallelism present in a super block. If a super block has little parallelism, then the critical path schedule will not saturate the processor, and little performance gain can be obtained since the schedule is not constrained by resources. On the other hand, if the super block has a lot of parallism in it, the critical path schedule will saturate the processor, and much performance gain can be had by rearranging the schedule in favor of high probability exits. A good measure of the parallelism available in a block is the processor utilization factor of the schedule for the block. This is essentially the the average load on the processor during the schedule expressed as a percentage. Formally, the *procesor utilization factor* is the number of cycles for which each functinal unit is busy, summed over all functional units, and expressed as a percentage of the product of the length of the schedule and the number of functional units.

Thus we have two independent factors that can affect the gains realized by our scheduling heuristic **(1)** The importance of the side exits as reflected in the critical path ratio and **(2)** the amount of parallelism available as reflected in the processor utilization. We will now examine the results of Table 7 in light of these two factors. To do so, let us extend the notion of the critical path ratio to benchmarks—the critical path ratio of a benchmark is the weighted sum of the critical path ratios of the blocks composing it, where the weights are the execution probabilities of each block. Similarly, the utilization factor of a benchmark is the weighted sum of the utilization factors of the blocks composing it, where the weights are the execution probabilities of each block. Our heuristic should perform well when the critical path ratio is small and the utilization factor is large. We test this hypothesis in Figure 3. The horizontal axis in the plot is the critical path ratio and the vertical axis is the processor utilization for critical path schedule on processor model u_4. Each box in the figure represents a benchmark, with the center of the box corresponding to its critical path ratio and processor utilization on the horizontal and vertical axes respectively.

The length of the side of each box is directly proportional to the improvement achieved by our heuristic on the benchmark, corresponding to the entry in column u_4 of Table 7. The benchmarks that have a high critical path ratio enjoy very little performance gain independent of their processor utilization. These benchmarks are shown as small box. Also, benchmarks that have little parallelism, manifested as low processor utilization, enjoy very little performance gain even if they have low critical path ratio. Thus, the performance gains of Table 7 are well explained by our intuition, and lends support to the conclusion that the heuristic exhibits gains where gains are possible.

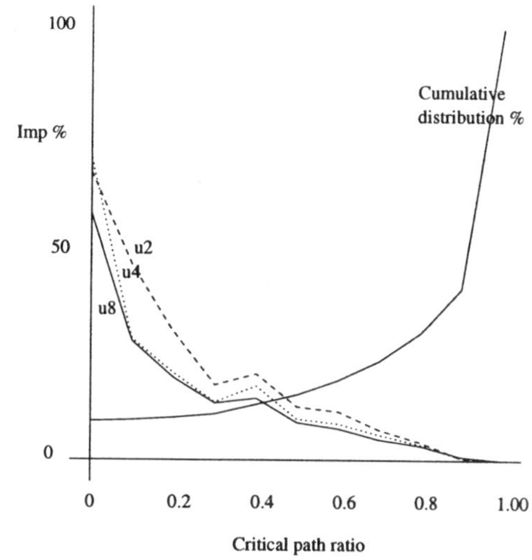

Figure 2. Performance gains of our heuristic over critical path scheduling, critical path scheduling is the profile-insensitive scheduler. Shown is improvement in run time of the blocks as a function of critical path ratio, and the distribution of the blocks as cumulative percentage against critical path ratio.

5. Conclusion

We presented a theoretical analysis of the general problem of scheduling with profile information–we gave a general lemma characterizing optimal sequential schedules for a weighted precedence graph. In a heuristic extension to this lemma, we presented a generic scheme for converting profile-insensitive list scheduling algorithms into profile-sensitive scheduling algorithms for super blocks. Experiments show that in some settings, our heuristic can offer substantial performance improvement over prior methods on a range of benchmarks. The sensity of the heuristic to the profile data remains a topic for study.

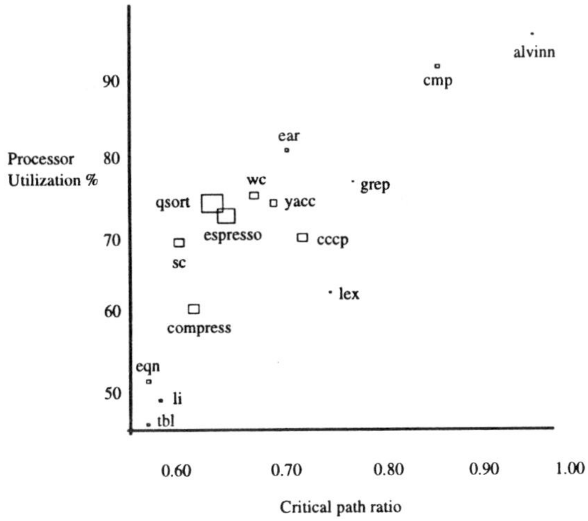

Figure 3. Scatter plot of performance gains of our heuristic over critical path scheduling on the u_4 processor model, critical path scheduling is the profile-insensitive scheduler. Each box corresponds to a benchmark, and the length of the side of the box is proportional to the percentage improvement in performance.

6. Acknowledgements

We thank the Impact group at the University of Illinois for permission to use the Impact compiler in this study. C. Chekuri was supported by NSF Award CCR-9357849, with matching funds from IBM, Mitsubishi, Schlumberger Foundation, Shell Foundation, and Xerox Corp. R. Motwani was supported by an Alfred P. Sloan Research Fellowship, an IBM Faculty Partnership Award, an ARO MURI Grant DAAH04-96-1-0007, and NSF Young Investigator Award CCR-9357849, with matching funds from IBM, Mitsubishi, Schlumberger Foundation, Shell Foundation, and Xerox Corp.

References

[1] D. Adolphson. Single machine job sequencing with precedence constraints. *SIAM J. on Computing*, 6:40–54 (1977).

[2] A. Aho, R. Sethi, and J.D. Ullman. *Compilers Principles, Techniques and Tools.* Addison Wesley, Reading, MA (1988).

[3] R. A. Bringmann, Enhancing instruction level parallelism through compiler controlled optimization. M.S Thesis, University of Illinois, 1992.

[4] J.C. Dehnert and R.A. Towle, Compiling for the Cydra-5 *J. of Supercomputing*, 7:181-228, (1993).

[5] J. Du, J.Y.T. Leung, and G.H. Young. Scheduling chain structured operations to minimize makespan and mean flow time. *Information and Computation*, 92:219–236 (1991).

[6] J. A. Fisher. Trace scheduling: A technique for global microcode compaction. IEEE Trans. on Computers, Vol C-30:478-490.

[7] J. A. Fisher. Global code generation for instruction level parallelism. Tech. Rep. HPL-93-43, Hewlett Packard Labs, June 1993.

[8] M.R. Garey. Optimal task sequencing with precedence constraints. *Discrete Math.*, 4:37–56 (1973).

[9] M.R. Garey and D.S. Johnson. *Computers and Intractability.* W.H. Freeman, San Francisco (1979).

[10] R. Graham. Bounds on multiprocessor timing anomalies. *SIAM J. on App. Math.*, 17:416-429 (1969).

[11] L.A. Hall, A.S. Schulz, D.B. Shmoys and J. Wein. Scheduling to minimize average completion time: offline and on-line algorithms. In *Proc. of the 7th ACM-SIAM Symp. on Discrete Algorithms*, 1996, 142–151.

[12] W.A. Horn. Single-machine job sequencing with treelike precedence ordering and linear delay penalties. *SIAM J. of App. Math.*, 23:189–202 (1972).

[13] T.C. Hu. Parallel sequencing and assembly line problems. *Operations Research*, 9:841–848 (1961).

[14] W.W. Hwu et al. The super block: An effective technique for VLIW and superscalar compilation. *J. of Supercomputing*, 7:229–248 (1993).

[15] E.L. Lawler. Sequencing jobs to minimize total weighted completion time. *Annals of Discrete Math.*, 2:75–90 (1978).

[16] S. A. Mahlke. Exploiting Instruction Level Parallelism in the Presence of Conditional Branches. Ph.D Thesis, U. of Illinois, Urbana, IL, (1996).

[17] S.A. Mahlke et al. Effective compiler support for predicated execution using the hyperblock. In *Proc. 25th Int. Symp. Microarchitecture (MICRO 25)*, 45–54 (1992)

[18] R. Ravi, A. Agrawal, and P. Klein. Ordering problems approximated: single-processor scheduling and interval graph completion. In *Proc. of ICALP* (Springer-Verlag), 751–762 (1991).

Session 3

Speculative Hedge: Regulating Compile-Time Speculation Against Profile Variations

Brian L. Deitrich Wen-mei W. Hwu
Center for Reliable and High-Performance Computing
University of Illinois
Urbana-Champaign, IL 61801
briand,hwu@crhc.uiuc.edu

Abstract

Path-oriented scheduling methods, such as trace scheduling and hyperblock scheduling, use speculation to extract instruction-level parallelism from control-intensive programs. These methods predict important execution paths in the current scheduling scope using execution profiling or frequency estimation. Aggressive speculation is then applied to the important execution paths, possibly at the cost of degraded performance along other paths. Therefore, the speed of the output code can be sensitive to the compiler's ability to accurately predict the important execution paths. Prior work in this area has utilized the speculative yield function by Fisher, coupled with dependence height, to distribute instruction priority among execution paths in the scheduling scope. While this technique provides more stability of performance by paying attention to the needs of all paths, it does not directly address the problem of mismatch between compile-time prediction and run-time behavior.

The work presented in this paper extends the speculative yield and dependence height heuristic to explicitly minimize the penalty suffered by other paths when instructions are speculated along a path. Since the execution time of a path is determined by the number of cycles spent between a path's entrance and exit in the scheduling scope, the heuristic attempts to eliminate unnecessary speculation that delays any path's exit. Such control of speculation makes the performance much less sensitive to the actual path taken at run time. The proposed method has a strong emphasis on achieving minimal delay to all exits. Thus the name, speculative hedge, is used. This paper presents the speculative hedge heuristic, and shows how it controls over-speculation in a superblock/hyperblock scheduler. The stability of output code performance in the presence of execution variation is demonstrated with six programs from the SPEC CINT92 benchmark suite.

1. Introduction

Path-oriented scheduling methods, such as trace scheduling [7] and superblock/hyperblock scheduling [10, 12], extract instruction-level parallelism from control-intensive programs by using speculation. Profile information or frequency estimation guides aggressive speculation, so that important execution paths can have their run time minimized. However, with limited execution resources, situations arise where one path will execute faster, only if another path gets delayed.

Fisher proposed the use of *speculative yield* to determine the profitability of speculating an instruction [8]. The speculative yield is an expected value function which is defined between basic blocks. It is the probability that an operation scheduled in basic block$_i$ produces useful work (meaning that its original basic block$_j$ executes when basic block$_i$ executes). Its use with dependence height has been shown to account for the needs of all paths during the scheduling process [2].

Speculative yield, coupled with dependence height, provides a good heuristic for path-oriented schedulers, but it does not address the problem of mismatches between compile-time prediction and run-time behavior. There is nothing inherent to speculative yield and dependence height that ensures that paths, which are shown by profile data to be unimportant, do not get delayed unnecessarily. This leads to execution-time slow-down when those paths are really executed at run time.

The *speculative hedge* heuristic, presented in this paper, attempts to ensure that no path gets delayed unnecessarily, even while performing aggressive speculation. Therefore, it *hedges* its reliance on the compile-time prediction data. It accomplishes this goal by accounting for different processor resources while scheduling, not just the common scheduling priority function of dependence height.

It should be noted that speculative hedge only solves part of the profile independence problem. Speculative hedge does not address the problem of determining what paths should be scheduled together. A poor selection of paths to schedule together will limit the amount of ILP that can be generated for a program, and cause a profile-dependence problem [5]. Speculative hedge limits the damage associated with a poor selection by ensuring that paths are not delayed unnecessarily. This property is especially important for any compiler which uses static analysis instead of profile information to determine which paths should be scheduled together [9].

1072-4451/96 $5.00 © 1996 IEEE

The usefulness of the speculative hedge heuristic is demonstrated in a superblock/hyperblock scheduler. The remainder of the paper describes the heuristic, its implementation in the superblock/hyperblock scheduler, and the results obtained when the heuristic is applied to six SPEC CINT92 benchmarks. The paper is organized as follows: Section 2 provides background on terms used in the paper and related work. Section 3 provides the details of the speculative hedge heuristic. The performance results are reported in Section 4. A summary and a description of future work is given in Section 5.

2. Background

2.1. Late Times and Dependence Height

Dependence height is an important measure in determining an operation's scheduling priority. Many heuristics depend on it exclusively during scheduling. Speculative hedge uses dependence height as one component when determining scheduling priority. *Late times* are used by the speculative hedge heuristic to account for dependence height while scheduling.

A late time for an operation is the latest time that an operation can be scheduled without delaying an exit. An operation has a set of late times associated with it, one for each exit. Late times are calculated based on the latencies associated with the dependence graph used for scheduling. Figure 1 shows the late time values for a simple dependence graph. The late times are a 2-tuple in the figure. The first entry in the tuple is the operation's late time for exit 0, and the second entry is the operation's late time for exit 1.

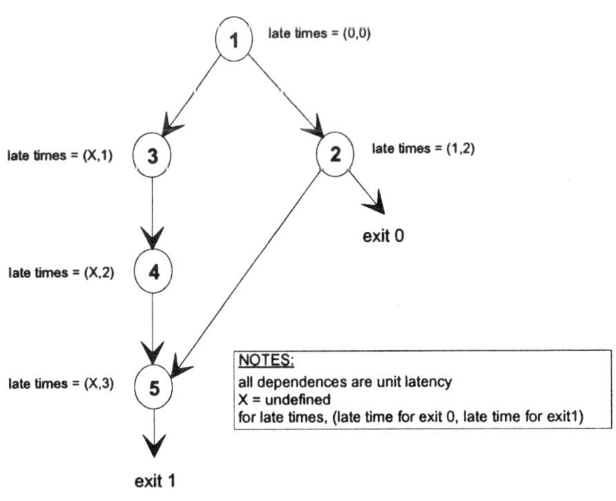

Figure 1. Dependence graph used for scheduling

Late times are computed via a bottom-up traversal of the dependence graph. The calculation is done once for every exit. An exit operation has its late time defined as the dependence height of the exit (which would have been determined with a top-down traversal of the dependence graph) minus one. In the example, operation 2's late time for exit 0 is 1, and operation 5's late time for exit 1 is 3. All other operations have their late times computed based on the exit late times of operations located later in the dependence graph. Operation$_x$'s late time for exit$_i$ (LT_x) is defined as:

For all dependence arcs exiting operation$_x$ and entering any operation$_y$, $LT_x = \min_{for\_all\_ops_y}(LT_y - lat_{xy})$[1]

LT_x = op$_x$_late_time_for_exit$_i$,

LT_y = op$_y$_late_time_for_exit$_i$,

lat_{xy} = latency_of_dep_arc_between_ops_x_and_y

If an operation does not reach an exit through a dependence chain, the operation does not contain a *valid late time* for that exit. Therefore, its late time for the exit is undefined.

Speculative hedge utilizes late times in the conventional manner, but allows an exit operation's late time for that exit to be defined by the most constraining resource height, instead of always using dependence height. In Figure 1, if the processor being scheduled is single-issue, the exit associated with operation 5 cannot be issued as quickly as the dependence height dictates. Since issue width is the limiting resource, operation 5's late time for exit 1 would actually be four (the issue width height minus one). Therefore, all the late times associated with exit 1 would be one greater than the values shown in the figure.

2.2. Previous Work and Other Heuristics

DEPENDENCE HEIGHT AND SPECULATIVE YIELD

Fisher suggests that the multiplication of dependence height by speculative yield is a good candidate for the scheduling priority function [8]. The appeal is that dependence height is commonly used as the priority function, and speculative yield allows it to take into account the probability of taken branches.

Bringmann utilized this concept in a list scheduler for superblocks [2]. In his method, a static heuristic utilizes the exit probabilities[2] and an operation's late times to generate the priority for that operation. The operations are then scheduled greedily, so that the highest priority operation that is available gets scheduled. The priority function used in this scheduler is:

$Priority_x = \sum_{ValLT_x}(Prob_i * (MaxLT + 1 - LT_x))$

$ValLT_x$ = for_all_valid_late_times$_i$_of_op$_x$

$Prob_i$ = probability_of_taking_exit$_i$

$MaxLT$ = max_late_time_in_dep_graph

LT_x = op$_x$_late_time_for_exit$_i$

To illustrate how the priority values are obtained, reference Figure 1. Assume exit 0 is taken 25% of the time and exit 1 is taken the other 75% of the time. The priority values obtained are:

operation$_1$ = $0.25 * (3 + 1 - 0) + 0.75 * (3 + 1 - 0) = 4$, operation$_2$ = 2.25, operation$_3$ = 2.25, operation$_4$ = 1.5, and operation$_5$ = 0.75.

Using only dependence height to guide the scheduler can delay exits unnecessarily though. This is shown in Figure 2.

[1]In a practical implementation, if all dependence arcs go in the forward direction relative to the original program order, the equation can be applied once for each operation by visiting the operations in the reverse program order.

[2]Since a superblock has only one entrance point, exit probabilities are equivalent to Fisher's speculative yield values

Assuming the latencies marked in the figure, the second branch, operation 7, can be retired in the third cycle when one only considers dependence height. If the profile information shows that exit 1 is always taken and dependence height guides the scheduling priority function, operations 1 and 2 would be scheduled in the first cycle. The earliest time exit 1 can actually be retired is in the fourth cycle because there are eight operations that must be issued on this two-issue machine. Since the issue width of the processor is the limiting factor, exit 0 should be retired right away (regardless of the profile information). This allows exit 0 to be retired immediately, and still allows exit 1 to be retired as soon as possible. This case illustrates the main concept behind speculative hedge—account for processor resources so exits are not delayed unnecessarily.

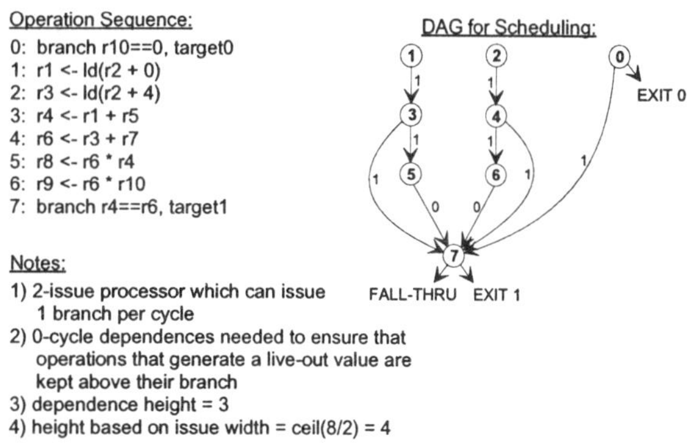

Figure 2. Example of dependence height not being a problem.

CRITICAL PATH

Critical path is a profile-independent scheduling heuristic that has been used in many types of schedulers [13, 6, 11]. Its application to superblock scheduling consists of using the dependence height associated with the last exit in a superblock.

The *dependence height and speculative yield* priority function creates identical schedules to *critical path* if the profile information shows that the last exit has a probability of one, and all other exits have a probability of zero. This scheduling heuristic suffers from over-speculation along the longest path of control, and the potential for delaying earlier side exits unnecessarily. Speculative hedge can use the same profile-independent assumption that the last exit is always taken, and create better schedules through its use of resource information, along with the dependence information.

SUCCESSIVE RETIREMENT

Successive retirement is another profile-independent scheduling heuristic which attempts to retire each exit in-order, as early as possible [4, 16]. This heuristic minimizes speculation, so that it only speculates when there are no non-speculative instructions available.

This scheduling method works well for narrow-issue processors, where speculation is not very important. However, it can potentially lose performance by not speculating enough for wide-issue processors. When a narrow-issue processor is scheduled for, successive retirement and speculative hedge create similar schedules. This results from speculative hedge's ability to understand when the processor's issue width is the limiting factor to the retirement of exits.

3. Speculative Hedge Heuristic

3.1. High-Level Overview

Speculative hedge takes both dependence height and resource constraints into account while scheduling. Many previous methods have considered only dependence height as the limiting factor. As shown previously, taking into account only dependence height can delay seemingly unimportant exits.

To account for the resources accurately, speculative hedge uses a dynamic-priority scheme. The dynamic-priority calculation is needed because exits can be constrained by different resources at various times during the scheduling process. The type of resource that constrains an exit's retirement has a direct effect on scheduling decisions. The compilation-time implications of this approach are addressed in Section 4.

In order to determine the best operation to schedule next, speculative hedge uses several priority values. The priority values used are:

- Helped weight - The sum of the taken probabilities for all exits having a *critical need* met by an operation.
- Helped count - The total number of exits having a *critical need* met by an operation.
- Minimum late time difference - The minimum difference between the current cycle time being scheduled and any of an operation's late times.
- Original program order - A unique number which is based on the original program location of an operation.

The first two priority values are utilized whenever the scheduling of an operation satisfies a *critical need* for an exit. A critical need can be dependence height, issue width, or any other restricted processor resource, which must be dealt with in order for an exit to be retired by its *retirement goal*. An exit's retirement goal is the earliest time that an exit can be retired based on dependence height or any resource constraint. An operation satisfies a critical need by having the properties necessary to retire an exit quickly. One example of satisfying a critical need occurs when an operation has a late time equal to the current cycle being scheduled and an exit is dependence height limited. Another example happens when an operation is an integer add operation and integer ALU issue width is the limiting factor for an exit. If an operation can satisfy a critical need, it *helps* an exit by allowing it to retire quickly.

Helped weight is the first criterion used to determine which operation should get scheduled. Helped weight's value is defined as the sum of all taken-exit profile weights that can be retired as soon as possible, if the current operation gets scheduled immediately. For example, if a superblock contains three exits (with each exit taken 25%, 40%, and 35% of the time respectively), an operation which helps the first two exits retire would have a helped weight of 0.65. An operation with the highest helped weight value gets scheduled next since it helps the most probable exits.

Of the four priority values, helped weight is the only one that depends on profile information. The other three priority values allow the speculative hedge heuristic to be less sensitive to profile variations. They allow fair decisions to be made for all exits, regardless of the compile-time predicted behavior.

The *helped count* priority value is used when operations share the same helped weight. Helped count is the number of exits having a critical need met by an operation. This criterion gives zero weight exits priority. If the weight of all the exits helped between two operations is equal, the operation helping the most exits should get scheduled first.

The helped weight and helped count priority values work together to prevent exits from being delayed unnecessarily. They accomplish this with the accurate accounting of resources. For example, if an important exit's retirement is issue-width limited, all operations located prior to the exit will meet the critical criteria for the exit. Therefore, operations helping an earlier, less important exit are critical for the important exit too. These operations would be chosen for scheduling because they will include both exits in their helped weight and helped count values. Even if the earlier exit was shown to never be taken based on the profile information, helped count would ensure the exit does not get delayed.

On the other hand, if dependence height is the limiting factor in an important exit's retirement, speculative hedge will work similar to the *dependence height and speculative yield* heuristic. Therefore, it will delay certain exits in favor of an exit that the profile information shows to be important. Speculative hedge does not keep exits from being delayed because of speculation. It only tries to minimize the number of exits and the penalty for exits that are delayed unnecessarily.

Another important aspect of speculative hedge is that it only looks at the exits that are helped by scheduling a particular operation. Speculative hedge's priority values do not directly deal with the condition where the scheduling of an operation might delay another exit. This is indirectly handled through the priority values for other operations. In order for the scheduling of operation$_x$ to delay an exit$_i$, there must exist another operation$_y$, whose scheduling would allow exit$_i$ to not be delayed. Since operation$_y$ helps exit$_i$, it gets exit$_i$'s contribution for helped weight and helped count. Therefore, the trade-off that needs to be made between the delaying of an exit$_i$ and another exit is done via the comparison of operations x and y's helped weight and helped count values.

If the helped weight and helped count values are equal, the next criterion used is *minimum late time difference*. As defined earlier, each operation has a set of late times, one for each exit. An operation's late time difference for an exit is defined as the difference between the current cycle being scheduled and the operation's late time for that exit. An operation's minimum late time difference is the minimum of all the exits' late time differences.

This criterion is important because it helps anticipate which operations are about to become critical. Its biggest benefit comes when the helped weight and helped count values are both zero. This condition occurs after several operations have already been scheduled for the current cycle, all the scheduled operations have met all the exits' critical needs, and there is still at least one open slot in the current cycle.

The final criterion, original program order, is used when all the previous criteria have tied. It is used so that an operation located earlier in the program order gets scheduled first. This keeps unnecessary speculation from occurring and allows a deterministic schedule.

The priority values are used by speculative hedge to determine which operation should be scheduled next. The speculative hedge heuristic computes the priority values in the following way. First, the retirement goals and critical needs for every exit that has not been retired are determined. Then, all the late times for unscheduled operations are computed using the exit retirement goals as the defined late times for their corresponding exit operations. Finally, the priority values for all operations available for scheduling are computed, and the operation with the highest priority gets scheduled.

The remainder of this section describes the details needed to utilize the speculative hedge heuristic effectively. First, the determination of exit retirement goals and critical needs is presented. Second, the application of the priority value calculation is shown. Finally, some potential problems with speculative hedge are discussed.

3.2. Exit Retirement Goals and Critical Needs

The key components of speculative hedge are the estimation on the number of cycles that remain before an exit can be retired, and the determination of which resources must be utilized in order to not delay the exit. This information is used directly by the dynamic priority function to determine if an exit has a critical need, and whether the scheduling of an operation will enable that need to be met. The scheduling of an operation meeting a critical need either shortens the unscheduled dependence height or consumes a resource so that resource need in the future is alleviated. As with the priority calculation, this information is recomputed dynamically during the scheduling process.

In speculative hedge, the estimation of when an exit can be retired is optimistic. It is a lower bound on how quickly an exit can be retired [14]. An estimate may change during the course of scheduling because conflicting needs between different exits force some exits to delay. It is the dynamic priority function's responsibility to effectively deal with the trade-offs that must be made during the scheduling process.

There are three main needs that are always considered,

independent of the processor that is targeted. They are dependence height, the branch unit, and issue width. Other processor resources that are restricted, such as memory operation issue width or special decoder requirements, are considered when they apply.

For each need, a cycle estimate is made which determines when an exit can be retired, based exclusively on that need. The maximum of all the cycle estimates for each need yields the retirement goal for an exit. Any need whose cycle estimate equals the exit retirement goal is considered critical.

The cycle estimate based on dependence height is a straight-forward computation which determines the dependence height that must be honored before an exit can be retired. It must account for unscheduled operations and latencies for already scheduled operations that have not been fully satisfied.

The cycle estimate based on the branch unit is a function of the number of branches that can be issued in the same cycle, and the retirement goals for previous exits sharing a common control path. Branches guarding a common control path cannot be reordered. Therefore, an exit with a branch must have a cycle estimate which is at least the same as the retirement goal for a preceding branch along a common control path. If an exit is a fall-thru, it must have a retirement goal that is at least the same as any preceding exit's retirement goal.

If the number of preceding branches having the same retirement goal is equal to the number of branches that can be issued in any cycle, the current exit's cycle estimate is the preceding retirement exit goal plus one. This happens because there are not enough branch units to retire all of those exits simultaneously. In the one branch-per-cycle case, the cycle estimate based on the branch unit is always one more than any preceding exit retirement goal.

Speculative hedge's cycle estimate based on issue width (ce_{iw}) could be:

$ce_{iw} = \lceil num\_ops\_to\_sched\_before\_exit / issue\_width \rceil$

This simple calculation does not detect enough issue-width problems though. Many times, an exit may have an issue-width problem early in its dependence chain, but contain few operations later in its dependence chain. This is illustrated in Figure 3. In this example, a two-issue machine needs to execute three loads which, based on dependence height, must be executed in cycle zero in order to not delay the exit. Since it is impossible to issue them all simultaneously, the exit is really issue width limited at the beginning of its dependence chain.

To deal with this effectively, speculative hedge detects these cases, and keeps track of the late times that are included in any issue-width problem. This allows the speculative hedge heuristic to ensure that the issue-width problem is taken care of properly. For an operation to help solve an issue-width problem, it must have a late time for the exit that is less than or equal to the late time where the issue-width problem ends.

The cycle estimates for other restricted resources, like a limited number of integer ALU operations that can be issued in any cycle, can be handled similarly to the general

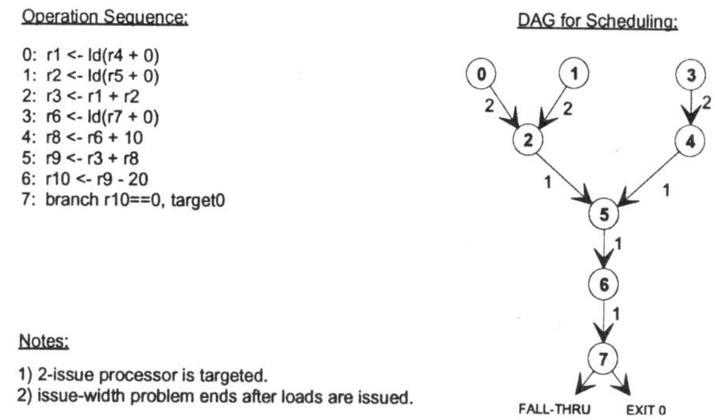

Figure 3. Example of an issue-width problem located at the beginning of a dependence chain.

issue-width problem just discussed.

3.3. Priority Calculation

Now that the exit retirement goals and critical needs have been determined, the dynamic priority calculation is performed. This dynamic scheme does require more computations than a static priority scheme, but is needed in order to account for all the changing resource requirements. The compilation-time implications of this method are discussed in the Section 4.

The priority calculation is performed for every operation that can be scheduled by evaluating each exit, and determining whether the operation meets a critical need for the exit. If the scheduling of an operation meets a critical need, the operation helps the exit retire quickly. The high-level view of the priority calculation is shown in Figure 4.

If an $exit_i$ has dependence height as its critical need, an $operation_x$ meets that need if it has a $late\_time_i$ which is equal to the current cycle being scheduled. If $operation_x$ meets the critical need, $operation_x$'s helped weight and helped count get incremented for $exit_i$. A check is also made to determine if the meeting of a critical need for the current $exit_i$ will help future exits meet a critical need.

The check is needed to accurately account for branch-to-branch dependence height. A future $exit_j$ is helped if the branch unit is a critical need for it, the current $exit_i$ precedes it, it shares a common control path with the branch for $exit_i$, and the delaying of the branch for $exit_i$ would cause the future $exit_j$ to also be delayed. The determination of whether delaying $exit_i$ will also delay a future $exit_j$ is not trivial. Figure 5 helps to illustrate the different cases that are handled by speculative hedge.

For each case, branch B1 is associated with $exit_i$. It is the exit that has a critical need met by $operation_x$. A determination is made to see if any future $exits_j$ will also be helped by $operation_x$. All branches shown are assumed to share a control path, and three branches can be issued in one cycle.

Case 1 is a basic example. In it, branch B2 is located after B1, and in the same cycle as B1. Therefore, if B1 gets delayed, B2 must be delayed too. B2's exit gets added to $operation_x$'s helped weight and helped count.

```
for (each unscheduled, available oper_x) {
   helped_weight_x = helped_count_x = 0
   for (each exit_i) helped_found_i = FALSE
   for (each exit_i where oper_x has a valid late time_i) {
      if (dependence_critical_for_i &&
         (oper_x's late time_i == current_cycle)) {
            helped_found_i = TRUE
            account_for_future_branches
      }
      if (issue_width_critical_for_i &&
         oper_x's late time is located before issue width
         problem ends) {
            helped_found_i = TRUE
            account_for_future_branches
      }
      /* the following is an example of what needs to be
            done for restricted resources */
      if (integer_alu_issue_width_critical_for_i &&
         oper_x is an integer alu operation &&
         oper_x's late time is located before integer alu
         issue width problem ends) {
            helped_found_i = TRUE
            account_for_future_branches
      }
   }
   for (each exit_i)
      if (helped_found_i) {
         helped_weight_x += profile_weight_i
         helped_count_x++
      }
   determine_min_late_time_diff_for_oper_x
}
```

Figure 4. Algorithm for dynamic priority calculation.

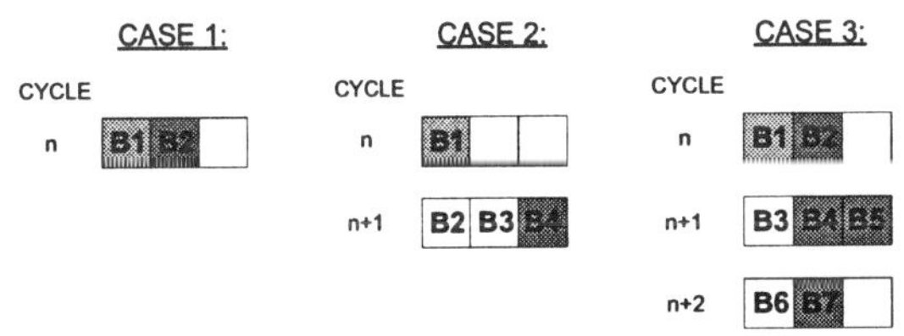

Figure 5. Cases for account_for_future_branches.

Case 2 is another basic example. Here, B1 is located by itself in a cycle, but the next cycle contains three branches. If B1 gets delayed, too many operations end up being located in the same cycle. So, B4 must be delayed also. B4's exit gets added to operation$_x$'s helped weight and helped count.

Case 3 is a combination of both cases 1 and 2. Here, the delay of B1, causes B2, B4, B5, and B7 to be delayed. Therefore, each one of them get their corresponding exit added into operation$_x$'s helped weight and helped count. In this cascading fashion, an operation$_x$ can help many exits just by meeting one exit's critical need.

The multiple branches-per-cycle problem is actually an important special case of a more general phenomenon. When predication is not used, branches have zero-cycle control dependences linking them. A similar case can also arise for other instructions. An example is a sequence of integer ALU operations that are linked by zero-cycle anti-dependences. If only one integer ALU operation can be issued in a single cycle, all the zero cycle anti-dependences can be changed to one cycle dependences in order to account for resource height. The fact making branches the most interesting case is that branches, when predication is not used, are always connected by these control dependences; no other instruction type has a zero-cycle dependence always linking them.

Operation$_x$ meets an exit's issue-width critical need, if the exit has issue width as a critical need, and operation$_x$'s late time is less than the late time associated with the issue width problem. The late time check is needed to ensure that the issue-width problem is really being addressed. As discussed in the previous section, an issue-width problem can be isolated to the beginning of an exit's dependence chain.

Finally, the checks needed for a restricted resource are also shown in Figure 4. They are identical to the issue width critical comparisons, with an extra check to ensure that operation$_x$ is the correct type of instruction. This same check can be replicated for any type of restricted resource that the scheduler should account for.

3.4. Potential Problems

As with any scheduling heuristic, there are some potential areas of concern with speculative hedge. Scheduling is an NP-complete problem, and obtaining an optimal solution for all cases is not feasible.

One problem area of speculative hedge has to do with the trade-offs made while selecting an operation to schedule. An operation may be chosen because it helps an important exit$_i$, but scheduling it may delay a less important exit$_j$. The problem arises, when a subsequent trade-off may mean that exit$_i$ gets delayed in order to help an even more important exit$_k$. Delaying exit$_j$, in hindsight, was unnecessary. Because the heuristic only looks at the situation for the current cycle, it may not always make the best decisions for the entire scheduling region as a whole.

This problem, while seen in practice, does not appear frequently enough to be a major issue. Also, it does not hurt the most frequently executed exits, and it causes only a short, unnecessary delay for the exits that it effects.

There is another problem related to scheduling trade-offs. This can happen when an important exit has dependence height as its critical need, and in the process of satisfying the dependence height need, it uses all the resources for a particular instruction type, like an integer ALU instruction. In addition, this situation lasts for several cycles. A less important exit can be retired immediately if it were allowed to issue an instruction whose type is being used up by the more important exit, but speculative hedge chooses to help the more important exit. When the problem is not solved for several cycles, the less important exit gets delayed several cycles.

This is an issue because a net loss may result. The cost of delaying the less important exit several cycles may not be offset by allowing the more important exit to be retired one cycle early. Speculative hedge only looks at the costs involved for the current cycle, and does not look at the costs that are involved in the future.

A final problem deals with speculative hedge's desire to not consciously schedule for an exit's retirement until it is absolutely necessary to do so. Speculative hedge will delay an operation on a path shown by profile information to be taken 100% of the time for an operation on a 0% path, if it determines that scheduling for the 0% path will not delay the 100% path. This works fine as long as the speculative hedge heuristic makes no misjudgments concerning the 100% path. If a misjudgment is made, the 100% path may get delayed unnecessarily.

This problem was seen in several places during the evolution of the speculative hedge heuristic. As the heuristic was improved, the problem became less pronounced. The main mechanism in the heuristic that helped alleviate the problem was the *determine_min_late_time_diff_for_oper* function. This function identifies operations that are most likely to be needed next, and helps ward off the potential problem.

4. Experimental Analysis

In this section, the effectiveness of the speculative hedge heuristic in minimizing the unnecessary delaying of exits is analyzed for a set of SPEC CINT92 benchmarks. First, speculative hedge's performance is compared against other scheduling heuristics on real input cases for a variety of machine configurations and compile-time assumptions. Then, an in-depth analysis is done to show exactly how well the speculative hedge heuristic controls unnecessary speculation for an exit that does not appear to be important based on the compile-time predicted data. Finally, the compilation-time implications of speculative hedge's dynamic priority scheme are addressed.

4.1. Methodology

The speculative hedge, dependence height and speculative yield, and successive retirement heuristics have been implemented in the IMPACT compiler [3]. This compiler inlined, coalesced into superblocks, and fully ILP optimized the six SPEC CINT92 benchmarks used in this testing. The benchmarks used are *espresso*, *li*, *eqntott*, *compress*, *sc*, and *cc1*.

To show the effectiveness of the speculative hedge heuristic for various issue width and functional unit constraints, four machine models are utilized. They are:

- 4_MIX – A 4-issue processor that contains 2-memory ports, 2-integer ALUs, 1-floating point ALU, and 1-branch unit. This machine model is similar to many of today's processors.

- 4_1BR – A fully-uniform 4-issue processor that contains only one branch unit. This machine model allows more scheduling freedom than 4_MIX, and shows how the scheduling heuristics perform when the functional units are not constraining resources.

Table 1. Instruction latencies.

Function	Latency	Function	Latency
Int ALU	1	FP ALU	2
memory load	2	FP multiply	2
memory store	1	FP divide(SGL)	8
branch	1 / 1 slot	FP divide(DBL)	15

- 4_2BR – A fully-uniform 4-issue processor that contains two branch units. This machine model forces the condition where branch resource height is tough to account for.

- SINGLE – A single-issue processor. This machine model forces issue width to be a major issue and speculation to be minimized in order to obtain good performance.

Each machine model's latencies match those of the HP PA-RISC PA7100 processor, and the latencies are shown in Table 1. An enhanced version of the HP PA-RISC processor instruction set is used with a non-trapping version of instructions added, so speculative instructions cannot cause program termination. This allows the general speculation model to be utilized by the scheduler [3]. This model gives the scheduler the freedom and choices during scheduling to help differentiate the performance of the heuristics.

The analysis focuses on prepass scheduling, and the effect that the compile-time predicted behavior has on the quality of the schedules produced. The effects of register allocation, cache misses, branch mispredictions, etc. are factored out, so that a fair comparison can be made between the different scheduling heuristics. This means that the execution time of programs is determined statically, by knowing the schedule time for a particular exit and the number of times that the profile information shows that the exit is taken.

4.2. Results

This section compares the schedules obtained for the different benchmarks. The first set of results analyze the schedules obtained by the speculative hedge, dependence height and speculative yield, and successive retirement heuristics for the four different machine models and different compile-time profile assumptions. The different schedules are compared assuming that the actual program input matches the exact input used to generate one of the compile-time profile assumptions. The second set of results analyze the effectiveness of the speculative hedge and dependence height and speculative yield heuristics to schedule the first exit when they both assume that the last exit is always taken. Finally, the time needed to schedule with the speculative hedge heuristic is compared against the time needed to schedule with dependence height and speculative yield.

Evaluation for Real Execution of Programs. In this test, the effectiveness of the speculative hedge heuristic in controlling unnecessary speculation is analyzed. This is done by scheduling each benchmark on four different machine models with the different scheduling heuristics. In addition, the two profile-dependent heuristics, speculative hedge (SH) and dependence height and speculative yield (DHASY), are given three different compile-time profile assumptions. The different assumptions will be used to show that SH is less sensitive to profile variations than DHASY.

The three different profile-time assumptions are *REAL* (the profile data matches the program behavior for the real data that is input), *ALL1* (the profile data shows that all exits are equally likely), and *LAST1* (the profile data shows that only the last exit in the superblock is ever taken). Note that the critical path scheduling heuristic is the same as scheduling DHASY with the LAST1 profile assumption.

The results for the four machine models after scheduling with the different scheduling heuristics are shown in Table 2. The cycle count for SH-REAL assumes the same profile input used to generate the SH-REAL schedule is used in the actual run. The *% Diff* columns represent the difference the column's scheduling heuristic cycle count had to the SH-REAL's cycle count for the same benchmark and input data (a negative value means the column's heuristic required more cycles to execute).

SH is less reliant on the compile-time profile assumption than DHASY. The largest difference between SH-REAL and SH-ALL1/SH-LAST1 for any machine model and benchmark is 2%. This is contrasted with DHASY-REAL and DHASY-LAST1 (which is critical path) which vary by over 5% for at least one benchmark in every machine model, and vary by over 10% for at least one benchmark for the 4_2BR and SINGLE machine models.

In addition, SH-ALL1 and SH-LAST1, which were scheduled with compile-time profile assumptions that differed from the run-time execution, outperformed DHASY-REAL for most of the test cases. SH-ALL1 and SH-LAST1 executed more cycles than DHASY-REAL for only one benchmark in each of the 4_MIX, 4_1BR, and 4_2BR machine models. SH-ALL1 and SH-LAST1 performed better because they were able to account for resources while scheduling, and minimize the effect of exits that were delayed unnecessarily. Even though SH-ALL1 and SH-LAST1 may not have helped some of the execution paths that were important at run-time (because they did not have that information), they were able to minimize unnecessary exit delays. On the other hand, DHASY-REAL did delay some less important exits unnecessarily, and this resulted in its schedule taking a few more cycles to execute than the schedules for SH-ALL1 and SH-LAST1.

To understand how speculative hedge performs for special cases, the SINGLE and 4_2BR machine models must be examined. The SINGLE machine model case shows how well speculative hedge performs when issue width is a severe problem. Speculative hedge generates schedules that are as good as, or better than successive retirement. This highlights speculative hedge's ability to control speculation, so exits are not delayed unnecessarily.

In the 2_BR machine model case, speculative hedge's method of accounting for the branch resource height allows it to be insensitive to the accounting problems for branch-to-branch dependences that effect DHASY. The zero cycle branch-to-branch dependence assumption made by DHASY leads to its profile sensitivity problems. For this machine model, DHASY-LAST1 (critical path) varies an average of over 5% when compared to DHASY-REAL, while SH-LAST1 only varies an average of 0.4% when compared to SH-REAL.

Evaluation of the unnecessary delaying of an exit. The results shown so far have been for real execution cases. These results can be affected by a minority of the superblocks present in the benchmarks. This makes it difficult to show how large a problem the dependence on profile information can be. To illustrate the potential problem, speculative hedge and DHASY are scheduled assuming that the last exit is always taken. Then, a comparison is made between their resulting schedules showing how well they handle the first exit for all the superblocks in the six benchmarks. The first exit was chosen because it has the best chance of being delayed unnecessarily by over-speculation.

The results are shown in Figure 6, and they were obtained for the 4_MIX machine model. The cycle difference subtracts the scheduled cycle for SH-LAST1's first exit to the cycle obtained for DHASY-LAST1's first exit. The zero cycle's column represents instances where SH-LAST1 and DHASY-LAST1 scheduled the first exit in the same cycle, and the cycle was later than could have been obtained if the first exit was scheduled to retire as quickly as possible. As shown in the figure, DHASY does a worse job in retiring the first exit of the superblocks for all the benchmarks.

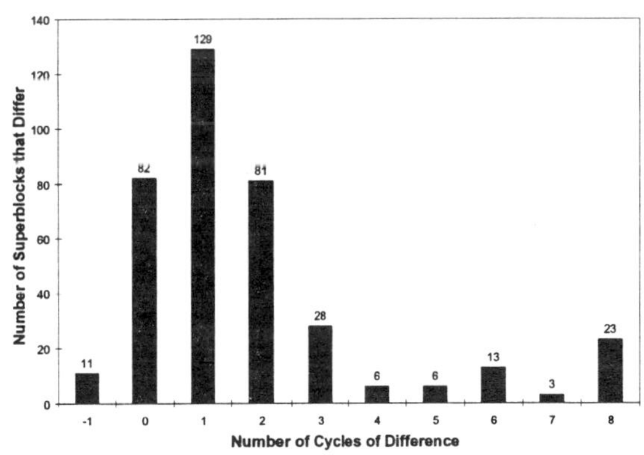

Figure 6. Cycle differences between SH-LAST1 and DHASY-LAST1 for the first exit.

An evaluation of speculative hedge's and DHASY's first exit schedule times to the earliest time that the first exit could be retired (which would be obtained if the profile information showed that it was the only exit ever taken) provides more insight into this issue. It confirms that not only does DHASY delay more exits unnecessarily, it also delays them longer than speculative hedge. An examination of the detailed data shows, that compared to the case where

Table 2. Results when input data matches input used for REAL profiling.

Machine Model	Benchmark	SH - REAL # of cycles	SH - ALL1 % diff	SH - LAST1 % diff	DHASY - REAL % diff	DHASY - ALL1 % diff	Crit. Path[a] % diff	Succ. Ret. % diff
4_MIX	espresso	152405400	-0.5	-0.9	-0.2	-0.6	-2.1	-0.7
	li	14486519	0.0	0.0	0.0	-0.7	-0.3	-0.4
	eqntott	423624658	0.0	0.0	0.0	0.0	0.0	0.0
	compress	25767022	-0.1	-0.1	-0.6	-3.1	-8.2	-2.6
	sc	38204165	0.0	0.0	-0.5	-0.9	-0.3	-3.7
	cc1	49349343	-0.2	-0.1	-0.3	-0.7	-0.2	-1.1
4_1BR	espresso	146674421	-0.1	0.0	-1.4	-1.2	-1.0	-1.6
	li	13702023	0.0	0.0	-0.8	-1.3	-0.2	-1.1
	eqntott	401064104	0.0	0.0	0.0	0.0	0.0	0.0
	compress	24174638	-0.5	-0.5	-0.4	-3.4	-6.3	-2.9
	sc	36938586	0.0	0.0	-0.1	-0.3	0.0	-2.5
	cc1	47497736	0.0	0.0	-0.1	-0.2	-0.1	-0.7
4_2BR[b]	espresso	129275735	-0.1	0.0	-1.0	-1.9	-7.2	-2.3
	li	12389729	-0.7	-0.7	0.0	-2.2	-1.3	-2.0
	eqntott	313622471	-0.4	-0.4	-1.0	-4.0	-6.4	-0.9
	compress	22011735	-0.3	-0.3	-0.6	-7.1	-11.4	-2.7
	sc	30904853	-1.2	-1.1	-1.4	-2.0	-5.8	-4.6
	cc1	41450987	0.0	0.0	-0.4	-0.6	-3.7	-1.3
SINGLE	espresso	330192736	-0.2	-0.2	-1.6	-3.1	-11.2	-0.2
	li	27242181	-0.6	-0.6	-0.3	-1.9	-4.4	-1.9
	eqntott	826767804	0.0	0.0	0.0	-0.1	-0.1	-0.1
	compress	56980582	-2.0	-2.0	-0.7	-6.3	-15.6	+0.1
	sc	84079061	-0.5	-0.4	+0.2	-0.8	-1.0	-0.7
	cc1	99468982	-0.3	-0.2	-0.1	-1.4	-3.1	-0.4

[a] Critical path is the same as DHASY-LAST1.

[b] All branch-to-branch dependences for DHASY are assumed to be 0.

the first exit was retired as soon as possible, speculative hedge delayed 125 first exits for an average of 1.3 cycles, while DHASY delayed 379 first exits for an average of 2.4 cycles.

Evaluation of compilation time. The compilation time for speculative hedge must be addressed because of its use of a dynamic priority calculation. The priority calculation is performed on every operation that can be scheduled (which means there are no resource conflicts and all the operation's incoming dependences have been satisfied), and gets recomputed before any operation is scheduled. In addition, the priority calculation's run time is proportional to the number of exits that have yet to be retired. This leads to a worst-case run time for speculative hedge of $O(n^2m)$, where n = number of operations and m = number of exits. Measurements, during prepass scheduling of the SPEC CINT92 benchmarks, showed that speculative hedge had to compute priorities for an average of 2.8 operations before an operation got scheduled. This leads to a run-time of $2.8nm$ in practice. The worst-case run time for DHASY's static priority calculation is $O(nm)$.

The speculative hedge heuristic was implemented in the IMPACT compiler. Timing measurements were made during prepass scheduling. Besides the calculation of operation priorities and the actual scheduling, the only other computationally-intensive functionality performed was the data-flow analysis required to compute the live-out variables. IMPACT uses a standard, iterative data-flow algorithm for the analysis which has a worst-case run time of $O(b^2)$, where b = number of basic blocks [1]. For the benchmarks used in this paper, prepass scheduling took 26% to 49% longer for speculative hedge than it did for DHASY.

5. Conclusion

5.1. Summary

This paper described a new path-oriented, scheduling heuristic, *speculative hedge*, which attempts to minimize speculation so paths of execution do not get delayed unnecessarily. This ensures that speculative hedge is much less sensitive to variations between compile-time predicted behavior and actual run-time behavior. This is done by accounting for dependence height and processor resources while scheduling. Previous scheduling heuristics that only accounted for dependence height while scheduling would delay exits unnecessarily, and perform poorly at run time when the program executed differently than expected. The speculative hedge heuristic was implemented in a superblock/hyperblock scheduler to illustrate its effectiveness.

The paper investigated the performance of speculative hedge for six programs from the SPEC CINT92 benchmark suite for four different machine models. Speculative hedge was scheduled with three different sets of compile-time predicted behaviors, and the largest variation for any combination of machine model and compile-time predicted behavior was 2%. In contrast, *dependence height and speculative yield*, using the same sets of compile-time predicted behavior, had variations of over 5% for at least one benchmark in every machine model, with three cases having variations of over 10%. In addition, an analysis of how the first exits of superblocks can be delayed for different profile inputs showed that *dependence height and speculative yield* delayed some superblock first exits by up to eight cycles more than speculative hedge.

5.2. Future Work

Future work includes fixing the speculative hedge heuristic so it can account for multiple, independent paths of control. This problem must be fixed so fully-resolved predicates [15] can be dealt with effectively. In addition, some of the potential problem areas discussed earlier may be tackled if new applications show that they are more of an issue than they were in SPEC CINT92.

Another area of future research will be a coupling of speculative hedge and register allocation. Currently, speculative hedge does not account for register pressure while scheduling. Allowing speculative hedge to control speculation and make intelligent decisions when register pressure is an issue should prove useful for a number of different situations.

A final area that needs to be addressed is making the path selection process done by the compiler less dependent on profile information. Speculative hedge makes the scheduling of paths within a scheduling scope less dependent on profile information, but it can only minimize the penalty incurred when path selection does a poor job. By lessening the profile sensitivity of path selection and utilizing speculative hedge, a complete solution to the profile sensitivity problem of scheduling can become reality.

Acknowledgments

The authors would like to thank John Gyllenhaal for his suggestions regarding the presentation of results. The authors would also like to thank all the members of the IMPACT research group and the anonymous referees whose comments and suggestions helped to improve the quality of this paper.

This research has been supported by the National Science Foundation (NSF) under grant MIP-9308013, Intel Corporation, Advanced Micro Devices, Hewlett-Packard, SUN Microsystems, NCR, and the National Aeronautics and Space Administration (NASA) under Contract NASA NAG 1-613 in cooperation with the Illinois Computer Laboratory for Aerospace Systems and Software (ICLASS).

References

[1] A. Aho, R. Sethi, and J. Ullman. *Compilers: Principles, Techniques, and Tools.* Addison-Wesley, Reading, MA, 1986.

[2] R. A. Bringmann. *Compiler-Controlled Speculation.* PhD thesis, Department of Computer Science, University of Illinois, Urbana, IL, 1995.

[3] P. P. Chang, S. A. Mahlke, W. Y. Chen, N. J. Warter, and W. W. Hwu. IMPACT: An architectural framework for multiple-instruction-issue processors. In *Proceedings of the 18th International Symposium on Computer Architecture*, pages 266–275, May 1991.

[4] C. Chekuri, R. Motwani, R. Johnson, B. Natarajan, B. R. Rau, and M. Schlansker. Profile-driven instruction level parallel scheduling with applications to super blocks. In *Proceedings of the 29th Annual International Symposium on Microarchitecture*, December 1996.

[5] T. M. Conte, B. A. Patel, K. N. Menezes, and J. S. Cox. Hardware-based profiling: An effective technique for profile-driven optimization. *International Journal of Parallel Programming*, 24(2):187–206, April 1996.

[6] S. Davidson, D. Landskov, B. D. Shriver, and P. W. Mallett. Some experiments in local microcode compaction for horizontal machines. *IEEE Transactions on Computers*, C-30:460–477, July 1981.

[7] J. A. Fisher. Trace scheduling: A technique for global microcode compaction. *IEEE Transactions on Computers*, C-30:478–490, July 1981.

[8] J. A. Fisher. Global code generation for instruction-level parallelism: Trace scheduling-2. Technical Report HPL-93-43, Hewlett-Packard Laboratory, 1501 Page Mill Road, Palo Alto, CA 94304, June 1993.

[9] R. E. Hank, S. A. Mahlke, R. A. Bringmann, J. C. Gyllenhaal, and W. W. Hwu. Superblock formation using static program analysis. In *Proceedings of the 26th Annual International Symposium on Microarchitecture*, December 1993.

[10] W. W. Hwu, S. A. Mahlke, W. Y. Chen, P. P. Chang, N. J. Warter, R. A. Bringmann, R. G. Ouellette, R. E. Hank, T. Kiyohara, G. E. Haab, J. G. Holm, and D. M. Lavery. The Superblock: An effective technique for VLIW and superscalar compilation. *The Journal of Supercomputing*, 7(1):229–248, January 1993.

[11] W. H. Kohler. A preliminary evaluation of the critical path method for scheduling tasks on multiprocessor systems. *IEEE Transactions on Computers*, C-24:1235–1238, December 1975.

[12] S. A. Mahlke, D. C. Lin, W. Y. Chen, R. E. Hank, and R. A. Bringmann. Effective compiler support for predicated execution using the hyperblock. In *Proceedings of the 25th International Symposium on Microarchitecture*, pages 45–54, December 1992.

[13] C. V. Ramamoorthy and M. Tsuchiya. A high level language for horizontal microprogramming. *IEEE Transactions on Computers*, C-23:791–802, August 1974.

[14] B. R. Rau. Iterative modulo scheduling: An algorithm for software pipelining loops. In *Proceedings of the 27th International Symposium on Microarchitecture*, pages 63–74, December 1994.

[15] M. Schlansker and V. Kathail. Critical path reduction for scalar programs. In *Proceedings of the 28th International Symposium on Microarchitecture*, pages 57–69, December 1995.

[16] M. D. Smith. Architectural support for compile-time speculation. In D. Lilja and P. Bird, editors, *The Interaction of Compilation Technology and Computer Architecture*, pages 13–49. Kluwer Academic Publishers, Boston, MA, 1994.

Hot Cold Optimization of Large Windows/NT Applications

Robert Cohn (rc@vssad.hlo.dec.com)
P. Geoffrey Lowney (lowney@vssad.hlo.dec.com)
Digital Equipment Corporation
Hudson, Massachusetts

Abstract

A dynamic instruction trace often contains many unnecessary instructions that are required only by the unexecuted portion of the program. Hot-cold optimization (HCO) is a technique that realizes this performance opportunity. HCO uses profile information to partition each routine into frequently executed (hot) and infrequently executed (cold) parts. Unnecessary operations in the hot portion are removed, and compensation code is added on transitions from hot to cold as needed. We evaluate HCO on a collection of large Windows NT applications. HCO is most effective on the programs that are call intensive and have flat profiles, providing a 3-8% reduction in path length beyond conventional optimization.

1. Introduction

Typically, compiler writers study code listings to look for optimization opportunities. However, we have found that a dynamic view, studying instruction traces, gives a very different perspective on code quality[Sites95]. High quality code often looks unoptimized when viewed as a dynamic instruction trace.

Below, we list an instruction trace fragment from the Windows NT kernel running on a Digital Alpha [Sites95]. The register `ra` is used to hold the return address when a call is made, `sp` is the stack pointer, `a0` is an argument register, `v0` is the return value, `t0` is a scratch register (caller saved), and `s0-s2` are preserved registers (callee saved).

```
bsr     ra,8009e3f0  ; call
lda     sp,-30(sp)   ; grow the stack
stq     s0,0(sp)     ; save the old value
stq     s1,8(sp)     ;  of some preserved
stq     s2,10(sp)    ;  registers
stq     ra,18(sp)    ;
bis     zero,a0,s0   ; copy a0 to s0
ldl     t0,9b8(gp)   ; load,..
cmpult  t0,#13,v0    ; compare, ...
bne     v0,8009e42   ; branch
bis     zero,zero,v0 ; clear v0
br      zero,8009e4f4 ; branch
ldq     s0,0(sp)     ; restore the old
ldq     s1,8(sp)     ;   value of some
ldq     s2,10(sp)    ;preserved registers
ldq     ra,18(sp)    ; load ret address
lda     sp,30(sp)    ; shrink the stack
ret     zero,(ra)    ; return
```

The trace appears to execute many unnecessary instructions. However, looking at the full function listing, they all are necessary. The return address (`ra`) is saved and restored but never modified. This function contains a call, but this code path does not execute it. The preserved registers `s1` and `s2` are also saved and restored but never used. Somewhere in the function, `s1` and `s2` are modified, but the trace does not go there. The function does modify the preserved register `s0` with a copy, but the value stored in `s0` is never read in the instruction trace so the copy and the save/restore of `s0` are unnecessary. The only truly necessary instructions is the load, compare, branch, copy sequence, which form an excellent inline candidate.

An insight into how an optimizer can take advantage of this type of situation came from a tool called NT OM, that arranges code for instruction cache performance[+]. Using profile information, NT OM lays out code so that the fall-through path is the common path and also splits routines into a frequently executed (hot) part and infrequently executed (cold) part [Pettis90, Calder94, Hwu89, McFarling89]. If there is only one path through a routine, the instruction trace and the hot part are identical. Usually, there are several common paths through the routine, and the hot part is the collection of these paths.

If we could optimize the hot part of the routine, ignoring the cold part, we could eliminate all the unnecessary instructions. We create a "hot" routine by copying the frequently executed basic blocks of a function. All calls to the original routine are redirected to the hot routine. Flow paths in the hot routine that target basic blocks that were not copied are redirected to the appropriate basic block in

[+] NT OM is Digital's executable optimization technology [Srivastava94,Wilson96] written for NT

1072-4451/96 $5.00 © 1996 IEEE

the original "cold" routine; that is, they jump into the middle of the original routine. We then optimize the hot routine, possibly at the expense of the flows that pass through the cold path. The process is called Hot Cold Optimization (HCO).

2. Overview of HCO optimization

We describe HCO in detail later; in this section we work through an example, a simplified version of the function associated with the above trace.

```
1.  foo:      lda sp,16(sp)  ; grow stack
2.             stq s0,0(sp)   ; save s0
3.             stq ra,8(sp)   ; save ra
4.             addl a0,1,s0   ; s0 = a0+1
5.             addl a0,a1,a0  ; a0= a0+a1
6.             bne s0,L2      ;brnch if s0!=0
7.      L1:    bsr f1         ; call f1
8.             addl s0,a0,t1  ; t1=a0+s0
9.             stl t1,40(gp)  ; store t1
10.     L2:    ldq s0,0(sp)   ; restore s0
11.            ldq ra,8(sp)   ; restore ra
12.            lda sp,-16(sp); pop stack
13.            ret (ra)       ; return
```

Assume that the branch in line 6 is almost always taken and that lines 7-9 are almost never executed. When we copy the hot part of the routine we exclude lines 7-9 as follows:

```
a)      foo2:  lda sp,16(sp)
b)             stq s0,0(sp)
c)             stq ra,8(sp)
d)             addl a0,1,s0
e)             addl a0,a1,a0
f)             beq s0,L1
g)             ldq s0,0(sp)
h)             ldq ra,8(sp)
i)             lda sp,-16(sp)
j)             ret (ra)
```

Note that the sense of the branch was reversed and its target was changed to L1 in the original routine. All calls to foo are redirected to the hot routine foo2, including indirect calls. If the branch in line f is taken, then control transfers to line 7, which is in the middle of the original routine. Once control passes to the original routine, it never passes back to the hot routine. This feature of HCO enables optimization; when optimizing the hot routine, we can relax some of the constraints imposed by the cold routine.

So far, we have set up the hot routine for optimization, but have not made it any faster. Now we show how to optimize the routine. The hot routine no longer contains a call; we can delete the save and restore of the return address in lines c and h. If the branch transfers control to L1 in the cold routine, we must arrange for ra to be saved on the stack. In general, whenever we enter the original routine from the hot routine, we must fix up the state to match the expected state. We call the fix-up operations compensation code. To insert compensation code, we create a stub, and redirect the branch in line f to branch to the stub. The stub saves ra on the stack and branches to L1.

Next, we see that the instruction in line e writes a0, but the value of a0 is never read in the hot routine. However, it is not truly dead because it is still read if the branch in line f is taken. We delete the instruction from the hot routine and place a copy on the stub.

HCO tries to eliminate the uses of preserved registers in a routine. Preserved registers can be more expensive than scratch registers because they must be saved and restored if they are used. Preserved registers are typically used when the lifetime of the value crosses a call. In the hot routine, no lifetime crosses a call and the use of a preserved register is unnecessary. We rename all uses of s0 in the hot routine to use a free scratch register t2. We insert a copy on the stub from t2 to s0. We can now eliminate the save and restore in lines b and g and place the save on the stub.

We have eliminated all references to the stack in the hot routine. The stack adjusts can be deleted from the hot routine and the initial stack adjust placed in the stub. The final code and the stub are listed below. The number of instructions executed in the frequent path has been reduced from 10 to 3. If the stub is taken, then the full 10 instructions and an extra copy and branch are executed.

```
1.      foo2.   addl a0,1,t2
2.              beq t2,stub1
3.              ret (ra)
4.      stub1:  lda sp,16(sp)
5.              stq s0,0(sp)
6.              stq ra,8(sp)
7.              addl a0,a1,a0
8.              mov t2,s0
9.              br L1
```

Finally, we would like to inline the hot function. Copies of instructions 1 and 2 can be placed inline. For the inlined branch, we must create a new stub that materializes the return address into ra before transferring control to stub1. Except for partial inlining, we have implemented all of these optimizations in our system.

In the following section, we present the NT applications we used to evaluate HCO and discuss the results. We then present the details of our method. We close the paper with a discussion of related work, and our conclusions.

3. Characteristics of NT Applications

For our experiments, we use programs that are representative of the types of applications run on high performance personal computers (PC's). We also include some programs from SpecInt95 for comparison, although our discussion in the paper focuses on the PC applications. Table 1 identifies the programs and the workloads used to exercise them. All programs are optimized versions of Digital Alpha binaries and are compiled with the same highly optimizing back end that is used on Unix and VMS[Blickstein92].

For our profile-directed optimization, we use the same input for training and timing so that we can know the limits of our approach. Others have shown that a reasonably chosen training input will give reliable speedups for other input sets [Calder95]. Our experience with program layout optimizations for our benchmark programs confirms this result.

Table 2 lists some static and dynamic characteristics of the single executable or dynamically linked library (DLL) responsible for a majority of the execution time for each application. The smallest PC application is three times larger than the largest SpecInt95 program in our list, and the largest PC application, ACAD, is twenty times larger. All of them have thousands of functions. Call overhead is high and ranges from 7%-16%, except for the more loop intensive TEXIM and MAXEDA. We approximate call overhead by measuring time spent in procedure prologs and epilogs, which is mostly stack adjusts and saving and restoring of preserved registers. The time spent in leaf routines is low, with the exception of WINWORD.

Program	Full Name	Type	Workload
VC	Microsoft Visual C	compiler backend	5000 lines of C code
SQLSERVR	Microsoft Sqlserver 6.5	database	cached TPC-B
ACAD	Autodesk Autocad	mechanical cad	SDUG benchmark
EXCEL	Microsoft Excel 5.0	spreadsheet	BAPCO
USTATION	Bentley Systems Microstation	mechanical cad	rendering
WINWORD	Microsoft Word 6.0	word processing	BAPCO
TEXIM	Welcom Software Texim 2.0	Project management	BAPCO
MAXEDA	OrCad MaxEDA 6.0	electronic cad	BAPCO
VORTEX	SpecInt95	database	SPEC ref
GO	SpecInt95	game	SPEC ref
M88KSIM	SpecInt95	simulator	SPEC ref
LI	SpecInt95	lisp interpreter	SPEC ref
COMPRESS	SpecInt95	compression	SPEC ref
IJPEG	SpecInt95	JPEG	SPEC ref

Table 1: Benchmark programs and their workloads

In Table 2, we list the percent of execution time spent in the top 5 routines for each routine. VC, SQLSERVR, ACAD, and EXCEL tend to have flat profiles, while the other PC applications have a single routine responsible for a large portion of the execution time.

The focus of our work is programs that have flat profiles and are more call intensive than loop intensive. In

Program	Text Size MB (static)	Routines (static)	Call overhead (dynamic)	Leaf routines (dynamic)	% time spent in the 5 most frequently executed routines				
					1st	2nd	3rd	4th	5th
VC	2.08	2139	11%	8%	10.9	5.5	5.5	2.6	2.5
SQLSERVR	3.11	3213	16%	2%	6.1	5.6	3.6	3.4	3.2
ACAD	9.29	22097	9%	16%	2.8	2.8	2.2	1.8	1.7
EXCEL	6.81	12129	13%	27%	10.4	4.3	3.9	3.7	3.2
USTATION	3.86	13302	12%	15%	34.4	10	9.9	6.2	6
WINWORD	6.97	12230	7%	50%	38.9	6.8	4.7	4.3	4
TEXIM	1.39	1953	2%	13%	77.1	7.4	3.2	1.3	1
MAXEDA	1.73	1807	2%	4%	34.4	10	9.9	6.2	6
VORTEX	.47	820	23%	2%	16.2	12.3	8.6	8.5	5.2
GO	.29	462	5%	30%	19.8	14.4	9.5	5.9	4
M88KSIM	.17	382	12%	43%	27.5	12.8	11.3	7.7	5.9
LI	.12	489	24%	10%	13.4	13.3	9.7	8.8	8.7
COMPRESS	.06	122	1%	28%	25.7	25.9	19.5	9.4	6.4
IJPEG	.18	408	2%	56%	14.5	14.3	13.4	11.6	10.7

Table 2: Static and dynamic characteristics of benchmark programs

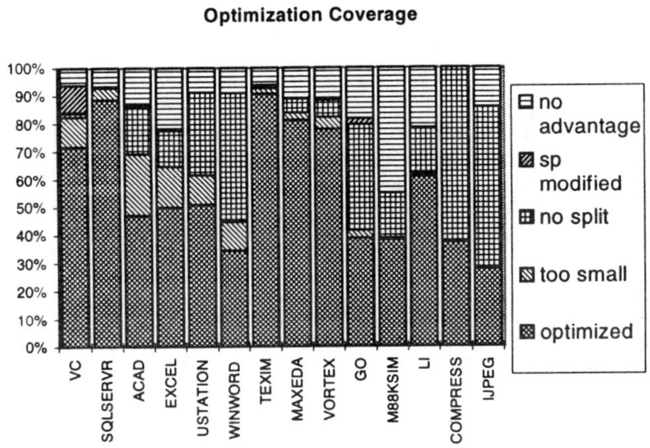

Figure 1: HCO coverage by execution time

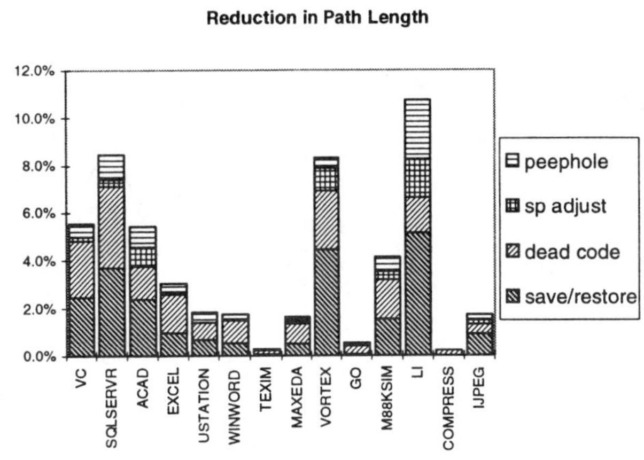

Figure 2: Reduction in path length

these programs, loops typically include function calls and span multiple procedures. The most frequently executed basic block in a function is often the entry point and call overhead tends to be high. Our experience with these programs has shown that optimizations that do not preserve the locality of the instruction stream can adversely affect performance. They all speed up from 5% to 15% when we apply code layout techniques [Pettis90, Calder94, Wilson96].

In this paper, all statistics based on execution time and speedups use path lengths (number of instructions executed) for the dominant executable or DLL. Path lengths are calculated by multiplying the number of instructions in a basic block by the number of times the block is executed. Using path lengths rather than measured times allows us to provide more detailed information about the contribution of each type of optimization. Since it is possible to reduce the path length at the expense of more cache misses, we used simulation and other techniques to verify that instruction cache misses were not affected for LI, VC, ACAD, and SQLSERVR. For the full set of HCO optimizations together, we verified that path length reductions resulted in equivalent run-time speedups for LI, VC, and ACAD. For SQLSERVR, the run-time speedup is less than the path length reduction (8%), and we continue to investigate this discrepancy.

4. Results

We present the results for the full suite of HCO optimizations, except for partial inlining, which has not yet been implemented. The optimizations are partial dead code elimination, which is the removal of code dead in the hot routine; stack pointer adjust elimination, which is the removal of the stack adjusts in the hot routine; preserved register elimination, which is the removal of the save and restore of preserved registers in the hot routine; and peephole optimization, which is the removal in the hot routine of self-assignments and conditional branches with an always-false condition. The optimizations were implemented in NT OM, an optimizer that operates on Alpha NT executables.

In Figure 1, we show coverage statistics for the HCO optimization. Coverage represents the percentage of execution time spent in each category. To compute coverage, we first assign each function to a category, and then for each category sum the execution time of its functions. The category "optimized" is the portion of the execution time that is in functions optimized by HCO. Optimization coverage is typically 60%, but is often higher. The category "too small" is the set of functions where the execution time is so small (< .1% of total time) it did not appear worthwhile to optimize them. Ignoring functions with small execution time allows us to optimize less than 5% of the program text, a significant reduction in optimizer time. The category "no split" represents the functions that we could not split into a hot and cold part because all basic blocks had similar execution counts. The category "sp modified" is for functions where the stack pointer is modified after the initial stack adjust in the prolog. We decided not to optimize these functions, but it is possible to do so with extra analysis. It was infrequent except for VC, where it is 7% of the program and occurs in 2 functions. Finally, the category "no advantage" is for the functions that were split but the optimizer wasn't able to make any faster.

In Figure 2, we show the overall reduction in path length for HCO, broken down by optimization. Most of the reduction in path length comes equally from removal of unnecessary save/restores and partial dead code.

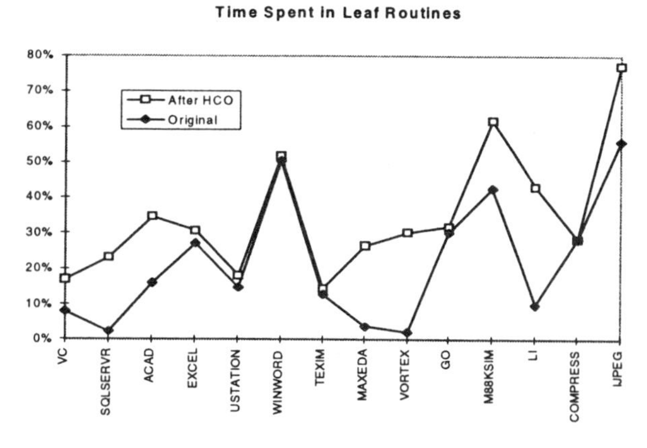

Figure 3: Time spent in leaf routines before and after HCO

Removing stack pointer adjusts and peephole optimizations are a smaller additional gain. When the peephole category is large it is usually because there is a save and restore of a preserved register that is made unnecessary by HCO, and the restore is converted to a self assignment by copy propagation, which is then removed by peephole optimization.

HCO is most effective on call intensive programs such as VC, SQLSERVR, and ACAD, where we eliminate calls when creating the hot routines. For WINWORD, the speedup is small because coverage is low; we could not find a way to split the routines. For EXCEL, HCO was able to split the routines, but there is often a call in the hot path. Inlining may help here, but frequently the call is to a shared library.

HCO is less effective on loop intensive programs such as USTATION, MAXEDA, and TEXIM. HCO provides a framework for optimizing loops, and Chang has shown that eliminating the infrequent paths in loops enables additional optimizations such as loop invariant removal [Chang91]. However, our current implementation has almost no information about the aliasing of memory operations and it can only optimize operations to local stack locations, such as spills of registers.

4.1 Leaf routines

Figure 3 compares the amount of time spent in leaf routines before and after HCO is applied. By eliminating infrequent code, HCO is able to eliminate all calls in functions that represent 10-20% of the execution time in VC, ACAD, SQLSERVR, and MAXEDA. The change in time spent in leaf routines for the other PC applications is very small. Most of the PC applications spend much less than half of the time in leaf routines. Since so much time

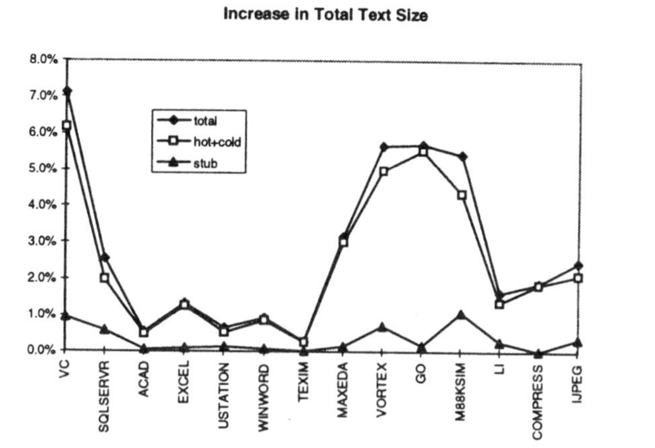

Figure 4: Overall increase in text size

is spent in code with calls in the frequent path, it is important to optimize well in the presence of calls.

4.2 Code size

Code size and its effect on cache behavior is a major concern for us. In large applications, locality for instructions is present but not high. If an optimization decreases path length but also decreases locality as a side effect, the net result can be a loss in performance.

Figure 4 shows the total increase in text size from optimization. "Hot+cold" is the part of increase that comes from replacing a single routine with the original routine plus a copy of the hot part. "Stub" is the increase attributed to stub routines. Overall the increase in size is small. The maximum increase is 7.1% for VC. Sqlservr has the best speedup and is only 2.6% bigger. Looking at the increase in total text size is misleading, however. HCO is not applied to routines that are executed infrequently, which typically accounts for more than 95%

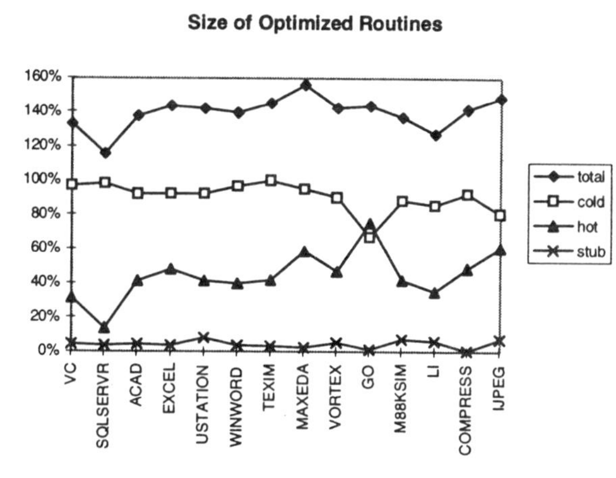

Figure 5: Size of optimized routines

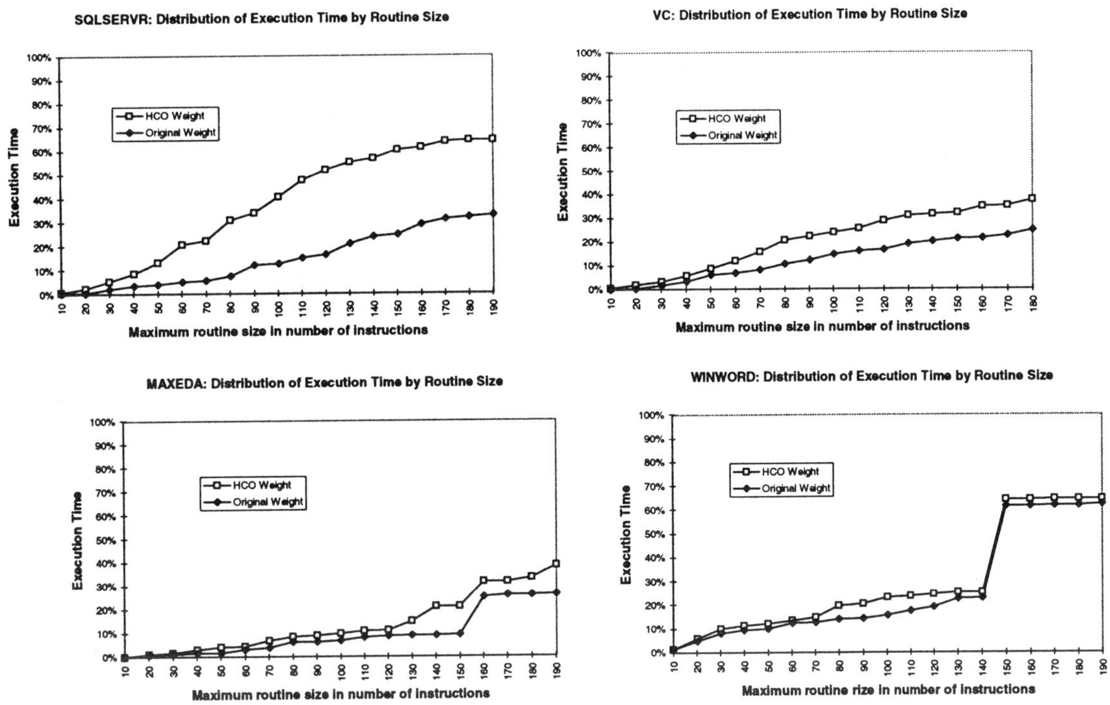

Figure 6: Distribution of routine size and execution time

of the program text, so tripling the size of optimized routines would only result in a modest increase in text size. However, tripling the size of the active part of an application will usually have a disastrous effect on performance.

For this reason, we also measure size increases based on the routines that are optimized. In Figure 5, we compare the total size of all the hot routines to the total size of the original routines they were derived from. By copying just the frequently executed part of the routine, we exclude about 50% of the original routine. Next, we eliminate code that is frequently executed, but is only reachable through an infrequently executed path and is therefore unreachable in the hot routine. This is usually only 1%. Finally, we optimize the hot routine, reducing the remaining code size by about 10% (5% of the size of the original routine). The final size of the hot routines as a percentage of the size of the original routines is shown in the line labeled "hot." By making the most frequently executed part of the program 50-80% smaller one would expect a big improvement in instruction cache behavior. It does; however, it would be misleading to attribute this improvement to HCO since a simpler optimization in NT OM already achieves the same result. As part of the optimization for instruction cache behavior, NT OM splits routines into two parts, one for the frequently executed code and another for infrequently executed code. The frequently executed parts are packed together so that they are less likely to conflict in a direct mapped cache. When HCO is turned on, the cache layout optimizations are run after HCO. The baseline we compare against also has cache optimizations turned on, so improvements attributed to HCO are improvements beyond what the other optimizations can do. HCO does make the frequently executed parts 10% smaller, but we did not see better instruction cache behavior when we ran programs with a cache simulator.

If we were to do partial inlining, only the hot routine would be copied. Since the hot routine is less than half the size of the original routine, this would greatly reduce the growth in code size due to inlining.

The line labeled "cold" in Figure 5 shows how the size of the cold routine is affected by HCO. When we redirect all calls to the hot routine, some of the code in the original routine becomes unreachable. This is usually less than 10%, which is much smaller than the 50% of the code we copied to create the hot routine. Apparently, the infrequent paths in a routine often rejoin the frequent paths, which makes it necessary to have a copy of both in the original routine.

The line labeled "stub" is the code size of the stubs, which is very small. We also implemented a variation of HCO that avoided stubs by re-executing the procedure from the beginning instead of trying to use a stub to fix up the state and jump into the middle. It usually isn't possible to re-execute the procedure because arguments had already been overwritten. Given the small cost of stubs, we did not pursue this method.

The line labeled "total" shows that HCO makes the total code(hot+cold+stub) 20-50% bigger. A routine is partitioned so that there is less than a 1% chance that the stub and cold part are executed so their size shouldn't have a significant effect on cache behavior as long as the profile is representative.

Figure 6 shows how splitting affects the distribution of time spent among different routine sizes for two programs where HCO is effective (VC and SQLSERVR), and two programs where it is not (MAXEDA and WINWORD). For each graph, the horizontal axis is the routine size in number of instructions and the vertical axis is the percentage of execution time spent in routines of the maximum size or smaller. The farther apart the two lines, the better HCO was at shifting the distribution from large routines to smaller routines. It is interesting to note that most of the programs spend a large percentage of the time in large functions, which suggests that compilers need to handle complex control flow well, even if profile information is used to eliminate infrequent paths.

5. Optimization

In this section, we describe in more detail how NT OM constructs the hot routine and how it is optimized. HCO was implemented as part of NT OM, a tool for optimizing executables and dynamically loaded libraries (DLLs) for Alpha Windows/NT [Srivastava94, Wilson96, Larus95]. NT OM reads in an executable, identifies the code and data, optimizes the code, and writes out a new executable. Because NT OM can examine the entire executable, it is able to do optimizations that a compiler cannot easily do. For example, NT OM can see the entire call graph, which makes it possible to lay out code to minimize instruction cache misses. However, NT OM does not have some information that is available to a compiler. Currently, NT OM derives the dataflow from the code itself; it does not use extra information from the compiler. The biggest limitation is the lack of memory alias information, which restricts the type of optimizations that can be done on instructions that touch memory.

NT OM can instrument executables to collect profile information in a manner similar to ATOM[Srivastava94b, Wilson96], and uses profile information when optimizing a program, as is done for code layout and HCO.

5.1 Partitioning a routine into hot and cold

Deciding what code to include in the hot routine is a tradeoff between two factors. When we exclude code from the hot routine (especially calls) we create opportunities for optimizations that decrease path length. However, the more code we exclude from the hot routine, the higher the probability that we enter the original routine. The transition from hot to cold is expensive because it is likely to cause cache misses.

We use the probability of exiting the hot routine through a stub to decide how much code to include in the hot routine. The exit probability is the number of times the program exits a hot routine through a stub for each time the routine is called. It is calculated from profile information.

Our experiments showed that path length reductions are not that sensitive to exit probability, but that cache misses and real performance are very sensitive. Doubling the exit probability results in a small improvement in cycles eliminated because of path length reduction but a large increase in additional cycles spent in cache misses. For this reason we tuned HCO to get the biggest reduction in path length that doesn't cause a significant increase in cache misses. We found that using a very low probability of 1% works best for most programs.

We tuned HCO to avoid cache misses by adjusting the exit probability for maximum measured speedup, rather than path length reduction. For the programs with short execution times, we confirmed that extra cache misses are not a problem through simulation.

5.2 Partially Dead Code

Sometimes, instructions are live on one path and dead on others. This is called partially dead code[Knoop94]. When an operation in the hot part computes a value that is only consumed in the cold part, we optimize this by moving the instruction from the hot routine to some or all of the stubs, which are less frequently executed.

The candidates for partially dead code are found by ignoring the branches to stubs when computing liveness. We do not eliminate dead stores or loads because we only have limited information on aliasing of memory operations.

Next, we find the set of stubs where the definition generated by the dead candidate may reach the stub, and

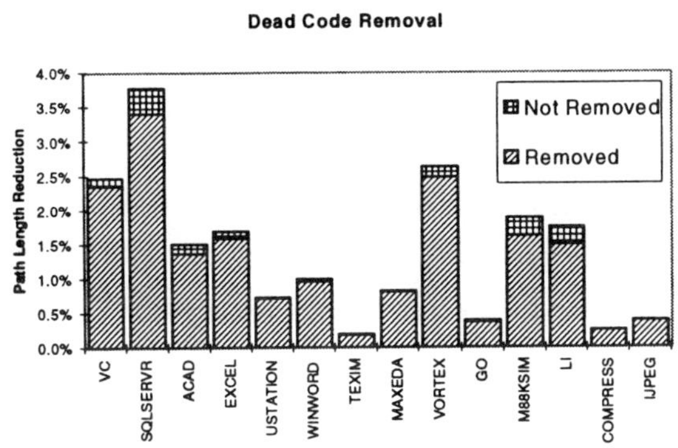

Figure 7: Potential improvements for dead code removal

the register holding the value is live at the stub. If the definition does not reach any stub where the register is live, then it is truly dead and we can eliminate it without any further work.

For all the stubs that the definition may reach, we check if the inputs or output of the dead candidate are possibly redefined on any path from the dead candidate to the stub. If this happens, the dead candidate cannot be removed. If not, then we eliminate the dead candidate in the hot routine and place a copy on every stub that the definition reaches.

With register reallocation, we could weaken the condition that requires that the inputs and output of the dead candidate not be overwritten in the path from the operation to the stub. To gauge how much better we could be doing, we estimated the path length reduction possible by assuming that all dead candidates could be eliminated. The results are in Figure 7. The bottom bar is what is actually achieved, and the top bar represents the results of this optimistic assumption. Our results slightly underestimate the gain, because we do not consider the effect of this optimization enabling other optimizations. The potential gain appears to be fairly small and we decided it was not worthwhile trying to remove these extra instructions. From looking at programs, the dead operations that cannot be eliminated are often copies of the argument registers into preserved registers. Interprocedural register allocation or inlining is probably the best way to attack this problem.

5.3 Lifetime Splitting

Often, a lifetime will start in the frequent part of the code and cross into the infrequent part. If the lifetime crosses a call, then it is typically assigned a preserved register, which requires a save and restore. If the call is only in the infrequent part, then it would be better to keep the value in a scratch register in the frequent part, then transfer it to a preserved register in the infrequent part. Then, the save and restore are not executed if the code stays in the frequent part.

5.4 Copy propagation

When we only copy the hot part of a routine, we eliminate some flow paths, making copy propagation legal where it was not before. For example, an argument register may be copied to a preserved register so that its value will be live across a call (e.g. mov a0,s0). However, if the call is eliminated because it is in the infrequent path, then applying copy propagation replaces uses of the preserved register with the original argument registers (e.g. addl s0,1,t0 becomes addl a0,1,t0). Copy propagation often eliminates all uses of a preserved register, which leads to further optimization.

5.5 Eliminating unnecessary preserved registers

Often HCO eliminates all uses of a preserved register by partitioning or by the optimizations described above. If the save and restore is made unnecessary, then it is eliminated in the hot routine and a copy of the save is placed on every stub.

5.6 Eliminating unnecessary stack adjusts

If all references to the stack pointer are removed from a routine, then the stack adjusts on entrance and exit can be removed. For compensation code, a stack adjust to grow the stack is placed on every stub.

5.7 Phase ordering

The order that the optimizations are applied is important for the final result. A sequence of copy propagation, dead code removal, and peephole optimizations is run repeatedly until no further progress is made. Each of these optimizations create opportunities for the others and themselves, and we have found that one to three passes is usually sufficient. Note that profile information allows us to apply optimization to less than 5% of the program text, so optimizer time is not large.

Next, lifetime splitting is applied once. Lifetime splitting uses an extra scratch register and introduces a copy on the stub, so it is better to eliminate the use of a preserved register with one of the previous optimizations than to split the lifetime.

Running the previous optimizations often eliminates all uses of a preserved register, and now the unnecessary saves and restores of preserved registers are eliminated. Finally, if all references to the stack pointer have been removed, we remove the stack adjusts.

6. Related work

Dead code elimination in HCO is closely related to partial dead code elimination[Knoop94], which uses code motions to move an instruction later to avoid computing it. When moving an instruction, partial dead code elimination finds the optimal points in the flow graph to minimize execution, while we take the simpler approach of using profile information to decide if it is profitable to move the instruction to a stub. There is a limited form of partial dead code elimination for superblocks[Chang91], but we have found that the scope of a superblock is too small for effective optimization, even when using techniques that expand their scope such as predication[Mahlke92].

Partial dead code elimination does not alter the flow graph when placing operations. This is done by HCO when it copies the hot part of a routine, which allows us to do better than the "optimal" method in some cases. For example, in Figure 8, the value of b is computed outside of a loop and is only used inside of the conditional inside of the loop. Techniques that don't alter the program structure can either leave the computation of b outside of the loop where it is always computed once, or put it inside of the conditional, where it is computed once for every time that p[i] is true. If the condition p[i] is rarely true, then HCO moves the computation of b to the stub. If p[i] is never true, b is never computed. The first time p[i] is true, we jump to the stub, compute b and then jump into the middle of the loop, so b is never computed again.

Much work has gone into profile directed interprocedural register allocation [Wall86, Santhanam90, Kurlander96]. We consider HCO to be a framework for optimization, and a register allocator for this framework is being implemented. Optimizations such as shrink wrapping [Chow88] and ORA [Goodwin96] have sought to reduce unnecessary spills and reloads by placing them in the program where they are executed less often. Many possible placements are not permitted by the Alpha NT run-time model[+]. HCO considers a smaller set of permissible locations, the stubs. Like partial dead code elimination, these techniques do not alter the flow graph, and the ability to alter the flow graph can enable HCO to find opportunities that other methods cannot.

Original routine

```
b = e + c * d
for (i = 0; i < n; i++)
      if (p[i])
         output(b);
return;
```

After HCO

```
for (i = 0; i < n; i++)
      if (p[i])
         goto stub;
return;
stub:
b = e + c * d;
goto inloop;

b = e + c * d;
for (i = 0; i < n; i++)
      if (p[i])
inloop:        output(b);
return;
```

Figure 8: Altering program structure gives HCO more flexibility

Region-based compilation[Hank95] uses profile information and aggressive inlining to expose more optimization candidates to the compiler. It then repartitions a program into regions to make compilation of the much larger program tractable. Our approach is similar in that we partition each routine into a hot and cold region. However, the subject of our work is optimizations that push work out of the hot region into the cold region and transformations that make it possible. If we were to add aggressive partial inlining to NT OM, we could use Hank's methods to partition the program into multiple hot regions.

7. Conclusions and future work

Many commonly used Alpha NT applications spend most of their time in non-leaf routines and in loops that span multiple procedures. For these applications, the most frequently executed basic block in a procedure is often the first basic block. Knowing this, it is not surprising that about 10% of the time is spent in procedure prologs and epilogs, which is essentially procedure call overhead.

The optimization in this paper is effective in eliminating path length from these types of programs. It does this by optimizing the frequently executed parts of a procedure at the expense of the less frequently executed parts. Much of the gain is dependent upon optimizations that eliminate partially dead code or change the register

[+] The Alpha NT software run-time model defines where in a routine the stack adjusts and the saving of preserved registers can be performed; this enables the exception handler to unwind the stack efficiently[CALLSTD].

assignment, splitting lifetimes and changing preserved registers into scratch registers.

HCO is an attractive framework for profile-directed optimization. In the future, we expect to add partial inlining, interprocedural register allocation, speculative scheduling, prefetching, and other optimizations. HCO also provides a practical solution for applying advanced compiler technology to large application programs. We can look beyond the SPECmarks and address the problems in real applications that are in day-to-day use.

Acknowledgments

The authors would like to thank David Goodwin for implementing the interprocedural dataflow in NT OM and to Mark Davis, Joel Emer, David Goodwin, Tryggve Fossum and the reviewers for their comments on this paper.

References

[Blickstein92] D. Blickstein, et al, "The GEM optimizing compiler system," *Digital Technical Journal*, 4(4):121-136.

[Calder94] B. Calder and D. Grunwald, "Reducing branch costs via branch alignment," *in ASPLOS VI Proc.*, San Jose, CA, Nov. 1994

[Calder95] B. Calder, D. Grunwald, and A. Srivastava, "The predictability of branches in libraries," *in Proc. of the 28th Annual Intl. Symp. on Microarchitecture*, pp. 24-34, Ann Arbor, MI, Nov. 1995

[CALLSTD] Alpha NT Calling Standard. http://www.partner.digital.com/www-swdev/pages/Home/TECH/documents/alpha_cookbook/biblio.htm

[Chang91] P.P. Chang, S.A. Mahlke, and W.W. Hwu, "Using profile information to assist classic code optimizations," *Software Prac. and Exp.*, 21(12): 1301-1321, 1991

[Chow88] F.C. Chow, "Minimizing register usage penalty at procedure calls," *in Proc. ACM SIGPLAN Conf. on Programming Language Design and Implementation '88, ACM pp.* 85-94, Atlanta, GA, June 1988

[Dragon] A.V. Aho, R. Sethi, and J.D. Ullman. *Compilers: Principles, Techniques, and Tools*. Addison-Wesley, 1985.

[Goodwin96] D. Goodwin and K. Wilken, "Optimal and near-optimal global register allocation using 0-1 integer programming," *Software-Practice & Exp.*, To appear 1996.

[Hank95] R.E. Hank, W.W. Hwu, and B.R. Rau, "Region-based compilation," *in Proc. of the 28th Annual Intl. Symp. on Microarchitecture*, pp. 158-168, Ann Arbor, MI, Nov. 1995

[Hwu89] W.W. Hwu and P.P. Chang, "Achieving high instruction cache performance with an optimizing compiler," *in Proc. 16th Annual Intl. Symp. on Computer Architecture,* Jerusalem, Israel, June 1989

[Knoop94] J. Knoop, O. Rüthing, B Steffen, "Partial dead code elimination," *in Proc. ACM SIGPLAN Conf. on Programming Language Design and Implementation '94, pp.* 147-158, Orlando, FL, June 1994

[Kurlander96] S.M. Kurlander and C.N. Fischer, "Minimum cost interprocedural register allocation," *in The 23rd ACM SIGPLAN SIGACT Symp. on Principles of Programming Languages*, pp. 230-241, St. Petersburg, Florida, Jan., 1996.

[Larus95] J.R. Larus and E. Schnarr, "EEL: Machine-independent executable editing," *in Proc. ACM SIGPLAN Conf. on Programming Language Design and Impl. '95, pp.* 291-300, La Jolla, CA, June 1995

[Mahlke92] S.A. Mahlke, et al., "Effective compiler support for predicated execution using the hyperblock," *in Proc. of the 25th Annual Intl. Symp. on Microarchitecture*, pp. 45-54, Dec. 1992.

[McFarling89] S. McFarling, "Program optimization for instruction caches," *in ASPLOS III Proc.*, pp. 183-193, Boston, MA, April 1989.

[Pettis90] K. Pettis and R.C. Hansen, "Profile Guided Code Positioning" *in Proc. ACM SIGPLAN Conf. on Programming Language Design and Implementation '90*, pp. 16-27, White Plains, NY, June 1990

[Santhanam90] V. Santhanam and D. Odnert, "Register allocation across procedure and module boundaries" *in Proc. ACM SIGPLAN Conf. on Programming Language Design and Implementation '90*, White Plains, NY, June 1990

[Sites95] R. L. Sites and S. Perl, "PatchWrx A dynamic execution tracing tool," http://www.research.digital.com/SRC/personal/Dick_Sites/patchwrx/PatchWrx.html.

[Srivastava94] A. Srivastava and D. Wall, "Link-time optimization of address calculation on a 64-bit architecture," *in Proc. ACM SIGPLAN Conf. on Programming Language Design and Implementation '94*, pp. 49-60, Orlando, FL, June 1994

[Srivastava94b] A. Srivastava and A. Eustace. "ATOM: A system for building customized program analysis tools," in Proc. SIGPLAN 94 Conf. on Programming Language Design and Implementation, pp. 85-96, Orlando, Florida, June 1994

[Wall86] D.W. Wall, "Global register allocation at link time" *in Proc. SIGPLAN 86 Symp. on Compiler Construction*, pp. 264-275, Palo Alto, CA, June 1986

[Wilson96] L.S. Wilson, C.A. Neth, M.J. Rickabaugh, "Delivering binary object modification tools for program analysis and optimization," volume 8,1 of *Digital Technical Journal*, pp. 18-31, 1996

Java Bytecode to Native Code Translation: The Caffeine Prototype and Preliminary Results

Cheng-Hsueh A. Hsieh John C. Gyllenhaal Wen-mei W. Hwu
Center for Reliable and High-Performance Computing
University of Illinois
Urbana-Champaign, IL 61801
ada, gyllen, hwu@crhc.uiuc.edu

Abstract

The Java bytecode language is emerging as a software distribution standard. With major vendors committed to porting the Java run-time environment to their platforms, programs in Java bytecode are expected to run without modification on multiple platforms. These first generation run-time environments rely on an interpreter to bridge the gap between the bytecode instructions and the native hardware. This interpreter approach is sufficient for specialized applications such as Internet browsers where application performance is often limited by network delays rather than processor speed. It is, however, not sufficient for executing general applications distributed in Java bytecode. This paper presents our initial prototyping experience with Caffeine, an optimizing translator from Java bytecode to native machine code. We discuss the major technical issues involved in stack to register mapping, run-time memory structure mapping, and exception handlers. Encouraging initial results based on our X86 port are presented.

1. Introduction

The software community has long desired a universal software distribution language. If such a language is widely supported across systems, software vendors can compile and validate their software products once in this distribution language, rather than repeating the process for multiple platforms. Software complexity is rapidly increasing and validation has become the deciding factor in software cost and time to market. Therefore, substantial economic motivation exists behind efforts to create such a software distribution language. The progress, however, has been very slow due to legal and technical difficulties.

On the legal side, many software vendors have been skeptical about the ability of the proposed software distribution languages to protect their intellectual property. In practice, such concern may have to be addressed empirically after a standard emerges. Although the protection of intellectual property in software distribution languages is an intriguing issue, it is not the topic addressed by this paper. For the purpose of our work, we expect Java to be accepted by a sufficient number of software vendors in the near future to make our work relevant.

On the technical side, the performance of programs distributed in a universal software distribution language has been a major concern. The problem lies in the mismatch between the virtual machine assumed by the software distribution language and the native machine architecture. The task of bridging the gap is made more difficult by the lack of source code information in the distributed code in order to protect intellectual property. As a result, software interpreters have been the main execution vehicles in the proposed standards. The disadvantage of software interpreters is poor performance. This disadvantage has been partially compensated for by the fast advance of microprocessor speed. For applications such as Internet browser applets where overall performance is often more limited by network delays than processor speed, sacrificing processor performance in favor of reducing software cost has become acceptable. This is, however, not true for general applications.

This paper presents our initial prototyping experience with *Caffeine,* an optimizing Java bytecode to native machine code translator. Although our techniques are presented in the context of handling Java, they are applicable to other software distribution languages such as Visual Basic P-code. We are by no means arguing that Java is the ultimate software distribution language. Rather, we intend to develop a strong portfolio of techniques from our Java implementation efforts that will contribute to the creation and acceptance of whatever language becomes the final standard. The objective of this work is to run the translated code at nearly the full performance of native code directly generated from a source representation such as the C programming language.

Due to space limitations, we will limit our discussion to three critical issues involved in the translation process. The first issue is the mapping of the stack computation model of the bytecode Virtual Machine to the register computation model of modern processors. A performance enhancing algorithm that

1072-4451/96 $5.00 © 1996 IEEE

takes advantage of the register computation model is presented. This algorithm requires analysis to identify the precise stack pointer contents at every point of the program. In addition, most compilation infrastructures require that each virtual register contains just one type of data, and that virtual registers do not overlap. We present a live-range-based register-renaming algorithm that can resolve such inconsistencies in non-pathological cases. The second issue is mapping the bytecode memory organization to the native architecture. A more efficient memory organization than the one used by the Java interpreter is introduced. The third issue is how to translate the exception handling semantics of Java. We describe the preliminary method used by *Caffeine* and some of the issues involved.

A prototype of *Caffeine* has been developed based on the IMPACT compilation infrastructure [1]. The prototype is sufficiently stable to handle Java bytecode programs of substantial size. This paper presents some initial experiments comparing the real machine execution time of Java bytecode programs using the SUN Java interpreter 1.0.2, the Symantec Java Just-in-time (JIT) compiler 1.0, and the IMPACT Java to X86 native code translator 1.0 running under Windows 95. Also included in the comparison is the execution time of equivalent C programs directly compiled by the Microsoft Visual C/C++ compiler 4.0 into X86 native code. Preliminary results show that the optimizing translator is currently capable of achieving, on average, 68% of the speed of the directly compiled native code.

The remaining sections are organized as follows. Section 2 introduces different approaches to execute Java bytecode programs and an overview of our translation steps. Section 3 presents the stack computation model used by Java followed by a proposed stack to register mapping. An overview of the stack analyses required to perform and validate this mapping is introduced in Section 4. Section 5 discusses the run-time memory model adopted by the SUN Java interpreter and presents a more efficient organization. Complications due to exception handling are discussed in Section 6. Preliminary performance results are presented in Section 7. Section 8 provides some concluding remarks and directions of future work.

2. Background

We will not cover the Java bytecode Virtual Machine model in this paper due to space limitations. Interested readers are referred to the Java web site [2] and a large collection of Java literature [3-11]. We will instead introduce three competing and sometimes complementary approaches to execute Java bytecode programs: interpreters, just-in-time compilers, and optimizing native code translators. A preliminary performance comparison between these approaches and native code execution are presented in Section 7.

Interpreters are the most widely understood approach to execute Java bytecode programs. A software interpreter emulates the Java bytecode Virtual Machine by fetching, decoding, and executing bytecode instructions. In the process, it faithfully maintains the contents of the computation stack, local memory state, and structure memory. The Java interpreter from SUN Microsystems is available to the public [2].

Just-in-time compilers do on-the-fly code generation and cache the native code sequences to speed up the processing of the original bytecode sequences in the future. The current generations of just-in-time compilers do not save the native code sequences in external files for future invocations of the same program. Rather, they keep the native code sequence to speed up the handling of the corresponding bytecode sequence during the same invocation of the program. Thus, they take advantage of iterative execution patterns such as loops and recursion. At the time of this work, Borland [12] and Symantec [13] had both announced just-in-time compiler products, and the Symantec JIT compiler is used in this paper. Due to the code generation overhead that occurs during program execution, just-in-time compilers are still intrinsically slower than executing native code programs.

Optimizing native code translators use compiler analysis to translate bytecode programs into native code programs off-line. This is the least understood approach among the three alternatives. Without extensive analysis and transformation capabilities, the native code generated may not be much better than that cached in the just-in-time compilers. Therefore, optimizing native code translators must perform extensive analysis and optimization in order to offer value beyond just-in-time compilers. Such analysis and transformations tend to make the translation process more expensive in time and space. In general, only those applications that will be repeatedly invoked or those applications whose execution time is much longer than the translation time should be translated. Thus, optimizing native code translators will not eliminate the need for interpreters and just-in-time compilers.

Figure 1 shows an overview of the steps in our prototype optimizing native code translator. The Java class files [4] required to execute the program are identified and decoded into sequences of bytecode operations, which are later used for construction of an internal representation (IR), called the Java IR, which is organized into functions and basic blocks. The construction of the Java IR is straightforward due to the absence of indirect jumps, indirect calls, self-modified code, embedded data, and branch target alignment "filler" code in bytecode. Due to the nature of the Java Virtual Machine specification [4] and the class file format, data recognition is also straightforward. Thus, the information recovered from Java bytecode ensures complete control flow graph construction.

The IMPACT low-level intermediate code (Lcode) serves as a machine-independent IR for our prototype translator. Translation from the Java IR to an efficient Lcode IR requires extensive analyses, as discussed in Section 4. The stack computation model is mapped to a more efficient register computation model. Bytecode operations which do not have corresponding Lcode operations are translated into sequences of Lcode operations or into function calls to the emulation library. After the Lcode IR is constructed, it is optimized by the X86 compilation path in the IMPACT compiler to generate assembly code and then an executable which runs under Windows 95. The Lcode IR construction phase is generic and will be retargeted to other code generation paths supported in IMPACT compiler in the future.

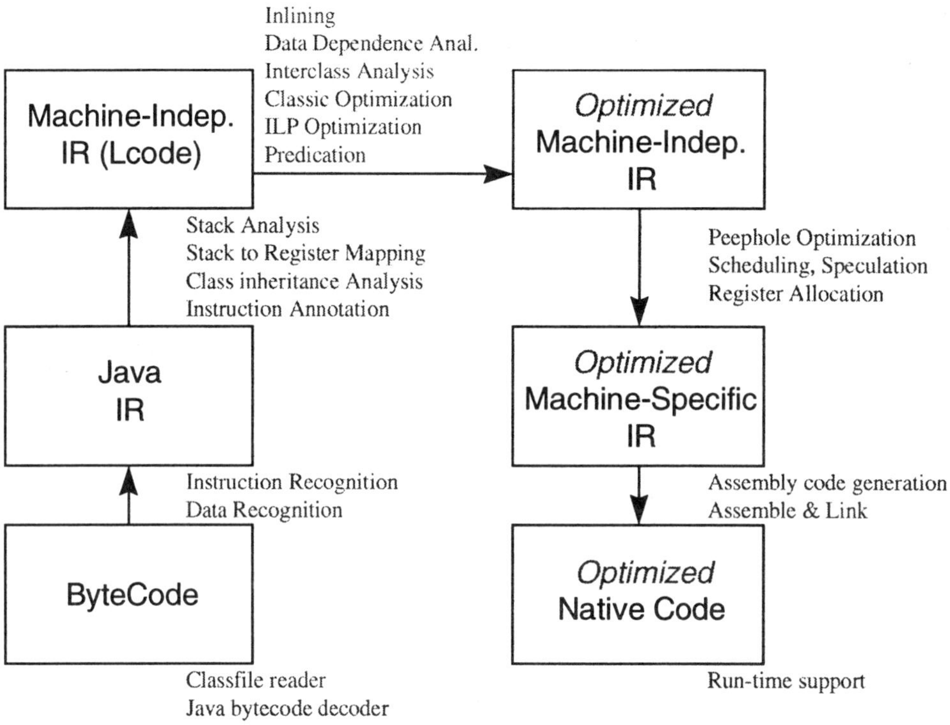

Figure 1. Java bytecode to native code translation steps.

Stack operations	Translated code
push A	push A
push B	push B
add	r2 ← pop (B)
	r1 ← pop (A)
	r3 ← r1 + r2
	push r3

Figure 2. Translated intermediate code example without stack to register mapping.

3. Stack to Virtual Register Mapping

3.1 Stack Computation Model

Java bytecode Virtual Machine uses a stack computation model to avoid making assumptions about the architectural register file size available to the interpreter [4]. Source operands are fetched from the top of *operand stack* and the result is pushed back on. The instruction size in this model is small since the operands are implicitly defined and require no operand fields in the instruction encoding, which facilitates efficient object code distribution over the Internet. Beside the operand stack, the Java Virtual Machine also provides a memory array, called the *local variable array*, for storage of local variables.

No stack analysis is required if the translated native code maintains a run-time operand stack in memory and manipulates it in the same way that the interpreter does. This straightforward approach is able to handle any situation that the interpreter can handle. The run-time cost of this straightforward approach, however, can be expensive due to the unnecessary memory traffic caused by inefficient register utilization. In Figure 2, the stack operations and the corresponding unoptimized translated intermediate code are presented side-by-side for an add operation to illustrate this approach. A load/store architecture is assumed in this example. Note that the original add operation pops two operands off the stack, adds them, and pushes the result back on.

Optimizations can be performed on the translated code to eliminate some of the loads (pops) and stores (pushes). However, many will still exist due to the use of stack operations across basic blocks. Global removal of unnecessary loads and stores requires an analysis equivalent to that discussed in Section 4 and is not the focus of this paper.

3.2 Register Mapping: Global Stack Location Register Mapping and Renaming

The performance of the translated code can be improved by mapping the run-time stack to the virtual register file. The approach used by *Caffeine* is to assign each stack location a unique virtual register number. Register allocation is later used to allocate the virtual registers to physical registers during the code generation phase. After this register mapping, a *push* to the operand stack is translated to a *move* to the register assigned to the stack location pointed to by the current stack pointer, and a *pop* is translated to a *move* from the register assigned to the stack location. This algorithm can only be applied when a constant stack offset can be determined for

Stack operation	Translated code	After copy prop. & Dead code removal
push A	r1 ← A	-
push B	r2 ← B	-
add	r1 ← r1 add r2	r1 ← A add B

Figure 3. Translated intermediate code example with stack to register mapping.

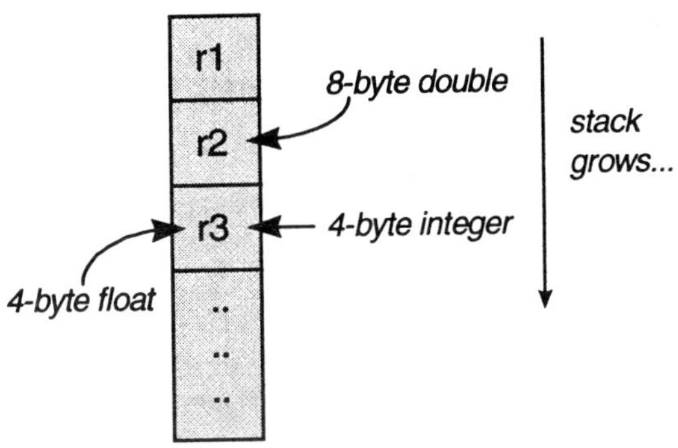

Figure 4. Example of type or size mismatch and register aliasing problems. A 32-bit architecture is assumed.

every push and pop at translation time. Algorithms to determine when this transformation can be applied are discussed in Section 4.1. The local variable array can be mapped to virtual registers using the array indices. Figure 3 shows the translated code using this approach for the same add operation as Figure 2. The moves of operands to virtual registers r1 and r2 before add will be forward copy propagated if possible. They are then removed as dead code if they are not live out.

There are two issues associated with this approach that need to be resolved. First, variables with different types or different sizes may be pushed to the same stack location and thus assigned to the same virtual register, causing some virtual registers to hold multiple types of operands or to alias with adjacent registers. In Figure 4, a push of 4-byte float onto stack location 3 is translated to "*r3 ← float_value*" in this register mapping scheme. At another point in the program, a 4-byte integer could be pushed to the same stack location and be translated to "*r3 ← integer_value*". As a result, register *r3* holds two different types, which is not allowed in many compiler infrastructures. Another conflict arises if an 8-byte double is pushed to stack location 2 and 3. The translated statement "*r2 ← double_value*" causes register *r2* to alias with neighboring register *r3*. Because Java has no union and all type conversions are made explicit, accesses to different types should never alias. Bytecode generated from a valid Java compiler should always have the *type state* property [6] that guarantees neither type conflict nor aliasing problems should occur. An algorithm presented in Section 4.2 is used to

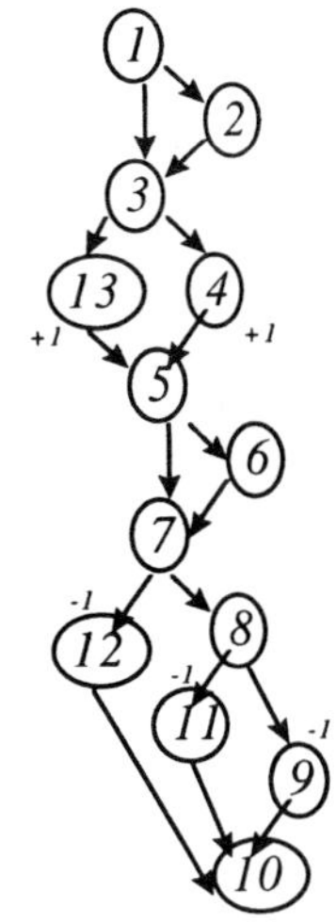

Figure 5. Stack balance analysis example.

validate this assumption and to disambiguate virtual registers which hold different types in this mapping scheme.

Second, parallelism may be lost for wide-issue machines because different variables use the same stack location in the original Java bytecode and get assigned to the same virtual register in this mapping scheme. This reuse of the virtual registers introduces artificial output and anti-dependencies. The same algorithm used to disambiguate virtual registers which hold different types can be applied to perform global virtual register renaming to remove the artificial dependencies.

4. Stack analysis

4.1 Stack balance analysis

For our register mapping scheme to function correctly, the position of the stack pointer must be a known constant for each operation at translation time. Although bytecode generated from valid Java compilers should satisfy this property [6], we can not assume all loaded bytecode came from valid sources.

A basic block may push more items on the stack than it consumes, and vice versa. The *residue* of each basic block, which is defined as the total number of pushes minus the total number of pops in the block, is computed first. The control flow graph is then traversed depth-first and each node is marked "visited" along the path from the first block. The stack pointer position upon entering a block is equal to the accumulated residue. If a marked basic block is revisited, the accumulated residue is checked against the stack pointer position in the revisited block. If they disagree, the stack to register mapping cannot be applied to this control flow graph. In such cases, *Caffeine* reverts to the stack model. The accumulated residue is also checked against zero whenever a leaf block (a block with no successor) is reached to ensure that the stack is balanced in each control flow graph. This algorithm runs in linear time in the number of basic blocks and control flow arcs. Figure 5 shows a control flow graph whose blocks are numbered in the order that they are visited by this algorithm. In this example, we assume blocks 4 and 13 have a

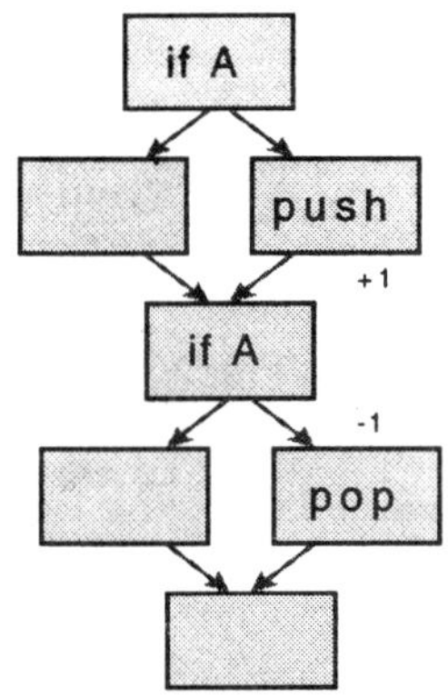

Figure 6. Example of where stack based approach must be used.

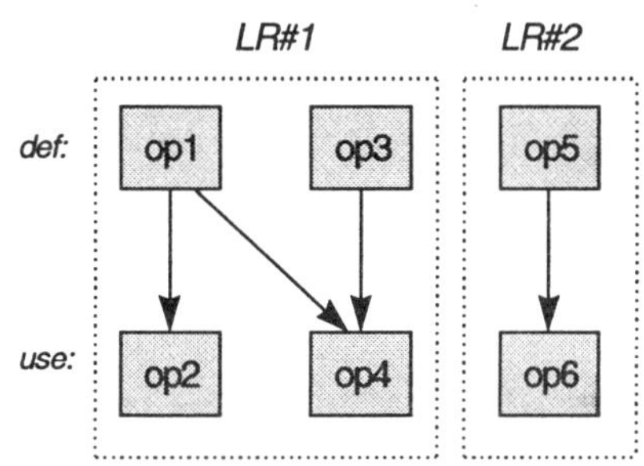

Figure 7. Def-use chains grouping.

residue of one, and blocks 9, 11, and 12 have a residue of minus one. All paths from block 1 to block 10 are stack balanced. The position of the stack pointer for each block is also a known constant. Specifically, the stack pointer at the entrance to blocks 5, 6, 7, 8, 9, 11, and 12 points to location one. For the rest of the blocks, the stack pointer initially points to location zero.

An example of when register mapping cannot be currently applied is shown in Figure 6. Depending on the path traversed, the stack offset for the pop is either zero or one. For this case, the stack based method needs to be used. However, since we are using a valid Java compiler, the register-based approach can always be used.

4.2 Live range disambiguation and register renaming

The mapping of stack locations and local variables to registers could have type and size conflicts as discussed in Section 3.2. Variables of different types which reside in the same virtual register are separated into separate registers, when possible, using the technique presented below. The live ranges of each register can be characterized by their def-use chains. Since the access of a double also takes the next contiguous memory word, the normal reaching-definition analysis [16] is slightly modified to take this effect into account. To be specific, the definition of *r2* by an 8-byte double in Figure 4 also reaches the contiguous register *r3*.

For each register *rx*, the identified def-use chains are grouped into non-overlapping live ranges. In Figure 7, operations op1, op3, and op5 define the register *rx* and operations op2, op4, and op6 use the same register *rx*. The def-use chains for register *rx* are 1→ 2, 1→ 4, 3→ 4, and 5→ 6 as shown. Each connected graph forms a non-overlapping live range of register *rx*. As a result, op1, op2, op3, and op4 form a live range (LR#1) while op5 and op6 form another (LR#2). Register *rx* in each live range is renamed to a different register id. If the type of register *rx* is not consistent inside a live range after this renaming, the stack to register mapping cannot be applied and the translation falls back to the stack computation model.

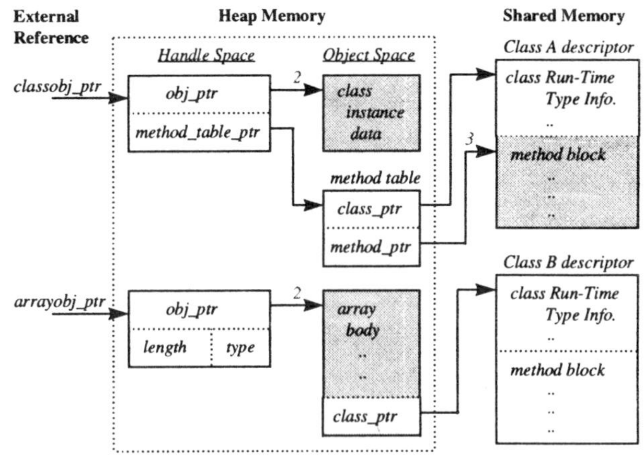

Figure 8. Run-time memory organization used by Java interpreter.

5. Run-time memory organization

Java programs are name-binding rather than address-binding and thus allow flexibility in the run-time memory organization implemented by the interpreter. Dynamically allocated objects in the heap can be roughly categorized into *class* objects and *array* objects. Figure 8 illustrates the heap memory organization used by the SUN Java interpreter. In this organization, neither a class object nor an array object points directly to its associated data. Rather, there is an 8-byte *handle* in between. Accesses to both *class instance data* and *array body* require two levels of indirection. Accesses to the *method block* for method invocation need three levels of indirection. Since these access events take place frequently during program execution, such high levels of indirection can cause significant performance degradation.

The enhanced memory model proposed in this paper (in Figure 9) reduces the amount of indirection by combining the *class instance data* block and the *method table* into one *object block*. The reference to *object block* now requires only one level of indirection. Since the class run-time type information in our implementation is of constant size, the method block can be accessed by a constant offset from a pointer to the class

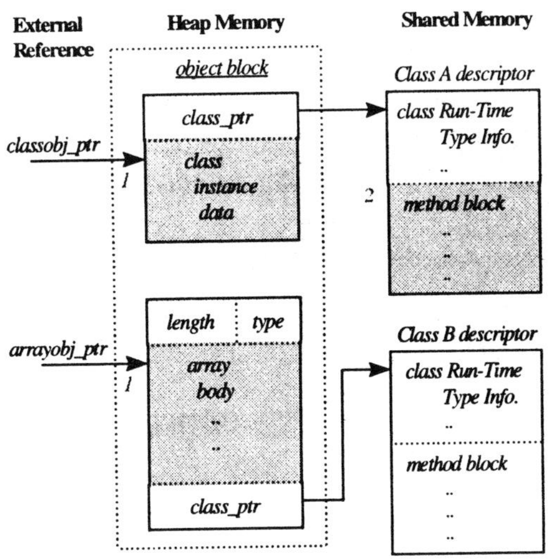

Figure 9. Run-time memory organization used by Java bytecode translator.

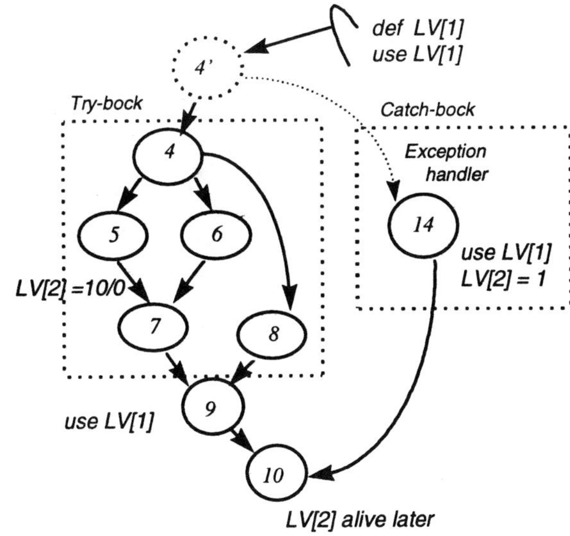

Figure 10. Example of exception handing.

descriptor. The *method_ptr* in Figure 8 is thus eliminated, which reduces a method block reference to two indirection levels. The enhanced model also consumes less memory. Changes made to the run-time library, which is source licensed from SUN, to support this enhanced memory model are minimal due to the library's heavy use of preprocessor macros for handle-to-object dereferencing.

6. Exception Handler Considerations

Exception handlers are sections of code that are reached when a run-time exception occurs. The *try-block* in Java is designed to enclose statements which may cause run-time exceptions. Exceptions which occur within a try-block are captured by an associated *catch*-block of the same exception type. A Java *method* can have many exception handlers cascaded together to guard ordinary code, or to guard other handlers. In Figure 10, block 14 is an exception handler that guards its try-block consisting of blocks 4 to 8. There are four issues that must be addressed during translation.

First, after exception handling, control may be transferred back to the original program (e.g. in Figure 10, block 14 → 10). As a result, exception handlers need to be connected to the control flow graph as shown in Figure 10.

Second, an exception handler might use local variables defined before its associated try-block. In Figure 10, the definition of local variable entry *LV[1]* reaches the use in exception handler block 14. A pseudo arc, shown as a dotted line, and a null block preceding the try-block are created to allow live variable information to be passed to the handler. Otherwise incomplete flow analysis may lead to incorrect optimizations.

Third, during optimization and scheduling, an instruction inside the try-block cannot be moved outside its try-block without enlarging the try-block in general. However, if the try-block has to be enlarged, to avoid changing the program behavior, the added instructions should not cause exceptions that can be captured by the try-block's handler.

Fourth, for maximum portability, exception handling support in the Java interpreter does not rely on the underlying architecture or operating system. Thus, the interpreter explicitly checks for null references, array index bounds, divide by zero, etc. It is expensive and often unnecessary for the translated code to do all of these explicit checks. *Caffeine* currently explicitly checks array index bounds in the translated code. This checking costs about 10% of the performance across our benchmark programs. Optimization opportunities exist to conduct analysis to eliminate unnecessary explicit checks. Previous work has shown that program analysis can be done to determine if it is possible for a load or store to ever have an address of zero or to ever access outside of its intended array, etc., for the purpose of speculative code motion [20].

The benchmarks presented in Section 7 do not cause exceptions and thus do not exercise the exception handler capabilities of Java. Although *Caffeine* does not currently support many of these capabilities, we believe that the underlying hardware architectures can be used to support the remaining exception-handling capabilities without affecting performance of these benchmarks.

7. Benchmarks and Preliminary Results

A suite of six integer programs was selected to evaluate our prototype translator. There were currently no standard Java benchmarks generally available at the time of this work. For each program, we hand translated the C source code into equivalent Java source code. By equivalence we mean that the algorithm, data structures, and operand types used in the Java code and the C code are the same. Due to the fundamental differences between C and Java with regard to the object-oriented concept, array accessing, array index bounds checking and library routines, an exact correspondence is not always feasible. When this occurred, we modified the C program so

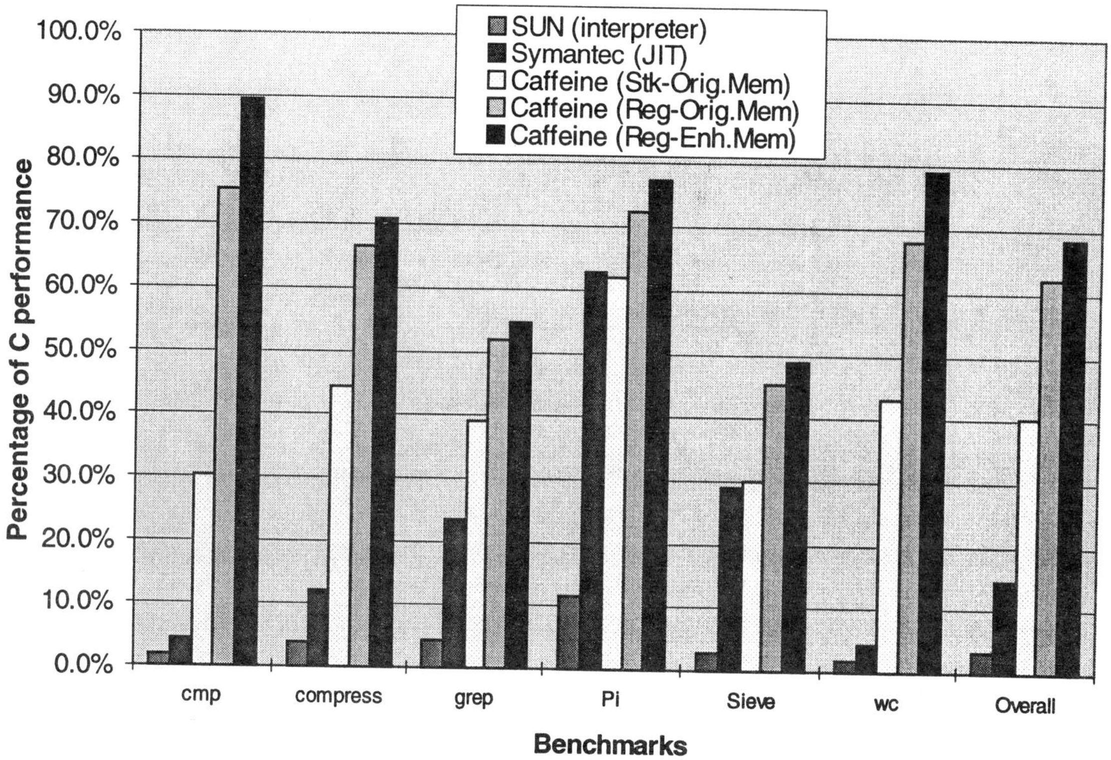

Figure 11. Experiment results on different approaches. All numbers are relative speed to the equivalent C code compiled by Microsoft Visual C/C++ compiler with optimization level two.

that it could be translated with close correspondence. The Java sources thus generated are then compiled into Java bytecode by the SUN Java compiler.

Figure 11 shows preliminary results that compare the real machine execution time of Java bytecode programs using the SUN Java interpreter, the Symantec Java Just-in-time compiler (JIT), and different configurations of the IMPACT Java to X86 native code translator *Caffeine*. All of the programs are executed on an Intel Pentium processor running Windows 95. Performance is shown in Figure 11 as a percentage of the benchmark performance for the equivalent C code compiled by the Microsoft Visual C/C++ compiler with optimization level two. The first *Caffeine* model (Stk.-Orig.Mem) uses the stack computation model and the interpreter's memory model. The performance is, on average, 2.8 times higher than the JIT compiler. This is because of the optimizations that remove unnecessary pushes and pops, and because no initial code-generation is required. The second *Caffeine* model (Reg.-Orig.Mem) uses the register computation model instead of the stack model. This results in 55% performance improvement over the stack model. The final *Caffeine* model (Reg.-Enh.Mem) also uses the proposed memory organization instead of the interpreter's memory organization. This results is a 7% performance improvement. This final model of our prototype Java native code translator *Caffeine* is capable of generating code that runs on average at 68% of the speed of the equivalent C code, 4.7 times faster than the Symantec Java JIT compiler, and more than 20 times faster than the Java interpreter. For these preliminary results, the *Caffeine* translated code is optimized using classic C code optimization techniques without profiling and inlining.

8. Conclusion and Future Work

In this paper, we presented our initial prototyping experience with *Caffeine*, a Java-bytecode-to-native-machine-code translator, to demonstrate the feasibility of efficient universal software distribution languages. The preliminary results show that it is capable of achieving 68% of the speed of the native code directly compiled from the equivalent C code. Besides the fact that it removes the interpretation overhead, much of the performance gain over the SUN Java interpreter comes from the stack to register mapping, which fully utilizes the register computation model of modern processors. The requirements and algorithms for the stack to register mapping were presented and discussed. Although these requirements will hold for all Java bytecode generated by a valid Java compiler, the stack computation model is kept as a fall-back when these requirements are not met. The penalty for using the stack model is about a 35% performance degradation.

We also presented and compared two different run-time memory organizations. Preliminary results showed that a 7% performance gain can be achieved by moving the data associated with dynamically allocated objects closer to their external references.

Several aspects of translating Java bytecode to native code that were not exercised by these benchmarks are now being investigated. These aspects include garbage collection, Java's extensive exception handling capabilities, threading support, and the use of the Java graphic library.

In addition, substantial ongoing efforts are focusing on removing indirection overhead for method invocation. By doing interclass reaching-definition analysis, we should be able to trace the class type of a current object from its definition and convert, if possible, the indirect method invocation to an absolute method invocation. Inlining is also made possible by this conversion. Another direction for research is to perform better memory disambiguation by taking advantage of well-protected class boundaries to eliminate dereferencing overhead. We also observe that the array index bounds checking as required by Java semantics is a major source of performance degradation. We feel that with aggressive analysis, most of these checks can be removed. We would also like to target other platforms and make use of more advanced instruction-level parallelism enhancing techniques such as predication and speculation.

Acknowledgments

The author would like to thank Daniel M. Lavery for proofreading the various versions of this paper, all the members of the IMPACT research group, and the anonymous reviewers whose comments and suggestions helped to improve the quality of this paper.

This research has been supported by the National Science Foundation (NSF) under grant MIP-9308013, Intel Corporation, Advanced Micro Devices, Hewlett-Packard, SUN Microsystems, NCR, and the National Aeronautics and Space Administration (NASA) under Contract NASA NAG 1-613 in cooperation with the Illinois Computer Laboratory for Aerospace Systems and Software (ICLASS).

Reference

[1] P.P. Chang, S. A. Mahlke, W. Y. Chen, N. J. Warter, and W. W. Hwu, *IMPACT: An architectural framework for multiple-instruction-issue processors*, Proc. 18th Ann. Int'l Symp. Computer Architecture, (Toronto, Canada), pp. 266-275, Jun 1991.

[2] *Java™ – Programming for the Internet,* Sun Microsystems, Inc., 1996, *http://java.sun.com/*

[3] James Gosling and Henry McGilton, *The Java Language Environment, A White Paper*, Sun Microsystems Computer Corporation, October, 1995.

[4] *The Java Virtual Machine Specification, Release 1.0 Beta DRAFT*, Sun Microsystems Computer Corporation, August 21, 1995.

[5] *The Java Language Specification, Version 1.0 Beta DRAFT*, Sun Microsystems Computer Corporation, October 30, 1995.

[6] James Gosling, *Java intermediate Bytecodes*, ACM SIGPLAN Workshop on Intermediate Representations, 1995.

[7] Arthur van Hoff, Sami Shaio, and Orca Starbuck, *Hooked on Java*, Addison-Wesley, December 1995.

[8] David Flanagan, *Java in a Nutshell*, O'Reilly & Associates, Inc, February 1996.

[9] Gary Cornell and Cay S. Horstmann, *Core Java*, The Sunsoft Press Java Series, March 1996.

[10] Michael C. Daconta, *Java for C/C++ Programmers*, Wiley Computer Publishing, March 1996.

[11] Ken Arnold and James Gosling, *The Java Programming Language*, Addison Wesley, May 1996.

[12] *Borland C++ Development Suite*, Borland International, Inc., 1996 , http://www.borland.com/

[13] *Café – Visual Java Development and Debugging Tools*, Symantec Corporation, 1996, http://www.symantec.com/

[14] Tim Wilkinson, *KAFFE – A JIT virtual machine to run Java code*, 1996, *http://web.soi.city.ac.uk/homes/tim/kaffe/kaffe.html*

[15] *Guava – High-performance Environment for Running Java Programs*, Softway Pty. Ltd., 1996, *http://www.softway.com.au/softway/products/guava/*

[16] Alfred V. Aho, Ravi Sethi, and Jeffery D. Ullman, *Compiler – Principles, Techniques, and Tools*, Addison Wesley, March, 1988.

[17] Jeffery Richter, *Advanced Windows - Chap.9 Thread Synchronization and Chap.14 Structured Exception Handling*, Microsoft Press, 1995.

[18] Matt Pietrek, *Windows 95 System Programming Secrets*, IDG Books Worldwide, 1995.

[19] Walter Oney, *Extend Your Application with Dynamically Loaded VxDs Under Windows 95*, MSJ, May 1995.

[20] Roger Alexander Bringmann, *Enhancing Instruction Level Parallelism Through Compiler-Controlled Speculation*, Ph.D. thesis, Department of Computer Science, University of Illinois, Urbana-Champaign, 1995.

Session 4

Analysis Techniques for Predicated Code

Richard Johnson and Michael Schlansker
{rjohnson,schlansk}@hpl.hp.com
Hewlett-Packard Laboratories
Palo Alto, CA 94304

Abstract

Predicated execution offers new approaches to exploiting instruction-level parallelism (ILP), but it also presents new challenges for compiler analysis and optimization. In predicated code, each operation is guarded by a boolean operand whose run-time value determines whether the operation is executed or nullified. While research has shown the utility of predication in enhancing ILP, there has been little discussion of the difficulties surrounding compiler support for predicated execution. Conventional program analysis tools (e.g. data flow analysis) assume that operations execute unconditionally within each basic block and thus make incorrect assumptions about the run-time behavior of predicated code. These tools can be modified to be correct without requiring predicate analysis, but this yields overly-conservative results in crucial areas such as scheduling and register allocation.

To generate high-quality code for machines offering predicated execution, a compiler must incorporate information about relations between predicates into its analysis. We present new techniques for analyzing predicated code. Operations which compute predicates are analyzed to determine relations between predicate values. These relations are captured in a graph-based data structure, which supports efficient manipulation of boolean expressions representing facts about predicated code. This approach forms the basis for predicate-sensitive *data flow analysis. Conventional data flow algorithms can be systematically upgraded to be predicate sensitive by incorporating information about predicates. Predicate-sensitive data flow analysis yields significantly more accurate results than conventional data flow analysis when applied to predicated code.*

1 Introduction

1.1 Predicated execution

Predicated execution [9, 15, 5, 10] is an architectural model in which each operation is guarded by a boolean operand whose value determines whether the operation is executed or nullified. From the viewpoint of the instruction set architecture, the main new features are an additional boolean operand guarding each operation and a set of compare operations used to compute predicates. Frequent and unpredictable branches present a major barrier to exploiting greater amounts of instruction-level parallelism. Predicated execution addresses this issue by generalizing the rules for code motion between basic blocks and by increasing the size of straight line code blocks by eliminating many branches completely. Often, an entire acyclic control flow region can be converted into a single, branch-free block of predicated code. This process of replacing branches with appropriate predicate computations and guards is called *if-conversion* [2, 4, 5, 14, 13].

Figure 1 illustrates the benefits of predicated execution and if-conversion. Conventional code for the program represented in Figure 1(a) is shown in Figure 1(b). Even assuming unit latencies, no mispredict penalty, and a sufficiently wide-issue machine, execution will take from four to six cycles depending on the path taken. If the branch latency increases or if there is a mispredict penalty, then execution time will increase. In Figure 1(c), the code has been if-converted. Explicit branches that control execution are replaced with guarding predicates on operations, together with compare operations which compute the appropriate guard values. The result is a single, branch-free block of predicated code. This code can be executed in three cycles, independent of branch latency or mispredict penalty.

The primary benefit of if-conversion is that it enlarges scheduling scope without dramatically increasing code size; thus, predication offers an attractive alternative to increasing block size through code replication [13]. A secondary benefit of predication is the elimination of unpredictable branches that would otherwise cause branch prediction stalls at run-time [17, 12].

1.2 Architectural model

Examples described in this paper are illustrated using the HPL PlayDoh research architecture [10]. This architecture provides support for predicated execution through an enhanced version of the predication capabilities of the Cydra 5 processor [4, 15]. In addition to guarded operations, PlayDoh introduces a family of compare operations which support efficient if-conversion of structured and unstructured control flow graphs, as well as parallel computation of high fan-in logical expressions. A compare operation has the following form.

```
p1,p2 = cmpp.<d1>.<d2> (r1 <cond> r2) if q
```

Each such operation is a two-target compare with the following interpretation.

- `p1`, `p2` are destination predicate register operands.
- `cmpp` is the generic compare opcode.
- `<d1>`, `<d2>` are two-letter descriptors that specify an action and mode for the compare operation. PlayDoh includes unconditional (`u`), conditional (`c`), parallel-or (`o`), and parallel-and (`a`) actions, specified by the first letter of the descriptor. Each action has both a normal mode (`n`) and a complement mode (`c`), specified by the second letter of the descriptor.

1072-4451/96 $5.00 © 1996 IEEE

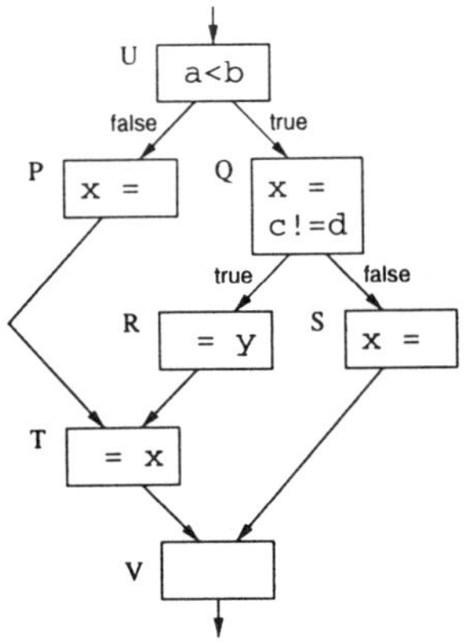

(a) control flow graph

```
U: l = cmp (a<b)
   branch l, Q
P: x =
   branch T
Q: x =
   m = cmp (c!=d)
   branch m, R
S: x =
   branch V
R:    = y
T:    = x
V: ...
```

(b) sequential code

```
U: p,q = cmpp.uc.un (a<b)
   t = cmpp.uc (a<b)
   x =            if p
   x =            if q
   r,s = cmpp.un.uc (c!=d) if q
   t = cmpp.on (c!=d) if q
   x =            if s
     = y          if r
     = x          if t
V: ...
```

(c) if-converted code

unit 1	unit 2	unit 3	unit 4
`p,q = cmpp.uc.un (a<b)`	`t = cmpp.uc (a<b)`		
`r,s = cmpp.un.uc (c!=d) if q`	`t = cmpp.on (c!=d) if q`	`x = if p`	`x = if q`
	`= y if r`	`x = if s`	`= x if t`

(d) scheduled code (predicate-sensitive analysis)

unit 1	unit 2	unit 3	unit 4
`p,q = cmpp.uc.un (a<b)`	`t = cmpp.uc (a<b)`		
`r,s = cmpp.un.uc (c!=d) if q`	`t = cmpp.on (c!=d) if q`	`x = if p`	
	`= y if r`		`x = if q`
		`x = if s`	
			`= x if t`

(e) scheduled code (conventional analysis)

Figure 1. Example of predicated code

- `r1 <cond> r2` specifies the actual comparison; the set of comparisons is the same as in the HP PA-RISC architecture [8].
- `q` is a source predicate register operand. Although `q` appears as a guarding predicate, it can be viewed as an input to the compare operation.

input predicate	result of compare	un	uc	on	oc
0	0	0	0	-	-
0	1	0	0	-	-
1	0	0	1	-	1
1	1	1	0	1	-

Table 1. Behavior of compare operations

These two-target compare operations support the generation of high-quality predicated code as produced by if-conversion of structured or unstructured regions, parallel computation of logical expressions, and height-reduction of control and boolean data expressions. For this paper, we are mainly concerned with unconditional and parallel-or actions, which are the actions used in if-conversion. Table 1 shows the execution behavior of the unconditional and parallel-or actions in both normal and complement modes. Each entry describes the result on the destination predicate; note that the destination may be assigned a value or may be left untouched (denoted as "-"). From the table, we see that an unconditional compare operation always writes a value into its destination register. The parallel-or compare operation only writes a value if both its guarding predicate and compare condition are satisfied. This form can be used to efficiently compute a disjunction by accumulating terms into a predicate register that was initially cleared. Since the operations computing the terms write the same value, they can execute in any order or even in parallel.

1.3 Predicate-sensitive analysis

To best exploit available instruction-level parallelism, the predicated code must be scheduled and its variables must be bound to physical registers. Both scheduling and allocation require predicate-sensitive analysis to generate the highest quality code. To illustrate this point, let's reconsider our example in Figure 1. Prior to scheduling, the compiler constructs precedence constraints between operations that are satisfied by any legal schedule.

This is done separately for each variable in the program. Consider the variable x in the if-converted code of Figure 1(c). There are three assignments to x (guarded by predicates p, q and s) and a single use of x guarded by predicate t. To achieve the schedule in Figure 1(d), the compiler must determine that the first two writes to variable x in Figure 1(c) are independent. Similarly, it must determine that the third write to x is independent of the read of x. Because predicates p and q cannot be true simultaneously, there is no output dependence edge between the first two assignments to x. Similarly, because predicates s and t cannot both be true, there is no flow dependence edge between the final assignment and the final use of x. We can see that data flow analysis must exploit relations between predicates in order to generate precise precedence edges, which are critical to ILP scheduling.

After precedence edges have been constructed, our compiler schedules code on actual machine resources to optimize the use of multiple pipelined function units. In this simple example, we show four functional units that execute any operation with unit latency. The scheduling process yields wide-word code similar to the code shown in Figure 1(d). This schedule is significantly better than the schedule formed without predicate-sensitive analysis, shown in Figure 1(e).

Once code is scheduled, variables must be bound to physical registers. A variable is live at a point if its value at that point can reach a subsequent use of the variable along some control flow path. In graph-coloring register allocation [3], two variables are said to *interfere* if one variable is live at a point where the other is written. Variables that interfere must be bound to separate physical registers, so that the writes to one variable do not overwrite live values of the other. In predicated code, overlapping lifetimes do not necessarily interfere. We augment the data flow information at each point to indicate the predicate conditions under which each variable is live. Overlapping variable lifetimes may share a common register provided the lifetimes conflict under predicate conditions which are mutually exclusive and therefore guaranteed not to occur.

1.4 Overview

In this paper, we discuss techniques for direct analysis of predicated code. This work has been motivated by a variety of tasks within Elcor, our research compiler for instruction-level parallel machines. In particular, we use predicate-sensitive analysis for optimization, scheduling, and register allocation of predicated code.

This work addresses two basic problems. First, we address the problem of analyzing predicated code to discover relations that exist between predicates. A typical relation is that two predicates are disjoint (i.e. they are never both true at the same time), or that a predicate p is true whenever a predicate q is true (this is analogous to control flow dominance). We will present a predicate query system that answers basic questions about predicate relations. The queries are used during predicate-sensitive data flow analysis as well as by optimizations on predicated code. Predicated code is analyzed directly, so that no correspondence to the original control flow is required.

The second problem we address is predicate-sensitive data flow analysis. Here, the objective is to extend conventional bitvector-style methods to predicated code. Our approach builds upon the analysis of predicate relations, using the predicate query system to manipulate predicate expressions, which represent executions for which each data flow property holds. We use the methods presented here to perform scheduling and register allocation on predicated code, achieving very high quality results using efficient analysis algorithms.

The rest of the paper is organized as follows. In Section 2 we sketch the outline of our approach and provide necessary terminology. In Section 3, we describe a simple translation of Play-Doh code to a sequential, single assignment form. This form facilitates analysis of predicate relations. We give an algorithm for extracting local predicate relations directly from the code. In Section 4, we define the partition graph, a data structure for representing predicate relations and for manipulating predicate expressions. Efficient partition graph algorithms appear in Section 5; these algorithms form the basis for predicate-sensitive data flow analysis. The extension of conventional bitvector data flow analysis to predicate-sensitive analysis is discussed in Section 6.

2 Terminology

In the introduction, we motivated the need for predicate-sensitive analysis, where relations between run-time values of predicates are incorporated into data flow analysis. In this section we introduce the basic ideas underlying our approach.

2.1 From paths to executions

Data flow analysis computes facts about a program at each point in a control flow graph representation. These facts are often of the form, "property W holds on all paths through point A," or "property W holds on some path through point A." For example, a definition of variable x in operation i reaches operation j provided there is some path from i to j containing no redefinition of x. In Figure 1(a), we see that the definitions in blocks P and Q reach the use in block T, but the definition in block S does not reach the use in block T. This analysis is used to determine precedence constraints between operations prior to instruction scheduling.

In Figure 1(c), there is a single control flow path through the block. To determine which definitions of x actually reach the use, we must consider the effect of predicated execution. For the definition of x under predicate p to reach the use of x under predicate t, we need to know whether there exists an execution such that (1) both p and t are assigned true; and (2) predicates q and s, which guard the intervening definitions of x, are assigned false.

Intuitively then, questions about whether a property holds on some or all paths through a control flow graph become questions about whether the property holds on some or all executions through a sequence of predicated operations. In the remainder of this section, we develop terminology for reasoning about executions of predicated code sequences.

2.2 Execution sets

Predicate analysis, as presented here, focuses on relations between predicate values within straight line sequences of operations.

Definition 1 *A **predicate block** is a straight line sequence of predicated operations.*

Predicate blocks are typically formed by if-conversion of single-entry single-exit control flow regions. To capture relations between run-time values of predicates, we look at relations between different possible executions of a predicate block.

Definition 2 *An **execution trace** is a record of boolean values assigned to predicate variables during an execution of a predicate block. We use* **1** *to denote the set of all possible execution traces. An **execution set** for a predicate* p*, denoted P, is the set of traces in which predicate* p *is assigned true. Note that $P \subseteq \mathbf{1}$ for any predicate* p*. Other non-empty subsets of* **1** *are also execution sets, although they are not explicitly named.*

Example: Consider the if-converted code in Figure 1(c). There are five predicate variables, and $2^5 = 32$ potential predicate assignments. Only three of these assignments are execution traces, corresponding to the three paths in the source control flow graph shown in Figure 1(a). These traces are listed below.

trace	p	q	r	s	t
e_1	1	0	0	0	1
e_2	0	1	1	0	1
e_3	0	1	0	1	0

All other combinations of predicate assignments are invalid, since they are not possible in any execution. For example, it is not possible for both p and q to be assigned true in a single execution; this fact can either be determined from correspondence to the original control flow graph or from the semantics of the compare operation which assigns values to p and q. The execution sets are as follows: $P = \{e_1\}$, $R = \{e_2\}$, $S = \{e_3\}$, $Q = \{e_2, e_3\}$, $T = \{e_1, e_2\}$, and $\mathbf{1} = \{e_1, e_2, e_3\}$. □

In the above example, we enumerated execution traces manually and then formed execution sets for each predicate. From the execution sets, we see simple run-time relations between predicates. For example, the fact that predicates s and t are never both true in any execution is evident from the fact that execution sets S and T are disjoint.

Clearly it is impractical to form execution sets and determine relations among them by enumerating a potentially exponential number of traces. Instead, we will derive relations between execution sets directly from the predicate-assigning operations. The algorithms for deriving relations between execution sets is given in Sections 3 and 4. The most basic relation is the partition relation.

2.3 The partition relation

Just as computing control dependence or dominance requires knowledge of control flow predecessors and successors (i.e. the graph connectivity), computing predicate relations requires basic information about local predicate properties. For example, consider the following code fragment.

```
m,n = cmpp.un.uc (i<k) if u
```

Locally, we can determine that several facts hold following execution of these statements.

- if m or n is true, then u must be true,
- if m is true, then n must be false and vice versa, and
- if u is true, then one of m or n is true.

These local facts are akin to knowing local connectivity in the control flow graph; for example, this code sequence would result from if-converting a basic block U having two successors M and N, where the condition i<k controls transfer to either M or N. From facts of this form, we will compute global relations akin to dominance and control dependence. The local relation between source and destination predicates induced by a compare operation can be expressed in terms of the predicates' execution sets:

- $M \cup N \subseteq U$,
- $M \cap N = \emptyset$, and
- $U \subseteq M \cup N$.

In other words, the execution set U is partitioned into disjoint sets M and N, denoted $U = M \mid N$.

2.4 Predicate expressions

During data flow analysis, we will need to reason about more general execution sets than the base executions sets corresponding to predicates. For example, during analysis we may need to represent the fact that a variable is live on all executions where either p or s is true. This set is represented by the union of sets P and S, denoted $P + S$. Such symbolic expressions representing general execution sets are called *predicate expressions*, defined below.

Definition 3 *A* **predicate expression** *is a symbolic expression that represents an execution set. The base symbols of predicate expressions are the names of execution sets for individual predicates. Base expressions are combined using the operators sum $(+)$, difference $(-)$, and product $(\cdot)$. A predicate expression is interpreted as the execution set formed by applying corresponding set operators to the base execution sets.*

In our example, the expression $P + S$ represents the execution set $P \cup S = \{e_1\} \cup \{e_3\} = \{e_1, e_3\}$. Whether P denotes a symbol or an execution set depends on the context of its usage.

3 Extracting local relations

Each predicate-assigning operation induces a local relation between the predicate variables being assigned. In general, each local relation can be represented symbolically as a partition relation between the predicates' execution sets. In this section, we describe an algorithm for directly analyzing predicated code and extracting local relations between predicates. The process has two steps. First, the code is translated to a sequential static single assignment intermediate form, which simplifies subsequent processing. Second, this intermediate form is processed to discover relations between predicates.

PlayDoh operation	sequential form
p = cmpp.un (r1 <cond> r2) if q	p = (r1 <cond> r2) · q
p = cmpp.uc (r1 <cond> r2) if q	p = !(r1 <cond> r2) · q
p = cmpp.on (r1 <cond> r2) if q	p = p + (r1 <cond> r2) · q
p = cmpp.oc (r1 <cond> r2) if q	p = p + !(r1 <cond> r2) · q

Table 2. Sequential forms of compare operations

```
U: p,q = cmpp.uc.un (a<b)
     t = cmpp.uc (a<b)
     x =         if p
     x =         if q
   r,s = cmpp.un.uc (c!=d) if q
     t = cmpp.on (c!=d) if q
     x =         if s
       = ..y..   if r
       = ..x..   if t
V: ...
```

(a) original predicated code

```
U:  p = !(a<b) · true
    q =   (a<b) · true
   t1 = !(a<b) · true
    x =         if p
    x =         if q
    r =  (c!=d) · q
    s = !(c!=d) · q
   t2 = t1 + (c!=d) · q
    x =         if s
      = ..y..   if r
      = ..x..   if t2
```

(b) sequential SSA form

Figure 2. Example of translation to sequential single assignment form

3.1 Translation to sequential SSA form

To simplify subsequent processing, we translate the PlayDoh compare operations to a single-target sequential form; this translation is performed before converting to static single assignment form. Foremost, this translation replaces conditional-overwrite parallel-or operations with a read-modify-write sequential version. Table 2 shows the translation to sequential form, which will be used in the remainder of the paper. In the sequential form, the destination predicate value is a boolean function of the predicate input value and the compare condition.

Since the sequential compare operations execute unconditionally, converting them into static single assignment form within an if-converted region is as simple as performing SSA renaming of scalars within a basic block: for each predicate variable, maintain a counter which is incremented at every definition of that predicate, and use the current counter value as the SSA subscript at every reference of the predicate.

Figure 2 shows the translation to single-target sequential SSA form applied to our running example. Note that `t1` and `p` are equivalent predicates. During the initial analysis of predicated code, we will detect such equivalences and map both predicates to a single symbolic predicate.

3.2 Gathering partition relations

Given a sequence of predicated operations in sequential SSA form, we scan the operations in order and perform a predicate-insensitive value numbering to match compare conditions and map predicate registers to predicate symbols. As compare operations are processed, we emit partition relations associated with the predicate symbols of the compare operands.

To perform value numbering, we maintain a counter for each variable. This counter is incremented at every definition and is appended as a suffix to subsequent uses of the variable. Compare conditions are normalized, with input operands being lexicographically ordered. The value number for an input operand consists of a variable name together with its counter. Note that PlayDoh compare operations have an additional degree of freedom during normalization, since negations can be pushed into the two-letter destination descriptor. For example, the comparisons $a < b$ and $a \geq b$ both normalize to the same form, although one will be complemented on output. Normalization allows us to detect equivalent and complementary compare conditions with hashing.

A hash table records the mapping between predicate names in the source and predicate symbols allocated during this phase. We use integers numbered from 1 as node names. Initially, the table contains the true predicate mapped to 1. Compare operations are processed in order, and the hash table is updated to keep track of the mappings from compare expressions to symbolic name and from symbolic names to predicate registers. At each compare operation, the right-hand side is reduced by normalizing the compare condition and replacing predicate operands with their symbolic name.

Figure 3 shows the algorithms for scanning a predicated block to extract local partition relations. The main routine is **scan_ops**, which iterates over compare operations in the block. As each operation is visited, the right-hand side compare operation and guarding predicate is normalized into a string that serves as a hash key. The functions **lookup_AND_string** and **lookup_OR_string** process keys from unconditional and parallel-or compare operations, respectively. Both functions return a symbolic name corresponding to the predicate variable computed by the compare operation. In both cases, if a name for the computation does not already exist in the hash table, an entry is created. As a result of adding

```
lookup_AND_string (String S)
  // S has form [!](r1<cond>r2)·i
  if S not in table then
     create entry for S, say m;
     create entry for complement of S, say n;
     emit partition relation i = m | n;
  endif
  return symbol for S;
```

```
scan_ops (List ops)
  for each compare operation in ops list do
     reduce the right-hand side to a normalized string S
     if compare is unconditional form then
        m = lookup_AND_string (S);
     else // compare is or-style
        m = lookup_OR_string (S);
     endif
     map destination predicate to m;
  endfor
```

```
lookup_OR_string (String S)
  if S not in table then
     if S has form j+[!](r1<cond>r2)·i then
        let S' be the right-hand subexpr of S;
        k = lookup_AND_string (S');
        further reduce S to j + k;
     endif
     // S has form j+k
     create entry for S, say m;
     emit partition relation m = j | k;
  endif
  return symbol for S;
```

Figure 3. Algorithm for gathering initial partition relations

entries to the hash table, new partition relations may be generated. Note that in the case of an parallel-or operation, we require that the previous predicate value and the new condition being "OR-ed" be disjoint. This is always the case for parallel-or compares generated by if-conversion.

3.3 Example

Below is our example from Figure 2(b), with the predicate computations reordered to make things more interesting. Compares are normalized; other operations are omitted to save space.

```
p  = !(a<b) · true
q  =  (a<b) · true
t1 = !(a<b) · true
t2 = t1 + !(c=d) · q
s  =  (c=d) · q
r  = !(c=d) · q
```

Operations are processed in order, producing the following effects.

- The initial table maps `true` to 1 and creates a symbolic name for the execution set.
- `p = !(a<b)·true`. Reduces to `p` = `!(a<b)` · 1. During lookup, the right-hand side and its complement are added to the table and a partition relation is emitted:

symbol	string	source names
1	true	true
2	!(a<b)·1	p
3	(a<b)·1	

$\Rightarrow 1 = 2 \mid 3$

- `q = (a<b)·true`. Reduces to `q` = `(a<b)` · 1, which further reduces to `q` = 3.

  Action: add `q` to list of source names for symbol 3.
- `t1 = !(a<b)·true`. Reduces to `t1` = 2.

  Action: add `t1` to list of source names for symbol 2.
- `t2 = t1 + !(c=d)·q`. Reduces to `t2` = 2+`!(c=d)`·3. During lookup, `!(c=d)` · 3 and its complement are added to the table and a partition relation is emitted. The outer expression further reduces to `t2` = 2+4, which is added to the table and a partition relation is emitted:

symbol	string	source names
1	true	true
2	!(a<b)·1	p, t1
3	(a<b)·1	q
4	!(c=d)·3	
5	(c=d)·3	
6	2+4	t2

$\Rightarrow 3 = 4 \mid 5.$
$\Rightarrow 6 = 2 \mid 4.$

- `s = (c=d)·q`. Reduces to `s` = 5.

  Action: add `s` to list of source names for symbol 5.
- `r = !(c=d)·q`. Reduces to `r` = 4.

  Action: add `r` to list of source names for symbol 4.
- The final table and the partitions emitted:

symbol	string	source names
1	true	true
2	(a<b)·1	p, t1
3	!(a<b)·1	q
4	!(c=d)·3	r
5	(c=d)·3	s
6	2+4	t2

Partitions: $1 = 2 \mid 3,\ \ 3 = 4 \mid 5,\ \ 6 = 2 \mid 4.$

4 The partition graph

Local partition relations must be combined to answer general questions about relations between predicates. For example, if we

```
if (a<b)
    S0;
else
    S1;
    if (m>n)
        S2;
if (i!=5)
    S3;
else
    S4;
```

(a) source code fragment

```
p =  (a<b) · true
q = !(a<b) · true
           S0          if p
           S1          if q
r =  (m>n) · q
           S2          if r
s =  (i!=5) · true
t = !(i!=5) · true
           S3          if s
           S4          if t
```

(b) sequential SSA form

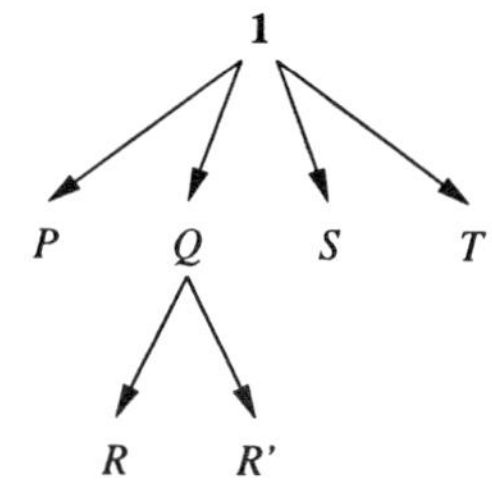

(c) partition graph

Figure 4. Example of partition graph for structured code

know the relations $\mathbf{1} = P \mid Q$ and $Q = R \mid S$, then we can deduce that P is disjoint from both R and S. The *partition graph* is a data structure that combines local partition relations in a form amenable to answering general queries about predicate relations. In this section, we define the partition graph and give its interpretation in terms of execution sets, and we show how the graph is built from local partition relations. Graph algorithms for answering general predicate queries are presented in Section 5.

4.1 Definition and interpretation

Definition 4 *A* **partition graph** *is a directed acyclic graph whose nodes represent execution sets and whose labeled edges represent partition relations between nodes. Specifically, a partition $U = M \mid N$ is represented by labeled edges $U \xrightarrow{r} M$ and $U \xrightarrow{r} N$, where the common label r indicates that these edges all belong to the same partition. A partition graph is* **complete** *if it contains a unique node having no predecessors from which all nodes are reachable.*

Figure 4 shows the partition graph for predicated code resulting from if-conversion of a structured program region. Nodes in the graph represent execution sets. To reduce clutter, we draw edges having the same label (representing a single partition) so that their tails touch, and then we omit edge labels. The root of the partition graph is the symbol **1**, which represents the universal set of valid executions through this code. This set is partitioned two different ways, with one partition for each of the two sequentially composed if-then-else statements: $\mathbf{1} = P \mid Q$ and $\mathbf{1} = S \mid T$. Set Q is partitioned as $Q = R \mid R'$, where R' is created to complete the partition, even though there is no corresponding predicate computed in the source code. This graph is complete.

We extend several familiar tree properties to partition graphs as follows.

Definition 5 *The* ***root*** *of a complete partition graph is the unique node having no predecessors. A* ***leaf*** *is any node having no successors. An* ***ancestor*** *of a node P is any node on a path from* **1** *to* ***P***. *A* ***descendant*** *of node P is any node reachable from P. The* ***level*** *of a node is its shortest-path distance from the root. The root has level zero. A lowest common ancestor of a set of nodes $\{Q_i\}$, denoted lca($\{Q_i\}$), is a node with greatest level number from the set of common ancestors of $\{Q_i\}$.*

Each node of the partition graph corresponds to an execution set for some predicate. A set of edges having the same label represents a partition relation. Each individual edge represents a subset relation, as does any path. Thus, we can test non-local relations by traversing paths in the partition graph. This technique underlies our algorithms for efficiently analyzing predicated code. For example, to determine that predicates `p` and `r` are disjoint in Figure 4(c), we simply show that execution sets P and R are disjoint in the partition graph. This is shown by finding a partition $X = Y \mid Z$ such that P is a descendant (i.e. subset) of Y and R is a descendant (i.e. subset) of Z. In this example, the partition $\mathbf{1} = P \mid Q$ suffices. In contrast, there is no partition that separates P and S, which are not disjoint.

4.2 Graph construction

In this section, we describe our approach to building a partition graph directly from predicated code. This approach frees us from incrementally maintaining the partition graph as the predicated code is transformed, and it also removes many phase-ordering constraints from the compiler. Fundamentally, we believe the facility to work with predicate code as effectively as we can with ordinary code is of paramount importance to ILP compilers for architectures supporting predication. The process has two parts: (1) building an initial graph from local partition relations, and (2) completing the partition graph. These steps are detailed below.

Building the initial graph

The initial partition graph is constructed from a list of partition relations, which can be generated either from the source control flow graph prior to if-conversion or from analysis of the predicated code itself. By inserting a set of labeled edges to represent each partition relation, we get a partition graph.

One source of local partition relations is the control flow graph itself. Suppose predicates are assigned to the basic blocks of an acyclic control flow region just prior to if-conversion. We assume empty basic blocks are inserted as necessary to prevent edges from directly connecting branch and merge points, such as happens on the false side of an if-then statement. We generate partition relations in a single traversal of the control flow region as follows. If a block with predicate `r` has successor (predecessor) blocks with predicates p_i through p_k, we generate the relation $R = P_i \mid \ldots \mid P_k$. During if-conversion, predicate computations are introduced to replace branches, and the predicates assigned to blocks are used in the predicate computations and as guards. The main advantage of this approach is the ease of generating partition relations; the main disadvantage is that the partition graph must be correctly maintained as the predicated code is transformed, since the correspondence to the original control flow region may be lost.

However, not all predicated code is generated via if-conversion. Predicated code may be introduced through inlining of hand-coded intrinsic functions, through schematic transformations such as control critical path reduction [16], and through optimizations that make use of predicated execution. In each of these cases, it is essential that we be able to analyze the predicated code directly, since no corresponding, predicate-free program representation exists. The approach presented here is to gather partition relations directly from predicated code. Other advantages of this direct approach are that it frees us from incrementally maintaining the partition graph as the code is further transformed, and it removes many phase-ordering constraints from the compiler.

Completing the partition graph

Each initial partition relation $r : P = Q_1|\ldots|Q_k$ translates into a set of labeled edges $U \xrightarrow{r} Q_i$ in the partition graph. The resulting graph may be incomplete, with not all nodes reachable from a unique root. In particular, nodes corresponding to unstructured control regions, whose partitions come from parallel-or compare operations, initially will not be reachable. To complete the partition graph, we synthesize additional partitions consistent with existing partitions so that all nodes are reachable from root.

Suppose $U = M \mid N$ is a partition and U is not reachable from $\mathbf{1}$. If M and N are reachable from $\mathbf{1}$, there exists a lowest common ancestor of M and N, denoted $lca(M, N)$, which is reachable from $\mathbf{1}$. Since $U = M \cup N$, $U \subseteq lca(M, N)$. Therefore, we can create the partition $lca(M, N) = U \mid Q_i$, where the union of Q_i's is the relative complement of U with respect to $lca(M, N)$. After inserting this new partition, U is reachable from $\mathbf{1}$. The algorithms for computing lowest common ancestors and relative complements is given in Section 5. Note that the least common ancestor and relative complement are computed in the partition subgraph consisting of nodes and edges reachable from the root.

Example: Figure 5 is our running example. The incomplete partition graph in Figure 5(b) is formed by inserting appropriately labeled edges to represent each partition relation extracted from the predicated code[1]. Node $T2$ is not reachable from $\mathbf{1}$, but its successors P and R are reachable from $\mathbf{1}$. Searching back through the rooted subgraph, we find that $\mathbf{1}$ itself is the lca of P and R. The relative complement of $T2$ with respect to $\mathbf{1}$ (i.e. $\mathbf{1} - T2$) can be computed as $(\mathbf{1} - R) - P$. The relative complement of a node N with respect to an ancestor M is found by collecting the union of siblings of nodes along any path from M to N. For example, P and S are the siblings of nodes on the path from $\mathbf{1}$ to R, so $\mathbf{1} - R = P + S$. Repeating this process, we compute $(P+S)-P = (P-P)+(S-P) = S$. The partition $\mathbf{1} = T2 \mid S$ is added, completing the partition graph. □

In general there may be multiple nodes requiring completion. These nodes can be processed in increasing order of their distance from the connected subgraph, so that when a node is processed it is guaranteed that its successors are reachable from the root.

[1] For sake of readability, we will continue to substitute execution set symbols in place of the arbitrary numeric names output by the local partition extraction process. As before, edge labels are omitted from the figure.

5 The predicate query system

The predicate query system (PQS) allows for manipulating predicate expressions and for testing general predicate relations. The query system builds a partition graph for each predicate block using the method from Section 4, and subsequently uses the partition graph to answer queries and perform operations on predicate expressions. The PQS interface is motivated by the needs of predicate-sensitive data flow analysis, described in Section 6. The interface includes the following functions.

- **true_expr** (): a predicate expression representing the universal set of executions.
- **false_expr** (): the null predicate expression representing the empty set of executions.

  These functions are used to initialize predicate expressions in data flow vectors to the appropriate default value. For example, in liveness analysis every point is initialized to the false expressions, representing no variables live.

- **lub_sum** $(P, \mathcal{E})$: an expression representing a smallest superset of the execution set $P \cup \mathcal{E}$.
- **glb_sum** $(P, \mathcal{E})$: an expression representing a greatest subset of the execution set $P \cup \mathcal{E}$.

  These functions are used to generate a property at a point under a guarding predicate. The functions need not be precise and may approximate the exact result from above and below respectively. This interface permits trade-offs between precision and efficiency of the solution. The choice between least upper bound and greatest lower bound is determined by the data flow problem being solved. For example, in liveness analysis, if variable x is live in executions represented by expression $\mathcal{E}$ just after an operation in which x is used under guarding predicate p, then x will be live in executions represented by $\mathcal{E} + P$ just before the operation. Since liveness is an "any path" problem, over-approximation of the execution set is conservative and so we compute $\mathcal{E} + P$ using **lub_sum** $(P, \mathcal{E})$.

- **lub_diff** $(\mathcal{E}, P)$: an expression representing a smallest superset of the execution set $\mathcal{E} - P$.
- **glb_diff** $(\mathcal{E}, P)$: an expression representing a greatest subset of the execution set $\mathcal{E} - P$.

  These functions are used to kill a property at a point under a guarding predicate. For example, in liveness analysis, if variable x is live in executions represented by expression $\mathcal{E}$ just after an operation in which x is defined under guarding predicate p, then x will be live in executions represented by $\mathcal{E} - P$ just before the operation. Since liveness is an "any path" problem, over-approximation of the execution set is conservative and we compute $\mathcal{E} - P$ using **lub_diff** $(\mathcal{E}, P)$.

```
U:  p = !(a<b) · true
    q =  (a<b) · true
   t1 = !(a<b) · true

    r =  (c!=d) · q
    s = !(c!=d) · q

   t2 = t1 + (c!=d) · q
```

(a) sequential SSA form

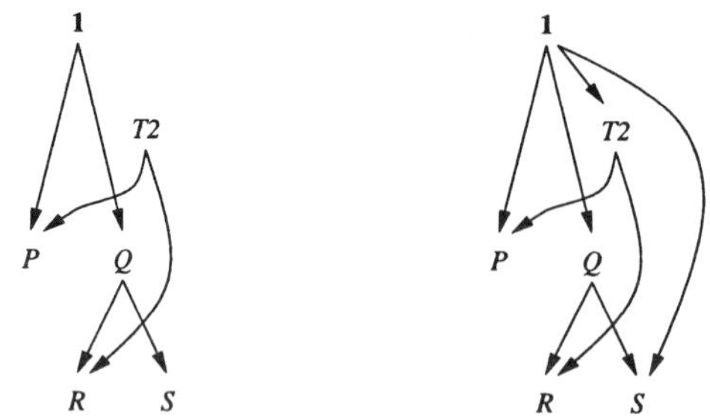

(b) initial partition graph (c) completed graph

Figure 5. Example of partition graph for unstructured code

- **is_disjoint** $(P, \mathcal{E})$: true if the execution set $P \cap \mathcal{E}$ is the empty set.

  Used to test whether a property holds in *some* execution at a point under a guarding predicate. For example, two variables interfere (i.e. they must be assigned to different physical registers) if one is live at a definition point of the other. If variable y is live in executions represented by $\mathcal{E}$ at a point where variable x is defined under predicate p, then the variables interfere if $\mathcal{E}$ is not disjoint from P. This is tested using **is_disjoint** $(P, \mathcal{E})$.

- **is_subset** $(p, \mathcal{E})$: true if P is a subset of the execution set represented by expression $\mathcal{E}$.

  Used to test whether a property holds in *all* executions at a point under a guarding predicate. For example, a computation of expression x/y is redundant if prior computations are available (i.e. computed after the most recent definition of either operand) on all executions to that point. If expression x/y is available in executions represented by $\mathcal{E}$ at a point where expression x/y is computed under predicate p, then the computation is redundant if P is a subset of $\mathcal{E}$. This is tested using **is_subset** $(P, \mathcal{E})$.

5.1 Expressions in 1-disjunctive normal form

In this section, we describe efficient partition graph algorithms for manipulating predicate expressions and for answering queries about predicate relations.. The approach we've taken is to restrict predicate expressions to a simple normal form that is easy to manipulate, making conservative approximations as necessary to ensure correctness. In our experience, this solution provides a good trade-off between accuracy and efficiency.

The variables of predicate expressions are symbols denoting execution sets for individual predicates, and they are represented explicitly by nodes in the partition graph. Since a predicate expression will be used to represent a set of executions for which some property holds, we can conservatively approximate this set by either taking a subset or a superset, depending on the kind of analysis being performed. For example, in an "any-path" problem such as liveness, we test liveness at a point under a predicate p by asking whether any execution in P is represented in the predicate expression for liveness at that point; i.e. we query whether P intersects $\mathcal{E}$. To make a conservative approximation, we must overestimate liveness, and thus any predicate expression $\mathcal{E}'$ representing a larger set than $\mathcal{E}$ is correct. Ideally, we would chose an expression that is both easy to represent and that is a good approximation, so that our analysis remains relatively precise. For other analysis problems, the correct approximation may require finding a representation of a set smaller than $\mathcal{E}$. When an algorithm may require performing an approximation, we provide both least upper bound (lub) and greatest lower bound (glb) versions. To save space, we restrict our attention to least upper bound algorithms; the greatest lower bound algorithms are similar, and differ only in the direction of their approximations.

We have explored a range of solutions, from simple (more approximate) to complex (more accurate) algorithms for predicate queries. Here, we present an efficient and accurate solution which restricts predicate expressions to disjunctions of individual symbols, known as 1-disjunctive normal form (1-dnf). Such expressions can be stored either as a list of symbols or as a bitvector having one bit per symbol (i.e. one bit per node in the partition graph). Since the number of predicate registers used within a predicate block is small, the bitvector usually fits in a single machine word and many of the algorithms can make use of bitvector operations for greater efficiency. The accuracy given up is minor; using a 1-dnf representation, only **lub_diff** requires any approximation.

5.2 Predicate query algorithms

We now describe algorithms for manipulating predicate expressions in 1-disjunctive normal form. We assume each predicate expression is a list of predicate symbols (possibly represented as a bitvector, where each bit position corresponds to a symbol). There are N symbols, where N is the number of nodes in the partition graph. The false expression, denoted $\mathcal{E}_{false}$, is simply an empty list. The true expression, denoted $\mathcal{E}_{true}$, is the list containing **1**, the root of the partition graph. Note that many predicate expressions are equivalent to $\mathcal{E}_{true}$; the algorithms in this section maintain predicate expressions in their reduced form.

Figure 6(a) shows the algorithms for testing disjointness between a pair of symbols, and between a symbol and a predicate expression (in reduced 1-dnf form). The algorithm attempts to show disjointness between two symbols P and Q by finding a partition such that P and Q are contained in disjoint parts. If no such partition exists, P and Q are assumed to intersect.

```
is_disjoint (Symbol P, Symbol Q)
if ∃ partition W = X | Y | Z_i
      s.t. P ⊆ X and Q ⊆ Y then
   return true;
else
   return false;
endif
```

```
is_disjoint (Symbol P, Expression ℰ)
// assumes ℰ is reduced
for each symbol Q in ℰ do
   if is_disjoint (P, Q) = false then
      return false;
endfor
return true;
```

(a) algorithms for **is_disjoint**

```
is_subset (Symbol P, Symbol Q)
if Q is an ancestor of P then
   return true;
else
   return false;
endif
```

```
is_subset (Symbol P, Expression ℰ)
// assumes ℰ is reduced
for each symbol Q in ℰ do
   if is_subset (P, Q) then
      return true;
endfor
return false;
```

(b) algorithms for **is_subset**

```
lub_sum (Symbol P, Expression ℰ)
ℰ' = ℰ_false;
for each symbol Q in ℰ do
   if Q ⊆ P then
      continue;
   else if P ⊆ Q then
      return ℰ;
   else
      ℰ' = ℰ' + Q;
   endif
endfor
return sum_reduce (P, ℰ');
```

```
sum_reduce (Symbol P, Expression ℰ)
add P to ℰ;
for each partition R = P | Q_i do
   if all Q_i are members of ℰ then
      ℰ = sum_reduce (R, ℰ);
      break;
   endif
endfor
if R is a member of ℰ then
   remove all proper descendents of R from ℰ;
endif
return ℰ;
```

(c) algorithms for **lub_sum**

```
lub_diff (Expression ℰ, Symbol P)
ℰ' = ℰ_false;
for each symbol Q in ℰ do
   if Q ⊆ P then
      continue;
   else if P ⊆ Q then
      ℰ' = ℰ' + rel_cmpl (P, Q);
   else if P disjoint from Q then
      ℰ' = ℰ' + Q;
   else
      ℰ' = ℰ' + approx_diff (P, Q);
   endif
endfor
return ℰ;
```

```
rel_cmpl (Symbol P, Symbol Q)
// return expression for Q − P
if is_subset (P, Q) = false then
   return false_expr ();
endif
find a path from Q to P;
let ℰ = ℰ_false;
for each edge R → S on path do
   let R = S | T_i be the partition
      containing edge R → S;
   add each T_i to ℰ;
endfor
return ℰ;
```

```
approx_diff (Symbol P, Symbol Q)
// over-approximate Q − P
return rel_cmpl (P, find_lca (P, Q));
```

```
find_lca (Symbol P, Symbol Q)
let S_P be the set of ancestors of P;
let S_Q be the set of ancestors of Q;
return member of S_P ∩ S_Q having the
   largest level number
```

(d) algorithms for **lub_diff**

Figure 6. Predicate Query System Algorithms

Figure 6(b) shows the algorithms for testing the subset relations. Set P is a subset of Q if there is a reverse path from node P to node Q in the partition graph. As we have mentioned, the subset relation is analogous to dominance and post-dominance, but is insensitive to temporal ordering of the predicate computations.

The algorithms for summing a single symbol into a predicate expression are shown in Figure 6(c). First, easy special cases are considered, such as the new symbol already being contained as a subset of one of the existing symbols in the expression. If the symbol needs to be added, it is added to the list and the resulting expression is recursively reduced. This step is performed by **sum_reduce**. Note that although we call this function **lub_sum**, no approximation is performed.

The algorithms for subtracting a symbol P from a predicate expression are shown in Figure 6(d). This is the only place where approximation is required. As in **lub_sum**, easy cases are handled first. If P is a subset of a symbol Q in the expression, we compute $Q - P$ by replacing Q with the relative complement of P with respect to Q, which can always be represented by a 1-dnf expression. If P intersects a symbol Q in the expression but is neither a subset or a superset, then approximation is required to represent the set difference. Any superset of the set difference is a valid approximation, and we use the relative complement of P with respect to the lowest-common ancestor of P and Q. We have found this approximation works well for liveness in real examples.

5.3 Treatment of the false predicate

Although rare, we must also be able to correctly analyze predicate operations whose guarding predicate is the constant false. Such code is dead; it is essentially the same as no-ops. The execution set for the false predicate is the empty set, because there are no execution traces in which an operation guarded by false is executed. Unlike other execution sets, the false set is not represented in the partition graph. This decision is motivated by the fact that the empty set has a special relation to all sets. Namely, the empty set is both a subset of every set and disjoint from every set.

We could represent the special relation of the empty set to other sets in the partition graph by creating a node for the false predicate, denoted as $\mathbf{0}$, and by adding partitions of the form $P = \mathbf{0} \mid P$ to the graph. This approach has two drawbacks. First, it makes the partition graph cyclic. Second, it roughly doubles the number of partitions; at minimum, we would add a new partition from the existing leaf nodes to the false node, making the false node the unique leaf node in the resulting graph. Because of these drawbacks, we choose to omit the false predicate from the partition graph and instead add special-case code to handle the false predicate in our partition graph algorithms. The extensions are straightforward and are not presented here.

6 Predicate-sensitive data flow analysis

We now have the tools needed to perform predicate-sensitive data flow analysis in if-converted regions. The techniques described in this paper have been implemented in our ILP research compiler and are used for computing data dependences prior to scheduling, for computing up and down exposed definitions and uses, and for computing live range and interference information during register allocation.

Conventional bitvector analysis computes whether some property holds for each variable (or expression) at every point in a control flow graph. Each variable maps to a particular position within all bitvectors. In predicate-sensitive analysis, this framework is extended so that a property holds at a point *for a set of executions*, i.e. at a point within an execution set. Each vector position is extended to hold a predicate expression instead of a single bit. When an operation generates a property under a predicate p, then the property holds for all executions in P at that point, and so set P is unioned with the execution set at that point. If an operation kills a property under predicate q, then Q is subtracted from the execution set at that point. The notion of testing a property at a point is extended to testing whether the property holds at a point in some subset of executions. These expression manipulations are performed efficiently using PQS functions. In the following section, we illustrate our approach by extending traditional liveness analysis to be predicate-sensitive.

6.1 Liveness: an example of local predicate-sensitive analysis

In traditional liveness analysis[2], a variable x is live at a point if there is a path containing no definition of x from that point to a use of x. Liveness is solved using a backward propagation of data flow information throughout the control flow graph. During this backward traversal, liveness is *generated* at each variable use (i.e. the bit position representing liveness for the variable is set to true), and liveness is *killed* at each variable definition (i.e. the bit position is set to false).

In a predicated block, we extend this notion to track the set of executions for which each variable is live. We use a vector of predicate expressions having one position for each variable in the code. Each predicate expression represents the set of executions in which the corresponding variable is live at that point. The predicate expressions are updated as each operation is visited in reverse order.

At an operation, we use $\mathcal{E}^-$ to denote an expression just prior to the operation, and $\mathcal{E}^+$ to denote an expression just after the operation. Consider a use of variable x guarded by predicate p. The use generates liveness in all executions in P just prior to the operation, i.e. at the operation, $\mathcal{E}_x^- = \mathcal{E}_x^+ + P$. A definition of x guarded by predicate q kills liveness of x in all executions in Q, i.e. at the operation, $\mathcal{E}_x^- = \mathcal{E}_x^+ - Q$. At a definition of y guarded by predicate r, y interferes with x if x is live under predicate r, i.e. if $\mathcal{E}_x^+ \cap R \neq \emptyset$. With respect to interference, it is conservative to overestimate the set of executions in which a variable is live. Therefore, we use **lub_sum** and **lub_diff** to manipulate predicate expressions. Interference is tested using **is_disjoint**.

Figure 7 shows the gen and kill schemata in detail. Operations are processed in reverse order. Within each operation, definitions are processed before uses. Figure 7(a) shows the gen and kill processing for ordinary predicated definitions and uses. Note that the use of the guarding predicate is different from other variable uses

[2]An introduction to standard data flow analysis can be found in the "Dragon Book" [1].

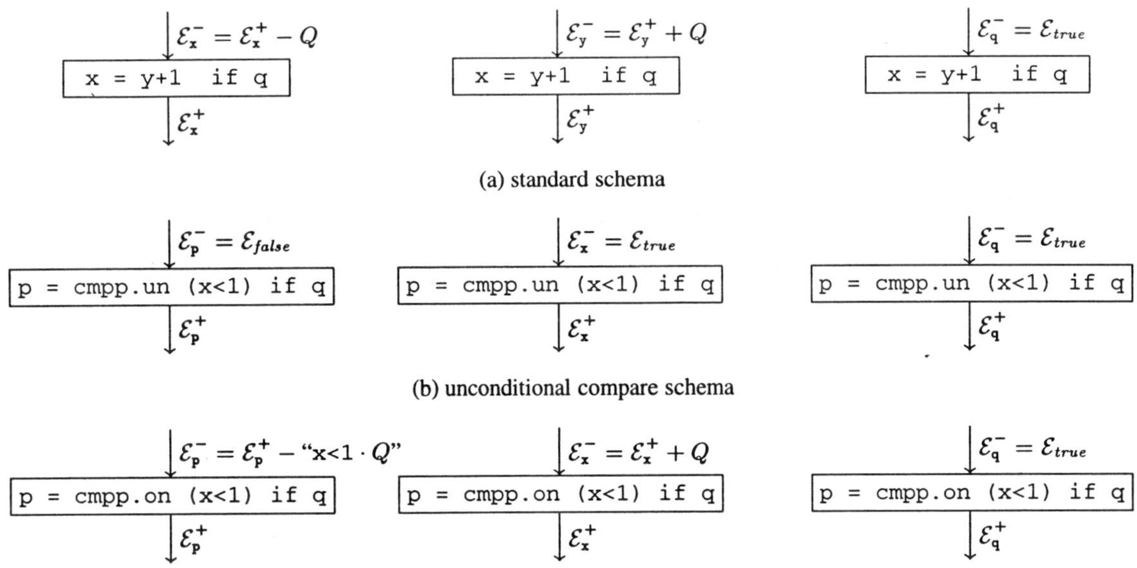

(a) standard schema

(b) unconditional compare schema

(c) parallel-or compare schema

Figure 7. Gen/Kill schemata for liveness analysis of predicated code

in an operation: it is used unconditionally and therefore generates liveness in all executions.

Compare operations require special attention. The unconditional compare operation always reads its source operands and always writes a value to its destination operand(s). Therefore, liveness is killed for destination operands in all executions, yielding the live set $\mathcal{E}_{false}$; liveness is generated for source operands in all executions, yielding the live set $\mathcal{E}_{true}$. This is the same result as for standard predicated operations when the guarding predicate is the constant true.

The parallel-or compare operation writes the value true whenever both the compare condition and guarding predicate are true. This conjunctive condition does not necessarily correspond to any predicate variable in the source code, however it is represented by a predicate symbol in the partition graph. This is due to the way partition relations are generated during extraction. Recall that the extraction algorithm performs a lookup of the string "`(r1<cond>r2)` · q" representing the right-hand subexpression from the sequential SSA form of the parallel-or compare operation. The resulting predicate symbol is the appropriate execution set for which liveness of the destination variable is killed. The gen conditions for source operands are the same as with standard predicated operations.

Now consider predicate-sensitive liveness analysis for variables m and n in Figure 8. Initially, both variables are dead on all executions at the bottom of the predicate block, so at end, $\mathcal{E}_{\mathtt{m}}^- = \mathcal{E}_{\mathtt{n}}^- = \mathcal{E}_{false}$. At the use of n under predicate t in operation k, n becomes live in all executions in set T:

$$\mathcal{E}_{\mathtt{n}}^- = \textbf{lub\_sum}\,(T, \mathcal{E}_{\mathtt{n}}^+) = \textbf{lub\_sum}\,(T, \mathcal{E}_{false}) = T.$$

At the definition of n under predicate r in operation j, n is killed in all of R:

$$\mathcal{E}_{\mathtt{n}}^- = \textbf{lub\_diff}\,(\mathcal{E}_{\mathtt{n}}^+, R) = \textbf{lub\_diff}\,(T, R) = P.$$

Finally, n is defined under p in operation i:

$$\mathcal{E}_{\mathtt{n}}^- = \textbf{lub\_diff}\,(\mathcal{E}_{\mathtt{n}}^+, P) = \textbf{lub\_diff}\,(P, P) = \mathcal{E}_{false}$$

We compute liveness for m in a similar way.

Figure 8(b) shows the live ranges for n and m annotated with predicate expressions. Although the live ranges overlap temporally, the two variables do not interfere. This is seen by examining predicate expressions at definition points. The only definition within both live ranges is the definition of n under predicate p in operation i. Since $P \cap \mathcal{E}_{\mathtt{m}}^+ = P \cap Q = \emptyset$, there is no execution in which both variables are live simultaneously. Therefore, m and n can be assigned the same physical register.

6.2 Global analysis

Predicate-sensitive analysis is performed within predicate blocks and can be used in conjunction with a conventional bitvector based solver. First, local predicate-sensitive analysis is performed on each block to compute transfer functions. These transfer functions summarize the effect of the block without exposing predicate expressions outside the block.

For liveness, a transfer function for a block consists of two bitvectors, GEN and KILL, which represent the overall effect of the block on liveness for each variable. We compute these bitvectors as follows. First, we assume all variables are dead at the block exit, i.e.

$$\mathcal{E}_{\mathtt{x}} = \mathcal{E}_{false}, \text{ for all x.}$$

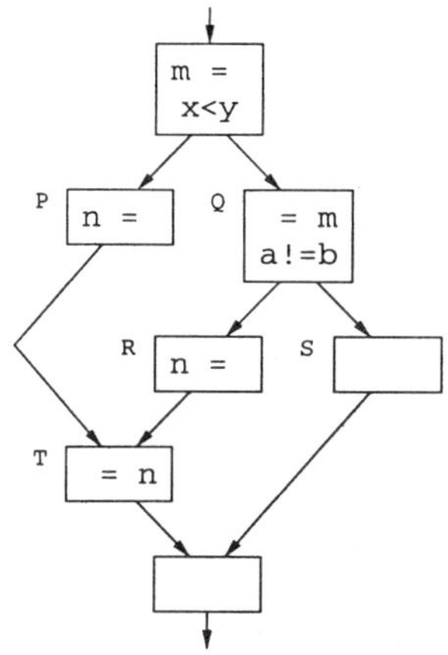

(a) original code

```
      t = false                 if true
      m =                       if true
    p,q = cmpp.un.uc (x<y)      if true
      t = cmpp.on (x<y)         if true
i:    n =                       if p
        = m                     if q
    r,s = cmpp.un.uc (a!=b)     if q
j:    n =                       if r
      t = cmpp.on (a!=b)        if q
k:      = n                     if t
```

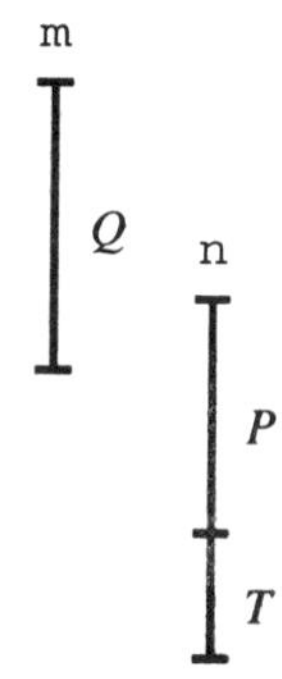

(b) liveness in if-converted code

Figure 8. Liveness analysis of predicated code

Starting with this initial vector of false expressions, we process the operations in reverse order, applying the operator-level liveness rules from Figure 7. At the entry, any variable whose predicate expression is not false is said to be generated by the block, since there is some definition free execution from the block entry to a use of the variable. The bit positions in GEN corresponding to such variables are set to true. Similarly, we compute KILL by assuming that all variables are live in all executions at the block exit, i.e.

$$\mathcal{E}_x = \mathcal{E}_{true}, \text{ for all x.}$$

Again, we perform predicate-sensitive analysis operation-by-operation in reverse order through the block. Any variable whose predicate expression is false is said to be killed, since on every execution a definition is encountered before reaching the first use or the block exit.

A conventional bitvector solver can now be used to compute the solution at block boundaries. Block transfer functions have the following form:

$$live_{in} = (live_{out} - KILL) + GEN.$$

Since predicate-sensitive analysis is localized within block, we retain the efficiency of the global solver. The solution at block boundaries is projected to points within the block by performing a final predicate-sensitive pass over the block, using the boundary values as the initial predicate expression values. More specifically, at each block exit, we assign $\mathcal{E}_X = \mathcal{E}_{true}$ if x is live out, else $\mathcal{E}_{false}$.

An alternative approach is to extend predicate-sensitive analysis beyond individual blocks. A more global predicate-sensitive analysis is beneficial when predicate lifetimes extend beyond predicate blocks. Additionally, global predicate-sensitive analysis can exploit correlations between branch conditions in control flow and therefore enhance the accuracy of analysis beyond traditional methods. Gillies et al [7] present an approach to global predicate-sensitive analysis and demonstrate its utility in register allocation.

7 Conclusion

New architectural features for high-performance computing continue to present new challenges and opportunities to compiler writers. Predicated execution offers substantial benefits to exploiting instruction-level parallelism, from enlarging scheduling scope and eliminating mispredicted branches to providing a means for parallelizing while loops and supporting software pipelining of loops containing complex control flow. To take full advantage of these opportunities, we must be able to work with predicated code as easily as existing compilers work with non-predicated code.

Some early work on understanding predicate relations has been done by Wen-mei Hwu's Impact compiler group at Illinois. They describe a data structure called the predicate hierarchy graph (PHG) [11], which represents the boolean equation under which each predicate is defined. The main use of PHG mentioned in Lin's thesis is to determine if a pair of predicate registers is disjoint. Two predicates are disjoint only if the conjunction of their associated boolean expressions can be simplified to false. Rather than perform predicate-sensitive live range analysis, the approach adopted in the Impact compiler is to apply reverse if-conversion [18] to predicated code, and then perform standard data flow analysis on the resulting control flow graph. This analysis can yield conservative results because the flow graph constructed by reverse if-conversion will in general contain paths that cannot be traversed during any execution.

Eichenberger and Davidson [6] perform local, predicate-sensitive live range analysis by reducing each pair-wise interference query to a satisfiability test of a conjunctive expression representing all the conditions under which the particular interference may occur. Each such query is solved using a powerful symbolic package. Their paper demonstrates the potential benefit of considering predicate relations during register allocation of predicated code, but we believe their approach is impractical for use in a production compiler.

In this paper, we have presented several techniques for analysis of predicated code. First, we addressed the problem of understanding relations between predicates. We model relations between predicates in terms of relations between execution sets, and we developed an algebra of predicate expressions to approximate execution sets. We introduced the predicate partition graph for representing and manipulating predicate expressions, and we showed how this graph can be built directly from predicated code.

We described the predicate query system, a system for manipulating predicate expressions to answer queries about predicate relations. The predicate query system makes use of partition graphs to perform these tasks efficiently. We have explored several classes of algorithms that trade-off accuracy for efficiency, and we presented one class of efficient algorithms that sacrifice little accuracy.

Finally, we showed how predicate expressions and the predicate query system are used to perform predicate-sensitive data flow analysis within predicate blocks. We use this analysis in our research compiler to perform data dependence and live range analysis to support hyperblock scheduling, software pipelining, and register allocation. By localizing predicate-sensitive analysis within predicate blocks, we retain the efficiency of bitvector solvers globally while performing high-quality analysis locally.

This work provides a starting point for further study of predicated code. In future work, we hope to show how performance of generated code varies as trade-offs are made between accuracy and efficiency of analysis. Predicated execution also opens up new opportunities in optimization; we intend to explore this area in detail.

Acknowledgments

The authors would like to thank Roy Ju and other members of the HP California Language Laboratory for their many interesting and useful discussions of predicates. We also thank the referees for their extensive comments.

References

[1] A. V. Aho, R. Sethi, and J. D. Ullman. *Compilers: Principles, Techniques, and Tools*. Addison-Wesley, Reading, MA, 1986.

[2] J. R. Allen, K. Kennedy, C. Portfield, and J. Warren. Conversion of control dependence to data dependence. In *Conference Record of the 10th Annual ACM Symposium on Principles of Programming Languages*, pages 177–189, Austin, Texas, Jan. 24–26, 1983.

[3] G. J. Chaitin. Register allocation and spilling via graph coloring. In *Proceedings of the 1982 SIGPLAN Symposium on Compiler Construction*, pages 98–105, Boston, Massachusetts, June 23–25, 1982. Published as ACM SIGPLAN Notices 17(6).

[4] J. C. Dehnert, P. Y.-T. Hsu, and J. P. Bratt. Overlapped loop support in the Cydra 5. In *Third International Conference on Architectural Support for Programming Languages and Operating Systems*, pages 26–38, Boston, Massachusetts, Apr. 3–6, 1989.

[5] J. C. Dehnert and R. A. Towle. Compiling for the Cydra 5. *IEEE Computer*, 7(1/2):181–227, 1993.

[6] A. E. Eichenberger and E. S. Davidson. Register allocation for predicated code. In *Proceedings of the 28th Annual International Symposium on Microarchitecture*, pages 180–191, Ann Arbor, Michigan, Nov. 29–Dec. 1, 1995.

[7] D. M. Gillies, D. R. Ju, R. Johnson, and M. Schlansker. Global predicate analysis and its application to register allocation. In *Proceedings of the 28th Annual International Symposium on Microarchitecture*, Paris, France, Dec. 2–4, 1996.

[8] Hewlett-Packard Company. *PA-RISC 1.1 Architecture and Instruction Set Reference Manual*. Prentice-Hall, second edition, 1992.

[9] P. Y. T. Hsu and E. S. Davidson. Highly concurrent scalar processing. In *Proceedings of the 13th Annual International Symposium on Computer Architecture*, pages 386–395, Tokyo, Japan, June 2–5, 1986.

[10] V. Kathail, M. Schlansker, and B. Rau. HPL PlayDoh architecture specification: Version 1.0. Technical Report HPL-93-80, Hewlett-Packard Laboratories, Feb. 1993.

[11] D. C. Lin. Compiler support for predicated execution in superscalar processors. Master's thesis, University of Illinois at Urbana-Champaign, 1990.

[12] S. A. Mahlke, R. E. Hank, R. A. Bringmann, J. C. Gyllenhaal, D. M. Gallagher, and W. Hwu. Characterizing the impact of predicated execution on branch predication. In *Proceedings of the 27th Annual International Symposium on Microarchitecture*, pages 217–227, San Jose, California, Nov. 30–Dec. 2, 1994.

[13] S. A. Mahlke, D. C. Lin, W. Y. Chen, R. E. Hank, and R. A. Bringmann. Effective compiler support for predicated execution using the hyperblock. In *Proceedings of the 25th Annual International Symposium on Microarchitecture*, pages 45–54, Portland, Oregon, Dec. 1–4, 1992.

[14] J. C. H. Park and M. Schlansker. On predicated execution. Technical Report HPL-91-58, Hewlett-Packard Software and Systems Laboratory, May 1991.

[15] B. Rau, D. Yen, W. Yen, and R. Towle. The Cydra 5 departmental supercomputer: Design philosophies, decisions, and trade-offs. *IEEE Computer*, 22(1):12–35, Jan. 1989.

[16] M. Schlansker and V. Kathail. Critical path reduction for scalar programs. In *Proceedings of the 28th Annual International Symposium on Microarchitecture*, pages 57–69, Ann Arbor, Michigan, Nov. 29–Dec. 1, 1995.

[17] G. S. Tyson. The effects of predicated execution on branch prediction. In *Proceedings of the 27th Annual International Symposium on Microarchitecture*, pages 196–206, San Jose, California, Nov. 30–Dec. 2, 1994.

[18] N. J. Warter, S. A. Mahlke, W. W. Hwu, and B. R. Rau. Reverse if-conversion. In *Proceedings of the SIGPLAN '93 Conference on Programming Language Design and Implementation*, pages 290–299, Albuquerque, New Mexico, June 23–25, 1993.

Global Predicate Analysis and its Application to Register Allocation

David M. Gillies, Dz-ching Roy Ju
Hewlett-Packard California Language Lab
11000 Wolfe Road, Cupertino, CA 95014
{ dgillies, royju }@cup.hp.com

Richard Johnson, Michael Schlansker
Hewlett-Packard Laboratories
1501 Page Mill Road, Palo Alto, CA 94304
{ rjohnson, schlansk }@hpl.hp.com

Abstract

To fully utilize the wide machine resources in modern high-performance microprocessors it is necessary to exploit parallelism beyond individual basic blocks. Architectural support for predicated execution increases the degree of instruction level parallelism by allowing instructions from different basic blocks to be converted to straight-line code guarded by boolean predicates. However, predicated execution also presents significant challenges to an optimizing compiler. For example, in live range analysis, a predicated definition does not necessarily end the live range of a virtual register.

This paper describes techniques to analyze the relations among predicates in order to improve the precision and effectiveness of various compiler analysis and transformation phases in the presence of predicated code. Our predicate analysis operates globally to obtain relations among predicates. Moreover, we analyze control flow and predication in a single unified framework. The result can be queried by subsequent optimization and analysis phases. Based on this framework, we extend a traditional method to a predicate-aware register allocator which takes global predicate relations into account. We have implemented the proposed algorithms to effectively reduce register pressure. Our experimental results show 24.6% of a large test suite obtain, on average, 20.71% better register allocation due to the algorithms presented in this paper.

1 Introduction

VLIW (Very Long Instruction Word) and superscalar architectures can exploit significant amounts of instruction level parallelism (ILP) to achieve improved performance in application programs. Parallelism within individual basic blocks are generally insufficient to fully utilize wide machine resources. Predicated execution [9, 11] is an architectural model to exploit parallelism across basic blocks. In this model instructions from different basic blocks are converted to straight-line code guarded by boolean predicates. Architectural support for predicated execution varies from general support for predication in the Cydra 5 [16] and HPL PlayDoh architectures [11] to conditional skip instructions in the HP PA-RISC architecture [8], conditional nullify instructions in the Sun SPARC architecture [19], and conditional move instructions in the DEC Alpha architecture [3]. In a general predicated execution model, the execution of an instruction is guarded by a boolean qualifying predicate. Each qualifying predicate can be regarded as a 1-bit predicate register. An example of a predicated instruction is

```
x = y + z        if p
```

where p is the qualifying predicate which controls whether the instruction executes and updates the architectural state. To explore predication, a compiler generally incorporates a technique called *if-conversion*, which eliminates branch instructions and converts affected instructions to appropriate predicated forms. If-conversion effectively converts control flow into data flow [1].

However, in order to achieve these benefits, predication presents a challenge to many conventional analysis and transformation phases performed in an optimizing compiler. For example, consider the code in Example 1.

Example 1:

```
S1:  p,q = cmpp.un.uc  (a < b)    if true
S2:  x = ..                       if p
S3:  y = ..                       if q
S4:  .. = x                       if p
S5:  .. = y                       if q
```

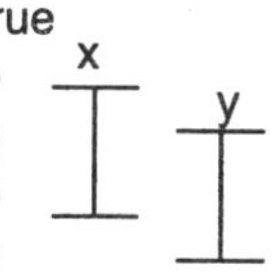

The cmpp instruction sets p true and q false if the condition (a < b) is true and reverses these values if the condition is false. (The details of the architectural model are described in Section 2.) Variable x is defined and used under p and variable y is defined and used under q. A conventional live range analysis would find the live range of x from S2 to S4 and the live range of y from S3 to S5. Based on this analysis, a traditional register allocator would conclude that x and y interfere with each other and subsequently assign different physical registers to them. However, since p and q are complementary, x and y will never hold valid values at the same time and thus they can share the same physical register. The focus of this work is to develop a practical and efficient mechanism to track global predicate relations in an entire procedure. This mechanism can be used to improve data flow analysis and optimizations in the presence of predicated code. As an important application, we demonstrate how a register allocator can benefit from understanding and utilizing the predicate relations.

1072-4451/96 $5.00 © 1996 IEEE

The IMPACT compiler uses a predicate hierarchy graph (PHG) to track the boolean equations for all of the predicates in a hyperblock [14]. The scope of their predicate analysis is a hyperblock and does not extend globally. When a companion data structure, like PHG, is maintained with the code, then it may require updating whenever the program is transformed. The work in [18] proposes a reverse if-conversion scheme to map predicates from the data flow domain back to the more familiar control flow domain. A major drawback of this approach is that, during the remapping process, some originally non-existent control paths may be created. This typically occurs when code is if-converted and then permuted by instruction scheduling. When this code is reverse if-converted, non-existent paths may cause conservative treatment in subsequent analyses and transformations. The work in [7] solves this register allocation problem by representing predicates as P-facts -- logically invariant expressions. The mechanism concludes that two live ranges do not interfere if the intersection of the two sets of P-facts can be simplified to false using a symbolic package. This approach is also restricted to the scope of a hyperblock, and may have limited practicality given the potential exponential compilation time behavior with respect to the number of predicates. The authors in [10] propose a representation called *predicate partition graph* to track the relations in predicates, and they describe how to construct a partition graph for the predicates in a hyperblock. Their work uses the partition graph to provide information to support data flow analysis.

The false interference in Example 1 can be avoided by a predicate analysis which analyzes the local predicate relations in the straight-line code between two branches. The code fragment in Example 2 shows the importance of recognizing predicate relations in a global scope, where code may be partially if-converted based on the profitability model in an if-converter. Both of x and y are defined and used in different basic blocks. To check for interferences, one would propagate the use of x under p to the else-clause towards the definition of x under r. While crossing the definition of y under s during this process, an interference will be assumed between x and y unless one can assert that p and s are disjoint. Since p and s are defined in the then- and else- clauses, respectively, p and s can never both be true at the same time. However, it requires global analysis to systematically take control flow into account to assert the disjointness between p and s. This relation cannot be captured by a hyperblock or basic block based analysis. Further, with global predicate analysis, one can also assert that p and r are disjoint. Therefore, the definition of x under r can never reach the use of x under p, and this definition is dead.

Our work is based on the predicate partition graph in [10]. The main contributions of our work are as follows: (1) We uniformly track relationships describing both control flow and explicit uses of predicates at a global scope by mapping them to a single partition graph. To the best of our knowledge, this is the first global predicate analysis framework. (2) We have developed and implemented practical algorithms for global predicate analysis and global predicate-aware register allocation using a generalized data flow framework. (3) We have demonstrated the effectiveness and practicality of this approach through experiments which show significant benefits of predicate-aware register allocation.

Example 2:

```
p, q, r, s = false
if ( .. ) then {
   p,q = cmpp.un.uc   (...)          if true
   x = ..                            if p
} else {
   r,s = cmpp.un.uc   (...)          if true
   x = ..                            if r
   y = ..                            if s
}
.. = x                               if p
.. = y                               if s
```

The rest of the paper has the following structure: Section 2 illustrates the architectural model for predication. Section 3 provides a brief overview of the predicate partition graph which is used to track the relations of predicates. Section 4 discusses the details on how to construct a single connected partition graph including both control flow and explicit predicates in an entire procedure. Section 5 presents the details of a predicate-aware register allocator, which exploits the relations of predicates during live range analysis and interference graph construction. Section 6 shows the experimental results in comparing the predicate-aware register allocator against a conventional register allocator. Section 7 provides conclusions.

2 Architectural Model

In this paper, we will assume the architectural support of general predicated execution model provided in the HPL PlayDoh architecture [11], in which the execution of an instruction can be guarded by a qualifying predicate. The following form of compare instructions is provided to set predicates.

```
p1, p2 = cmpp.<d1><d2> (a rel b)   if qp
```

Predicates p1 and p2 are two destination predicates. Each of <d1> and <d2> is a two-letter descriptor that specifies a type and mode for the compare instruction. There are four comparison types: *unconditional* (u), *conditional* (c), *parallel-or* (o), and *parallel-and* (a), specified by the first letter of the descriptor. Each type has both a normal mode (n) and a complement mode (c), specified by the second letter of the descriptor. Descriptors <d1> and <d2> control destination predicates p1 and p2, respectively. The condition, (a rel b), is in the form of a logical comparison of two variables a and b, where *rel* can be eq, ne, lt, etc. Predicate qp is the qualifying predicate.

To simplify the discussion, for the unconditional and conditional types, we assume they are always generated in form of cmpp.un.uc and cmpp.cn.cc, respectively. Therefore, for a comparison with the unconditional type, the values of p1 and p2 are complementary. If the comparison type is *and* (*or*) and qp is true, the *an* (*on*) target predicate (say p1) is equal to the result of (a rel b) "*and*"ed ("*or*"ed) with the old value of p1.

Table 1. Behaviors of predicates in compare instructions

qp	(a rel b)	un	uc	cn	cc	on	oc	an	ac
F	X	F	F	nc	nc	nc	nc	nc	nc
T	T	T	F	T	F	T	nc	nc	F
T	F	F	T	F	T	nc	T	F	nc

Table 1 is the summary on how the destination predicates are set in these compare instructions. In the table, T and F stand for true and false values, respectively. X means "don't care" and nc means that the result is unchanged. We also assume that there is a special predicate register p0, where any read is always true and any write is discarded.

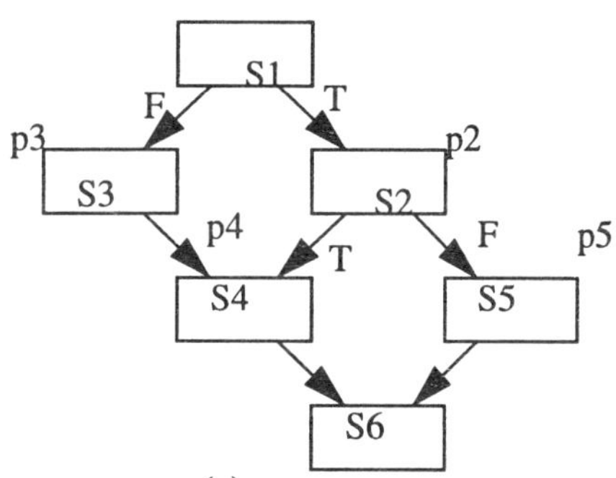

(a)

```
I1: p2, p3 = cmpp.un.uc  (s1 cond)  if true
I2: p4 = cmpp.uc  (s1 cond)         if true
I3: S2                              if p2
I4: p5 = cmpp.uc (s2 cond)          if p2
I5: p4 = cmpp.on  (s2 cond)         if p2
I6: S3                              if p3
I7: S5                              if p5
I8: S4                              if p4
I9: S6                              if true
```

(b)

Figure 1. (a) Control flow graph and (b) if-converted code.

Figure 1 shows an example, which contains the original control flow graph and the if-converted code. The branch condition of basic block containing S*n* is represented as (S*n* cond). If-conversion converts all six basic blocks into a single basic block with predicated code. Each of the switch points at the respective basic blocks containing S1 and S2 is converted to a compare instruction with an unconditional type. The merge (or confluence) point at the basic block containing S4 is converted to the combination of one compare instruction with an unconditional type and one compare instruction with an *or* type.

3 Overview of Predicate Partition Graph

In this work, we use the notion of predicate partition graph proposed in [10] to track the relations among predicates. To simplify the discussion, we assume that predicates are in static single assignment (SSA) form, where each predicate is statically defined no more than once. However, this is not required by our implementation. For the example in Figure 1, p4 is defined twice. To describe references to p4 in SSA form, the related definitions and uses are translated into the following intermediate form.

```
...
p4_1 = cmpp.uc (...)          if true
...
px = cmpp.un(s2 cond)         if p2
p4_2 = p4_1 | px              if true
...
S4                            if p4_2
...
```

We use the concept of an execution set to describe the relations among predicates. We first define the following notations for straight-line code and extend them to incorporate control flow in the next section. An execution *trace* includes all of the instructions being executed from the beginning to the end in straight-line code. A trace belongs to the *domain* of predicate p, if all of the instructions on this trace are executed when p is true. The domain of p includes all such traces. If unambiguous, we will simply use p to mean the domain of p. A *partition* of a predicate is a division of the domain of the predicate into multiple disjoint subsets, where the union of these subsets is equal to the domain. For example, the pictorial view of the relations among the predicates in instruction `p1,p2=cmpp.un.uc (...) if p3` is in Figure 2. When p3 is true, the values of p1 and p2 are always complementary. In another words, no trace exists where p1 and p2 are both true. One can also derive that if p1 or p2 is true, p3 must be true.

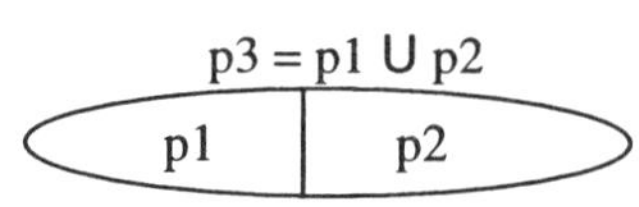

Figure 2. Set relations between predicate domains.

In a *predicate partition graph*, G=(V, E), each node p in V represents predicate p and each edge (p, q) represents that there exists a partition in p such that q is a subset in this partition. An edge in G is directed and the edges created from the same partition are given the same label. For example, partition p0 = p1 U p2 would be represented by two edges: p0->p1 and p0->p2, where both edges are assigned the same label. G is a directed acyclic graph, and there may be multiple edges between two given nodes due to different partitions. A partition graph is *complete* if the universal set, p0, is the unique root. This makes every node reachable from the root as is required by the algorithms used in predicate analysis. Because the partition graph approximates predicate relations, one may construct different partition graphs with varying accuracy for a single code sequence.

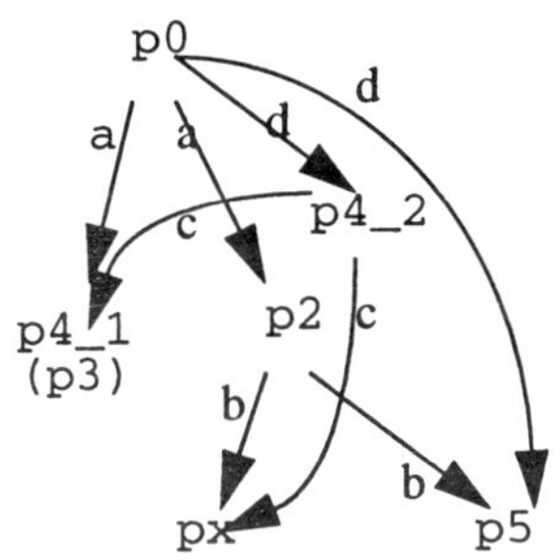

Figure 3. A partition graph for the example in Figure 1.

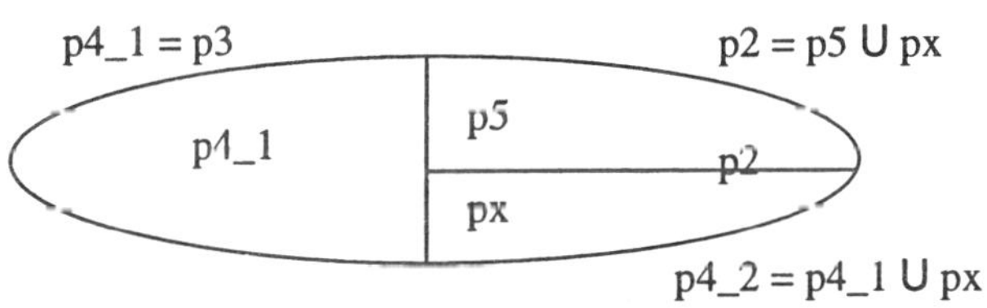

Figure 4. Domains of predicates in Figure 1.

A partition graph for the if-converted code in Figure 1(b) is shown in Figure 3. The pictorial view of the partitions shown in Figure 4 helps understand how domains are partitioned. The root of the partition graph, p0, is partitioned into p2 and p3 in instruction I1. Since instructions I1 and I2 both have an unconditional compare type and check for the same condition, these two instructions are essentially value congruent. Therefore, p3 and p4_1 always have the same value and can be mapped to the same predicate node. In I4, p2 is partitioned into p5 and an implicit predicate px, which is created to complete this partition. In I5, the union of px and p4_1 makes up the domain for p4_2. We can also find that the complement of p4_2 is p5 and generate another partition with p0 as the parent predicate and p4_2 and p5 as the child predicates. This step is necessary to make p4_2 reachable from the root.

Once a partition graph is constructed, one can use simple graph traversal algorithms to support a number of different queries on predicate relations. Readers are referred to [10] for further details on the properties of the partition graph and the implementation of various queries. We list below only the queries used in our predicate-aware register allocator.

`IsDisjoint(p,q)`: asks whether the domain of predicate p overlaps with that of predicate q. Two predicates are disjoint if they can reach a common ancestor through different edges of the same partition. For example, in Figure 3, p3 and p5 are disjoint, but p2 and p4_2 are not. Note this is obvious from the domain relations in Figure 4, where px is a subset of both p2 and p4_2. It is straightforward to extend this query to `IsDisjoint`(p, Q), where Q is a set of predicates, and the answer is true if p is disjoint from every predicate in Q.

`LeastUpperBoundSum(p,Q)` : adds predicate p to a set of predicates, Q. The domain of the resultant set is the smallest superset of the union of the domain of p and the domain of Q. The resultant set is expected to be simplified in the way that if all of the child predicates in a partition appear in the union of p and Q, these child predicates are replaced with their parent predicate.

`LeastUpperBoundDiff(p,Q)` : subtracts predicate p from a set of predicates, Q. The domain of the resultant set is the smallest superset of the domain of Q subtracted by the domain of p. For the example in Figure 3, px is equal to `LeastUpperBoundDiff`(p5, p2).

4 Global Predicate Partition Graph and its Construction

Previous work in predicate analysis are generally based on the scope of a *hyperblock*, which is an if-converted single-entry multiple-exit control flow region. In our work, each node in a control flow graph (CFG) is still a basic block, which is a single-entry single-exit straight line sequence of possibly predicated code. One advantage of this representation is that this is the most familiar representation to compiler analyses and optimizations. We assume that a CFG has a single start node and a single stop node. Our global predicate analysis operates on an entire procedure. Global predicate analysis provides more precise predicate relations when predicates are defined and used in different basic blocks.

We now extend previously defined notations to an entire procedure. A *trace* includes all of the executed instructions on an acyclic path from the start node to the end node in a CFG. A trace belongs to the *domain* of predicate p, if all of the instructions on this trace are executed when p is true. Analogous to predicates, we define the domain of a basic block to be all of the traces such that the basic block is executed. Therefore, when a basic block can be reached from another basic block (or vice versa), the domains of these two basic blocks are not disjoint. This control flow reachability information is expressed in a global partition graph to track relations among basic blocks regardless of the existence of predicates.

In order to uniformly treat control flow and predication, we assign a predicate to each basic block. We call a predicate assigned to a basic block a *control predicate* and a predicate which explicitly appears in the instruction stream a *materialized predicate*. A control predicate of a basic block is viewed as a predicate combining all of the conditions which control whether the basic block will be executed or not. We perform global predicate analysis based on building a single *complete* predicate partition graph which includes both control predicates and materialized predicates. This single partition graph allows us to uniformly track the semantics of conditional execution through program branches as well as predicated execution. Note that our if-converter assures that if a control predicate is also materialized to a materialized predicate, they share the same domain and are mapped to the same node in the partition graph. This further improves the precision of the predicate analysis.

The graph construction mechanism described below can be invoked anywhere throughout an optimizer. This can be done either before or after if-conversion. This flexibility is again due to that fact that we treat control flow and materialized predicates in a uniform way. Although if-conversion is the major source of creating materialized predicates, phases like expanding high level pseudo code may also emit predicated code. Data flow analyses both before and after if-conversion can be more precise for predicated code by knowing the global relations among materialized predicates.

The above discussion associates the control flow and data flow aspects of predicates. The following two subsections illustrate the construction of a partition graph for control predicates and materialized predicates, respectively.

4.1 Handling Control Predicates

In order to analyze control flow, control predicates are assigned to basic blocks and partitions are formed at control flow switch and merge points. Although special attention is given to the following control flow structures, our predicate analysis handles any arbitrary control flow graph including irreducible graphs.

Critical Edges - A critical edge is defined as an edge whose source has more than one successor and whose destination has more than one predecessor. For example, the edge from S2 to S4 in Figure 1(a) is a critical edge. At a switch (merge) point, a critical edge prevents the use of the destination (source) node's control predicate as a child predicate in the partition. This occurs because, on this critical edge, the source (destination) node does not dominate (post-dominate) the destination (source) node. To resolve this problem, we conceptually create a node on a critical edge and assign an implicit predicate to the node. Note that this edge splitting is only done at a conceptual level without actually changing the CFG. With this virtual edge splitting, all predecessors dominate their successors at switch points and all successors post-dominate their predecessors at merge points. This simplifies the creation of partitions. Note that if node p dominates or post-dominates node q, p can always be an ancestor of q in the partition graph.

Back Edges - Back edges are those edges which complete cycles in a CFG. With current techniques, if we were to take back edges into account in predicate analysis, there is little useful information that we can derive for predicates. For example, for an if-then-else construct enclosed in a loop, the then- and else- clauses will never both be executed in the same iteration, but they may be in different iterations. Therefore, the predicates assigned to the two clauses are disjoint within a particular iteration, but not necessarily across iterations. The results of this predicate analysis are interpreted with back edges ignored. This has little impact on the accuracy of the analysis. This is partially due to the fact that the if-converter is already restricted to acyclic regions. Section 5 will discuss the approximation of data flow information through back edges.

During partition graph construction, back edges are also split by assigning virtual nodes to them. Our analysis is also applicable to irreducible graphs. However, because the back edges are selected rather arbitrarily for an irreducible graph, the results may be less precise.

Figure 5 presents an algorithm to construct a partition graph based on control predicates. The input is a CFG. Edge splitting is first performed on critical edges and back edges. Finding control equivalent nodes is not essential for correctness, but instead improves the accuracy of predicate analysis as predicates with equivalent domains are mapped to the same node. We then create partitions at all program switch and merge points to track the predicate relations. Finally, if any non-start node does not have a parent node, a partition is created to link it to its immediate dominator to make the partition graph *complete*.

We now demonstrate how to construct the partition graph in Figure 3 based on the CFG in Figure 1(a) in analogy to an earlier discussion in Section 3 on constructing the same graph based on the if-converted code. Node S1 is the start node in the CFG and is given p0 as its control predicate. Node S6 is control equivalent to S1 and is assigned with p0 as well. The control predicates assigned to the rest of nodes are as shown in Figure 1(a). The a partition (as marked in Figure 3) is created due to the switch point at S1. The edge from S2 to S4 is a critical edge, and px is assigned to this edge to achieve edge splitting. The b partition is created due to the switch point at S2. The c and d partitions are created due to the merge points at S4 and S6, respectively.

```
ConstructPartitionGraphForControlPredicates(CFG) {
  Create a virtual node on each critical edge or back edge
  Find control equivalent nodes
  Assign a predicate to each set of control equivalent nodes

  for every node in the CFG {
    v = current node
    p = control predicate assigned to v
    if( number of successors > 1)
      Create a partition with p as the parent predicate and
      predicates assigned to the successors as the child
      predicates
    if( number of predecessors > 1)
      Create a partition with p as the parent predicate and
      predicates assigned to the predecessors as the child
      predicates, if this partition has not been generated yet
  }
  if a non-start node, u, has no parent, create a partition with
  the immediate dominator of u as the parent predicate, and
  u and an implicit predicate as the child predicates
}
```

Figure 5. Algorithm of constructing partition graph for control predicates.

4.2 Handling Materialized Predicates

This subsection discusses the details of constructing a partition graph which captures local relations among materialized predicates. The relations among materialized predicates are created at each point where predicates are defined, i.e. compare instructions. Figure 6 presents an algorithm to construct a partition graph for materialized predicates. The most common case of defining materialized predicates is a compare instruction with an unconditional type. In Figure 6, a partition is created with pp as the parent predicate and p1 and p2 as the disjoint child predicates. If qp is p0, we can view that the current instruction is guarded by bp which is the control predicate of the basic block, and the union of the domains of p1 and p2 is the domain of bp. Therefore, we build a partition with control predicate bp as the parent predicate. This is the key to establish the relations between control predicates and materialized predicates and to allow predicate analysis at a global scope. If qp is not p0, all of the control conditions affecting whether this instruction will be executed have been synthesized into the definition of qp. This is ensured in our implementation. Therefore, if qp is not p0, the union of p1 and p2 is qp and there is no need to build a partition to link p1 and p2 to bp. One can conclude that the domain of the actual predicate (pp) guarding the compare instruction is always a subset of the domain of bp.

The other three types of compare instructions involve updating a predicate, where the previous value of a predicate affects the new predicate result. We treat these compare types conservatively because they appear infrequently and are not easily modeled by the partition graph. For a compare instruction with a conditional type, if qp is p0, this instruction is effectively an unconditional type and is treated in the same way as the unconditional type. If qp is not p0, we simply map p1 and p2 to a dummy predicate node and during queries to the predicate analysis they are treated in a conservative manner. Note that if both of *on* and *oc* (or *an* and *ac*) target predicates appear in a compare instruction, we treat them being split into two single-target cmpp's, which are then processed separately. For an *and* type compare instruction, the domain of p1 is always a subset of that of p1_old. For an *or* type compare instruction, the domain of p1 is always a superset of that of p1_old and a partition is created to link p1 to control predicate cp to make the partition graph *complete*.

```
ConstructPartitionGraphForMaterializedPredicates
(instruction stream + CFG) {
  for every compare instruction in CFG {
    cinst = current compare instruction
    qp = qualifying predicate of cinst
    bp = control predicate assigned to the basic block
      containing cinst
    p1 = the first destination predicate
    p1_old = the old definition of p1 if p1 is an update
    p2 = the second destination predicate if exists
    pp = parent predicate
    If( qp == p0 )  pp = bp  else  pp = qp

    switch (compare type) {
      case .un.uc:
        Create a partition with pp as the parent predicate
        and p1 and p2 as child predicates
      case .cn.cc:
        if( qp == p0 )  process in the same way as a
          .un.uc case
        else   map p1 and p2 to a dummy predicate node
      case .an (.ac):
        Create a partition with p1_old as the parent predi-
        cate and p1 and an implicit predicate as child pred-
        icates
      case .on (.oc):
        Create a partition with p1 as the parent predicate
        and p1_old and an implicit predicate as child predi-
        cates
        Create a partition with pp as the parent  predicate
        and p1 and an implicit predicate as child predicates
    }
  }
}
```

Figure 6. Algorithm of constructing partition graph for materialized predicates.

Based on the algorithms in Figures 5 and 6, the partition graph in Figure 7 is constructed to capture the global relations for predicates in Example 2. The basic block containing the if-clause is assigned with p0 as its control predicate to become the root of the partition graph. The then- and else- clauses are assigned with p_then and p_else as their control predicates, respectively. The initialization of predicates to false does not create any predicate node in the partition graph. The a partition is created at the switch point in the control flow due to the if-then-else construct. The b partition is created due to the compare instruction assigning the materialized predicates, p and q, in the then-clause. The c partition is created due to the compare instruction assigning the materialized predicates, r and s, in the else-clause. This partition graph tracks the global predicate relation that p, q, r, and s are disjoint, which is necessary to assert that x and y do not interfere with each other.

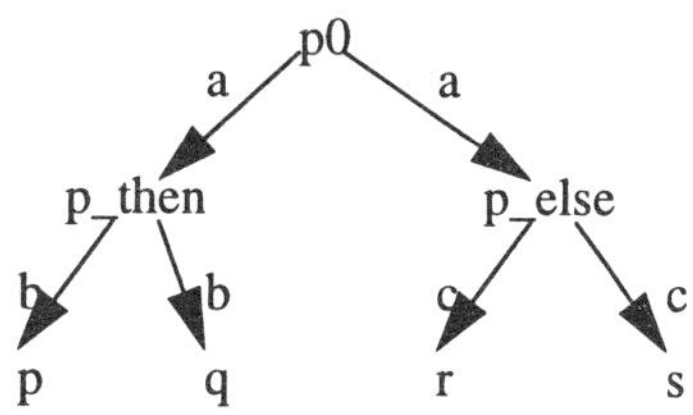

Figure 7. The partition graph for Example 2.

We have implemented the algorithms in Figures 5 and 6 and used them in our predicate-aware register allocator to obtain the experimental results in Section 6. There are two common patterns of compare instructions generated by our if-converter. For a program switch point, a cmpp.un.uc instruction is generated, and the algorithm in Figure 6 models this precisely. For an unstructured program merge point (often due to a critical edge), a combination of cmpp.un.uc and cmpp.on (or cmpp.oc) instructions is generated. The algorithm in Figure 6 is always correct but may be conservative for a comparison instruction with an *or* type. This is because in this initial implementation we did not track the compare conditions controlling predicates nor apply value numbering on predicates as proposed in [10]. For example, for the if-converted code in Figure 1(b), without value numbering we do not recognize that p3 and p4_1 can be mapped to the same predicate node and are unable to obtain that p4_2 is the union of p4_1 and px. However, this type of unstructured merge only accounts for a small portion (< 10% in our experience) of the if-converted compare instructions. In the future, we will model comparison instructions with an *or* type more precisely.

5 Predicate-aware Register Allocation

The problem of global register allocation is well known [4, 5, 6] and good heuristic approximations have been developed to solve the problem. However, predication creates new challenges for the established techniques. In the quest for greater instruction level parallelism through predication many register live ranges are created which, with current analysis techniques, will appear to overlap. Without applying knowledge of the relationships among predicates a large number of false interferences will arise. Our experiments show the resulting register allocation will conservatively allocate far more registers than are necessary.

Example 3:

```
loop:
S1:    p, q = cmpp.un.uc (a<b)   if true
S2:    x = ...                   if p
S3:    y = ...                   if q
S4:    ... = x                   if p
S5:    ... = y                   if q
S6:    z = ...                   if true
S7:    ... = z                   if true
S8:    w = ...                   if true
S9:    ... = w                   if true
       Branch loop
```

Example 3 illustrates the need for predicate-aware register allocation. This code sequence arises from if-conversion and simple list scheduling. As was pointed out in Section 1, without any knowledge of the relationship between p and q we will conservatively infer that x and y interfere. Additionally, it is difficult to conclude that a predicated definition ends a live range. To do so we must know that the definition's qualifying predicate is a superset of all predicates under which it is currently live. In this example, the live range of y begins at S5 but, without tracking all the predicates under which y is live, we cannot deduce that it is ended at S3. Conservative data flow analysis will then cause the live range for y to extend around the back-edge of the loop to interfere with w at S8 and z at S6. This originally short live range now interferes with every other live range defined in the loop. If the number of live ranges within a loop body of this type is greater than n, where n is the number of registers available on the target machine, spilling must occur. This example is presented in terms of liveness around the back-edge of a loop but the same situation also occurs in straight-line code.

When predicates cannot be accurately analyzed, the spilling of predicated code must be handled carefully to ensure that the graph coloring algorithm terminates. That is, if we are not able to infer the end of a predicated live range x correctly then we cannot do so for x's predicated spill code either.

Figure 8(b) shows the desired spill code for the two instruction sequence shown in Figure 8(a). To allow coloring to progress after spilling, without predicate analysis and from the code stream alone, we must arrange for each component of the spilled live range to be definitively ended by an unpredicated definition. To this end we insert unpredicated *kill* pseudo-ops to mark the end of live ranges.

```
x = ...    if m             y = ...          if m
                            st[spill] = y    if m
. . .                       . . .
                            ld z = [spill]   if n
... = x    if n             ... = z          if n
     (a)                        (b)

S1:    <Kill y>             if true
S2:    y = ...              if m
S3:    st [spill] = y       if m
       . . .
S4:    <Kill z>             if true
S5:    ld z = [spill]       if n
S6:    ... = z              if n
              (c)
```

Figure 8. Spill code difficulties: (a) Sequence to be spilled. (b) Desired spill code. (c) Worst case spill code.

There are a great number of practical problems in performing register allocation for predicated code. We have enhanced traditional global data flow analysis and interference graph construction to address these problems. Section 5.1 describes extensions necessary to enhance a traditional register allocation scheme to build a predicate-aware interference graph for a single basic block using conservative data flow information. Section 5.2 describes enhancements to the traditional global liveness data flow calculation, procedure-wide interference graph construction and the benefit of using global scheduling regions as boundaries for predicated live range analysis. Section 5.3 discusses approximations which may occur in live range analysis.

5.1 Local Analysis

Register allocators typically construct an interference graph by first calculating a bit-vector of all currently live registers at each point in the CFG. The bit-vector is initialized at the bottom of each basic block to all those registers which were computed to be *live out* by a previous pass of data flow analysis. The bit-vector is then propagated through the instruction stream to the top of the basic block. At each instruction an interference is recorded between each *def* and all elements of the bit-vector, then the *defs* are removed from the bit-vector and all *uses* added.

Our technique builds upon the standard bit-vector style interference graph construction algorithm. We first scan the basic block and collect the set of predicates used in the code stream and then augment the set with p0, the always true predicate. This set is termed the *basis of analysis* for the basic block or, more simply, the *basis*. We then allocate a bit-vector for each (predicate) element in the basis. This bit-vector represents liveness with respect to each of its basis elements. We call this data structure a *LiveSet*. We augment each LiveSet with an identifying basis *tag* to ease data flow propagation. In the absence of predicated code this scheme reduces to the traditional unpredicated case, since the basis contains only p0, and a LiveSet is a single bit-vector.

	w	x	y	z
p0	0	0	0	0
p	0	1	0	0
q	0	0	1	0

Figure 9. LiveSet for example in Example 3 after processing S4.

Figure 9 depicts the LiveSet for Example 3 after processing the instruction marked S4 in the backward traversal. Liveness is indicated by the bit value 1. This LiveSet represents the fact that x is live only under p and y is live only under q at this point. At S3, y is defined under q. Since x is live under p, and p and q are disjoint, we discover there is no interference between x and y.

In the next few subsections we will develop the machinery necessary to build the interference graph in the presence of predication. This machinery naturally extends from single basic blocks to arbitrary regions or entire procedures.

```
AssertLiveUnderPredicate(x, qp) {
    let A = { p in the basis | x is live under p }
    // Already live
    if qp is a member of A return
    // Minimize the liveness information
    B = leastUpperBoundSum(qp, A)
    mark x as dead under all predicates in
          the basis
    for each element r in B {
        if r is in the basis
            // Add x to the LiveSet
            liveSet[r] += x
        else
            for each element s in the basis
                if (!isDisjoint(r, s))
                    // Approximation
                    liveSet[s] += x
    }
}
```

Figure 10. Algorithm for asserting register liveness.

AssertLiveUnderPredicate - For each register x used in an instruction we will update liveness under the qualifying predicate qp. Instructions guarded by predicate true are treated as if they were predicated with the control predicate of the containing basic block. AssertLiveUnderPredicate is a function which asserts the liveness of a virtual register under a predicate. Pseudo code for this operation is shown in Figure 10 (All the pseudo code is written in an object-oriented manner: each method is assumed to be operating on a LiveSet). If x is already live under qp then no work is necessary. If x is not currently live under qp then we compute a minimal set of predicates which encapsulate the liveness of x by a call to leastUpperBoundSum. This allows us to keep the underlying representation compact. In the event that the minimal set contains a predicate which is not part of the basis we will conservatively update the liveness information to conform to the basis by checking disjointness with each basis element. This situation may arise due to the limiting the size of a basis.

AssertDeadUnderPredicate - For each register x defined in an instruction we will update deadness under the qualifying predicate qp. AssetDeadUnderPredicate is a function which asserts that a virtual register has *gone dead* under a predicate. The pseudo code for this operation is shown in Figure 11. We always minimize the number of basis elements required to represent the liveness of a variable. Therefore, if x is already live under qp we simply remove liveness under qp and return. Otherwise, we form a set of all predicates under which x is currently live and subtract qp from the set by using leastUpperBoundDiff to keep the number of predicates involved to a minimum. As is the case with AssertLiveUnderPredicate, some approximation may be introduced.

```
AssertDeadUnderPredicate(x, qp) {
        let A = { p in the basis | x is live under p}
        if qp is an element of A {
          // Remove x from the liveSet
          liveSet[qp] -= x
          return
        }
        // Call to predicate analysis
        B = leastUpperBoundDiff(qp, A)
        mark x as dead under all predicates in  the basis
        for each element r in B
          if r is in the basis
            // Add x to the liveSet
            liveSet[r] += x
          else
            for each element s in the basis
              if (!isDisjoint(r, s))
                liveSet[s] += x   // Approximation
}
```

Figure 11. Algorithm for recording register deadness.

AllCurrentlyLive - In order to compute interferences or conservatively conduct an analysis across basic block boundaries we need to be able to produce a set of all registers which are currently live under a given predicate qp. For example, each def of an instruction interferes with the set of registers given by AllCurrentlyLive(qp), where qp is the qualifying predicate of the instruction. Data flow information can be propagated conservatively across basic blocks by use of AllCurrentlyLive(p0). The pseudo code for this operation is shown in Figure 12. AllCurrentlyLive computes a single bit-vector which is the union of all bit-vectors within a LiveSet whose basis element is not disjoint from qp.

```
AllCurrentlyLive(qp) {
   S = {}
   for each p in the basis
      if (!isDisjoint(p, qp))
         S += liveSet[p]   // Set union
   return S
}
```

Figure 12. Algorithm for producing a list of all registers live with respect to a given predicate.

Interference Graph Construction - The algorithm in Figure 13 describes, in general terms, how the interference graph is constructed in the presence of predicates. The method is quite similar to the traditional method of interference graph construction -- it is simply augmented by the use of LiveSet's and the support routines described above. By controlling the widths of the LiveSet's, the runtime of this method is kept in harmony with compile speed requirements[1].

```
BuildInterferenceGraph() {
   for each basic block bb in the program {
     // work is a LiveSet
     work = dataflowLiveOut[bb]
     for each instruction inst in bb in
     backward order {
       qp = inst.qualifyingPredicate()
       if (qp == P0) qp=bb.homePredicate()
       S = work.AllCurrentlyLive(qp)
       for each def d in inst
           interfere(d, S)   // Add edge to d from set S
       for each def d in inst
         work.AssertDeadUnderPredicate(d, qp)
       for each use u in inst
         work.AssertLiveUnderPredicate(u, qp)
     }
   }
}
```

Figure 13. Algorithm for building the predicate-aware interference graph.

1. In some cases the coloring algorithm as a whole can even be faster due to the simpler interference graph.

5.2 Global Analysis

The local framework allows for detailed analysis of single basic blocks and is sufficient to analyze Example 3. However, to obtain higher degrees of ILP, aggressive optimizations, such as global scheduling [2] or trace scheduling [13], must be employed to move instructions into ILP-poor basic blocks. In this section we extend the local framework to a global framework. The scheduling techniques cited above generally restrict their region of analysis to sub-regions of the CFG. Our approach recursively merges the bases of analysis of basic blocks within *global scheduling regions* (GSR's) to form a single common basis for data flow analysis.

```
RegionSelection() {
   for each interval I in the procedure
       in depth-first order {
       A = {}
        for each GSR R in I {
        B = {basis for R}
         if I A+B I <= LIMIT {
          mark R as merged
           A += B
         }
     }
     for each direct descendent interval J of I {
         C = {basis of J}
         if I A+C I <= LIMIT {
            mark J as merged
            A += C
          }
     }
     set the basis of I and all merged GSR's
          and intervals to A
   }
}
```

Figure 14. Algorithm for selecting analysis regions.

Region Selection - Our approach is aimed at analyzing entire procedures. However, global analysis of predicated live ranges can be very expensive if limits are not placed on the algorithm. In practice, it may not be desirable to always analyze an entire procedure in an aggressive manner. We accommodate such cases by hierarchically building the regions of analysis from the most deeply nested portions of the CFG. That is, bases for several basic blocks are merged only if the size of the resulting basis does not exceed some limit[1].

Good predication can be accomplished only with intimate familiarity with the underlying machine architecture. In our approach we assume that most interesting predicated live ranges will be created by an if-converter and transported across basic blocks by a global instruction scheduler. Therefore, the scheduling regions used by a global scheduler will limit the scope of predicated code motion and hence the extent of predicated live-ranges[2]. Therefore, GSR's are a natural building block for basis construction for register allocation.

While GSR's limit scheduling induced code motion and thus the length of live ranges, naturally occurring (e.g. programmer created) live ranges will span many GSR's. Limiting the scope of analysis strictly to GSR's is too conservative. We recursively build-up the basis, first by attempting to coalesce the basis of all GSR's within an interval [12], and then coalescing the bases of inner intervals into a single basis of analysis. Intervals are coalesced in a depth-first traversal of the interval tree. In the best case this recursive selection will result in the entire procedure being analyzed with a single basis. In the event that multiple regions are selected, data flow calculations can then be performed accurately within each region and summarized at region boundaries. Figure 14 shows pseudo-code for the region selection process.

Finally, the basis used by each basic block in the program is recorded by *tagging* its LiveSet with a unique basis identifier. A bit-vector style data flow analysis can now be performed by extending traditional techniques.

```
LiveSetUnion(Target, Source) {
   If (Target.tag == Source.tag)
      for i=0 to Target.setCount - 1
         // Set union
            Target.liveSet[i] += Source.liveSet[i]
   else
     // Conservative
      Target.liveSet[p0] +=
            Source.AllCurrentlyLive(p0)
}
```

Figure 15. Algorithm for computing the union of LiveSet's.

Data Flow Transfer Functions - Standard bit-vector liveness calculation techniques can be used by extending the algorithm to use LiveSet's rather than simple bit-vectors. Some additional complication arises when propagating the information across basic block boundaries. To pass predicated liveness information across basic blocks boundaries we need two pieces of information about the source and target basic blocks:

1.The current liveness information.

2.The analysis basis used.

Information to identify identical bases is kept with each LiveSet as its basis tag. The liveness information is contained in the bit-vectors of each LiveSet. If the two

1.We used 32 as the limit in this study.

2.Recursive motion between nested GSR's may also occur. The recursive nature of our region selection attempts to address this issue.

LiveSet's use the same basis then data flow information can be transferred without approximation. Conservative liveness information is used otherwise. Figure 15 shows pseudo-code for a data flow LiveSet *union* operation. Other data flow operations are quite similar.

5.3 Approximation

In some cases the predicate analysis may return an answer containing predicates outside of the present basis. This can arise from levels of nesting outside the current region or from asymmetries in the CFG requiring internal predicate nodes to be generated (e.g. a critical edge) to represent the missing symmetrical relationship. These cases are handled conservatively.

Secondly, the analysis of predicate relations ignores back edges. Consequently, we cannot accurately analyze predicated live ranges which are defined on one iteration of a loop and consumed on a subsequent iteration. We detect such live ranges and use conservative data flow information for them at loop back edges.

6 Experimental Results

This section contains experimental measurements which show the effects of predicate-aware register allocation on a large number of procedures. Several benchmarks from the SPECint-92 suite were compiled and the number of *colors* required for procedure-wide graph coloring register allocation with and without our technique were recorded. In all, we compiled 1009 procedures and observed that 248 cases (24.6%) showed improved register allocation when using our technique. Of those cases which improved, the average improvement was a 20.71% decrease in the number of colors required. The standard deviation was 15.10%. Figure 16 graphically depicts the distribution of improvement. While most procedures saw improvements in the 1-35% range some procedures improved by as much as 75%. Some results of the experiments are shown in Table 2. The first column of Table 2 shows the name of the function compiled. The second column lists the number of colors required when using a traditional predicate-unaware graph coloring register allocator on the predicated code. The third column shows the number of colors required when using our predicate-aware register allocator. The fourth column shows the percentage of improvement.

While many procedures improved with our technique the majority did not. The dominant cause was absence of any predicated code in the procedure due to the simple nature of the if-converter [15]. With a more aggressive if-conversion technique [17] more programs should benefit from our work. Also, even when predicated code was present, it was sometimes of such a simple form as to allow the predicate-unaware method to achieve good results.

Since graph coloring based register allocation is a heuristic approximation to an optimal solution we expected to see some cases which degraded simply due to the different structures of the interference graphs. That is, the heuristic approximation used to color the predicate-unaware interference graph could use fewer colors than the same heuristic approximation used to color the predicate-aware interference graph. However, we have not observed any such case to date.

As the number of predicated live ranges increase in proportion to the number of unpredicated live ranges the impact of our approach should be even more beneficial. Furthermore, predicate-aware register allocation will be even more important when register pressure is increased by aggressive function inlining.

7 Conclusion

To maximize the effectiveness of predicated execution, it is very important to take into account the semantics of predicates during compilation analysis, such as data flow analysis. In this paper, we have proposed global techniques to analyze the relations among predicates, and these relations can then be queried by a subsequent compilation analysis or transformation phase. In contrast to previous work, our predicate analysis integrates the relations among control flow and predication. We have also developed a predicate-aware register allocator by naturally extending a traditional method. The precision of data flow analyses supporting this register allocator is greatly enhanced by taking into account global predicate relations. The importance of a predicate-aware register allocator is demonstrated by the significant reduction in register pressure as shown in our extensive experimental results. For cases which show improvement, on average, our predicate-aware register allocator reduces the number of colors by 20.71%.

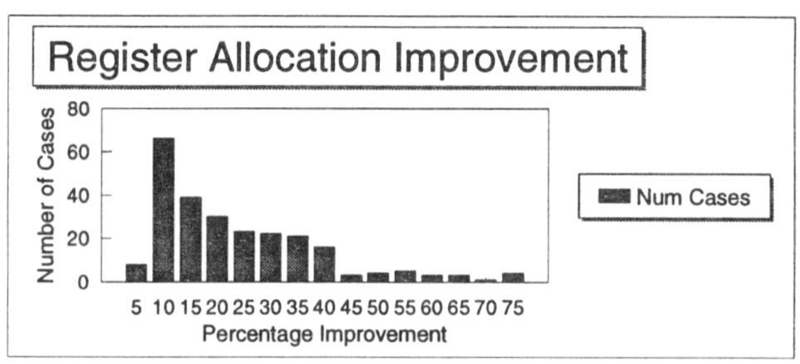

Figure 16. Distribution of register allocation improvement.

Table 2: Experimental results for register allocation

Function	Predicate-Unaware	Predicate-Aware	Improvement
set_dist	30	9	70.00%
xlremprop	13	4	69.23%
mv_reduce	102	42	58.82%
massive_count	101	44	56.44%
cdist	32	14	56.25%
explode	25	15	40.00%
map	63	39	38.10%
tagblock	19	12	36.84%
doprod	22	14	36.36%
yyparse	94	63	32.98%
sharp	29	20	31.03%
opo_leaf	31	22	29.03%
xlgo	14	10	28.57%
sweep	25	18	28.00%
closerow	22	16	27.27%
rmcvd	12	9	25.00%
opo	45	34	24.44%
openrow	29	22	24.14%
OpenConnection	22	17	22.73%
printfile	94	73	22.34%
xload	18	14	22.22%
dobindings	34	27	20.59%
duple	25	20	20.00%

Acknowledgements - We would like to thank the compiler optimization teams at California Language Lab and HP Labs for their support and comments on this work.

References

[1] J.R. Allen, K. Kennedy, C. Portfield, and J. Warren, "Conversion of Control Dependence to Data Dependence," In Conf. Record of the 10th Annual ACM Symp. on Principles of Programming Languages, pp. 177-189, January 1983.

[2] David Bernstein and Michael Rodeh, "Global Instruction Scheduling for Superscalar Machines," SIGPLAN Notices 26(6):241-255. Proc. of the ACM SIGPLAN '91 Conference on Programming Languages and Implementation.

[3] D.P. Bhandarkar, *Alpha Implementations and Architecture*, Digital Press, Butterworth Heinemann, Newton, MA, 1996.

[4] Preston Briggs, *Register Allocation via Graph Coloring*, Ph.D Thesis, TR92-183, Rice University, 1992.

[5] Gregory J. Chaitin, "Register Allocation and Spilling via Graph Coloring," SIGPLAN Notices 17(6):98-105, June 1982. Proc. of the ACM SIGPLAN '82 Symp. on Compiler Construction.

[6] Fred C. Chow and John L. Hennessy, "The Priority-Based Coloring Approach to Register Allocation," ACM Trans. on Programming Languages and Systems, 12(4):501-536, October 1990.

[7] Alexandre E. Eichenberger and Edward S. Davidson, "Register Allocation for Predicated Code," In Proc. of the 28th Annual Int'l Symp. on Microarchitecture, November 1995.

[8] Hewlett-Packard Company. *PA-RISC 1.1 Architecture and Instruction Set Reference Manual*, Second edition, 1992.

[9] P.Y. Hsu and E.S. Davidson, "Highly Concurrent Scalar Processing," In Proc. of the 13th Annual Int'l Symp. on Computer Architecture, pp. 386-395, June 1986.

[10] Richard Johnson and Michael Schlansker, "Analysis Techniques for Predicated Code," In Proc. of the 29th Annual Int'l Symp. on Microarchitecture, December 1996.

[11] V. Kathail, M. Schlansker, B. Rau, *HPL PlayDoh Architecture Specification: Version 1.0*, Hewlett-Packard Laboratories Technical Report, HPL-93-80, Feb. 1993.

[12] T. Lengauer and R. E. Tarjan, "A Fast Algorithm for Finding Dominators in a Flow Graph", ACM Trans. on Prog. Languages and Systems, 1:1, pp 121-141, July 1979.

[13] P. G. Lowney, S.M. Freudenberger, T.J. Karzes, W.D. Lichtenstein, R.P. Nix, J.S. O'Donnell and J.C. Ruttenberg, "The Multiflow Trace Scheduling Compiler," The Journal of Supercomputing, 7, 51-142, 1993.

[14] S.A. Mahlke, D.C. Lin, W. Y. Chen, R.E. Hank, and R.A. Bringmann, "Effective Compiler Support for Predicated Execution Using Hyperblock," In Proc. of the 25th Annual Int'l Symp. on Microarchitecture, pp. 45-54, Dec. 1992.

[15] J.C.H. Park and M. Schlansker, *On Predicated Execution*, Technical Report HPL-91-58, Hewlett-Packard Laboratories, May 1991.

[16] B.R. Rau, D. Yen, W. Yen, and R. Towle, "The Cydra 5 Departmental Supercomputer: Design Philosophies, Decisions, and Trade-offs," IEEE Computer, 22(1):12-35, Jan. 1989.

[17] Michael Schlansker and Vinod Kathail, "Critical Path Reduction for Scalar Programs", In Proc. of the 28th Annual Int'l Symp. on Microarchitecture, November 1995.

[18] N.J. Waters, S.A. Mahlke, W.-M. W. Hwu, and B.R. Rau, "Reverse If-conversion," In Proc. of the SIGPLAN'93 Conf. on Programming Language Design and Implementation, pp. 290-299, June 1993.

[19] D. Weaver and T. Germond, *The SPARC Architecture Manual - Version 9.* Prentice-Hall, Englewood Cliffs, NJ 1993.

Modulo Scheduling of Loops in Control-Intensive Non-Numeric Programs

Daniel M. Lavery   Wen-mei W. Hwu

Center for Reliable and High-Performance Computing
University of Illinois, Urbana-Champaign, IL 61801
lavery@crhc.uiuc.edu, hwu@crhc.uiuc.edu

Abstract

Much of the previous work on modulo scheduling has targeted numeric programs, in which, often, the majority of the loops are well-behaved loop-counter-based loops without early exits. In control-intensive non-numeric programs, the loops frequently have characteristics that make it more difficult to effectively apply modulo scheduling. These characteristics include multiple control flow paths, loops that are not based on a loop counter, and multiple exits. In these loops, the presence of unimportant paths with high resource usage or long dependence chains can penalize the important paths. A path that contains a hazard such as another nested loop can prohibit modulo scheduling of the loop. Control dependences can severely restrict the overlap of the blocks within and across iterations.

This paper describes a set of methods that allow effective modulo scheduling of loops with multiple exits. The techniques include removal of control dependences to enable speculation, extensions to modulo variable expansion, and a new epilogue generation scheme. These methods can be used with superblock and hyperblock techniques to allow modulo scheduling of the selected paths of loops with arbitrary control flow. A case study is presented to show how these methods, combined with superblock techniques, enable modulo scheduling to be effectively applied to control-intensive non-numeric programs. Performance results for several SPEC CINT92 benchmarks and Unix utility programs are reported and demonstrate the applicability of modulo scheduling to this class of programs.

1. Introduction

The scheduling of instructions in loops is of great interest because many programs spend the majority of their execution time in loops. It is often necessary for the scheduler to overlap successive iterations of a loop in order to find sufficient instruction-level parallelism (ILP) to effectively utilize the resources of high-performance processors.

Software pipelining [18, 6, 1, 15], is a loop scheduling scheme that allows motion of instructions from one iteration to another and maintains the overlap of loop iterations throughout the execution of the loop. A description of the various approaches to software pipelining is given in [17]. This paper focuses on a class of software pipelining methods called *modulo scheduling* [16].

Modulo scheduling simplifies the generation of overlapped schedules by initiating iterations at a constant rate and by requiring all iterations of the loop to have a common schedule. The constant interval between the start of successive iterations is called the *initiation interval* (II). The initial candidate II is chosen as the maximum of two lower bounds. The resource-constrained lower bound on the II (ResMII) [16] is equal to the number of cycles that the most heavily used resource is used by a single iteration. The worst-case constraint among all the cycles in the dependence graph determines the recurrence-constrained lower bound on the II (RecMII) [16].

Most of the previous work on modulo scheduling has targeted numeric programs, in which, often, the majority of the loops are well-behaved "DO" loops (loop-counter-based loops) without early exits. All of the more extensive performance evaluations of modulo scheduling techniques have been for such loops. There seems to exist a perception that modulo scheduling is primarily applicable only to numeric programs.

In control-intensive non-numeric programs, the loops frequently have characteristics that make it more difficult to apply modulo scheduling and to obtain significant speedup. These characteristics include multiple control flow paths, loops that are not based on a loop counter, and multiple exits. Several techniques have been developed to allow modulo scheduling of loops with intra-iteration control flow such as hierarchical reduction [11], predicated execution [5], and reverse if-conversion [21]. The above work has assumed that all of the paths through the loop body are included for scheduling. Including all of the paths can be detrimental to overall loop performance. The presence of unimportant paths with high resource usage or long dependence chains can result in a schedule that penalizes the important paths. An infrequent path that contains a hazard, such as another nested loop or a function call, can prohibit modulo scheduling of the loop.

Previous work has also been done on modulo schedul-

1072-4451/96 $5.00 © 1996 IEEE

ing of loops that are not based on a loop counter [20, 19]. The key difficulty with this type of loop is that it may take many cycles to determine whether or not to start the next iteration, limiting the overlap of the iterations. This difficulty is overcome by speculatively initiating the next iteration. The work in [20] also mentions a source-to-source transformation to convert a loop with multiple exits into a single-exit loop. The resulting loop contains multiple paths of control and is dealt with using one of the methods for modulo scheduling of loops with intra-iteration control flow referred to above. However this method adds extra instructions and delays the early exits until the end of the loop body. More work is needed to evaluate the performance of this approach, especially for architectures without predicated execution.

This paper describes a new set of methods that allow effective modulo scheduling of loops with multiple paths of control and multiple exits. We use superblock [10] (and in the future hyperblock [14]) techniques to exclude the unimportant and detrimental paths from the loop. Loops with multiple exits often occur naturally in control-intensive programs and the beneficial exclusion of paths via the formation of superblock and hyperblock loops creates many more of them. Thus, an effective method for handling multiple exits is essential.

Rather than transform the loop into a single exit loop, the proposed methods modulo schedule the loop "as is", with the multiple exits present. A new code generation scheme is described which creates correct epilogues for the early exits. Speculation is used to increase both the overlap of the basic blocks within each iteration and the overlap of successive iterations. We extend modulo variable expansion to allow the speculation of instructions that write to variables that are live at the loop exits. Altogether, the methods described in this paper allow effective modulo scheduling of the selected paths of loops with arbitrary control flow.

This paper reports speedup results for several SPEC CINT92 benchmarks and Unix utilities. These are the first reported performance results for modulo scheduling on control-intensive non-numeric programs, and they demonstrate the applicability of modulo scheduling to this class of programs and validate the correctness of the proposed methods.

The paper is organized as follows: Section 2 describes the methods developed and presents a case study to show how these methods, when combined with superblock techniques, enable modulo scheduling to be effectively applied to control-intensive loops. Section 3 reports the performance results, and Section 4 provides a summary and directions for future work.

2. Modulo Scheduling of Control-Intensive Loops

A detailed example is used to illustrate the difficulties caused by control-intensive loops and the benefits of the techniques developed. The loop chosen for this case study is one of the frequently executed loops in *lex*, the lexical analyzer generator. The source code for the loop is shown in Figure 1.

```
for (i = n; i >= 0; i--) {
     j = state[i];
S1:  if (count == *j++) {
          for (k = 0; k < count; k++)
               if (!temp[*j++]) break;
          if (k >= count)
               return (i);
     }
}
```

Figure 1. Source code for example loop from *lex*.

Loops in general purpose non-numeric programs frequently have complex control flow, and this is evident in the example loop. The outer loop contains an if-statement, an inner loop, and an early exit via a return statement. The inner loop contains an if-statement and an early exit via a break statement.

Obviously, this loop contains a number of hazards for modulo scheduling. Modulo scheduling would ordinarily target the inner loop. However, profile information indicates that the inner loop is infrequently invoked and usually has few iterations. The condition for the if-statement S1 evaluates to false more than 90% of the time. Figure 2a shows a simplified version of the control flow graph for the loop. Block X contains the code to load **state[i]** and ***j** and do the comparison for statement S1. Block Y consists of the post-increment of the pointer **j** and all the code in the body of the if-statement S1. The control flow within block Y has been omitted for clarity. Block Z contains the code to update **i** and to test the exit condition.

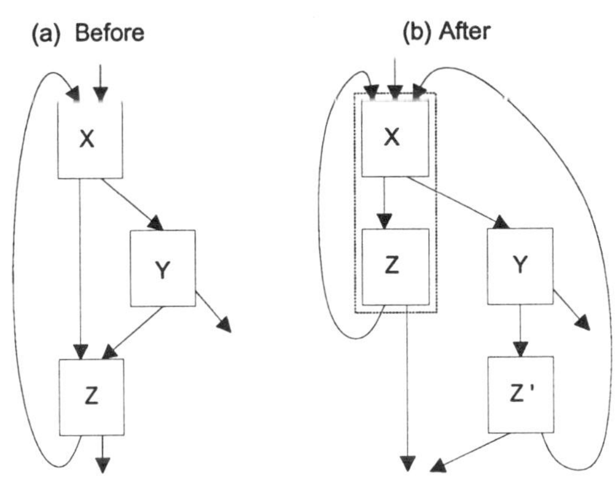

Figure 2. Superblock formation for example loop.

The detrimental path containing the inner loop can be excluded from the loop via superblock formation. Effective superblock formation can be done using profile information [3] and/or static analysis of the structure and hazards in the program [9]. A superblock loop consisting of the most frequent path through the outer loop (blocks X and Z) is formed as shown in Figure 2b. The path through block

Y has been excluded via tail duplication of block Z. A superblock loop consists of a single path through a loop, with a single entrance and one or more exits. The loop consisting of blocks X and Z now appears to be an inner loop with multiple exits and can be targeted for modulo scheduling. For a detailed description of superblock formation, see [10, 3].

It has been shown that superblock optimization and acyclic scheduling techniques provide substantial speedup [10]. In general, the ability of superblocks (and similarly hyperblocks) to exclude undesirable paths of execution can provide the following benefits for modulo scheduling:

- Decrease ResMII by excluding unimportant paths with high resource usage.
- Decrease RecMII by excluding unimportant paths that contribute to long dependence cycles.
- Increase the number of loops that can be modulo scheduled by excluding paths containing hazards such as nested loops and function calls.

Although the modulo scheduling methods developed in this paper are described using superblock examples, they are equally applicable to hyperblock code.

Figure 3 shows the assembly code for the example superblock loop. Each instruction is numbered for later reference. Block X in the control flow graph consists of instructions 1 through 3. Instructions 4 through 6 are in block Z. The assembly code shown is that produced by the IMPACT compiler after classic optimizations have been applied. The elements of the array **state** are four bytes in size. The registers shown are virtual registers. Register allocation is done after modulo scheduling.

Inst.		Assembly	Register Contents
1	L1:	r12 = MEM(r34+r8)	r8 = state
2		r13 = MEM(r12+0)	r34 = i*4
3		beq (r6 r13) L2	r12 = j
4		r4 = r4 - 1	r13 = *j
5		r34 = r34 - 4	r6 = count
6		ble (0 r4) L1	r4 = i

Figure 3. Assembly code for superblock loop.

Control exits the superblock loop if instruction 3 is taken, or if instruction 6 is not taken. In this paper, the exit associated with the fall-through path of the loop back branch is termed the *final exit*. Any other exits from a superblock loop are via taken branches and are termed *early exits*.

The virtual registers r34, r4, and r12 are live out when the early exit to **L2** (block Y) is taken. The values in r34 and r4 are decremented in block Z′. The value in r12 is incremented in block Y. No virtual registers are live out when the loop exits via the final exit (instruction 6).

Loops with complex control flow occur frequently in general purpose non-numeric programs. Table 1 shows statistics on the percentage of dynamic instructions that are in single basic block loops (*Basic Block*) and multiple exit superblock loops (*Superblock*) for the SPEC CINT92 benchmarks and several Unix utility programs. The column labeled *Total* is the sum of the other two columns. The time not spent in these two types of loops is spent in the excluded paths of inner and outer loops and in acyclic code.

Table 1. Percentage of dynamic instructions in single basic block and superblock loops.

Benchmark	Basic Block	Superblock	Total
008.espresso	5.6	57.8	63.4
022.li	0.7	21.4	22.1
023.eqntott	1.8	70.5	72.3
026.compress	0.6	49.8	50.4
072.sc	4.4	34.6	39.0
085.gcc	14.1	28.5	42.6
cmp	0.0	94.5	94.5
eqn	2.6	20.9	23.5
lex	2.0	86.2	88.2
tbl	17.4	9.6	27
wc	0.0	64.7	64.7
yacc	3.2	45.5	48.7

For all the programs except *gcc* and *tbl*, little or no time is spent in single basic block loops. For all the programs except *tbl*, more time (usually much more) is spent in multiple exit superblock loops than in single basic block loops. From this table, it is clear that modulo scheduling must be able to effectively handle loops with control flow to be applicable to these programs. The remainder of this section describes how the proposed techniques overcome the control dependences and register anti-dependences associated with loops that have multiple exits and live-out virtual registers. A code generation scheme for loops with multiple exits is also presented.

2.1. Overcoming control dependence using speculative code motion

Control dependences are a major impediment to the exploitation of ILP in the loops of general-purpose non-numeric programs. Cross-iteration control dependences restrict the overlap of loop iterations by delaying the start of subsequent iterations until all the branches from the current iteration have been executed. Frequently the branches are dependent on earlier computations in the loop body and cannot be executed until late in the iteration, severely limiting any overlap.

Intra-iteration control dependences combined with cross-iteration data dependences create recurrences which limit the throughput of the modulo scheduled loop. They also increase the length of the critical paths through a single iteration, resulting in a longer schedule for each iteration, an important consideration for short trip count loops.

As described in [20, 19], the cross-iteration control dependences from the loop back branch to the instructions in the next iteration can be relaxed, allowing speculative code motion and overlap of the iterations. For loops with multiple exits, this concept must be extended to the early exit branches. It is often necessary to remove the cross-iteration control dependences from an early exit branch to the instructions in subsequent iterations to achieve the desired level of overlap. It is also often necessary to remove intra-iteration control dependences to allow overlap of the blocks within an iteration and to achieve good performance for short trip count loops.

Removal of either type of control dependence is not quite so simple however. We currently assume that stores and branches are not speculatively executed. The reordering of branches will be the subject of future work. In order to speculatively execute loads and other instructions that can cause exceptions, either the processor architecture must contain support for speculative execution [4, 13] or the compiler must be able to prove via program analysis that the speculatively executed instruction will not except [2]. In this paper, we assume an instruction set architecture that contains silent (non-trapping) versions of the instructions that can cause exceptions [4]. Furthermore, instructions that write to virtual registers that are live at the loop exits require special attention when removing control dependences. This issue will be discussed in Section 2.2. We now show the effect of control dependences on the example superblock loop.

Figure 4a shows the dependence graph. Each node is numbered with the ID (from Figure 3) of the instruction it represents. The branch nodes are shaded. The data and control dependences are shown with solid and dashed lines respectively. Some of the transitive dependences are not shown. None of the register anti-dependences are shown, assuming that they can be removed. Removal of anti-dependences is discussed in Section 2.2.

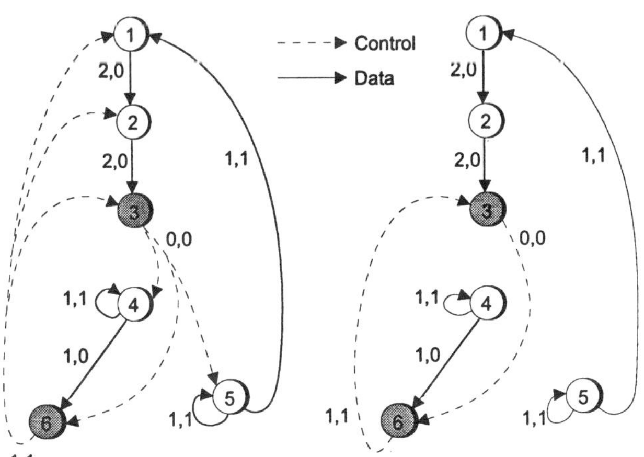

Figure 4. Dependence graph for example loop.

Each arc is labeled with two numbers. The first is the minimum delay in cycles required between the start of the two instructions. The second number is the distance, which is the number of iterations between the two dependent instructions. Arcs with a distance of zero are intra-iteration dependences and those with a distance greater than zero are cross-iteration dependences. The instruction set assumed is similar to HP's PA-RISC 1.1 but has no branch delay slots. Except for the branches, the delays shown are those of the PA7100. It is assumed that the instructions in the fall-through path of a branch can potentially be executed in the same cycle as the branch and that instructions in the taken path are executed the cycle following the branch.

There are several non-trivial recurrences apparent in the graph. The longest recurrence circuit runs through instructions 1, 2, 3, 4, 6, and back to 1. It has a total delay of six and spans one iteration, resulting in a RecMII of six. If the loop is scheduled using this dependence graph, there is no overlap of the iterations. The cross-iteration control dependences from the loop back branch to the instructions in the next iteration (except instruction 3) can be removed, allowing speculative code motion and overlap of the iterations. However, there are still limiting control dependences present. The recurrence circuit consisting of instructions 1, 2, 3, and 5 limits the RecMII to five. To break this recurrence, the intra-iteration control dependence between instructions 3 and 5 must be removed, enabling speculative execution of instruction 5. The control dependence from instruction 3 to instruction 4 must also be removed to break the remaining limiting recurrence. Figure 4b shows the dependence graph after all of the limiting control dependences have been removed, reducing the RecMII to one.

An instruction can legally be moved during modulo scheduling from above to below a branch if the branch is not data dependent on the instruction. For example, instruction 5 could legally be scheduled after instruction 6. When an instruction is moved from above to below a branch, it is automatically moved into both paths of the branch during the generation of epilogues which follows the actual modulo scheduling process. In Sections 2.2 and 2.4, it is shown that special attention must be paid to this type of code motion for correct code generation in multiple exit loops.

Assuming a 4-issue processor that can execute one branch per cycle, the ResMII for the example loop is two. The RecMII was one, resulting in an II of two. This is a speedup of three over modulo scheduling using the dependence graph of Figure 4a.

2.2. Overcoming anti-dependence using modulo variable expansion

Thus far, nothing has been said about anti-dependences and the constraints imposed by the virtual registers that are live out of the loop exits. In its original form, an instruction **I** that writes a virtual register **V** that is live out of an exit branch **B** cannot be moved from below to above **B**, because it overwrites the value in **V** that is used when exit **B** is taken. This constraint on upward code motion is exactly the same as if **V** was one of the operands of **B** (i.e. it is an anti-dependence constraint) but is represented differently in many compilers. Instead of adding an explicit anti-dependence arc, many compilers, including IMPACT, overload the control dependence arc to represent both the control dependence and the anti-dependence.

There are several examples of anti-dependence in the case study loop. Instruction 1 uses r34 which is later defined by instruction 5. Virtual register r34 is live out when the branch to **L2** (instruction 3) is taken, so there is an anti-dependence between instruction 3 and instruction 5.

Anti-dependences can be removed by renaming. Modulo variable expansion [11, 19] unrolls the kernel and renames the successive lifetimes corresponding to the same loop-variant so that they no longer overlap in time. This allows register anti-dependences to be removed before scheduling, knowing that modulo variable expansion will correct the overlap of lifetimes that the lack of these dependences allows. The modulo variable expansion algorithm, as originally described [11], allows the removal of cross-iteration anti-dependences. However, intra-iteration anti-dependences can also be removed if the lifetime analysis and the renaming algorithms are extended to include lifetimes that cross iterations. It is assumed that this can be done in [19]. In this paper, we describe the changes needed.

Figure 5 illustrates the relaxation of a cross-iteration anti-dependence using modulo variable expansion, as described in [11]. Three iterations of an abstract loop body containing a definition and a use of a virtual register r1 are shown. There is an intra-iteration flow dependence (marked with an f) and a cross-iteration anti-dependence (marked with an a). The cycle in which each instruction is issued is shown in square brackets to the right of the abstract instruction, assuming the delay for the flow dependence is two and the anti-dependence is zero. In its original form as shown on the left, the minimum II that can be achieved is two. Using modulo variable expansion, the anti-dependence can be removed prior to scheduling, reducing the II to one. Two virtual registers are now used as shown on the right.

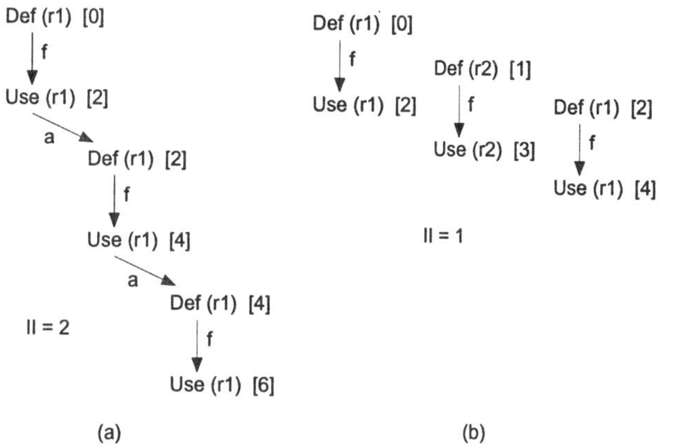

Figure 5. Relaxation of cross-iteration anti-dependence.

Figure 6 shows the relaxation of an intra-iteration anti-dependence. In this case, the use appears before the definition in the original iteration, and the lifetime of r1 now crosses the iterations. Removal of the intra-iteration anti-dependence prior to scheduling allows the definition to be moved above the use within the iteration as shown on the right. As in the previous case, two registers are used and the II is reduced from 2 to 1.

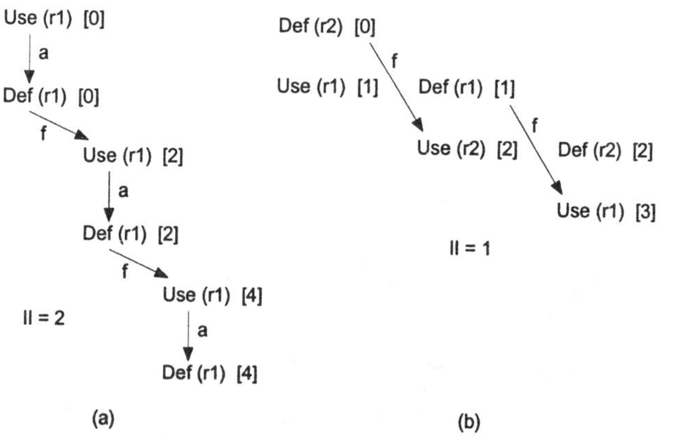

Figure 6. Relaxation of intra-iteration anti-dependence.

The lifetime of a virtual register extends from its first definition to its last use. The lifetime of a loop-variant virtual register **V** from a definition **D** to a use **U** is computed using the following equation, assuming that the lifetime starts when **D** is issued and ends when **U** is issued.

$$Lifetime(\mathbf{V}) = Issue(\mathbf{U}) - Issue(\mathbf{D}) + II * Dist(\mathbf{V}) \quad (1)$$

Issue(**D**) and Issue(**U**) are the issue time of the instances of **D** and **U** from the same original iteration [1]. Dist(**V**) is the number of iterations separating **D** and the instance of **U** that uses the value defined by **D** in the original loop.

Note that in equation 1, use **U** could be a branch for which **V** is live out. For correct renaming, the lifetime analysis must be extended to include such uses. There is an additional consideration for live out virtual registers. Instruction **D** can be moved downward across the branch **B**. If such code motion occurs, the definition is moved into both paths of the branch during epilogue generation, **V** is no longer live-out, and Lifetime(**V**) as computed by equation 1 becomes less than or equal to 0. Thus, the lifetime of **V** is computed for all the uses except those associated with the exits that **D** has been moved down across.

Figure 7 shows the execution of two iterations of the case study loop after modulo scheduling. The first iteration starts at time 0 and its instructions are denoted with the subscript 1. The second iteration starts at time 2 and its instructions are denoted with subscript 2. The second iteration's instructions are also shaded to further distinguish the two iterations. The lifetimes of all the virtual registers written in the loop are shown to the right of the execution record. Each virtual register's lifetime begins with its

[1] Modulo scheduling generates a schedule for a single iteration of the original loop. It is this schedule that we are working with when analyzing the lifetimes for modulo variable expansion.

definition in the first iteration. Each of the subsequent tic marks denotes either an explicit use of the virtual register as a source operand, or a branch for which the register is live-out. The lifetime extends until the last use of the register.

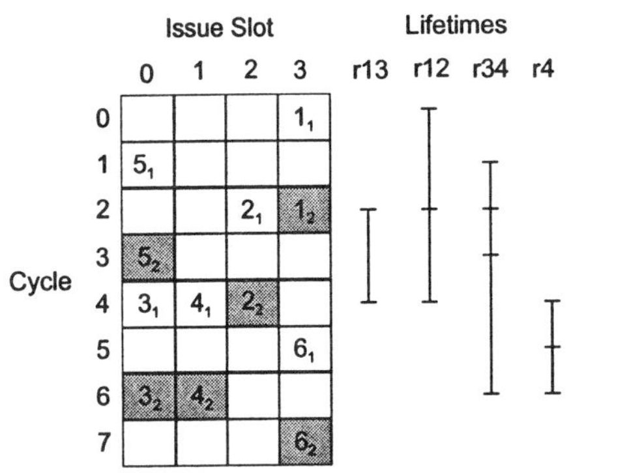

Figure 7. Execution record and lifetimes for two iterations.

The lifetime of r13 is entirely contained within one iteration. It is defined by instruction 2 and used by instruction 3. $Issue(2)$ is 2, $Issue(3)$ is 4, $Dist(r13)$ is 0, and II is 2. Using equation 1, the length of the lifetime is 2. The lifetime of r34 crosses iterations. It is defined by instruction 5, used by instruction 1 and 5 of the next iteration, and live out of instruction 3 of the next iteration. $Issue(5)$ is 1, $Issue(3)$ is 4, and $Dist(r34)$ is 1. Using equation 1, the total length of the lifetime is 5.

The definitions of **V** are renamed by cycling through the set of virtual registers assigned for **V**. Each use of **V** is renamed by first finding the iteration that contains the corresponding definition of **V** (the current iteration if Distance(**V**) is zero or the previous iteration if Distance(**V**) is one) and using the same virtual register name as the definition from that iteration.

The longest lifetime, that of r34, is 5 cycles so the loop must be unrolled three times for modulo variable expansion. Figure 8 shows the unrolled kernel of the modulo scheduled loop after modulo variable expansion. The instructions have been renumbered. When renaming, one of the names used is the original virtual register name. The set of registers used for r34 is r34, r342, and r343. The set of registers used for r12 is r12, r122, and r123. The instructions have been put into sequential order, as would be done when generating code for a superscalar processor. The target and fall-through path for the first two copies of the loop back branch (instructions 6 and 12) have been reversed in preparation for epilogue generation. Block **L3** is the original fall through path of the loop.

Inst.		Assembly	Cycle
1	L1:	beq (r6 r13) L2	0
2		r4 = r4 - 1	0
3		r13 = MEM(r123+0)	0
4		r12 = MEM(r343+r8)	0
5		r34 = r343 - 4	1
6		bgt (0 r4) L3	1
7		beq (r6 r13) L2	2
8		r4 = r4 - 1	2
9		r13 = MEM(r12+0)	2
10		r122 = MEM(r34+r8)	2
11		r342 = r34 - 4	3
12		bgt (0 r4) L3	3
13		beq (r6 r13) L2	4
14		r4 = r4 - 1	4
15		r13 = MEM(r122+0)	4
16		r123 = MEM(r342+r8)	4
17		r343 = r342 - 4	5
18		ble (0 r4) L1	5
	L3:		

Figure 8. Unrolled kernel for superscalar processor.

2.3. Review of a code generation scheme for single exit loops

In this subsection, we review an existing code generation scheme for single exit loops in preparation for introducing a modified scheme for multiple exit loops. For a complete discussion of this and other possible code schemes for single exit loops, see [19]. We use the abstract code representation of [19] to reduce the complexity of the examples. Figure 9a shows a single iteration of a generic single-exit loop after modulo scheduling. Each square represents the code from one stage, or II cycles, of a single iteration of the original source loop. The number of stages is called the *stage count*.

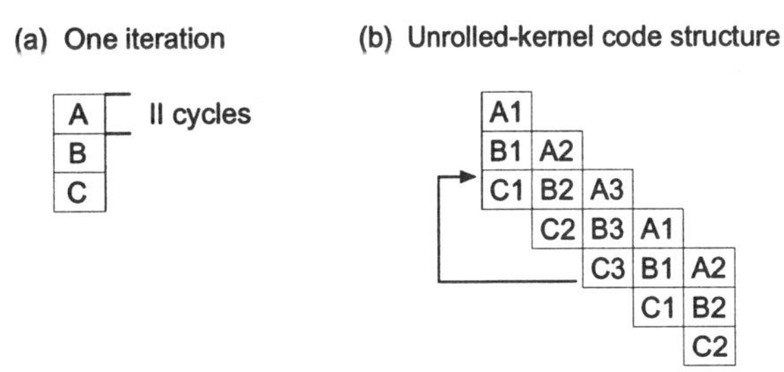

Figure 9. Abstract representation of iterations.

Figure 9b shows the code structure for the modulo scheduled loop after kernel unrolling and generation of the prologue and epilogue. The iterations progress from left to right with each one starting one stage after the previous one. The back-edge arrow from row 6 to row 3 identifies the start and end of the unrolled kernel (the degree of unrolling is unrelated to the stage count). The squares before the kernel represent the prologue and the squares afterward represent the epilogue. Each square is now also given a number to specify which version of the code is being used.

Each version uses different names for the registers to avoid overwriting live values. The code structure in Figure 9b is simplistic and does not allow an arbitrary number of iterations to be correctly executed [19], but it illustrates some of the basic concepts and prepares the reader for the more complex (and correct) code schemes described later in this section.

In this paper, *loop back branch* refers to the loop back branch in the original loop body. There are multiple copies of this branch after modulo scheduling because of the kernel unrolling and prologue generation. For all the copies except the one that becomes the loop back branch of the kernel, the target and fall-through path are reversed, as was shown in Figure 8, so that the loop is exited when the branch is taken rather than when it falls through. All the exits associated with the copies of the loop back branch are called *final exits.* All other exits are *early exits.*

The chain of dependences leading up to the loop back branch determines the earliest stage in which the loop back branch can be placed. The stage in which the loop back branch is scheduled determines the number of iterations that are speculatively initiated. Assume the stages of an iteration are numbered such that stage A corresponds to 0, stage B corresponds to 1, and so on. Using the terminology of [19], if the loop back branch is scheduled in stage θ, then there are θ speculatively executed stages for each iteration after the first. For example, in Figure 9b, if the loop back branch is scheduled in stage B, then stage A of every iteration after the first is executed speculatively. In this paper, the *last* iteration refers to the last iteration that would have been executed in the original non-pipelined loop. When the exit from the last iteration is taken, any speculative iterations are aborted.

Figure 10 shows the structure of the code that is generated for each of the possible stages in which the loop back branch could be placed for a three-stage schedule. In Figure 10a, b, and c, the loop back branch is scheduled at the end of stage A, B, and C respectively.

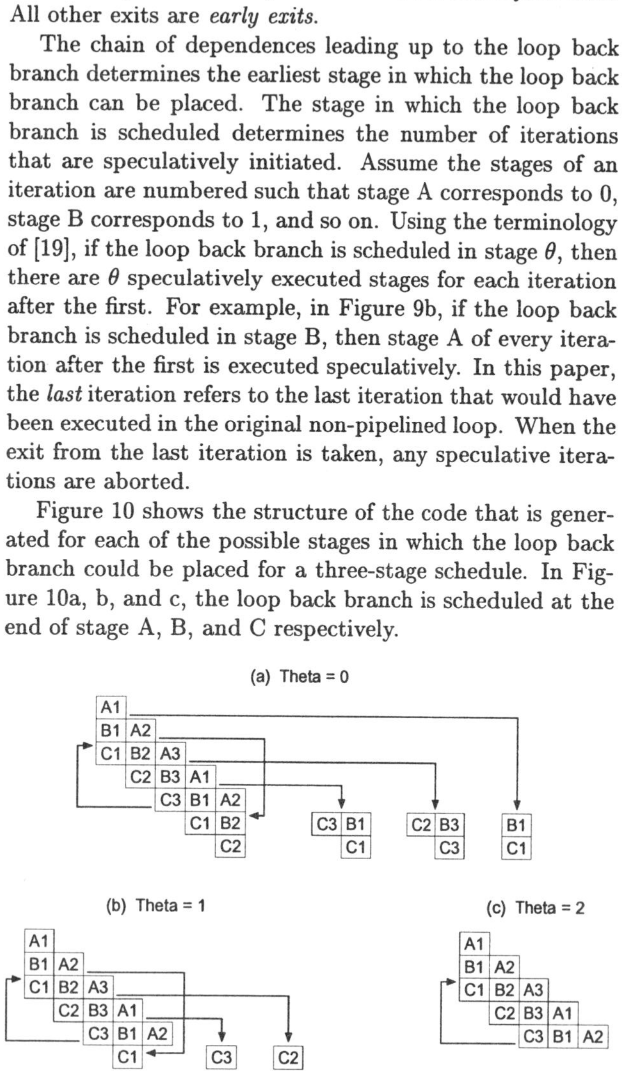

Figure 10. Code generation scheme for single exit loops.

The arrows (except the back-edge) represent control transfers from the prologue and kernel to the epilogues shown. Because the final exits are scheduled at the end of the stage, the arrows originate very close to the bottom of each row of squares. Each epilogue contains the code to complete the non-speculative iterations that are in progress at the time the exit is taken. Although it is not explicitly shown, at the end of each epilogue there exists code to move any live out values to the registers in which the code outside the loop expects to find them and to jump to the original target block of the exit.

By comparing Figure 10a and b, one can see how the structure of the generated code changes when the loop back branch is scheduled at the end of stage B instead of stage A. Because the loop back branch is executed one stage later, there are fewer stages left to execute in the epilogues for the last iteration and its predecessors. Thus, the epilogues all have one less row. The one speculative iteration that is in progress when the loop exits is aborted and so there is one less column in each epilogue. There is one less exit from the prologue, so one of the epilogues has disappeared altogether. In general, when the loop back branch is placed in stage θ instead of stage 0, the θ rightmost columns of each epilogue are removed, corresponding to the θ aborted speculative iterations [19]. The resulting epilogues have $\mathbf{SC} - \theta - 1$ rows where $\mathbf{SC}$ is the stage count.

In Figure 10c, the loop back branch is scheduled at the end of the last stage. Thus, the last iteration and its predecessors are complete when the loop exits. The epilogues consist only of the code needed to move the live values and are not shown.

2.4. A code generation scheme for multiple exit loops

Figure 11 illustrates the changes to the code generation scheme for multiple exit loops. The figure assumes a loop with two exits, where both the early exit and the loop back branch are scheduled in the same stage. In Figure 11a, b, and c, the branches are scheduled in stage A, B, and C respectively. There are now more exits from the modulo scheduled loop and thus more epilogues. The arrows associated with the early exits originate very close to the top of each row and have dashed lines to distinguish them from the final exits.

There are two key differences between a final exit and an early exit. First, the final exit is scheduled at the very end of the stage, but an early exit branch can be in the middle of a stage. Thus, for a final exit, the epilogue starts at the beginning of the stage following the one containing the final exit branch. For an early exit, the remainder of the row containing the exit branch in the kernel must be examined for copying to the epilogue. For all the iterations before the last one, the remainder of that iteration's stage in the row containing the exit branch is copied to the epilogue. The treatment of the last iteration will be discussed shortly. In Figure 11, small letters are used to denote a partial stage resulting from an exit branch from the middle of a stage.

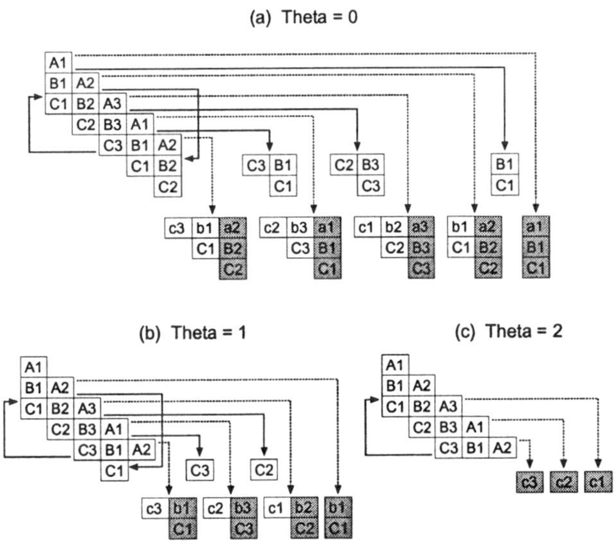

Figure 11. Code generation scheme for multiple exit loops.

The second key difference is that the loop back branch is always the last instruction in the original loop body, but an early exit branch is somewhere in the middle of the original loop body. When a final exit is taken, the last iteration is always fully executed. The remaining stages for the last iteration are copied to the epilogue in their entirety. However after an early exit is taken, only the instructions from the last iteration that appeared before the exit branch in the original loop body should be executed.

Assume the basic blocks in a superblock are assigned numerical IDs sequentially from zero to $\mathbf{SC} - 1$. Define the *home block* for an instruction to be the basic block in which the instruction resides in the original loop body. For an early exit, an instruction from the remaining stages of the last iteration is copied to the epilogue only if the ID of its home block is less than or equal to the home block ID of the exit branch. In Figure 11, shaded squares are used to denote the stages for which the home block is checked before copying the instruction.

In Figure 11, the epilogues for the final exits are all the same as in Figure 10. The epilogues for the early exits always have one more row and usually have one more column than the corresponding final exit from the same stage. The extra row consists of the remainder of the row in the kernel in which the early exit branch resides. Thus, all the squares in the extra row are marked with small letters. The extra column corresponds to the last stage of the oldest iteration in progress at the time the exit is taken. For a final exit, this iteration is just finished when the exit is taken. For an early exit, part of the last stage remains and is completed in the epilogue. The epilogues for the early exits from the prologue do not have an extra column because none of the iterations have started execution of the last stage. The rightmost column of each early exit epilogue is shaded. This column corresponds to the last iteration. For the last iteration, only the instructions that appeared before the exit branch in the original loop body are copied to the epilogue.

Figure 12 shows the algorithm for generating an epilogue for an exit branch. The algorithm starts with the instructions following the exit branch and copies rows of instructions from the unrolled kernel to the epilogue, wrapping around the kernel until the last row of the epilogue is complete. Squares are not copied if they correspond to instructions from iterations after the last or to instructions from the last iteration that appeared after the exit branch in the original loop body. The algorithm as shown assumes a processor that does not have branch delay slots. The following paragraphs describe the data structures and concepts needed to understand the algorithm.

The unrolled kernel is divided into sections of II cycles each called *kernel rows*. There are **kmin** rows where **kmin** is the degree of unrolling of the kernel. Each row contains a linked list of the instructions contained in that row. The data structure for each instruction contains a pointer to an information structure which contains among other items: the stage in which the instruction is scheduled, the instruction's home block ID, and the row of the kernel that contains the instruction.

There are $\mathbf{SC} - \theta$ rows in each epilogue (numbered zero to $\mathbf{SC} - \theta - 1$) where θ is the stage in which the exit branch is scheduled. Row zero is the partial row and is empty for a final exit (the linked list for each kernel row ends with a final exit). In row **epi_row** of the epilogue, the last iteration is executing in stage $\mathbf{epi\_row} + \theta$. Instructions from stages less than $\mathbf{epi\_row} + \theta$ must be from iterations after the last, and thus are not copied.

For simplicity, the algorithm shown generates correct epilogues for exits from the kernel, but not for exits from the prologue. In practice, the algorithm contains additional code to map an exit in the prologue to the corresponding exit in the kernel. The prologue is generated in a similar manner to the epilogues, by copying selected instructions from the rows of the unrolled kernel. Mapping a prologue exit to a corresponding kernel exit facilitates the copying of rows for the epilogue. Also in practice, if the epilogue is for an exit from the prologue, the algorithm does not copy an instruction that is from a later stage than the stage that the very first iteration is executing. Such instructions correspond to the non-existent iterations prior to the first one.

We now apply the code generation scheme to the example loop. The schedule for a single iteration of the example loop contains 3 stages. Stage A consists of instructions 1 and 5 from the original loop (see Figure 7). Stage B contains instruction 2. Instructions 3 (early exit), 4, and 6 (final exit) are in stage C. The code scheme in Figure 11c is similar to what would be generated for the example loop. Because of the dependence structure of the loop, there is no opportunity for downward code motion across the early exit branch. Thus, when the early exit branch is taken there are no remaining instructions from the last iteration that appeared before the exit branch in the original loop body

```
Algorithm gen_epi(exit branch) {

  create epilogue block
  sc = stage count
  theta = exit->info->stage
  row = exit->info->row
  exit_home_block = exit->info->home_block

  /* Generate all rows of epilogue */
  for (epi_row = 0 to sc - theta - 1) do {

    /* Determine where to start copying */
    if (epi_row == 0)
      /* Partial row.  If exit is a final exit,
         exit->next_op is NULL and no instructions
         will be copied to the partial row. */
      oper = exit->next_op
    else
      /* Full row */
      oper = kernel[row]->first_op

    /* Generate one full or partial row */
    while (oper != NULL) {

      oper_stage = oper->info->stage
      oper_home_block = oper->info->home_block

      /* Copy instruction if it is from an
         iteration previous to the last iteration,
         or if it is from the last iteration and
         appears before the exit branch in the
         original loop body */
      if ( (oper_stage > epi_row + theta) or
           (oper_stage == epi_row + theta and
            oper_home_block <= exit_home_block) ) {
        new_op = copy_operation(oper)
        insert_op_after(epilogue->last_op, new_op)
      }
      oper = oper->next_op
    }
    /* Rotate through the rows of the kernel */
    row = (row + 1) mod kmin
  }

  /* insert moves at end of epilogue for variants
     that are live out of exit */
  insert_moves_for_live_variants(epilogue, exit)

  /* Last exit branch falls through to epilogue */
  if (exit is not last exit in unrolled kernel) {
    jump = create jump to target of exit branch
    insert_op_after(epilogue->last_op, jump)
    make epilogue block the target of exit branch
  }
}
```

Figure 12. Epilogue generation algorithm.

and the shaded epilogues are empty.

2.5. Insertion of moves for live-out values

As mentioned earlier, code must be appended to the end of each epilogue to move the values that are live-out of the corresponding exit into the register in which the code outside the loop expects to find them. For single exit superblock loops, the value used outside the loop must have been defined in the last iteration. Thus, for each final exit, the instructions from the last iteration are examined in the corresponding epilogue and in the kernel. If the value produced by the instruction is live-out and the destination register is not the one expected outside the loop, a move instruction is inserted at the end of the epilogue.

For multiple exit loops, the procedure is the same for the final exits. However, for the early exits there is an additional consideration. The live out value could be defined in the last iteration by one of the instructions that preceded the exit branch in the original loop body, or it could be defined in the second-to-last iteration by one of the instructions that followed the exit branch in the original loop body. Thus, the last iteration is examined for instructions that originally resided in the same or earlier home block as the early exit branch and the second-to-last iteration is examined for instructions that originally resided in a later home block than the exit.

In the example loop, when the early exit (instruction 3 from Figure 3) is taken, the live out values of r34 and r4 are from the second-to-last iteration and the live out value of r12 is from the last iteration. There are no values live out of the final exit. Figure 13 shows the code generated for the example loop using the multiple epilogue code scheme of Figure 11c. The instructions have again been renumbered. The moves for the live out values (instructions 25, 27, 28, and 30) are also shown.

The blocks labeled **Pro** and **L1** are the prologue and the unrolled kernel respectively. The blocks labeled **LE1, LE3** and **LE5** are epilogues. The block immediately following the kernel is the epilogue reached by falling through the loop back branch. Block **L3** is the original fall through path of the loop. Label **L2** is the start of block Y. The epilogues for the final exits (instructions 11, 17, and 23) are all empty because no code was moved downward across the loop back branch and there are no virtual registers live out of the final exits. Rather than branching to empty epilogues, the final exits branch directly to **L3**. The exception is the loop back branch, which falls through into its epilogue and then jumps to **L3**.

The early exits (instructions 6, 12, and 18) all require moves for one or more of the live virtual registers, so all branch to epilogues. As mentioned at the end of 2.2, when renaming, one of the names used is the original virtual register name. Thus, if the live out value is already in the correct register, a move is not necessary. This is the case for r34 in epilogue **LE1** and r12 in epilogue **LE5**. A jump is placed at the end of each early exit epilogue to transfer control to Block Y.

Inst.		Assembly	Cycle
1	Pro:	r122 = MEM(r34+r8)	0
2		r342 = r34 - 4	1
3		r13 = MEM(r122+0)	2
4		r123 = MEM(r342+r8)	2
5		r343 = r342 - 4	3
6	L1:	beq (r6 r13) LE1	0
7		r4 = r4 - 1	0
8		r13 = MEM(r123+0)	0
9		r12 = MEM(r343+r8)	0
10		r34 = r343 - 4	1
11		bgt (0 r4) L3	1
12		beq (r6 r13) LE3	2
13		r4 = r4 - 1	2
14		r13 = MEM(r12+0)	2
15		r122 = MEM(r34+r8)	2
16		r342 = r34 - 4	3
17		bgt (0 r4) L3	3
18		beq (r6 r13) LE5	4
19		r4 = r4 - 1	4
20		r13 = MEM(r122+0)	4
21		r123 = MEM(r342+r8)	4
22		r343 = r342 - 4	5
23		ble (0 r4) L1	5
24		jump L3	0
25	LE1:	r12 = r122	0
26		jump L2	0
27	LE3:	r12 = r123	0
28		r34 = r342	0
29		jump L2	0
30	LE5:	r34 = r343	0
31		jump L2	0
	L3:		

Figure 13. Final assembly code for the example loop.

The virtual registers are renamed during modulo variable expansion such that the uses of a live-in virtual register in the first iteration refer to the original virtual register name. Thus, no moves are required for live-in values. For example, virtual register r34 is live-in and the first iteration in the prologue uses r34 (instructions 1 and 2) rather than one of the renamed versions (r342 and r343).

3. Experimental Results

In this section, we report experimental results on the applicability of modulo scheduling to control-intensive non-numeric programs. The results were obtained using the IMPACT compiler. Inter-procedural alias analysis [7] and data dependence analysis are done in the front end and memory dependence arcs are passed to the back end, giving the optimizer and the schedulers accurate dependence information. In addition to the classic optimizations, optimizations are performed in the back end to increase the ILP of the code [10].

Modulo scheduling is done before prepass acyclic scheduling and global register allocation. The modulo scheduler is an implementation of Rau's Iterative Modulo Scheduling [16]. It uses a machine description system [8] to get information on instruction latencies and resource requirements. The modulo scheduler has been used to pipeline loops for high issue rate versions of the PA-RISC (in this paper) and SPARC architectures. Loops are eligible for modulo scheduling if they are inner loops (outer loops may become inner loops after superblock formation), are single basic block or superblock loops, and do not contain function calls on the included path (function calls may be excluded from the loop by superblock formation, enabling modulo scheduling).

The target processors for these experiments are multiple issue processors with issue rates between 4 and 8 with varying resource constraints. Table 2 shows the functional unit mix for each processor. All processors are assumed to have 32 integer registers and 32 double-precision floating-point registers. The latencies used are those of the HP PA7100 processor.

Table 2. Processor characteristics.

Name	Number of				
	Issue Slots	Integer ALUs	Memory Ports	Branch Units	FP ALUs
Base	1	1	1	1	1
A	4	2	2	1	1
B	4	4	4	1	4
C	4	4	4	4	4
D	8	8	8	8	8

All speedups are reported over the single-issue base processor. For the base processor, ILP optimizations and modulo scheduling are not applied. For the multiple issue processors, code is generated three ways, once without modulo scheduling, once with modulo scheduling of only the single basic block loops, and once with modulo scheduling of superblock loops using the techniques described in this paper. All the code that is not software pipelined is scheduled using acyclic superblock scheduling [10].

None of the loops are unrolled before acyclic scheduling or modulo scheduling. In general, prior unrolling improves the performance of both acyclicly scheduled and modulo scheduled loops [12]. However, there are complex interactions between unrolling, optimization, and scheduling, which add another variable when we are trying to focus on the effect of modulo scheduling. The purpose of the paper is primarily to describe an effective method for modulo scheduling loops in control-intensive non-numeric programs. The results in this paper are used to demonstrate the applicability of modulo scheduling to this class of programs and to validate the correctness of the method. The effects of unrolling prior to scheduling and performance comparisons of modulo scheduling and acyclic scheduling of unrolled loops in control-intensive non-numeric programs are the subject of future work as described in Section 4.

The execution times of the whole programs are calculated using scheduler cycle counts for each basic block and profile information. A 100% cache hit rate is assumed. The benchmarks are profiled after all transformations to insure accuracy. The profiling is done by instrumenting the target (virtual) processor's assembly code and then emulating it

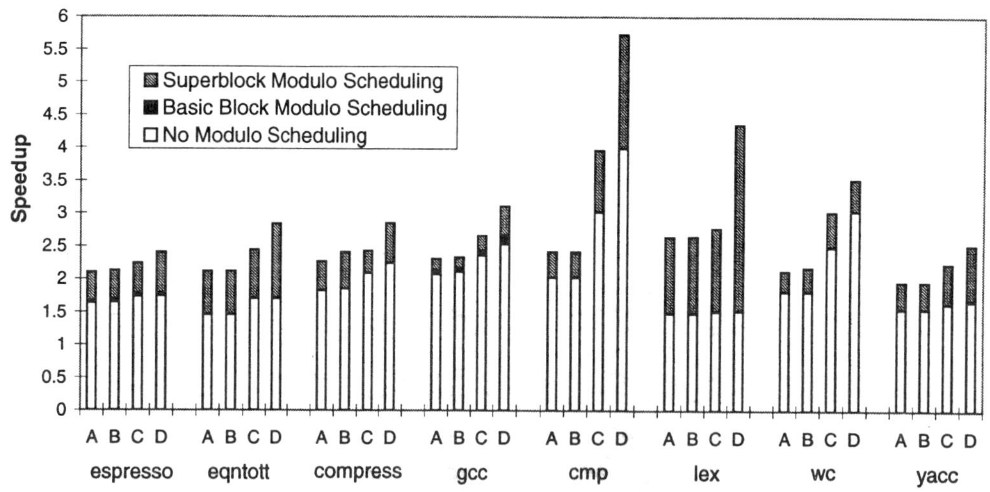

Figure 14. Speedup over single issue processor with and without modulo scheduling.

on an HP Series 700 workstation. This execution produces benchmark output which is used to verify the correctness of the target processor's assembly code.

The benchmarks chosen for the experiments are the four SPEC CINT92 and four Unix programs from Table 1 (espresso, eqntott, compress, gcc, cmp, lex, wc, and yacc) that spend the most time in basic block and superblock loops, loops to which we apply modulo scheduling. For all of the chosen programs, over 40% of the dynamic instructions were in such loops. A total of 305 loops were modulo scheduled.

Figure 14 shows the speedup results. The white part of the bars show the speedup over the base processor when acyclic scheduling is applied to all of the code. For *espresso, eqntott, lex,* and *yacc,* the performance is flat as resources are increased. Without overlapping the iterations, the ILP that can be exploited is limited. The black part of the bars show the slightly increased performance when modulo scheduling is applied to the single basic block loops. For all of the benchmarks except *gcc*, less than 6% of the dynamic instructions are in basic block loops. Thus only a slight performance improvement can be expected. The benchmark *gcc* spends about half as much time (14%) in single basic block loops as it does in superblock loops and shows speedups of about 5%.

The cross-hatched part of the bars show the increased performance when superblock modulo scheduling is applied to the eligible loops. Modulo scheduling almost doubles the performance of *lex* for the 4-issue processor and almost triples performance for the 8-issue processor. As was shown in the case study, there is very limited ILP within a single iteration of the loops in that program. Modulo scheduling provides good speedup across all the benchmarks and processors. In particular, speedups of 25% or more are obtained across all the processors for *espresso, eqntott, compress, lex,* and *yacc.* For the most aggressive processor, performance is improved by 30% or more for all the benchmarks except *gcc* and *wc.*

With superblock modulo scheduling, the performance of *espresso, eqntott, lex,* and *yacc* is no longer flat as the processor resources are increased. More ILP is being exploited by overlapping the loop iterations. The results clearly show that modulo scheduling, using the techniques described in this paper, is applicable to control-intensive, non-numeric programs.

4. Conclusion

This paper has described a set of methods that allow effective modulo scheduling of loops with multiple exits. These methods can be used to allow modulo scheduling of the selected paths of loops with arbitrary control flow. A case study was presented to show how these methods enable modulo scheduling to be effectively applied to control-intensive non-numeric programs. Performance results for several SPEC CINT92 benchmarks and Unix utility programs demonstrated that modulo scheduling can significantly accelerate loops in this class of programs.

Previous work has shown that unrolling prior to modulo scheduling improves performance for numeric programs [12]. Unrolling enables additional optimization and an effective II that is not an integer. For acyclic scheduling, unrolling is done to allow both optimization and overlap of iterations. For modulo scheduling, unrolling is done to optimize the effective ResMII and RecMII. Much research needs to be done to study the effect of unrolling prior to modulo scheduling for non-numeric programs and to understand the amount of unrolling necessary to achieve the minimum II possible for a given loop. This will be the next step in our effort to apply modulo scheduling to control-intensive non-numeric programs. One result of the next step will be the ability compare modulo scheduling and global acyclic scheduling of unrolled loops within a common framework.

Acknowledgments

The research for this paper has benefited from conversations with Mike Schlansker and Bob Rau at HP Labs. Thanks to Bob Rau, Scott Mahlke, and Grant Haab for providing feedback on a very early version of this paper and to Brian Deitrich, John Gyllenhaal, and the anonymous referees for their suggestions on the submitted version. The authors would also like to thank Jurgen Mihm, whose work inspired some of our thoughts on modulo variable expansion, and Nancy Warter-Perez, Noubar Partamian, and the past and present members of the IMPACT research group for providing the underlying technology on which the modulo scheduler is built.

This research has been supported by the National Science Foundation (NSF) under grant MIP-9308013, Intel Corporation, Advanced Micro Devices, Hewlett-Packard, SUN Microsystems, NCR, and the National Aeronautics and Space Administration (NASA) under Contract NASA NAG 1-613 in cooperation with the Illinois Computer Laboratory for Aerospace Systems and Software (ICLASS).

References

[1] A. Aiken and A. Nicolau. A realistic resource-constrained software pipelining algorithm. In A. Nicolau, D. Galernter, T. Gross, and D. Padua, editors, *Advances in Languages and Compilers for Parallel Processing*, pages 274–290. Pitman/The MIT Press, London, 1991.

[2] R. A. Bringmann. *Compiler-Controlled Speculation.* PhD thesis, Department of Computer Science, University of Illinois, Urbana, IL, 1995.

[3] P. P. Chang, S. A. Mahlke, and W. W. Hwu. Using profile information to assist classic code optimizations. *Software Practice and Experience*, 21(12):1301–1321, December 1991.

[4] P. P. Chang, N. Warter, S. A. Mahlke, W. Y. Chen, and W. W. Hwu. Three architectural models for compiler-controlled speculative execution. *IEEE Transactions on Computers*, 44(4):481–494, April 1995.

[5] J. C. Dehnert, P. Y. Hsu, and J. P. Bratt. Overlapped loop support in the Cydra 5. In *Proceedings of the Third International Conference on Architectural Support for Programming Languages and Operating Systems*, pages 26–38, April 1989.

[6] K. Ebcioglu and T. Nakatani. A new compilation technique for parallelizing loops with unpredictable branches on a VLIW architecture. In *Languages and Compilers for Parallel Computing*, pages 213–229, 1989.

[7] D. M. Gallagher. *Memory Disambiguation to Facilitate Instruction-Level Parallelism Compilation.* PhD thesis, Department of Electrical and Computer Engineering, University of Illinois, Urbana, IL, 1995.

[8] J. C. Gyllenhaal. A machine description language for compilation. Master's thesis, Department of Electrical and Computer Engineering, University of Illinois, Urbana, IL, 1994.

[9] R. E. Hank, S. A. Mahlke, R. A. Bringmann, J. C. Gyllenhaal, and W. W. Hwu. Superblock formation using static program analysis. In *Proceedings of the 26th Annual International Symposium on Microarchitecture*, December 1993.

[10] W. W. Hwu, S. A. Mahlke, W. Y. Chen, P. P. Chang, N. J. Warter, R. A. Bringmann, R. G. Ouellette, R. E. Hank, T. Kiyohara, G. E. Haab, J. G. Holm, and D. M. Lavery. The Superblock: An effective technique for VLIW and superscalar compilation. *The Journal of Supercomputing*, 7(1):229–248, January 1993.

[11] M. S. Lam. Software pipelining: An effective scheduling technique for VLIW machines. In *Proceedings of the ACM SIGPLAN 1988 Conference on Programming Language Design and Implementation*, pages 318–328, June 1988.

[12] D. M. Lavery and W. W. Hwu. Unrolling-based optimizations for modulo scheduling. In *Proceedings of the 28th International Symposium on Microarchitecture*, pages 327–337, Nov. 1995.

[13] S. A. Mahlke, W. Y. Chen, R. A. Bringmann, R. E. Hank, W. W. Hwu, B. R. Rau, and M. S. Schlansker. Sentinel scheduling: A model for compiler-controlled speculative execution. *Transactions on Computer Systems*, 11(4), November 1993.

[14] S. A. Mahlke, D. C. Lin, W. Y. Chen, R. E. Hank, and R. A. Bringmann. Effective compiler support for predicated execution using the hyperblock. In *Proceedings of the 25th International Symposium on Microarchitecture*, pages 45–54, December 1992.

[15] M. Rajagopalan and V. H. Allan. Efficient scheduling of fine grain parallelism in loops. In *Proceedings of the 26th International Symposium on Microarchitecture*, pages 2–11, December 1993.

[16] B. R. Rau. Iterative modulo scheduling: An algorithm for software pipelining loops. In *Proceedings of the 27th International Symposium on Microarchitecture*, pages 63–74, December 1994.

[17] B. R. Rau and J. A. Fisher. Instruction-level parallel processing: History, overview, and perspective. *The Journal of Supercomputing*, 7(1):9–50, January 1993.

[18] B. R. Rau and C. D. Glaeser. Some scheduling techniques and an easily schedulable horizontal architecture for high performance scientific computing. In *Proceedings of the 20th Annual Workshop on Microprogramming and Microarchitecture*, pages 183–198, October 1981.

[19] B. R. Rau, M. S. Schlansker, and P. P. Tirumalai. Code generation schema for modulo scheduled loops. In *Proceedings of the 25th Annual International Symposium on Microarchitecture*, pages 158–169, December 1992.

[20] P. Tirumalai, M. Lee, and M. Schlansker. Parallelization of loops with exits on pipelined architectures. In *Supercomputing*, November 1990.

[21] N. J. Warter, G. E. Haab, K. Subramanian, and J. W. Bockhaus. Enhanced modulo scheduling for loops with conditional branches. In *Proceedings of the 25th Annual International Symposium on Microarchitecture*, pages 170–179, December 1992.

Featured Speaker

Robert Montoye,
IBM Austin

"Migration of Functions to the Main CPU"

Session 5

Assigning Confidence to Conditional Branch Predictions

Erik Jacobsen, Eric Rotenberg†, and J. E. Smith
Departments of Electrical and Computer Engineering and
† Computer Sciences
University of Wisconsin-Madison
Madison, WI 53706
jacobsen@cae.wisc.edu, ericro@cs.wisc.edu, jes@ece.wisc.edu

Abstract

Many high performance processors predict conditional branches and consume processor resources based on the prediction. In some situations, resource allocation can be better optimized if a confidence level is assigned to a branch prediction; i.e. if the quantity of resources allocated is a function of the confidence level. To support such optimizations, we consider hardware mechanisms that partition conditional branch predictions into two sets: those which are accurate a relatively high percentage of the time, and those which are accurate a relatively low percentage of the time. The objective is to concentrate as many of the mispredictions as practical into a relatively small set of low confidence dynamic branches.

We first study an ideal method that profiles branch predictions and sorts static branches into high and low confidence sets, depending on the accuracy with which they are dynamically predicted. We find that about 63 percent of the mispredictions can be localized to a set of static branches that account for 20 percent of the dynamic branches. We then study idealized dynamic confidence methods using both one and two levels of branch correctness history. We find that the single level method performs at least as well as the more complex two level method and is able to isolate 89 percent of the mispredictions into a set containing 20 percent of the dynamic branches. Finally, we study practical, less expensive implementations and find that they achieve most of the performance of the idealized methods.

1. Introduction

It is becoming common practice in high performance processors to predict conditional branches [4, 7, 9, 13] and speculatively execute instructions based on the prediction [2, 8]. Typically, when speculation is used, all branch predictions are acted upon because there is low penalty for speculating incorrectly. I.e. most resources available to speculative instructions would be unused anyway. And, on average, a branch prediction will be correct a high percentage of the time.

However, as processors become more advanced, we can envision implementations where the penalty for an incorrect speculation may be high enough that it may be better not to speculate in those instances where the likelihood of a branch misprediction is relatively high. That is, it may be desirable to vary behavior depending on the likelihood of a misprediction. Consequently, we would like to develop hardware methods for assessing the likelihood that a conditional branch prediction is correct; we refer to these as *branch prediction confidence mechanisms*. Consider the following potential applications.

1) Selective Dual Path Execution: Resources may be made available for simultaneously executing instructions down both paths following a conditional branch. However, it will likely be too expensive to follow both paths after all branches, especially when several conditional branches may be unresolved at any given time. Consequently, it may be desirable to set a limit of two threads at any given time and to fork a second execution thread for the non-predicted path only in those instances when a branch prediction is made with relatively low confidence. After most predicted branches only the predicted path would be speculatively followed, but occasionally, both paths would be followed.

2) Guiding instruction fetching in simultaneous multithreading (SMT): In SMT, instruction fetching has been identified as a critical resource [10]. This resource can be more efficiently used by fetching instructions only down predicted paths that have a high likelihood of being correctly predicted. That is, threads predicted with a high confidence should be given priority over those with low confidence. This will reduce the number of wasted instruction fetches caused by following the wrong speculative path.

3) Dynamic Selector for a hybrid branch predictor: Hybrid branch predictors [1, 5] use more than one predictor and select the prediction made by one of them based on the history of prediction accuracies of the constituent predictors. The methods proposed in [1, 5] are basically *ad hoc* confidence mechanisms developed for this specific application. By studying confidence mechanisms in general, we may be able to arrive at more accurate hybrid selectors.

4) Branch Prediction Reverser: If the confidence in a branch prediction can be determined to be less than 50%,

1072-4451/96 $5.00 © 1996 IEEE

then the prediction should be reversed. Hence, a confidence mechanism could be used to generate a "reverse prediction" signal for those branch predictions with a less than 50% accuracy.

In theory, one could focus on developing hardware that computes probabilities that individual branch predictions are correct (or incorrect). However, in practice this could be rather complex (because a division is implied), and a computed probability for each branch is not what is really wanted, anyway. Rather, we attempt to divide branch predictions into two sets: those in which there is high confidence, and those in which there is low confidence. A binary signal is generated simultaneously with a branch prediction to indicate the confidence set to which the prediction belongs. The pair of prediction and confidence signals are illustrated in Fig. 1. To see how a confidence signal could be used, consider again the four applications listed above.

1) For Selective Dual Path Execution, the confidence signal can be used to trigger the forking of a second thread for low confidence branch predictions.

2) For the SMT instruction fetching application, the confidence signal can be used to enable instruction fetching for speculative threads in which there is high confidence.

3) For designing a hybrid prediction selector, confidence signals from the multiple predictors can be compared to select the prediction to be used.

4) For the reverser application, if the confidence threshold can be set at approximately 50% accuracy, then the confidence signal can be used to reverse a prediction.

For each of these applications, we would like to divide the predictions into high and low confidence sets and concentrate as many of the mispredicted branches as possible into the low confidence set -- while at the same time keeping the low confidence set relatively small. Note that in general, one could divide the branches into multiple sets with a range of confidence levels. To date, we have not pursued this generalization and consider only two confidence sets in this paper.

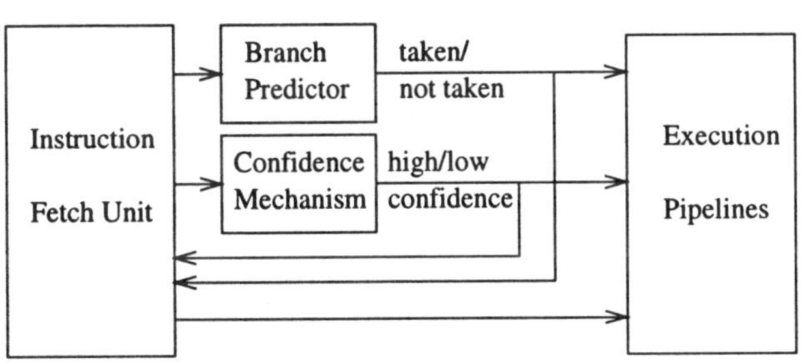

Fig. 1. A generic speculative processor containing a branch prediction signal paired with high/low confidence signal.

To generate the signal that separates the two confidence sets, we propose using benchmarks to collect prediction accuracy data. This data can then be used to design logic so that the high and low confidence sets have the characteristics we desire. Note that this logic is designed using data *for our selected benchmarks*. However, once implemented, the confidence logic is used for all programs. That is, to simplify the hardware design, we do not dynamically adjust the criteria for determining the high and low confidence sets.

1.1. Previous Work

In [9] there is a proposal for assigning confidence levels to different counter values in predictors based on saturating counters. There is also a relatively abstract example of optimizing performance by speculating to different degrees based on the confidence level.

In [12] the authors use branch probability levels to guide disjoint eager execution when forking multiple threads. Multiple threads are forked, with the most probable being forked first. Because of the difficulties with dynamically computing the probabilities, static profile-based probabilities are used in the suggested implementation.

Regarding the specific application to reversing predictions, some processors have static "prediction reversal" bits. The Livermore S-1 [3] made a static branch prediction, but had a dynamic "reverse" bit in the instruction cache that was used to reverse the static prediction after it was found to be incorrect. The more recent PowerPC 601 microprocessor [6] makes a prediction based on the opcode and direction of the branch, but allows the compiler to place a "reverse" bit in the instruction to change the default prediction.

1.2. Simulation Methodology

We collected branch prediction accuracy data using trace-driven simulation. For benchmarks, we used the Mach version of the IBS benchmark suite [11] -- chosen because they more accurately represent branch characteristics of real programs than the commonly used SPEC benchmarks, and, because they include kernel code.

We arrive at composite data for the collection of benchmarks by averaging. We do this by weighting the results so that each benchmark, in effect, executes the same number of conditional branches.

An important part of the study is the underlying branch predictor. In most of our simulations, we use a fairly aggressive predictor. It is the gshare predictor [5] with 2^{16} entries -- each of which is a saturating 2-bit counter. The counter array is addressed with the exclusive-OR of bits 17 through 2 of the program counter and the most recent 16 branch outcomes held in a branch history register (BHR). In Section 5 we consider performance using less expensive predictors.

1.3. Paper Overview

We focus on methods of assigning confidence to branch predictions -- not the applications of the confidence methods. We are currently investigating some of the more interesting applications, and our goal here is to establish a set of base confidence methods to use as a starting point for other studies. In Section 2, we collect branch prediction accuracy statistics and relate them to static branches. This exercise establishes the general method we will use to display confidence results, and it suggests an optimal static confidence method that we use as a baseline for comparing the dynamic methods to follow. In Section 3, we look at a number of general dynamic confidence methods, using both one and two levels of tables. In Section 4, we give some experimental results for the dynamic methods using the IBS benchmark suite. In Section 5, we consider some practical implementation issues for dynamic confidence methods with a goal of reducing logic complexity and cost. Section 6 concludes the paper.

2. Analysis of Static Branches

We first consider an idealized method where all static branches are assigned either high or low confidence levels, based on the accuracy with which they can be predicted. We begin with the relatively powerful gshare dynamic predictor described in Section 1.2 and collect statistics for each static branch: 1) the number of times the branch is executed, and 2) the number of incorrect predictions. Consequently, the misprediction rate for each static branch can be generated.

Then we combine the branches for all the benchmarks and normalize them so that each benchmark effectively contributes the same number of dynamic branches. Next, we sort the static branches according to their misprediction rates, highest rate first. This concentrates the most difficult to predict static branches at the top of the sorted list, and the sorted list can then be used to divide the predicted branches into low and high confidence sets.

Of course, many such sets are possible, depending on what we define to be "low" and "high" -- we have thus far been vague on this point. To understand the range of possibilities, we go down the the sorted list of branch statistics and plot accumulated fractions of mispredicted branches versus the accumulated fractions of executed branches that produce them. For the IBS benchmarks, Fig. 2 is the resulting plot.

Note that the graph has discrete data points (although they run together when plotted), corresponding to each static branch that occurs in the sorted list. Each such point defines a pair of high and low confidence branch prediction sets. To interpret the graph, consider

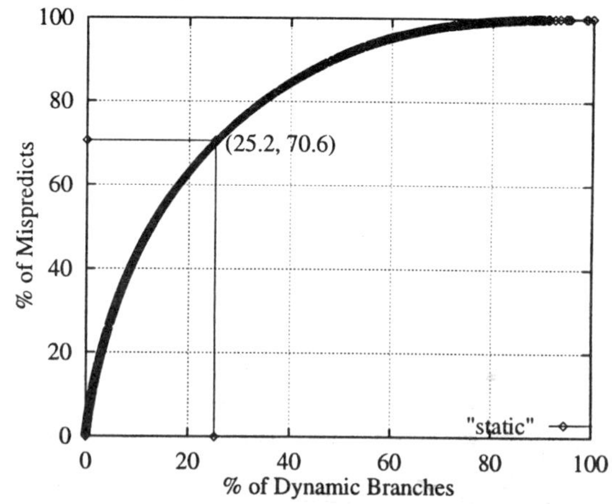

Fig. 2. Cumulative mispredictions versus cumulative dynamic branches.

the data point (25.2,70.6), marked on the graph. At this point, 25.2 percent of the dynamic branches have been accumulated by the time we reach the static branch in question, and 70.6 of the mispredictions are included. That is, we can separate the branches so that 25.2 percent of executed branches are placed in the low confidence set and account for 70.6 percent of the mispredictions.

The general shape of the curve is a steep rise that rounds a "knee" into a nearly horizontal line. This particular curve for static branches has a rather gentle knee; some of the dynamic methods given in the next section have much sharper knees. The steeper the initial slope and the farther to the left the knee occurs, the better. With a curve of this shape, more mispredictions are concentrated within a smaller set of low confidence predictions. Or, in other words, the branches in the lower confidence set have a higher misprediction rate, and, conversely, the branches in the higher confidence set have a lower misprediction rate. The ideal low confidence set would consist solely of mispredicted branches. The corresponding graph would have a straight line parallel to the y-axis shifted to the right from the origin by the mispredict rate.

One could develop a static branch confidence method based on the procedure just followed. That is, one could profile branches as we have just done. Then a threshold misprediction rate could be set, with all static branches above the threshold being tagged one way (low confidence), and those below tagged another (high confidence). Or, alternatively, a fraction of mispredictions could be chosen, and the corresponding set of static branches could be selected as the low confidence ones.

For the static confidence method just described, the graph in Fig. 2 provides an optimistic estimate of the performance. The method is optimistic because it represents "perfect" profiling -- we are executing the programs with exactly the same data as for the profile. Nevertheless, we use the results from this optimistic static method for comparison with the dynamic methods we consider in the following sections. At a minimum, we would like the dynamic methods to exceed the performance of the static method.

3. Dynamic Confidence Mechanisms

In the previous section we partitioned static branches into high and low confidence sets. That is, all dynamic predictions of the same static branch are assigned to the same confidence set. However, we can also partition branches so that dynamic predictions of the same static branch can be assigned to different confidence sets. This partitioning is done based on dynamic history, and we refer to these as *dynamic confidence mechanisms*. There are a large number of dynamic confidence mechanisms available. They are first cousins of dynamic branch predictors, and many such branch predictors have been proposed over the years [4,7,9,13]. In this paper, we cannot explore the entire design space. But we select some representative confidence methods -- those that preliminary experiments indicated as being more interesting variations.

We begin with generic confidence mechanisms that are somewhat idealized. In Section 5 we refine them to more practical implementations.

3.1. One-Level Confidence Methods

The one level dynamic confidence methods are so-named because they use a single level of table lookup; this is illustrated in Fig. 3. The table contains the n most recent correct/incorrect indications for the given table entry. These n-bit entries are essentially shift registers. We call each of these a Correct/Incorrect Register (CIR, pronounced "sir"), and we refer to the entire table as the CIR Table (CT). We use the convention that a 1 in a CIR indicates an incorrect prediction, and a 0 indicates correct prediction. For example if a prediction is correct 3 times, followed by an incorrect prediction, followed by 4 correct predictions, then an 8-bit CIR contains 00010000.

There are a number of possibilities for accessing the table. In one, the (truncated) program counter for a branch instruction is used as an index into the CT. Alternatively, one could keep track of global branch outcomes in a branch history register (BHR) and use it to index into the CT. A third alternative is to maintain a global CIR (i.e. correct/incorrect status collected for the most recent dynamic branches) and use it to index into the CT.

Beginning with these three basic methods of indexing into the CT (PC, global BHR, global CIR), one can construct a number of others by concatenating portions of each or exclusive-ORing them. Preliminary studies we have done indicate that exclusive-ORing is more effective than concatenating sub-fields. However, this can be

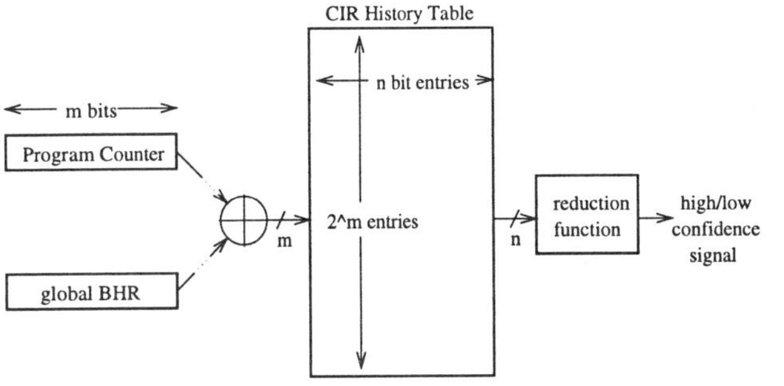

Fig. 3. One Level Dynamic Confidence Mechanism(s).

influenced by the table size and deserves further study. Our preliminary studies also indicate that indexing with a global CIR is of little value -- it gives low performance when used alone and typically reduces performance when added to the others. Consequently, we will report results only for implementations using the PC and global BHR. This leads to three variations for indexing into the CT: PC alone, global BHR alone, and PC xor BHR.

Now, to divide the branches into two sets, we have to take the CIR accessed from the table and reduce it to a single binary signal. In general, we do this by passing the CIR through a combinational logic block, named the "reduction" function in Fig. 3. For example, the reduction function could perform a ones count on the CIR: more ones indicate a higher number of recent mispredictions which would tend to indicate lower accuracy. In Section 5, we will consider this ones count reduction function, along with some others.

In an actual implementation, complete CIRs could be kept in the CT, with a separate logic block implementing the reduction function, exactly as shown in Fig. 3. However, one might also use implementations that maintain a compressed form of the CIRs in the CT along with a simplified reduction function. These will be discussed more in Section 5.

3.2. Two Level methods

With two level dynamic confidence methods, we index into a first level CT in a manner similar to the one level methods, then combine the CIR read from the table with some combination of the PC and global BHR to index into a second level CT. The second level table contains the Correct/Incorrect values for the p most recent times the first level CIR/PC/BHR combination occurred. Finally, the CIR read out of the second level table passes through a combinational reduction function as in the previous one level methods.

There are several variations of the two-level method (refer to Fig. 4). In general, one can hash some

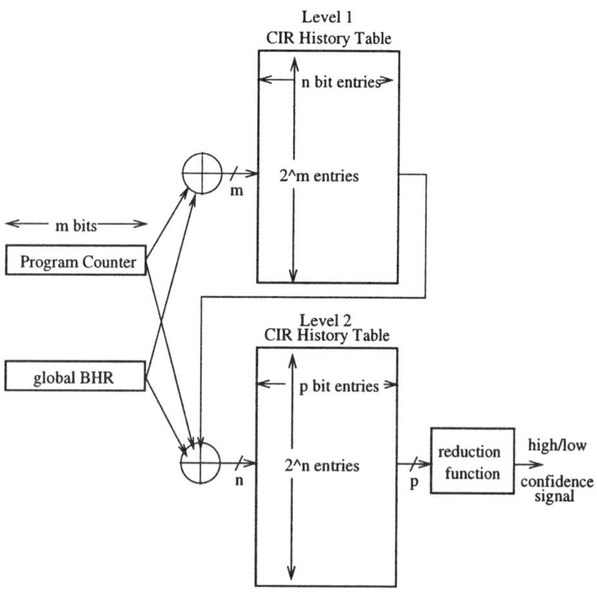

Fig. 4. Two Level Dynamic Confidence Mechanism(s).

combination of PC and global BHR for the first table, then hash the output of the first table with some combination of PC and global BHR. This leads to 12 different possibilities -- and other two level structures could probably be made (one could consider using the global CIR when computing the index into the second level table, for example). After some preliminary exploration, we settle on only three representative methods.

In the first variation, the PC alone is used to read the first table, and the CIR alone is used to access the second level table. In the second variation, the PC xor BHR is used to read the first level table, and the CIR read from the table is used to read the second level table. The third variation is like the second except the PC and BHR are exclusive-ORed with the CIR read from the first level table before indexing into the second level table.

4. Experimental Results

We now use trace-driven simulation to study the dynamic confidence methods outlined in the previous section. As stated earlier, the underlying branch predictor is a gshare predictor using a table with 2^{16} two-bit counters. The prediction table is accessed with the exclusive-OR of the 16 low order PC bits and a 16 bit global BHR. For the one level confidence methods, the CIR tables also have 2^{16} entries, each of which contains a 16 bit CIR. We simulate the IBS benchmark suite. Results are averaged by weighting the individual benchmarks so that each contributes the same total number of dynamic branches. For the relatively large underlying branch predictor we use, the overall misprediction rate is 3.85 percent.

For all methods, we initialize the branch predictor table to "weakly taken" and the CIR tables to all ones. All ones was found to give better results than other initial CT values we studied; additional information on initial values will be given in Section 5.

Initially, we will collect separate statistics for each CIR value read from the CT (the second level CT in the case of the two level methods). For each CIR pattern we keep track of number of times the pattern appears and the fraction of incorrect predictions that occurred when that CIR pattern was read.

After collecting this data for each CIR pattern, we sort and construct a graph similar to that used for the static method in section 2. In particular, we sort the CIR patterns according to misprediction rates, highest rate at the top. The sorted list is used to plot data points -- one per CIR. For each point the X axis value is the fraction of accumulated conditional branches corresponding to this CIR and those higher on the list; the Y axis value is the fraction of mispredictions the conditional branches account for. Now, each point can be used to define high and low confidence prediction sets. A combinational reduction function that detects the sets selects only those CIRs above (low confidence) or below (high confidence) the CIR in question. The CIRs define minterms for the reduction function.

As in the static method, this method of determining the confidence sets is idealized because the reduction function is tuned to a specific set of data input values. In addition, the combinational reduction function could be very complicated, i.e. it could have many prime implicants -- many of which could conceivably be minterms. In Section 5 we look at more practical reduction functions.

4.1. One Level Methods

Fig. 5 gives performance graphs for one level methods: indexing with PC alone, global BHR alone, and PC xor BHR. Note that in order to avoid the data points running together (as they do in Fig. 2) we only plot those points that differ from a previous point by 2.5 percent. The best method (the one that concentrates the largest set of mispredictions into the smallest set of predictions) uses PC xor BHR to index into the table. The reason is that the PC and the BHR together more precisely establish a context for the branch in question than either alone (essentially the same reasoning that leads to the gshare predictor). A close second in performance indexes with the global BHR alone, and the worst performance is provided by using the PC alone. Consider the points in the curves that correspond to a low confidence set containing 20 percent of all the branch predictions (20 percent is chosen rather arbitrarily for illustrative purposes). Indexing with PC xor BHR concentrates 89 percent of the mispredictions into the low confidence set; BHR alone concentrates 85 percent, and the PC concentrates 72 percent.

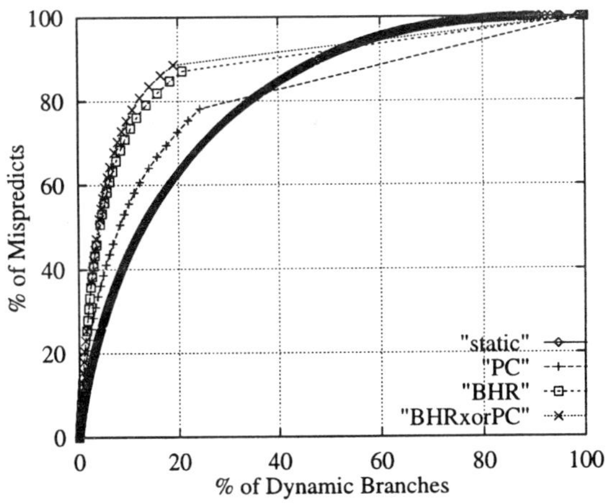

Fig. 5. Cumulative mispredictions versus cumulative dynamic branches for one level dynamic confidence methods.

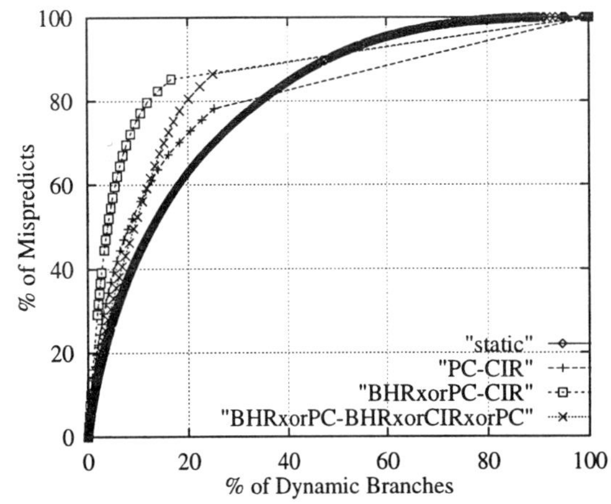

Fig. 6. Cumulative mispredictions versus cumulative dynamic branches for two level dynamic confidence methods.

Also shown in the Fig. 5 graph is a curve for the static method given in Section 2. We see that the dynamic methods are capable of performing much better than the optimistic static method. For comparison, with the static method 20 percent of the branches concentrate only about 63 percent of the mispredictions.

For the dynamic methods, the all zeros CIR occurs frequently, and we refer to this all zeros CT entry as the "zero bucket". The zero bucket corresponds to the case where the table entry has seen a correct prediction the last 16 times in a row. It is not surprising that the zero bucket is accessed frequently, given that the overall prediction accuracy is 96.15 percent. The large zero bucket explains the long gap between data points for the dynamic methods in the right side of the graph. For example, with the two better dynamic methods, about 80 percent of the branch predictions lead to the all zeros CIR, and 12-15 percent of the mispredictions occur with the all zeros CIR. Hence, in the 20 to 100 percent dynamic branch region of the graph, the dynamic methods have no data points. The static method does have data points, however, and these points allow the static curve to arc above the interpolated curves for the dynamic methods in this region.

Finally, we note once again that the dynamic results are idealized in a way similar to the way the static branches are. In particular, we sort the CIRs from worst to best based on their performance for the IBS benchmarks, and effectively use an optimal reduction function for the resulting CT. When we look at practical reduction functions, this level of optimism will be mitigated.

4.2. Two Level Methods

Now, we consider the two level confidence methods. The results are shown in Fig. 6 The best method accesses the first level table with PC xor BHR, and the second level table is accessed only with the CIR read from the first level table. The method that accesses the first level table with PC xor BHR and the second level table with the first level CIR xor PC xor BHR is generally the second best performer. However, there is a region in the 5 to 10 percent range (X-axis) where the third method -- PC accessing the first level, CIR the second level -- is slightly better. Otherwise the third method is worse than the other two level methods we chose to simulate. As with the one level methods, the all zeros CT entry is very large and leads to no data points from the 10-30 percent region to the 100 percent point on the X-axis.

In Fig. 7, we compare our best one level method (from Fig. 5) with our best two level method (from Fig. 6) and the static method (from Fig. 2). We see that the one and two level methods give very similar performance. If anything, the two level method performs very slightly worse. The main difference is the presence or absence of the second level table; the first level tables are identical. Consequently we conclude that the extra hardware in the second level table is not worth the cost, at least when we use ideal reduction functions. Additional studies with realistic reduction functions tend to reinforce this conclusion, so we do not consider two level tables further in this paper.

5. Implementation Issues

In this section we apply the results from the previous section to arrive at actual implementations. First, we look at reduction functions, then consider what we call the "granularity" issue, cost considerations, and initialization issues.

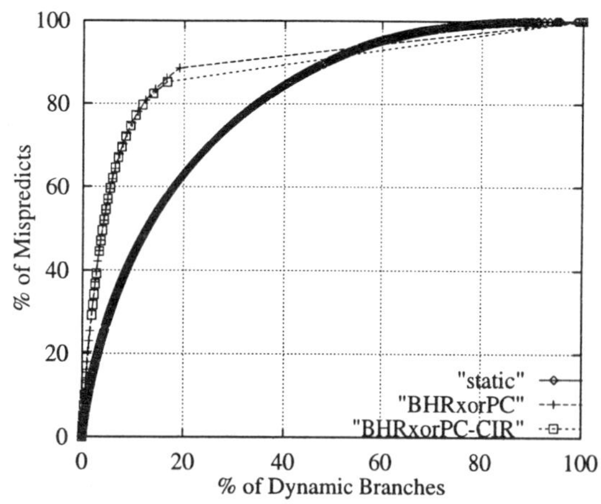

Fig. 7. Comparison of best one level, two level, and static methods.

5.1. Reduction Functions

We now propose some simple reduction functions and compare results they provide with the relatively optimistic results from the previous section. For the obvious reasons of reducing cost and/or logic complexity, we would like simple reduction functions. We have arrived at three by inspection of the sorted lists of CIRs, guided by our intuition.

We have already observed that PC xor BHR indexing performs best of the one level methods we studied. Consequently, in this section, we focus on this method. Note that we will occasionally refer to this method simply as the "best", even though it is only the best *of those we studied.*

Ones Counting. First, we consider counting the ones in the CIRs read from the table. The reasoning is that the more ones in the CIR, the higher the number of recent mispredictions, and therefore the more likely there will be a future mispredict. Because the CIRs are length 16 in the study given above, we have 17 data points (0 ones, i.e. no mispredictions out of the last 16, a single one, i.e. one mispredict, etc. up to 16 ones). The results for ones counting and for the other reduction methods considered in this section are plotted in Fig. 8. On the same graph is the plot for the optimistic reduction function we are trying to approximate; the optimistic curve does not have the discrete data points plotted to make the other points easier to read. Note that for ones counting the zero bucket lines up with the optimistic zero bucket (as it should). The one level method with ones counting falls short of optimum for other data points, however.

The reason is that with a one level table, there is significant time ordering in the CIR, with the most recent 16 predictions being represented, in time sequence. However, recent mispredictions, e.g. the most recent, correlate better than the older ones, e.g. 16 predictions ago. Yet, with ones counting, they are all given equal weight.

Saturating Counters. A second reduction function that we consider is a saturating ones count on the CIR values. We do not expect this method to perform any better than ones counting. However, it could lead to a less costly confidence method because the saturating counters can be embedded into the CT in place of the CIRs -- leading to an essentially logarithmic reduction in table space. Using counters that count from 0 to 16 allow us to compare directly with the ones counters from the preceding subsection (although a slightly less expensive implementation would count from 0 to 15). We count up for each correct prediction and down for each incorrect one, saturating at the extremes of 0 and 16. We once again have 17 data points which we plot in Fig. 8. We see that saturating counters have a potential deficiency. In particular, the equivalent of the zero bucket, the maximum saturated counter, becomes significantly larger; i.e. it contains more mispredicted branches. This happens because branches that are correctly predicted a vast majority of the time usually access a maximum saturated counter. If there is a single misprediction, followed by a correct prediction, then the saturating count will be non-maximum for only one branch. On the other hand, if the full CIR is kept and a ones count is used, the single misprediction will lead to a nonzero CIR for the next 16 branches. This means many non-zero CIRs containing a single one are "converted" to the maximum saturated count value.

For the portions of the curves at the extreme left of the graph, i.e. before the zero bucket region is reached,

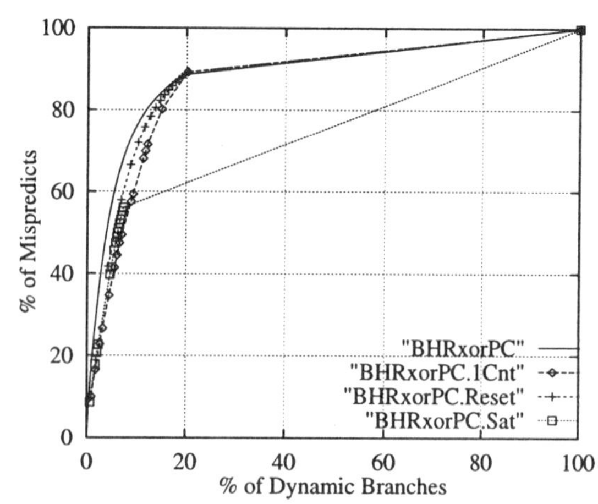

Fig. 8. Confidence graph for one level method with reduction via ones counting, saturating counting, and resetting counting.

saturating counters behave about as well as ones counting. Consequently, if we choose to partition the confidence sets in this region, i.e. with 10 percent or fewer of the dynamic branches in a low confidence set containing about 60 percent of the mispredictions, then saturating counters appear to be adequate. However, the large maximum saturated counter region makes it impossible to partition with a larger low confidence set -- i.e. containing more than 60 percent or more of the mispredictions. Consequently, we might like to find a better method for cost-saving than saturating counters that maintains the zero bucket characteristics of the optimal curve.

Resetting Counters. A third algorithm was arrived at by examining the sorted lists of CIRs. In doing so, we observed that a few CIR patterns account for most of the dynamic branches. In particular those containing all zeros or a single one -- this reflects the high accuracy of the underlying branch predictor. This suggests that we can capture most of the information of full-length CIRs by only keeping track of the time the most recent misprediction has occurred, and this can be accomplished by incrementing a counter held in the CT each time the corresponding branch is predicted correctly, and resetting the counter to zero on any misprediction. The counter saturates at 16 -- to match the CIR and counter sizes used in the preceding subsections.

Fig. 8 shows the results with a resetting counter, as compared with the ideal reduction function, ones counting, and saturating counters. We see that the resetting counter works quite well. It tracks the ideal curve closely, and has the same zero bucket. In addition, as observed earlier for saturating counters, a resetting counters can replace the full-length CIRs in the CT, yielding a logarithmic cost savings. We conclude that resetting counters are probably the best choice for implementing confidence methods in a practical manner.

5.2. Threshold Granularity

For producing the confidence sets in practice, we note we are at the mercy of the natural "buckets" that result from the reduced CIRs. For example, if we were using resetting counters, we can only establish confidence sets at data points determined by the 17 resetting counter values. Table 1 contains the 17 data points defined by the best single level method using resetting counters that count from 0 to 16. These counters saturate at 16. The first column contains the counter value; the second is the misprediction rate when the counter has the shown in the first column. The third and fourth columns are the percentages of references and mispredictions that occur for the counter value, and the fifth and sixth columns are the cumulative reference and misprediction percentages from the top of the table. If we were to use a count value of 0 to define the low confidence set, then we could isolate 41.7 percent of the mispredictions to a set of 4.28 percent of the branch predictions. Of course, we would only need

Table 1: Statistics for Resetting Counter Values

Count	Mis-pred. Rate	% Refs.	% Mis-preds.	Cum. % Refs.	Cum.% Mis-preds.
0	.376	4.28	41.7	4.28	41.7
1	.241	2.58	16.2	6.85	57.9
2	.174	1.91	8.64	8.76	66.5
3	.136	1.54	5.45	10.3	72.0
4	.112	1.31	3.80	11.6	75.8
5	.090	1.14	2.66	12.8	78.5
6	.079	1.03	2.12	13.8	80.6
7	.071	.936	1.73	14.7	82.3
8	.062	.860	1.39	15.6	83.7
9	.058	.798	1.19	16.4	84.9
10	.053	.744	1.02	17.1	85.9
11	.045	.699	.817	17.8	86.7
12	.043	.662	.746	18.5	87.5
13	.040	.628	.645	19.1	88.1
14	.039	.598	.599	19.7	88.7
15	.037	.571	.550	20.3	89.3
16	.005	79.7	10.7	100.	100.

a single-bit "counter" to accomplish this. Similarly, if we were to use a count of 0 or 1, then we could isolate 57.9 percent of the mispredictions to within a set of 6.85 percent of the branch predictions, etc. The maximum count, 16, is equivalent to the zero bucket for full-length CIRs. Consequently, if we use counter values from 0 to 15, we can isolate 89.3 percent of the mispredictions to a set of 20.3 percent of the branches. In the relatively large zero bucket region defined by the saturated counter, we can not achieve any finer granularity. We could, however, use larger counters to get somewhat better granularity, but this approach is limited.

Finally, note that we are using the same tables and reduction functions for all programs, yet we have been discussing confidence levels for a particular set of benchmarks. There can be variation in the confidence sets depending on the individual benchmark or program. Considering just the IBS benchmarks, Fig. 9 shows the confidence curves for the best (JPEG) and worst (GCC) performing IBS benchmarks using the best single level method with ideal reduction. We see that there is considerable variation. The zero buckets appear to contain approximately the same fractions of mispredictions, but the total number of branches in the zero bucket varies considerably. The importance of this characteristic will depend on the application to which the confidence mechanism is applied.

5.3. Cost Considerations

The study thus far has assumed fairly large (and relatively expensive) predictors and confidence methods. We did this to reduce aliasing effects so that we could get

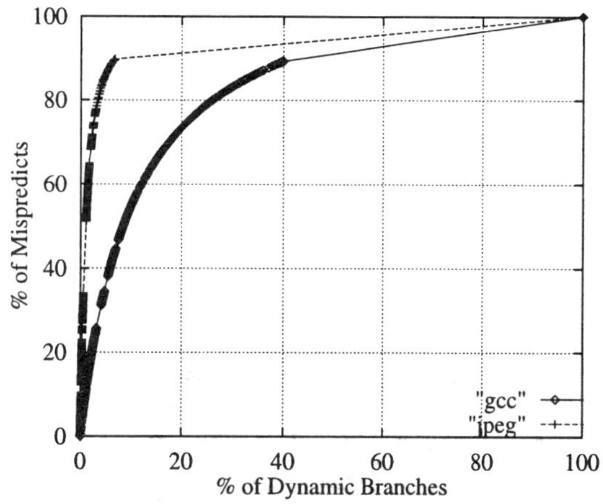

Fig. 9. Confidence graphs for best (JPEG) and worst (GCC) performing benchmarks. The best one level confidence method with ideal reduction is used.

an idea of how a more pure implementation might perform. However, we should also consider smaller, less expensive implementations. We do not fully explore the design space here. Rather, we choose a particular small predictor and investigate the performance of the single level confidence method when aliasing is present. We use a series of small confidence history tables to illustrate the fall-off in performance as we reduce the table size.

For the smaller underlying branch predictor we use a gshare branch predictor with 4K entries consisting of saturating 2-bit counters. The predictor is accessed with the exclusive-OR of bits 13-2 of the branch program counter and 12 bits of global branch history. The misprediction rate of this predictor for the IBS benchmarks is 8.6 percent.

We implemented a confidence mechanism that uses the best single level method, which is accessed the same way as the gshare predictor. Resetting counters are held in the CT. We simulate tables that are the same size as the predictor, 4K entries, down to 128 entries. The results are plotted in Fig. 10.

We see that for the case where the confidence table is the same size as the predictor, relative performance is somewhat less than for the larger table studied. We note that the zero bucket regions -- i.e. where counters are at their maximum values -- contain about the same fraction of mispredictions as before, but there are fewer overall branches in this region. To put it another way, the low confidence sets contain about the same fraction of mispredictions, but they are larger sets. This occurs because of the aliasing that takes place. If any branch accessing the same table entry suffers a misprediction, then the counter resets, and it will take at least 16 correct predictions for the the counter to re-enter the saturated state. Hence, aliased counters are likely to spend more of their time in the non-saturated state. Nevertheless, the performance is still fairly good with 75 percent of the mispredictions being identified with 20 percent of the conditional branches. This suggests that the confidence method can be applied when smaller, less costly predictors are used. For the case where the prediction and confidence tables have the same number of entries, the cost of the confidence method is twice the underlying predictor (4-bit resetting counters versus 2-bit saturating counters).

From Fig. 10, we also see that performance diminishes in a well-behaved manner as the confidence table is reduced in size. Again, this loss is no doubt due to aliasing. We can not make any definite statement about any one table size being more cost-effective than another, however, because to do so would require some knowledge of the application where the confidence method is to be used. That is, a performance/simulation model of the application for which we are using the confidence method would have to be used to determine actual performance impact of the confidence sets.

5.4. The Effect of Initial State

In the course of this study, we found that the initial state of the CIRs held in the CT is important, because it takes a long time for the tables to build up history. There are a number of possibilities for initializing the CIRs. For example, one could initialize the CIRs to all 0s, all 1s, and random. Another alternative is to not initialize the CIRs between context switches, but we did not study this alternative.

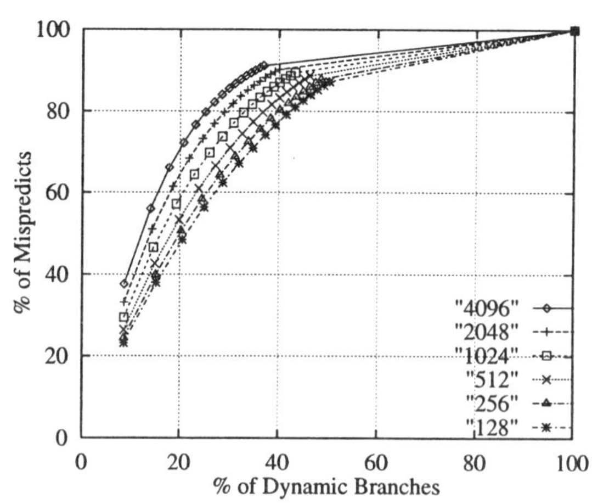

Fig. 10. Performance with small CIR tables; tables hold resetting counters, accessed with PC xor BHR.

Fig. 11 shows results for the ideal one level method using a CT with 2^{16} entries. We see that all 1's and random perform similarly, but all 0s does not perform nearly as well. As mentioned above, there are differences because the CT has a fairly "deep" memory, and initial state effects still appear even when the benchmarks are run to their full length. The all 0's initialization increases the number of branches in the zero bucket when a benchmark begins. At startup there is likely to be a higher number of mispredictions, but the initially zero CIRs will assign them a high confidence. On the other hand, a non-zero initial value will tend to assign a lower confidence. However, exactly which non-zero initial value is used does not seem to make much difference.

If better performance is provided by avoiding all zeros, then a reasonable alternative is to initialize only the "oldest" bit in the CIR to 1 and the others to zero. We refer to this as "lastbit", and the results are shown in Fig. 11 along with the other initial values. We see that the performance is essentially the same as for the other nonzero methods. From this experiment, we conjecture that one could probably leave the CIRs at their current values at the time of a context switch, except the oldest bit which should be initialized at 1. This would tend to simplify the initialization hardware and provide good performance.

6. Conclusions

For implementing confidence methods, there is a large design space -- probably as large as for branch prediction, and many branch prediction methods have been proposed and studied over the years. Consequently, the methods proposed here are by no means comprehensive.

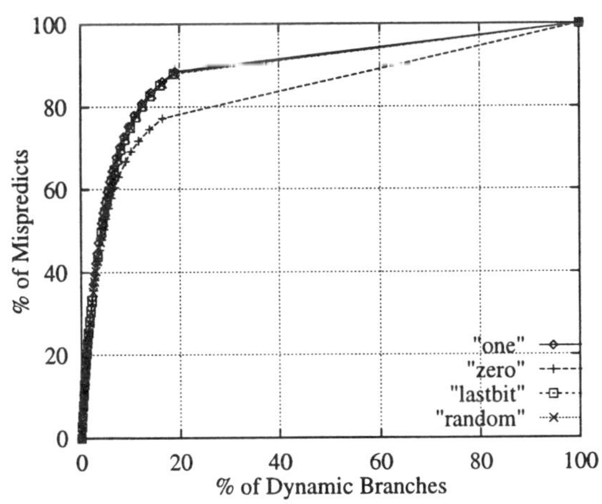

Fig. 11. The effect of different CT initializations; the best one level confidence method with ideal reduction is used.

Our goal has been to introduce the concept of assigning confidence to branch predictions and to look at the characteristics of some methods. There are no doubt many other possible methods that can (and should) be explored.

Just looking at static branches indicates that some are predicted with higher confidence than others; but to better separate the low and high confidence predictions one must look at dynamic information. This is similar to the case with branch prediction where predictors taking the dynamic context into account perform better than static predictors.

Dynamic confidence methods are indeed better than static ones -- even the ideal static method. In general, it appears that the single level dynamic methods work as well as the two level methods and are less expensive. Of reduction functions, we found that resetting counters work well, and these counters can be embedded into the CIR table to reduce cost.

Most of our study was for large (64K) predictors and confidence tables. When using smaller (4K) predictors and smaller confidence tables (4K and smaller), we found that the confidence methods performed relatively worse -- the reason is that the use of resetting counters tends to amplify the negative effects of aliasing.

Of the applications we mentioned above, we are currently researching three out of the four. We are studying potential performance benefits of selective dual thread forking as well as aspects of the implementation. For this application, data for the single level methods indicate that if we fork a dual thread following 20 percent of the conditional branch predictions, we can capture over 80 percent of the mispredictions. We conjecture that this will be adequate to provide worthwhile performance gains.

We also have studies for the reverser and the hybrid prediction selector underway. The reverser application looks promising, but a key issue will be whether the cost/performance of a predictor plus reverser is better than the cost/performance of a more powerful predictor -- indeed, the predictor/reverser model could be considered a method of decomposing the design of a powerful predictor. The study of the hybrid prediction selector has just begun, but we are optimistic that work on branch confidence will lead to a systematic way of developing near-optimal selectors.

Acknowledgements

This work was supported in part by NSF Grant MIP-9505853 and by the U.S. Army Intelligence Center and Fort Huachuca under Contract DABT63-95-C-0127 and ARPA order no. D346. The views and conclusions contained herein are those of the authors and should not be interpreted as necessarily representing the official policies or endorsements, either expressed or implied, of the U.S. Army Intelligence Center and Fort Huachuca, or the

U.S. Government. Eric Rotenberg is funded by an IBM graduate fellowship. Erik Jacobsen was funded by a Wisconsin/Hilldale undergraduate research scholarship

The authors would like to thank Joel Emer for helpful discussions while this work was in progress and for suggesting potential applications.

References

[1] M. Evers, P. Chang, and Y. Patt, ''Using Hybrid Branch Predictors to Improve Branch Prediction Accuracy in the Presence of Context Switches,'' *International Symposium on Computer Architecture*, pp. 3-11 , May 1996.

[2] Linley Gwennap, ''MIPS R10000 Uses Decoupled Architecture,'' *Microprocessor Report*, vol. 8, pp. 18-22, October 24, 1994.

[3] B. T. Hailpern and B. L. Hitson, ''S-1 Architecture Manual,'' CSL Report STAN-CS-79-715., Stanford University, January 1979.

[4] J. K. F. Lee and A. J. Smith, ''Branch Prediction Strategies and Branch Target Buffer Design,'' *Computer*, vol. 17, pp. 6 - 22, January 1984.

[5] S. McFarling, ''Combining Branch Predictors,'' Digital Western Research Lab Technical Note TN-36, June 1993.

[6] Motorola, ''PowerPC 601 User's Manual,'' 1993, No. MPC601UM/AD.

[7] S.-T. Pan, K. So, and J. T. Rahmeh, ''Improving the Accuracy of Dynamic Branch Prediction Using Branch Correlation,'' *Proc. Architectural Support for Programming Languages and Operating Systems (ASPLOS-V)*, pp. 76-84, October 1992.

[8] Michael Slater, ''AMD's K5 Designed to Outrun Pentium,'' *Microprocessor Report*, vol. 8, pp. 1,6-11, October 24, 1994.

[9] J. E. Smith, ''A Study of Branch Prediction Strategies,'' *Proc. Eighth Annual Symposium on Computer Architecture*, pp. 135-148, May 1981.

[10] D. Tullsen, S. Eggers, J. Emer, H. Levy, J. Lo, and R. Stamm, ''Exploiting Choice: Instruction Fetch and Issue on an Implementable Simultaneous Multithreading Processor,'' *Proc. 23rd Annual International Symposium on Computer Architecture*, pp. 191-202, May 1996.

[11] Richard Uhlig, David Nagle, Trevor Mudge, Stuart Sechrest, and Joel Emer, ''Instruction Fetching: Coping with Code Bloat,'' *Proc. 22nd Annual Symposium on Computer Architecture*, pp. 345-356, June 1995.

[12] A. K. Uht and V. Sindagi, ''Disjoint Eager Execution: An Optimal Form of Speculative Execution,'' *Proc. 28th Annual International Symposium on Microarchitecture*, pp. 313-325, November 1995.

[13] T. Y. Yeh and Y. N. Patt, ''Two-Level Adaptive Branch Prediction,'' *Proc. 24th Annual International Symposium on Microarchitecture*, November 1991.

Compiler Synthesized Dynamic Branch Prediction

Scott Mahlke Balas Natarajan
Hewlett-Packard Laboratories
Palo Alto, CA 94304
E-mail: {mahlke,balas}@hpl.hp.com

Abstract

Branch prediction is the predominant approach for minimizing the pipeline breaks caused by branch instructions. Traditionally, branch prediction is accomplished in one of two ways, static prediction at compile-time via compiler analysis or dynamic prediction at run-time via special hardware structures. In this paper, we propose a novel technique that aims to combine the strengths of the two approaches – the lower cost of compile-time analysis with the effectiveness of dynamic prediction. Specifically, we propose that the compiler use profile feedback to define a prediction function for each branch and insert a few explicit instructions per branch into the compiled code to compute the prediction function. These instructions are carefully selected to predict the direction of the branch using any information available during run-time. A strength of this approach is that information beyond branch history can be used to make predictions, such as the contents of the architectural registers. To substantiate our proposal, we present an algorithm for selecting the prediction instructions, and demonstrate the performance of the approach against contemporary static and dynamic branch prediction strategies.

1 Introduction

The performance of pipelined processors depends strongly on the efficiency with which branch instructions are handled. Branches cause lengthy breaks in the pipeline by redirecting instruction flow during program execution. In a simple pipelined processor, instructions proceed sequentially through fetch, decode, execute, and write-back stages of the pipeline. When a branch is fetched, the address of the instruction that will execute next is not immediately known. Hence, the fetch stage must stall and wait for the branch target to be calculated. The target of a branch is generally resolved during the execute stage. Therefore, the fetch unit stalls while the branch advances through the decode and execute stages of the pipeline. After the branch instruction has completed execution, the branch direction is known and instruction fetch can safely resume at the correct target address. Stalling the instruction fetch for each branch introduces a large number of empty cycles, referred to as bubbles, into the pipeline. These bubbles severely limit the performance of pipelined processors by restricting the utilization of the processor resources. The performance problem becomes amplified as pipeline depth and instruction issue width of processors are increased.

Branch prediction is a highly effective approach for dealing with branches in pipelined processors. Branch prediction guesses the targets of branches in order to speculatively continue executing instructions while a branch target is being calculated. In the cases where the prediction is correct, all the speculative instructions are useful instructions, and pipeline bubbles are completely eliminated. On the other hand, incorrect prediction results in both the normal pipeline bubbles while the branch target is resolved, as well as additional delay to remove all instructions that were improperly executed. Clearly, the accuracy of the branch prediction strategy is central to processor performance.

There are two basic classes of branch prediction strategies: static and dynamic. Static branch prediction utilizes information available at compile time to make predictions. In general, the compiler is responsible for static branch prediction. The most common static branch prediction approach is to use profile information [8],[5]. Other static branch prediction approaches include deriving and applying heuristics based on program structure [2],[6], and utilizing machine-learning techniques to determine static feature sets of branches that are correlated with branch direction [3]. Static branch prediction can also be done with simple hardware such as prediction using branch direction (backward taken, forward not taken) [15]. The major advantage of static branch prediction is the low cost. Branch state information is not required since the prediction is explicitly specified by the program itself. The fundamental limitation of static branch prediction is the prediction is fixed at compile-time, thus it cannot vary during program execution. As a result, the accuracy of static branch prediction is inherently limited for unbiased branches.

The second class of branch prediction strategies is dynamic branch prediction. Dynamic branch prediction utilizes run-time behavior to make predictions. In general, a hardware structure is provided to maintain branch history. Based on the current history, a prediction is made for each branch encountered in the program. Example dynamic branch prediction schemes are the branch target buffer (BTB) with a 2-bit saturating counter [15] [11] and two-level adaptive branch prediction [16],[17],[14]. More recently, hybrid branch predictors which allow different dynamic predictors to be selected for different branches, have been proposed [13],[4]. The major advantage of dynamic prediction is the increased accuracy. The use of run-time information and the ability to predict a branch differently during various phases of execution, allows dynamic techniques to enjoy significantly higher accuracy than static techniques. For superscalar and VLIW processors, this increased accuracy translates into large performance gains. The primary disadvantage of the dynamic prediction techniques is the cost. Dynamic branch prediction techniques utilize relatively large amounts of hardware and provide difficult challenges for circuit

1072-4451/96 $5.00 © 1996 IEEE

designers to meet cycle time goals.

In this paper, we propose a new approach for dynamic branch prediction, referred to as compiler synthesized prediction, that is not hardware based. Rather, the compiler is completely responsible for defining and realizing a prediction function for each branch. The technique is based on the following observation. When a branch is executed, the contents of the registers offer complete information on the outcome of the branch. In particular, evaluating the branch comparison on the source register values would perfectly predict the branch. As we go backwards in time from the branch, this information becomes gradually less complete. Thus, the contents of the registers offer a path to predicting the branch, although the prediction may not be perfect eight or sixteen cycles in advance of the branch. With this in mind, we propose that the compiler add a few instructions to the compiled code ahead of each branch to be predicted. The role of these instructions would be to predict the branch. These instructions will be standard operations from the instruction set of the processor, such as arithmetic, comparison, and logical instructions. The only hardware support needed for these instructions is that the instructions be allowed to write their predictions into a "branch predict register" that will later be used by the processor's instruction pipeline.

There are two major advantages to this approach. First, the flexibility of selecting a predictor function is vastly increased. The compiler is free to realize almost any function including standard hardware prediction functions (such as a 2-bit counter) as well as new functions involving the processor register values. These new predictor functions offer the potential to substantially increase the prediction accuracy where branch history is not effective. Furthermore, a specific prediction function can be tailored for each branch which minimizes cost and maximizes performance, as is utilized with the hybrid predictor strategy [4]. However with this approach, the number of predictors is not limited to a preselected group which are available in the hardware. The second advantage of this approach is the reduced hardware overhead. Branch prediction state information is no longer maintained and manipulated by a separate hardware structure. Rather, the compiler uses architecturally visible registers and explicit instructions to compute the branch prediction values.

Two important questions arise with compiler synthesized prediction. How is the compiler to determine the predictor, and how complex should the predictor be? Clearly, there is a tradeoff between the complexity of the predictor and its effectiveness. We give an algorithm that automatically generates a predictor for a branch from profile information — history of the machine register values and the branch outcome. The complexity of the predictor can be explicitly controlled in terms of the number of instructions involved. We close with experimental results obtained by applying our algorithm to some sample benchmarks. For each benchmark, we selected the branches that are most frequently mispredicted by the profile-based static predictor. Our results show that our proposed method can offer significantly improved prediction on these branches. In addition, we compare our results with popular hardware-based dynamic predictors, namely a 2-bit counter BTB and a two-level branch predictor.

2 Branch Architecture

The major architectural feature that is required to support compiler synthesized dynamic branch prediction is a branch prediction mechanism that is visible in the instruction set. By visible, it is meant that the compiler can generate instructions which manipulate the prediction values for a particular branch. In this manner, new prediction functions can be realized by inserting additional instructions into the program to compute prediction values and write them into the appropriate predictor locations. An additional requirement is that there must be a known way to associate branch predictor locations with the branches themselves. This is necessary to be able to selectively modify prediction values for specific branches.

The PlayDoh branch architecture is chosen as the baseline architecture for this paper [10]. PlayDoh is an experimental architecture specification that serves as a vehicle for ILP research. While PlayDoh provides general branch prediction and instruction prefetch mechanisms exposed to the compiler, it is not sufficient in its current form to support compiler synthesized dynamic branch prediction. Therefore, we extend it to support dynamic branch prediction. This section summarizes the baseline PlayDoh branch architecture and our extensions. The application of compiler synthesized branch prediction is not limited in any way to architectures such as PlayDoh. This section closes with a brief discussion of several strategies to incorporate compiler synthesized prediction into more traditional branch architectures.

2.1 PlayDoh branch architecture

In the PlayDoh architecture, a branch is broken down into its basic components [10]. The purpose of this strategy is to allow different pieces of information regarding a branch to be specified as soon as they become available. The processor can then utilize this early information to reduce the performance overhead of the branch. Branches consist of three components in PlayDoh:

1. Specification of the target address - Prepare-to-branch instructions specify the branch target address in advance of the branch point allowing a prefetch of the instructions from the target address to be performed [18]. A static prediction bit is also provided at this step to indicate the direction the compiler believes the branch will go.

2. Computation of the branch condition - The branch condition is computed by a compare-to-predicate instruction and stored in a predicate register. For an unconditional branch, this condition computation is not required. Hence, this component does not exist for unconditional branches.

3. Transfer of control - The actual redirection of control flow occurs if the branch is taken. The true branch in PlayDoh performs this action. The architecture provides several types of branch instructions including conditional, unconditional, branch and link, and special branches to support loop execution.

The PlayDoh instructions and their functionality are best described with an example. For simplicity, the guarding predicates

```
blt  r2, r3, L1          pbra                 b2, L1, 1
                         cmpp_w_lt_un_un      p2, -, r2, r3
                         brct                 b2, p2

      (a)                         (b)
```

Figure 1: Representation of a compare-and-branch instruction in PlayDoh, (a) conventional branch, (b) PlayDoh equivalent.

```
              Original branch:   blt  r2, r3, L1

                  p9 = f(···)    cmpp_w_lt_un_un   p2, -, r2, r3
pbra              b2, L1, p9, 0  pbra              b2, L1, p2, 1
cmpp_w_lt_un_un   p2, -, r2, r3  brct              b2, p2
brct              b2, p2

            (a)                           (b)
```

Figure 2: Representation of a compare-and-branch in PlayDoh with dynamic prediction, (a) dynamic prediction realization, (b) early comparison operand availability realization.

for each PlayDoh instruction are ignored in this discussion. Figure 1 contains an example compare-and-branch instruction for a general RISC architecture along with its realization in the PlayDoh architecture. The original branch, *blt*, branches to label *L1* if $r2$ is less than $r3$. Otherwise, execution falls through to the next sequential instruction. In the PlayDoh architecture, the branch is split up into its 3 components. The first instruction, *pbra*, specifies the potential target of the branch if it is taken, namely label *L1*. In addition, a 1-bit literal is specified to indicate the static prediction direction for the branch. In this example, the compiler expects the branch to be taken, so a '1' is used. The prepare-to-branch instruction writes the computed effective target address and prediction bit into a special set of registers, referred to as the branch target registers (BTRs). For the example, $b2$ is the BTR that is utilized. The BTRs are the medium to communicate the target and prediction information to the subsequent branch as well as the instruction prefetch unit.

The second instruction performs the actual comparison operation, computing $r2 < r3$ and storing the result into a predicate register ($p2$ in the example). The final instruction performs the actual branch. Each branch specifies a source BTR, which contains the branch target address. Furthermore, all branches which are conditional specify a source predicate operand as the condition. In this example, a branch on condition true (*brct*) is utilized, which indicates if p2 contains a 1, the branch should transfer control to the target address in $b2$.

The usage and functionality of the PlayDoh branch instructions is still a subject of open research, but some general statements can be made. Ideally, a prepare-to-branch instruction should be scheduled so that there is enough time between the prepare and the corresponding branch to prefetch instructions from the target address. Therefore, when the actual branch is encountered, instruction fetch can be immediately switched to the predicted target. The compiler must also manage the prefetch resources so they are not over-committed by a number of prepare instructions. There are no ordering restrictions placed between the prepare-to-branch and comparison instructions, so they can be scheduled in any order. However, the comparison instruction normally has limited code motion freedom because it must wait for the comparison operands to become available. In contrast, the prepare instruction uses only immediate operands, so it can be scheduled much earlier to allow the prefetch to complete.

2.2 Extensions to PlayDoh

As it stands, the PlayDoh architecture only supports static branch prediction. To enhance it to support compiler synthesized dynamic branch prediction, two simple extensions are made to the operation of the prepare-to-branch instruction. First, the 1-bit literal field used for static prediction is generalized to be a predicate register operand. In this manner, a prediction value may be computed by an arbitrary set of machine instructions with the final result placed in a predicate register. The prepare-to-branch instruction subsequently reads the particular predicate register to obtain the prediction value.

The second extension is to efficiently handle the case where a prediction is not required. Rather, the exact direction of the branch is known when the prepare-to-branch instruction is issued. For this case, the comparison operands are available very early, which allows the comparison to be computed in advance of the prepare. To support this mode of operation, a new 1-bit literal field is added to the prepare-to-branch instruction which specifies whether the predicate operand is the actual branch direction or simply a prediction. In the case where the predicate is the actual branch condition, the processor can be much more aggressive in terms of fetching and executing instructions after the branch since there is no ambiguity as to whether the prediction may turn out to be wrong. In the opposite case where the predicate utilized by the prepare is a prediction, the normal operation of the prepare is observed.

Instruction sequences illustrating the usage of the enhanced prepare-to-branch instruction are shown in Figure 2. The most common use is prepending the previous three instruction sequence with a set of instructions to compute a dynamic prediction for the branch. In the example (Figure 2a), the prediction value is computed by the function f and the result is stored into $p9$. The prepare-to-branch instruction explicitly sources the predicate register containing the prediction value along with the target of branch. In addition, the literal field specifying whether the predicate is the actual or a predicted value is set to 0, indicating the predicate is only a prediction. The prepare-to-branch instruction writes all this information into its destination BTR, $b2$. The two remaining instructions are the same as the conventional PlayDoh architecture.

The second case is where the branch comparison can be performed before the prepare. For this case (Figure 2b), the predicate operand for the prepare-to-branch is just specified as the destination of the comparison instruction, $p2$ in the example. In addition, the 1-bit field in the prepare is set to 1 to indicate the value in $p2$ is the actual branch direction. Again, the other instructions are unchanged from the baseline PlayDoh architecture.

2.3 Use in traditional branch architectures

The applicability of compiler synthesized dynamic branch prediction is not limited to architectures employing static branch prediction, such as PlayDoh. It can be efficiently incorporated into more conventional architectures that utilize hardware-based dynamic branch prediction. In [1], two schemes to accomplish compiler synthesis are proposed: Predicate Only Prediction (POP) and Predicate Enhanced Prediction (PEP). For these schemes, a traditional BTB is extended with an additional field for each entry. The new field holds the register number for the condition value of the branch. When a branch is allocated an entry in the BTB, the condition register number is recorded. Subsequent predictions of the branch fetch and utilize the contents of the condition register to assist with the prediction. In the POP scheme, the contents of the condition register fully specify the value of the prediction. In contrast for the PEP scheme, the contents of the condition registers are used to select among two potential prediction values.

These schemes offer two important advantages for a processor that utilizes hardware-based dynamic branch prediction. First, in cases where the comparison instruction for a particular branch can be hoisted sufficiently early, all mispredictions associated with the branch are eliminated. The branch predictor effectively communicates the known branch condition value to the instruction pipeline. The second advantage is that they efficiently support compiler synthesis of branch prediction functions. As with the PlayDoh model, the compiler inserts instructions into the program sufficiently in advance of the branch to compute prediction values. The only additional requirement is the condition value be stored in the branch condition register. Additionally with the PEP scheme, the compiler is free to selectively utilize its own synthesized prediction functions for certain branches and rely on the hardware-based predictor for the remaining branches.

3 The Prediction Algorithm

With support for compiler synthesized dynamic branch prediction available, the compiler is free to choose almost any prediction function for a branch. For the purposes of this paper, we have selected one class of predictor functions for investigation. Specifically, prediction functions are synthesized which correlate the values contained in architecture registers with the direction of the branch. Register contents and branch directions are obtained by profiling the target program. Of course, many other classes of prediction functions are interesting and will likely be the subject of future research.

For this section, a brief description of the general approach to obtain the information to be utilized by the compiler is first described. Then, the algorithms used to derive the branch prediction function are presented. The algorithm is best described in its basic form, i.e., in the context of infinite resources, assuming that the predictor can be arbitrarily complex. Later we describe a practical version of the algorithm that takes into account the fact that any real predictor will be restricted to consist of a few instructions. Otherwise, the cost of evaluating the predictor will outweigh the gains from the increased prediction accuracy.

3.1 General approach

The synthesis of branch prediction functions which correlate the values in architecture registers with the branch direction require two sets of information. First, for each branch a record of the direction taken for each execution is needed. This is identical to the information obtained with standard control flow profiling. The second set of information is a dump of the contents of the register file some predetermined distance before the branch. These register values are those that are available at run-time to compute a prediction. For the purposes of this paper, the register values 16 cycles before the branch are used. The procedure for collecting this information fits into the standard three step process used for almost all profile-based compilation:

Phase (1) Precompile: Compile the program without attempting any synthesis of branch prediction functions. Instrumentation code is inserted to collect branch direction information as well as the contents of the architectural registers a specified number of machine cycles prior to each branch.

Phase (2) Profile: Run the compiled code on sample inputs. The program will output the branch profile information as well as the register dump information.

Phase (3) Recompile: The register dumps are analyzed to identify correlations between branch directions and the contents of the registers. Based on the analysis, predictors are constructed for each branch. The operations for these predictors are added back to the intermediate code, and the intermediate code is then rescheduled to generate the final compiled code.

3.2 Basic prediction algorithm

Figure 3 gives our basic algorithm for constructing a predictor for a single branch. The algorithm limits itself to constructing predictors that are based on at most two registers in that the predictor will predict the branch predicate using the value of some two registers, at a predetermined number of cycles prior to the branch. This restriction on the number of registers is not inherent to the algorithm, and is only in the interest of pragmatics. Apart from this restriction, the algorithm pays no attention to resource constraints. Let the processor have n registers $r_1, r_2, ...r_n$. Let us focus on a specific branch b, and assume that the branch predicate value resides in a branch register r_b. At any particular execution of the branch, let $v_1, v_2, ..., v_n$ denote the values of the registers at a fixed number of cycles prior to branch b, and let v_b denote the value of the branch predicate after it is evaluated during that run. In other words, $v_1, v_2, ..., v_n$ and v_b constitute the entries in the register dump, for a particular pass through the branch, with the values $v_1 - v_n$ for the registers $r_1 - r_n$ being a fixed number of cycles prior to the branch, and the value v_b of the branch predicate register r_b just after the branch.

The algorithm maintains integer valued arrays, C_i for each register r_i and $C_{i,j}$ for each pair of registers r_i, r_j. There is one entry in C_i for each of the values r_i could take, and one entry in $C_{i,j}$ for each possible pair of values for r_i and r_j. This is an impracticable demand and is solely in the interest of expository clarity. Later, the algorithm will be modified to respect practical resource constraints. All the entries in the arrays are initialized to zero. For each pass through the branch b, if the branch predicate evaluated

```
for i = 1, 2, ..., n do
  for all register values v do C_i[v] = 0;
for i = 1, 2, ..., n do
  for i = 1, 2, ..., n do
    for all register values u, v do C_{i,j}[u][v] = 0;
for each pass through branch b do
  if v_b = 1 then
    for i = 1, 2, ..., n do increment C_i[v_i];
    for i, j = 1, 2, ..., n do increment C_{i,j}[v_i][v_j];
  else
    for i = 1, 2, ..., n do decrement C_i[v_i];
    for i, j = 1, 2, ..., n do decrement C_{i,j}[v_i][v_j];
for i = 1, 2, ..., n do S_i = Σ_v |C_i[v]|;
for i, j = 1, 2, ..., n do S_{i,j} = Σ_{u,v} |C_{i,j}[u][v]|;
let k be such that S_k is maximum over all S_i.
let l, m be such that S_{l,m} is maximum over all S_{i,j}.
if S_{l,m} > S_k then
  output the two-register predictor based on r_l and r_m.
else output the one-register predictor based on r_k;

One-register predictor based on r_k
  predict (C_k[v_k] > 0)

Two-register predictor based on r_l, r_m
  predict (C_{l,m}[v_l][v_m] > 0)
```

Figure 3: The basic algorithm for branch prediction synthesis.

to true (v_b has the value 1), the arrays entries incremented. In particular, if register r_i had value v_i, then entry $C_i[v_i]$ is incremented. Similarly, $C_{i,j}[v_i][v_j]$ is incremented for the pair of registers i, j. If the branch predicate evaluated to false (v_b has the value 0), the corresponding array entries are decremented. In essence, the entries in the array estimate the usefulness of knowing the values of the registers towards predicting the branch. If for a given value v of register r_i, the branch predicate evaluates to true much of the time, the array entry $C_i[v]$ will be strongly positive. Conversely, if the branch predicate evaluates to false much of the time, the array entry $C_i[v]$ will be strongly negative. If the branch predicate is evenly distributed between true and false, $C_i[v]$ will be close to zero.

With this in view, after all the passes through the branch have been processed, the absolute values of the array entries are summed up to assign scores S_i and $S_{i,j}$ to each register r_i and register pair r_i, r_j. The register or register pair with the highest score is the best predictor for the branch.

Once the register or register pair with the highest score has been selected, constructing a predictor is straightforward. Suppose a single register r_k has the highest score. A predictor involving r_k would take the value v_k of r_k, and check to see whether the array entry $C_k[v_k]$ is positive. If so, the branch is predicted to be 1, else not. If a pair of registers r_l, r_m have the highest score, the predictor would be similar. If $C_{l,m}[v_l][v_m]$ is positive, the branch predicate would be predicted to be 1, else 0.

Reg	Pass #						
	1	2	3	4	5	6	7
v_b	1	1	0	1	0	0	1
v_1	17	17	19	13	14	19	17
v_2	15	12	15	12	0	8	8

Table 1: Register dump for 7 passes of a branch, two-register machine of Example 1. Values for r_1 and r_2 are at 16 cycles ahead of the value for branch register r_b.

3.3 Example 1

To illustrate the working of the basic algorithm, we consider a processor with two registers r_1 and r_2, and one-branch register r_b. Suppose that for a sample execution in a certain program, a particular branch was executed seven times. The register dump for these seven passes is show in Table 1, where the values of r_1 and r_2 are at 16 cycles prior to the value of r_b.

Applying the basic algorithm, we get the following values for the array entries.

$C_1[17] = 3; C_1[19] = -2; C_1[13] = 1; C_1[14] = -1;$
$C_2[15] = 0; C_2[12] = 2; C_2[0] = -1; C_2[8] = 0;$
$C_{1,2}[17][15] = 1; C_{1,2}[17][12] = 1; C_{1,2}[19][15] = -1;$
$C_{1,2}[13][12] = 1; C_{1,2}[14][0] = -1;$
$C_{1,2}[19][8] = -1; C_{1,2}[17][8] = 1;$

From the above array values, we get that $S_1 = 7$, $S_2 = 3$ and $S_{1,2} = 7$. Taking S_1 to be the maximum of S_1, S_2 and $S_{1,2}$, the algorithm will output the one-register predictor based on r_1. The predictor is shown below in simplified form.

if $v_1 = 17$ or $v_1 = 13$ **then** predict 1
else predict 0

3.4 Practical prediction algorithm

We now discuss modifications to the basic algorithm to make it practical. Two issues must be addressed. (1) The range of the register values must be quantized so that the arrays C_i and $C_{i,j}$ are feasibly small. (2) The complexity of the predictors constructed should be small and controllable. In order to reduce the range of the register values, we quantize them to fit within a predetermined interval. We consider two quantizers, a linear quantizer and a logarithmic quantizer. The linear quantizer would scale the register values linearly to lie between 0 and 256, so that the arrays C_i would have 256 entries and the arrays $C_{i,j}$ would have 65536 entries. The logarithmic quantizer would simply take the logarithm of the register content in base 2, yielding a range from 0 to 32, assuming 32-bit registers. We will use one of these two quantizers for each register, depending on the distribution of values in the register dumps – for values that are widely dispersed we use the logarithmic quantizer and for values that are concentrated, the linear quantizer. A less ad hoc procedure for quantizer design is

for $i = 1, 2, ..., n$ **do**
  for all quantized register values v **do** $C_i[v] = 0$;
for $i = 1, 2, ..., n$ **do**
  for $i = 1, 2, ..., n$ **do**
    for all register values u, v **do** $C_{i,j}[u][v] = 0$;
for each pass through branch b **do**
  Quantize $v_1, v_2, ..., v_n$;
  if $v_b = 1$ **then**
    for $i = 1, 2, ..., n$ **do** increment $C_i[v_i]$;
    for $i, j = 1, 2, ..., n$ **do** increment $C_{i,j}[v_i][v_j]$;
  else
    for $i = 1, 2, ..., n$ **do** decrement $C_i[v_i]$;
    for $i, j = 1, 2, ..., n$ **do** decrement $C_{i,j}[v_i][v_j]$;
for $i = 1, 2, ..., n$ **do**
  $S_i = \max_{v^*} \left|\sum_{v<v*} C_i[v]\right| + \left|\sum_{v \geq v^*} C_i[v]\right|$;
for $i, j = 1, 2, ..., n$ **do**
  $S_{i,j} = \max_{u^*,v^*}$
  $\left|\sum_{u<u^*,v<v^*} C_{i,j}[u][v]\right| + \left|\sum_{u \geq u^*,v<v^*} C_{i,j}[u][v]\right| +$
  $\left|\sum_{u<u^*,v \geq v^*} C_{i,j}[u][v]\right| + \left|\sum_{u \geq u^*,v \geq v^*} C_{i,j}[u][v]\right|$;

let k be such that S_k is maximum over all S_i.
let l, m be such that $S_{l,m}$ is maximum over all $S_{i,j}$.

if $S_{l,m} > S_k$ **then**
  output the two-register predictor based on r_l and r_m.
else output the one-register predictor based on r_k;

One-register/One-compare predictor based on r_k
  if $v_k < v^*$ **then** predict $(\sum_{v<v*} C_k[v] > 0)$;
  else predict $(\sum_{v \geq v^*} C_k[v] > 0)$;

Two-register/Two-compare predictor based on r_l, r_m
  let $u = v_l; v = v_m$;
  if $u < u^*, v < v^*$ **then**
    predict $(\sum_{u<u^*,v<v^*} C_{l,m}[u][v] > 0)$;
  else if $u \geq u^*, v < v^*$ **then**
    predict $(\sum_{u \geq u^*,v<v^*} C_{l,m}[u][v] > 0)$;
  else if $u < u^*, v \geq v^*$ **then**
    predict $(\sum_{u<u^*,v \geq v^*} C_{l,m}[u][v] > 0)$;
  else predict $(\sum_{u \geq u^*,v \geq v^*} C_{l,m}[u][v] > 0)$;

Figure 4: The practical algorithm for branch prediction synthesis.

deferred to a later paper. There is a considerable body of literature on optimal quantizer design for prediction, see [12] for instance.

We restrict the complexity of the constructed predictors as follows. A one-register predictor is only allowed to compare the contents of the register with a single literal. If the register value is less than the literal, it predicts the branch predicate to be true (false), else the branch predicate is predicted to be false (true). A three-way comparison involving *less than, equal to, and greater than* can be handled by a simple modification of the algorithm, but is not considered in this paper. Thus, the practical one-register predictor requires one operation for its implementation. Similarly, a two-register predictor is allowed to compare the contents of each of the registers with literals, and combine the results of the comparison with logical operators. There are four possible outcomes for the combinations of these comparisons, and each combination will be awarded an independent prediction. Since the four combinations can be obtained as the logical AND, OR or XOR of the outcomes of the two comparisons, the practical two-register predictor requires three operations for its implementation.

In light of the above, the practical algorithm of Figure 4 works in much the same was as the basic algorithm, with two exceptions. Firstly, the arrays C_i and $C_{i,j}$ are constructed using quantized register values. Secondly, the score values S_i and $S_{i,j}$ are computed in the context of the one-compare predictor. Specifically, for each array C_i, the algorithm finds the best cut-point v^* that optimally partitions the values of r_i, in the sense that predicting the branch predicate to be true (false) for all values that lie below v^* and to be false (true) for all other values is optimal over all cut-points. Similarly, for each array $C_{i,j}$, the algorithm finds the best cut-point (u^*, v^*) yielding the optimal rectilinear partition of the values of registers r_i and r_j.

3.5 Example 2

Let us reexamine Example 1 in the context of the practical algorithm. Since the values of the registers are all small positive integers, using the linear quantizer to scale the values between 0 and 256 will leave them unaltered. Thus, we can ignore the quantization step, and the arrays C_1, C_2 and $C_{1,2}$ will be the same as in Example 1. We now compute the scores S_1, S_2 and $S_{1,2}$. For r_1, $v^* = 18$ is the best cut-point, yielding a score $S_1 = 5$. For r_2, $v^* = 1$ is the best cut-point, yielding a score $S_2 = 3$. For the register pair r_1, r_2, the best cut-point is $u^* = 18, v^* = 1$ with a score $S_{1,2} = 7$. See Figure 5. Since $S_{1,2}$ is the maximum among these scores, the algorithm outputs the two-register/two-compare predictor based on registers r_1 and r_2. The predictor is shown below in simplified form.

Two-register/Two-compare predictor based on r_1, r_2
  if $v_1 < 18, v_2 \geq 1$ **then** predict 1
  else predict 0;

4 Experimental Results

The effectiveness of compiler synthesized dynamic branch prediction is analyzed in this section. Branch prediction accuracy results are presented and compared to four other branch prediction strategies: static prediction based on profile information, dynamic prediction using a 2-bit counter BTB, and two configurations of dynamic prediction using a two-level adaptive predictor.

4.1 Methodology

In order to accomplish compiler synthesized dynamic branch prediction, the PlayDoh emulation facilities in the IMPACT compiler were modified. The modifications were two fold. First, the

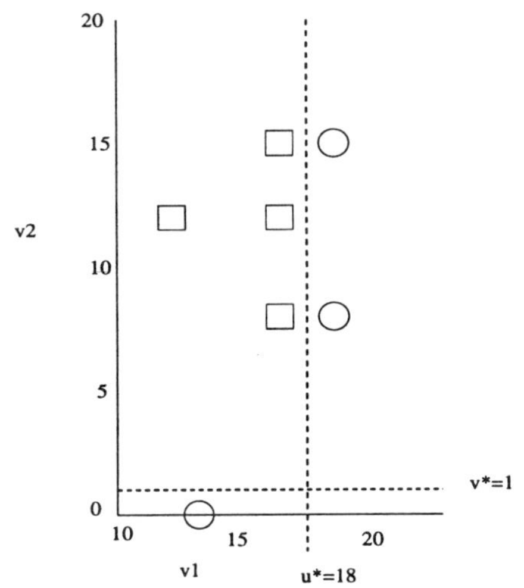

Figure 5: Pictorial view of the optimal cut-point for the two-register case of Example 2. The circles shown are (v_1, v_2) pairs for which $v_b = 0$, and the squares are (v_1, v_2) pairs for which $v_b = 1$. The optimal cut-point is selected so that the four quadrants formed by them best separate the circles from the squares.

synthesis algorithms require dumps of the register file contents to identify correlations. Instrumentation code was added into the PlayDoh emulation facility to provide such dumps a user specified number of cycles before the branch. Thus, when the program is executed for the profiling phase, the emulator maintains a running history of the register file contents for the last several cycles of execution. Then, for each instrumented branch, the register file contents the specified number of cycles before the branch are dumped into the profile database. For all the experiments presented in this paper, a 16 cycle distance is utilized unless otherwise specified.

The second modification was the insertion of new instructions to realize the derived branch prediction functions by the compiler backend. The compiler attempts to place the prediction instructions approximately 16 cycles ahead of the branch. In general, the compiler must insert these instructions along all paths of control leading to the branch to ensure the prediction is always available. For our experiments, this task was simplified by utilizing the superblock compilation approach in the IMPACT compiler [9]. For most cases, superblock construction ensures a single path leading to each important branch. Therefore, a single copy of the prediction instructions is inserted into each superblock with a branch targeted for prediction synthesis. With other scheduling frameworks, multiple copies of the prediction instructions may be required to cover all paths leading to a branch.

The benchmarks studied in this paper were compiled with superblock compilation techniques for the PlayDoh architecture [9]. The benchmarks consist of 11 integer programs collectively from the SPEC-92 suite (*008.espresso*, *023.eqntott*, *026.compress*, and *072.sc*); SPEC-95 suite (*099.go* and *124.m88ksim*); and several common Unix utilities (*grep*, *lex*, *qsort*, *wc* and *yacc*). The processor model chosen is an 8-issue VLIW processor. The processor has no restrictions on the combination of instructions that may be issued each cycle, except for branches. At most one branch per cycle is allowed. Further, perfect caches and instruction latencies for the HP PA-RISC 7100 are assumed [7].

Four alternative branch prediction models are considered in the evaluation. The first is the conventional static branch prediction approach using profile information ("Profile"). The second model is dynamic branch prediction utilizing a BTB with a 2-bit saturating counter ("2bit-Ctr"). The BTB is assumed to be direct-mapped and have 1024 entries. The final models are two alternative implementations of dynamic branch prediction using two-level branch prediction. One is a PAg configuration with a direct-mapped, 1024 entry branch history table with a history length of 8 bits ("2lv-PAg(8)"). The other is a PAs configuration with a direct-mapped, 1024 entry branch history table with a history length of 10 bits and 64 pattern history tables ("2lv-PAs(10,64)").

As it currently stands, our synthesis procedure is not fully automated. In order to reduce experimentation time, all branches in the benchmarks were not subject to the prediction synthesis. Instead, the branches were ranked according to the mispredictions that are suffered by a static predictor based on profile information. Then, the top fraction of the branches were treated by the synthesis algorithm. To permit an estimate of full performance results for the compiler synthesized approach, branches that are not subject to synthesis utilize the static prediction based on profile information. More details regarding the branches selected are presented in the next section.

An important component of the experiments for any profile-based compilation technique are inputs for each benchmark that are used for profiling (training) and those for measurement (reference). For this paper, the effectiveness of compiler synthesized branch prediction is first evaluated without any profiling uncertainties. Therefore, the reference input is chosen as the training input. After these measurements, a second set of data is presented to assess the profiling sensitivity of the technique. In this experiment, separate training and reference inputs are used.

As previously mentioned, the distance chosen to obtain the register dumps was 16 cycles. The basis for this choice is that we assume the prepare-to-branch instruction must be issued at least 12 cycles before the actual branch to provide sufficient time to communicate the branch prediction value to the processor as well as to initiate the appropriate instruction prefetch requests. Since the prepare communicates the prediction value to the hardware, the prediction computation must be performed prior to this 12 cycle distance. Using register values available 16 cycles before the branch provides a reasonably accurate view of the processor state when the actual prediction must be computed. Note that having register dumps for the exact distance at which prediction instructions will be issued is not required. Although, the prediction functions will likely lose accuracy if the register dumps are not indicative of the register values available when prediction instructions are issued.

A consequence of the 16 cycle distance and the 8-issue processor used in these experiments is that in no case could the actual branch comparison instruction be scheduled ahead of the prepare. As was described in Section 2.2, in situations where the compare can be issued before the prepare, no prediction is required since the true direction of the branch is known. However, for the processor models and branches studied in this paper, this situation never oc-

Benchmark	No. br	Br Cov (%)	Mp Cov (%)
008.espresso	14	25.9	67.8
023.eqntott	4	90.9	97.0
026.compress	6	58.9	92.8
072.sc	9	30.2	79.0
099.go	14	7.2	9.7
124.m88ksim	1	3.7	33.8
grep	5	42.1	97.8
lex	12	46.1	71.4
qsort	6	70.2	93.5
wc	4	44.7	99.9
yacc	12	24.7	62.2

Table 2: Characteristics of the branches selected for compiler synthesized branch prediction.

curred. Consequently, all results reported in the next section are based completely on prediction results.

4.2 Results

Selected branches. Table 2 presents the details of the branches selected for synthesizing branch prediction functions. As previously mentioned, for each benchmark, we treated a select subset of the branches with our algorithm, and used the static predictor to predict the remainder. Column 2 of the table shows the number of branches treated for each benchmark. Columns 3 and 4 show the dynamic fraction of branches and mispredictions with a profile-based static predictor that were accounted for by the treated branches, respectively. For instance, for *008.espresso*, the 14 branches treated accounted for 25.9% of the dynamic branches and 67.8% of the dynamic mispredictions. In general, we selected branches in order of their static misprediction rate, from most mispredicted to least, until we covered 90% of the dynamic total mispredictions. This was difficult to achieve for some of the benchmarks since the number of branches involved was large. For these benchmarks, a smaller coverage of branches predicted by compiler synthesized branch predictions is the consequence. If our technique were fully automated into a compiler, this would have not been an obstacle.

Comparison of branch prediction models. The overall performance of the compiler synthesized dynamic branch prediction method compared with other common branch prediction schemes is presented in Table 3. The branch prediction schemes compared against are: a 2-bit counter BTB, a PAg two-level predictor, a PAs two-level predictor, and a profile-based static predictor. The results in the table only consider the prediction accuracy for conditional branch instructions in the application. The last two columns of the table, marked *CS-Practical* and *CS-Theoretical*, correspond to the misprediction rate of the compiler synthesized practical and theoretical algorithms, respectively. We remind the reader that in both cases, we applied our algorithms to a select subset of the branches as outlined in Table 2, with the remaining branches being treated with the static predictor. Furthermore, the practical variant of our algorithm restricts itself to one-compare per register, with at most two registers being involved in the prediction, requiring one instruction for a one-register predictor and three instructions for a two-register predictor. The theoretical predictor is an upper bound on the performance of the synthesis algorithm, and is shown solely as a reference point.

From Table 3, it is clear that the practical compiler synthesized predictor achieves an extremely competitive prediction rate. For every benchmark tested, the compiler synthesized predictor outperforms both profile-based prediction and the 2-bit counter BTB. The most notable improvements occur for *023.eqntott* and *wc* in which the 2-bit counter misprediction rate is cut in half by the compiler synthesized predictor. The two-level predictors and the compiler synthesized predictor achieve similar performance levels. On six of the eleven benchmarks, the compiler synthesized predictor outperforms the PAg predictor. Similarly, the compiler synthesized predictor outperforms the PAs predictor on five of the eleven benchmarks. For the remaining benchmarks, the two-level predictors achieve a better misprediction rate. The major advantage the two-level and the compiler synthesized predictors have over the other predictors is exploiting correlation information to compute a more accurate prediction value. Neither the 2-bit counter nor the profile-based predictor utilize any correlation information. On the other hand, the correlation information utilized by the two-level and compiler synthesized predictors is quite different. The two-level predictors use branch history information exclusively. In contrast, the compiler synthesized predictor uses the contents of architecture registers.

Comparing the practical and theoretical misprediction rates for the compiler synthesized predictors in Table 3 shows that generally a near upper bound result can be achieved with the practical realization of the prediction function. The one real exception to this statement occurs for *026.compress*, in which a 9.808% miss rate is achieved with the practical while a 7.408% is theoretically feasible. In general, it is believed there is a large room for improvement in both the practical and theoretical performance levels by using more careful quantizer designs, and allowing a broader range of operations within the predictor.

Table 4 is similar to Table 3, but compares the performance of the various predictors only over the branches that were treated by the synthesis algorithm. In general, the performance differences between the branch prediction schemes become more apparent in this experiment. The smoothing effect of utilizing profile-based prediction for the untreated branches is removed. As a result, the performance differences between the compiler synthesized model and the 2-bit counter and profile-based static model becomes quite substantial. On average, the misprediction rate is reduced by approximately 50% with the compiler synthesized model on the selected branches. The largest improvement is observed for *124.m88ksim*, in which the misprediction rate is reduced from approximately 50% for the profile and 2-bit counter models to less than 1% with the compiler synthesized model.

Interestingly, the relative performance distinction between the two-level model and the compiler synthesized model is increased when only the selected branches are considered. The benchmarks in which each model outperforms the other model remain unchanged. However, the performance difference is noticeably larger. For example, with *072.sc* the misprediction difference has substantially increased to favor both two-level prediction schemes

Benchmark	Misprediction Rate (%)					
	2bit-Ctr	2lv-PAg(8)	2lv-PAs(10,64)	Profile	CS-Practical	CS-Theoretical
008.espresso	9.449	5.025	4.497	12.703	6.942	6.833
023.eqntott	17.561	6.115	5.455	13.381	8.214	7.961
026.compress	12.795	11.946	10.947	13.933	9.808	7.408
072.sc	6.783	2.667	1.601	11.000	5.399	5.084
099.go	26.880	28.507	25.157	24.853	24.317	23.996
124.m88ksim	5.840	4.202	2.300	5.463	3.630	3.622
grep	1.611	1.374	1.377	1.333	1.164	0.975
lex	2.268	1.413	0.964	2.660	1.863	1.659
qsort	17.652	16.619	15.568	16.249	14.117	14.011
wc	9.961	10.889	10.621	9.394	4.822	3.534
yacc	5.636	4.118	3.275	7.783	5.620	5.385
A-mean	10.585	8.443	7.433	10.796	7.809	7.315

Table 3: Comparison of the overall dynamic branch misprediction rate for all of the prediction schemes.

Benchmark	Misprediction Rate (%)					
	2bit-Ctr	2lv-PAg(8)	2lv-PAs(10,64)	Profile	CS-Practical	CS-Theoretical
008.espresso	22.472	9.580	8.752	33.302	11.036	10.614
023.eqntott	18.834	6.062	5.567	14.279	8.595	8.316
026.compress	20.393	19.363	18.092	21.958	14.955	10.880
072.sc	17.030	2.871	1.771	28.748	10.213	9.170
099.go	35.015	36.610	29.998	33.238	25.827	21.391
124.m88ksim	49.891	0.528	0.513	49.861	0.386	0.174
grep	3.748	3.173	3.130	3.097	2.695	2.245
lex	3.611	2.053	1.298	4.124	2.395	1.952
qsort	23.269	21.080	19.811	21.650	18.612	18.459
wc	22.255	24.018	23.641	20.993	10.767	7.884
yacc	12.280	8.228	6.485	19.627	10.857	9.902
A-mean	20.800	12.142	10.823	22.807	10.576	9.181

Table 4: Comparison of the dynamic branch misprediction rate across all of the prediction schemes over just the branches treated by the prediction synthesis algorithm.

for only the selected branches. In contrast, for *099.go* and *wc*, the misprediction difference is increased to distinctly favor the compiler synthesized model. Clearly, for *072.sc* branch directions correlate very strongly with branch history. In contrast, for *099.go* and *wc* the correlation of the branch directions with branch history is rather weak. Branch prediction using correlation with the contents of the register file provides distinct performance improvements. One potential strength of compiler synthesized branch prediction is the ability to tailor branch prediction functions to distinct branches to take advantage of the strongest correlations.

Effect of prediction distance. One important parameter that has been kept constant up to this point is the distance ahead of the branch in which the prediction is computed. Figure 6 shows the misprediction rate achieved with compiler synthesized dynamic branch prediction for the most frequently executed branch in *026.compress* as the branch prediction distance is varied from 1 to 64 cycles. Recall, that a 16 cycle distance has been assumed throughout all the previous experiments. The figure also contains data points for the four alternative branch prediction models for reference purposes. For these models, the specified prediction distance is not applicable. From the figure, the prediction accuracy is perfect for the compiler synthesized model for up to two cycles before the branch. At this distance, the branch comparison operands are available and can be used directly to determine the outcome of the branch.

As the distance is increased, the misprediction rate of the practical compiler synthesized model increases steadily, crossing both two-level misprediction rates between 16 and 32 cycles. This result reflects the information loss in the register file as earlier and earlier points in time are considered. However, even at 64 cycles before the branch, the compiler synthesized model achieves nearly the performance of the PAg two-level predictor and out performs both the 2-bit counter and profile models. Its encouraging to observe that the theoretical compiler synthesized predictor maintains

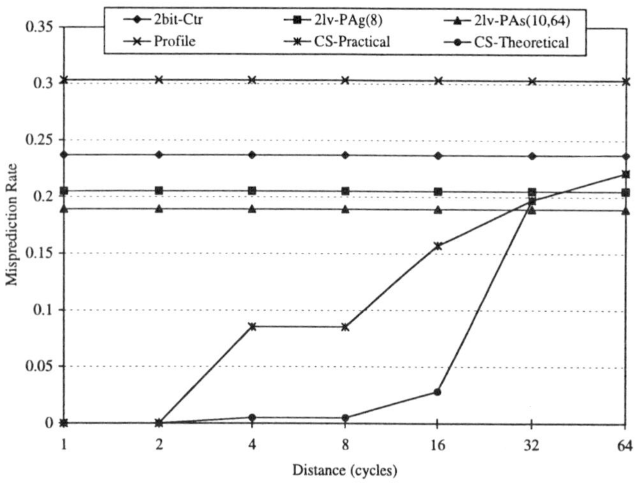

Figure 6: Effect of prediction distance on the accuracy of compiler synthesized branch prediction.

Benchmark	Static (%)	Dynamic (%)
008.espresso	0.03	8.06
023.eqntott	0.05	25.53
026.compress	0.17	14.33
072.sc	0.04	8.94
099.go	0.03	2.33
124.m88ksim	0.00	1.43
grep	0.25	9.14
lex	0.12	10.40
qsort	2.44	7.32
wc	2.15	14.65
yacc	0.16	8.69
A-mean	0.49	10.07

Table 5: Static and dynamic instruction overhead to accomplish compiler synthesized branch prediction.

nearly a 0% misprediction rate through 16 cycles for this branch. With a more sophisticated algorithm for computing practical predictors, it is expected the real performance can more closely track the theoretical performance.

Overhead of prediction synthesis. The primary overhead associated with compiler synthesized dynamic branch prediction is the additional instructions that the compiler inserts to realize the prediction functions. Table 5 presents the static and dynamic instruction overhead incurred with prediction synthesis. From the table, the static code size is not appreciably effected by the prediction instructions. On average, the prediction instructions increase the static code size by only 0.49%. The dynamic instruction count is more noticeably increased by the prediction instructions. The average increase across the benchmarks is 10.07% with the largest increases occurring for *023.eqntott*, *026.compress*, and *wc*. These large increases generally occur in cases where the benchmark contains a small loop which dominates the dynamic execution. Inserting several instructions into this loop to realize a branch prediction function substantially increases the dynamic instruction count. For larger benchmarks with a more dispersed execution pattern, a more modest increase in dynamic instruction count is observed.

Benchmark	Misprediction Rate (%)			
	Training = Ref		Training ≠ Ref	
	Overall	Selected	Overall	Selected
008.espresso	6.942	11.036	7.808	12.821
023.eqntott	8.214	8.595	8.300	8.678
026.compress	9.808	14.955	10.642	16.042
072.sc	5.399	10.213	8.784	16.121
099.go	24.317	25.827	24.752	27.521
124.m88ksim	3.630	0.386	3.720	0.386
grep	1.164	2.695	1.139	2.635
lex	1.863	2.395	2.153	2.911
qsort	14.117	18.612	14.136	18.639
wc	4.822	10.767	4.988	11.136
yacc	5.620	10.857	6.365	11.475
A-mean	7.809	10.576	8.435	11.669

Table 6: Effect of the training input on the dynamic branch misprediction rate for compiler synthesized branch prediction.

The relationship between the increase in the dynamic instruction count and the associated increase in the dynamic cycle count is highly dependent on the processor model. For our experiments, sufficient empty instruction slots were generally available to place the prediction instructions. Therefore, only negligible increases in dynamic execution cycles were observed. For a processor with fewer available instruction slots, larger increases are possible. Note that the prediction functions exclusively utilize ALU instructions. Thus, the dynamic execution overhead will be highly dependent on the available ALU execution bandwidth.

Profile sensitivity. Up to this point, all of the results presented in this section utilize the same input for reference and training. Clearly, this approach provides optimistic results for any profile-driven compilation technique. To provide a better understanding of the profile sensitivity of the synthesized prediction functions, the branch prediction accuracy results are regenerated using different inputs for reference and training. The misprediction rates for the compiler synthesized predictors are compared for different training inputs in Table 6. The first two columns of the table are the previously presented misprediction rates for the practical prediction algorithm over the entire application and over just the selected branches (column 5 of Tables 3 and 4). The last two columns correspond to the same data with an input different from the reference input used for training.

Across the benchmarks, the use of a different training input produces only small losses of accuracy for the synthesized predictor functions. As an example with *008.espresso*, the misprediction rate for the selected branch increases from 11.0% to 12.8% with the different training input. In correspondence, the overall misprediction rate increases from 6.9% to 7.8%. The loss of accuracy occurs for several reasons. First, some of the branches may behave differently across different runs of the application. Second, the register values that are correlated with branch direction in one run, may have a weaker correlation in a different run. However, in general, the synthesized prediction functions appear to be rather stable with a different training input. In fact, for all cases where the compiler synthesized predictor achieved better performance than the two-level predictors in the original experiment, this relation still holds in this experiment.

The one notable exception is *072.sc*. For this benchmark, rather large increases in the misprediction rates are observed. The prediction functions synthesized from the training input were not effective for predicting the branches with the reference input. Clearly, a more suitable training input or set of training inputs are required for this benchmark. It is important to note that by no means is this profile sensitivity experiment complete. More detailed analysis of the profile sensitivity of compiler synthesized branch prediction is required to make any definitive conclusions.

5 Concluding Remarks

A novel branch prediction technique called *compiler synthesized dynamic branch prediction* has been proposed in this paper. Our technique combines the lower cost of static compile-time prediction with the greater accuracy of dynamic prediction. Specifically, we proposed that the compiler use profile feedback to define a prediction function for each branch and insert a few explicit instructions per branch into the compiled code to compute the prediction function. These instructions are carefully selected to predict the direction of the branch using any information available during run-time. To substantiate our proposal, we presented an algorithm for selecting the prediction instructions. Using simulation experiments on a range of benchmark programs, we demonstrated the performance of the approach against contemporary static and dynamic branch prediction strategies. Our experiments showed that the performance of our algorithm is significantly better than that of the 2-bit counter BTB, and is comparable to that of the more sophisticated two-level hardware predictors.

These encouraging early results point us towards further research to improve the effectiveness of the technique. One important issue that warrants investigation is more general branch prediction functions. Currently, the algorithms are limited to a specific class of prediction functions. Extensions to support other classes may provide significant increases in prediction accuracy.

Acknowledgments

The authors thank Rick Hank and Dan Connors for all their effort developing and debugging the PlayDoh emulation tools in the IMPACT compiler; Richard Johnson for all the discussions he took part in where the concepts for this paper were developed; David August, Bob Rau, and the anonymous referees whose comments and suggestions substantially improved this paper.

References

[1] D. I. August, D. A. Connors, J. C. Gyllenhaal, and W. W. Hwu. Architectural support for compiler-synthesized dynamic branch prediction strategies: Rationale and initial results. To Appear *Proceedings of HPCA-3*, February 1997.

[2] T. Ball and J. R. Larus. Branch prediction for free. In *Proceedings of the ACM SIGPLAN 1993 Conference on Programming Language Design and Implementation*, pages 300–313, June 1993.

[3] B. Calder, D. Grunwald, D. Lindsay, J. Martin, M. Mozer, and B. Zorn. Corpus-based static branch prediction. In *Proceedings of the ACM SIGPLAN 1995 Conference on Programming Language Design and Implementation*, pages 79–92, June 1995.

[4] P. Y. Chang, E. Hao, T. Y. Yeh, and Y. N. Patt. Branch classification: A new mechanism for improving branch predictor performance. In *Proceedings of the 27th Annual International Symposium on Microarchitecture*, November 1994.

[5] J. A. Fisher and S. M. Freudenberger. Predicting conditional branch directions from previous runs of a program. In *Proceedings of ASPLOS-V*, pages 85–95, October 1992.

[6] R. E. Hank, S. A. Mahlke, R. A. Bringmann, J. C. Gyllenhaal, and W. W. Hwu. Superblock formation using static program analysis. In *Proceedings of the 26th Annual International Symposium on Microarchitecture*, December 1993.

[7] Hewlett-Packard Company, Cupertino, CA. *PA-RISC 1.1 Architecture and Instruction Set Reference Manual*, 1990.

[8] W. W. Hwu, T. M. Conte, and P. P. Chang. Comparing software and hardware schemes for reducing the cost of branches. In *Proceedings of the 16th International Symposium on Computer Architecture*, pages 224–233, May 1989.

[9] W. W. Hwu et al. The Superblock: An effective technique for VLIW and superscalar compilation. *The Journal of Supercomputing*, 7(1):229–248, January 1993.

[10] V. Kathail, M. S. Schlansker, and B. R. Rau. HPL playdoh architecture specification: Version 1.0. Technical Report HPL-93-80, Hewlett-Packard Laboratories, Palo Alto, CA 94303, February 1994.

[11] J. Lee and A. J. Smith. Branch prediction strategies and branch target buffer design. *IEEE Computer*, pages 6–22, January 1984.

[12] S. P. Lloyd. Least squares quantization in PCM. *IEEE Transactions on Information Theory*, 28(3):129–137, March 1982.

[13] S. McFarling. Combining branch predictors. Technical Report TN-36, Digital Equipment Corporation WRL, Palo Alto, CA, June 1993.

[14] S. Pan, K. So, and J. T. Rahmeh. Improving the accuracy of dynamic branch prediction using branch correlation. In *Proceedings of ASPLOS-V*, pages 76–84, October 1992.

[15] J. E. Smith. A study of branch prediction strategies. In *Proceedings of the 8th International Symposium on Computer Architecture*, pages 135–148, May 1981.

[16] T. Y. Yeh and Y. N. Patt. Two-level adaptive training branch prediction. In *Proceedings of the 24th Annual International Symposium on Microarchitecture*, pages 51–61, November 1991.

[17] T. Y. Yeh and Y. N. Patt. Alternative implementations of two-level adaptive branch prediction. In *Proceedings of the 19th Annual International Symposium on Computer Architecture*, pages 124–134, May 1992.

[18] H. C. Young and J. R. Goodman. A simulation study of architectural data queues and prepare-to-branch instructions. In *Proceedings of the IEEE International Conference on Computer Design: VLSI in Computers ICCD '84*, pages 544–549, 1984.

[8] W.-C. Hsu and J. Smith, "Prefetching in supercomputer instruction caches," *Supercomputing '92*, pp. 588-597, Nov. 1992.

[9] A. Klaiber and H. Levy, "An architecture for software-controlled data prefetching," In *Proceedings of the 18th Int. Symp. on Computer Architecture*, pp. 43-53, May 1991.

[10] D. Kroft, "Lockup-free instruction fetch/prefetch cache organization," In *Proceedings of the 8th Int. Symp. on Computer Architecture*, pp. 81-87, May 1981.

[11] D. Lee, J.-L. Baer, B. Calder, and D. Grunwald, "Instruction cache fetch policies for speculative execution," In *Proceedings of the 22rd Int. Symp. on Computer Architecture*, pp. 357-367, June 1995.

[12] D. Nagle, R. Uhlig, and T. Mudge, *Monster: A Tool for Analyzing the Interaction Between Operating Systems and Computer Architectures*, Technical Report TR-147-92, The University of Michigan, 1992.

[13] J. Pierce, *Cache Behavior in the Presence of Speculative Execution—The Benefits of Misprediction*, Ph.D. Thesis, The University of Michigan, 1995.

[14] J. Pierce and T. Mudge, "The effect of speculative execution on cache performance," *IPPS 94, Int. Parallel Processing Symp.*, Cancun Mexico, pp. 172-179, Apr. 1994.

[15] A.J. Smith, "Cache memories," *ACM Computing Surveys*, pp. 473-530, Sep. 1982.

Wrong-Path Instruction Prefetching

Jim Pierce
Intel Corporation

Trevor Mudge
University of Michigan

Abstract

Instruction cache misses can severely limit the performance of both superscalar processors and high speed sequential machines. Instruction prefetch algorithms attempt to reduce the performance degradation by bringing lines into the instruction cache before they are needed by the CPU fetch unit. There have been several algorithms proposed to do this, most notably next line prefetching and target prefetching. We propose a new scheme called wrong-path prefetching which combines next-line prefetching with the prefetching of all control instruction targets regardless of the predicted direction of conditional branches. The algorithm substantially reduces the cycles lost to instruction cache misses while somewhat increasing the amount of memory traffic. Wrong-path prefetching performs better than the other prefetch algorithms studied in all of the cache configurations examined while requiring little additional hardware. For example, the best wrong-path prefetch algorithm can result in a speed up of 16% when using an 8K instruction cache. In fact, an 8K wrong-path prefetched instruction cache is shown to achieve the same miss rate as a 32K non-prefetch cache. Finally, it is shown that wrong-path prefetching is applicable to both multi-issue and long L1 miss latency machines.

1 Introduction

Instruction cache misses are detrimental to the performance of high-speed microprocessors. As the differential between processor cycle time and memory access time grows and the degree of instruction-level parallelism in superscalar architectures increases, the performance degradation caused by cache misses will become even more apparent. Designers have proposed several strategies to increase the performance of the cache memory systems which will be implemented in next-generation microprocessors. The option often used is to increase the cache size and/or its associativity. However, an increasingly important set of techniques are to prefetch instructions and data into the cache [2][3][5][6][8].

In the case of instruction caches, the focus of this paper, prefetching is an attempt to fetch lines from memory into the cache before the instructions in the line are referenced by the processor's fetch unit. To be effective, the prefetch strategy must accomplish two things. It must be able to guess which cache lines will soon be referenced and it must initiate the prefetch requests far enough in advance of instruction fetch so that the miss latencies are significantly reduced or eliminated entirely. Theoretically, an optimal prefetch algorithm could remove all cache misses by prefetching all instructions immediately before they are needed. Unfortunately, non-sequential program flow makes it impossible for the prefetcher to always predict the correct execution direction. Much work has been done to develop methods which anticipate the direction of program flow and to prefetch instructions in this direction. In this chapter, a new prefetching algorithm is proposed which makes no attempt to predict the correct direction. In fact, it relies heavily on prefetching the wrong direction. This method outperforms several previously proposed prefetching schemes, but it does so at a lower hardware cost. It's simplicity also makes it suitable for combining with more sophisticated prefetch techniques.

The work in this paper grew out of a study of instruction prefetching in [13], where the idea of wrong path prefetching was first proposed. It was further discussed in [11]. Proposals have also been made for prefetching data from data caches [1][9][14] however, this paper does not address data prefetching issues.

2 Prefetching Methods

Instruction prefetching can be done passively by modifying the cache organization to promote prefetching through line size or by including additional hardware mechanisms to execute an explicit prefetching algorithm.

1072-4451/96 $5.00 © 1996 IEEE

2.1 Long Cache Lines

The simplest form of prefetching is the use of long cache lines [15]. When a line is replaced, new instructions are brought into the cache in advance of their use by the CPU, thereby reducing or eliminating miss delays. Longer cache lines also reduce the amount of space required for tag storage. The disadvantages are that longer lines take longer to fill, they increase memory traffic, and they contribute to cache pollution due to the larger replacement granularity.

2.2 Next-Line Prefetching

Another approach to instruction prefetching is next-line prefetching. It tries to prefetch sequential cache lines before they are needed by the CPU's fetch unit. In this scheme, the current cache line is defined as the line containing the instruction currently being fetched by the CPU. The next line is the cache line located sequentially after the current line. If the next line is not resident in the cache, it will be prefetched when an instruction located some distance into the current line is accessed. This specified distance is measured from the end of the cache line and is called the fetchahead distance. Next-line prefetching predicts that execution will fall-through any conditional branches in the current line and continue along the sequential path. The scheme requires little additional hardware since the next line address is easily computed. Unfortunately, next-line prefetching is unlikely to reduce misses when execution proceeds down non-sequential execution paths caused by conditional branches, jumps, and subroutine calls. In these cases, the next line guess will be incorrect except in the case of short branches and the correct execution path will not be prefetched. Performance of the scheme is dependent upon the choice of fetchahead distance. If the fetchahead distance is large, the prefetch is initiated early and the next line is likely to have been received from memory in time for the CPU to access it. However, increasing the fetchahead distance increases the probability that a branch will be encountered in the current line after the prefetch begins, rendering the next-line prefetch ineffectual. This useless prefetch increases both memory traffic and cache pollution. In spite of these shortcomings, next-line prefetching has been shown to be an effective strategy, sometimes reducing cache misses by 20-50% [7].

2.3 Target-Line Prefetching

Target-line prefetching addresses next-line prefetching's inability to correctly prefetch non-sequential cache lines. When instructions in the current line are being executed, the next cache line accessed might be the next sequential cache line or it might be a line containing the target of a control instruction found in the current line. Since unconditional jump and subroutine call instructions have a fixed target and conditional branch instructions are often resolved in the same direction as they were when last executed, a good heuristic is to base the prefetch on the previous behavior of the current line, i.e., prefetch the line which was referenced next the last time the current line was executed. Target-line prefetching uses a target prefetch table maintained in hardware to supply the address of the next line to prefetch when the current line is accessed. The table contains current line and successor line pairs. When instruction execution transfers from one cache line to another line, two things happen in the prefetch table. The successor entry of the previous line is updated to be the address of the new current line. Also, a lookup is done in the table to find the successor line of the new line. If a successor line entry exists in the table and that line does not currently reside in the cache, the line is prefetched from memory. By using this scheme, instruction cache misses will be avoided or at least their miss penalty will be reduced if the execution flow follows the path of the previous execution.

2.4 Hybrid Schemes

A hybrid scheme which combines both next-line and target prefetching was proposed in Hsu and Smith [8]. In this scheme, both a target line and next line can be prefetched, offering double protection against a cache line miss. Next-line prefetching works as previously described. Target-line prefetching is similar to that above except that if the successor line is the next sequential line, it is not added to the target table. This saves table space thus enabling the table to hold more non-sequential successor lines. They compared the performance of this scheme with next-line and target-line algorithms using supercomputer reference traces and their results were impressive—miss rates are reduced by 50-60%. In addition, they showed that the performance gain of the hybrid method was roughly the sum of the gains achieved by implementing next-line and target prefetching separately.

Performing target prefetching with the help of a prefetch target table is not without drawbacks, however. First, significant hardware is required for the table and the associated logic which performs the table lookups and updates. This requires additional chip area that has the potential to increase CPU cycle time. Secondly, the extra hardware has only limited effectiveness in that it cannot be used to remove certain types of misses. First time accessed code does not profit from table-based target prefetching since the table must first be set up with the proper links or current-successor pairs. Thus, compulsory misses are unaffected by target prefetching. Furthermore, unlike a branch prediction table, even when the correct information does exist in the table it cannot always be utilized. Upon re-execution of the code when the links are properly set, prefetching will only occur if the target line has been previously displaced from the cache. In the likely event that the line is still in the cache, the table entry space and lookup are wasted because prefetching is not needed. This suggests that target prefetching using a table is best suited for small caches with low associativity where lines are often displaced and then rereferenced. This was the proposed application environment in [8].

It is interesting to note several points common to the above schemes. One is that prefetch decisions are made at the cache line level. No instruction-specific information is used. This makes sense because a prefetch decision must be made early and many cycles may pass before instruction recognition can take place in the decode stage of the pipeline. Another point is that the above schemes try to predict the correct execution path and then prefetch only down the predicted path. For instance, using a small fetchahead distance will bias the next-line prefetching scheme toward the correct path by lowering the probability of a control instruction being within the fetchahead distance. Target prefetching predicts that the correct direction in which to prefetch is the direction of the previous execution. Even though the hybrid algorithm may prefetch lines down the wrong path, since it sometimes prefetches both a next line and a target line for the current line, such actions are unintentional and rarely occur. Prefetching the correct path satisfies intuition because only lines soon to be executed should be prefetched. The alternative, fetching wrong path lines into the cache, would seem to increase memory traffic and cause cache pollution.

2.5 Wrong-Path Prefetching

We will show that the intuition expressed above is partially false. Our earlier studies have shown that executing instructions down mispredicted paths actually reduced the number of cache misses occurring during correct path execution [13]. This suggests that prefetching instruction cache lines down mispredicted paths might have a positive result. Accordingly, we have termed this new prefetch algorithm *wrong-path prefetching.* It is similar to the hybrid scheme in the sense that it combines both target and next-line prefetching. The next line is prefetched whenever instructions are accessed inside the fetchahead distance as described earlier. The major difference is in the target prefetching component. No target line addresses are saved and no attempt is made to prefetch only the correct execution path. Instead, the line containing the target of a conditional branch is prefetched immediately after the branch instruction is recognized in the decode stage. Thus, both paths of conditional branches are always prefetched: the fall-through direction with next-line prefetching, and the target path with target prefetching. Unfortunately, because the target is computed at such a late stage, prefetching the target line when the branch is taken is unproductive. In this case, if the target address is not in the cache, a fetch miss and a prefetch request of the same line will be generated simultaneously. Similarly, prefetching unconditional jump or subroutine call targets is useless since the targets are always taken and the prefetch address would be produced too late. To reiterate, the target prefetching part of the algorithm can only perform a potentially useful prefetch for a branch which is not taken. This is why the algorithm is called wrong-path prefetching. However, if execution returns to the branch in the near future, and the branch is then taken, the target line will probably reside in the cache because of the prefetch.

The hardware requirements for wrong-path prefetching are roughly equivalent to what is required for next-line prefetching since the target prefetch addresses are generated by the existing decoder and no target addresses are saved. The obvious advantage of wrong-path prefetching over the hybrid algorithm is that there is a lower hardware cost. The performance of wrong path prefetching might also compare favorably with other schemes. Wrong-path prefetching can prefetch target paths which have yet to be executed unlike the table-based schemes which require a first execution pass to create the cache line links. In addition, wrong-path prefetching should perform better than correct-path only schemes when there exists a large disparity between the CPU cycle time and the memory speed. This is because other algorithms try to prefetch down target paths which will be executed almost immediately, and if memory has a long latency, the prefetch may not be initiated soon enough. Conversely, wrong-path prefetching prefetches lines down a path which is not immediately taken thus it potentially has more time to prefetch the line from a slow memory before the path is executed.

The potential advantages of wrong-path prefetching would not come without cost. Prefetching down not-taken paths will put some lines into the cache that are never accessed. This will increase both memory traffic and cache pollution. For the algorithm to be successful, the benefits of prefetching must overcome the added pollution misses. The extra traffic cannot be reduced, but memory bandwidth can be viewed as a hardware resource to be utilized to reduce the performance degradation caused by instruction cache misses.

3 Experimental Method

This section details the experimental procedure used to study the performance characteristics of the previously mentioned prefetching algorithms. A detailed, trace-driven memory system simulator was written to model the performance of the instruction cache, memory bus, prefetch unit, and processor fetch unit in typical current and next-generation microprocessors. The simulator can model the behavior of a wide range of system configurations.

3.1 Memory System Model

The base model is a single issue pipelined processor with RISC-like properties. Each instruction takes one cycle to execute and all instructions are of uniform 4 byte length. The CPU clock speed is assumed to be high so the disparity between clock speed and memory access time is large. Conventional split L1 instruction and data caches are implemented which connect directly to memory or to a second-level, L2, cache. Instruction cache accesses are not pipelined and cache hits complete in one cycle. The base cache model is a 16K direct-mapped cache with 32 byte lines and a 16 byte/cycle refill rate. Four wait cycles are required before the first byte is transferred into the cache. These parameters will be varied in the experiments described in Section 4.

To handle both instruction fetch and multiple outstanding prefetches, a non-blocking instruction cache is necessary [1][10].

The prefetch unit suggests when a line should be prefetched, computes the line's address, and performs a cache tag lookup to see if the line is resident in the cache. If the line is not resident, the prefetch is initiated and a memory request is sent to the non-blocking cache handler. The cache tag structure can be accessed simultaneously by both the fetch and prefetch units. This requires that the tag structure be either dual-ported or replicated. Only one prefetch cache tag lookup can occur per cycle. If both a next-line and target-line prefetch is suggested in one cycle, the target-line address takes precedence. The next-line prefetch will be suggested during the next cycle if necessary.

For the next-line prefetching component of all algorithms, the default fetchahead distance is 3/4 of the line size. For table-based target prefetching, the default target table is direct-mapped and has 128 2-word entries. For wrong-path prefetching, a target prefetch is suggested during the cycle in which a conditional branch is decoded. The instruction decoder forwards the target address to the prefetch unit where the cache tag lookup occurs. To summarize the changes necessary for prefetching, the following hardware additions are required:

- Structures for a non-blocking instruction cache.
- Cache tag replication (or two tag ports) and tag comparison logic.
- Next-line prefetching requires logic for fetchahead distance calculation and next address calculation.
- Target-line prefetching requires next-line hardware, target table, logic to compare and update table entries, and data paths between table and cache tags.
- Wrong-path prefetching requires next-line hardware and a data path between instruction decoder and prefetch unit.

Further micro-architecture details can be found in [13].

3.2 Traces Used in Simulation

The traces were taken from the IBS traces obtained by Nagle and Uhlig using a hardware monitoring setup [12]. The platform is a MIPS R3000-based DECstation 5000/200 running a Mach 3.0 operating system kernel. The traces contain physical instruction and data addresses gathered directly from the system bus while executing between 40 and 130 million kernel and user mode instructions. The benchmark programs are listed with sample cache activity in Table 1.

Trace	Description	Instr	Misses	Traffic
gcc	Gnu C compiler	126M	111	16
gs	PS file viewer	86M	110	16
mpeg-play	Video displayer	111M	94	15
sdet	From SPEC SDM suite	43M	139	16
verilog	HDL tool	52M	115	17

Table 1 Trace Benchmark Descriptions. The miss column is the number of misses per thousand instructions. The traffic column is the percentage of time the bus is active with instruction information. The cache is 8Kbytes.

3.3 Performance Measurement

Most cache studies use the number of cache misses or miss ratio as the performance measure. However, miss reduction is not a sufficient measure of the performance of prefetched caches because it does not account for changes in miss latencies produced by prefetching. For instance, suppose the full miss latency for a processor is five cycles and one algorithm initiates a prefetch three cycles before the fetch while the other initiates a prefetch only one cycle before the fetch. An instruction miss will occur in both cases but the net result is not the same. The first prefetch algorithm will have reduced the miss penalty by two more cycles, thus giving better performance. Two statistics are used to compare the algorithms: total CPU cycles and miss cycles. The latter is the number of cycles wasted due to instruction misses, i.e.,

Total CPU cycles = Instructions executed + Miss cycles

The measures of memory bus traffic are the total bus cycles and the bus utilization. The former is the number of cycles during which the bus is busy sending or receiving memory requests. The bus is deemed not busy during wait cycles. The bus utilization is the percentage of total CPU cycles during which the bus is busy. The results are based upon the sum of the cycle counts for all five of the IBS benchmarks.

4 Comparison Experiments

This section summarizes the results of a comprehensive empirical study of the aforementioned prefetching algorithms using the trace driven simulator. The complete results can be found in [13]. The first 2 subsections compare algorithm performance for different cache sizes, line sizes, refill rates, and cache associativity. Section 4.3 explains the reasons behind the hybrid algorithm's ineffectiveness and why these results differ from those found in [8]. Section 4.4 examines the effect of increased latency. Finally, Section 4.5 shows the effects of prefetching on multi-issue microprocessors.

4.1 Cache Size

The left graph in Figure 1 shows the number of CPU cycles needed to execute the system traces with no prefetching and with different prefetch algorithms. The right graph shows the percentage reduction in the execution cycles due to the prefetching algorithm. Wrong-path prefetching performed the best in terms of CPU cycles for all cache sizes, producing up to a 16% speedup over that of no prefetching. It performs up to 4% better than the other algorithms.The hybrid algorithm performed only slightly better than next-line prefetching. It seems to extract little performance gain from its additional hardware.

It is interesting to note in the left graph that a wrong-path prefetched 8K cache gives better performance than a non-prefetched 32K cache and a next-line or hybrid prefetched 16K cache.

Since prefetching can only reduce the miss latency cycles, which in the above caches comprise 20-40% of the total execution cycles, the prefetching algorithms must be removing a high percentage of miss cycles. We found that wrong-path prefetching reduces miss cycles by almost 40% in an 8K cache.

The major disadvantage of prefetching is the additional memory traffic it generates as can be seen in Figure 2. Two factors combine to cause this increased bus utilization. The first is that prefetching generates unnecessary references which increases the bus traffic. The second is that prefetching reduces the total CPU cycle count. More traffic in a shorter time period translates into higher bus utilization.

Bus bandwidth should be viewed as a resource just as a functional unit or memory port. For instance, if the bus bandwidth is allowed to grow by doubling the refill rate, implementing a prefetching scheme can significantly reduce the required cache size without greatly increasing the bus traffic. Figure 3 shows the effect of this resource allocation. Cache A, B, and C are non-prefetched 32K caches with a 32 byte line size and 8, 16, and 32 byte/cycle refill rates respectively. Cache E is a wrong path prefetched 8K cache with a 32 byte line and 32 byte/cycle refill. Cache E has the best CPU cycle performance and its bus traffic is only slightly higher than that of Cache A. Caches B and C are included in the graph to verify that the performance improvement is a result of prefetching and not of the increased refill rate.

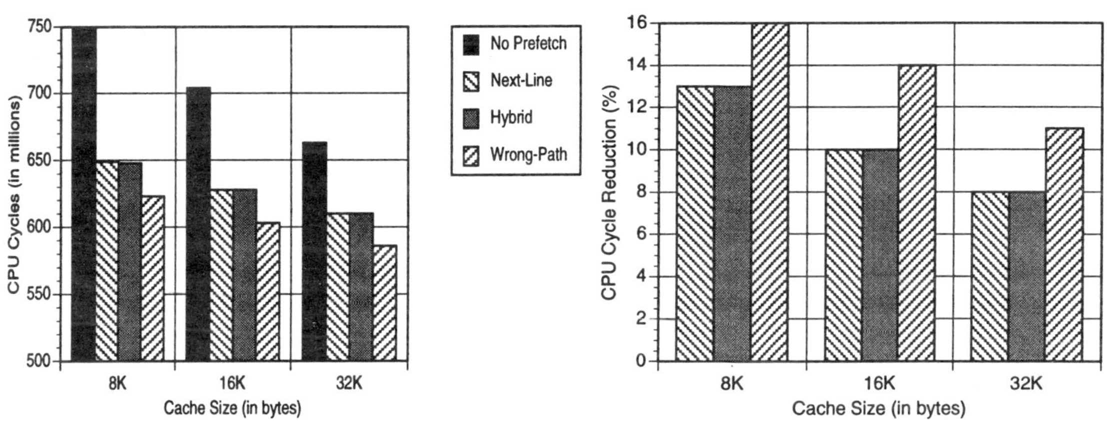

Figure 1 Cycle Time for Different Cache Sizes - The left graph shows total CPU cycles and the right graph shows the cycle improvement gained by prefetching.

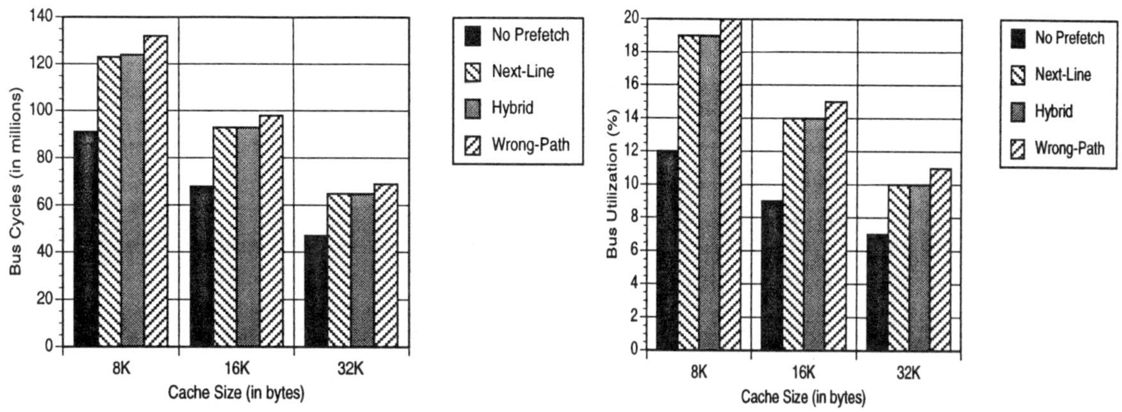

Figure 2 Bus Traffic For Different Cache Sizes - The left graph is the total bus cycles and the right graph is the bus utilization. System traces are used for simulation input.

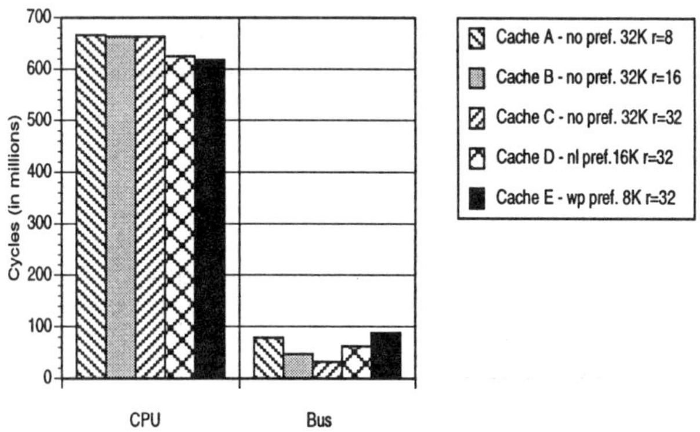

Figure 3 Prefetching Allows Better Performance with Smaller Cache - Caches A, B, and C are non-prefetched 32K caches with 8, 16, and 32 byte/cycle refill rates. Cache D is a next-line prefetched 16K cache with 32 byte/ cycle refill rate. Cache E is a wrong-path prefetched 8K cache with 32 byte/cycle refill rate.

4.2 Cache Associativity and Refill Size

The cache line refill rate plays an important role in the effectiveness of prefetching. A small refill rate means that many bus cycles are required to transfer a line from memory to the cache. This exacerbates two detrimental effects. First, prefetching inevitably causes unnecessary lines to be transferred to the cache. A small refill rate puts a high cost, in terms of bus cycles, on these wasted transfers. Secondly, longer miss handling increases the fetch memory request delay. When a fetch miss occurs during the service of a prefetch request, the memory request cannot be sent until the prefetch is completed. Increased line segment transfer cycles, caused by the smaller refill rate, increase the fetch delay and thus the execution time. Our results show that the higher the prefetch rate, the better the prefetch performance.

An anticipated problem of prefetching, especially wrong-path prefetching, is its potential to pollute the cache with non-accessed lines. Caches with higher associativity can absorb this pollution and will improve prefetching performance. However, although overall performance improved with higher associativity, miss cycle reduction actually declines as associativity increases. Prefetching algorithms excel at bringing lines back into the cache which were previously displaced. Much of their performance benefit is derived from this behavior. High associativity takes a chunk out of the prefetch gain by reducing the number of line displacements in the cache. One might then suggest that higher associativity be used in place of prefetching. We found however that prefetching works in conjunction with increased associativity. Furthermore, prefetching is unlikely to affect the cache hit access times, while highly associative caches are likely to increase the CPU cycle time or require pipelined cache accesses which would negate its perceived advantages [4].

4.3 Prefetch Effectiveness

To summarize the results thus far, prefetching is effective in reducing CPU cycle times in all of our studied cache configurations obtained by varying cache size, line size, associativity, and refill rate [13]. The cost is an increase in bus traffic. Wrong-path prefetching performed slightly better than next-line prefetching in all cases, sometimes by as much as 4%, and the difference in hardware cost difference between the two methods is small. On the other hand, the hybrid scheme gives almost equivalent performance to that of next-line prefetching but at considerable additional hardware cost. This was not the result found by Hsu and Smith in their comparison study in which the performance gain from the hybrid algorithm was approximately the sum of the gains individually achieved by next-line and table-based target prefetching.

We believe the differences in results are mainly due to the difference in cache sizes and associativities modeled. They studied supercomputer cache behavior with cache sizes ranging from 128 to 2K bytes in size. To be effective, table-based target prefetching requires a high line turnover rate in the cache. The larger caches and high associativity of today's microprocessor caches limit the turnover rate and subsequently limit the effectiveness of table-based prefetching. These conclusions are verified by several experiments in [13]. We found that in the hybrid scheme, the miss reduction due to table-based target prefetching was negligible compared to that of next-line prefetching. This is due to a combination of two factors:

- Compulsory misses are not eliminated since a previous execution is required to add the necessary link in the target table.
- After the first miss and the table is updated, the line will be cache resident. In order for the line to be prefetched, the line will first have to be displaced by the cache. This is less likely to occur in a larger cache.

In wrong-path prefetching, target address prefetching accounted for roughly 1/3 of the reduction in miss cycles. Furthermore, it is interesting to note that target prefetches in wrong-path prefetching were useful over 75 percent of time. In other words, 75% of the lines prefetched because they were targets of not-taken branch were referenced before they were displaced. The affects of target table size and fetchahead distance were also measured and recorded in [13].

4.4 Effect of Higher L1 Miss Latency

How do the prefetch algorithms scale to increased memory latency? As the memory latency increases, prefetching algorithms must prefetch farther in advance of the current execution point in order to cover the latency period. Therefore, it might be expected that the performance advantage of prefetching will diminish as the latency increases. Nevertheless, of the three algorithms studied, the wrong-path algorithm might still be expected to suffer the least from increased latency since its target prefetching component does not prefetch immediately used instructions. Figure 4 shows the results of varying the number of memory wait cycles. As expected, the CPU cycle time increases as the number of wait cycles is increased. Unexpectedly, the CPU cycle reduction due to prefetching also increases as the number of wait cycles is increased. As memory latency increases, prefetching becomes more effective.

The reason for this is that the reduction in the number of instruction miss cycles becomes more visible as the portion of total CPU cycles due to instruction misses increases. Higher latency causes more instruction miss cycles which, in turn, allows the prefetching algorithm to have a greater overall effect as Figure 4 shows.

To investigate the effect of memory latency on each prefetching component, we define the *prefetch distance* to be the number of cycles between a prefetch initiation and the first instruction fetch request to the prefetched line. By having the simulator record these values for every next-line and target-line prefetch gain in the wrong-path algorithm, we verify that target-line prefetches do indeed prefetch farther ahead of the current execution point. Figure 5 shows the results. For both a high and a low fetchahead value, the target line prefetch gains have statistically higher prefetch distances.

4.5 Effect on Multi-Issue Machines

It has been shown that prefetching allows increased performance on single issue architectures. To what extent does it also demonstrate performance gains in superscalar or VLIW machines with higher IPC? There are two opposing factors which are similar to those concerning the

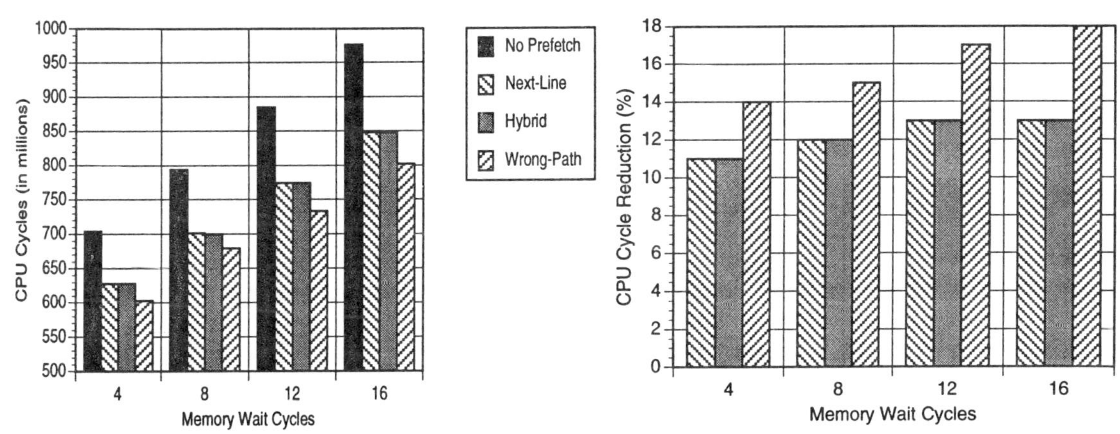

Figure 4 CPU Cycles for Different Memory Latencies.

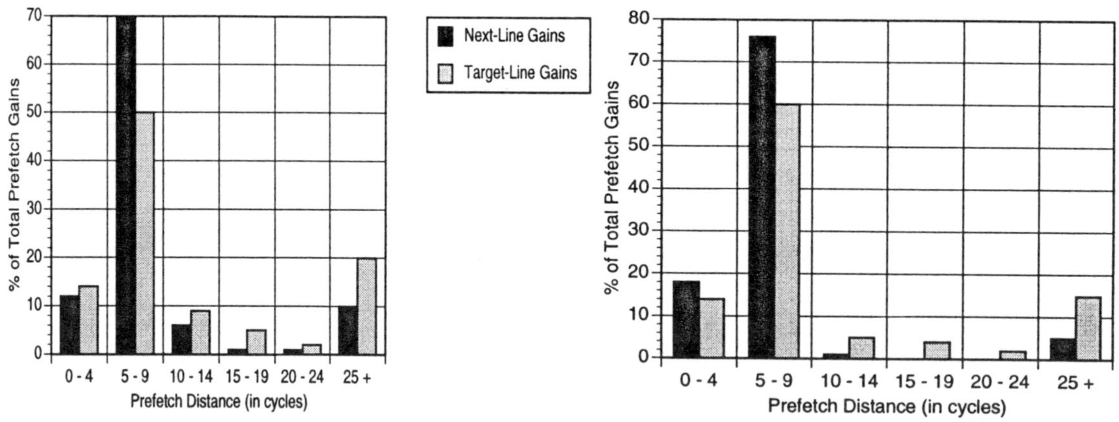

Figure 5 Prefetch Distance Distribution - The graphs show the distribution of prefetch distances for all next-line and target-line prefetch gains within the wrong-path algorithm. The caches are 16K, direct-mapped, line size 32, and refill rate 16 bytes/cycle. In the left graph, the next-line fetchahead distance is 24 while on the right it is 8.

variation in the number of memory wait cycles. In multi-issue machines, since the execution rate is higher, the prefetch algorithm must prefetch farther in advance of the current execution point. This will degrade prefetch performance since a larger portion of the prefetches will not arrive in time. Conversely, increasing the issue rate reduces the time spent executing instructions and makes the effects of misses more pronounced. In multi-issue machines, a larger fraction of the total execution time is due to miss latency cycles. Since prefetching removes a portion of the miss cycles, the effects of prefetching could be greater than in single-issue microprocessors.

Another element of design complexity which goes hand in hand with issue rate is the number of memory ports, i.e, the number of memory requests which can be processed concurrently. Adding memory ports will expand the memory-to-cache bandwidth so the seriousness of prefetch-induced traffic should be lessened. In addition, multiple ports will reduce the backlog of waiting memory requests which will have two positive effects. The first is a reduction in fetch miss request delays caused by in progress prefetches. With only a single port, if a previous prefetch is receiving a cache line on the bus, a fetch miss memory request will be stalled until the line is transferred. Multiple ports will often allow the fetch request to be initiated immediately. Secondly, prefetches will be initiated earlier which will increase the prefetch distance.

The effects of increasing the instruction issue rate and adding additional memory ports to the cache are examined in this section. Multiple instruction issue is simulated by maintaining a fetch window which, at the beginning of each cycle, contains the maximum number of instructions which can be issued per cycle. Each instruction which does not cause a fetch miss is removed from the window. At the beginning of the next cycle, the fetch window is refilled from the trace. This is only an approximation to that of an actual processor since number of instructions retired per cycle also depends upon data dependencies, exceptions, and branch mispredictions. The model for multiple memory ports is an interleaved memory with the same number of banks as ports. As long as two memory requests do not address the same bank, they can be handled in parallel. Each port has its own memory bus so request operations are truly independent if no bank conflicts occur. If a conflict does occur, one request waits in the non-blocking cache structure until the port is available. The memory is partitioned into banks at the cache line level, i.e., one memory bank contains every word in the cache line. Consecutive cache lines are stored in consecutive banks.

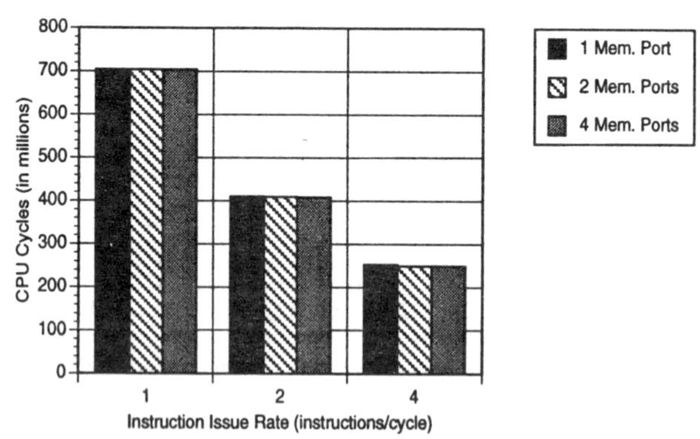

Figure 6 Effect of Issue Rate and Memory Ports with No Prefetching - The graph shows the cycles required to execute the system traces for different issue rates and

The following graphs show the results of varying the issue rate and the number of ports when using the system traces as input to the simulator. Notice that in Figure 6 when the issue rate is doubled the CPU cycles does not decrease by a factor of two. This is because the miss latency cycles are not reduced. Figures 7 and 8 show that

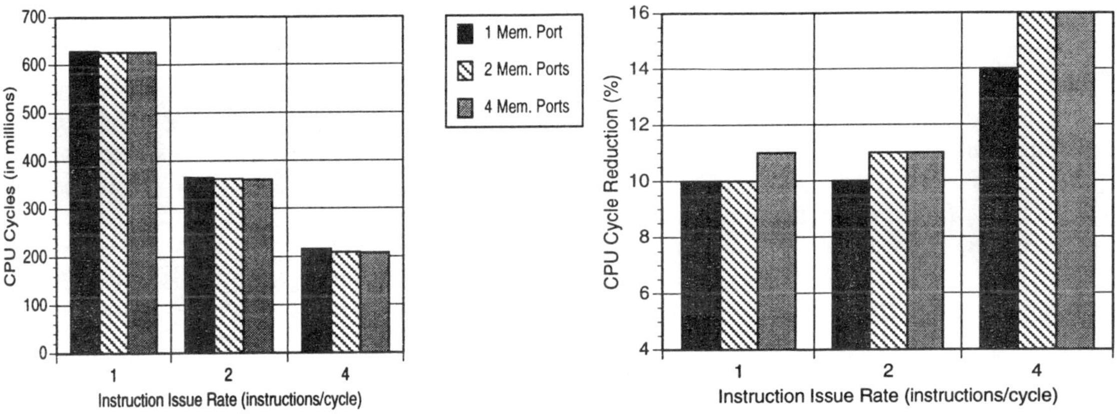

Figure 7 Effect of Issue Rate and Memory Ports with Next-Line Prefetching - The left graph shows the CPU cycles required to execute the system traces. The right graph shows the percent reduction in CPU cycles over the case when no prefetching is done.

the effectiveness of prefetching increases as the issue rate increases. Next-line prefetching improves performance by up to 16% and wrong-path prefetching by 21% in a machine with an issue rate of 4.

The graphs seem to show that the number of memory ports is rather unimportant but this is misleading. First, as mentioned previously, multiple memory ports are probably necessary to achieve an average IPC of 2 or 4. In addition, multiple ports are also required to handle the memory traffic. With superscalar execution, the same amount of memory traffic will occur in a shorter amount of time. Figure 9 shows the port utilization which is defined as the percentage of CPU cycles during which the port is busy sending or receiving information. For multiple port configurations, the highest utilization percentage is given but, since the requests are relatively randomly distributed over all the banks, there is little variation in the utilizations between the ports. It can be observed that even when no prefetching is used, additional ports are necessary to keep the traffic down to a reasonable level. If prefetching is implemented, multiple ports are a must.

5 Summary and Conclusions

The work reported here sheds light on the applicability of instruction cache prefetching schemes in current and next-generation microprocessor designs where memory latencies are likely to be longer. In particular, a new prefetching algorithm is examined that was inspired by previous studies of the effect of speculation down mispredicted paths. The highlights of the experimental results are:

- Prefetching achieves significant performance gains in terms of CPU cycle reduction - up to 14% reduction with standard cache configurations.
- Wrong-path prefetching achieves higher performance than other algorithms in all studied cache configurations. At the same time, its hardware

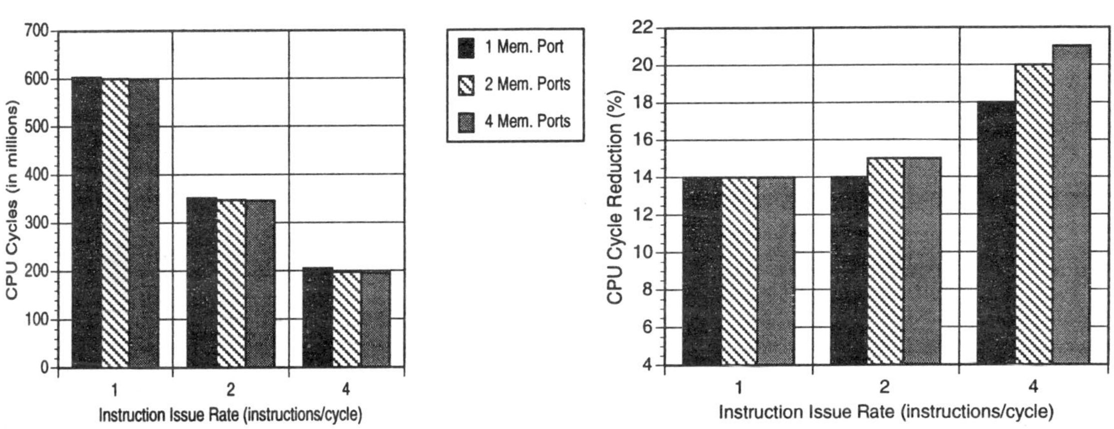

Figure 8 Effect of Issue Rate and Memory Ports with Wrong-Path Prefetching - The left graph shows the CPU cycles required to execute the system traces. The right graph shows the percent reduction in CPU cycles over the case when no prefetching is done.

cost is equivalent to next-line prefetching. Somewhat surprisingly, 75% of all not-taken path prefetches result in miss reductions.

- The cost of prefetching is the increased bus traffic. Bus utilization rises from 12% for no prefetching to up to 25% for prefetching with standard cache configurations. Bus bandwidth may be viewed as a resource which can be employed to reduce miss cycles. By implementing prefetching and adding hardware to increase refill rate, equivalent memory performance can be achieved with a much smaller cache.
- Table-based target prefetching performs poorly with current generation instruction cache sizes rendering the hybrid algorithm performance equivalent to that of next-line prefetching. The negligible performance gain is not worth the cost of the additional hardware required to implement the target table.
- Prefetching is more effective as memory latencies increase. Wrong-path prefetching reduced CPU cycles by 18% when the wait cycles rose to 16.
- Wrong-path prefetching becomes even more effective as instruction issue width increases. Our results show a greater than 20% cycle reduction is some cases.

6 Acknowledgments

Jim Pierce was supported by a grant from the Intel Corporation while pursuing this work at The University of Michigan. The work was also supported in part by ARPA under Grant DAAH04-94-G-0327.

7 Bibliography

[1] T. Chen and J. Baer, "Reducing memory latency via non-blocking and prefetching caches," In *Proceedings of the 5th Int. Conf. Architectural Support for Programming Languages and Operating Systems*, pp. 51-61, Oct. 1992.

[2] M. K. Farrens and A. R. Pleszkun, "Improving performance of small on-chip instruction caches," In *Proceedings of 16th Annual Symposium on Computer Architecture*, pp. 234-241, June 1989.

[3] G. F. Grohoski and J. H. Patel, "A performance model for instruction prefetch in pipelined instruction units," In *Proceedings of the 9th International Symposium on Parallel Processing*, pp. 248-252, Aug. 1982.

[4] M. D. Hill, "A Case for Direct Mapped Caches," *Computer*, pp. 25-40, 1988.

[5] M. D. Hill, *Aspects of Cache Memory and Instruction Buffer Performance*, Doctoral Thesis, Department of Computer Sciences, University of California, Berkeley, 1987.

[6] M. Horowitz, M. Martonosi, T. Mowry, and M. Smith, "Informing memory operations: Providing memory performance feedback in modern processors," In *Proceedings of the 23rd Int. Symp. on Computer Architecture*, pp. 260 -270, May 1996.

[7] P. Hsu, "Design of the TFP microprocessor," *IEEE Micro*, 1993.

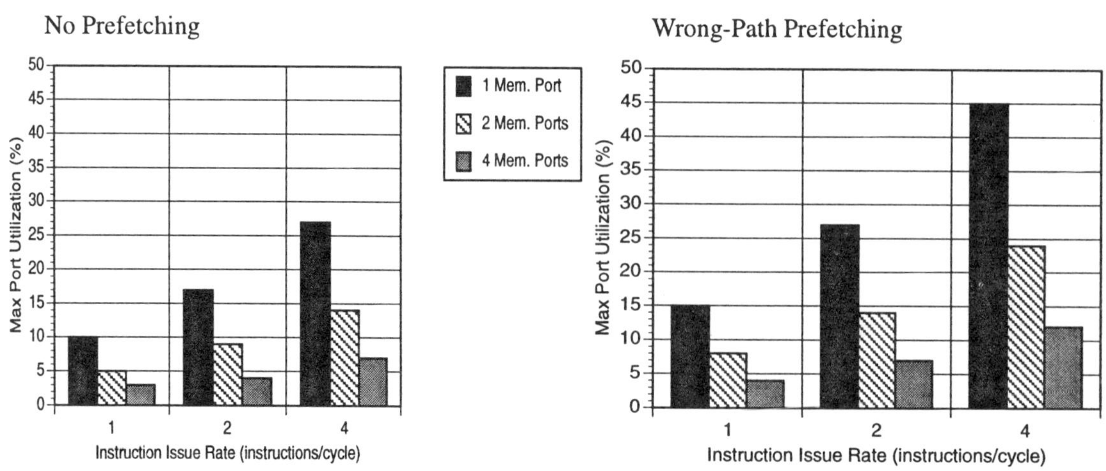

Figure 9 Port Utilization - These graphs show the percentage of cycles the busiest memory port spends transferring information during the execution of the system traces. The left graph is with no prefetching, the right graph with wrong-path prefetching.

[8] W.-C. Hsu and J. Smith, "Prefetching in supercomputer instruction caches," *Supercomputing '92*, pp. 588-597, Nov. 1992.

[9] A. Klaiber and H. Levy, "An architecture for software-controlled data prefetching," In *Proceedings of the 18th Int. Symp. on Computer Architecture*, pp. 43-53, May 1991.

[10] D. Kroft, "Lockup-free instruction fetch/prefetch cache organization," In *Proceedings of the 8th Int. Symp. on Computer Architecture*, pp. 81-87, May 1981.

[11] D. Lee, J.-L. Baer, B. Calder, and D. Grunwald, "Instruction cache fetch policies for speculative execution," In *Proceedings of the 22rd Int. Symp. on Computer Architecture*, pp. 357-367, June 1995.

[12] D. Nagle, R. Uhlig, and T. Mudge, *Monster: A Tool for Analyzing the Interaction Between Operating Systems and Computer Architectures*, Technical Report TR-147-92, The University of Michigan, 1992.

[13] J. Pierce, *Cache Behavior in the Presence of Speculative Execution—The Benefits of Misprediction*, Ph.D. Thesis, The University of Michigan, 1995.

[14] J. Pierce and T. Mudge, "The effect of speculative execution on cache performance," *IPPS 94, Int. Parallel Processing Symp.*, Cancun Mexico, pp. 172-179, Apr. 1994.

[15] A.J. Smith, "Cache memories," *ACM Computing Surveys*, pp. 473-530, Sep. 1982.

Session 6

Design Decisions Influencing the UltraSPARC's Instruction Fetch Architecture

Robert Yung
Sun Microsystems Laboratories
Sun Microsystems Inc.
yung@sun.com

ABSTRACT

Designing a modern microprocessor is a complex task that demands careful balance between cycle time, cycle-per-instruction and area costs. In particular, the instruction fetch unit greatly affects the performance of a multi-issue processor. It must provide adequate bandwidth to sustain peak instruction issue rate and must predict future instruction sequences with high accuracy. In the UltraSPARC prefetch and dispatch unit design, we examined a technique that combined two prediction methods: predictive set-associative cache and in-cache prediction. This combination was compared with alternative designs such as direct-mapped and set-associative caches, and a branch history table and a branch target buffer. We chose the combined prediction technique for its fast cycle time, lower cycle-per-instruction, and lower area costs. This paper summarizes the trade-off decisions made in the design of the UltraSPARC instruction prefetch and dispatch unit.

1. Introduction

Designing an instruction prefetch and dispatch unit (PDU) has become a critical and complex task in a modern processor such as Sun Microsystem UltraSPARC™ [8]. It is critical because the throughput of a processor depends on the ability of the processor's PDU to fetch and issue needed instructions. It is complex for two reasons. As the speed gap between a processor and its memory system widens, there is greater reliance on high speed caches to sustain peak instruction dispatch bandwidth. A first level cache should utilize only a small fraction of the integrated circuit area to reduce cost and minimize access speed, but still provide most of the instructions needed by the PDU. The second complexity arises with increases in instruction issue width and pipeline depth. An efficient PDU should anticipate, with high accuracy, the outcome of issued yet pending branches, and prefetch and issue in the predicted execution path. If a prediction is later found to be incorrect, a PDU should quickly invalidate incorrectly issued instructions and restart fetching from the right instruction addresses.

The design of the UltraSPARC prefetch and dispatch unit centered around two questions:

- What is the optimal cache organization to sustain peak instruction dispatch rates?
- What branch prediction technique achieves high prediction accuracy with small misprediction penalties?

The answer to the first question is typically a choice of a direct-mapped or a set-associative cache; both have been thoroughly researched in academia and industry in the last thirty years with no definitive preference to either [1, 4, 5, 10, 12, 13]. Neither cache organization offered the best trade-offs for the UltraSPARC design. Instead, we proposed a new technique called the ***predictive set-associative cache (PSAC)*** [20], implemented in the UltraSPARC processor, in an attempt to combine the benefits of higher cache hit rates associated with set-associative caches and the shorter access time of direct-mapped caches.

The second question was how to handle branches. Two factors that make instruction fetching difficult are high dynamic branch density in programs and the large number of pending branches possible in a multi-issue processor. Percentages of dynamic branches in integer and commercial programs are usually over 20%, with more than half being taken branches [18]. High scalarity and deep pipelining increase the number of pending branches in a multi-issue processor. In search of a branch prediction solution for the UltraSPARC design, static prediction and software prediction were rejected because of their low prediction accuracy or difficulties in applying them to all programs. The combination of a branch history table (BHT) and a branch target buffer (BTB) offers good prediction accuracy [9]. Unfortunately, a BTB access could not be completed within the target cycle time without incurring a one cycle predicted taken branch penalty. Instead, a new branch prediction technique, ***in-cache prediction (ICP)*** [19],

1072-4451/96 $5.00 © 1996 IEEE

integrated into the instruction cache was proposed and implemented in the UltraSPARC. An ICP provides high branch prediction accuracy and no branch following latency; it can be implemented within the UltraSPARC target cycle time.

Solutions to these two questions were complicated by further tradeoffs such as area, power dissipation, design complexity and scalability for future enhancement. This paper offers some insight into the choices made in the UltraSPARC prefetch and dispatch unit design. Section 2 surveys instruction fetch unit organization in recent microprocessors. Section 3 describes the UltraSPARC instruction prefetch and dispatch unit and summarizes its design goals. Section 4 discusses the benchmarks and methodology used to drive the design process. Section 5 presents miss rates and cycle-per-instruction (CPI) costs for the PSAC and ICP schemes and some alternatives. These results include design alternatives not examined in the original UltraSPARC design. They show quantitatively the consequences of choices made in the design and point out possible future improvements. Section 6 examines area cost to implement the PSAC and ICP, and some alternatives. Section 7 concludes with a summary and suggests possible future work.

2. Related Work

With increases in transistor budget and performance goals, eight recent microprocessors, shown in Table 1, incorporate large and fast instruction caches and advanced branch prediction techniques to sustain high instruction dispatch and execution rates. Many microprocessors contain an on-chip, direct-mapped, single cycle access, level one instruction cache, as recommended in [10]. [5] suggested a hashing scheme to minimize conflict misses in a direct-mapped cache, but its complexity and cycle time impacts prohibit its use in a commercial design. [6] outlined a scheme similar to PSAC with its benefits but did not include data specifying its miss rates and miss causes.

All eight microprocessors implement branch prediction. The most popular scheme is a branch history table combined with either a branch target address buffer or dynamic target address calculation in parallel with instruction cache access. If a branch is predicted not taken in the BHT or is absent from the BTB, it is presumed to be not taken and its address is calculated. The combination of a BHT and a BTB provides high accuracy in branch direction and target address prediction but has two disadvantages. First, because the next fetch address selection depends on the outcome of the BTB search, it may add to the critical path of a design. Second, if the current cache line contains more than one branch, the branch history and branch target address of each branch must be accessed and prioritized to determine the next fetch address. This most likely adds to the critical path of a design. In this case, the next fetch may be assumed not taken and if wrong, the target address can be refetched in the following cycle. This approach reduces cycle time at the expense of a two cycle taken branch latency which leads to increased CPI for taken branches.

Except for the UltraSPARC and the AMD 5K86, all the BHTs and BTBs are implemented with RAM structures separate from the instruction cache. Incorporating the ***next fetch address (NFA)*** into a cache was described in [6] and [11]. Both schemes store only target addresses in the NFA, while sequential addresses of predict-not-taken branches are calculated. Our study in [22] shows that there is little difference in prediction accuracy between storing only target addresses in the NFA and storing either a branch target or a sequential address in the NFA. Storing only target addresses in the NFA has both the BTB disadvantages, while the alternate does not.

	Sun UltraSPARC	DEC 21164	HAL R1	HP PA-8000
Clock Frequency	167 / 250 Mhz	300 / 366 Mhz	154 Mhz	160 / 275Mhz
Level 1 Instruction cache (L1IC)	16KB predictive 2-way	8KB direct-mapped	4KB direct-mapped	external 1MB direct-mapped
L1IC thruput/latency	1 / 1	1 / 1	1 / 1	1 / 2
Icache bandwidth	16B per cycle	16B per cycle	16B per cycle	16B per cycle
branch history	2048-entry 2-bit BHT in L1IC	2048-entry 2-bit BHT	1024-entry 2-bit BHT	256-entry 3-bit BHT
branch target address	1024 11-bit NFA in L1IC	computed and stored in L1IC on miss	computed 1 cycle after L1IC fetch	32-entry BTB
return addr stack	4-entry	none	4-entry	none
taken branch latency	none	1 cycle	none if hit L1 Icache	none
mispredict penalty	4 cycles	5 cycles	3 to 6 cycles	5 cycles

Table 1: Summary of instruction fetch unit in recent microprocessors [1,4,12].

	IBM PPC620	SGI R10000	AMD 5K86	Intel Pentium Pro
Clock Frequency	133 Mhz	200 Mhz (estimated)	90 Mhz	133 / 200 Mhz
Level 1 Instruction cache (L1IC)	32KB effective 8-way	32KB 2-way	16KB direct-mapped	8KB 4-way
L1IC thruput/latency	1 / 2	1 / 2	1 / 1	1 / 3
L1IC bandwidth	16B per cycle	16B per cycle	16B per cycle	16B per cycle
branch history	2048-entry 2-bit BHT	512-entry 2-bit BHT	1024-entry 1-bit BHT in L1IC	512-entry 4-way 4-bit BHT
branch target address	256-entry BTB	computed 1 cycle after L1IC fetch	1024-entry BTB in L1IC	512-entry, 4-way BTB
return addr stack	none	4-entry branch stack	none	16-entry
taken branch latency	1 cycle	1 cycle	none	1 cycle
mispredict penalty	2 cycles	> 4 cycles	> 3 cycles	> 10, 15 cycles (typ)

Table 1: Summary of instruction fetch unit in recent microprocessors [1,4,12].

3. Instruction prefetch and dispatch

Features	UltraSPARC (US-I,-II) PDU implementation
Cycle time	single cycle instruction cache access. 6ns in US-I; 4ns in US-II
Capacity, Associativity	16KB, predictive 2-way set-associative, 32B block size
Physical organization	direct-mapped, 32 bytes per line, delivers up to 4 out of 8 instructions in a cache line each cycle
Set prediction	1024-entry 1-bit dynamic set predictors (SP), 1 for 4 instructions
Branch prediction	2048-entry 2-bit dynamic history (PRED), 1 for 2 instructions
Address prediction	1024-entry 11-bit next-fetch-address (NFA), 1 for 4 instructions, 4-entry subroutine return stack
Decoded instruction bits	One 4-bit instruction class field (ICLASS) per instruction
Address translation	single cycle access, 64-entry fully associative TLB. single cycle check, one 1-entry micro-TLB, 41-bit physical address
Instruction buffer	12-entry instruction buffer
Transistors, Area	1.6 million transistors; <10% chip area

Table 2: Summary of the UltraSPARC PDU.

To limit the number of design choices for the UltraSPARC PDU, the following goals were set [17]:

- single cycle cache access sets the cycle time.
- contributes to less than 30% of total CPI cost.
- sustains instruction issue rate above three for integer and four for floating point and graphic code.
- instruction cache miss rate below 2% per instruction.
- branch and target prediction accuracy above 85% per branch with minimal misprediction penalties.
- consumes less than 20% of chip area.

All the PDU goals were achieved in the UltraSPARC design. Highlights of the UltraSPARC PDU are summarized in Table 2. Two key PDU design decisions are its cache organization and branch prediction technique. In the remainder of this paper, the choices made in the UltraSPARC design, predictive set-associative cache and in-cache prediction, are evaluated.

4. Evaluation metric

4.1. Methodology

Two approaches were taken in the design of the UltraSPARC prefetch and dispatch unit. Results from three analytical models set the six PDU goals. A cycle accurate simulator finalized the UltraSPARC organization.

Three analytical models were coded in a spread sheet program. The CPI model estimates CPI costs for a wide range of superscalar pipelines with different numbers and types of functional units, branch predictors, and cache and memory organizations. Two sets of inputs used by the CPI model are processor-independent statistics such as cache miss rates and dynamic instruction and dependency counts, and pipeline and cache configurations for the target design. A speed model was created to estimate cycle time by calculating worst case delay of critical paths using a delay file for the target process technology. The delay file contains estimation of delays, produced by HSPICE, for the most commonly used components such as the ALU, registers and cache array. An area model estimates die size by summing the estimated cell sizes for each component with consideration given to cache array efficiency, routing and input/output overhead. The results from the analytical models set the six PDU goals.

Although the six goals limited the number of choices, the remaining PDU alternatives needed a thorough and detailed analysis. A cycle accurate simulator, *spitfire_per*, was written which contains 26,000 lines of C code [16] (Spitfire was the code name of UltraSPARC). The simulator includes parameterized components such as pipelines, multi-level cache, load and store buffers, instruction prefetch and dispatch front-end, and a simple memory and bus model. The final UltraSPARC organization was based on the results from *spitfire_per.*

The results reported in this paper are based on a faster PDU simulator, *Cachesim7* [21], and confirmed with *spitfire_per* results. *Cachesim7* has been generalized for evaluation of a wider spectrum of alternatives based on in-cache prediction schemes. Results of alternative branch designs are based on *predl* [21], a generic BHT and BTB simulator.

4.2. Benchmarks

SPEC92Int was one of the benchmarks used to evaluate architectural alternatives for the UltraSPARC. Its analysis formed the basis of this paper. The results from the SPEC95Int benchmark was also included, with the hope that it is more representative of the programs we use today. What we found was that the two sets of benchmarks behaved similarly and most of their programs did not exercise the instruction cache nor the branch prediction mechanism typical in a modern microprocessor.

All the performance results were obtained from trace-driven simulations for the six SPEC92Int and eight SPEC95Int benchmark programs [2,3]. *The results from gcc, the only program in the benchmark suite that exercises a substantial number of static branches similar to larger programs [13], are presented along with the geometric means of the six SPEC92Int and eight SPEC95Int programs.* The SPEC92Int and SPEC95Int programs were compiled with the SunSoft compiler SC3.0 and SC4.2 respectively. The binaries were traced with *shade* [7] running on Solaris 2.5. *Shade* produces dynamic instruction traces for the simulators described above. Due to *shade's* limitations, only user level instructions were simulated. Branch statistics for the benchmarks are shown in Table 3.

Benchmarks	programs	Dynamic instructions (excluding annulled instruction)	Dynamic Branches (% dynamic instruction)			static instr.	Static Branches (% static instruction)			num. of static branches constituting 90% of dynamic branches
			uncond	return	cond		uncond	return	cond	
SPEC92Int	espresso	931,034,624	1.6%	0.7%	17.9%	74,848	9.3%	1.3%	8.9%	191
	li	4,764,766,826	4.3%	2.4%	16.3%	53,506	10.1%	1.6%	9.4%	120
	eqntott	579,705,590	2.8%	2.0%	19.8%	26,212	5.9%	1.9%	12.5%	77
	compress	126,826,068	1.3%	0.7%	14.4%	42,968	8.3%	1.7%	9.1%	17
	sc	315,481,376	3.5%	1.1%	18.8%	67,579	9.3%	1.4%	9.4%	235
	gcc	1,127,468,030	2.9%	1.8%	15.7%	208,283	9.3%	2.0%	11.1%	2427
SPEC95Int	go	94,271,363,517	2.3%	0.9%	12.7%	104,537	6.1%	1.0%	10.0%	1137
	m88ksim	65,618,372,090	2.1%	1.4%	13.9%	53,098	8.1%	2.2%	10.3%	170
	gcc	1,814,616,506	2.5%	1.8%	19.0%	326,220	9.0%	1.7%	12.8%	4240
	compress	14,048,170,148	2.9%	0.0%	13.4%	29,030	8.1%	1.4%	10.7%	6
	li	51,761,814,700	4.5%	2.0%	17.0%	42,799	9.9%	1.7%	10.0%	114
	ijpeg	82,707,620,515	5.3%	5.3%	12.3%	80,675	5.6%	2.8%	9.4%	63
	perl	35,450,862,596	2.9%	2.4%	16.4%	99,313	9.8%	1.2%	10.6%	188
	vortex	165,162,278,043	2.8%	2.1%	16.7%	150,792	9.2%	1.3%	9.5%	267

Table 3: Branch statistics for the SPEC92Int and SPEC95Int benchmarks.

Note: Espresso and sc SPEC92Int results are based on tial.in and loada1 respectively. Gcc SPEC95Int results are based on inputs amtjp.i, gcc.i, integrate.i, and varasm.i. All results based on the average of the first one billion dynamic instructions of each input. Unconditional branches (uncond) include call, branch_always and branch_never. Returns are JMPL used as returns. Conditional branches (cond) are PC-relative conditional branches.

5. Performance evaluation

In this section, predictive set-associative cache and in-cache prediction techniques are described. Miss rates and CPI costs for each are presented and analyzed.

5.1. Predictive set-associative cache (PSAC)

A direct-mapped cache has a higher miss rate than a set-associative cache but is faster because instructions from a cache access can be used while the tag comparison takes place, thus reducing cache cycle time. A set-associative cache reduces conflict misses, and overall cache misses, by providing two or more sets to which a cache block can be stored. The disadvantages of a set-associative cache are higher area cost and longer access time than a direct-mapped cache of the same size. If a set-associative cache were implemented, UltraSPARC would have a 30% increase in cycle time, or else two-cycle cache accesses.

A PSAC enables a direct-mapped cache to achieve the same higher cache hit rate of a multi-way set-associative cache with minimal area overhead. A PSAC is divided into N logical sets (N=2 in the UltraSPARC) implemented with a direct-mapped SRAM array. Each cache line contains one or more dynamic set predictors (SP). When a cache line is fetched, the corresponding SP selects the set for the next fetch. If a set prediction is correct, the access time of a PSAC is the same as a direct-mapped cache. In the event that an SP misses, the needed set is refetched in a subsequent cycle and the incorrect SP is updated. During a cache miss, a most recently used history bit, mru, is used to decide the placement or replacement of a cache line, just as in a set-associative cache. If the set size does not exceed the smallest page size, a PSAC enables a further speed improvement by allowing a cache access to proceed in parallel with TLB translation. Although the translation outcome is needed to determine a cache hit or miss, the likely cache entry can be used in the interim.

The UltraSPARC uses a 2-way PSAC and there is a one-bit SP for every four instructions in the UltraSPARC instruction cache. The instructions of only the predicted set are accessed in each four-instruction fetch, thus saving power and cache cycle time. To minimize SP miss cost to one cycle, tags of both sets are read in parallel.

The efficiency of a PSAC depends on miss rate differences between a direct-mapped and a set-associative cache of equal size, and set prediction accuracy. If the working set of programs fits in a direct-mapped cache, PSAC does not help. A PSAC is useful when conflict misses dominate cache misses. Figure 1 to Figure 4 show cache miss rates for direct-mapped and predictive 2-way PSAC, and SP miss rates. Three reasons for set prediction misses are explained below and their breakdowns are shown in Table 4. Table 5 shows the CPI costs for several possible UltraSPARC cache organizations.

Fetch size is the number of instructions, four in the UltraSPARC, read in each cache access. Although fetch size does not affect the cache miss rate, it affects the SP miss rate in two ways. First, there is a great increase in SP sharing misses, discussed below, if the number of instructions per fetch is less than the number of instructions per SP. Figure 1 to Figure 4 show that eight instructions per SP is always much worse than four or fewer instructions per SP because the UltraSPARC is a four instruction per fetch design. Second, larger fetch sizes reduce SP miss rates because there are more instructions in each fetch and fewer set predictions are needed for a given number of instructions fetched. Another indirect contributor to SP misses is a cache's block size. The UltraSPARC has a 32 byte cache block. As the block size increases, there are fewer blocks in a given sized cache which causes an increase in conflict misses.

During a cache fill, SPs in the current cache line are initialized to the current set. ***First use misses*** occur when the initial set predictions are wrong. The SP of the last cache line leading to the missed fetch may be updated to avoid a future miss. If a cache line has multiple callers, each of the callers' accesses may result in a first use miss. Table 4 shows that first use misses decrease with larger caches. ***Branch misses*** happen because conditional branches change between taken and not taken directions during execution. If only a single SP is used to hold set history for a branch, changes in branch direction may cause a future set prediction miss. A design that has separate or *dual SPs*, one for each of taken and not taken directions, can avoid this class of misses but requires branch prediction information before set selection for the next fetch. ***Sharing misses*** are a *major* component of total set prediction misses. Sharing misses occur when an SP is shared between two or more instructions and one of the earlier instructions is a branch. The latter instruction may be the delay instruction of the branch. For example, if the set of a CALL target address is different from the set of the sequential address, an SP can hold either, but not both of them. Sharing misses also occur when a fetched block has one or more entry points after a branch. A branch miss is a form of sharing miss.

As cache size increases, total cache misses decrease and conflict misses dominate over capacity and compulsory misses. Because mispredictions are irrelevant during cache misses, set prediction miss rates increase initially for small cache sizes as cache hits increase. Despite these initial increases in set prediction miss rates, Table 5 shows that a PSAC with fewer than eight instructions per SP has a lower or comparable CPI than the alternatives. When working sets fit in the larger caches, set prediction miss rates drop as well.

The UltraSPARC design point, 16KB cache size, four instructions per SP, is highlighted in Table 4 and Table 5. Figure 1 shows that a 16KB direct-mapped cache has only a 0.6% higher cache miss rate than a 2-way PSAC in gcc92, but the CPI, shown in Table 5, is increased by 0.03 or 3% for a design with 1.00 original CPI. Similarly, Figure 2 showed that a 0.7% higher direct-mapped cache miss rate in gcc95 increased the CPI by 0.02. A 2-cycle, 2-way design is worse than the others because of its multi-cycle access. Table 5 also shows that the SPEC92Int and SPEC95Int CPI differences between a direct-mapped and a 2-way PSAC design are minimal because many programs fit in small, direct-mapped caches and a PSAC offers little benefit in CPI reduction.

The UltraSPARC design could be improved by having one instruction per SP and most importantly, by reducing the instruction cache miss cost. A one predictor per instruction design would decrease set prediction miss cost by 0.02 for SPEC92Int and 0.01 for SPEC95Int.

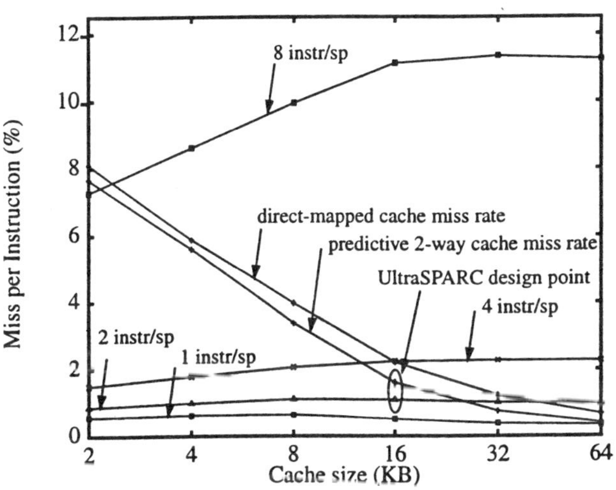

Figure 1. Icache and SP miss rates (gcc92)

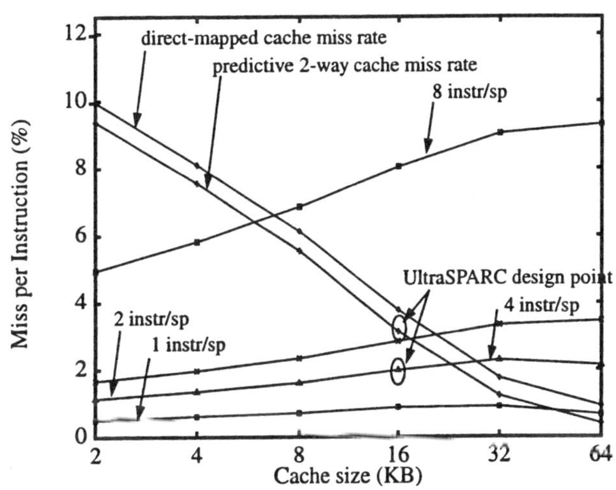

Figure 3. Icache and SP miss rates (gcc95)

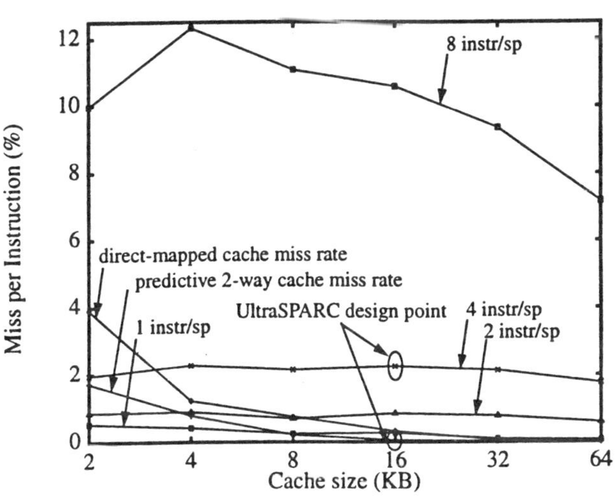

Figure 2. Icache and SP miss rates (SPEC92Int)

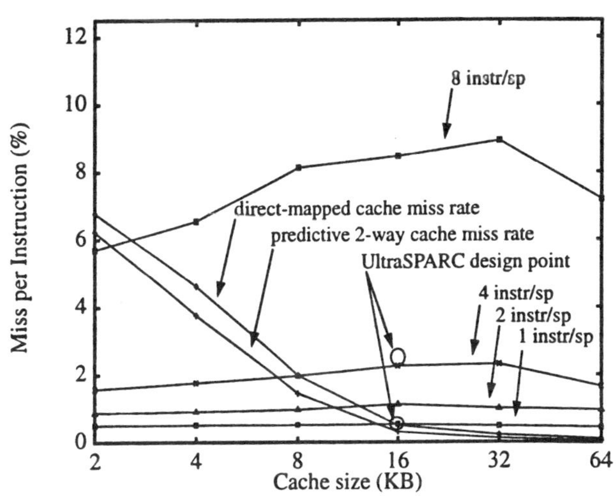

Figure 4. Icache and SP miss rates (SPEC95Int, excluding 129.compress. Icache and SP miss rates for 129.compress are nearly zero.)

cache size	Predictive-2-way, single sp							
	1 instr/sp		2 instr/sp		4-instr/sp		8 instr/sp	
	1st_use	brmiss + sharing	1st_use	brmiss + sharing	1st_use	brmiss + sharing	1st_use	brmiss + sharing
	gcc92							
2KB	0.36% 64%	0.20% 36%	0.32% 37%	0.54% 63%	0.29% 19%	1.21% 81%	0.11% 2%	7.16% 98%
4KB	0.34% 56%	0.27% 44%	0.30% 30%	0.69% 70%	0.27% 15%	1.52% 85%	0.10% 1%	8.51% 99%
8KB	0.28% 44%	0.35% 56%	0.26% 23%	0.85% 77%	0.22% 11%	1.84% 89%	0.08% 1%	9.87% 99%
16KB	0.16% 31%	0.35% 69%	0.14% 13%	0.95% 87%	**0.13% 6%**	**2.11% 94%**	0.05% 0%	11.08% 100%
32KB	0.07% 18%	0.32% 82%	0.06% 6%	0.96% 94%	0.05% 2%	2.22% 98%	0.02% 0%	11.33% 100%
64KB	0.04% 12%	0.30% 88%	0.03% 3%	0.96% 97%	0.02% 1%	2.24% 99%	0.00% 0%	11.25% 100%
	gcc95							
2KB	0.26% 52%	0.24% 48%	0.23% 20%	0.91% 80%	0.21% 13%	1.46% 87%	0.10% 2%	4.85% 98%
4KB	0.26% 43%	0.35% 57%	0.23% 17%	1.12% 83%	0.21% 11%	1.76% 89%	0.09% 2%	5.73% 98%
8KB	0.28% 39%	0.43% 61%	0.25% 16%	1.36% 84%	0.23% 10%	2.11% 90%	0.09% 1%	6.76% 99%
16KB	0.26% 30%	0.62% 70%	0.23% 12%	1.75% 88%	**0.22% 8%**	**2.62% 92%**	0.08% 1%	7.97% 99%
32KB	0.13% 14%	0.77% 86%	0.12% 5%	2.16% 95%	0.11% 3%	3.23% 97%	0.04% 0%	9.00% 100%
64KB	0.04% 6%	0.63% 94%	0.03% 1%	2.10% 99%	0.03% 1%	3.43% 99%	0.01% 0%	9.30% 100%

Table 4: Types of set prediction misses. The first percentage in each pair is the SP miss rate per instruction. The second percentage is the portion of total SP misses for the miss type.

cache size	Direct-mapped	2-way, 2 cycles	Predictive-2-way, single sp				Direct-mapped	2-way, 2 cycles	Predictive-2-way, single sp			
			1 instr/sp	2 instr/sp	4-instr/sp	8 instr/sp			1 instr/sp	2 instr/sp	4-instr/sp	8 instr/sp
	gcc92						SPEC92Int					
2KB	0.67	0.87	0.64	0.64	0.65	0.71	0.33	0.40	0.16	0.16	0.17	0.25
4KB	0.49	0.71	0.48	0.48	0.49	0.56	0.11	0.32	0.08	0.08	0.10	0.20
8KB	0.34	0.53	0.30	0.30	0.31	0.39	0.07	0.28	0.03	0.04	0.05	0.14
16KB	0.20	0.40	0.15	0.16	**0.17**	0.26	0.04	0.27	0.02	0.03	**0.04**	0.12
32KB	0.12	0.33	0.09	0.09	0.10	0.20	0.02	0.27	0.02	0.02	0.04	0.11
64KB	0.08	0.30	0.06	0.06	0.08	0.17	0.02	0.26	0.01	0.02	0.03	0.08
	gcc95						SPEC95Int					
2KB	0.84	1.02	0.79	0.80	0.81	0.84	0.34	0.67	0.32	0.32	0.32	0.35
4KB	0.69	0.87	0.65	0.66	0.66	0.70	0.24	0.54	0.20	0.21	0.22	0.26
8KB	0.53	0.72	0.49	0.50	0.51	0.55	0.12	0.41	0.10	0.10	0.11	0.18
16KB	0.34	0.53	0.30	0.31	**0.32**	0.37	0.06	0.34	0.05	0.06	**0.06**	0.12
32KB	0.18	0.38	0.15	0.16	0.17	0.23	0.04	0.30	0.03	0.03	0.05	0.10
64KB	0.11	0.32	0.08	0.09	0.11	0.16	0.03	0.28	0.02	0.03	0.03	0.07

Table 5: Icache miss CPI costs. Miss costs are 8 cycles for Icache, 30 cycles for Ecache and 1 cycle for SP. The 512KB unified Ecache miss rates are 0.11% and 0.06% for gcc92 and SPEC92Int, and 0.19% and 0.01% for gcc95 and SPEC95Int respectively.

5.2. Branch History: PRED field vs. BHT

The PRED and BHT results are based on single cycle access, predictive 2-way PRED and direct-mapped BHT with single level 2-bit predictors and four cycle miss penalty. The UltraSPARC 16KB instruction cache contains 2048 2-bit dynamic PRED fields, or one PRED field for every two instructions. The PRED fields do not directly affect next instruction fetches but are used by the PDU to determine whether to update the NFA and SP fields when PRED misses occur. The breakdown of three PRED miss types are shown in Table 6. During a cache fill, PRED fields are initialized to likely-not-taken state unless there is a likely-taken software hint. A ***first use miss*** occurs the first time a PRED field is used and the initial prediction is wrong. First use misses decrease with larger caches and can also be reduced by preserving history in the next level cache. ***Direction misses*** occur when a branch changes direction and constitute the majority of PRED misses. ***Sharing misses*** occur when a PRED field is shared between two or more branches. Although fewer than 30% of all instructions are branches, some branches are clustered together which results in sharing misses.

Several observations can be drawn from the miss rates and CPI results shown in Figure 5 to Figure 8, Table 6 and Table 7. First, as the number of predictors or cache size increases, PRED miss rates decrease because more branch history is maintained. Second, most SPARC branches have a delay slot and the delay slot rarely contains another branch instruction. The delay slot is the reason for the negligible miss rate differences between one instruction per PRED with 2N predictors and two instructions per PRED with N predictors. Third, BHT, with 2048 or fewer entries, has lower miss rates than PRED because victimization of a BHT entry affects only one entry but victimization of a cache line may lose several PREDs. With more than 2048 entries, the working set fits in the PRED as evidenced in the small first use miss rates in Table 6. Fourth, the optimal design point, the lowest point in each curve, shifts from four to two instructions per PRED as the number of PREDs increases. With fewer PREDs, PRED misses are dominated by cache misses; with more PREDs, direction and sharing misses are the major component of the PRED misses. Fifth, Table 7 shows that a design with fewer than eight instructions per PRED has similar miss rates and CPI costs as a BHT but a PRED implementation uses less area. The UltraSPARC design is at or near the optimal.

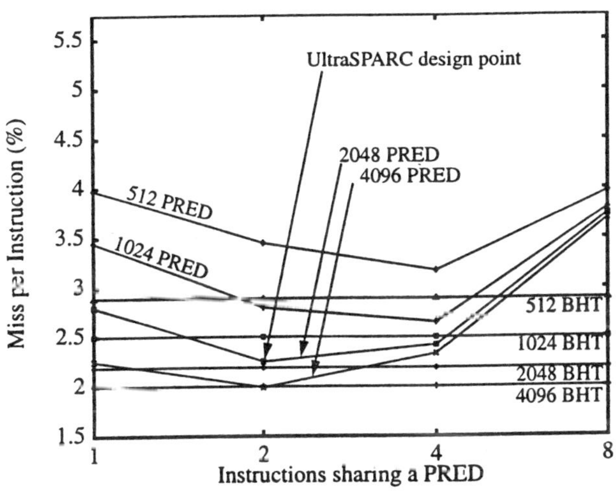

Figure 5. PRED and BHT miss rates (gcc92).

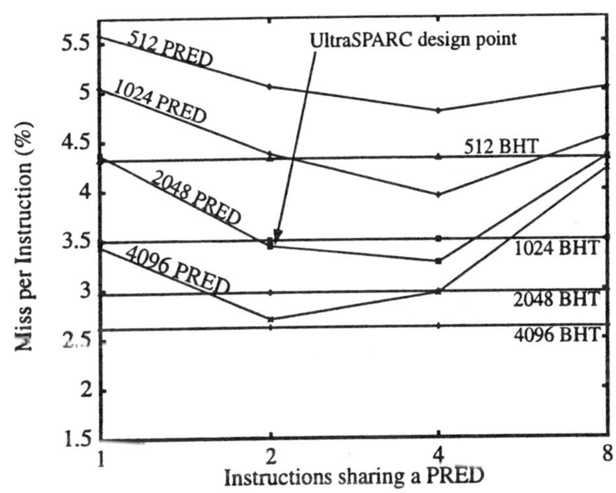

Figure 7. PRED and BHT miss rates (gcc95).

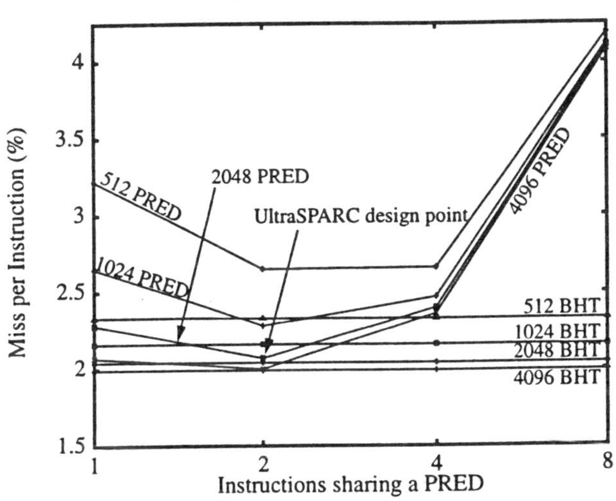

Figure 6. PRED and BHT miss rates (SPEC92Int).

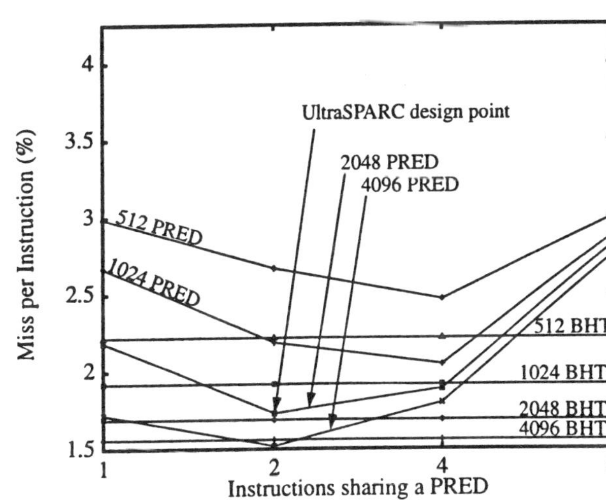

Figure 8. PRED and BHT miss rates (SPEC95Int).

number of PRED	1 instr/pred		2 instr/pred		4-instr/pred		8 instr/pred	
	1st_use	direction + sharing	1st_use	direction + sharing	1st_use	direction + sharing	1st_use	direction + sharing
	gcc92							
512	2.72% 68%	1.26% 32%	2.03% 59%	1.42% 41%	1.14% 36%	2.03% 64%	0.43% 11%	3.54% 89%
1024	2.03% 59%	1.42% 41%	1.23% 44%	1.57% 56%	0.53% 20%	2.12% 80%	0.20% 5%	3.60% 95%
2048	1.23% 44%	1.57% 56%	**0.58% 26%**	**1.67% 74%**	0.25% 10%	2.17% 90%	0.11% 3%	3.63% 97%
4096	0.58% 26%	1.67% 74%	0.28% 14%	1.71% 86%	0.14% 6%	2.19% 94%	0.04% 1%	3.65% 99%
	gcc95							
512	4.16% 75%	1.42% 25%	3.44% 68%	1.61% 32%	2.40% 50%	2.39% 50%	1.05% 21%	3.98% 79%
1024	3.44% 68%	1.61% 32%	2.58% 59%	1.79% 41%	1.35% 34%	2.59% 66%	0.41% 9%	4.12% 91%
2048	2.58% 59%	1.79% 41%	**1.46% 42%**	**1.98% 58%**	0.54% 17%	2.73% 83%	0.13% 3%	4.20% 97%
4096	1.46% 42%	1.98% 58%	0.58% 21%	2.12% 79%	0.17% 6%	2.79% 94%	0.01% 0%	4.20% 100%

Table 6: Breakdown of PRED misses by type for gcc. The first percentage in each pair is the PRED miss rate per instruction. The second percentage is the portion of total PRED misses for the miss type.

# history entries	BHT	PRED				BHT	PRED			
		1 instr/ pred	2 instr/ pred	4-instr/ pred	8 instr/ pred		1 instr/ pred	2 instr/ pred	4-instr/ pred	8 instr/ pred
	gcc92					SPEC92Int				
512	0.12	0.16	0.14	0.13	0.16	0.09	0.13	0.11	0.11	0.17
1024	0.10	0.14	0.11	0.11	0.15	0.09	0.11	0.09	0.10	0.16
2048	0.09	0.11	**0.09**	0.10	0.15	0.08	0.09	**0.08**	0.10	0.16
4096	0.08	0.09	0.08	0.09	0.15	0.08	0.08	0.08	0.09	0.16
	gcc95					SPEC95Int				
512	0.17	0.22	0.20	0.19	0.20	0.09	0.12	0.11	0.10	0.12
1024	0.14	0.20	0.17	0.16	0.18	0.08	0.11	0.09	0.08	0.12
2048	0.12	0.17	**0.14**	0.13	0.17	0.06	0.09	**0.07**	0.07	0.11
4096	0.10	0.14	0.11	0.12	0.17	0.06	0.07	0.06	0.07	0.10

Table 7: Branch history miss CPI costs: BHT vs. PRED.

5.2.1. Branch Target Address: NFA vs. BTB

In the absence of a branch misprediction, the PDU uses the next fetch address (NFA) field in the current cache line for the next fetch without examining the instruction types or branch direction history in the current cache line. Because the NFA is part of the instruction cache, next fetch address prediction does not lengthen the cycle time of the cache or the PDU. The NFA also enables the PDU to follow one or more branches in the next fetch or ***1-cycle branch following***, which is crucial in wide-issue designs. An NFA design does not have the cycle time and branch following disadvantages of a BTB. The branch following disadvantage may greatly degrade the efficiency of a wide-issue instruction fetch unit design with frequent back-to-back taken branches.

Predicted NFAs are verified with either the sequential address of an actually-not-taken branch or the target address of an actually-taken branch. If an NFA misprediction occurs, the NFA is updated according to an update policy and the corrected address is refetched within two cycles. Updating an NFA only on PRED misprediction and branch direction change yields the lowest NFA miss rates [22] and is assumed in this paper. There are three types of NFA misses. ***First use misses*** are caused by initial predicted-not-taken but actually-taken branches. A ***PRED miss*** happens when branch history is incorrect; a PRED miss most likely leads to an NFA miss. Misprediction penalties for these two NFA miss types are accounted for in the PRED miss cost and are not included in Table 8. ***Sharing misses*** occur when an NFA is shared between two or more instructions and one of the earlier instructions is a branch or the delay slot of a branch.

To improve target address prediction accuracy for subroutine returns, a BTB or an NFA may be supplemented with a subroutine return address stack. There is a four-entry return address stack implemented in the UltraSPARC. When a return instruction is fetched, the next fetch based on the NFA is discarded. The PDU refetches with the return address at the top of the return stack. Refetching causes a one cycle penalty for subroutine return but improves the overall CPI.

The PRED and BHT results are based on single cycle access, predictive 2-way NFA and direct-mapped BTB. Several observations can be drawn from Figure 9 to Figure 12 and Table 8. First, NFA miss rates are dominated by sharing misses; NFA sharing should be avoided. Second, unlike PRED miss rates which decrease with more PRED entries, the NFA miss rates may increase with more NFA entries, as shown near the UltraSPARC design point in the figures. Despite there are more NFA misses, the combined CPI cost for a PRED and an NFA decreases with more PRED and NFA entries. The NFA misses caused by PRED misses are irrelevant and are not included in the figures and Table 8. Third, miss rates increase rapidly when the fetch size, four instructions per fetch, is less than the number of instructions per NFA.

Table 8 shows the CPI impacts of NFA and BTB misses. An NFA is a better choice than a BTB for the UltraSPARC design because a BTB design would have a two cycle taken branch latency or else longer cycle time. The NFA miss cost may be reduced for a given sized cache at the expense of increased area if there are less sharing between instructions. For example, a design with one NFA field per instruction would have 0.05 and 0.08 lower CPI costs for gcc92 and SPEC92Int, and 0.07 and 0.08 lower CPI costs for gcc95 and SPEC95Int than the UltraSPARC design point respectively.

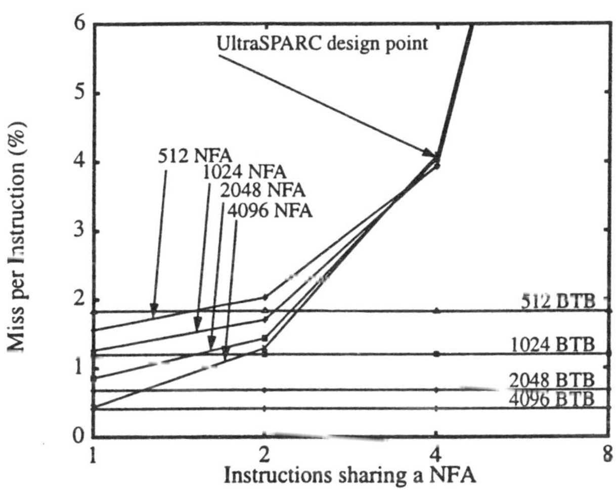

Figure 9. NFA and BTB miss rates (gcc92).

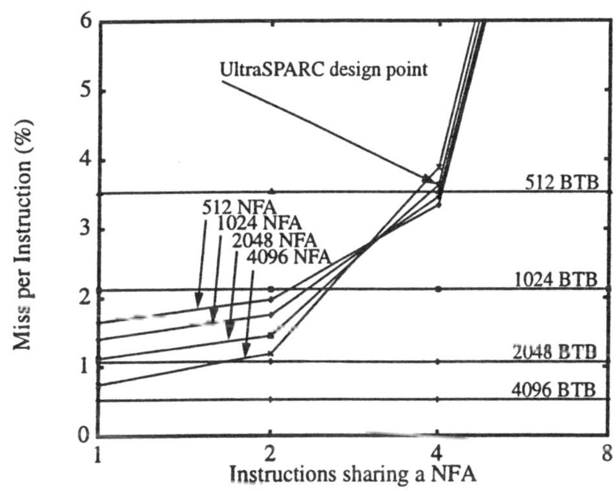

Figure 11. NFA and BTB miss rates (gcc95).

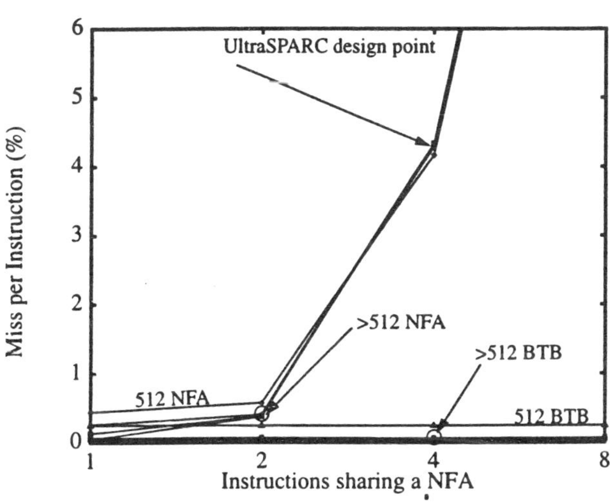

Figure 10. NFA and BTB miss rates (SPEC92Int).

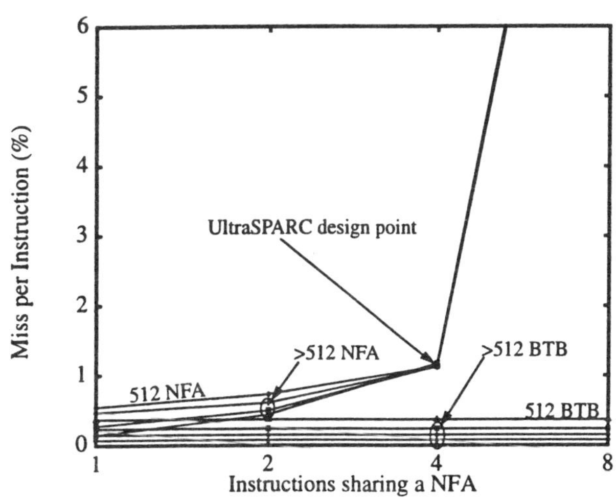

Figure 12. NFA and BTB miss rates (SPEC95Int).

num of predictors	BTB	NFA+ret_stack				BTB	NFA+ret_stack			
		1 instr/ nfa	2 instr/ nfa	4-instr/ nfa	8 instr/ nfa		1 instr/ nfa	2 instr/ nfa	4-instr/ nfa	8 instr/ nfa
	gcc92					SPEC92Int				
512	0.19	0.05	0.06	0.10	0.30	0.14	0.02	0.03	0.10	0.33
1024	0.16	0.05	0.06	**0.10**	0.30	0.13	0.02	0.02	**0.10**	0.33
2048	0.14	0.04	0.05	0.10	0.30	0.12	0.01	0.02	0.10	0.33
4096	0.13	0.03	0.05	0.10	0.30	0.12	0.01	0.02	0.10	0.33
	gcc95					SPEC95Int				
512	0.17	0.05	0.06	0.09	0.29	0.14	0.04	0.04	0.06	0.29
1024	0.16	0.05	0.06	**0.09**	0.29	0.14	0.04	0.04	**0.06**	0.29
2048	0.16	0.04	0.05	0.09	0.30	0.14	0.03	0.04	0.06	0.30
4096	0.16	0.04	0.05	0.10	0.31	0.14	0.03	0.04	0.06	0.30

Table 8: CPI costs for NFA and BTB misses. There are 1.8%, 1.3%, 1.8%, 1.8% subroutine returns per instruction in gcc92, SPEC92Int, gcc95 and SPEC95Int respectively. The return stack hit rates are 92%, 95% 93%, 94% for gcc92, SPEC92Int, gcc95, and SPEC95Int respectively.

6. Area Estimates

To evaluate the merits of architectural ideas in a processor design, it is necessary to analyze the cycle time, cycle-per-instruction and area impacts together. In the early stage of the UltraSPARC design, area estimates for many cache and branch prediction organizations were obtained from the formula, *area = num_SRAM_bits * um^2_per_bit / efficiency + random logic*. A 6-transistor SRAM cell, based on the Texas Instrument 0.5um CMOS process used for UltraSPARC fabrication, is 63 um^2. Efficiency factors for SRAM arrays are provided to account for overhead such as decoders, word line drivers, sense amps, comparators and other control logic. For example, excluding the Iclass field in Table 2, there are 162048 6-transistor SRAM cells in the UltraSPARC 16KB, predictive 2-way in-cache prediction design. The estimated area for the SRAM array is 10.21 mm^2; total area estimates including overhead for the entire ICP design is 21.27 mm^2, which has an efficiency factor of 48%. The actual area measured from the layout is 22.3 mm^2. The high correlation between the estimate and the layout shows that the above formula provides an accurate first order estimation of area cost.

Table 9 illustrates area estimates for various possible PDU organizations of the UltraSPARC design, assuming a 41-bit physical address and a 32-byte cache block size. The UltraSPARC design point is highlighted in Table 9. The area required for the UltraSPARC PDU design, the predictive 2-way ICP, and its alternative are estimated to be 21.27 mm^2 and 32.79 mm^2 respectively, or a 54% saving for the ICP design. Most of the savings in the in-cache prediction design are due to the sharing of existing decoder, word lines and tags in the cache array made possible by the incorporation of the prediction information in the instruction cache. Because the contents in a BHT and a BTB are predictions, it may be possible to eliminate their tags, at an expense of higher CPI costs, to save area.

cache size	branch history entries	branch target entries	Direct-mapped+BHT+BTB		Predictive-2-way ICP	
			# bits	mm^2	# bits	mm^2
2KB	256	128	31,424	4.36	20,064	2.81
4KB	512	256	62,208	8.55	40,256	5.51
8KB	1024	512	123,136	16.74	80,768	10.83
16KB	2048	1024	243,712	32.79	162,048	21.27
32KB	4096	2048	482,304	64.23	325,120	41.80
64KB	8192	4096	954,368	125.82	652,288	82.19

Table 9: Area estimates for direct-mapped, BHT and BTB vs. predictive 2-way ICP.

7. Conclusions and future work

In the UltraSPARC PDU design, we examined a technique that combined two prediction methods: predictive set-associative cache and in-cache prediction. This combination was compared with alternative designs such as direct-mapped and set-associative caches, and BHT and BTB. Two possible organizations for the UltraSPARC PDU are shown in Table 10. They were chosen for three reasons. They both met the cycle time, area budget and were the highest performance techniques known to the UltraSPARC design team in 1991. We chose the ICP design for its fast cycle time, lower CPI and lower area costs.

A predictive set-associative cache was a better choice than a direct-mapped or a set-associative cache for the high clock rate design of UltraSPARC. A PSAC is more effective when cache misses are dominated by conflict misses. The sharing of set predictors in a PSAC should be avoided for any size cache. For example, the UltraSPARC design could have a lower CPI if there were one SP for each instruction. This change would have negligible increase in area and would not impact cycle time. We would have incorporated this change if we had learned about its impact early in the UltraSPARC design.

Branch prediction has been the focus of much micro-architectural research today and most of the efforts are concentrated on improving branch history prediction accuracy, as in [15]. This alone is not adequate in optimizing a PDU design. Other factors that may impact PDU performance are branch target prediction, taken branch latency, misprediction costs, and most importantly, cycle time of the design. We chose the in-cache prediction technique to perform branch prediction in the UltraSPARC design. This technique offers high accuracy in history and target address prediction, no branch following latency and fast cycle time. Moreover, in-cache prediction can directly support multi-branch following per cycle with no cycle time or area impact. In-cache prediction is sensitive to sharing misses when a next fetch address is shared between two or more instructions. The UltraSPARC design would have lower CPI, at the expense of increased area, if additional NFA fields were added to minimize sharing misses.

Results in this paper show that interactions between cache size, sharing of predictors and update policy are complex. Further studies, in particular with a larger set of programs, are needed to better understand their interactions, to improve prediction accuracy and to reduce miss penalty. It will also be an interesting and possibly rewarding exercise to apply multi-level and collating schemes to the integrated prediction techniques.

Advances in process technology offer more transistors on an integrated circuit and enable higher clock speed. As the transistor budget increases, a microprocessor may incorporate a second level cache on the same die. To meet the faster cycle time, the first level cache size may be reduced. A smaller cache size has negative impact on both the PSAC and the ICP because of higher CPI costs due to first use misses. One way to minimize the impact is to save the prediction information in the next level cache when a cache line is victimized. If the victim is needed in the future, the saved information can be used to initialize the cache line and minimize first use misses. This organization deserves further investigation.

cache size	branch history entries	branch target entries	direct-mapped cache, BHT, BTB, 4-entry return stack					ICP predictive 2-way cache, 2 instr/PRED, 4 instr/NFA, 4 instr/SP (single predictor), 4-entry return stack				
			mm^2	CPI cost				mm^2	CPI cost			
				gcc92	SPEC92Int	gcc95	SPEC95Int		gcc92	SPEC92Int	gcc95	SPEC95Int
8KB	1024	512	16.74	0.63	0.30	0.84	0.34	10.83	0.52	0.24	0.77	0.21
16KB	2048	1024	32.79	0.45	0.25	0.62	0.26	**21.27**	**0.36**	**0.22**	**0.55**	**0.18**
32KB	4096	2048	64.23	0.34	0.22	0.44	0.24	41.80	0.28	0.22	0.37	0.15

Table 10: Area estimates and CPI costs for ICP and an alternative.

8. Acknowledgments

There is a popular quote that says "Failure is an orphan...but success has many fathers." The UltraSPARC is a success by any industry standard. If this paper turns out to be useful to the readers, it will be due to the vision and support of many. First, Dave Patterson and Neil Wilhelm were strongly supportive of this work. They encouraged the author to tell the what, how and why, and what we would have done differently if we had the present knowledge in 1991. Hindsight is useful if we learn from it.

The author acknowledged the contributions of Kit Tam, Alfred Yeung, and Bill Joy in defining the UltraSPARC instruction fetch architecture. When we started the UltraSPARC program, popular opinion was that it could not be done and let alone be on time. Special thanks go to the UltraSPARC-Spitfire-team whose hard work and dedication not only brought us the UltraSPARC microprocessor, but disproved the myth.

The author thanks his colleagues, Neil Wilhelm, John Ousterhout, Ivan Sutherland, Charles Molnar, Tom McWilliams, Brent Welch, Jon Bertoni, James Rose, Jon Lexau, Bill Coates, C.C. Lee and Bob Coldwell, and the anonymous reviewers, for reading and commenting on early drafts of this paper. Special thanks go to Dave Patterson who has done an unenviable job of reading and commenting on many early drafts.

Finally, the author would like to thank Sun Microsystems Laboratories and Sun Microelectronics for their support.

9. Bibliography

[1] *Microprocessor Report* (Sept. 12, 1994 - Mar 6, 1995)

[2] SPEC CINT92, Release V1.1, Dec. 1992

[3] SPEC CINT95, Release V1.0, Sept. 1995

[4] R10000 Microprocessor User's Manual, Release v1.1, Jan. 22, 1996

[5] A. Agarwal and S.D. Dydar, "A Technique for Reducing the Miss Rate of Direct-mapped Caches", Proceeding of the 20th International Symposium on Computer Architecture, May 1993

[6] B. Calder and D. Grunwald, "Next Cache Line and Set Prediction", Proceeding of the 22nd International Symposium on Computer Architecture, May 1995

[7] R. Cmelik R. and D. Keppel, "Shade: A Fast Instruction-Set Simulator for Execution Profiling", Sun Microsystems Laboratories Technical Report TR-93-12

[8] D. Greenley et al, "UltraSPARC: The Next Generation Superscalar 64-bit SPARC", The Proceedings of COMPCON-95, March 1995

[9] J. Lee, A. Smith, "Branch Prediction Strategies and Branch Target Buffer Designs", *IEEE Computer,* 17:6-22, January 1984

[10] M. Hill, "A Case for Direct-mapped Caches", *Computer 21*, 12 (Dec 1988)

[11] M. Johnson, "Superscalar Microprocessor Design", Prentice Hall. Inc., Englewood Cliffs, NJ

[12] N. Patkar et al, "Microarchitecture of HAL's CPU", The Proceedings of COMPCON-95, March 1995

[13] S. Sechrest, C. Lee, T. Mudge, "Correlation and Aliasing in Dynamic Branch Predictors", To appear in the Proceeding of the 23nd International Symposium on Computer Architecture, May 1996

[14] A. Smith, "Cache Memories", *ACM Computer Survey 14*, 3 (Sept. 1982), 473-530.

[15] T-Y Yeh, and Y. Patt," A Comparison of Dynamic Branch Predictors that use Two Levels of Branch History", Proceedings of the 20th International Symposium on Computer Architecture, 257-266, May 1993.

[16] R. Yung, A. Yeung, M. Maturana, *Spitfire_per* simulator, Sun Microsystems Inc, Apr. 1991.

[17] R. Yung, "In-Cache Prediction: Instruction Cache And PDU Design To Shorten Sequential and Target Fetch Delay", Technical Memo, Sun Microsystems, Inc., Oct. 23 1991

[18] R. Yung, "Instruction Dependencies of the SPEC92 Integer Programs", Sun Microsystems Laboratories Technical Report #94-0059, March 1994

[19] R. Yung, A. Yeung, K. Tam, W. Joy, "Rapid Instruction Prefetching and Dispatching Using Prior Prefetching Predictive Annotations", U.S. Patent, Jun. 1992

[20] R. Yung, "Rapid Data Retrieval From Data Storage Structures Using Prior Access Predictive Annotations", U.S. Patent, Oct. 1994

[21] R. Yung, *Cachesim7* and *Pred1* simulators, Sun Microsystems Laboratories, Nov. 1995.

[22] R. Yung, "Design of the UltraSPARC's Instruction Fetch Unit", Sun Microsystems Laboratories Technical Report, In Preparation.

Increasing the Instruction Fetch Rate via Block-Structured Instruction Set Architectures

Eric Hao, Po-Yung Chang, Marius Evers, and Yale N. Patt
Advanced Computer Architecture Laboratory
Department of Electrical Engineering and Computer Science
The University of Michigan
Ann Arbor, MI 48109-2122
ehao@eecs.umich.edu

Abstract

To exploit larger amounts of instruction level parallelism, processors are being built with wider issue widths and larger numbers of functional units. Instruction fetch rate must also be increased in order to effectively exploit the performance potential of such processors. Block-structured ISAs provide an effective means of increasing the instruction fetch rate. We define an optimization, called block enlargement, that can be applied to a block-structured ISA to increase the instruction fetch rate of a processor that implements that ISA. We have constructed a compiler that generates block-structured ISA code, and a simulator that models the execution of that code on a block-structured ISA processor. We show that for the SPECint95 benchmarks, the block-structured ISA processor executing enlarged atomic blocks outperforms a conventional ISA processor by 12% while using simpler microarchitectural mechanisms to support wide-issue and dynamic scheduling.

1. Introduction

To achieve higher levels of performance, processors are being built with wider issue widths and larger numbers of functional units. In the past ten years, instruction issue width has grown from one (MIPS R2000, Sun MicroSparc, Motorola 68020), to two (Intel Pentium, Alpha 21064) to four (MIPS R10000, Sun UltraSparc, Alpha 21164, PowerPC 604). This increase in issue width will continue as processors attempt to exploit even higher levels of instruction level parallelism. To effectively exploit the performance potential of such processors, instruction fetch rate must also be increased. Because the average basic block size for integer programs is four to five instructions, processors that aim to exploit higher levels of instruction level parallelism must be able to fetch multiple basic blocks each cycle.

Various approaches have been proposed for increasing instruction fetch rate from that of a single basic block per cycle. Some approaches [24, 1, 2, 20] extend the branch predictor and icache so that multiple branch predictions can be made each cycle and multiple, non-consecutive cache lines can be fetched each cycle. However, this extra hardware requires extra stages in the pipeline which will increase the branch misprediction penalty, decreasing performance. Other approaches [5, 8] statically predict the direction to be taken by a program's branches and then based on those predictions, use the compiler to arrange the blocks so that the multiple blocks to be fetched are always placed in consecutive cache lines. Although they eliminate the need for extra hardware, these approaches must rely on the branch predictions made by a static branch predictor which is usually significantly less accurate than those made by a dynamic branch predictor.

This paper presents a solution using block-structured ISAs that exploits the advantages of both compiler-based and hardware-based solutions by merging basic blocks together statically and providing support for dynamic branch prediction. Block-structured ISAs [14, 13, 22] are a new class of instruction set architectures that were designed to address the performance obstacles faced by processors attempting to exploit high levels of instruction level parallelism. The major distinguishing feature of a block-structured ISA is that it defines the architectural atomic unit (i.e. the instruction) to be a group of operations. These groups of operations are called atomic blocks. Each operation within the atomic block corresponds roughly to an instruction in a conventional ISA. This redefinition of the atomic unit enables the block-structured ISA to simplify many implementation issues for wide-issue processors.

Block-structured ISAs increase the instruction fetch rate of a processor through the use of an optimization called

1072-4451/96 $5.00 © 1996 IEEE

block enlargement. Block enlargement combines separate atomic blocks into a single atomic block, increasing the average size of the program's atomic blocks. By increasing the sizes of the atomic blocks, the instruction fetch rate of the processor is increased without having to fetch multiple blocks each cycle. Furthermore, the semantics of the block-structured ISA enable the processor to use a dynamic branch predictor to predict the successor for each block fetched. As a result, block-structured ISAs increase the instruction fetch rate without relying on extra hardware to fetch non-consecutive blocks out of the icache or foregoing the use of dynamic branch prediction.

In this paper, we define one instance of a block-structured ISA for a wide-issue, dynamically scheduled processor. We have constructed a compiler that generates block-structured ISA code, and a simulator that models the execution of that code on a processor with a real branch predictor and a real icache. We show that for the SPECint95 benchmarks, the block-structured ISA processor executing enlarged atomic blocks outperforms a conventional ISA processor by 12% while using simpler hardware to support wide-issue and dynamic scheduling.

This paper is organized into five sections. Section 2 gives an overview of block-structured ISAs, explaining how the block enlargement optimization works and how it increases instruction fetch rate. Section 3 discusses other approaches to increasing instruction fetch rate. Section 4 describes our block-structured ISA and the compiler and microarchitectural support needed to implement that ISA. Section 5 presents experimental results comparing the performance of our block-structured ISA to that of a conventional ISA. Concluding remarks are given in section 6.

2. Block-Structured ISAs

Block-structured ISAs [14, 13, 22] were designed to help solve the performance obstacles faced by wide-issue processors. Their major distinguishing feature is that the architectural atomic unit is defined to be a group of operations. These groups, known as atomic blocks, are specified by the compiler. When an atomic block is issued into the machine, either every operation in the block is executed or none of the operations in the block are executed. The semantics of the atomic block enable the block-structured ISA to explicitly represent the dependencies among the operations within a block and to list the operations within the block in any order without affecting the semantics of the block. These features simplify the implementation of a wide-issue processor by simplifying the logic required for recording architectural state, checking dependencies, accessing the register file, and routing operations to the appropriate reservation stations. By reducing hardware complexity, wide-issue implementations of a block-structured ISA will require fewer hardware resources than that of a wide-issue implementation of a conventional ISA, resulting in a faster cycle time or a shallower pipeline. In addition to these benefits, block-structured ISAs can increase the instruction fetch rate of a processor via the block enlargement optimization.

Block enlargement is a compiler optimization that increases the size of an atomic block by combining the block with its control flow successors. Figure 1 illustrates how block enlargement works. The control flow graph on the left consists of the atomic blocks A–E, each one ending with a branch that specifies its successor blocks. These branches are called trap operations to differentiate them from fault operations which will be described below. These blocks are analogous to the basic blocks in a control flow graph for a conventional ISA. The control flow graph on the right shows the result of combining atomic block B with its control flow successors C and D to form the enlarged atomic blocks BC and BD. Both blocks BC and BD are now control flow successors to block A.

To support the block enlargement optimization, a new class of branch operations, the fault operation, is included in block-structured ISAs. The fault operation takes a condition and a target. If the condition evaluates to false, the fault operation has no effect. If the condition evaluates to true, the execution of the atomic block to which it belongs is suppressed and the instruction stream is redirected to its target. When two blocks are combined, the trap operation at the end of the first block is converted into a fault operation. If a block is combined with its fall-through successor, then the condition of the resulting fault operation is the same as the original trap operation's condition. If a block is combined with the target of its trap operation, then the condition of the resulting fault operation is the complement of the original trap operation's condition. The target of the fault operation is the enlarged block that results from combining the first block with its other control flow successor. In figure 1, when blocks B and C are combined, the trap at the end of B is converted into a fault in block BC. The fault's condition is true whenever block D is suppose to follow block B in the dynamic instruction stream and the fault's target is BD. Block BD contains a corresponding fault operation with a complementary condition and a target that points back to BC.

The block enlargement optimization requires that the processor support speculative execution [1]. This is required because the operations which compute a fault operation's condition may be in the same block as the fault operation. For example, in figure 1, the operations which compute the condition for block B's trap operation may be in block B

[1] Satisfying this requirement does not necessarily require that the block-structured ISA processor include hardware not already found in a conventional ISA processor because any processor that uses dynamic branch prediction must also support speculative execution, regardless of the ISA implemented by that processor.

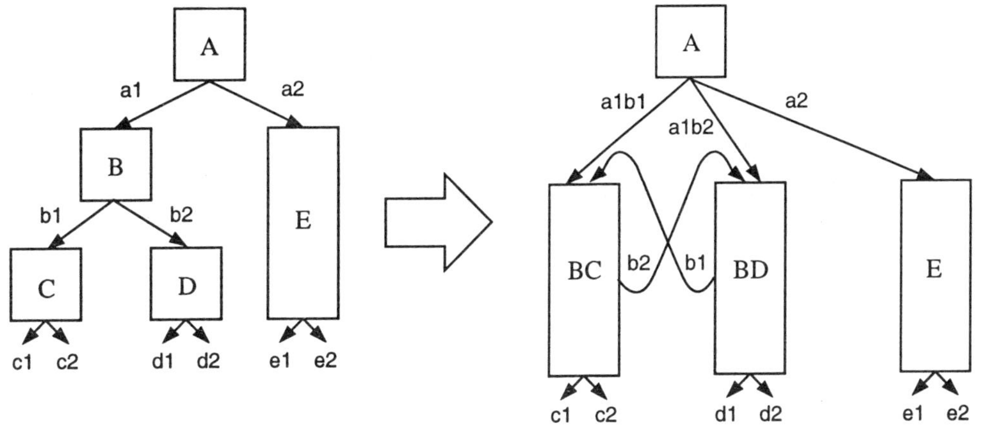

Figure 1. Combining atomic blocks into an enlarged atomic block.

itself. As a result, the operations which compute the conditions for block BC and block BD's fault operations are in block BC and block BD. To determine the correct successor to block A, the processor must speculatively execute either block BC or block BD and rely on the fault operations to correct the control flow if the speculation was incorrect. This assumes that block A's trap operation specifies that the $a1$ direction is to be taken.

Using the block enlargement optimization and the fault operation, block-structured ISAs are able to increase the instruction fetch rate without suffering the disadvantages associated with traditional approaches. By combining multiple basic blocks into a single, enlarged atomic block, the block enlargement optimization increases the instruction fetch rate without requiring the processor to fetch multiple non-consecutive cache lines. Furthermore, the use of fault operations enables the processor to use a dynamic branch predictor to choose which enlarged block is to be fetched next. However, for the block enlargement optimization to be effective, the optimization's effect on branch prediction accuracy and icache performance must be carefully considered. As more basic blocks are combined into an enlarged block, the probability that a fault operation within that block is mispredicted increases. Mispredicted fault operations incur an extra penalty not associated with ordinary branch mispredictions, because they cause all the work in their block to be discarded. Some of this work may have to be issued and executed again after the correct block is fetched. In addition, each time a block is combined with its successors, a separate copy of it is created for each successor. This duplication may increase the number of icache capacity misses during program execution and lower performance. This assumes that all the enlarged blocks formed from combining the block with its successors are accessed with sufficient frequency. If an enlarged block is never accessed, then it is never brought into the icache. The duplication incurred by such a block has no effect on the icache miss rate or the memory bandwidth used by the icache.

3. Related work

The majority of the approaches previously proposed for increasing the instruction fetch rate can be divided into two categories, compiler-based and hardware-based. The compiler-based schemes place the basic blocks to be fetched next to each other in the icache, eliminating the need for extra hardware. These schemes include trace and superblock scheduling [5, 8], predicated execution [7, 12, 18], and the VLIW multi-way jump mechanism [4, 10, 3, 15]. The hardware-based schemes extend the branch predictor and icache so that multiple branch predictions can be made each cycle and multiple non-consecutive cache lines can be fetched each cycle. They include the branch address cache [24], the collapsing buffer [1], the subgraph-level predictor [2], the multiple-block ahead branch predictor [20], and the trace cache [19].

Trace scheduling [5] and superblock scheduling [8] are compiler optimizations that enlarge the scope in which the compiler can schedule instructions. They use static branch prediction to determine the frequently executed program paths and place the basic blocks along these paths into consecutive locations, forming a superblock. The instructions within the superblock can then by optimized as if they were in a single basic block. The manner in which superblock scheduling combines blocks into superblocks is on the surface similar to that of the block enlargement optimization. The significant difference between the two approaches is that

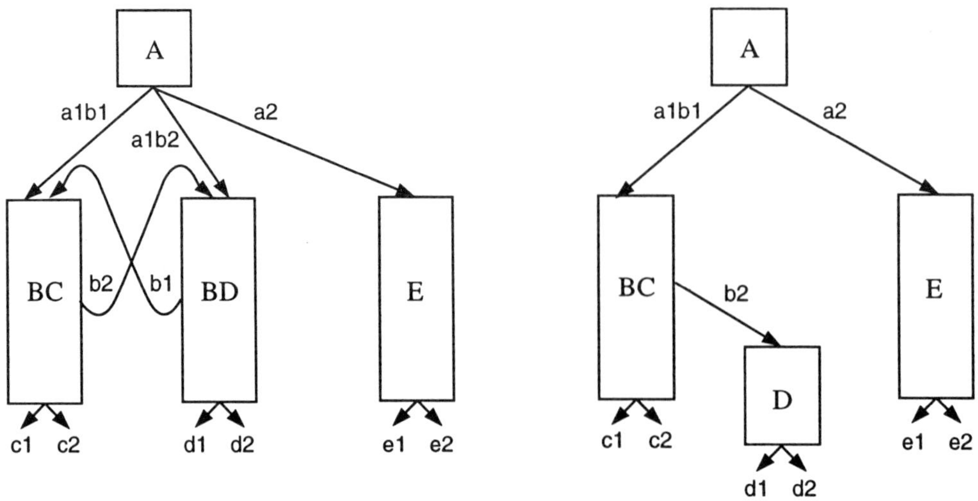

Figure 2. Using trace scheduling to combine basic blocks into a trace.

the block enlargement optimization uses dynamic branch prediction instead of static branch prediction to determine which basic blocks to fetch together. To illustrate this difference, figure 2 shows the results of applying block enlargement and superblock scheduling to the control flow graph from figure 1. The control flow graph on the left is the result of applying the block enlargement optimization and is identical to the one in figure 1. The control flow graph on the right is the result of applying superblock scheduling. The static branch predictor has predicted that block C is the most likely successor to block B so blocks B and C are combined to form a superblock. As a result, block B can only be fetched with block C. It can never be fetched with block D. In the block enlargement case, block B is combined with both of its successors to form enlarged atomic blocks BC and BD, allowing the dynamic predictor to choose the most likely combination. This extra degree of freedom provides a performance advantage for the block enlargement optimization over superblock scheduling because dynamic branch predictors usually achieve significantly higher prediction accuracies than static branch predictors.

Predicated execution [7, 12, 18] eliminates program branches by converting their control dependencies into data dependencies. Once a basic block's branch has been eliminated, it can be combined with its control flow successors to form a single basic block. Predicated execution has two disadvantages. First, it wastes fetch and issue bandwidth fetching and issuing instructions that are suppressed because their predicates evaluate to false. Second, by converting an instruction's control dependency into a data dependency, the program's critical paths may be lengthened. The processor must now wait for the new data dependency to be resolved instead of speculatively resolving the control dependency at fetch time. While predicated execution by itself may not be an effective mechanism for increasing instruction fetch rate, it can provide a significant performance benefit when used in conjunction with speculative execution [11] and other schemes for increasing fetch rate.

The VLIW multi-way jump mechanism [4, 10, 3, 15] combines multiple branches from multiple paths in the control flow graph into a single branch. Using this mechanism, basic blocks which form a rooted subgraph in the control flow graph can be combined into a single VLIW instruction. The branches for these basic blocks are combined into a single multi-way branch operation. This approach gives VLIW processors the means to fetch instructions from multiple basic blocks each cycle. However, because the operations within a VLIW instruction must be independent, it is critical that the compiler be able to find enough independent instructions to fill each VLIW instruction and be able to schedule the operations which evaluate the condition codes for the multi-way jump early enough so that the condition codes are available when the multi-way jump is issued. The compiler may have to delay the scheduling of certain operations in order to meet these requirements, lowering the instruction fetch rate of the processor.

The branch address cache [24], the collapsing buffer [1], the subgraph-level predictor [2], and the multiple-block ahead branch predictor [20] are hardware schemes that propose different ways to extend the dynamic branch predictor so that it can make multiple branch predictions each cycle. Because some of the branches may be predicted to be taken, these schemes all require the ability to fetch multiple non-consecutive lines from the icache each cycle. They all propose to meet this requirement by interleaving the icache. This general approach has two disadvantages. First, bank conflicts will arise in the icache when fetching multiple lines from the same bank. To handle this conflict, the fetch for all but one of the conflicting lines must be delayed. This first disadvantage can be minimized if the icache is interleaved with a large enough number of banks. Second, because it is fetching multiple non-consecutive blocks from the icache, the processor must determine which instructions from the fetched cache lines correspond to the desired basic blocks and reorder the instructions so that they correspond to the order of those basic blocks. The processor will require at least one additional stage in the pipeline in order to accomplish these tasks. This additional stage will increase the branch misprediction penalty, decreasing overall performance.

The trace cache [19] is a hardware-based scheme that does not require fetching non-consecutive blocks from the icache. Its fetch unit consists of two parts, a core fetch unit and a trace cache. The core fetch unit fetches one basic block each cycle from the icache. The trace cache is a small cache that records sequences of basic blocks fetched by the core fetch unit, combining them into a single trace. If the branch predictor indicates that the sequence of basic blocks to be fetched matches a trace stored in the trace cache, then the processor is able to fetch multiple blocks that cycle by using the specified trace from the trace cache. If no matching trace is found, the processor is able to fetch only one basic block that cycle via the core fetch unit. As long as the processor is fetching its instructions from the trace cache, the trace cache is an effective means for fetching multiple basic blocks each cycle without incurring the costs associated with the other hardware-based approaches.

The trace cache and the block enlargement optimization are two very similar approaches to increasing instruction fetch rate. They both combine basic blocks into a single enlarged block (or trace) and use dynamic branch prediction to decide which enlarged block to fetch next. The key difference between them is that the trace cache combines its basic blocks at run-time while the block enlargement optimization combines its basic blocks at compile-time. By combining the blocks at run-time, the trace cache does not require changes to the instruction set architecture and does not increase the size of the executable. By combining the blocks at compile-time, the block enlargement optimization has the advantage of being able to use the entire icache to store its enlarged blocks instead of the small cache used in the trace cache approach.

Multiscalar processors [6, 21] are a new processing paradigm that does not fall into either the compiler-based or hardware-based categories. Multiscalar processors consist of a set of processing elements connected in a ring. Each processing element executes a task, a set of basic blocks specified by the compiler. The connecting logic among the processing elements forwards needed values along the ring and guarantees that the dependencies among the tasks are honored. Multiscalar processors eliminate the problem of fetching multiple cache lines from the icache each cycle by associating a L1 icache with each processing element. Each processing element accesses its own L1 icache for its task's instructions. As long as each icache achieves a sufficient hit rate, the multiscalar processor is able to fetch the equivalent work of multiple basic blocks each cycle. However, the multiscalar model raises new performance issues not found in traditional wide-issue processors. It is important that the compiler create tasks so that the work is evenly distributed and the communication among the tasks does not exceed the ring bandwidth.

4. Implementation details

4.1. The Block-Structured ISA Specification

We have defined a block-structured ISA that incorporates a subset of the features described in section 2. This ISA's architectural unit is the atomic block. The operations that can be found in an atomic block correspond to the instructions of a load/store architecture with the exception of conditional branches with direct targets. These branches are implemented as trap and fault operations. Each atomic block can contain any number of fault operations, but can contain at most one trap operation. Although an atomic block that ends in a trap operation may have more than two control flow successors, each trap operation specifies only two targets. The first target points to a block from the set of potential successor blocks given that the trap condition is true. The second target points to a block from the set of potential successor blocks given that the trap condition is false. Each trap operation also specifies the log of the total number of control flow successors for the trap's atomic block. Section 4.3 describes how the dynamic branch predictor uses this information to accurately predict the control flow successor for each atomic block.

4.2. The Block-Structured ISA Compiler

We implemented a compiler that is targeted for the block-structured ISA described above. This compiler is based on the Intel Reference C Compiler [9] with the back end appropriately retargeted. The Intel Reference C Compiler generates an intermediate representation of the program being compiled and applies the standard set of optimizations to that representation. We implemented a back end that takes this representation and applies a set of target-specific optimizations, allocates registers, and executes the block enlargement pass. During the block enlargement pass, the compiler attempts to combine as many different combinations of blocks as possible. The compiler begins with the first block of each function and continues until one of the termination conditions listed below is met. The process is recursively repeated with the successor blocks of the newly formed enlarged block. The five termination conditions for the enlargement process are:

1. Atomic blocks can continue to expand until further expansion would cause the size of the enlarged block to exceed processor issue width. We restrict the maximum block size to the issue width in this block-structured ISA so as to avoid the complexity of supporting atomic blocks that require more than one cycle to issue. For our experiments the maximum block size will always be sixteen.

2. Each atomic block can contain at most two fault operations, which restricts the number of successor blocks for each block to at most eight. This restriction helps reduce the size of the branch predictor (see section 4.3) without significantly reducing the fetch bandwidth used.

3. Blocks that are connected via a call, return, or indirect jump cannot be combined. Mechanisms to support multiple successor candidates for such operations have not yet been developed.

4. Separate loop iterations are not combined into enlarged blocks. This restriction helps reduce the code expansion due to block enlargement without significantly affecting performance.

5. Blocks in library functions are not combined. Currently, we do not have the source code for our system library functions so we are not able to recompile them with the block enlargement optimization.

4.3. The Block-Structured ISA Processor

The block-structured ISA processor modeled in our experiments is a sixteen-wide issue, dynamically scheduled processor that implements the HPS execution model [16, 17]. The processor supports speculative execution as required by block-structured ISAs (see section 2). It can fetch and issue one atomic block each cycle. Each atomic block can contain up to sixteen operations. Dynamic register renaming removes any anti and output dependencies in the dynamic instruction stream. The processor can hold up to 32 atomic blocks at a time, equaling a maximum of 512 operations. As soon as its operands are all ready, an issued operation is scheduled for execution on one of sixteen uniform functional units whose latencies are listed in table 1. The processor has a 16KB L1 dcache and a perfect L2 dcache with a six cycle access time. The size of the processor's L1 icache is varied in our experiments, but the L2 icache is always modeled as perfect with a six cycle access time.

Instruction Class	Exec. Lat.	Description
Integer	1	INT add, sub and logic OPs
FP Add	3	FP add, sub, and convert
FP/INT Mul	3	FP mul and INT mul
FP/INT Div	8	FP div and INT div
Load	2	Memory loads
Store	-	Memory stores
Bit Field	1	Shift, and bit testing
Branch	1	Control instructions

Table 1. Instruction classes and latencies

To predict the next atomic block to be fetched, the block-structured ISA processor uses a predictor based on the Two-Level Adaptive Branch Predictor [25]. Because each atomic block may contain multiple branches, the block-structured ISA predictor must be able to implicitly make multiple branch predictions each cycle. To do this, the Two-Level Adaptive Branch Predictor must be modified in three ways:

1. The size of each BTB entry must be increased so that it can store all the possible control flow successors for an atomic block.. For our simulations, this number will be eight. When the atomic block is first encountered, the two explicitly specified targets in its trap operation are stored in the BTB. The remaining six targets are filled in to the BTB as they are encountered due to fault mispredictions.

2. Because each block can have up to eight control flow successors, the predictor must now produce a three bit prediction instead of a one bit prediction to select the predicted successor block. To do this, the pattern history table (PHT) entry is modified to hold additional counters to predict the fault operations in addition to the normal two-bit counter which will now be used to predict the trap direction.

3. The branch history register (BHR) should be updated each cycle with a varying number of history bits, because the number of branches predicted each cycle varies. When predicting the control flow successor to an atomic block with only two control flow successors, the branch predictor is predicting the direction taken by exactly one branch and only one bit is needed to uniquely identify that prediction. However, if the BHR is updated with the entire three bit prediction value, then two potentially useful history bits will be unnecessarily shifted out of the BHR. To prevent this unnecessary loss of branch history, the

block-structured ISA predictor shifts in the minimum number of history bits required to uniquely identify the current prediction. This number is specified in the corresponding trap operation (see section 4.1) and stored in the BTB.

5. Experimental results

To evaluate the performance advantages of block-structured ISAs, we compared the performance of the implementation of our block-structured ISA described in section 4.3 to an identically configured implementation of a conventional ISA. The two implementations had the same number of functional units, cycle times, icache size, and dcache size. In reality, the reduction in hardware complexity provided by block-structured ISAs would have enabled the implementation for the block-structured ISA to either have had a faster cycle time or a shallower pipeline than that of the conventional ISA implementation. As a result, the performance gains measured were more conservative than they otherwise would have been.

The conventional ISA implemented was the load/store ISA that formed the basis of our block-structured ISA. This eliminated any architectural advantages the block-structured ISA may have had over the conventional ISA with the exception of those due to block-structuring. To generate the conventional ISA executables, we used a variant of the block-structured ISA compiler that was retargeted to the conventional ISA. This eliminated any unfair compiler advantages one ISA may have had over the other.

Table 2 lists the eight SPECint95 benchmarks used for our comparison [2], along with the input data sets, and the number of conventional ISA instructions required to run each benchmark to completion.

Figure 3 compares the performance of the block-structured ISA executables to the performance of the conventional ISA executables when using a 64KB, four-way set associative L1 icache. Although current day L1 icache sizes are on the order of 8–16KB, advances in device densities will make 64KB L1 icaches feasible for future processors. The graph shows the total number of cycles required to execute each benchmark. With the exception of the go benchmark, each block-structured ISA executable outperformed the corresponding conventional ISA executable. The block enlargement optimization reduced the execution time on average by 12.3%, with reductions that ranged from 7.2% for gcc to 19.9% for m88ksim. The go benchmark showed a 1.5% increase in execution time which was due to increased icache misses, as will be shown below.

Benchmark	Input	# of Instructions
compress	test.in*	103,015,025
gcc	jump.i	154,450,036
go	2stone9.in*	125,637,006
ijpeg	specmun.ppm*	206,802,135
m88sim	dcrand.train	120,738,195
perl	scrabbl.pl*	78,148,849
vortex	vortex.big*	232,003,378
xlisp	train.lsp	187,727,922

Table 2. The SPECint95 benchmarks and their input data sets. * indicates the input set is an abbreviated version of the SPECint95 reference input set.

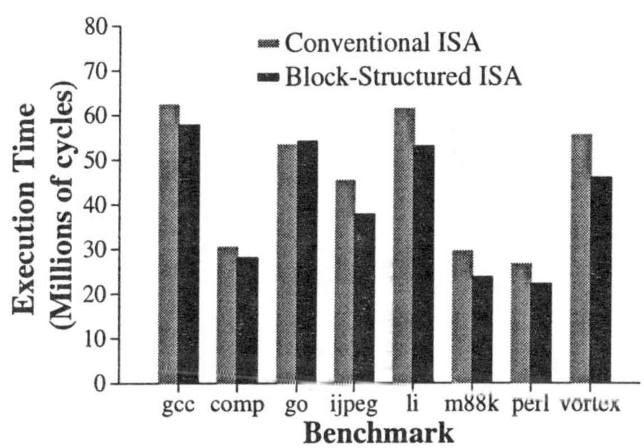

Figure 3. Performance comparison of block-structured ISA executables and conventional ISA executables.

To measure the performance impact of branch mispredictions on block-structured ISAs, figure 4 shows the same performance comparison as figure 3 except that perfect branch prediction is assumed. With perfect branch prediction, the average reduction in execution time is increased to 19.1%. Because both block-structured and conventional ISA executables incur about the same number of branch mispredictions, the increase in performance difference between the two ISAs indicates that branch mispredictions are more costly for block-structured ISAs. This is because good work must be removed from the machine for a fault misprediction and because the block-structured ISA is capable of fetching and issuing more work each cycle, increasing the performance loss for each cycle of branch misprediction penalty.

Figure 5 shows the average block size issued during exe-

[2] The SPECfp95 floating point benchmarks were omitted from the study because our work has focused on extracting instruction level parallelism from non-scientific programs that represent everyday applications, where the parallelism is irregularly distributed and harder to extract. We note that block-structured ISAs should be able to achieve even larger performance gains for the floating point benchmarks.

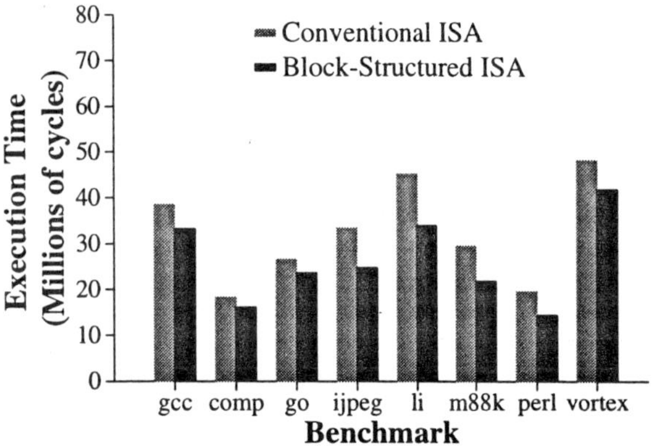

Figure 4. Performance comparison of block-structured ISA executables and conventional ISA executables while assuming perfect branch prediction.

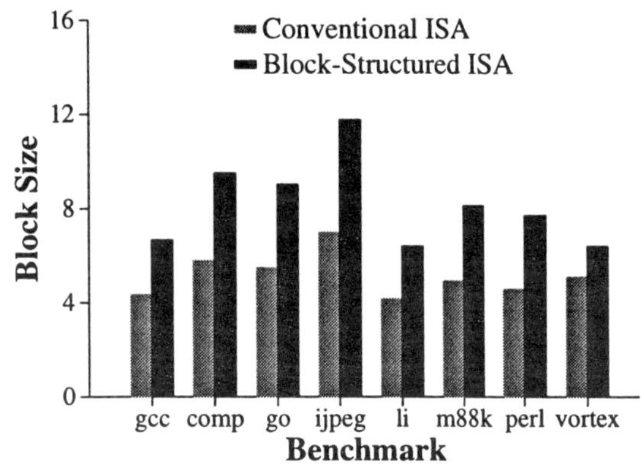

Figure 5. Average block sizes for block-structured and conventional ISA executables.

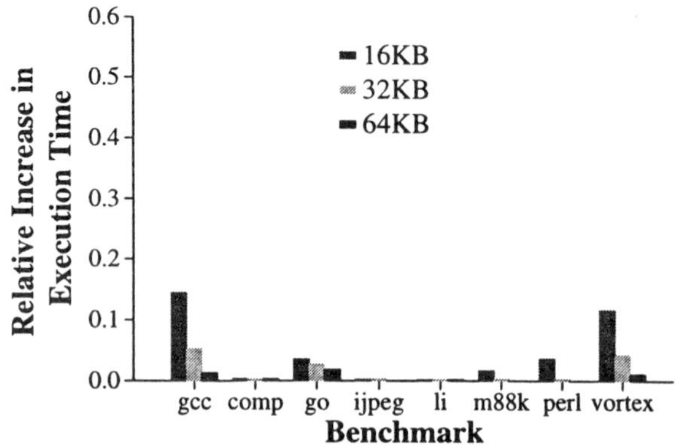

Figure 6. Relative increase in execution times for the conventional ISA executables over the execution time with a perfect icache.

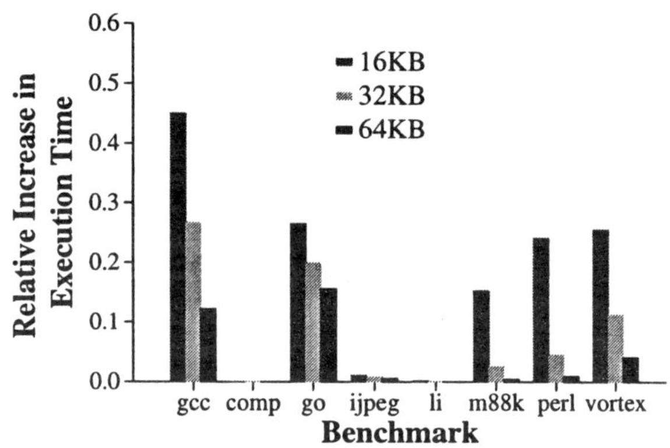

Figure 7. Relative increase in execution times for the block-structured ISA executables over the execution time with a perfect icache.

cution of each of the block-structured ISA and conventional ISA executables. Blocks that were not retired (i.e. that were issued after a branch misprediction) were not counted toward the average. Across all eight benchmarks, the average block sizes for the conventional ISA and block-structured ISA executables were 5.2 and 8.2 instructions. Despite increasing the block size by 58%, the block enlargement optimization still has left almost half the processors fetch bandwidth unused. The major reason why block enlargement was unable to create larger blocks was the occurrence of procedure calls and returns (see section 4.2). Their occurrence eliminated many opportunities for further block enlargement.

As discussed in section 2, by duplicating blocks, the block enlargement optimization may decrease the performance of the icache. To quantify this effect, we measured for each benchmark, the relative increase in execution time for a given icache size as compared to a perfect icache. This study did not model the icache effects due to operating system code. These effects may further decrease icache performance [23]. Figures 6 and 7 show the results of these comparisons for icache sizes from 16KB to 64KB. With the exception of the small benchmarks (compress, li, and ijpeg), the block-structured ISA executables show much larger performance decreases due to icache misses than the conventional ISA executables. The decrease is greatest in the gcc and go benchmarks which have many small basic blocks and many unbiased branches. As a result, by combining all the frequently executed combinations of basic blocks into enlarged blocks, the block-structured ISA executables for these benchmarks use significantly more icache space than the conventional ISA executables.

6. Conclusions

In this paper, we examined the performance benefits of using a block-structured ISA to increase the processor instruction fetch rate. Through the block enlargement optimization, the atomic blocks of the block-structured ISA could be combined to form larger blocks. As a result, larger units of work could be fetched from the icache each cycle without having to fetch non-consecutive cache lines. Furthermore, the block-structured ISA provides support for the use of dynamic branch prediction in selecting the successor block, rather than restricting the processor to static branch prediction.

We defined one instance of a block-structured ISA and implemented a compiler targeted to that ISA and a simulator to model the performance of a sixteen wide issue, dynamically scheduled processor that implements that ISA. Using this compiler and simulator, we compared the performance of programs executing on a block-structured ISA processor to the performance of programs executing on a conventional ISA processor for the SPECint95 benchmarks. The block-structured ISA processors achieved a 12% performance improvement over conventional ISA processors. This performance difference increased to 20% when perfect branch prediction was assumed. These performance improvements were due to the block enlargement optimization increasing the average block size from 5.2 instructions to 8.2 instructions. We also examined the block enlargement optimization's effect on icache performance. Because the block enlargement optimization duplicates blocks, the number of icache misses was larger for the block-structured ISA executables than for the conventional ISA executables. The difference was most significant for the gcc and go benchmarks.

The experimental results point to future directions in which the performance of processors implementing block-structured ISAs can be improved. Improving the branch prediction accuracy and icache hit rate and more fully utilizing the fetch bandwidth of the processor will further increase the performance difference between block-structured ISAs and conventional ISAs. Possibilities for achieving these goals include predicated execution, profiling, and inlining. Predicated execution can reduce the performance lost due to mispredicted branches by eliminating hard to predict branches. In addition, predicated execution can increase the fetch bandwidth used by eliminating branches that jump around small sections of the code. This optimization will create larger basic blocks which in turn will allow the block enlargement optimization to create even larger enlarged atomic blocks. Profiling can improve the icache hit rate by guiding the compiler's use of the block enlargement optimization. The amount of code duplication caused by the block enlargement optimization can be reduced if this optimization does not combine blocks that contain unbiased branches with their successors, thereby reducing the icache miss rate in exchange for smaller enlarged atomic blocks. Inlining can increase the fetch bandwidth used by eliminating procedure calls and returns, allowing the block enlargement optimization to combine blocks that previously could not be combined. In addition, using block-structured ISAs in conjunction with another fetch rate enhancing mechanism, such as the trace cache [19], may lead to even higher fetch rates without sacrificing icache performance.

We also plan to measure the performance gains that can be achieved by block-structured ISAs for scientific code. Those performance gains should be even greater than the gains achieved for the SPECint95 benchmarks because the branches that occur in scientific code are more predictable and the basic blocks are larger. These differences will reduce the performance penalty suffered by block-structured ISAs for branch mispredictions and increase the size of the blocks formed by the block enlargement optimization, resulting in even higher levels of performance.

This study focused on the improvements in instruction fetch rate provided by block-structured ISAs, ignoring the implementation benefits provided by block-structured ISAs. By reducing the hardware complexity of various microarchitectural mechanisms, block-structured ISAs enable the implementation of extremely wide issue processors. The performance benefits of these features would further increase the performance advantage of block-structured ISA processors over conventional ISA processors. In addition, as new algorithms are developed that increase the instruction level parallelism in programs that use them, the ability to implement wide issue processors will become even more important.

Acknowledgments

This paper is one result of our ongoing research in high performance computer implementation at the University of Michigan. The support of our industrial partners: Intel, Motorola, Hewlett-Packard, and NCR is greatly appreciated. We would also like to thank all the members of the HPS group for their contributions to this paper and the reviewers for their helpful suggestions.

References

[1] T. M. Conte, K. N. Menezes, P. M. Mills, and B. Patel. Optimization of instruction fetch mechanisms for high issue rates. In *Proceedings of the 22st Annual International Symposium on Computer Architecture*, pages 333–344, 1995.

[2] S. Dutta and M. Franklin. Control flow prediction with tree-like subgraphs for superscalar processors. In *Proceedings of the 28th Annual ACM/IEEE International Symposium on Microarchitecture*, pages 258–263, 1995.

[3] K. Ebcioğlu. Some design ideas for a VLIW architecture for sequential natured software. *Parallel Processing (Proceedings of IFIP WG 10.3 Working Conference on Parallel Processing*, pages 3–21, Apr. 1988.

[4] J. A. Fisher. 2^n-way jump microinstruction hardware and an effective instruction binding method. In *Proceedings of the 13th Annual Microprogramming Workshop*, pages 64–75, 1980.

[5] J. A. Fisher. Trace scheduling: A technique for global microcode compaction. *IEEE Transactions on Computers*, C-30(7):478–490, July 1981.

[6] M. Franklin and G. S. Sohi. The expandable split window paradigm for exploiting fine-grain parallelism. In *Proceedings of the 19th Annual International Symposium on Computer Architecture*, pages 58–67, 1992.

[7] P. Hsu and E. Davidson. Highly concurrent scalar processing. In *Proceedings of the 13th Annual International Symposium on Computer Architecture*, 1986.

[8] W. W. Hwu, S. A. Mahlke, W. Y. Chen, P. P. Chang, N. J. Warter, R. A. Bringmann, R. G. Ouellette, R. E. Hank, T. Kiyohara, G. E. Haab, J. G. Holm, and D. M. Lavery. The superblock: An effective technique for VLIW and superscalar compilation. *Journal of Supercomputing*, 7(9-50), 1993.

[9] Intel Corporation. *Intel Reference C Compiler User's Guide for UNIX Systems*, 1993.

[10] K. Karplus and A. Nicolau. Efficient hardware for multi-way jumps and prefetches. In *Proceedings of the 18th Annual Microprogramming Workshop*, pages 11–18, 1985.

[11] S. A. Mahlke, R. E. Hank, R. A. Bringmann, J. C. Gyllenhaal, D. M. Gallagher, and W. W. Hwu. Characterizing the impact of predicated execution on branch prediction. In *Proceedings of the 27th Annual ACM/IEEE International Symposium on Microarchitecture*, pages 217–227, 1994.

[12] S. A. Mahlke, D. C. Lin, W. Y. Chen, R. E. Hank, and R. A. Bringmann. Effective compiler support for predicated execution using the hyperblock. In *Proceedings of the 25th Annual ACM/IEEE International Symposium on Microarchitecture*, pages 45–54, 1992.

[13] S. Melvin and Y. Patt. Enhancing instruction scheduling with a block-structured ISA. *International Journal on Parallel Processing*, 23(3):221–243, 1995.

[14] S. Melvin and Y. N. Patt. Exploiting fine-grained parallelism through a combination of hardware and software techniques. In *Proceedings of the 18th Annual International Symposium on Computer Architecture*, pages 287–297, 1991.

[15] S.-M. Moon and K. Ebcioğlu. An efficient resource-constrained global scheduling technique for superscalar and VLIW processors. In *Proceedings of the 25th Annual ACM/IEEE International Symposium on Microarchitecture*, pages 55–71, 1992.

[16] Y. Patt, W. Hwu, and M. Shebanow. HPS, a new microarchitecture: Rationale and introduction. In *Proceedings of the 18th Annual Microprogramming Workshop*, pages 103–107, 1985.

[17] Y. N. Patt, S. W. Melvin, W. Hwu, and M. C. Shebanow. Critical issues regarding HPS, a high performance microarchitecture. In *Proceedings of the 18th Annual Microprogramming Workshop*, pages 109–116, 1985.

[18] D. N. Pnevmatikatos and G. S. Sohi. Guarded execution and dynamic branch prediction in dynamic ILP processors. In *Proceedings of the 21st Annual International Symposium on Computer Architecture*, pages 120–129, 1994.

[19] E. Rotenberg, S. Bennett, and J. E. Smith. Trace cache: A low latency approach to high bandwidth instruction fetching. Technical Report 1310, University of Wisconsin - Madison, Apr. 1996.

[20] A. Seznec, S. Jourdan, P. Sainrat, and P. Michaud. Multiple-block ahead branch predictors. In *Proceedings of the 7th International Conference on Architectural Support for Programming Languages and Operating Systems*, 1996. To appear.

[21] G. S. Sohi, S. E. Breach, and T. N. Vijaykumar. Multiscalar processors. In *Proceedings of the 22st Annual International Symposium on Computer Architecture*, 1995.

[22] E. Sprangle and Y. Patt. Facilitating superscalar processing via a combined static/dynamic register renaming scheme. In *Proceedings of the 27th Annual ACM/IEEE International Symposium on Microarchitecture*, pages 143–147, 1994.

[23] R. Uhlig, D. Nagle, T. Mudge, S. Sechrest, and J. Emer. Instruction fetching: Coping with code bloat. In *Proceedings of the 22st Annual International Symposium on Computer Architecture*, pages 345–356, 1995.

[24] T.-Y. Yeh, D. Marr, and Y. N. Patt. Increasing the instruction fetch rate via multiple branch prediction and branch address cache. In *Proceedings of the International Conference on Supercomputing*, pages 67–76, 1993.

[25] T.-Y. Yeh and Y. N. Patt. Two-level adaptive branch prediction. In *Proceedings of the 24th Annual ACM/IEEE International Symposium on Microarchitecture*, pages 51–61, 1991.

Instruction Fetch Mechanisms for VLIW Architectures with Compressed Encodings

Thomas M. Conte Sanjeev Banerjia Sergei Y. Larin Kishore N. Menezes
Sumedh W. Sathaye

Department of Electrical and Computer Engineering
North Carolina State University
Raleigh, North Carolina 27695-7911
(919)-515-5067
{conte,sbanerj,sylarin,knmeneze,swsathay}@eos.ncsu.edu

Abstract

VLIW architectures use very wide instruction words in conjunction with high bandwidth to the instruction cache to achieve multiple instruction issue. This report uses the TINKER experimental testbed to examine instruction fetch and instruction cache mechanisms for VLIWs. A compressed instruction encoding for VLIWs is defined, and a classification scheme for i-fetch hardware for such an encoding is introduced. Several interesting cache and i-fetch organizations are described and evaluated through trace-driven simulations. A new i-fetch mechanism using a silo cache is found to have the best performance.

1. Introduction

VLIW architectures use very wide instruction words to achieve multiple instruction issue. These architectures require high bandwidth instruction fetch (i-fetch) mechanisms to transport instruction words from the cache to the execution pipeline. The complexity of the hardware support required for i-fetch is related to the type of instruction encoding used. In general, VLIW instructions are horizontally encoded wide words that issue an operation on every clock cycle to functional units (FUs) in the machine. The sequence of instruction words that compose a program is the *schedule* for the program. The instruction words can be encoded in several ways, and the choice of encoding can greatly influence the hardware required for i-fetch. A VLIW with an *uncompressed encoding* is one that explicitly stores NOP operations in the instruction word. The VLIW instruction stores a NOP in the operation slot for a particular FU if this FU is not scheduled to execute an operation at that point in the schedule. Use of an uncompressed encoding yields a fixed length instruction word, which can simplify the i-fetch hardware but at the expense of the potentially poor memory utilization.

Another class of encodings are *compressed encodings*, which do not store NOPs. VLIW instructions encoded using a compressed encoding are variably sized. The size of an instruction is dependent on the number of FUs that will receive an operation at that point in the schedule. This type of encoding has a higher memory utilization and allows greater effective memory bandwidth than an uncompressed encoding. A compressed encoding also aids in object–code compatibility for VLIWs, such as in the dynamic rescheduling algorithm that has been proposed in the TINKER VLIW testbed [9]. A drawback is that such an encoding requires more complicated i-fetch to handle the variable length instructions.

This paper focuses on the requirements of i-fetch imposed by a compressed encoding. Several mechanisms for i-fetch are presented, and the effect of each mechanism on instruction cache (i-cache) design is described. The paper is organized as follows: Section 2 introduces a basic instruction fetch mechanism and details the implementation of a compressed encoding; previous work in the area is also discussed. Section 3 presents a scheme for classifying i-caches for a compressed encoding and introduces four different organizations: the uncompressed cache, the banked cache, the rigid silo cache, and the flexible silo cache. Sections 4.1-4.3 describe each of the i-cache designs in detail, including their respective performance. Section 5 discusses the performance of the designs and also discusses directions for future research.

1072-4451/96 $5.00 © 1996 IEEE

2. A Basic Instruction Fetch Model

2.1. Instruction Fetch with a Compressed Encoding

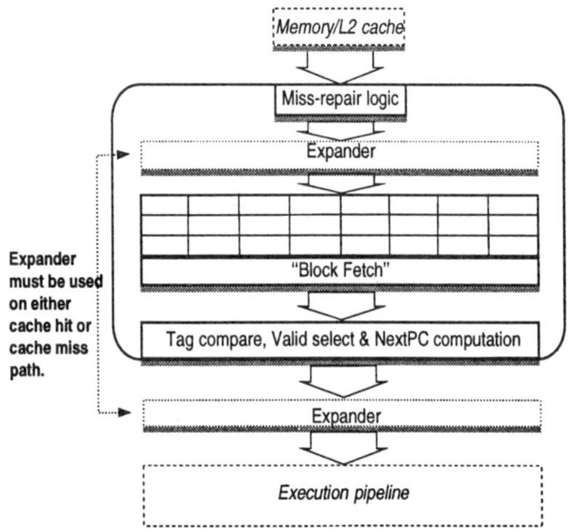

Figure 1. The basic instruction fetch model. All of the necessary stages for i-fetch for a compressed encoding are shown.

A simplified instruction fetch model for compressed encodings is shown in Figure 1. The solid lower borders in the diagram indicate pipeline latches that delineate the stages of the fetch pipeline. The main blocks in this model are the miss-repair logic, the pipelined instruction cache, and the *expander*, which is discussed below. The miss-repair logic handles cache miss repair requests, and could be implemented as a pipelined interface to the next level in the memory hierarchy. Inside the instruction cache, each cache block holds one or more VLIW instructions. This is dependent on the instruction fetch mechanism and is explained in depth in Section 3. The cache is pipelined and consists of a *"block fetch"* stage that selects and fetches a cache block when presented with an address, and a *"tag compare & valid select"* stage that performs tag comparisons in parallel with selecting the Ops in the block that belong to the requested VLIW instruction.

A compressed instruction encoding using the TINKER VLIW experimental testbed is used for this study [8]. The compressed encoding combines individual operations (Ops) that can be issued in parallel into a unit of parallel issue called a MultiOp. A TINKER Op is a RISC-like instruction that is 64 bits in length. A TINKER Op can execute on one of four types of functional units (*FUType*): integer (integer computation and predicate handling), memory (loads and stores), FP (floating point add/mul/div/convert) and branch. An example of a TINKER integer add Op is shown in Figure 2. The TINKER encoding uses *header* and *tail* bits within an Op to delineate the beginning and end of a

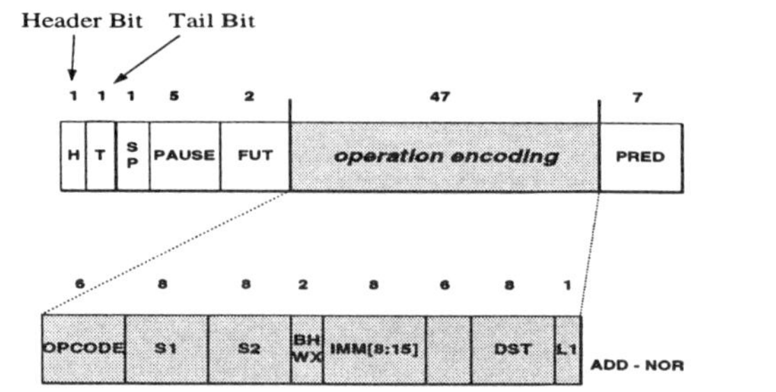

Figure 2. An integer add Op in the TINKER encoding.

MultiOp i.e., the first Op in a MultiOp has its header bit set, and the last Op in a MultiOp has its tail bit set. The branch architecture is compiler-directed, similar to that of the Play-Doh specification from Hewlett Packard Laboratories [16]. For a n issue machine (TINKER-n), the maximum MultiOp size is $n * 64$ bits. A maximum-sized MultiOp contains an Op for each functional unit in the machine.

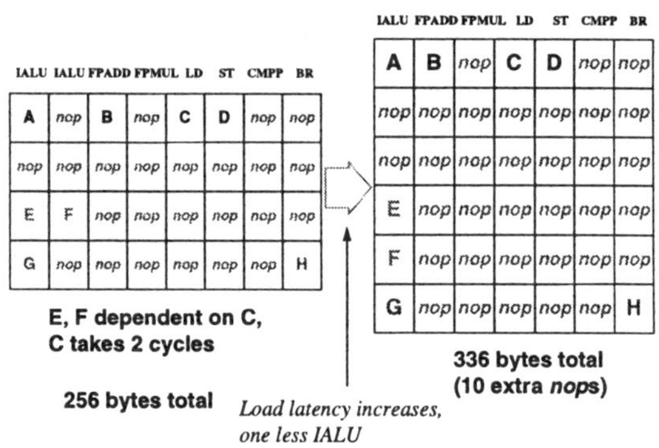

Figure 3. Object code compatibility using an uncompressed encoding.

The size of the code changes when it is rescheduled for a different machine organization.

A useful property of compressed encodings is *rescheduling size invariance (RSI)*. RSI means that the size of a program does not vary across different generations of a VLIW architecture. Figure 3 shows that when using an uncompressed (non-RSI) encoding the size of an executable image can change. A change in code size can cause problems, such as branch target invalidation and constrained speculation [9]. A solution to the code size change problem is to use a RSI encoding like TINKER. The result of using the TINKER encoding to reschedule the code of Figure 3 is shown in Figure 4. Manipulation of the header and tail bits and the pause fields is the only requirement for modification of the schedule to execute correctly on different generations of an architecture[1].

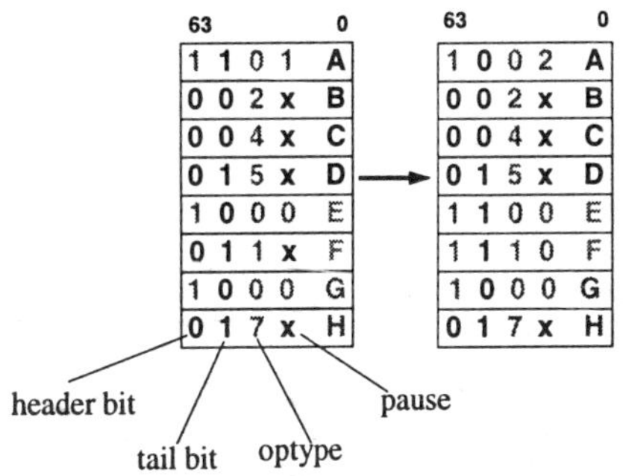

Figure 4. Object code compatibility using the TINKER compressed encoding.

The size of the binary remains the same. The pause field for the first MultiOp is incremented by one, and the MultiOp originally consisting of Ops E and F has been made into two MultiOps.

Although a compressed encoding has several advantages, it also requires a complex i-fetch mechanism. One step of i-fetch is NextPC generation, during which a PC is generated for the subsequent i-cache access. NextPC generation for an uncompressed encoding consists of adding a constant (the size of the fixed instruction) to the PC and using the new quantity (NextPC) to address the i-cache in the next cycle. Architectures that use variable length instructions have to first determine the length of current instruction being fetched to determine what quantity to add to the PC to get NextPC. Another step of i-fetch is to determine how individual Ops in a MultiOp should be routed to FUs. For an uncompressed encoding, the FU is fixed by the position of the Op in the MultiOp, but this is not the case for a compressed encoding. A TINKER Op contains an FUT field indicating for what FUType it is destined. An Op destined for a particular FUType can reside anywhere in a MultiOp, depending on the other types of Ops in the same MultiOp. This is intrinsic to a compressed encoding, and requires that Ops must be partially decoded and then *routed* to the appropriate functional unit. For example, if the instruction issue logic expects only integer Ops in Op position one in a MultiOp, and a one Op MultiOp is composed of a floating point Op, the Op must be routed to the floating point unit and not the integer unit. The *expander stage* performs this routing by routing all Ops in one MultiOp in parallel. An expander should have the functionality of a full crossbar; that is, route any type of Op to any FU (this requirement can be relaxed somewhat if the compiler enforces a partial ordering of Ops based on FUType).

An expander can be placed either on the cache hit path or the cache miss path as shown in Figure 1. A *miss path expander* is used only when a cache miss occurs and operates as follows: (1) As a MultiOp is fetched from memory, it is placed into the expander. (2) When the entire MultiOp has been received, the expander routes the Ops to specific positions in the cache, as selected by the miss address (i.e., the cache holds Ops in specific positions corresponding to their FUTypes).

Miss path expansion adds extra stages to the miss penalty. The number of extra stages is equal to the number of stages needed for expansion. In contrast, a *hit path expander* is used on every cache access. After a MultiOp has been fetched from the cache, it is processed by the expander for Op-to-functional-unit routing. The expander is not on the cache miss path and therefore does not affect the miss penalty. However, the number of cycles needed for expansion is now in the fetch path and therefore adds to the branch misprediction penalty. For this reason, hit path expansion should be performed in one cycle, requiring a complex and potentially costly implementation to meet the single cycle constraint.

2.2. Related Work

Other classes of encodings can also be used for VLIW architectures. The 4S architecture proposed by Sun Microsystems used a *frame encoding* which grouped MultiOps into instruction *frames*. An instruction frame is the same size as the i-fetch width of the machine. A frame encoding supports variable size instructions but enforces the restriction that all Ops in a MultiOp must reside in the same frame to ease the requirements on the i-fetch mechanism [3]. This requires NOPs, thereby violating RSI. The Cydrome Cydra 5 VLIW machine used a *split encoding* such that instruction cache blocks were composed of either one MultiOp or multiple one Op MultiOps called UniOps [20], [5]. Cache blocks composed of one MultiOp are in an uncompressed form, and those composed of UniOps are padded with NOPs, if needed for cache block alignment. It is also non-RSI. Another commercial VLIW architecture, the Multiflow TRACE family of machines, used a compressed encoding [17]. Nops were not stored in instruction words in memory. Instructions were expanded as they were fetched from memory into the instruction cache (TRACE machines used cache miss expansion).

Much of the related work in instruction fetch mechanisms has concentrated on superscalar or CISC architectures, especially in the arena of x86 architectures. Patt, *et al.*, studied the use of the fill buffer and a decoded instruction cache to break down CISC instructions into microoperations which can then be efficiently scheduled using dynamic scheduling

[1] In general, the relative Op ordering may also change without ill effects, although this is not demonstrated in this example.

hardware [18]. Smotherman and Franklin adapted the fill unit and decoded instruction cache for use in decoding x86 instructions [23]. Their design associates a NextPC field with each cache block. The Intel Pentium Pro processor employs a multi-stage i-fetch that fetches 16 bytes per cycle from the i-cache and then uses three stages to align the instructions [19]. NextPC is PC+16 in the absence of a branch instruction. The AMD K5 stores decode information related to instruction length in the L1 instruction cache which is later used for NextPC computation in the i-fetch stage [7]. Like the Pentium Pro, the K5 uses multiple stages to fetch and align an x86 instruction stream. An x86 processor design from NexGen uses a different approach for NextPC generation. It has dedicated logic that performs instruction alignment at fetch time to compute NextPC [11]. In the arena of RISC architectures, the CRISP processor used a decoded instruction cache [10]. CRISP instructions were converted from their in–memory format of 16-80 bits to a 192 bit expanded form in the i-cache. Each expanded instruction occupied a cache block by itself and had associated with it a NextPC field. The effect of encoding instructions in a compressed manner was studied by Wolfe and Chanin [24]. Their Compressed Code RISC Processor was designed to conserve memory bandwidth and did so by storing instructions in a compressed format in memory and decompressing them into the instruction cache at cache miss time. The R1 SPARC processor from HaL performs limited decoding between memory and the L1 i-cache to aid in decoding during i-fetch [21].

3. A Classification for VLIW I-Caches

VLIW cache organizations can be classified based on two factors, the *degree of partitioning (DoP)* and the *NOPs policy* of the cache. The DoP describes the number of independent memory units (partitions) that are used to implement the cache and the placement of Ops into those memory units (an independent memory unit is a tag and data array that can be searched in parallel with other independent memories). A traditional cache is a cache with one partition: all Ops can be stored at any location within the entire cache and only one tag or set of tags is searched[2]. An alternative is a cache that uses multiple partitions, such that an Op maps into a particular partition based on its FUType. As described in Section 2.1, the TINKER encoding uses four FUTypes: integer (I), floating point (F), memory (M) and branch (B). A cache organization that assigns each FUType to a separate partition is represented as (I) (F) (M) (B) and is labeled *fully partitioned* (using this notation, a unified partition cache – a traditional cache – is represented as (I F M B)). Between the extremes of the unified partition and fully partitioned designs are *flexible* designs that permit multiple FUTypes to reside in a partition. For example, a design that allows integer and floating point Ops to share a partition and assigns other FUTypes to their own partitions is represented as (I F) (M) (B).

In implementation, a fully partitioned cache for a TINKER-n machine has n partitions, where every partition is the same size. A flexible partitioned cache combines the partitions for the sharing FUTypes and is the same size overall as a fully partitioned cache. Also, a flexible design allows the sharing FUTypes to reside at arbitrary locations within the combined partition.

The second factor for classification is whether the cache explicitly contains NOPs (a *NOP cache*) or not (a *NOPs-free cache*). The MultiOps held in a NOP cache are in uncompressed form, whereas in a NOPs-free cache they are in compressed form. The NOPs policy of a cache is closely tied to the placement of the expander in i-cache pipeline (this is explained further in Section 4).

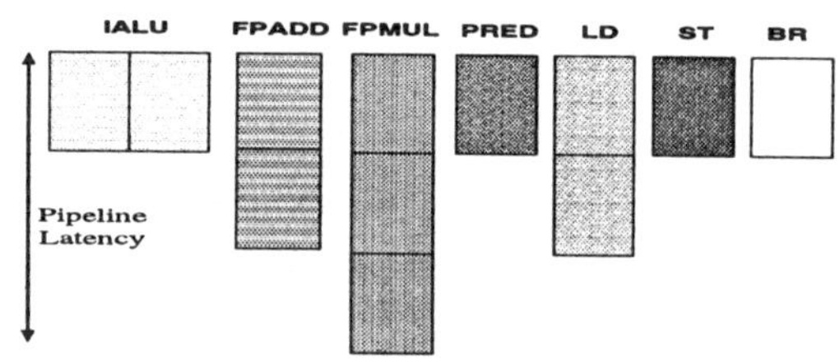

Figure 5. The TINKER-8 machine model.

Table 1. Benchmarks used for evaluation.

Benchmark Programs	
Integer	Floating point
085.gcc	039.wave5
124.m88ksim	048.ora
129.compress	052.alvinn
130.li	056.ear
134.perl	089.su2cor
147.vortex	090.hydro2d

A permutation of the DoP and NOPs policies yields a wide variety of cache configurations. In this paper, four representative organizations are explored. The **uncompressed cache** has a DoP = (I F M B) (all Ops are stored in one partition), and a NOP policy. The **banked cache** has a DoP = (I F M B), and uses a NOPs-free policy. The **silo cache** has a DoP = (I) (F) (M) (B) (fully partitioned), and a NOP policy. Lastly, the **flexible silo cache** uses a combined partition for two FUTypes and separate partitions for the remaining two FUTypes, and a NOP policy. The four designs are assumed to have the same cycle time. Trace driven

[2] Set associativity permits parallel tag compares, but this is orthogonal to partitioning, as is shown in Section 4.3.

simulations were used to evaluate the performance of the schemes. The IMPACT compiler employing superblock-based scheduling was used to compile benchmark programs using the TINKER compressed encoding for the TINKER-8 machine organization [13]. The functional unit configuration and pipeline latencies are shown in Figure 5, with each functional unit pipelined to the depth indicated. A pipelined L1 cache/memory interface with a three cycle latency and a one Op bandwidth was assumed (the three cycle latency was chosen as it is similar to the L2 latency in contemporary microprocessors [19], [6]). A perfect L1 data cache and L2 cache was assumed to prevent data cache effects from coloring the performance measurements. Integer and floating point programs from the SPEC92 and SPEC95 suiteswere used as benchmarks for the evaluations and are listed in Table 1[3]. Two million Ops were sampled across the entire program for each simulation run.

4. Instruction Fetch Mechanisms

4.1. I-Fetch using the Uncompressed Cache

Figure 6 shows the organization of the *uncompressed cache*. The cache block size is the same as the machine width. A miss path expander is used with the cache miss-repair mechanism (a two cycle expander is assumed). The branch misprediction penalty is one cycle.

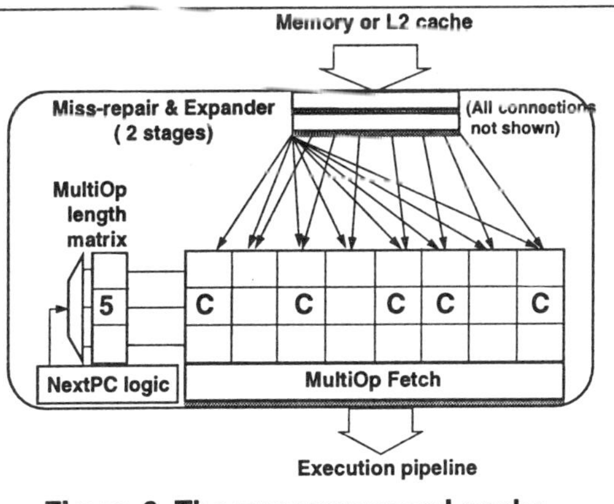

Figure 6. The uncompressed cache.
A two cycle miss path expander is used to place Ops into positions within a cache block. A length field is associated with every cache block.

A modified direct mapped addressing scheme is used for the uncompressed cache. An example illustrates why traditional direct-mapped addressing (bit selection) cannot be used. Assume a TINKER-4 machine with a 32 KB i-cache that uses 32 bit addresses. Consider the two MultiOps in Figure 7, shown as they would appear in memory. All Ops in the first MultiOp are marked "A", and those in the second MultiOp are marked "B". MultiOp A has 2 Ops, while MultiOp B has a single Op. Assume that A does not contain a branch Op. If the cache were addressed as a normal direct-mapped cache, with the physical addresses of MultiOps A and B as 0x80000000 and 0x80000080, respectively, both would have the same tag and index, and hence map onto the same cache block (depicted in Figure 8(a)). For a sequential access pattern, a conflict miss is generated for the second MultiOp access i.e., for B. Not only do MultiOps A and B create contention for a cache block, but because their tags are identical it cannot be determined which one is resident in the cache.

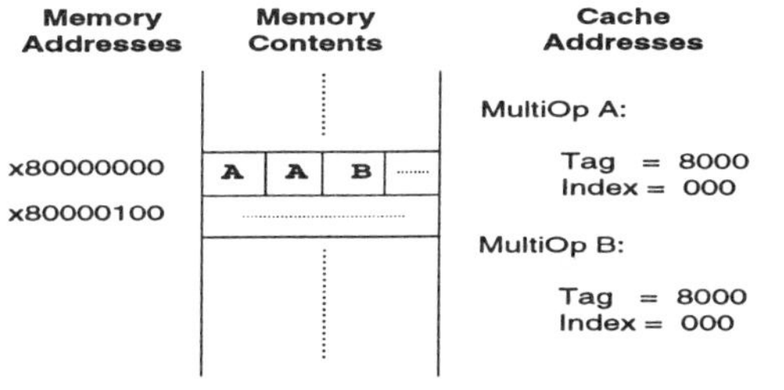

Figure 7. A traditional address mapping for the uncompressed cache.

One way to differentiate between such sequential Ops is to use some of the offset bits as part of the index. Figure 8(b) depicts how the cache interprets the address when using such a scheme. This *offset reduced* addressing maps each individual MultiOp from a memory block frame into a separate cache block. Associativity is not required because the possibility of sequential MultiOps mapping to the same cache block is eliminated.

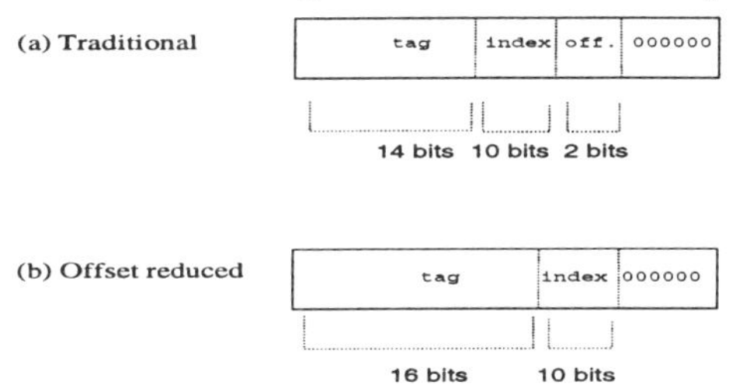

Figure 8. Interpreting a cache address – (a) traditional scheme, (b) reduced offset scheme.

The uncompressed cache holds the MultiOp in uncompressed form, hence the valid select logic and the hit path expander that were shown as a stage in the basic model

[3]Results presented for floating point programs are lower than normal due to the lack of software pipelining of those programs.

(Figure 1) are unnecessary. NextPC computation still needs to be performed. The fetch hardware must add the length of the current MultiOp to the PC to generate the NextPC. Computation of the length can be performed at run-time, after the block containing the MultiOp is fetched out of the cache matrix. But this places the NextPC computation *after* the block fetch, adding sequential computation at the end of fetch cycle and possibly increasing the cycle time. To avoid this situation, a MultiOp length field can be associated with every cache block. The length field can be accessed in parallel with the tag and data, and the addition of the length to the PC can be done before the beginning of the tag compare stage.

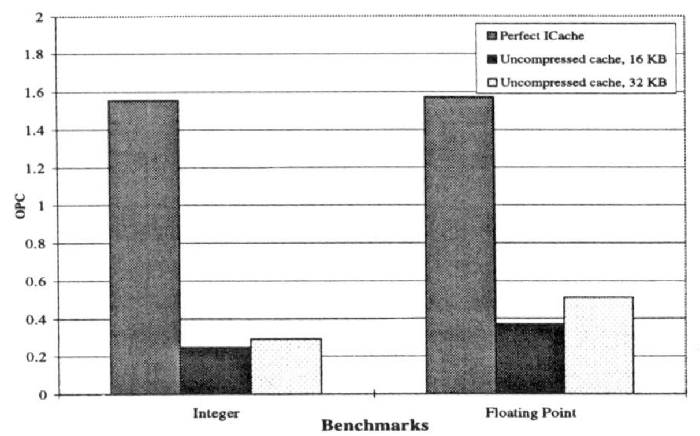

Figure 9. Performance of the uncompressed cache.

The metric used in useful Ops completed per cycle (OPC). Each individual bar represents the harmonic mean for the combination of cache size and benchmark programs.

The graph in Figure 9 presents the results of simulations for the performance of the uncompressed cache as compared to a perfect i-cache (a cache that never misses). The metric used here – and for all simulations in this report – is useful Ops completed per cycle (OPC). OPC is used because it captures the effect of i-cache performance on overall performance. The results are grouped based on cache size and the type of benchmarks. The uncompressed cache performs very poorly when compared to a perfect i-cache. Although increasing the cache size from 16 KB to 32 KB yields better performance, the resulting OPCs are still much smaller than the perfect cache. For the integer benchmarks, increasing the cache size yields 22% better performance but is still more than five times slower than a perfect i-cache. For the floating point benchmarks, the larger cache performed 19% better but is still four times slower than the perfect i-cache. The reason for this is the extremely low space utilization of the uncompressed design. The maximum OPC of < 2 for the perfect cache indicates that only two out of eight words in a cache block are typically used. A possible solution to this is a design that can place more than one MultiOp in a cache block, and this is explored in the next section.

4.2. I-Fetch using the Banked Cache

Figure 10 shows the organization of the instruction fetch mechanism when using a *banked cache*. The cache is organized as two data and tag arrays, as in the Intel Pentium processor [2]. The cache block size is the same as the machine width n. A MultiOp can span two cache blocks. For this reason, on every clock cycle, two cache blocks are accessed: the block in which the requested MultiOp could reside (the *current block*) and the next sequential block (the *successor block*). In contrast to the uncompressed cache, the expander is on the cache hit path and adds an extra stage to the processor pipeline. The extra stage increases the branch misprediction penalty to two cycles.

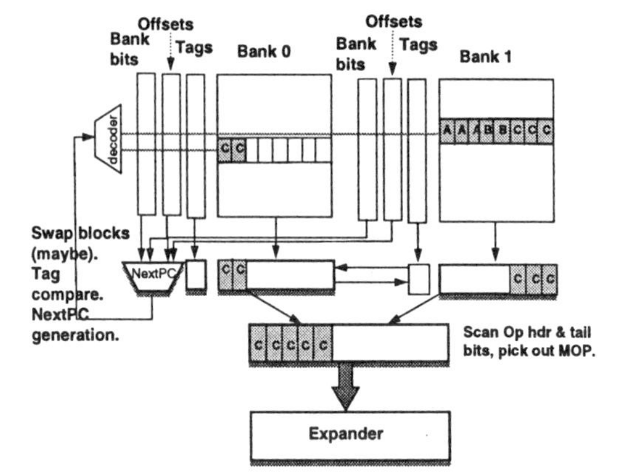

Figure 10. The banked cache.

A fetch for MultiOp C is shown. Blocks from both banks are fetched and then swapped (if needed) before being passed to the single-cycle expander. NextPC computation is performed in parallel with cache access.

Addressing in the banked cache is similar to a traditional cache. The high order bits of the address are used as a tag, and the middle bits are used as an index. Because a MultiOp is variable length and does not always begin on a n-word boundary in memory, the low order bits are used as an offset to index to the start of the MultiOp in the cache block. When a PC is presented to address the cache, the cache address decoder selects consecutive blocks in both cache banks.

The fetch mechanism is shown in Figure 10 with an example fetch operation. The first three Ops of MultiOp C occupy the last three Ops of the cache block in bank one, and the last two Ops of C occupy the first two Ops of the next cache block in bank zero. The PC is the address of the first Op of C at the beginning of fetch cycle. There are three sequential steps required to fetch MultiOp C. These are also shown in Figure 10 and detailed below.

1. The current block containing the first three Ops and the successor block containing the fourth and fifth Ops are requested from the cache.

2. For correct alignment of the MultiOp, the fetch hardware must know where the last Op of MultiOp C lies in the successor cache block. To do this, it searches for the tail bit of the last Op in C. This information permits the cache fetch stage to perform correct alignment by swapping the two MultiOp fragments. Note that a banking factor of two facilitates such an exchange.

3. The header bits for all Ops in the blocks are scanned to determine the Ops belonging to MultiOp C, starting from the location of the first Op in the requested MultiOp. Valid select lines are then enabled to pass only the requested Ops to the expander stage.

While fetching the current MultiOp, NextPC must also be computed. In the absence of an Op that changes the control flow of the program, this is be accomplished by using extra bits to store offset information for MultiOps in the cache. Details of the hardware are pictured in Figure 11. An offset field and a bank bit are maintained for every Op in a cache block. The offset field indicates the offset within the cache block of the next MultiOp, and the bank bit indicates if the next MultiOp resides in the same bank as the current MultiOp or in the next bank. The values for these fields are set as Ops are received in the cache–memory interface at cache miss time. (The complete algorithm for NextPC computation is available in a technical report [4].) Offset fields and bank bits can also be used in a two-way set associative design, in tandem with way prediction techniques [15]. The use of dedicated storage within the cache to aid in NextPC computation is similar to the use of successor indices initially proposed by Johnson [14] and implemented in the AMD K5 [7], although that scheme is for an unbanked cache. For a TINKER-n banked cache, $\log_2 n$ offset bits per word (Op) are needed, plus a valid bit and a bank bit. For a 32 KB direct-mapped configuration, the total size of the cache (tag and data arrays) is increased by approximately 8% over that of a traditional cache.

Figure 12 presents the results for simulations of the banked cache compared against a perfect i-cache. The banked design performs at least an order of magnitude better than the uncompressed design. The greater utilization of the data storage area by the banked design offsets the greater branch misprediction penalty. The performance is still lower than the perfect cache, by as much as 25%. Some of this penalty may be due to overfetching an entire cache block when only a portion of the block is requested. This hypothesis is tested in the next section.

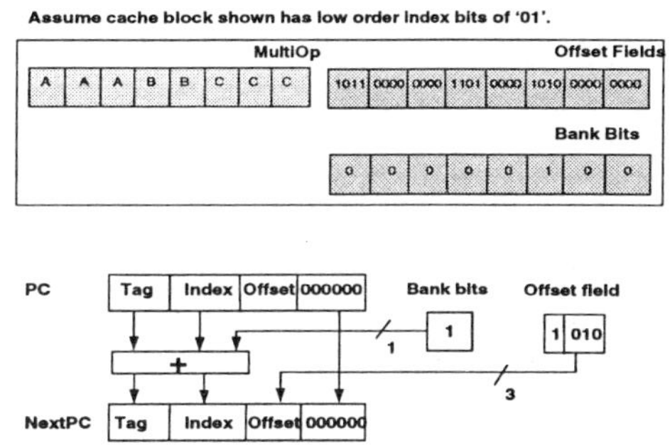

Figure 11. NextPC computation for the banked cache.

A cache access for MultiOp C is shown. The offset field for C is placed into the appropriate positions and the bank bit is added to the remaining high order bits to form a new index and tag.

4.2.1. Sub–blocking in the banked cache

A variant of the banked cache is to use *sub-blocking* [22]. Sub-blocking partitions each cache block into smaller units (sub-blocks). Sub-blocking usually increases the miss ratio of a cache but reduces the amount of memory traffic as each sub-block in a block can be independently filled and replaced. For miss repair with sub-blocking, Ops are retrieved starting from the address of the beginning of the MultiOp, not the address of the beginning of the cache block, as is done without sub-blocking (this is called *block fetching*). The advantage is reduction of the time for miss repair, at the expense of a small increase in the miss ratio because instructions preceding the requested instruction are not filled in the cache block. When a miss occurs, the length of the missing MultiOp is not known. Unless the miss occurs on a cache block boundary, enough memory fetches are generated to fill to the end of the successor block (this is required because a MultiOp can span two blocks). If the MultiOp resides entirely within the current block, the successor block is not filled. A valid bit is associated with each sub-block and is set when the sub-block is filled (sub-block valid bits for all preceding Ops in the current block are unset). Offset fields and bank bits can be used for NextPC computation.

Prefetching can be used in a sub-blocked banked cache. Block fetching performs *implicit prefetching*: as the requested MultiOp is loaded into the cache, fragments of other MultiOps that reside in the same block(s) are also loaded. A sub–blocked cache can employ a form of prefetching termed *load forwarding* [12]. Load forwarding for an instruction cache consists of fetching the sub-block in which the requested MultiOp X lies and all subsequent sub-blocks to the end of the cache block.

A banked i-cache with a one Op sub-block size was sim-

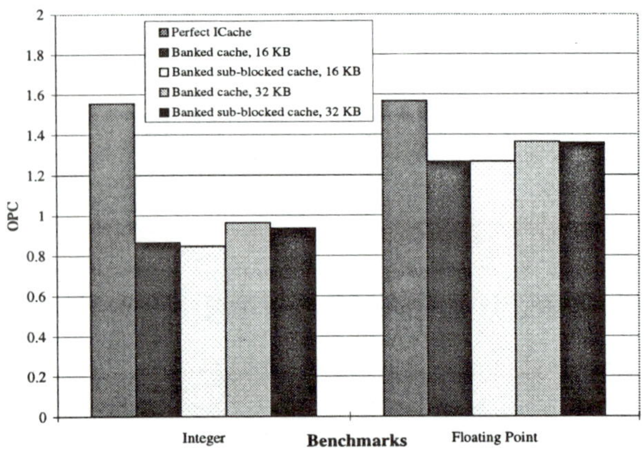

Figure 12. Performance of the banked cache. The metric used is useful Ops completed per cycle (OPC). Each individual bar represents the harmonic mean for the combination of cache size and benchmarks programs.

ulated and the results are presented in Figure 12. The performance of the sub-blocked design was very benchmark dependent. Sub-blocking was very effective for the integer programs, outperforming the non-sub-blocked design by 9% and 45% for 16 KB and 32 KB sizes, respectively. For the floating point benchmarks, the performance was slightly lower than that of the non-sub-blocked design. Examining the behavior of the programs revealed the reasons for the differences in performance. The integer programs have many branches that branch to the latter half of a cache block. When such a branch causes a cache miss, only the latter half of the block and the next block are filled. Contrast this with a block fetch design in which both blocks in their entirety are fetched. The fill time for the sub-blocked design is potentially up to almost 50% less. For the floating point programs, the total number of stall cycles due to i-cache misses were slightly higher. Much of the code involved backward branches that branched to the beginning of cache blocks. Although the latter part of the block had been filled during an earlier demand request, the beginning words had not. Contrast this with the block fetch design in which the entire block is filled when a miss occurs. The sub-blocked designs therefore generated memory requests in situations where the block fetch designs did not.

4.3. I-Fetch using the Silo Cache

The silo cache is organized as a series of partitions or *silos*, where each silo holds Ops for a particular FU or set of FUs, as shown in Figure 13. The DoP can range from a unified partition to one-FUType-per-partition. Each entry in a silo can hold one Op, and has associated with it a tag and and a length field and a valid bit for NextPC computation. The silos can be organized in a direct-mapped or set-associative manner. When set-associativity is used, not only are the silos independently searched, but within each silo, parallel tag compares are performed among the sets.

4.3.1. The Rigid Silo Cache

The *rigid silo cache* is pictured in Figure 13. The cache block size is the same as the machine width. The design uses a miss path expander (two cycle expansion is assumed). The branch misprediction penalty is one cycle.

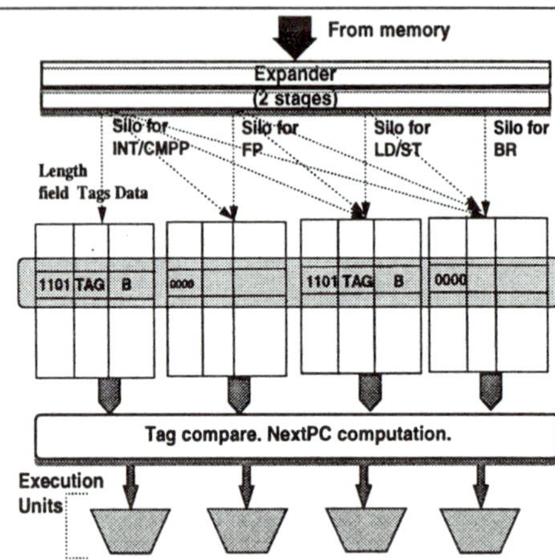

Figure 13. Instruction fetch for the rigid silo cache.

Each silo is searched independently on each cycle. Each silo holds Ops destined for only one FUType. A two cycle expander between the cache and lower levels of memory routes Ops to their appropriate silo.

As with the uncompressed cache, in a silo cache sequential MultiOps of a size less than the machine width can map into the same cache block and cause conflict misses if the address is interpreted in a traditional manner, as shown in Figure 8(a). For this reason, the silo cache uses the offset–reduced scheme to interpret the address (see Section 4.1). The index bits are used to address the silos and map to the same location in each silo. Tag comparisons for all silos are done in parallel. A hit is signaled by a tag match and a valid length field, similar to the banked cache (as shown for MultiOp B in Figure 13, the tags and length bits for all Ops in MultiOp are identical). For a cache hit, the Ops for the MultiOp are directed to the functional units associated with their specific silos. The silos can be organized in a direct–mapped or set–associative manner. LRU replacement is used for set–associative silos.

A miss occurs when either none of the tags in any of silos match or a tag match occurs but the length is invalid. A fetch for the missing MultiOp is then initiated to the next level of the memory hierarchy. After the MultiOp has been fetched into the cache–memory interface, it is expanded, and each Op is routed to an appropriate silo. Values for the length fields are computed in parallel with expansion. For each silo that receives an Op, the corresponding tag and length fields are updated. A situation can occur where some but not all of the Ops for a MultiOp are replaced during a cache fill. The Ops that are not replaced need to be flagged to indicate that the entire "parent" MultiOp is not present. This is accomplished by searching for all Ops that have the same tags as the Ops being replaced, and un-setting the length valid bits for those Ops. The next cache access for the partially displaced MultiOp results in a miss, due to the un-set length valid bits.

During a cache fill, if a particular silo does not have an Op routed to it by the expander, the Op position corresponding to the fill address in that silo is left empty. In this respect, the silo cache uses a NOP policy. However, several MultiOps can reside at the same address across all silos, which is a hybrid between the NOP and NOPs-free policies. To understand this, note that each silo is addressed individually and perform placements/replacements with some degree of autonomy. As shown in Figure 13, MultiOp B consists of a integer/compare-to-predicate Op and a memory Op. It does not place Ops into the silos for floating point or branch operations, and in fact these silos are currently empty as indicated by their valid bits. If a MultiOp X, containing only a single floating point operation, maps to the same cache location, it can be placed into the floating point silo and can update the tag and length fields for the proper location in that silo. MultiOps B and X can coexist at the same address across the silos.

The silo cache has a tag for every Op that is stored in the cache, in contrast to the uncompressed cache and the banked cache, all of which use a tag for a cache block. The tag storage requirements for a silo cache are obviously higher. However, the data array for a silo cache need not hold all of the bits in a Op. Header and tail bits and the FUT field (see Figure 2) are no longer needed. For a TINKER-8 machine, a 32 KB silo cache requires approximately 10 KB (or 30%) more storage than a traditional cache.

Performance results for the rigid silo cache are shown in Figure 14. Even at low degrees of associativity (direct-mapped and two-way), the silo cache outperforms the banked cache by 6-18%. For the integer programs, higher degrees of associativity reduces the number of conflict misses and yields further improvements.

4.3.2. The Flexible Silo Cache

The performance of a silo cache is dependent on the FU-Type distribution in the workload. A program that does not contain any Ops mapping to a silo does not utilize that silo

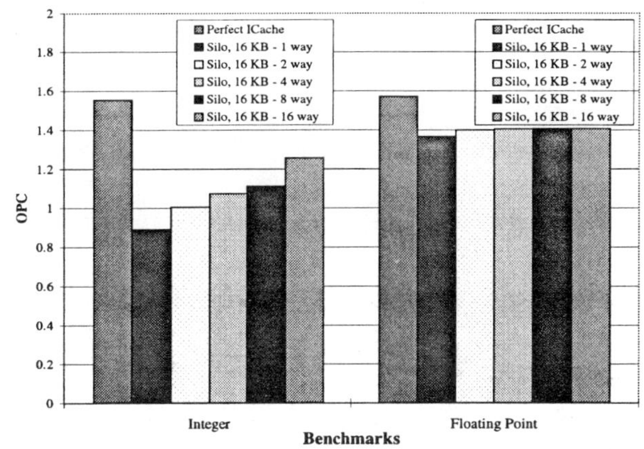

Figure 14. Performance of the rigid silo cache.

The metric used is useful Ops completed per cycle (OPC). Each individual bar represents the harmonic mean for the combination of cache size and benchmarks programs.

at all. In effect, the program sees a smaller i-cache, and the silos that are not used starve. For example, this behavior could occur in an integer-intensive application that starves the floating point silos. If the 1-FUType-to-1-silo requirement is relaxed so that complimentary types of Ops (those that typically do not execute together) are allowed to share a silo, the starvation problem might be eased. For example, if floating point and integer operations are placed in the same silo – an (I F) (M) (B) partitioning – the silo would be well utilized by programs that are floating point or integer intensive as well as by programs that have a mix of both types of Ops. A small hit-path expander is required to route Ops from the silo to the appropriate functional units. This is in addition to the miss-path expander that is required for Op placement. The hit-path expander increases the branch misprediction penalty to two cycles.

A silo that allows multiple FUTypes per silo is termed a *flexible silo cache*, and a silo that holds multiple FUTypes is a *flexible silo*. A flexible silo that supplies Ops for n FUs has a tag array of the same size as the n silos for those FUs in a rigid silo cache. The data array is slightly larger because the FUT field is stored in the flexible silo, for use by the miss-path expander, but not in the rigid design. A flexible silo holds Ops in a compressed fashion, but the overall design is nominally a NOP cache. The offset bits of Ops that map to a flexible silo are used to determine their cache locations. A flexible silo that holds m FUTypes has the same size tag and data arrays as the m silos for those FUTypes in a rigid silo cache. Of particular interest is a design that stores two FUTypes in a flexible silo and assigns the remaining two FUTypes to 1-FUType-per-partition silos.

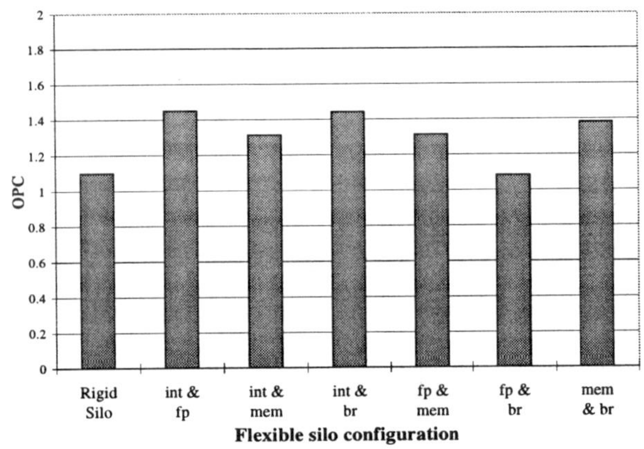

Figure 15. Evaluation of shared silos for integer programs.

The metric used is useful Ops completed per cycle (OPC). With the exception of the first bar on the chart, each individual bar represents the harmonic mean for the combination of benchmarks programs using one flexible silo for the FUTypes indicated and private silos for the remaining FUTypes. The caches simulated were 16 KB with associativities of 1, 2, 4, 8, and 16. The first bar represents the harmonic mean for all benchmarks using the same cache size and associativity parameters but with a rigid silo design.

Simulations were performed for the integer benchmark programs for a 16 KB cache with a variety of flexible partitions to determine which FUTypes were best suited to share a flexible silo. The results are presented in Figure 15. With the exception of the floating point/branch combination, all of the shared silo designs performed better than the rigid silo design. The performance gains ranged from 19% for the integer/memory combination to 31% for the integer/floating point combination. Based on these preliminary results, the flexible silo design clearly outperforms the rigid silo design as well as the uncompressed and banked cache designs.

5. Conclusion

This study investigated the issues involved in i-fetch support for VLIW architectures that use compressed encodings. The effect of i-fetch mechanisms on i-cache architecture was discussed, and a taxonomy for classifying VLIW i-caches based on degree of partitioning and the NOPs policy was introduced. Four cache designs were presented and evaluated: the uncompressed cache, the banked cache, the rigid silo cache, and the flexible silo cache.

Among the cache designs examined, the uncompressed cache can be viewed as the simplest i-fetch mechanism. MultiOp placement and access and NextPC computation are done in a straightforward manner, and no prefetching is used. The drawback of this simplicity is that the NOP policy causes low cache utilization which is reflected by poor performance. The banked cache uses a different approach as it is a NOPs-free cache, can place multiple MultiOps in a cache block and does implicit prefetching. NextPC generation is performed differently than for the uncompressed cache but the hardware requirements of both mechanisms (an adder and extra storage for length/offset information) are equivalent. Overall, the banked cache requires more complex logic than the uncompressed cache. However, the performance is substantially better which indicates that the extra complexity may be warranted.

The third design examined was the rigid silo cache. It is nominally a NOP cache but allows limited sharing of cache locations by multiple MultiOps. The rigid silo cache requires considerably more storage than either of the previous designs as each Op-wide storage location has associated with it a tag and a length field. A direct–mapped design performs roughly equivalent to a banked cache. As associativity is increased, however, the rigid silo cache outperforms the banked cache.

Individual silos in the rigid silo cache can be underutilized when workloads are run that do not contain Ops mapping to those silos. The flexible silo design attempts to alleviate this problem by allowing multiple FUTypes to reside in a silo. The flexible design outperformed all of the other designs even when using low associativity. Based on the results, the plan for the TINKER testbed is to complete the evaluation of the flexible silo design and investigate the implementation details and tradeoffs for the rigid silo and flexible silo cache designs.

Acknowledgments

Discussions with the other members of the TINKER group proved useful to the development of ideas in this paper. This work was supported by the Intel corporation and the National Science Foundation under grants MIP-9696010 and MIP-9625007. The authors would like to express their gratitude to the University of Illinois IMPACT group for the use of the IMPACT compiler system. The comments from the anonymous referees are also appreciated.

References

[1] *Proc. 1995 International Solid-State Circuits Conference*, San Francisco, CA, Feb. 1995.

[2] D. Alpert and D. Avnon. Architecture of the Pentium microprocessor. *IEEE Micro*, 13(3):11–21, June 1993.

[3] S. Arya, H. Sachs, and S. Duvvuru. An architecture for high instruction level parallelism. In *Proc. 28th Hawaii Int'l.*

Conf. on System Sciences, pages 153–161, Maui, HI, Jan. 1995.

[4] S. Banerjia, K. N. Menezes, and T. M. Conte. NextPC computation for a banked instruction cache. Technical report, Department of Electrical and Computer Engineering, North Carolina State University, Raleigh, NC 27695-7911, June 1996.

[5] G. R. Beck, D. W. L. Yen, and T. L. Anderson. The Cydra 5 minisupercomputer: architecture and implementation. *J. Supercomputing*, 7(1):143–180, Jan. 1993.

[6] W. J. Bowhill et al. A 300 mhz 64b quad-issue CMOS RISC processor. In *Proc. 1995 International Solid-State Circuits Conference* [1], pages 182–183.

[7] D. Christie. Developing the AMD–K5 architecture. *IEEE Micro*, 9(2):16–26, 1996.

[8] T. M. Conte et al. *The TINKER Machine Language Manual*. North Carolina State University, Raleigh, NC 27695-7911, Apr. 1995.

[9] T. M. Conte and S. W. Sathaye. Dynamic rescheduling: A technique for object code compatibility in VLIW architectures. In *Proc. 28th Ann. International Symposium on Microarchitecture*, Ann Arbor, MI, Nov. 1995.

[10] D. R. Ditzel and H. R. McLellan. Branch folding in the CRISP microprocessor: Reducing branch delay to zero. In *Proc. 14th Ann. International Symposium Computer Architecture*, pages 2–9, Pittsburgh, PA, June 1987.

[11] D. Draper et al. A 93 mhz, x86 microprocessor with on–chip L2 cache controller. In *Proc. 1995 International Solid-State Circuits Conference* [1], pages 172–173.

[12] M. D. Hill and A. J. Smith. Experimental evaluation of on–chip microprocessor cache memories. In *Proc. 11th Ann. International Symposium Computer Architecture*, pages 158–166, Ann Arbor, MI, June 1984.

[13] W. W. Hwu, S. A. Mahlke, W. Y. Chen, P. P. Chang, N. J. Warter, R. A. Bringmann, R. G. Ouellette, R. E. Hank, T Kiyohara, G. E. Haab, J. G. Holm, and D. M. Lavery. The superblock: An effective structure for VLIW and superscalar compilation. *The Journal of Supercomputing*, 7(1):229–248, Jan. 1993.

[14] W. M. Johnson. *Super-scalar processor design*. PhD thesis, Department of Electrical Engineering, Stanford University, Stanford, California, June 1989.

[15] T. Juan, T. Lang, and J. J. Navarro. The difference–bit cache. In *Proc. 23nd Ann. International Symposium Computer Architecture*, pages 114–120, Philadelphia, PA, May 1996.

[16] V. Kathail, M. Schlansker, and B. R. Rau. HPL PlayDoh architecture specification: version 1.0. Technical Report HPL-93-80, Hewlett-Packard Laboratories, Technical Publications Department, 1501 Page Mill Road, Palo Alto, CA 94304, Feb. 1994.

[17] P. G. Lowney, S. M. Freudenberger, T. J. Karzes, W. D. Lichtenstein, R. P. Nix, J. S. O'Donell, and J. C. Ruttenberg. The Multiflow Trace scheduling compiler. *J. Supercomputing*, 7(1):51–142, Jan. 1993.

[18] S. Melvin, M. Shebanow, and Y. Patt. Hardware support for large atomic units in dynamically scheduled machines. In *Proc. 21th Ann. International Symposium on Microarchitecture*, pages 60–66, San Diego, CA, Dec. 1988.

[19] D. B. Papworth. Tuning the Pentium Pro microarchitecture. *IEEE Micro*, 16(2):8–15, Apr. 1996.

[20] B. R. Rau, D. W. L. Yen, W. Yen, and R. A. Towle. The Cydra 5 departmental supercomputer. *Computer*, 22(1):12–35, Jan. 1989.

[21] G. Shen et al. A 64b 4–issue out–of–order execution RISC processor. In *Proc. 1995 International Solid-State Circuits Conference* [1], pages 170–171.

[22] A. J. Smith. Cache memories. *ACM Comput. Surv.*, 14(3):473–530, 1982.

[23] M. Smotherman and M. Franklin. Improving CISC Instruction Decoding Performance Using a Fill Unit. In *Proc. 28th Ann. International Symposium on Microarchitecture*, pages 313–323, Ann Arbor, MI, Dec. 1995.

[24] A. Wolfe and A. Chanin. Executing compressed programs on an embedded RISC architecture. In *Proc. 25th Ann. International Symposium on Microarchitecture*, pages 81–91, Portland, OR, Dec. 1992.

Session 7

Tango: a Hardware-based Data Prefetching Technique for Superscalar Processors

Shlomit S. Pinter
IBM Science and Technology
MATAM Advance Technology ctr.
Haifa 31905, Israel
E-mail: shlomit@haifa.vnet.ibm.com

Adi Yoaz
Intel Israel (74)
MATAM Advance Technology ctr.
Haifa 31905, Israel
E-mail: ayoaz@iil.intel.com

Abstract

We present a new hardware-based data prefetching mechanism for enhancing instruction level parallelism and improving the performance of superscalar processors. The emphasis in our scheme is on the effective utilization of slack time and hardware resources not used for the main computation. The scheme suggests a new hardware construct, the Program Progress Graph (PPG), as a simple extension to the Branch Target Buffer (BTB). We use the PPG for implementing a fast pre-program counter, pre-PC, that travels only through memory reference instructions (rather than scanning all the instructions sequentially). In a single clock cycle the pre-PC extracts all the predicted memory references in some future block of instructions, to obtain early data prefetching. In addition, the PPG can be used for implementing a pre-processor and for instruction prefetching. The prefetch requests are scheduled to "tango" with the core requests from the data cache, by using only free time slots on the existing data cache tag ports. Employing special methods for removing prefetch requests that are already in the cache (without utilizing the cache-tag ports bandwidth) and a simple optimization on the cache LRU mechanism reduce the number of prefetch requests sent to the core–cache bus and to the memory (second level) bus. Simulation results on the SPEC92 benchmark for the base line architecture (32K-byte data cache and 12 cycles fetch latency) show an average speedup of 1.36 (CPI ratio).

1. Introduction

The demand on the performance of memory subsystems is rapidly increasing with the advances in microprocessor architecture. The growing gap between processor and memory speeds further increases the *memory access penalty* problem. Data prefetching is an effective technique for hiding memory latency.

Timely and correct prediction of data accesses are the key issues in both software and hardware based prefetching techniques. In hardware based schemes the timely generation of a data prefetch and the additional traffic on both the memory bus and the cache-tag ports can potentially be controlled in order not to interfere with the main computation process. In addition, the amount of prefetching done can be tuned to the cache parameters using dynamic information. Prediction in hardware can recognize constant memory strides (resulting from integer valued linear functions of loop variables) [6, 1, 7]. For speculative data prefetching the hardware based techniques can improve on software approaches by using information from the branch prediction unit.

Hardware based off-chip schemes, like the stream buffer [5], are driven by cache miss accesses, whereas with on-chip schemes all the memory accesses instructions are sampled and more prediction information is available [6, 1]. Prediction on-chip is not influenced by out of order computations and the data cache status can be used for controlling the prefetch rate. However, the known on-chip prefetch schemes are not suitable for superscalar processors. Specifically, they cannot generate and issue predictions fast enough. Another problem studied in [13] and noted by [5] is the cache bandwidth problem. The problem is manifested by the heavy load on the data ports and tag ports of the data cache. In superscalar processors the cache-tag ports are one of the most critical resources and extra prefetch requests (especially with aggressive on-chip prediction) cannot directly use this resource. In our scheme we provide an effective and simple solution to these problems.

In software based prefetching extra prefetch instructions are inserted. The new instructions may increase the length of the critical path since there are not enough "open" slots (in the load functional units), especially for data intensive programs, or when prefetching most of the memory access instructions [13]. The extra prefetch instructions also occupy space in the I-cache and increase the traffic on the memory bus. Whereas extensive software analysis can generate accurate static predictions, the timely generation of the

1072-4451/96 $5.00 © 1996 IEEE

prefetch requests is a problem. In [10] the number of iterations to prefetch ahead was chosen to be the prefetch latency divided by the length of the shortest path through the loop. To reduce redundant insertions of prefetch instructions the compiler must be tuned to the data cache parameters. Such tuning has no effect on existing code and is very intricate for the compiler (see [2, 10] for some heuristics).

In this paper we present the design and simulation results of a new on-chip hardware based data prefetching scheme called Tango. The scheme uses a pre-PC[1] component that exploits only instructions that use the data cache (rather than scanning the instructions sequentially). At each clock cycle, all the memory references in some future block of instructions are exposed with the help of the Program Progress Graph (PPG) table. The pre-P mechanism uses the data prediction component to generate prefecth requests for these instructions. The scheme thus provides data fast enough for future multi-functional processors that can employ out-of-order execution. The prefetch requests do not interfere with the main computation and are scheduled to *tango* with the core requests from the cache (they only use the free time slots on the existing data cache tag ports). Tango employs a new simple method that — without cache-tag ports bandwidth consumption — removes prefetch requests for data already in the cache; this mechanism can be used by other schemes as well. Another simple optimization on the cache LRU mechanism lets us further reduce the number of prefetch requests sent to the core–cache bus and to the memory bus. The cost incurred by Tango involves chip space, which is smaller than a 4K-byte dual ported cache.

The PPG, which is implemented as a small and simple extension to a BTB, provides an efficient and fast method for lookahead on instructions. Thus, in addition to data prefetching, it can be used as a pre-processor for decoding instructions early enough on their way to the core or for instruction prefetching.

Our investigations show that the Tango prefetching scheme significantly improves the overall system performance and extensively reduces the memory access miss penalty. In most of the programs tested, the speedup gained is over 1.33 (average of 1.36 for the base line architecture), and the reduction in the memory penalty is 96% to 43%.

We first discuss related work in Section 2. Then, in Section 3 we present our scheme and discuss its properties. Section 4 includes the machine model, and experimental results are brought in Section 5. Conclusions and discussion are presented in Section 6.

2 Related Work

Most simple hardware data prefetching schemes are based on data misses that can trigger the prefetch of the next data line. Such schemes were investigated in [4] and with the help of special prefetch buffers (stream buffers) by [8]. For improving the prediction [6] uses a history table for keeping the previous memory address. The difference between the current address and the previous one is used to calculate the memory stride. The prefetch is issued for the next iteration based on the calculated stride. Similar off-chip schemes that use more elaborate strides are studied in [11] and in [5].

Even with good prediction, data can be prefetched too early or too late to be useful. One way for solving this problem is a lookahead scheme. The lookahead scheme in [9] is based on generating data prefetch for operands simultaneously with the decoding of the instruction.

Prediction and lookahead are integrated in [1, 3] to support prefetch for scalar processors. In this on-chip scheme the stride prediction is calculated with a reference prediction (history) table (RPT) indexed by load/store instruction addresses. The lookahead mechanism implements a lookahead program counter (LA-PC) that advances at the same pace as the PC. The time wasted for checking all the instructions prevents the possibility to adapt this method for superscalar processors. Our pre-PC mechanism skips over instructions that are not memory references (it goes only through memory reference instructions). Thus, it can progress in a higher pace and may use more of the precious free time slots on the core–cache bus (cache-tag ports). In [3] branches are chosen for the LA-PC by using the BTB with a duplicated branch address field (indexing field) for the use of the lookahead PC. Instead, we added extra information to the BTB with the same amount of extra hardware. Furthermore, in [3] whenever an incorrect branch prediction occurs the distance between the LA-PC and the PC is reset and has to build up by waiting to a data miss. During such a period, prefetches may not be issued early enough. In our scheme the pre-PC can build the distance from the PC immediately after a wrong branch prediction, without waiting for a data miss.

3. The Tango Data Prefetching Scheme

The Tango hardware predicts when data is likely to be needed and generates requests to bring it into the data cache. To accomplish this goal, memory access instructions are saved in the Reference Prediction Table for Superscalar Processors (SRPT) together with some history information is used to generate memory access predictions. In order to bring the predicted data on time, Tango employs a fast pre-program counter, pre-PC, that uses the branch prediction information and the PPG (a graph representing the predicted future of the execution flow). With the PPG information the pre-PC searches the predicted memory access instructions in the SRPT and generates the prefetch requests. The stream of prefetch requests is then filtered in the prefetch requests

[1] Pre-program counter.

controller (PRC) and redundant requests are removed. This is done before the requests query the cache, thus reducing primary cache-tag ports bandwidth consumption as well as memory bus bandwidth.

In this section we describe our data prefetching mechanism and discuss its hardware considerations. We start with motivation and functional presentation of the design, and then provide the details of the components.

The Tango scheme exploits the advantages of the lookahead scheme presented for scalar processors by [1] and extends it further to superscalar processors. In [5] it is suggested that lookahead schemes are not efficient for superscalar processors due to the need for extra ports to the data cache tag. Indeed, in our simulations the tag ports are heavily used by the core (demand fetches). Thus, Tango filters out prefetch requests for data in the cache before the requests consume data cache-tag ports bandwidth and it uses only open slots on the cache-tag ports.

The scheme comprises three functional parts. The first is a special lookahead mechanism. Our pre-PC mechanism jumps from a branch point to its predicted successor branch point and in each block it searches only through the memory reference instructions. It is implemented as a simple extension to the BTB — called PPG — and a special field in the SRPT. The second functional part generates data access predictions. This mechanism is based on the Reference Prediction Table of [1] designed for scalar processors. The table is enhanced to support the fast pre-PC which extracts the reference predictions. The third part, the Prefetch Requests Controller (PRC), is a mechanism for filtering out redundant prefetch requests. The SRPT and the lookahead mechanism (pre-PC) generate prefetch requests for most of the future memory access instructions. With software prefetching some extra analysis is done in order to remove prefetch requests whenever it is predicted that the data is already in the cache [10, 2]. In our scheme this task is very simple.

3.1. PPG: The Program Progress Graph

The first hardware component is the Program Progress Graph (PPG) generated from the instructions currently viewed by the processor. In this directed graph every node corresponds to a branch instruction and an edge to a block of instructions on the path between the corresponding two branch instructions. A number on every edge indicates the number of instructions in that block. Figure 1 is an example of a program fragment and its PPG. The br-num values are the entry numbers of the branch instructions in the PPG table. For example, the marking T,3 on the edge from br-num 18 to br-num 15 corresponds to instructions 1,2,3 of the taken block following instruction 17.

The PPG is stored as an extension to the BTB by adding

```
               1  ...
               2  ...
br-num 15      3  beqz 40
               4  load
               5  load
               6  ...
               7  store
               8  ...
               9  ...
              10  ...
              11  ...
              12  load
br-num 30     13  bnez 3
              14  ...
              15  ...
              16  load
br-num 18     17  beqz 1
```

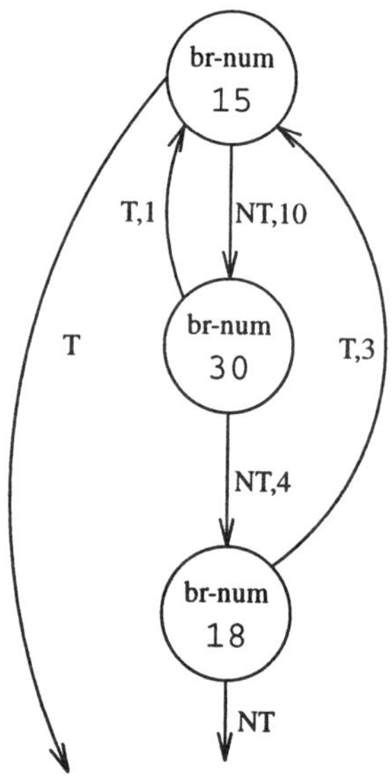

Figure 1. A sample program fragment and its PPG.

four new columns. An entry in the BTB/PPG table has 7 fields:

branch-pc	target	prediction-info

and

T-entry	NT-entry	T-size	NT-size

The first three are the address of the branch instruction (branch tag), the branch target address, and the branch prediction information of the BTB. The T-entry field contains the entry number (in the BTB/PPG table) of the next branch on the taken path, and NT-entry is the entry number of the next branch along the not-taken path. Each of the T-size and NT-size fields holds the size of the block (number of instructions) following the branch on the taken and not-taken paths, respectively.

The relevant parts of entries number 15, 18, and 30 of the BTB/PPG table for the example in Figure 1 are given in Table 1.

entry	BTB	T-en	NT-en	T-s	NT-s
15	...	...	30	...	10
18	...	15	...	3	...
30	...	15	18	1	4

Table 1. Entries number 15, 18, and 30 of the BTB/PPG table for the example in Figure 1.

A simple BTB has two large fields: the address of the branch instruction (part of it is used as a tag), and the branch target address. For implementing parallel lookup for the PC and a simple pre-PC there is a need for an extra tag of size similar to the address size. Instead, in our scheme each of the two extra entry fields, `T-entry` and `NT-entry`, contains an entry number in the PPG table, which take 9 bits each for a 512 entry table. The size fields (`T-size` and `NT-size`) of 7 bits each are used for controlling the distance between the PC and the pre-PC. As a result 32 bits per entry are needed to keep the extra information independent of the processor's address size.

3.1.1 Hardware Design Considerations of the PPG Table

The PPG design has to consider the case in which an entry is removed when allocating a new entry in a full table set. In such a case, the `T-size` and/or `NT-size` fields of the entries pointing to the entry being removed need to be reset (set to 0). We could avoid this reset by keeping the branch address in the `T-entry` and the `NT-entry` fields, and by adding an extra tag field for the pre-PC search; but this will double the area of a standard BTB. Since evicting a BTB entry is a relatively rare event[2], and the PC is stalling in this case, due to a miss predicted branch, we decided instead to keep the table small and stop the pre-PC during the updates. The `T-entry` and `NT-entry` fields are stored in an associative memory, thus, when removing an entry from the table an associative search is done on the two fields with the removed entry number. For every match the corresponding size field is reset to 0; this operation may consume a few cycles for a big table. We note that the delay thus incurred to the pre-PC is negligible compared with the cost of the alternative.

The updates of the BTB and PPG fields are done together following a branch resolution. Since different fields are changed in each table no extra write port is needed. Only one bit (taken/not-taken) from the BTB is used by both the PC and pre-PC (when reading the BTB/PPG predictions). A dual read port to this bit can solve the problem. Altogether, with four bytes per entry (two of which use associative memory), a table of 512 entries is equivalent to a 2K-byte cache.

3.2. SRPT: a Reference Prediction Table for Superscalar Processors

The second hardware component is a Reference Prediction Table for Superscalar processors (SRPT). This table stores the access history information of the memory reference instructions, so that whenever a memory reference has a steady access pattern it is possible to predict the future memory accesses. The table is managed as a cache. An entry is allocated for a memory reference instruction accessed by the PC and the relevant information is kept and updated on the following accesses. A special tag field is used to generate predictions based on the information stored in the table.

The RPT of [3] has two `pc-tag` fields (or two ports to the same `pc-tag`); one is used for the PC search (set-associative) and the second for the lookahead PC (which is incremented and maintained in the same fashion as the PC). Instead, in the SRPT, which is an extension to the RPT, the PC search uses the pc-tag as above, but the search with the second index (called `pre-pc-tag`) is fully associative and is tuned for superscalar processors. The pre-PC uses the second index to identify all the access instructions in a block predicted for execution. An entry in the SRPT contains the following fields:

pre-pc-tag	pc-tag	last-ea

and

stride	times	fsm	dist

The `pc-tag` field holds the address of the load/store instruction. The `last-ea` field stores the last effective address accessed by this instruction. The `stride` field holds the difference between the last two effective addresses accessed by the memory instruction, and the counter `times` keeps track of how many iterations (with respect to that instruction) the pre-PC is ahead of the PC. The fields `stride` and `times` together with `fsm` are used to generate the predicted address as in [3].

The `dist` field contains the distance of the memory reference instruction from the last branch and is used to control the distance between the PC and the pre-PC. The `pre-pc-tag` field stores the following three values:

br-entry-num	T/NT	mem-ref-num

The 9 bits `br-entry-num` field holds the BTB/PPG entry number of the last branch executed before reaching the memory access instruction; the `T/NT` bit indicates if the instruction is on the taken or not-taken path, and the last 7 bits, called `mem-ref-num`, are the ordinal number of the instruction within the load/store instructions of the block.

The SRPT is updated whenever the CPU core (PC) executes a load/store instruction. The pre-PC uses the SRPT information in order to predict future accesses addressed by this instruction. The predicted effective address is equal to `last-ea` + (`stride` x `times`) and the decision to generate the prediction is made by a four state finite state machine (`fsm`).

The hardware needed to implement a 128 entry SRPT is equivalent to a 2K-byte data cache where the pc-tag size is equivalent to the tag field of the cache and the memory needed for the `pre-pc-tag` is counted twice its actual size.

[2] In our simulations it happens, on average, only once per 7000 instructions – 99.9% BTB hit rate, and 1/7 branch instruction rate.

3.2.1 SRPT Updates and Management

In our simulations we assume the possibility of issuing multiple instructions per cycle with no more than two memory accesses per cycle (dual ported cache); thus, to support the updates of the memory reference instructions, the SRPT must be dual ported. An entry in the SRPT is allocated on the first execution of a memory access instruction. At that point the prediction fields (`stride, times` and `fsm`) are set to zero. When an entry is removed from the BTB/PPG there is a need to update the SRPT entries for which the `br-entry-num` field is equal to the number of the entry being removed. This is done by setting the `dist` field to zero (invalidate the `pre-pc-tag` field of the SRPT entry). Note that the PC is stalling in this case (due to a mispredicted branch penalty) for a few cycles and the pre-PC is not progressing until all updates complete.

3.3. The pre-PC — Using the PPG and SRPT Structures

In this section we describe the pre-PC mechanism. In the beginning of the program execution, and following a misprediction in the direction taken by the pre-PC, the PC and pre-PC are equal. The pre-PC can depart from the PC at each branch entry whose size field is not 0. Within one clock cycle the pre-PC can now advance a full block ahead of the PC. Using the entry of the next branch (according to the branch prediction) the pre-PC can move directly to the next block without the need for a lookup on the BTB tag field. Thus, the PPG provides an efficient method for supporting a pre-PC that can be used in many places.

During a data cache access, a lookup and update are conducted on the SRPT with the pc-tag. In parallel, the pre-PC is looking for future memory reference instructions in the SRPT. With the example in Figure 1 we illustrate the pre-PC progress assuming that branch instructions 3, 13, and 17 are kept in entries 15, 30, and 18 of the BTB/PPG table, respectively (as in Table 1). For a given execution of the code fragment in Figure 1 we next discuss the contents of the `pre-pc-tag` of the SRPT entries for all five memory reference instructions.

The `mem-ref-num` fields of the two first memory reference Instructions (in block 15), 4 and 5 (denoted by `I4, I5`), have value 1 when the memory is dual ported. The value of that field for `I7` and `I12` is 2 and it is 1 for I16 (first in block 30). The `br-entry-num` values for `I4, I5, I7`, and `I12` are 15 and it is 30 for `I16`. The `T/NT` values for all five instructions are zero since they are on the not-taken path of there respective branches, 15 and 30. At some point when the pre-PC value is (15,0,1) its lookup in the SRPT on the `pre-pc-tag` field (`br-entry-num,T/NT,mem-ref-num`) matches `I4` and `I5` and partially matches `I7`, and `I12`. A partial match is given for the SRPT entries for which the `br-entry-num` and `T/NT` fields of the `pre-pc-tag` have the same values as in the lookup operation, e.g. (15,0,). In the next clock cycle the pre-PC value is (15,0,2) and it matches `I7` and `I12`. Thus, the pre-PC jumps over irrelevant instructions without losing cycles between consecutive accesses to the SRPT. Once `I7` and `I12` are found (matched), with the help of the PPG, in the next cycle the pre-PC value is (30,0,1) (described latter). The new pre-PC value causes the next block to be scanned and the load of `I16` is found. Whenever a match occurs the reference prediction is computed and a prefetch request can be issued.

In the following example we discuss the progress of the pre-PC in a few scenarios for the example in Figure 1. Assume we are at clock cycle x and a lookup is done on entry 15 of the PPG (see PPG:LU column in the first row of Tables 2). By the end of cycle x the PPG:LU results are: T/NT=0 (branch 15 is not taken) and next-br=30.

cycle	`PPG:LU`	`PPG:LU results`
x	15	T/NT=0, next-br=30
$x+1$	30	T/NT=0, next-br=18
$x+2$		
$x+3$	18	T/NT=1, next-br=15
$x+4$	15	T/NT=0, next-br=30
$x+5$	30	T/NT=0, next-br=18

cycle	`SRPT:LU`	`SRPT:LU results`
x	...	...
$x+1$	(15,0,1)	FM={`I4, I5`}, PM={`I12`}
$x+2$	(15,0,2)	FM={`I12`}
$x+3$	(30,0,1)	FM={`I16`}
$x+4$	(18,1,1)	no match
$x+5$	(15,0,1)	FM={`I4, I5`}, PM={`I12`}

Table 2. The pre-PC progress (a possible scenario for Figure 1).

To make the example more general, assume at this stage that `I4, I5, I12` and `I16` are in the SRPT and the entry for `I7` was removed. During cycle $x+1$, in parallel to a direct lookup on PPG entry 30, the pre-PC searches the SRPT pre-pc-tag with (15,0,1) (see SRPT:LU column of Table 2). The SRPT:LU results are two full matches for `I4, I5`, and a partial match for `I12`. The partial match on `I12` indicates the need to continue and search this block by the pre-PC. Thus, during cycle $x+2$ the SRPT is searched with values (15,0,2). By the end of cycle $x+2$ instruction `I12` is fully matched (last in the block). The next predicted block is 30 and T/NT=0, thus, during cycle $x+3$ a SRPT:LU search for (30,0,1) is generated and `I16` is fully matched. In parallel, a PPG:LU search on branch entry 18 is generated. At the next cycle a SRPT:LU with (18,1,1) yields no match since block

18 has no memory access instructions. From the PPG:LU results of cycle $x+3$ the next branch is 15, this branch is not taken (due to PPG:LU results at the end of cycle $x+4$). Thus, the next SRPT:LU search (cycle $x+5$) is for (15,0,1).

The pre-PC search in the SRPT is fully associative and can take a full clock cycle[3]. Thus, this search is pipelined with the calculation of the predicted effective address and the prefetch dispatch.

The example above shows the progress of the pre-PC in a few special cases. The pre-PC searches the SRPT and the PPG in parallel and thus, in one clock cycle, it can jump over a block that has two or less memory reference instructions. If a block has more than two memory reference instructions the pre-PC's progress through the block is not slower than that of the PC.

3.4. PRC: a Prefetch Requests Controller

The third part of our scheme, the Prefetch Requests Controller (PRC), is a mechanism for controlling and scheduling the prefetch requests. Due to the heavy traffic on the core–cache bus, the number of open slots for prefetching queries in the cache is very small. In addition, the timing when open slots occur may not be the right one for prefetching. Minimizing the prefetching overhead traffic in this bus and on the memory bus calls for optimizations on the prefetch requests in two places. The PRC mechanism filters out redundant prefetch requests and controls the scheduling of the prefetch requests on the core–cache bus (it always gives priority to the core requests). In addition, the data cache LRU is touched (following reference predictions) in order to reduce the number of requests on the memory bus and for improving Tango performance.

When the pre-PC scans a memory reference instruction its predicted effective address is supplied by the SRPT. In the next step the address can be looked up in the data cache. Since the ports to the data cache-tag may be occupied by requests from the core we added a FIFO buffer, `Req-Q`, of four entries for keeping the prefetch requests (see Figure 2). Thus, the pre-PC can advance before the request is served. When `Req-Q` is full, the pre-PC must wait. The queue is flushed if the pre-PC took the wrong direction (wrong branch prediction). Due to the locality of reference principle it is very likely that within short time periods more than a single request for data in a cache line (block) can occur. Thus, an associative search on `Req-Q` is done in order to avoid a double insertion of a prefetch request.

At every clock cycle it is possible to issue up to two prefetch requests on the cache-tag ports not used by the core.

[3] If more than a single clock cycle is needed (128 entries) the depth of the associativity can be reduced by partitioning the SRPT (e.g. instructions of blocks in the upper and lower halves of the PPG are mapped into two different parts of the SRPT).

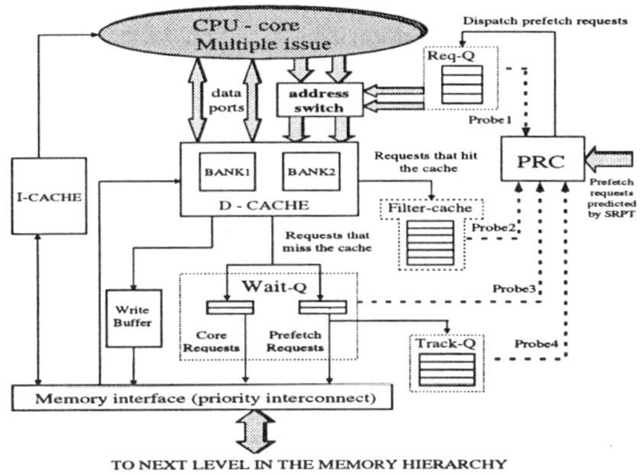

Figure 2. Scheduling and controlling prefetch requests.

A prefetch request which misses the cache is directed to the next level in the memory hierarchy. If the memory bus is busy the request is stored in a second small buffer, `Wait-Q`, of which two entries (with top priority) are dedicated to requests generated by the core (see Figure 2). The prefetch requests are flushed from the buffer when the pre-PC took the wrong direction (on a branch). A `Track-Q` is served for tracking prefetch requests issued to the memory bus, and for preserving system consistency.

Lastly, Tango uses a unique buffer, `Filter-cache`, in order to track requests that were found (hit) in the data cache. The idea behind this action is to minimize the dispatching of prefetch requests to `Req-Q`, and thus to decrease the traffic on the core–cache bus. The `Filter-cache` behaves like a FIFO queue (for more details see [12]). This filter provides a simple way to dynamically remove redundant prefetch requests and is suitable for various prefetch scheme.

Only prefetch requests that are not in either `Req-Q`, `Wait-Q`, `Track-Q` or `Filter-cache` are directed to the `Req-Q` buffer. Thus, the Tango scheme minimizes the number of requests sent to `Req-Q` and prevents loading the core–cache bus by leaving out most (about 2/3) of the requests generated by the SRPT. About 80% of the requests removed were filtered by a `Filter-cache` of six entries.

Avoiding the prefetch of data found in the data cache without indicating that it may be needed soon can result in purging it out before its actual use. This indeed happened in our early simulations and indicated that due to the distance between the pre-PC and the PC many lines residing in the cache following the pre-PC lookup were not there when the PC looked for them. This problem was solved by a simple modification to the data cache LRU scheme. The Tango scheme generates LRU touch whenever a prefetch request is a hit, thus indicating that it may be needed soon (rather than leaving it an early used). This *internal prefetching* prevents an erroneous purging on one hand and saves us the cost of issuing redundant requests to the next memory level on the other hand. The simulation results showed significant improvement along this avenue for both the performance and the memory bus traffic.

The prediction done by the SRPT is very aggressive since the majority of the references are of constant stride. An extreme example is the dnasa7 program in the SPEC92 benchmark. For this program the SRPT generated predictions for 98% of the memory accesses. Since 46% of all the instructions are memory reference instructions, the cache tag ports were occupied by the core 60% of the execution time. Without an addition optimization the prefetch requests will also need 60% of the cache-tag ports bandwidth; since only 40% of the bus bandwidth is available — and not always at the right moment, the prefetch performance was impaired. With the above PRC optimizations only 1/3 of the SRPT requests remained. In addition, the internal prefetch (touching the LRU) reduces the traffic on the memory bus. The improvement to the total performance and the reduction in buses utilization show the effectiveness of the above optimizations.

4. Architectural Models for the Simulations

Our investigated architecture consists of a modern processor that can issue up to four instructions per cycle (base line architecture). The physical limitations on this rate are: at most two memory reference instructions per cycle (i.e. two loads, two stores, or one of each), and a single conditional or unconditional control flow operation. All execution units are fully pipelined with one cycle throughput and one cycle execution stage (latency).

The instruction cache size is 32K-byte organized as 4-way set-associative with 32-byte cache line size. No penalty is charged for a hit and the miss penalty in this cache is 6-cycles (the instruction cache miss penalty is relatively small to compensate for the lack of instruction prefetching mechanism in the simulations). In addition to the I-cache miss penalty (and the following use of memory bus bandwidth), a misprediction of a branch can also stall the execution.

In our simulated architecture (described in Figure 3) we use a branch prediction mechanism based on the two-level adaptive training scheme suggested by Yeh and Patt [14]. In our simulations the automata are initialized with non-zero values and branches that are not in the table are predicted as not-taken. A mispredicted branch stalls the execution for 2-cycles. This happened in case that the BTB generates a wrong prediction (direction or target address) or for a taken branch which is not in the table. The base line BTB configuration for our simulations comprises a 512-entry 4-way set-associative table. Each entry has a 2-bit history register which is used for selecting one of four 2-bit Lee & Smith automata.

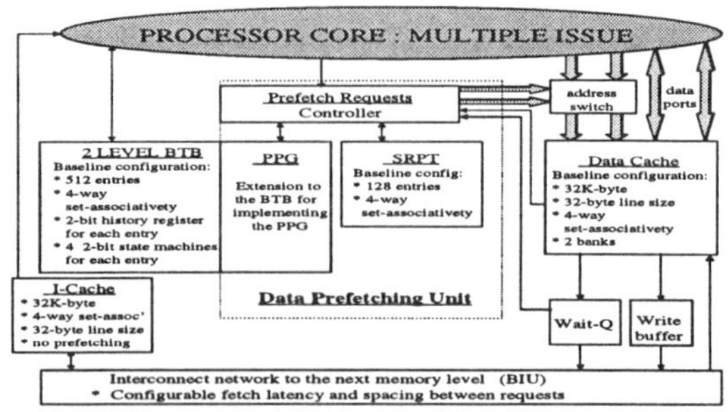

Figure 3. Simulated architecture model.

The data cache is an interleaved (2 banks) write-back cache with write-allocate policy and a write-back buffer (for replacing dirty data lines) of 8 entries. Each bank has a separate data port that can serve either a load or a store in every cycle (i.e. no write "blockage" between a store and a subsequent load). The two ports are accessible from all four execution units and two memory reference operations may access the cache in parallel if they address the different banks. The bank selection is made at the switching point, with the low order bit of the line address. The base line configuration for the data cache is 32K-byte organized as 4-way set-associative with 32-byte cache line size. The write buffer has the lowest priority on the memory bus unless it is full and a dirty cache line is replaced. A prefetch request that may cause a dirty cache line replacement when the write buffer is full will not be entered to the cache. The size of the PRC buffers are those presented in Figure 2 (4, 6, and 4 entries for `Req-Q`, `Filter-cache`, and `Track-Q` respectively).

The interface with the memory is parameterized in two ways. First, the bandwidth is constrained by controlling the number of cycles, *fetch spacing*, between two consecutive launches of memory fetch requests. The second parameter, *fetch latency*, specifies the number of cycles needed for fetching the data. When the fetch spacing is one, the memory interface is pipelined, and at the other extreme, when fetch spacing equals to the fetch latency, only one memory fetch is allowed at a time. In our base configuration the fetch spacing is 4 cycles and the fetch latency is 12 cycles.

We tested the Tango prefetching scheme by running programs from the SPEC benchmarks. In each simulation we used the same environment parameters with two system architectures: the reference (no data prefetching) and the Tango prefetching scheme.

5 Simulation Results

In this section we explore our prefetching design for various architecture parameters. We ran trace driven simulations with five programs from the SPEC92 benchmark and matrix from SPEC89. We used matrix mainly for investigating the load on the cache-tag ports (data intensive program). Every simulation included the first 100 Million instructions and results were inspected every 10 Million instructions. The behavior of five programs (all but espresso) reached a steady phase already at 50 Million instructions, hence, some of the detailed simulations (starting from Section 5.2) were carried out for the first 50 Million instructions.

5.1 Programs Characteristics and General Results

Table 3 shows the dynamic characteristics of the programs.

program	*Data ref. rate*		*Corr BTB*
	write	*read*	*pred (%)*
matrix	0.115	0.338	98.71
dnasa7	0.049	0.418	85.87
xlisp	0.094	0.216	83.30
tomcatv	0.116	0.296	99.41
espresso	0.038	0.235	91.52
spice2g6	0.059	0.193	96.54

program	*Stride distribution*			
	zero	*large*	*small*	*irreg.*
matrix	0.243	0.724	0.0002	0.032
dnasa7	0.386	0.575	0.001	0.037
xlisp	0.335	0.0004	0.101	0.564
tomcatv	0.525	0.054	0.416	0.009
espresso	0.332	0.008	0.239	0.421
spice2g6	0.413	0.173	0.268	0.146

Table 3. Programs Characteristics for 100 million Instructions

The column "Data ref rate" shows the percentage of writes and reads in each application. As expected, the reads are more frequent than the writes and the portion of read misses from the total misses is also larger than that of the writes (see Table 4, first 2 columns). The Corr BTB column presents the percentage of correct BTB predictions for the base line BTB. This information can help in further estimating the success of our prefetching mechanism.

The next four columns in Table 3 indicate the predictability of memory references. The stride distribution information tells us the proportions of data references that behave according to one of four categories. Data references with zero stride are steady references directed to the same memory location, large and small are those references with strides larger/equal than 32-byte (line size in the base line architecture) and smaller than 32-byte, respectively[4]. The data cache can be very helpful with zero and small stride references, but the prefetching mechanism further improved in these cases when there was no temporal locality. Large and irregular stride references can be the main source for cache misses; while the prefetching mechanism is useful for large strides it must also identify irregular memory references so as to avoid unnecessarily initiation of erroneous prefetch requests.

Table 4 summarizes the results obtained for the base line architecture (with pipelined memory bus).

program	*misses (%)*		*ref hit*	*Prefetch*	*C-tag used*	*M bus extra*	*M penalty*	*speedup*
	read	*write*	*ratio*	*C-hit rat.*	*by core (%)*	*band (%)*	*reduced (%)*	*CPI ratio*
matrix	97.26	2.74	0.936	0.998	56.96	0.339	96.57	1.834
dnasa7	96.28	3.72	0.972	0.998	60.20	0.949	94.11	1.381
xlisp	64.18	35.82	0.993	0.996	35.48	23.16	43.64	1.026
tomcatv	74.35	25.65	0.948	0.990	50.70	0.404	81.45	1.515
espresso	96.08	3.92	0.974	0.989	33.93	28.94	57.59	1.120
spice2g6	96.64	3.36	0.838	0.912	21.56	15.55	45.88	1.386

Table 4. Simulation Results of the Base Architecture (100 million instructions); Tango vs. the reference system.

The misses (read/write) columns of Table 4 represent the distribution of read and write misses. The ref hit ratio column shows the hit ratio of the reference data cache followed by the data cache hit ratio column of the prefetch enhanced architecture. For the Tango architecture we incorporated the relative portions of the penalty for those miss requests that were on their way (due to a late prefetch). In this calculated hit ratio, the sum of all the partial penalties was divided by the fetch latency value to generate the relative number of misses. In five out of the six programs the C-hit ratio was 99% and only for spice2g6 the change is from 83.8% to 91.2% in the Tango system.

Instruction scheduling and out of order execution exposed most of the available parallelism (this is implied by the relatively small ideal CPI in Figure 4). Such parallelism exploits the hardware resources most of the time. In the "C-tag used by core" column of Table 4 we present the

[4] We gathered this data with infinite size SRPT.

percentage of time in which the data cache tag ports were busy due to core accesses (demand fetches). On the average, the cache-tag ports are used by the core 43.34 percent of the time. Thus, the remaining bandwidth for prefetch requests is small and must be used wisely.

The "M bus extra bandwidth" column presents the percentage of extra requests imposed by Tango on the memory bus. For xlisp and espresso this number is significant. Nevertheless, in xlisp the total number of prefetch requests was small since the hit ratio (for the reference system) is 99.3%.

The last two columns summarize the performance of the Tango scheme. The percentage of memory penalty reduction is correlated with low irregular strides and high BTB prediction rate (see matrix, dnasa7, and tomcatv). The other programs too exhibit significant improvements. For matrix and dnasa7 programs 96.57% and 94.11% of the memory penalty were removed, respectively, witnessing an efficient prefetching scheme in spite of the small bandwidth left on the core–cache bus (45.3% and 46.7% of the dynamic code access the data cache respectively). On the other side of the scale we find xlisp with a very high hit ratio (99.3%) and a large irregular stride percentage. Nevertheless, the performance of this program is improved as well.

Figure 4 summarizes the performance in three bars for each application. The I-CPI is the ideal CPI derived for the case in which every memory access reference is a hit. The R-CPI bar is the result found for the reference system, and the T-CPI bar presents the Tango performance.

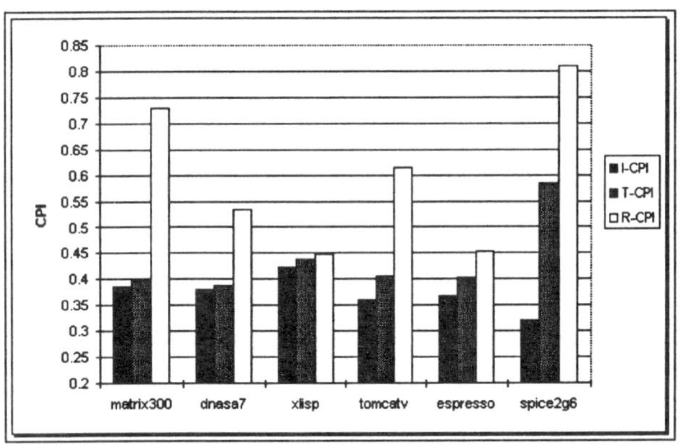

Figure 4. Comparing performance results; I-CPI — ideal CPI, T-CPI — CPI with prefetching (Tango), R-CPI — CPI with out prefetching (reference).

5.2 The Effect of Data Cache Parameters

Next we investigate the effect of the data cache size, associativity, and line sizes on the prefetching scheme.

5.2.1 The Effect of Data Cache size and Associativity

In Figures 6, and 5 the performance is plotted as a function of the cache size. For all cache sizes the line size is 32-byte and the associativities tested are 2, 4, and 8. In addition, the number of memory bus transactions (Num of bus trans.) are plotted versus the cache size. Due to page limitation only part of the results are presented.

The results shown for tomcatv and dnasa7 are for 8-way set associative data caches. The speedup improvements for tomcatv are from 1.48 to 1.60, and the reduction of the memory penalty is 60-80%. For dnasa7 the improvements are huge for all cache sizes and every possible associativity; the memory penalties are reduced by up to 95% and the speedups are 2.53 for 1K to 8K bytes and more than 1.33 for bigger caches..

The small difference between the number of transactions generated by Tango compared to the reference system indicates the effectiveness of the Tango predictions and LRU touch mechanism. In some cases (like dnasa7, and for tomcatv with cache size of 2K-byte to 32K-byte) the number of memory bus transactions generated by Tango is even smaller than that generated by the reference system. These results are unique to Tango and proves the effectiveness of the special LRU touch (a change to the replacement algorithm).

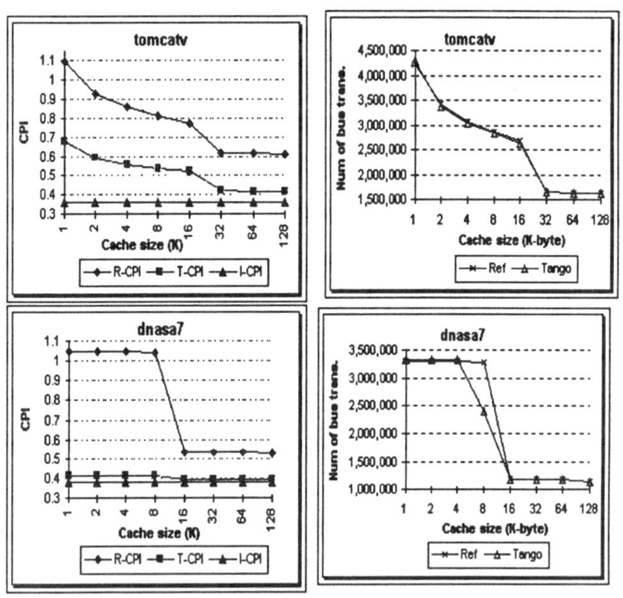

Figure 5. Investigating the data cache size (8-way set associativity).

The data caches presented for xlisp, spice2g6, and matrix300 are 4-way set associative and the improvements are from 1.001 to 1.041 (15% to 75% reduction in memory penalty), 1.1 to 1.4 (about 42% reduction in memory

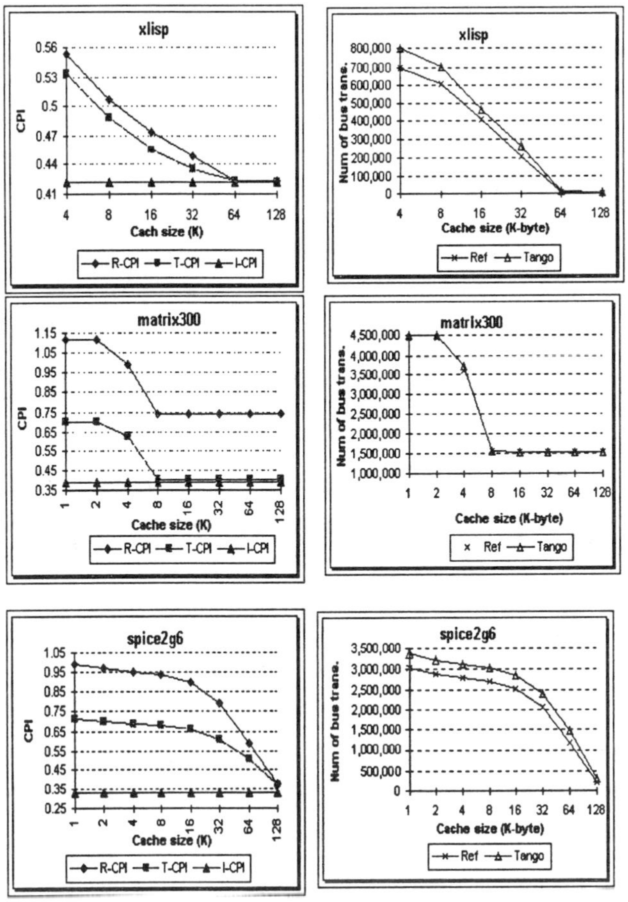

Figure 6. Investigating data cache size (4-way set associativity).

penalty), and 1.59 to 1.83 (about 95% reduction in the memory penalty), respectively.

With caches of 8K-byte to 128K-byte for matrix300, and 32K-byte to 128K-byte for tomcatv the reduction in the memory penalty is about 95% and 80%, respectively, for every cache associativity. Improvements in both the reference and the Tango architectures are obtained for each program until the working set is contained in the cache. Since the hardware cost incurred by Tango is about 4K-byte cache, its use is preferable over the increase in the cache size.

The net effect of the LRU touch on the overall performance improvements reached 20% with small cache size (8K-byte) and its influence drooped with larger caches (32K-byte).

5.2.2 The Effect of Data Cache Line Size

In Figure 7 we see the influence of the cache line size on the performance with prefetching (T-CPI) and without it (R-CPI). The lowest graph (I-CPI) presents the values for a processor with ideal data cache memory (every access is a hit). Even in the ideal case two accesses to the same bank in the same clock cycle are not permitted and its (small) effect is shown in the changes to the I-CPI graph. The T-CPI and R-CPI are also influenced by the change in the access time as a function of the cache line size. For 32-byte cache line size we used a 10-clock-cycle fetch latency and fetch spacing 2. In general, when line size is changed the memory bus parameters are configured according to the following equations:

$$\texttt{fetch spacing} = \frac{\texttt{cache line size}}{\texttt{bus width}},$$

$$\texttt{fetch latency} = \texttt{memory access time} + \texttt{fetch spacing},$$

where the bus width is 16 bytes and the memory access time is 8 clock cycles.

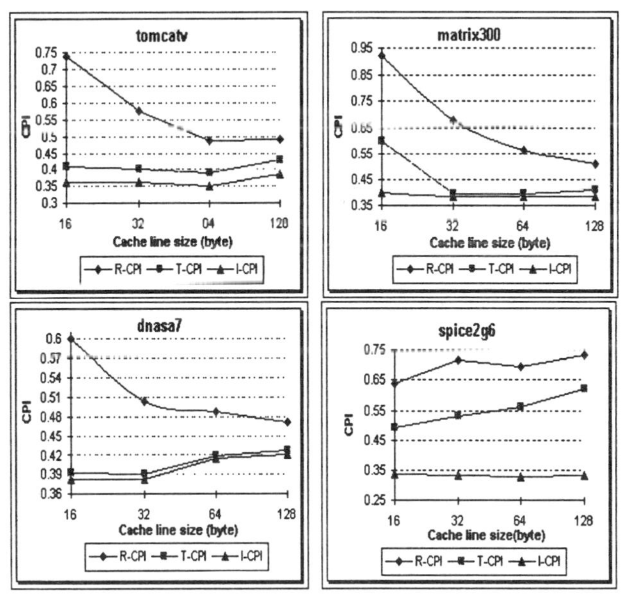

Figure 7. Investigating the data cache line size.

From Figure 7 we can conclude that without the prefetching mechanism a cache with a big line size (64 byte) is preferable. For Tango, the best choice of line size is 32 bytes. A large cache line size reduces compulsory misses as suggested by the locality principle. At the same time, large lines also reduce the number of cache lines, thus increasing conflict misses. As a result, using a prefetch mechanism and avoiding the increase of the line size reduce both conflict and compulsory misses.

Analyzes of the Memory Bus and Interface Parameters can be found in [12].

5.3 Exploring Tango Parameters

The successful operation of the prefetching scheme depends, among other things, on the quality of the reference prediction, the quantity and timing for issuing the prefetch requests. This, in turn, depends on the size and associativity of the SRPT, the size of the buffers in the PRC unit and the distance kept between the PC and pre-PC. Analyzes of the SRPT parameters can be found in [12].

5.3.1 The Impact of the PRC Buffers

The quality of the prediction and the performance of the Tango scheme depends heavily on the size of the PRC queues and the limit on the possible distance between the PC and the pre-PC. In Figure 8 we observe the influence of the `Req-Q` size on the reduction in the memory penalty.

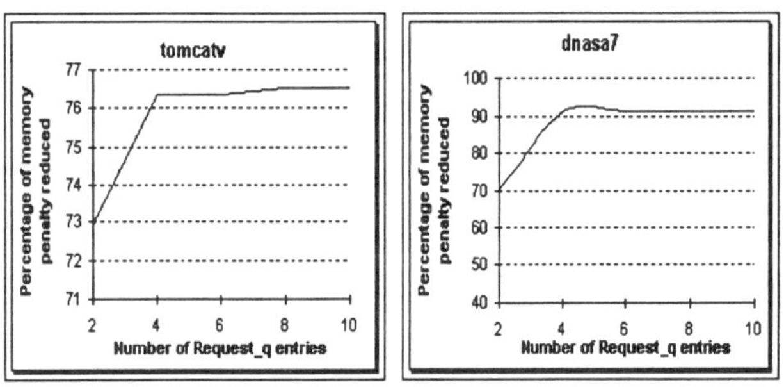

Figure 8. Analyzing the request queue size.

The most effective filter mechanism is the `Filter-cache` that reduces the number of requests destined to `Req-Q` by remembering the last few hits in the cache. As we see in Figure 9 six entries suffice. On the average over all 6 programs about 80% of the requests removed were filtered by a `Filter-cache` of 6 entries and 10% were removed with `Req-Q` of 4 entries.

The pre-PC extracts the prefetch requests from the SRPT. If the data address requested is in `Filter-cache` or any of `Request-Q`, `Track-Q` or `Wait-Q` buffers then the request is removed; otherwise it is inserted into `Request-Q`. A request in `Request-Q` will be looked up in the cache unless it waited too long, or the pre-PC took the wrong direction in some branch; In such a case the request is marked as `lost_req`. In Figure 10 we see for each program the distribution of requests removed by each PRC component out of the total number of request removed by the PRC. The

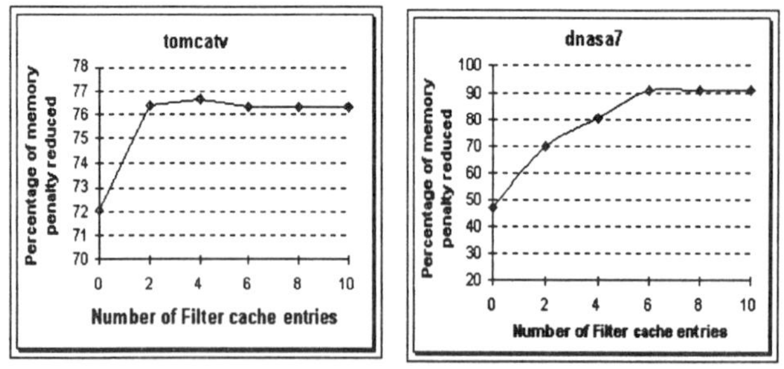

Figure 9. Analyzing the Filter-cache size.

total percentage of requests removed by the PRC is provided under each column.

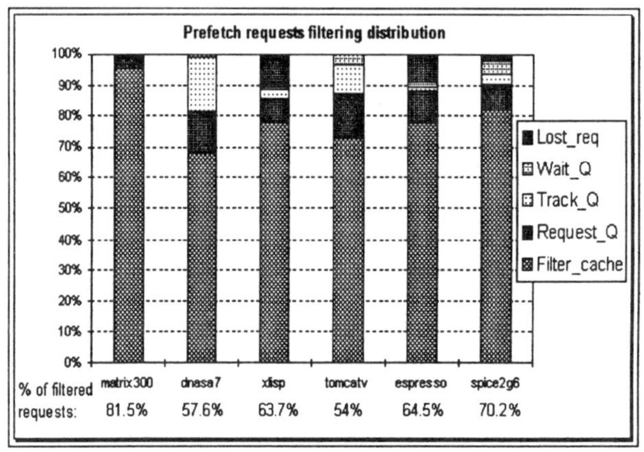

Figure 10. Distribution of prefetch requests filtered by the PRC components.

The PRC removes about two thirds of the requests before they are looked up in the cache. The most effective component is the filter cache which is responsible for 80% of the filtering job.

5.3.2 Controlling the Distance between the PC and the pre-PC

In Figure 11 we observe the influence of the bound on the maximum distance between the PC and the pre-PC. In general, a maximum distance of 60 to 70 instructions is the best. For dnasa7 a maximum value of 30 already reduced most of the memory penalty. In our simulations we used maximum distance of 70 instructions.

When the distance between the PC and Pre-PC is small, prefetch requests arrive too late. With large distance the predictions (of branches and addresses) are not as accurate. In both cases, the prefetching mechanism is not reaching its peek performance. In xlisp the average distance is 25 instructions thus, large limits on the distance has no influence.

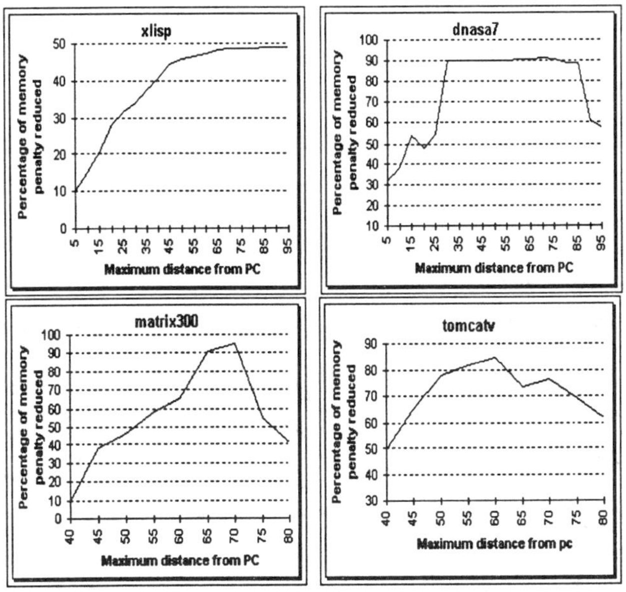

Figure 11. Analyzing the PC pre-PC distance.

We tried some dynamic mechanisms for limiting the distance (like the maximal number of blocks between the PC and pre-PC) but the results were similar.

6 Conclusions

In the design of the Tango prefetching scheme we provide a solution to the memory access penalty problem for superscalar processors. The emphasis in our scheme is on the effective utilization of slack time and hardware resources not used for the main computation. The main characteristics of Tango are:

- A data prefetching scheme for superscalar processors.
- A PPG table that "spread out" the predicted progress of the execution, thus enabling the pre-PC to freely advance in the predicted execution flow.
- A pre-PC that "jumps" and scans only predicted memory references in the SRPT.
- A prefetch requests controller for filtering out prefetch requests without consuming cache-tag bandwidth.
- An improvement to the data cache LRU replacement algorithm which indicates that a datum will be needed soon (due to a prediction) rather than leaving it an early use. In some cases this internal prefetching causes the total number of transactions in a Tango system to be smaller than in the reference system. We note that the touching mechanism of the LRU can be used with software prefetching as well.

References

[1] J. Baer and T. Chen. An effective on-chip preloading scheme to reduce data access penalty. In *Supercomputing '91*, pages 178–186, November 1991.

[2] D. Bernstein, D. Cohen, A. Freund, and D. Maydan. Compiler techniques for data prefetching on the powerpc. In *International Conference of Parallel Architectures and Compilation Techniques*, 1995.

[3] T. Chen and J. Baer. Effective hardware-based data prefetching for high-performance processors. *IEEE Transactions on Computers*, 44(5):609 – 623, May. 1995.

[4] F. Dahlgren, M. Dubois, and P. Stenstrom. Fixed and adaptive sequential prefetching in shared memory multiprocessors. In *International Conference on Parallel Processing*. CRC Press, Inc., 1993.

[5] K. I. Farkas, N. P. Jouppi, and P. Chow. How useful are non-blocking loads, stream buffers, and speculative execution in multiple issue processors? In *First International Symposium on High Performance Computer Architecture*, pages 78–89, Raleigh, North Carolina, January 1995. IEEE Computer Society.

[6] J. W. C. Fu and J. H. Patel. Data prefetching in multiprocessor vector cache memories. In *The* 18th *International Symposium on Computer Architecture*, pages 54–63, Toronto, Canada, May 1991. ACM SIGARCH.

[7] J. W. C. Fu and J. H. Patel. Stride directed prefetching in scalar processors. In *25th Annual International Symposium on Microarchitecture*, pages 102–110, Portland, Oregon, December 1992.

[8] N. P. Jouppi. Improving direct-mapped cache performance by the addition of small fully associative cache and prefetching buffers. In *The* 17th *International Symposium on Computer Architecture*, pages 364–373, May 1990.

[9] R. L. Lee, P. C. Yew, and D. H. Lawrie. Data prefetching in shared memory multiprocessors. In *International Conference on Parallel Processing*, pages 28–31. CRC Press, Inc., 1987.

[10] T. C. Mowry, M. S. Lam, and A. Gupta. Design and evaluation a compiler algorithm for prefetching. In *The* 5th *International Conference on Architectural Support for Programming Languages and Operating Systems*, pages 62–73, September 1992.

[11] S. Palacharla and R. E. Kessler. Evaluating stream buffers as a secondary cache replacement. In *The* 21th *International Symposium on Computer Architecture*, pages 24–33. ACM SIGARCH, 1994.

[12] S. S. Pinter and A. Yoaz. Tango: a hardware-based data prefetching technique for superscalar processors. Technical Report TR88.371, IBM Israel Research Center, Haifa, Israel, September 1996.

[13] G. S. Sohi and M. Franklin. High-bandwidth data memory systems for superscalar processors. In *The* 4th *International Conference on Architectural Support for Programming Languages and Operating Systems*, pages 53–62, April 1991.

[14] T. Yeh and Y. N. Patt. Two-level adaptive training branch prediction. In *24th Annual International Symposium on Microarchitecture*, pages 51–61, Albuquerque, NM, November 1991.

Exceeding the Dataflow Limit via Value Prediction

Mikko H. Lipasti and John Paul Shen
Department of Electrical and Computer Engineering
Carnegie Mellon University
Pittsburgh PA, 15213
{mhl,shen}@ece.cmu.edu

Abstract

For decades, the serialization constraints imposed by true data dependences have been regarded as an absolute limit--the dataflow limit--on the parallel execution of serial programs. This paper proposes a new technique--value prediction--for exceeding that limit that allows data dependent instructions to issue and execute in parallel without violating program semantics. This technique is built on the concept of value locality, which describes the likelihood of the recurrence of a previously-seen value within a storage location inside a computer system. Value prediction consists of predicting entire 32- and 64-bit register values based on previously-seen values. We find that such register values being written by machine instructions are frequently predictable. Furthermore, we show that simple microarchitectural enhancements to a modern microprocessor implementation based on the PowerPC 620 that enable value prediction can effectively exploit value locality to collapse true dependences, reduce average result latency, and provide performance gains of 4.5%-23% (depending on machine model) by exceeding the dataflow limit.

1. Motivation and Related Work

There are two fundamental restrictions that limit the amount of *instruction level parallelism* (*ILP*) that can be extracted from sequential programs: *control flow* and *data flow. Control flow* limits *ILP* by imposing serialization constraints at forks and joins in a program's control flow graph [1]. *Data flow* limits *ILP* by imposing serialization constraints on pairs of instructions that are data dependent (i.e. one needs the result of another to compute its own result, and hence must wait for the other to complete before beginning to execute). Examining the extent and effect of these limits has been a popular and important area of research, particularly in the case of control flow [2,3,4,5]. Continuing advances in the development of accurate branch predictors (e.g. [6]) have led to increasingly-aggressive control-speculative microarchitectures (e.g. the Intel Pentium Pro [7]), which undertake aggressive measures to overcome control-flow restrictions by using branch prediction and speculative execution to bypass control dependences and expose additional instruction-level parallelism to the microarchitecture. Meanwhile, numerous mechanisms have been proposed and implemented to eliminate false data dependences and tolerate the latencies induced by true data dependences by allowing instructions to execute out of program order (see [8] for an overview).

Surprisingly, in light of the extensive energies focused on eliminating control-flow restrictions on parallel instruction issue, less attention has been paid to eliminating data-flow restrictions on parallel issue. Recent work has focused primarily on reducing the latency of specific types of instructions (usually loads from memory) by rearranging pipeline stages [9, 10], initiating memory accesses earlier [11], or speculating that dependences to earlier stores do not exist [12, 13, 14, 15].

The most relevant prior work in the area of eliminating data-flow dependences consists of the *Tree Machine* [16,17], which uses a *value cache* to store and look up the results of recurring arithmetic expressions to eliminate redundant computation (the *value cache*, in effect, performs *common subexpression elimination* [1] in hardware). Richardson follows up on this concept in [18] by introducing the concepts of *trivial computation*, which is defined as the trivialization of potentially complex operations by the occurrence of simple operands; and *redundant computation*, where an operation repeatedly performs the same computation because it sees the same operands. He proposes a hardware mechanism (the *result cache*) which reduces the latency of such trivial or redundant complex arithmetic operations by storing and looking up their results in the *result cache*. In [19], we introduced *value locality*, a concept related to *redundant computation*, and demonstrated a technique--*Load Value Prediction*, or *LVP*--for predicting the results of load instructions at dispatch by exploiting the affinity between load instruction addresses and the values the loads produce. *LVP* differs from Harbison's *value cache* and Richardson's *result cache* in two important ways: first, the LVP table is indexed by instruction address, and hence value lookups can occur very early in the pipeline; second, it is speculative in nature, and relies on a verification mechanism to guarantee correctness. In contrast, both Harbison and Richardson use table indices that are only available later in the pipeline (Harbison uses data addresses, while Richardson uses actual operand values); and require their predictions to be correct, hence requiring mechanisms for keeping

1072-4451/96 $5.00 © 1996 IEEE

their tables coherent with all other computation.

In this paper, we extend the LVP approach for predicting the results of load instructions to apply to all instructions that write an integer or floating point register; show that a significant proportion of such writes are trivially predictable; describe a *value prediction* hardware mechanism that allows dependent instructions to execute in parallel; and present results that demonstrate significant performance increases over our baseline machine models.

2. Taxonomy of Speculative Execution

In order to place our work on value prediction into a meaningful historical context, we introduce a taxonomy of speculative execution. This taxonomy, summarized in Figure 1, categorizes ours as well as previously-introduced techniques based on which types of dependences are being bypassed (control vs. data), whether the speculation relates to storage location or value, and what type of decision must be made to enable the speculation (binary vs. multi-valued).

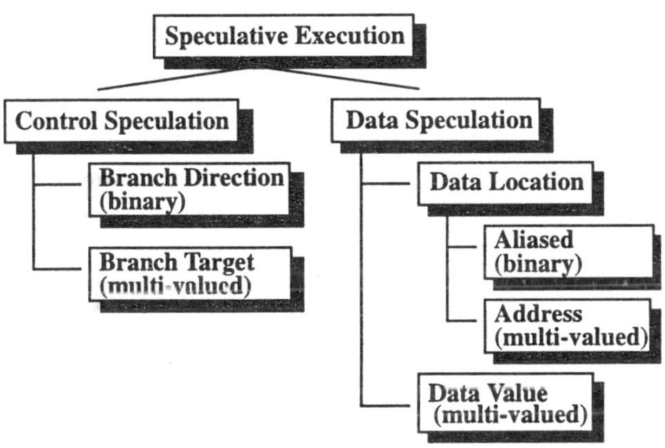

FIGURE 1. Taxonomy of Speculative Execution Techniques.

2.1. Control Speculation

There are essentially two types of control speculation: speculating on the direction of a branch, which requires a binary decision (taken vs. not-taken); and speculating on the target of a branch, which requires a multi-valued decision (the target can potentially be anywhere in the program's address space). Examples of the former are any of the many branch prediction schemes explored in the literature (e.g. [20,6]), while examples of the latter are the Branch Target Buffer (*BTB*) or Branch Target Address Cache (*BTAC*) units included on most modern high-end microprocessors (e.g. the PowerPC 620 [15] or the Intel Pentium Pro [7]).

2.2. Data Speculation

Data speculation techniques break down logically into two categories: those that speculate on the storage location of the data, and those that speculate on the actual value of the data. Furthermore, techniques that speculate on the location come in two fundamentally different flavors: those that speculate on a specific attribute of the storage location (e.g. whether or not it is aliased with an earlier definition), and those that speculate on the address of the storage location. An example of the former is *speculative disambiguation*, which optimistically assumes that an earlier definition does not alias with a current use, and provides a mechanism for checking the accuracy of that assumption. Speculative disambiguation has been implemented both in software [13] as well as in hardware [12, 14, 15]. Another example of this type of speculation occurs implicitly in most control-speculative processors, whenever execution proceeds speculatively past a join in the control-flow graph where multiple reaching definitions for a storage location are live [1]. By speculating past that join, the processor hardware is implicitly speculating that the definition on the predicted path to the join in question is in fact the correct one (as opposed to the definition on an alternate path).

There are a large number of techniques that speculate on data address. Most prefetching techniques, for example, are speculative in nature and rely on some heuristic for generating addresses of future memory references (e.g. [21, 22, 23, 24, 25]). Of course, since prefetching has no architected side effects, no mechanism is needed for verifying the accuracy of the prediction or for recovering from mispredictions. Another example of a technique that speculates on data address is *fast address calculation* [26, 11], which enables early initiation of memory loads by speculatively generating addresses early in the pipeline.

The final category in our taxonomy, techniques that speculate on data value, has received little attention in the literature. The only prior work we are aware of is the LVP structure described in [19]. This paper also falls squarely into the data-value-speculative category, since it is an extension of the LVP approach. Note that neither the *Tree Machine* [16,17] or Richardson's work [18] qualify since they are not speculative.

3. Value Locality

In this paper, we revisit the concept of *value locality*, which we first introduced in [19] as the likelihood of a previously-seen value recurring repeatedly within a storage location. Although the concept is general and can be applied to any storage location within a computer system, we have limited our current study to examine only the value locality of general-purpose or floating point registers immediately following instructions that write to those registers. A plethora of previous work on static and dynamic branch prediction (e.g. [20,6]) has focused on an even more restricted application of value locality, namely the prediction of a single condition bit based on its past behavior. In [19], we examined the value locality of registers being targeted by loads from memory. This paper can be viewed as a logical continuation of that work, extending the prediction of load values to the prediction of all integer and floating point register values.

TABLE 1. Benchmark Descriptions.

Bench-mark	Description	Input Set	Instr. Count
cc1-271	GCC 2.7.1	SPEC95 genoutput.i	102M
cc1	SPEC92 GCC 1.35	SPEC92 insn-recog.i	146M
cjpeg	JPEG encoder	128x128 BW image	2.8M
compress	SPEC92 compression	1 iter. w/ 1/2 input	38.8M
eqntott	SPEC92 eqn to tr tbl	SPEC92 mod. input	25.5M
gawk	GNU awk	Parse 1.7M output	25.0M
gperf	GNU hash fn gen	-a -k 1-13 -D -o dict	7.8M
grep	GNU grep -c "st*mo"	Same as compress	2.3M
mpeg	MPEG decoder	4 frames	8.8M
perl	SPEC95 anagram srch	"admits" in 1/8 input	105M
quick	Recursive quick sort	5,000 elements	688K
sc	SPEC92 spreadsheet	SPEC92 short input	78.5M
xlisp	SPEC92 LISP	6 queens	52.1M
doduc	SPEC92 Nucl sim	SPEC92 tiny input	35.8M
hydro2d	SPEC92 galactic jets	SPEC92 short input	4.3M
swm256	SPEC92 water model	5 iterations	43.7M
tomcatv	SPEC92 mesh gen	4 iterations (vs. 100)	30.0M
Total			720M

Intuitively, it seems that it would be a very difficult task to discover any useful amount of value locality in a general purpose register. After all, a 32-bit register can contain any one of over four billion values--how could one possibly predict which of those is even somewhat likely to occur next? As it turns out, if we narrow the scope of our prediction mechanism by considering each static instruction individually, the task becomes much easier and we are able to accurately predict a significant fraction of register values being written by machine instructions.

What is it that makes these values predictable? After examining a number of real-world programs, we assert that value locality exists primarily for the same reason that *partial evaluation* [27] is such an effective compile-time optimization; namely, that real-world programs, run-time environments, and operating systems incur severe performance penalties because they are *general by design*. That is, they are implemented to handle not only contingencies, exceptional conditions, and erroneous inputs, all of which occur relatively rarely in real life, but they are also often designed with future expansion and code reuse in mind. Our results--which agree with Richardson's persuasive arguments and results in [18]--show that even code that is aggressively optimized by modern, state-of-the-art compilers exhibits these tendencies.

The benchmark set we use to explore value locality and quantify its performance impact is summarized in Table 1. We have chosen thirteen integer benchmarks, five of them from SPEC '92, one from SPEC '95, along with two image-processing applications (cjpeg and mpeg), two commonly-used Unix utilities (gawk and grep), GNU's perfect hash function generator (gperf), a more recent version of GCC (cc1-271), and a recursive quicksort. In addition, we have chosen four of the SPEC '92 floating-point benchmarks. All benchmarks are compiled at full optimization with the IBM CSET reference compilers, and are run to completion with the input sets described, but do not include supervisor-state instructions, which our tracing tool is unable to capture.

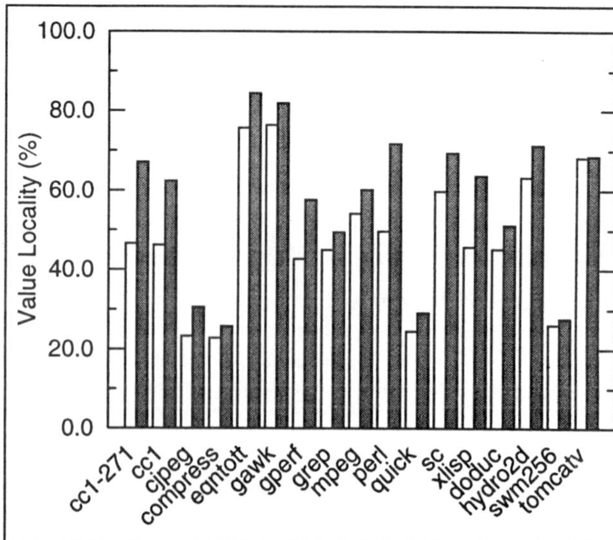

FIGURE 2. Register Value Locality. The light bars show value locality for a history depth of one, and dark bars show it for a history depth of four.

Figure 2 shows the *register value locality* for all instructions that write an integer or floating point register in each of the benchmarks. The register value locality for each benchmark is measured by counting the number of times each static instruction writes a register value that matches a previously-seen value for that static instruction and dividing by the total number of dynamic register writes in the benchmark. Two sets of numbers are shown, one (light bars) for a history depth of one (i.e. we check for matches against only the most-recently-written value), while the second set (dark bars) has a history depth of four (i.e. we check against the last four unique values).[1] We see that even with a history depth of one, most of the programs exhibit value locality in the 40-50% range (average 49%), while extending the history depth to four (along with a perfect mechanism for choosing the right one of the four values) can improve that to the 60-70% range (average 61%). What that means is that a majority of static instructions exhibit very little variation in the values that they write during the course of a program's execution.

To further explore the notion of value locality, we collected value predictability data that classifies register writes based on instruction type (the types are summarized in Table 2). These results are summarized in Figure 3. Once

1. The history values are stored in a direct-mapped table with 16K entries indexed but not tagged by instruction address, and the values (up to four) stored at each entry are replaced with an LRU policy. Hence, the potential exists for both constructive and destructive interference between instructions that map to the same entry.

TABLE 2. Instruction Types.

Instr Type	Description	Freq (%)
SC_A	Single-cycle arithmetic, 2 reg. operands	5.45
SC_A_I	Single-cycle arithmetic, 1 reg. operand	23.55
SC_L	Single-cycle logical, 2 reg. operands	1.86
SC_L_I	Single-cycle logical, 1 reg. operand	9.89
MC_A	Multi-cycle arithmetic, 2 reg. operands	0.14
MC_A_I	Multi-cycle arithmetic, 1 reg. operand	0.06
MC_MV	Multi-cycle register move	1.86
I_LD	Integer load instructions	33.00
ST_U	Store with base reg. update	5.14
FP_LD	FP load single	3.16
FPD_LD	FP load double	4.76
FP_A	FP instructions other than multiply	3.52
FP_M	FP multiply instructions	2.11
FP_MA	FP multiply-add instructions	3.65
FP_OTH	FP div,abs,neg,round to single precision	1.61
FP_MV	FP register move instructions	0.26

again, two sets of numbers are shown; one for a history depth of one, and another for a history depth of four. Integer and floating-point double loads (I_LD and FPD_LD) are the most predictable frequently-occurring instructions. FP_OTH, FP_MV, MC_MV are also very predictable but make up an insignificant portion of the dynamic instruction mix. For the single-cycle instructions, fewer input operands (one vs. two) correlate with higher value locality. For the multi-cycle instructions, however, the opposite is true.

The worst value locality is exhibited by the floating-point-single instructions. We attribute this to the fact that the floating-point benchmarks we used initialize input arrays with pseudo-random numbers, resulting in poor value locality for loads from these arrays.

The store-with-update (ST_U) instruction type also has poor value locality. This makes sense, since the ST_U instruction is used to step through an array at a fixed stride (hence the base address register is updated with a different value every time the instruction executes, and history-based value prediction will fail). On the other hand, ST_U is also used in function prologues to update the stack frame pointer, where, given the same call-depth, the value is predictable from one call to the next. Hence, some of our call-intensive benchmarks report higher value locality for ST_U. However, the former effect dominates and lowers the overall value locality for ST_U.

4. Exploiting Value Locality

The fact that the register writes in many programs demonstrate a significant degree of value locality opens up exciting new possibilities for the microarchitect. Since the results of many instructions can be accurately predicted before they are issued or executed, dependent instructions are no longer bound by the serialization constraints imposed by operand

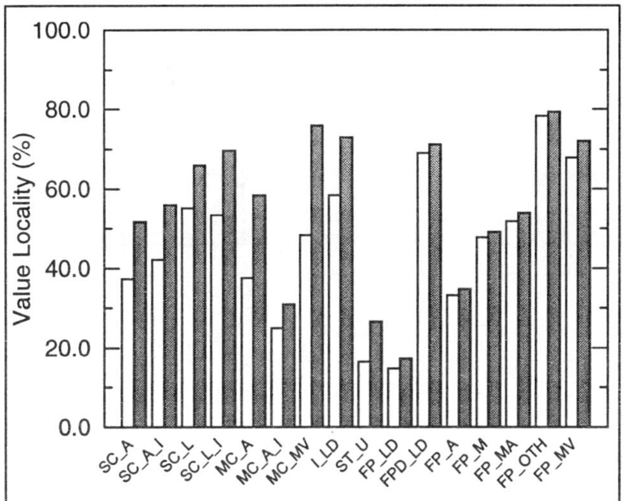

FIGURE 3. Register Value Locality by Instruction Type.

data flow. Instructions can now be scheduled speculatively with additional degrees of freedom to better utilize existing functional units and hardware buffers, and are frequently able to complete execution sooner since the critical paths through dependence graphs have been collapsed. However, in order to exploit value locality and bring about all of these benefits, two mechanisms must be implemented: one for accurately predicting values--the VP (value prediction) unit--and one for verifying these predictions.

4.1. The Value Prediction Unit

Value prediction is useful only if it can be done accurately, since incorrect predictions can lead to increased structural hazards and longer latency (the misprediction penalty is described in greater detail in Section 5.3). Hence, we propose a two-level prediction structure for the VP Unit: the first level is used to generate the prediction values, and the second level is used to decide whether or not the predictions are likely to be accurate.

The internal structure of the VP Unit is summarized in Figure 4. The VP Unit consists of two tables: the *Classification Table* (CT) and the *Value Prediction Table* (VPT), both of which are direct-mapped and indexed by the instruction address (PC) of the instruction being predicted. Entries in the CT contain two fields: the *valid* field, which consists of either a single bit that indicates a valid entry or a partial or complete tag field that is matched against the upper bits of the PC to indicate a valid field; and the *prediction history*, which is a saturating counter of 1 or more bits. The prediction history is incremented or decremented whenever a prediction is correct or incorrect, respectively, and is used to classify instructions as either predictable or unpredictable. This classification is used to decide whether or not the result of a particular instruction should be predicted. Increasing the number of bits in the saturating counter adds hysteresis to the classification process and can help avoid erroneous classifications by ignoring anomalous values and/or

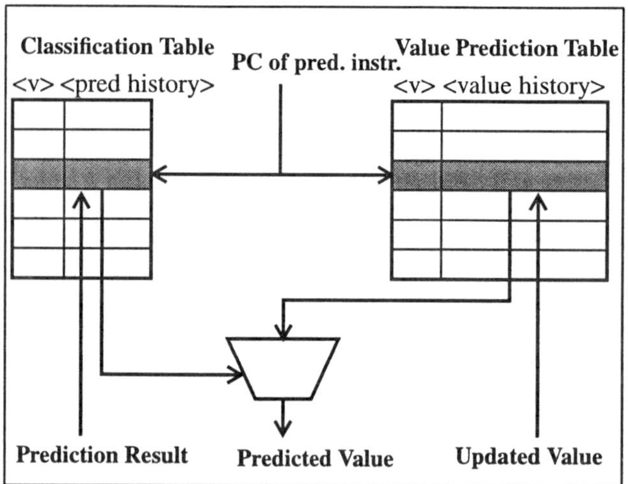

FIGURE 4. Value Prediction Unit. The PC of the instruction being predicted is used to index into the VPT to find a value to predict. At the same time, the CT is also indexed with the PC to determine whether or not a prediction should be made. When the instruction completes, both the prediction history and value history are updated.

destructive interference.

The VPT entries also consist of two fields: a *valid* field, which, again, can consist of a single valid bit or a full or partial tag; and a *value history* field, which contains one or more 32- or 64-bit values that are maintained with an LRU policy. The *value history* fields are replaced when an instruction is first encountered (by its result) or whenever a prediction is incorrect (by the actual result). The VPT replacement policy is also governed by the CT prediction history to introduce hysteresis and avoid replacing useful values with less useful ones.

As a preliminary exploration of the VP Unit design space, we analyzed sensitivity to a few key parameters, and then selected a specific design point to use with our microarchitectural studies (see Section 7). However, the intent of this paper is not to explore the details of such a design; rather, our intent is to explore the larger issue of the impact of value prediction on microarchitecture and instruction-level parallelism, and to leave such details to future work.

In Figure 5, we show the sensitivity of the VPT hit rate to size for each of our benchmarks. We see that for most benchmarks, the hit rate levels off at or around 4096 entries, though in several cases significant improvements are possible beyond that size. Nevertheless, we chose 4096 as our design point, since going beyond that size (i.e. 4096 entries x 8 bytes/entry = 32KB) seemed unreasonable without severely impacting processor cycle time.

The purpose of the CT is to partition instructions into two classes: those that are predictable by the VPT, and those that are not.To measure its effectiveness at accomplishing this purpose, we simulated six different CT configurations, which are summarized in Table 3. The state descriptions specify the effect of each state on both value prediction as well as the replacement of values in the VPT when new val-

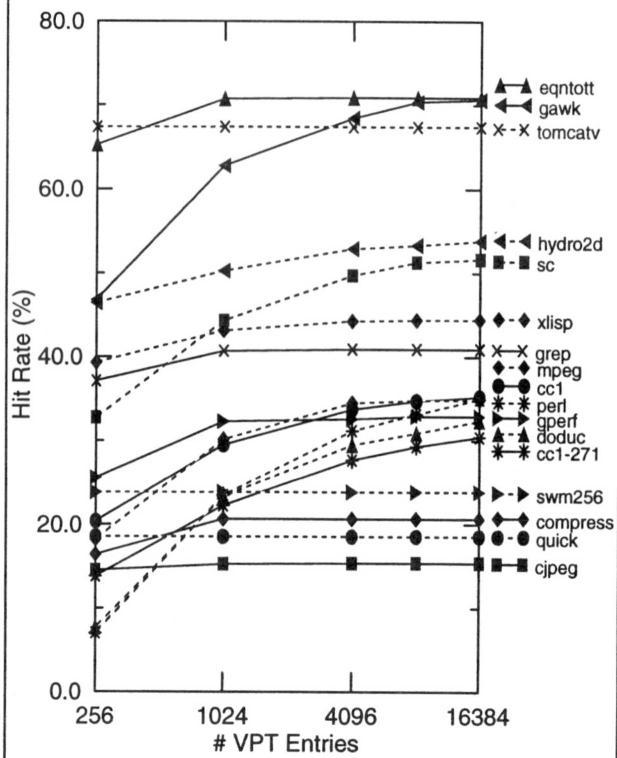

FIGURE 5. VPT Hit Rate Sensitivity to Size.

ues are encountered. The results for each configuration are summarized in Figure 6. From the results, we conclude that the best choice for maximizing both the predictable and unpredictable hit rates is the *1024/3-bit* configuration (this is not surprising, since it has the highest hardware cost). However, since the *1024/2-bit* configuration is only slightly worse at identifying predictable instructions and is actually better at identifying unpredictable ones (hence minimizing misprediction penalty), and is significantly cheaper to implement (it uses 1/3 fewer bits), we decided to use the latter in our microarchitectural simulation studies.[1] We note that the unpredictable hit rates of the 3-bit configurations are worse (relative to the 1- bit and 2-bit configurations) than their predictable hit rates, and conclude that this must be because the 3-bit state assignments heavily favor prediction (see Table 3). Changing the state assignments might improve these hit rates.

4.2. Verifying Predictions

Since value prediction is by nature speculative, we need a mechanism for verifying the correctness of the predictions and efficiently recovering from mispredictions. This mechanism is summarized in the example of Figure 7, which

1. Note that we do not claim that the hit rates shown in Figure 6 are a reliable predictor of system performance. Just as in branch prediction, higher hit rates may not necessarily translate into fewer execution cycles. Rather, detailed cycle-by-cycle simulation of the entire microarchitecture is needed to verify performance improvements.

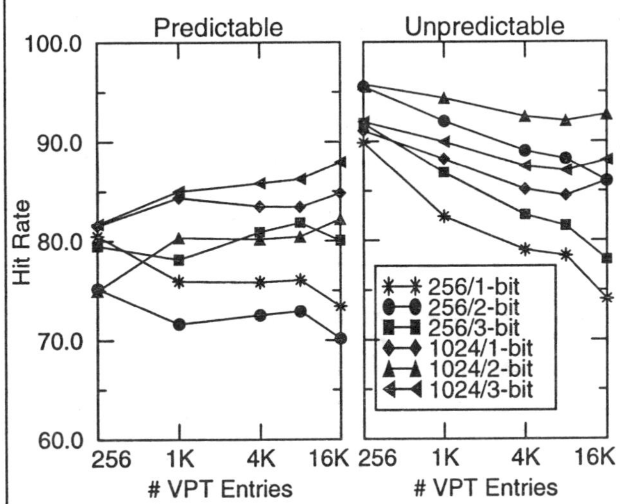

FIGURE 6. CT Hit Rates. The Predictable Hit Rate is the number of correct value predictions that were identified as such by the CT divided by the total number of correct predictions, while the Unpredictable Hit Rate is the number of incorrect predictions that were identified as such by the CT divided by the number of incorrect predictions.

TABLE 3. Classification Table Configurations.

Configuration (entries/bits)	State Descriptions
256/1-bit	{0=no pred, 1=pred & no repl}
256/2-bit	{0,1=no pred, 2,3=pred, 3=no repl}
256/3-bit	{0,1=no pred, 2-7=pred, 5-7= no repl}
1024/1-bit	{0=no pred, 1=pred & no repl}
1024/2-bit	{0,1=no pred, 2,3=pred, 3=no repl}
1024/3-bit	{0,1=no pred, 2-7=pred, 5-7= no repl}

shows the parallel execution of two data-dependent instructions. The producer instruction, shown on the left, has its value predicted and written to its rename buffer during the *fetch* and *dispatch* cycles. The consumer instruction, shown on the right, reads the predicted value from the rename buffer at the beginning of the *execute* cycle, and is able to issue and execute normally, but is forced to retain its reservation station. Meanwhile, the predicted instruction also executes, and its computed result is compared with the predicted result during its *completion* stage. If the values match, the consumer instruction releases its reservation station. If not, completion of the first instance of the consumer instruction is invalidated, and a second instance reissues with the correct value.

5. Microarchitectural Models

In order to validate and quantify the performance impact of the Value Prediction Unit, we implemented three cycle-accurate simulation models, two of them based on the Pow-

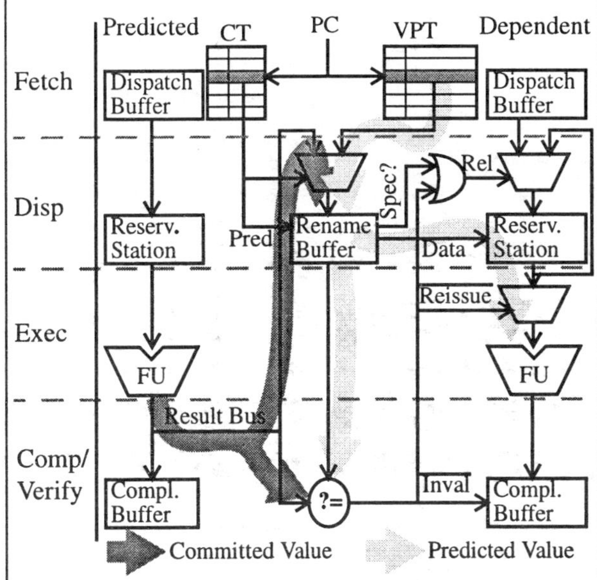

FIGURE 7. Example use of Value Prediction Mechanism. The dependent instruction shown on the right uses the predicted result of the instruction on the left, and is able to issue and execute in the same cycle.

erPC 620 [28, 15]--one which matches the current 620 closely, and one, termed the 620+, which alleviates some of its known bottlenecks--and an additional idealized model which removes all structural dependences[1]. The number of functional units and issue and result latencies for common instruction types on the three machines are summarized in Table 4. Our idealized *infinite* model also implements the following assumptions:

- Perfect caches
- Perfect alias detection and store-to-load forwarding
- Perfect instruction fetching (limited to one taken branch per cycle).
- Unit latency for mispredicted branches with no fetch bubble (i.e. instructions following a mispredicted branch are able to execute in the cycle following resolution of the mispredicted branch).

It is our intent that the *infinite* model match the *SP* machine model presented in [4], except for the branch prediction mechanism, which is a 2048-entry BHT design with a 2-bit saturating counter per entry, copied exactly from our 620 model. Table 5 summarizes the performance of each of our benchmarks on each of the three baseline machine models without value prediction.

5.1. PowerPC 620 Microarchitecture

The microarchitecture of the PowerPC 620 is summarized in Figure 8. Our model is based on published reports

1. For reasons of efficiency, the instruction window of our simulator is limited to 4096 active instructions. Hence, we did not truly model an infinite number of resources, only one that approaches that number.

TABLE 4. Machine Model Specifications.

Instruction Class	PowerPC 620/620+				Infinite
	# FU/RS		Issue Lat	Result Lat	I&R Lat
	620	620+			
Simple Int	2/4	2/8	1	1	1,1
Complex Int	1/2	1/4	1-35	1-35	1,1
Load/Store	1/3	2/6	1	2	1,1
Simple FP	1/2	1/4	1	3	1,1
Complex FP	shared	shared	18	18	11,
Br (pr/mispr)	1/4	1/8	1	0/1+	1,0/1+

TABLE 5. Baseline Performance (IPC).

Bench mark	620	620+	Infinite
cc1-271	1.05540	1.07260	6.40244
cc1	1.20880	1.30892	6.81969
cjpeg	0.99308	1.10503	10.11820
compress	1.15508	1.22739	5.66520
eqntott	1.35984	1.41655	5.58084
gawk	1.22254	1.23106	4.05087
gperf	1.61187	1.82027	7.00588
grep	1.07909	1.06635	2.02673
mpeg	1.62410	1.86998	7.99286
perl	1.00018	1.05241	8.03310
quick	0.97000	0.99904	4.91123
sc	1.24365	1.31691	6.75335
xlisp	1.15722	1.21509	8.30155
doduc	0.81249	0.83851	5.80629
hydro2d	0.80267	0.82059	5.53410
swm256	0.85172	0.88852	4.15299
tomcatv	0.91337	0.93081	5.77235
GM	1.09757	1.15473	5.84794

on the PowerPC 620 [28, 15], and accurately models all aspects of the microarchitecture, including branch prediction, fetching, dispatching, register renaming, out-of-order issue and execution, result forwarding, the non-blocking cache hierarchy, store-to-load alias detection, and in-order completion. To alleviate some of the bottlenecks we found in the 620 design, we also modeled an aggressive "next-generation" version of the 620, which we termed the 620+. The 620+ differs from the 620 by doubling the number of reservation stations, FPR and GPR rename buffers, and completion buffer entries; adding an additional load/store unit (LSU) without an additional cache port (the base 620 already has a dual-banked data cache); and relaxing dispatching requirements to allow up to two loads or stores to dispatch and issue per cycle. In addition, we added a VP Unit that predicts register writes by keeping a value history indexed by instruction addresses.

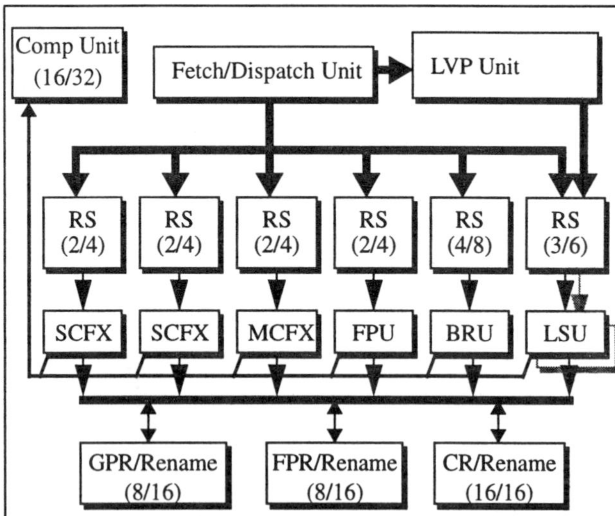

FIGURE 8. PPC 620 and 620+ Block Diagram. Buffer sizes are shown as (620/620+).

5.2. VP Unit Operation

The VP Unit predicts the values during fetch and dispatch, then forwards them speculatively to subsequent dependent instructions via the 620's rename buffers. Up to four predictions can be made per cycle on our 620/620+ models, while the infinite model can make up to 4096 predictions per cycle. Dependent instructions are able to issue and execute immediately, but are prevented from completing architecturally and are forced to retain possession of their reservation stations until their inputs are no longer speculative. Speculatively forwarded values are tagged with the uncommitted register writes they depend on, and these tags are propagated to the results of any subsequent dependent instructions. Meanwhile, uncommitted instructions execute in their respective functional units, and the predicted values are verified by a comparison against the actual values computed by the instructions. Once a prediction is verified, its tag gets broadcast to all active instructions, and all the dependent instructions can either release their reservation stations and proceed into the completion unit (in the case of a correct prediction), or restart execution with the correct register values (if the prediction was incorrect). Since a large number of instructions can be in flight at the same time (16 on the base 620, 32 on the 620+, and up to 4096 in our *infinite* model), verifying a predicted value can take dozens of cycles or more, allowing the processor to speculate multiple levels down the dependence chain beyond the write, executing instructions and resolving branches that would otherwise be blocked by data-flow dependences.

5.3. Misprediction Penalty

The worst-case penalty for an incorrect value prediction in this scheme, as compared to not predicting the value in question, is one additional cycle of latency along with struc-

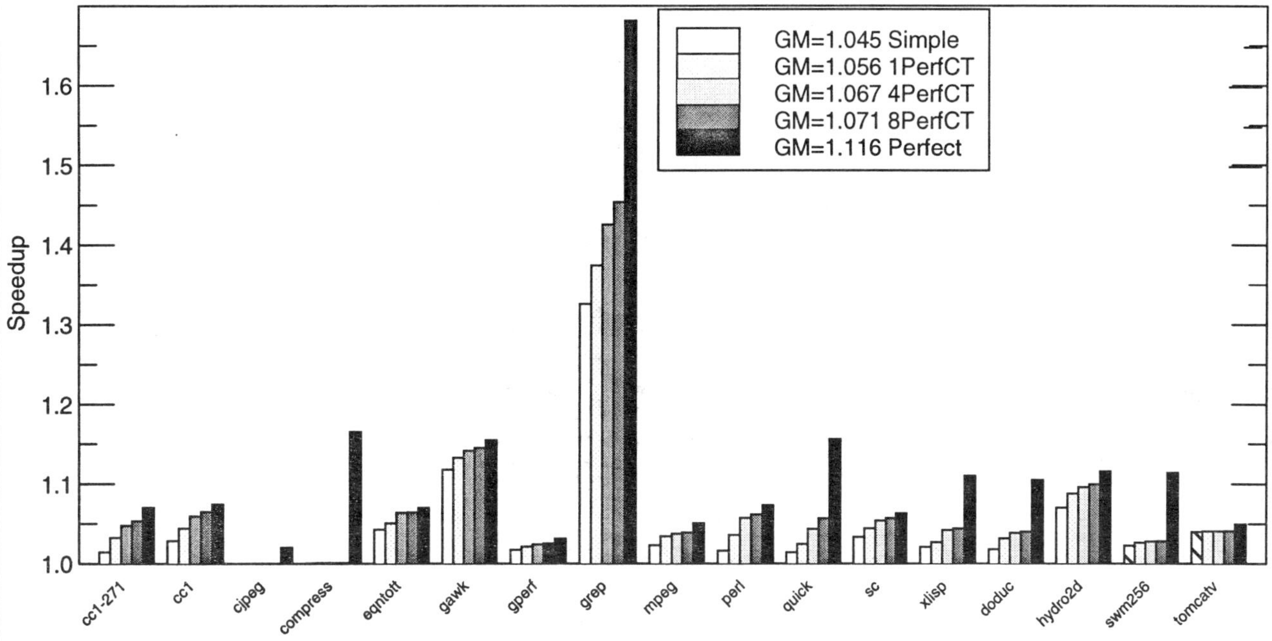

FIGURE 9. 620 Speedups.

tural hazards that might not have occurred otherwise. The penalty occurs only when a dependent instruction has already executed speculatively, but is waiting in its reservation station for one of its predicted inputs to be verified. Since the value comparison takes an extra cycle beyond the pipeline result latency, the dependent instruction will reissue and execute with the correct value one cycle later than it would have had there been no prediction. In addition, the earlier incorrect speculative issue may have caused a structural hazard that prevented other useful instructions from dispatching or executing. In those cases where the dependent instruction has not yet executed (due to structural or other unresolved data dependences), there is no penalty, since the dependent instruction can issue as soon as the actual computed value is available, in parallel with the value comparison that verifies the prediction. In any case, due to the CT which accurately prevents incorrect predictions (see Figure 6), the misprediction penalty does not significantly affect performance.

There can also be a structural hazard penalty even in the case of a correct prediction. Since speculative values are not verified until one cycle after the actual values become available, speculatively issued dependent instructions end up occupying their reservation stations for one cycle longer than they would have had there been no prediction.

6. Experimental Framework

Our experimental framework consists of three main phases: trace generation, VP Unit simulation, and microarchitectural simulation. Traces are collected and generated with the TRIP6000 instruction tracing tool, which is an early version of a software tool developed for the IBM RS/6000 that captures all instruction, value and address references made by the CPU while in user state. Supervisor state references between the initiating system call and the corresponding return to user state are lost. The instruction, address, and value traces are fed to a model of the VP Unit described earlier, which annotates each instruction in the trace with one of three value prediction states: no prediction, incorrect prediction, or correct prediction. The annotated trace is then fed to a cycle-accurate microarchitectural simulator that correctly accounts for the behavior of each type of instruction. All of our microarchitectural models are implemented using the VMW framework [29], which enables significant productivity gains by allowing us to reuse and retarget existing models. The VP Unit model is separated from the microarchitectural models for two reasons: to shift complexity out of the microarchitectural models and thus better distribute our simulations across multiple CPUs; and to conserve trace bandwidth by passing only two bits of state per instruction to the microarchitectural simulator, rather than the full 32/64 bit values being written.

One of the well-known shortcomings of trace-driven simulation is that the non-architected side effects of speculative instructions that never complete are not accurately modeled. For our machine models, these side effects include instruction and data cache perturbation due to speculative fetches and loads as well as perturbation of the branch history table, return address stack, and branch target address cache by speculative branch instructions. Fortunately, the VPT and CT structures are modeled accurately since they are never updated until completion. Our model also properly accounts for all other structural resource contention caused

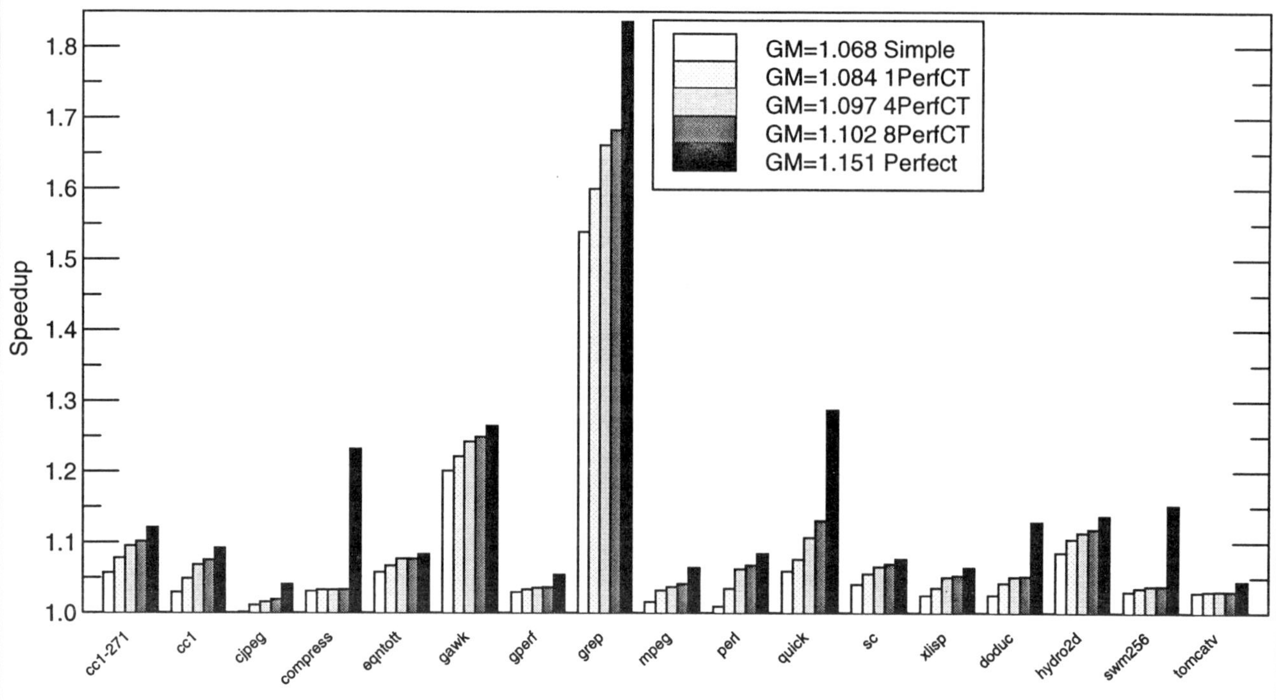

FIGURE 10. 620+ Speedups.

by speculative execution.

TABLE 6. VP Unit Configurations.

Configuration	VPT		CT	
	Entries	History Depth	Entries	Bits/ Entry
Simple	4096	1	1024	2
1PerfCT	4096	1	∞	Perfect
4PerfCT	4096	4/Perfect	∞	Perfect
8PerfCT	4096	8/Perfect	∞	Perfect
Perfect	∞	Perfect	∞	Perfect

7. Experimental Results

We collected performance results for each of the three machine models described in Section 5 (base *620*, enhanced *620+*, and *infinite*) in conjunction with five different VP Unit configurations, which are summarized in Table 6. Attributes that are marked *perfect* in Table 6 indicate behavior that is analogous to *perfect caches*; that is, a mechanism that always produces the right result is assumed. More specifically, in the 1PerfCT, 4PerfCT and 8PerfCT configurations, we assume an *oracle CT* that is able to correctly identify all predictable and unpredictable register writes. Furthermore, in the 4PerfCT and 8PerfCT configurations, we assume a perfect mechanism for choosing which of the 4 (or 8) values stored in the value history is the correct one. Moreover, we assume that the Perfect configuration can always correctly predict a value for every register write. We point out that the only VP Unit configuration that we know how to build today is the *Simple* one, while the other four are merely included to measure the potential contribution of improvements to both VPT and CT prediction accuracy.

7.1. PowerPC 620 Machine Model Speedups

In Figure 9 we show the speedups that the VP Unit configurations of Table 6 obtain over the base PowerPC 620 machine model. The *Simple* configuration achieves an average speedup of 4.5% (geometric mean), the *1PerfCT* configuration improves that to 5.6%, *4PerfCT* to 6.7%, *8PerfCT* to 7.1%, and *Perfect* all the way to 11.6%. Two benchmarks, *gawk* and *grep*, demonstrate outstanding performance gains, even with the imperfect configurations, while the gains for *cjpeg* and *compress* are nonexistent, even with perfect CTs. We attribute the poor showing of *cjpeg* and *compress* to their lack of register value locality (see Figure 2).

Detailed profiling of *grep* and *gawk* revealed that both spend a significant portion of their time in the *bmexec()* and *dfaexec()* routines, which implement string search routines in loops with long dependence chains. For both benchmarks, value prediction is frequently able to break these dependence chains, resulting in significant additional parallelism.

The speedups for several benchmarks (*cc1-271, grep, perl, doduc,* and *hydro2d*) are quite sensitive to CT accuracy (i.e. a perfect CT produces significantly more speedup), indicating a need for a more accurate classification mechanism. In general, however, we are pleased with our results, which show that value prediction is able to produce measur-

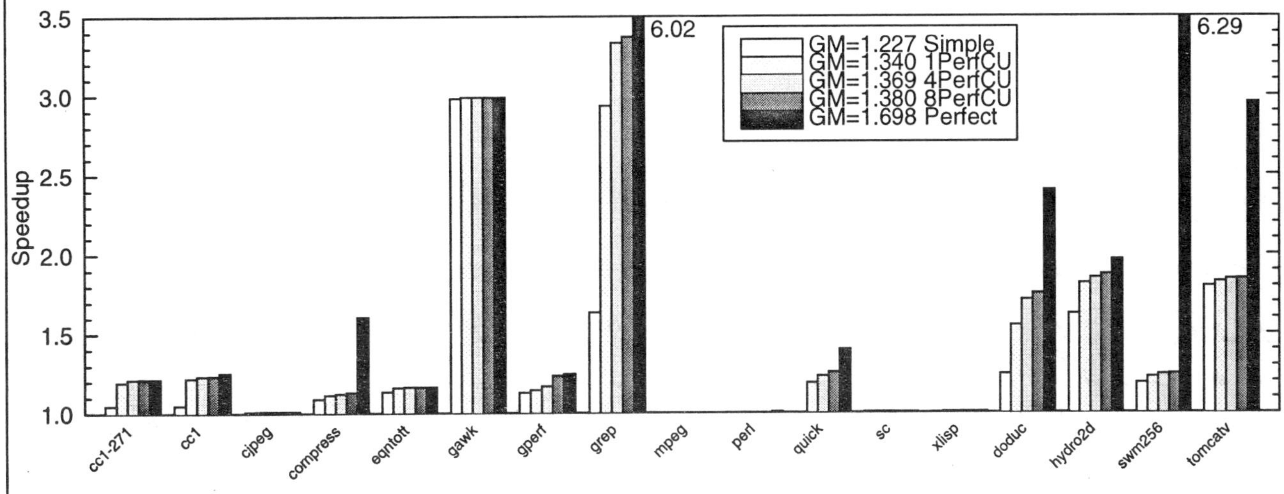

FIGURE 11. Infinite Machine Model Speedups.

able speedups on a current-generation microprocessor design.

7.2. PowerPC 620+ Machine Model Speedups

In Figure 10 we show the value prediction speedups over the baseline 620+ machine model. The *Simple* configuration achieves an average speedup of 6.8% (geometric mean), the *1PerfCT* configuration improves that to 8.4%, *4PerfCT* to 9.7%, *8PerfCT* to 10.2%, and *Perfect* all the way to 15.1%. While the trends are similar to the speedups for the base 620 model, the speedups are higher across the board. We attribute this to the fact that the increased machine parallelism and additional hardware resources provided by this model better match the additional instruction-level parallelism exposed by value prediction. Furthermore, the hardware is better able to tolerate the increase in structural hazards caused by value prediction

Perhaps the most interesting observation about Figure 10 (which applies to Figure 9 as well) is the lack of any obvious correlation to Figure 2, which shows the value locality for each benchmark. This underscores our earlier point that a high hit rate (i.e. high value locality) does not necessarily translate into a proportional reduction in execution cycles. This follows from the fact that benchmarks with high value locality may not necessarily be sensitive to result latency (i.e. they are not data-flow-limited), whereas benchmarks with lower value locality may be very sensitive, and hence may derive significant performance benefits even if only a small fraction of register writes are predictable. For example, *eqntott* has significantly better value locality than *grep*, yet *grep* obtains significantly more speedup from value prediction..

7.3. Infinite Machine Model Speedups

In Figure 11 we show the value prediction speedups over the *Infinite* machine model. The *Simple* configuration achieves an average speedup of 22.7% (geometric mean), the *1PerfCT* configuration improves that to 34.0%, *4PerfCT* to 36.9%, *8PerfCT* to 38.0%, and *Perfect* all the way to 69.8%. These numbers are very encouraging to us, since they demonstrate that the ultimate performance potential of value prediction remains largely untapped by current and even reasonably-extrapolated next generation processors, and that much work remains to be done to find more effective ways to apply it to realistic microarchitectures.

Several benchmarks that displayed measurable speedups with the finite models show negligible speedup with the infinite model (e.g. *mpeg, perl, sc, xlisp*), which leads us to believe that they are not dataflow-limited by nature. However, the fact that they do show speedups with the finite models highlights the fact that value prediction, by removing serialization constraints, allows a processor to more efficiently utilize a limited number of execution resources.

We included the infinite model results to support our assertion that value prediction can be used to exceed the dataflow limit. Our infinite machine model measures a dataflow limit, since, for all practical purposes (ignoring our limit of 4096 active instructions), parallel issue in the *infinite* model is restricted only by the following three factors:

- Branch prediction accuracy
- Fetch bandwidth (single taken branch per cycle)
- Data-flow dependences

Value prediction directly impacts only the last of these, and yet we are able to demonstrate average and peak speedups of 22.7% and 198% (2.98x speedup for *gawk*) using our *Simple* VP Unit configuration. Hence, we lay claim to exceeding the dataflow limit.

8. VP Unit Implementation

An exhaustive design study of VP Unit design parameters and implementation details is beyond the scope of this

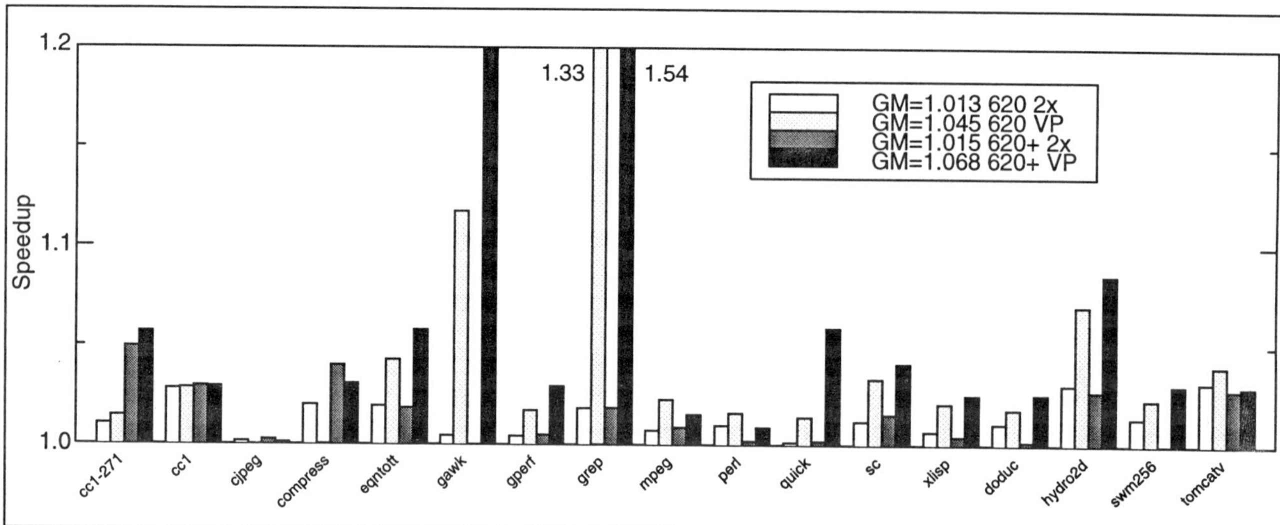

FIGURE 12. Doubling Data Cache vs. VP.

paper. As stated earlier, some preliminary exploration of the design space was conducted by analyzing sensitivity to a few key parameters. We realize that the design selected is by no means optimal, minimal, or even reasonably efficient, and could be improved significantly with some effort. For example, we reserve a full 64 bits per value entry in the VPT, while most instructions generate only 32 or fewer bits, and space in the table could certainly be shared between such entries with some clever engineering.

However, to evaluate the feasibility of implementing a VP Unit in a real-world processor, we compare it against one alternative approach that consumes roughly the same amount of chip space: doubling the first-level data cache to 64K by increasing the line size from 64 bytes to 128 bytes. The results of this comparison, which are shown in Figure 12, make clear that, at least for this benchmark set, value prediction delivers three to four times more speedup than doubling the data cache for both the 620 and 620+ machine models.

Furthermore, the VP Unit has several characteristics that make it attractive to a CPU designer. First of all, since the VPT and CT lookup indices are available very early, at the beginning of the instruction fetch stage, access to these tables can be superpipelined over two or more stages. Hence, given the necessary chip space, even relatively large tables could be built without impacting cycle time. Second, the design adds little or no complexity to critical delay paths in the microarchitecture. Rather, table lookups and verifications are done in parallel with existing activities or are serialized with a separate pipeline stage (value comparison). Hence, it is unlikely that VP would have an adverse effect on processor cycle time, whereas doubling the data cache would quite likely do just that.

9. Conclusions and Future Work

We make four major contributions in this paper. First, we present a taxonomy of speculative execution techniques. Second, we demonstrate that many instructions that write general purpose or floating point registers, when examined on a per-instruction-address basis, exhibit significant amounts of value locality. Third, we describe value prediction, a data-speculative microarchitectural technique for capturing and exploiting value locality to reduce data-flow restrictions on parallel instruction issue. Fourth, we demonstrate that value prediction can be used to exceed the data-flow limit by 23% (geometric mean), as measured on a processor model with no structural hazards. We are very encouraged by our results. We have shown that measurable (5% on average for the 620, 7% on average for the 620+) and in some cases dramatic (up to 33% on the 620 and 54% on the 620+) performance gains are achievable with simple microarchitectural extensions to current-generation and reasonably-extrapolated next-generation microprocessor implementations.

We envision future work proceeding on several different fronts. First of all, we believe that the relatively simple techniques we employed for capturing value locality could be refined and extended to effectively predict a larger share of register values. Those refinements and extensions might include allowing multiple values per static instruction in the prediction table by including branch history bits or other readily available processor state in the lookup index; or moving beyond history-based prediction to computed predictions through techniques like value stride detection. Second, our classification mechanism could also be refined to correctly classify more instructions and extended to control pollution in the value table (e.g. removing instructions that are not latency-critical from the table). Third, significant engineering work is needed to optimize our VP Unit design and reduce its implementation cost and potential impact on processor cycle time. Fourth, the microarchitectural design space should be explored more extensively, since *value prediction* appears to dramatically alter the available program parallelism in ways that may not match current levels of machine parallelism very well. Fifth, feedback-directed compiler support for rescheduling instructions for different latencies based on their value locality may also prove beneficial. Finally, more aggressive approaches to *value prediction* could be investigated (e.g. speculating down multiple paths in the value space, or predicting writes to condition code and other special purpose registers). In short, there is a great deal of interesting future work that is related to value prediction and the exploitation of value locality.

Acknowledgments

This work was supported in part by ONR grant no. N00014-96-1-0928. We also gratefully acknowledge the generosity of the Intel Corporation for donating numerous fast Pentium Pro-based workstations for our use. These systems reduced our simulation turnaround-time by more than an order of magnitude. We also wish to thank the IBM Corporation for letting us use the TRIP6000 instruction tracing tool in our work.

References

[1] A. Aho, R. Sethi, and J. Ullman. *Compilers principles, techniques, and tools*. Addison-Wesley, Reading, MA, 1986.

[2] E. M. Riseman and C. C. Foster. "The inhibition of potential parallelism by conditional jumps." *IEEE Transactions on Computers*, pages 1405–1411, December 1972.

[3] D. W. Wall. "Limits of instruction-level parallelism." In *em Proceedings of the Fourth International Conference on Architectural Support for Programming Languages and Operating Systems*, pages 176–189, Santa Clara, California, 1991.

[4] M. Lam and R. Wilson. "Limits of control flow on parallelism." In *Proceedings of the 19th International Symposium on Computer Architecture*, pages 46–57, 1992.

[5] K. B. Theobald, G. R. Gao, and L. J. Hendren. "On the limits of program parallelism and its smoothability." In *Proceedings of the 25th Annual ACM/IEEE International Symposium on Microarchitecture*, December 1992.

[6] T. Y. Yeh and Y. N. Patt. "Two-level adaptive training branch prediction." In *Proceedings of the 24th Annual International Symposium on Microarchitecture*, pages 51–61, November 1991.

[7] R. P. Colwell and R. Steck. "A 0.6um BiCMOS process with Dynamic Eexecution." In *Proceedings of ISSCC*, 1995.

[8] M. Johnson. *Superscalar Microprocessor Design*. Prentice Hall, Englewood Cliffs, NJ, 1991.

[9] N. P. Jouppi. "Architectural and organizational tradeoffs in the design of the MultiTitan CPU." Technical Report TN-8, DEC-wrl, December 1988.

[10] M. Golden and T. Mudge. "Hardware support for hiding cache latency." Technical report, University of Michigan, 1993.

[11] T. M. Austin and G. S. Sohi. "Zero-cycle loads: Microarchitecture support for reducing load latency." In *Proceedings of the 28th Annual ACM/IEEE International Symposium on Microarchitecture*, pages 82–92, December 1995.

[12] M. Franklin. *The Multiscalar Architecture*. PhD thesis, University of Wisconsin-Madison, 1993.

[13] A. S. Huang, G. Slavenburg, and J. P. Shen. "Speculative disambiguation: A compilation technique for dynamic memory disambiguation." In *Proceedings of the 21st International Symposium on Computer Architecture*, pages 200–210, Chicago, IL, April 1994.

[14] D. M. Gallagher, W. Y. Chen, S. A. Mahlke, J. C. Gyllenhaal, and W. mei W. Hwu. "Dynamic memory disambiguation using the memory conflict buffer." In *Proceedings of the Sixth International Conference on Architectural Support for Programming Languages and Operating Systems*, pages 183–193, San Jose, California, October 4–7, 1994.

[15] D. Levitan, T. Thomas, and P. Tu. "The PowerPC 620 microprocessor: A high performance superscalar RISC processor." *COMPCON 95*, 1995.

[16] S. P. Harbison. *A Computer Architecture for the Dynamic Optimization of High-Level Language Programs*. PhD thesis, Carnegie Mellon University, September 1980.

[17] S. P. Harbison. "An architectural alternative to optimizing compilers." In *em Proceedings of the Symposium on Architectural Support for Programming Languages and Operating Systems*, pages 57–65, Palo Alto, California, 1982.

[18] S. E. Richardson. "Caching function results: Faster arithmetic by avoiding unnecessary computation." Technical report, Sun Microsystems Laboratories, 1992.

[19] M. H. Lipasti, C. B. Wilkerson, and J. P. Shen. "Value locality and load value prediction." In *Proceedings of the Seventh International Conference on Architectural Support for Programming Languages and Operating Systems (ASPLOS-VII)*, October 1996.

[20] J. E. Smith. "A study of branch prediction techniques." In *Proceedings of the 8th Annual Symposium on Computer Architecture*, pages 135–147, June 1981.

[21] W. Y. Chen, S. A. Mahlke, P. P. Chang, and W.-M. Hwu. "Data access microarchitecture for superscalar processors with compiler-assisted data prefetching." In *Proceedings of the 24th International Symposium on Microarchitecture*, 1991.

[22] T.-F. Chen and J.-L. Baer. "A performance study of software and hardware data prefetching schemes." In *21st Annual International Symposium on Computer Architecture*, pages 223–232, 1994.

[23] D. Callahan, K. Kennedy, and A. Porterfield. "Software prefetching." In *Fourth International Conference on Architectural Support for Programming Languages and Operating Systems*, pages 40–52, Santa Clara, April 1991.

[24] T. C. Mowry, M. S. Lam, and A. Gupta. "Design and evaluation of a compiler algorithm for prefetching." In *Fifth International Conference on Architectural Support for Programming Languages and Operating Systems*, pages 62–73, 1992.

[25] M. H. Lipasti, W. J. Schmidt, R. R. Roediger, and S. R. Kunkel. "SPAID: Software prefetching in in pointer- and call-intensive environments." In *Proceedings of the 28th Annual ACM/IEEE International Symposium on Microarchitecture*, 1995.

[26] T. M. Austin, D. N. Pnevmatikatos, and G. S. Sohi. "Streamlining data cache access with fast address calculation." In *Proceedings of the 22nd Annual International Symposium on Computer Architecture*, pages 369–380, Santa Margherita Ligure, Italy, June 22–24, 1995.

[27] SIGPLAN. *Proceedings of the Symposium on Partial Evaluation and Semantics-Based Program Manipulation*, volume 26, Cambridge, MA, September 1991. SIGPLAN Notices.

[28] T. A. Diep, C. Nelson, and J. P. Shen. "Performance evaluation of the PowerPC 620 microarchitecture." In *Proceedings of the 22nd International Symposium on Computer Architecture*, Santa Margherita Ligure, Italy, June 1995.

[29] T. A. Diep and J. P. Shen. "VMW: A visualization-based microarchitecture workbench." *IEEE Computer*, 28(12):57–64, 1995.

The Performance Potential of Data Dependence Speculation & Collapsing

Yiannakis Sazeides
Department of Electrical and Computer Engineering
University of Wisconsin-Madison
1415 Engr. Dr.
Madison, WI 53706
yanos@ece.wisc.edu

Stamatis Vassiliadis
Department of Electrical Engineering
Delft University of Technology
Mekelweg 4, 2628 CD Delft
The Netherlands
stamatis@duteca.et.tudelft.nl

James E. Smith
Department of Electrical and Computer Engineering
University of Wisconsin-Madison
1415 Engr. Dr.
Madison, WI 53706
jes@ece.wisc.edu

Abstract

Two hardware methods for remedying the effects of true data dependences are studied. The first method, dependence speculation, is used to eliminate address generation-load dependences. This is enabled by address prediction that permits load instructions to proceed speculatively without waiting for their address operands. The second technique, dependence collapsing, is used to eliminate data dependences by combining a dependence among multiple instructions into one instruction. The potential of these techniques for improving processor performance is demonstrated via trace-driven simulation. When both techniques are used with maximum issue widths of 4, 8, 16, and 32, the overall speedups in comparison to a base instruction level parallel machine are 1.20, 1.35, 1.51, and 1.66, respectively. In general, dependence collapsing contributes the majority of the improvement in performance. Under the dependence collapsing model, 29% to 47% of the total number of instructions in a trace may be collapsed. The distance separating the collapsed instructions is nearly always less than 8. Our experimentation also suggests that further performance improvements can be achieved by incorporating mechanisms that increase the address prediction rate.

1. Introduction

An execution of a computer program defines a dynamic dataflow or dependence graph, that reflects the true data and control dependences. That is, the dynamic dependence graph contains all the dynamic instructions as nodes, with an arc from one instruction to another if there is a true data or control dependence. If we label an arc with a time equal to the execution time of the instruction producing the result, then, in theory, the minimum execution time of the program is the length of the longest path (i.e. the "critical path") through the dependence graph.

Driving towards the critical path execution time requires discovery of parallelism among instructions. Consequently, many techniques for instruction level parallelism (ILP) are aimed at discovering and executing parallel instructions, both in hardware and software – e.g. multiple reservations stations, issuing multiple instructions out of order, software pipelining, loop unrolling, etc. A different approach is the use of techniques that improve performance by essentially "restructuring" the dependence graph. There are two basic ways hardware can be used to do this:

- The first method effectively removes a dependence arc by predicting the value carrying the dependence and proceeding with speculative execution. If the prediction is correct, then the critical path is decreased – possibly below the theoretical minimum (at least locally). If the prediction is incorrect, then recovery is imperative and the critical path is not decreased; execution time can in fact be increased in a real implementation by using resources needlessly. This technique has been used for branches (control dependences) for some time, but has also been proposed for memory addresses [5] and for data loaded from memory [9].

1072-4451/96 $5.00 © 1996 IEEE

- The second method can reduce the latency by combining a dependence among multiple dependent instructions into a single instruction. Functionality for the collapsing of multiple operations has been advanced in a number of proposals for floating point and fixed point instructions [14, 16, 19].

The performance limit studies published in the literature [1, 3, 6, 7, 20] are primarily based on the assumption that true dependence paths through the dynamic dependence graph place a limit on performance. In addition to theoretical limits under ideal assumptions, limit studies also explore the envelope of practical performance by placing some constraints on hardware execution resources, for example by limiting the "window" of instructions that may simultaneously be considered for parallel execution. Significant performance is achieved with perfect branch prediction, but gains are diminished when using realistic prediction. Furthermore, though predicting branches removes some control dependences, data dependences remain as an impediment for increased performance.

In this work, we investigate the potential performance improvements that can be achieved by the combined use of two hardware approaches that restructure the dynamic dependence graph: data dependence speculation (*d-speculation*) and data dependence collapsing (*d-collapsing*). To illustrate the two approaches, consider the code segment and its dynamic dependence graph shown in Figures 1.a-b. The d-speculation approach can be used to predict the addresses for memory instructions, thus enabling the removal of the arc(s) between dependent address generation and load instruction (in Figure 1.c this results in the removal of the arc between instructions 1 and 2). D-speculation can also be used to predict data values such as those loaded from memory (in Figure 1.d this results in the removal of the arc between instructions 2 and 3) and in general the data result of any instruction. The d-collapsing approach can be used to combine the dependence of multiple instructions. In the above example the dependence between instructions 3 and 4 can be collapsed by executing *4'. [8+Ra+Rd] = Re* instead of *4. [8+Rc] = Re*. The effect on the dependence graph is shown in Figure 1.e. Note that the dependence to instruction 4' comes from node 2 instead of node 3.

It is worthwhile to observe that it is sometimes possible to eliminate nodes in a dynamic dependence graph. For instance, with the collapsing of the dependence between instructions 3 and 4, if the result of instruction 3 is not needed elsewhere then 3 need not be executed. This restructuring is shown in Figure 1.f. Instructions whose execution is necessary to verify a prediction always need to be executed (such as instruction 1 in 1.c).

The remainder of the paper is organized into the following sections. Section 2 reviews related work. In Section 3, we discuss the speculation and collapsing mechanisms

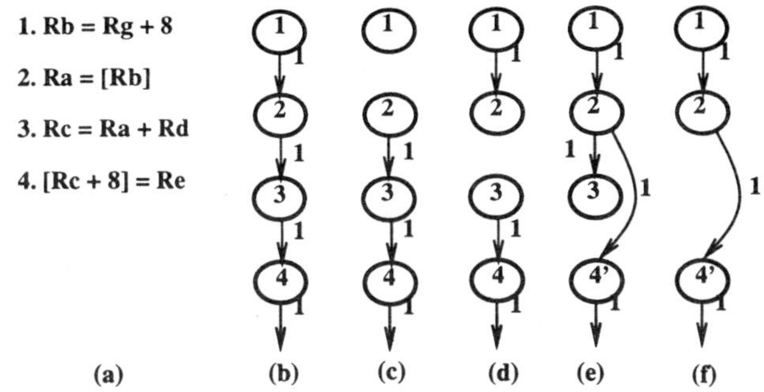

Figure 1. (a) Sample Dynamic Instruction Stream (b) Dynamic Dependence Graph (c) D-Speculation Predict Address (d) D-Speculation Predict Value to be Loaded (e) D-Collapsing (f) Node Elimination

studied in this paper. Section 4 addresses the experimental framework and assumptions. Section 5 contains the discussion of the obtained results. Section 6 will conclude the study.

2. Related Work

Several schemes for reducing the effects of execution and memory dependences have been proposed [2, 5, 9, 19]. These techniques are claimed to have minimal or no impact on the clock cycle. Mechanisms for remedying the effects of memory dependences using early memory loads were introduced in [2, 5]. In [5] the combination of three strategies is proposed. The first identifies data dependences required for address generation that can be resolved immediately. The second is used for the case in which dependences can not be resolved immediately; it predicts the address using a table where memory access patterns are stored. The third strategy removes load operations from the instruction stream in advance (possibly multiple cycles before the actual issue of loads). This approach allows the processor to execute load instructions in parallel with instructions preceding the loads, achieving a zero cycle load execution time when the speculation is found to be correct. Austin [2] exploits the fact that small offsets are suitable for simple fast address calculation and determines memory addresses early in the pipeline for those cases. This enables the load instructions to issue early and effectively hide the load-use latency. A different approach that predicts data values instead of addresses has been proposed in [9] for invariant data values loaded from memory. Numerous other schemes for prefetching data in the memory hierarchy have been proposed – for further references see [4, 12]. Prefetching schemes do not consider the possibility of speculative instruction execution using predicted addresses. The address prediction techniques used for prefetching can be applicable for prediction in d-speculation, however.

Data dependence collapsing functionality has been advanced in a number of proposals. Collapsing for specific instances of floating point operations with new instruction definitions has been proposed and implemented in a number of processors. The multiply-add operation was used in the RS/6000 [14, 16] and since then it has been incorporated in other superscalar pipelined processors [21]. A general scheme capable of collapsing a dependence pair involving fixed point arithmetic and logical instructions was proposed in [19]. The proposed solution takes into account a general CISC instruction set that includes the functionality of RISC and post-RISC based instruction sets. The performance of such a proposal for some realistic machine organizations was reported in [10] and a single cycle implementation of a subset of this proposal was implemented in POWER 2 [21]. A device that includes the majority of the functions a collapsing fixed point unit can perform, was proposed in [17].

Several studies have examined the limits of instruction level parallelism with a variety of control and resource models [1, 3, 6, 7, 20]. However, no limit study has examined the impact of data dependence collapsing and speculation on instruction parallelism. A related work [15] used static program representation and profiling weights to calculate the frequencies of sequences (pairs, triples and quads) of dependent instructions within and across basic blocks. This work however did not examine the impact on latency/parallelism. In [10, 18], performance studies were conducted to characterize the effects of interlock (dependence) collapsing functionality on parallelism for a variety of resource and control models. The dependence collapsing performed in these studies was restricted to collapsing only consecutive instructions within a single basic block.

The models used in the work presented here differentiate from previous studies of data speculation and collapsing in the following ways:

- **D-Speculation:**
  - Load speculation is performed selectively based on a confidence indication.
- **D-Collapsing:**
  - Non-consecutive instructions can be collapsed.
  - Dependence collapsing may be performed across basic block boundaries.
  - Shift operations can be collapsed in addition to fixed point arithmetic and logic operations.
  - Three dependent instructions may be collapsed, in addition to two dependent instructions as in previous work.
  - Zero operands are detected and used to enable further collapsing.
- **Combining speculation and collapsing:**
  - We study the combination and interaction of d-speculation and d-collapsing techniques.

3. Speculation and Collapsing Mechanisms

In this section we provide some information regarding the specific mechanisms as they are modeled in the simulator used to collect the results.

D-Speculation Mechanisms: Data speculation can be used to predict data and address values. In this study one mechanism, called **load-speculation,** is directed at memory dependences. The aim of load-speculation is to reduce the effect of the latency of *load-use* dependences. This is achieved by predicting addresses and speculatively issuing load operations.

A realistic method for address prediction uses a table for maintaining information about strides used for memory accesses. The table we consider is a 4096 entry direct mapped table. The 14 least significant bits of a load instruction address is the index into the table. The algorithm used for prediction and the table entry information is identical to the *two delta strategy* in [5][1]. The delta size in our table is 32 bits. To the previously proposed table, we add a 2 bit saturating counter for each table entry to represent the confidence in issuing a load with a predicted address. The counter in each table entry is initialized to zero and incremented by 1 (decremented by 2) on a correct (wrong) address prediction. The predicted address is used only when the counter value is greater than 1. This means that as long as the counter indicates low confidence in a prediction, predicted addresses are not used for speculative load issue.

A load calculating its address early enough that it does not require a predicted address is called a *ready* load. All loads update the table state but only not ready loads (i.e. loads that take advantage of speculation) use the table. Therefore, a not ready load will either speculatively issue using the predicted address from the table (if the confidence table value is greater than 1) or wait to issue until its address can be calculated (if the confidence table value is less than or equal to 1). Speculatively issued loads can be divided further into two categories: those that were *predicted correctly* and those *predicted incorrectly*. Subsequent instructions that depend on a speculative load can issue as soon as the data are available from the memory without having to wait for the determination of the correct address. When the correct address becomes available and a misprediction

[1] Note that the load speculation mechanism uses a subset of the mechanisms presented in [5].

is detected, only the instructions dependent on the load are affected. In the simulator, these instructions can not issue before the cycle that the load with the correct address completes execution. No restriction on the number of loads that can be load-speculated is imposed. We report the distribution of loads sorted into the four categories: ready, not predicted, predicted correctly, predicted incorrectly.

For the purpose of comparison with an ideal case, we also simulated the case where all load addresses are predicted correctly (*ideal load-speculation*).

D-Collapsing Mechanisms: Computational data dependences are resolved using the d-collapsing approach. The collapsing of data dependences, theoretically, can be applied to any sequence of dependent instructions. In this study we enabled only the collapsing of dependences between pairs and triples of instructions (in some cases as explained below four dependent instructions can also be collapsed). A dependent sequence of instructions can be described by a n-1 (n to 1) dependence expression where n is the number of operands in the expression. For instance in the following sequence:

```
1.  Rb =     Rd << Rh
2.  Rg =     Rb +  Re
3.  Ra =     Rf -  Rg
```

the dependence expression between instructions 1 and 2 is a 3-1:

```
Rg = (Rd << Rh) + Re
```

and the dependence expression between instructions 1, 2 and 3 a 4-1:

```
Ra = Rf - ((Rd << Rh) + Re).
```

As a result of the collapsing assumed in this paper, the above serial sequence is transformed to the following with all dependences eliminated.

```
1.  Rb = Rd << Rh
2.  Rg = (Rd << Rh) + Re
3.  Ra = Rf - ((Rd << Rh) + Re)
```

It should be noted that it is possible for a dependence between two or three instructions to result in a dependence expression greater than 3-1 or 4-1. A dependence between a pair of instructions can result to a 4-1 dependence, for example, if the instructions are Rb = Ra + Rd and Rc = Rb + Rb, then the computation of Rb requires (Ra + Rd) + (Ra + Rd) which is a 4-1 dependence. A dependence between three operations can result in up to an 8-1 dependence expression. In this study we assume the performance of a collapsing devices for 3-1 and 4-1 dependence expressions that involve the following operation types: shift, arithmetic (not multiply or divide), logical, move, address generation (for loads and stores), and condition code generation for branch instructions. This is a relatively optimistic approach intended to explore the envelope of the performance potential.

The assumed mechanisms extend proposed devices [17] with the ability of collapsing shift operations and 4-1 dependence expressions. Shift operations are added in our study because they appear frequently in the instruction mix of programs (about 6%) and shift distances are dominated by a few values. We believe the potential exists for collapsing shifts with ALU operations – at least for the commonly occurring shift distances. We also consider collapsing performed between consecutive and non-consecutive instructions, within and across basic block boundaries. Furthermore, zero operands are detected in loads and stores operations and reduce the size of the dependence expressions. For instance, in the fragment code below, the dependence expression for instruction 4 is a 5-1 which is not collapsible with the assumed functionality. However, the detection of the zero reduces the expression to a collapsible 4-1 expression. In general the detection of zero operands can reduce the expression size and hence the complexity of the device required to resolve a dependence.

```
1.  Rf =     Rg or 0x288
2.  Rh =     Ra -  1
3.  Rd =     Rf >> Rh
4.  Ra =     [Rd + 0]
```

We divide the dependences collapsed in three broad categories: *3-1*, *4-1* and zero operand detection (*0-op*). We report the contribution for each collapsing category as well as the distance between collapsed instructions.

4. Simulation Framework

To measure the impact of data speculation and dependence collapsing on parallelism we developed a trace driven simulator for the SPARC v.8 Architecture [13]. Our test set includes the benchmarks shown in Table 1. The benchmarks 026.compress, 008.espresso, 0.23 eqntott and 022.li are from the SPECINT92 suite and 099.go and 132.ijpeg are from the SPECINT95 suite. The benchmarks were compiled using the gcc version 2.6.3 at -O4 optimization level (go and ijpeg benchmarks compiled at -O3 optimization). The traces were generated by *qpt2* [8] and do not include system code. For those benchmarks longer than 250 million instructions, only the first 250 million instructions of each benchmark trace were simulated due to time constraints. Nop operations were ignored and are not included in the simulations.

Simulation Methodology: Our simulation methodology is similar to that used by Wall[20]. Instructions are fetched and placed in a "window", from which instructions are chosen to issue. The maximum window size is fixed, and in-

Name	Input File	Flags	Trace Size (Millions)
026.compress	in		88
008.espresso	bca.in		250
023.eqntott	int_pri_3.eqn	-s -.ioplte	250
022.li	li-input.lsp (7 queens)		207
099.go		9 9	122
132.ijpeg	vigo.ppm		250

Table 1. Benchmark Characteristics

Name	Conditional Branches (%)	Predicted Correctly (%)
026.compress	13.2	89.7
008.espresso	18.5	94.1
023.eqntott	27.5	96.0
022.li	15.8	96.8
099.go	13.5	83.7
132.ijpeg	8.97	92.8

Table 2. Benchmark Branch Characteristics

structions are placed into the window to replace instructions as they issue – i.e. the window is kept full. The latency of the different operations is 1 cycle with the following exceptions: loads and multiplications require 2 cycles and divides require 12 cycles.

Simulation Parameters: The simulation model contains a number of parameters that characterize important processor characteristics. These parameters include the maximum number of instructions allowed in the scheduling window, the maximum issue width and the types of data speculation and collapsing schemes used. The maximum issue width establishes the maximum attainable instruction level parallelism. For all configurations simulated, conditional branches are predicted using the bimodalN/gshareN+1 scheme proposed in [11] with 8kByte cost. All other branches and jumps (indirect, unconditional, call and return) are assumed to be always predicted correctly. The performance of the predictor is shown in Table 2. We show the percentage of branch instructions in each trace and the percent of the branches that were predicted correctly.

We assume zero cycle penalty for fetching instructions from the path of correctly predicted branches. In the case of misprediction, instructions following a branch can not issue before or during the cycle the branch instruction issues.

All simulated configurations use ideal register renaming and perfect memory disambiguation. No resource limit was set for the different operation types.

Real load-speculation uses the address prediction table described in the previous section. *Ideal* load-speculation is assumed to speculate correctly every load instruction. Load-speculation in the context of memory disambiguation is modeled as follows. With no load-speculation a load can issue as soon as all its dependences are satisfied; a load-speculated load needs to respect all dependences with the exception of address generation dependences. In the case of address misprediction, or no prediction, a load will issue as if no load-speculation is employed. A speculatively issued load instruction may require resources for both speculation and verification. In this study we account for the resources during the verification phase only.

The simulations were conducted for a base and four different data speculation and dependence collapsing configurations. The different configurations simulated are outlined below. The uppercase letter in parentheses will be used to identify the configurations in graphs to follow.

- base, *(A)*,
- base + real load-speculation, *(B)*,
- base + d-collapsing, *(C)*,
- base + d-collapsing + real load-speculation *(D)*
- base + d-collapsing + ideal load-speculation *(E)*

For each of the above configurations simulations were performed for instruction issue widths of 4, 8, 16, 32 and 2048 (2k). In each case the window size was set to twice the issue width.

5. Simulation Results

This section contains results of our performance simulations. We present results both in terms of instructions per cycle (IPC) and speedup versus the base superscalar machine. The speedups are with respect to the base configuration with same issue width. For both measures, we summarize results by taking the harmonic mean over the benchmark set.

5.1. Overall Performance

For the five machine configurations studied (A through E), Figures 2 and 3 show the harmonic mean instructions per cycle and speedups versus the base machine. Results for maximum issue widths 4, 8, 16, 32, and 2K per cycle are plotted. The results suggest the following:

- The maximum potential of d-speculation and d-collapsing (point E) is quite high, with speedups from 1.25 (issue width 4) to 2.95 (issue width 2K). Note that these are compared with base superscalar implementations that are quite optimistic – with the major (non-ideal) limitation being realistic branch prediction.
- If a realistic load-speculation mechanism is used with d-collapsing (point D), speedups are still significant (1.2–1.9).

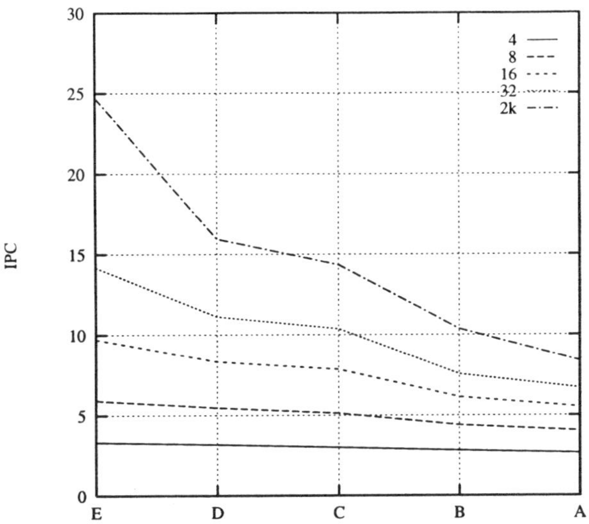

Figure 2. IPC for the Different Configurations and Issue Widths

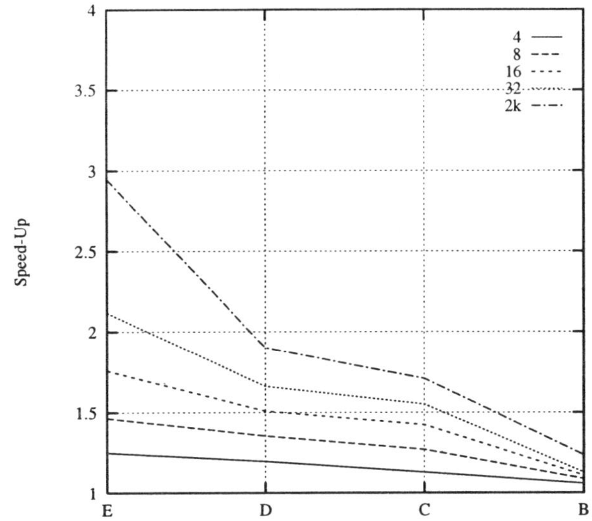

Figure 3. SpeedUp over the Superscalar Base Machine (A)

- The combined use of d-collapsing and d-speculation provide speedups roughly equal to the sum of the individual speedups of d-collapsing and d-speculation (compare point D and the sum of points B and C in Figure 3).

Although the use of realistic load-speculation and d-collapsing provide significant speedup, as pointed out above, there is also significant performance drop when going from ideal load-speculation (i.e. always load speculate correctly) to the realistic stride-based load-speculation mechanism. In fact, when using realistic load-speculation, it is apparent that d-collapsing provides the biggest portion of the performance gain. This leads us to study load-speculation in more detail to determine means of capturing more of the ideal performance.

5.2. The effect of pointers on load-speculation performance

Given that the load-speculation mechanism is based on detecting strides, we decided it would be useful to divide the benchmarks into two categories, namely *pointer chasing* benchmarks and *non pointer chasing* benchmarks – under the assumption that the stride-based load-speculation mechanism would be relatively ineffective for the pointer chasing benchmarks. A program was classified as pointer chasing if a large fraction of its loads are indirect. We categorized the benchmarks by profiling and inspection of code. The pointer chasing benchmark set consists of the benchmarks go and li and the other set contains the remaining benchmarks. Figures 4 - 7 report the overall IPC and speedups for the two sets.

The following can be observed regarding pointer chasing benchmarks (Figures 4 and 5):

- With ideal load-speculation (point E), the speedup is about the same as when all the benchmarks are considered. However, the performance drop with realistic load-speculation is more pronounced than in the complete set of benchmarks.
- Furthermore, for issue widths 4, 8, 16 and 32, realistic load-speculation has a very small performance effect (speedups of 5%-9%, see B in Figure 5).
- The d-collapsing gains are smaller as compared to the means for all benchmarks (points C in Figures 3 and 5). This can be attributed to the instruction mix of those benchmarks that consist of non-collapsible instructions (for 022.li, 7% of the instructions are calls and returns) and higher branch misprediction rates (go has branch prediction rate of 83.6%).

The most important observation regarding realistic load-speculation for pointer chasing benchmarks is that by itself (with no d-collapsing) it provides negligible performance gains. This is understandable because the load-speculation mechanism is based on stride prediction, and it does not perform well with pointer-based codes. Special load units for pointer-based codes have been proposed [12], however, there is no scheme known to us that combines load-speculation mechanisms for both pointer chasing and non pointer chasing codes. It is of interest, therefore, as a future research topic to investigate load-speculation mecha-

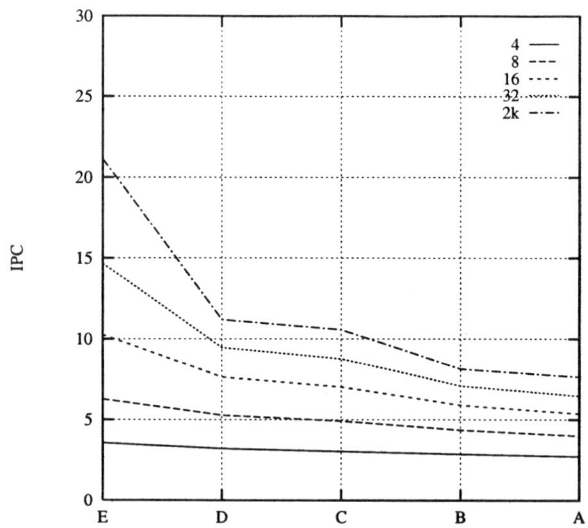

Figure 4. IPC for the "Pointer Chasing" Benchmarks

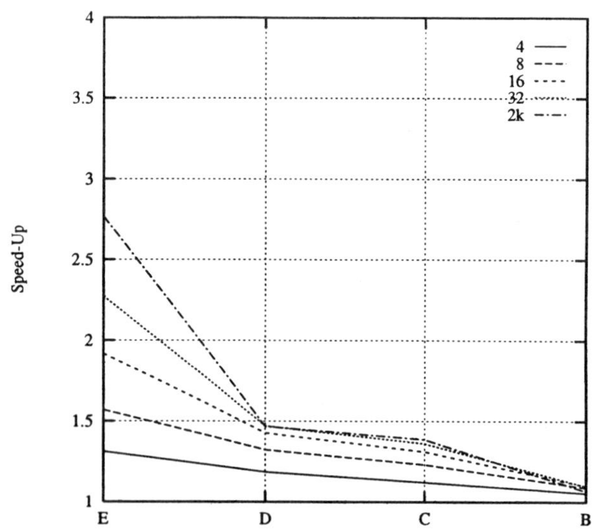

Figure 5. SpeedUp over the Superscalar Base Machine (A) for the "Pointer Chasing" Benchmarks

nisms that can provide satisfactory performance for both non-pointer and pointer chasing benchmarks.

To better understand the issues caused by pointer chasing we investigated in more detail the performance of the load-speculation mechanism we used. Table 3 suggests the following.

- For pointer chasing benchmarks, the success rate of address prediction is low (12.4-26.7%).
- Low prediction rate is mainly because a very large percentage of loads (around 38-44%) are not predicted at all – they simply do not demonstrate stride behavior.
- On the positive side, the percentage of incorrect predictions is very small implying that the counter scheme can capture the predictability of loads. Possible variations are currently being explored to determine even more accurate confidence measurements.

Issue Width	Ready (%)	Predicted Correctly (%)	Predicted Incorrectly (%)	Not Predicted (%)
4	30.16	26.73	4.76	38.34
8	35.94	20.87	5.16	38.02
16	39.79	15.13	5.13	39.95
32	40.29	12.42	5.35	41.94
2k	36.20	14.90	5.41	43.50

Table 3. Load-Speculation Behavior for Pointer Chasing Benchmarks with Configuration D

The increase in the number of ready (non-speculated) loads, with increasing window size (Table 3), is attributed to a corresponding increase of collapsed instructions.

Turning to the benchmarks that do not rely on pointer chasing, we have plotted the expected IPC and speedups over the base superscalar machine in Figures 6 and 7. The following can be observed:

- The overall speedups are higher when using realistic load-speculation than for the entire mix of benchmarks.
- Collapsing with realistic load-speculation (point D in Figure 7 for windows of 4, 8, 16 and 32) speedups between 1.23–1.8 are reached.
- The difference between speedups with ideal and realistic load-speculation is smaller when compared with the pointer chasing programs.
- The major contribution is still due to d-collapsing, but a significant contribution is made by load-speculation.

Table 4 is the counterpart of Table 3 for the non pointer chasing benchmarks. The behavior of the loads in Table 4 in comparison to the behavior of the loads for pointer chasing benchmarks (Table 3) indicates a significant reduction in the number of mispredicted loads and similar reduction of the number of not predicted loads. A significant number of loads remain not predicted, nevertheless. These results suggest that even the stride-based load-speculation method can be improved. We intend to investigate such approaches as part of our continuing research.

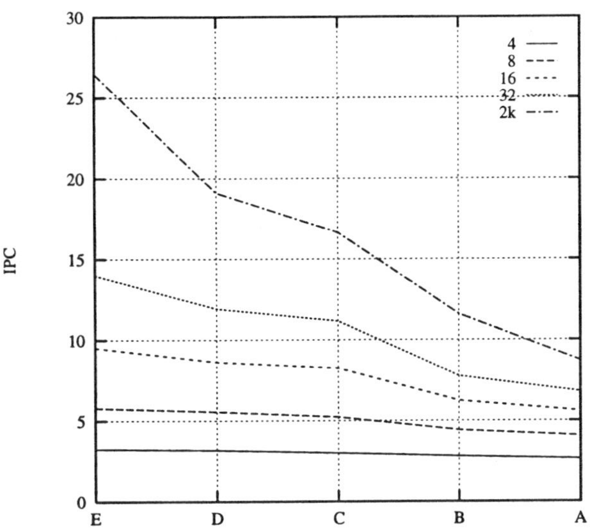

Figure 6. IPC for the non "Pointer Chasing" Benchmarks

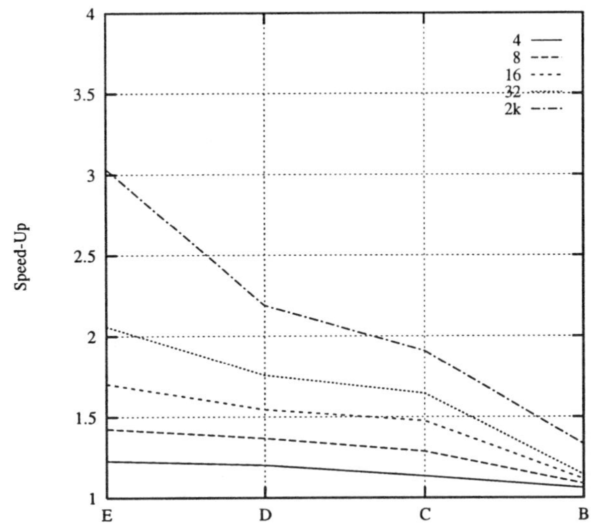

Figure 7. SpeedUp over the Superscalar Base Machine (A) for non "Pointer Chasing" Benchmarks

Issue Width	Ready (%)	Predicted Correctly (%)	Predicted Incorrectly (%)	Not Predicted (%)
4	20.67	56.95	2.17	20.21
8	39.23	39.99	1.91	18.87
16	49.94	28.16	1.97	19.93
32	47.80	30.13	1.96	20.11
2k	38.13	39.85	2.02	20.00

Table 4. Load-Speculation Behavior for non-Chasing Pointer for Configuration D

5.3. A Closer Look at D-Collapsing

As indicated earlier, d-collapsing plays an important role in the speedup gains over a base superscalar machine. To analyze in more depth the various contributions and behavior of such mechanisms we plot in Figures 8 - 10: the percentage of instructions that have been collapsed in all benchmarks, the contribution of the 3-1, 4-1, and 0 operand detection, and distance between collapsed instructions. The following conclusions are suggested by the figures.

- A large percentage of the instructions are collapsed (from 29-47% with increasing issue width - Figure 8).
- The biggest collapsing contributor is the 3-1 (Figure 9). For example, with issue windows equal to or less than 32 instructions, 3-1 collapsing accounts for 65-82% of the d-collapsing instructions.
- 4-1 collapsing mechanisms account for 13-30% of the collapsed instructions. This indicates that 4-1 collapsing may hold important performance benefits and the design of such units may need to be considered. However, doing this without adding latency will be a major issue. The results also suggests that collapsing greater than 4-1 dependences may offer very little performance benefit.
- The zero value operand detection has a contribution of 5–10%. If the implementation of such a mechanism is not expensive it could offer some performance improvements.
- An interesting statistic is the distance among the instructions that are collapsed (Figure 10). For issue widths larger than 8 instructions the majority of the collapsed instructions are not consecutive. This suggests that a wide-issue implementation will need to consider non-consecutive instruction collapsing in order to exploit the available performance gains. We also observe most of the instructions collapsed have a distance of less than 8 instructions even for the 2k issue width. This indicates that we may not need to implement across basic blocks since the average basic block size is expected to be around 6 - 8 instructions. The performance pay off versus the complexity of collapsing across basic blocks is currently being investigated.

In Tables 5 and 6 we show the average for the most frequently collapsed 3-1 and 4-1 dependence sequences for the D configuration. The following encodings are used in Tables 5 and 6, the instruction types are ar: arithmetic, lg: logic, sh: shift, mv: move, ld: load, st: store, brc: conditional branch; the source operand types are r: register, i: imme-

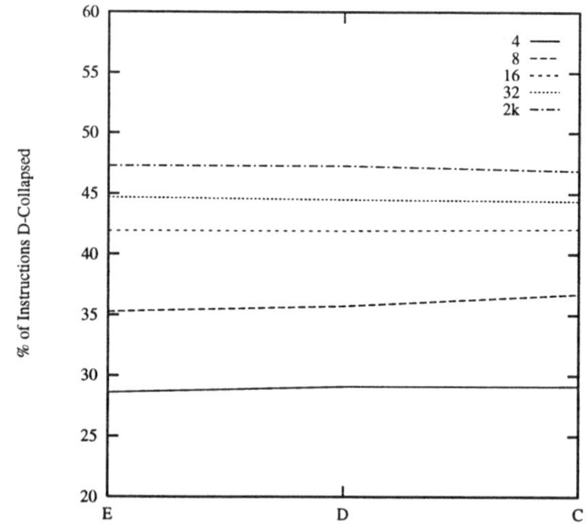

Figure 8. Instructions D-Collapsed

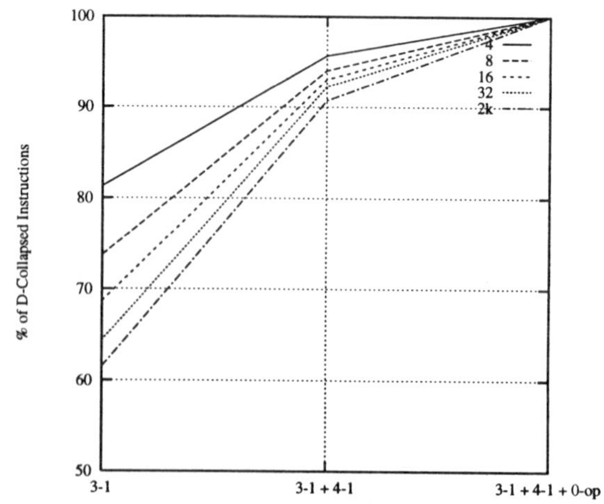

Figure 9. Contribution of the three Collapsing Mechanisms for the D Configuration

diate, 0: zero immediate or zero register. For example, the collapsing of Rb = Rd + Rh and Rg = Rb + 8 to Rg = Rd + Rh + 8, corresponds to an arrr – arri collapsed pair. The average for each 3-1(4-1) dependence sequence is the sum of all such collapsed dependences over the total number of 3-1(4-1) collapsed dependences in all benchmarks.

6. Conclusions

In this paper we considered two hardware based schemes that enable the elimination of true data dependences: **d-speculation** and **d-collapsing**. The separate and combined use of the mechanisms that implement the different schemes was investigated. Trace driven simulation was the means used for demonstrating the potential of these methods. Several experiments were conducted for a number of machine configurations and issue widths.

The results show consistently that a substantial increase in performance is possible by using d-collapsing and realistic load-speculation (configuration D). We observed that d-collapsing is responsible for the majority of the gains though d-speculation still provides significant gains for non-pointer chasing programs. It is also established that there are large benefits to be gained if the load-speculation scheme is improved.

With regard to the behavior of d-collapsing, a large fraction of instructions, 29% to 47%, can potentially be collapsed. The number of collapsed instructions increases as windows grow larger. The distance between collapsed instructions increase marginally even for larger windows, but is usually less than 8.

Overall, the results are quite promising and suggest that data dependence speculation and collapsing can potentially have a significant impact on performance. This study reveals interesting information about the behavior of dependences that can be of value during the implementation of data speculating and collapsing mechanisms. Further research is currently undertaken in several directions that include: development of mechanisms to support data dependence speculation and collapsing, determination of ways to use compilers to increase ILP under this paradigm, and additional performance studies for more realistic environments.

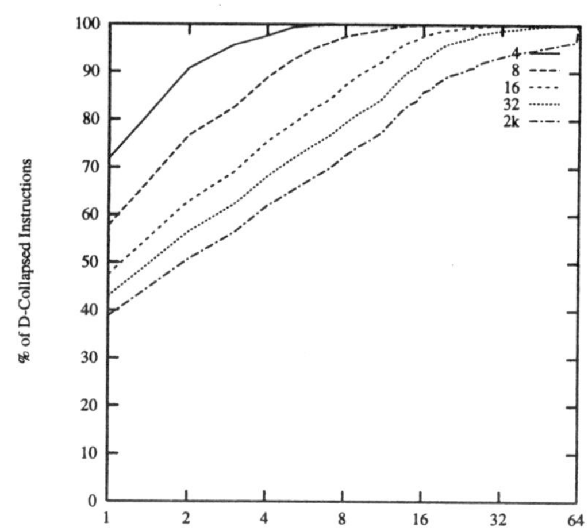

Figure 10. Distance between D-Collapsed Instructions for the D Configuration

7. Acknowledgements

This work was supported in part by NSF Grants MIP-9505853 and MIP-9307830 and by the U.S. Army Intelligence Center and Fort Huachuca under Contract DABT63-

Operation Types		Issue Width				
Op1	Op2	2k	32	16	8	4
arrr	brc	12.68	12.67	12.25	13.62	17.08
arri	brc	12.37	12.72	12.87	14.00	15.71
arri	arri	8.04	7.12	7.01	3.35	1.75
arr0	brc	7.13	7.47	7.76	8.95	10.05
shri	ldrr	5.07	5.42	5.43	5.31	5.75
mvi	lgri	4.99	4.81	4.62	4.34	3.96
mvi	ldri	4.87	4.88	4.80	4.77	4.07
arrr	arrr	4.43	3.80	3.78	4.10	3.31
arri	ldrr	3.16	3.54	4.66	3.31	1.56
shri	arrr	3.01	3.90	3.94	4.54	4.07
arrr	shri	2.77	2.38	2.24	2.46	3.32
arri	arrr	2.02	2.37	3.56	4.81	4.38

Table 5. Collapsed 3-1 Dependences

Operation Types			Issue Width				
Op1	Op2	Op3	2k	32	16	8	4
arri	arri	arri	17.97	14.55	7.27	0.46	0.00
lgr0	lgr0	arrr	6.59	6.52	8.32	10.89	0.50
arri	arri	ldrr	6.19	7.25	4.38	0.02	0.00
arrr	arrr	arrr	5.97	6.05	5.56	4.09	2.38
arrr	shri	arrr	4.84	4.73	5.86	7.83	13.70
arri	arri	arrr	4.16	4.57	3.88	0.08	0.02
lgri	shri	ldrr	3.37	4.12	5.25	7.80	7.72
arrr	arrr	shri	3.15	2.76	3.68	4.33	5.63
shri	arrr	shri	2.88	4.39	5.66	8.28	12.17
lgrr	lgrr	lgrr	2.51	2.87	3.28	3.13	3.20
shri	arrr	ldrr	2.22	2.50	0.82	0.76	0.15
shri	arrr	ldri	2.16	2.49	3.17	4.47	5.57
shri	arrr	arrr	1.72	3.04	5.41	8.00	12.55

Table 6. Collapsed 4-1 Dependences

95-C-0127 and ARPA order no. D346. The views and conclusions contained herein are those of the authors and should not be interpreted as necessarily representing the official policies or endorsements, either expressed or implied, of the U. S. Army Intelligence Center and Fort Huachuca, or the U.S. Government.

The authors would like to thank Rajiv Jain and Andreas Moshovos for their helpful suggestions and constructive critique while this work was in progress.

References

[1] T. M. Austin and G. S. Sohi. Dynamic dependency analysis of ordinary programs. In *Proceedings of the 19th International Symposium on Computer Architecture*, pages 342–351, May 1992.

[2] T. M. Austin and G. S. Sohi. Zero-cycle loads: Microarchitecture support for reducing load latency. In *Proceedings of the 28th Annual ACM/IEEE International Symposium and Workshop on Microarchitecture*, pages 82–92, June 1995.

[3] M. Butler, T.-Y. Yeh, Y. N. Patt, M. Alsup, H. Scales, and M. Shebanow. Single instruction stream parallelism is greater than two. In *Proceedings of the 18th International Symposium on Computer Architecture*, May 1991.

[4] T. F. Chen and J. L. Baer. Effective hardware-based data prefetching for high performance processors. *IEEE Transactions on Computers*, 44(5):609–623, May 1995.

[5] R. J. Eickemeyer and S. Vassiliadis. A load instruction unit for pipelined processors. *IBM Journal of Research and Development*, 37(4):547–564, July 1993.

[6] N. P. Jouppi and D. Wall. Available instruction-level parallelism for superscalar and superpipelined machines. In *Proceedings of the 3rd International Conference on Architectural Support for Programming Languages and Operating Systems*, April 1989.

[7] M. S. Lam and R. P. Wilson. Limits of control flow on parallelism. In *Proceedings of the 19th International Symposium on Computer Architecture*, pages 46–57, May 1992.

[8] J. R. Larus. Efficient program tracing. *IEEE Computer*, 26(5):52–61, May 1993.

[9] M. H. Lipasti, C. B. Wilkerson, and J. P. Shen. Value locality and data speculation. In *Proceedings of the 7th International Conference on Architectural Support for Programming Languages and Operating Systems*, October 1996.

[10] N. Malik, R. J. Eickemeyer, and S. Vassiliadis. Interlock collapsing alu for increased instruction-level parallelism. In *Proceedings of the 25th Annual ACM/IEEE International Symposium and Workshop on Microarchitecture*, September 1992.

[11] S. McFarling. Combining branch predictors. In *DEC WRL TN-36*, June 1993.

[12] S. Mehrotra and L. Harrison. Examination of a memory access classification scheme for pointer intensive and numeric programs. In *Proceedings of the 10th International Conference on Supercomputing*, May 1996.

[13] S. MICROSYSTEMS. *The SPARC Architecture Manual.* Prentice Hall, 1992.

[14] R. K. Montoye, E. Hokenek, and S. L. Runyon. Design of the ibm risc system/6000 floating-point execution unit. *IBM Journal of Research and Development*, 34(1):59–70, January 1990.

[15] A. Moshovos. Increasing instruction level parallelism through instruction coallescing. *private communication*, 1995.

[16] R. R. Oehler and R. D. Groves. Ibm risc system/6000 processor architecture. *IBM Journal of Research and Development*, 34(1):23–36, January 1990.

[17] J. Phillips and S. Vassiliadis. High performance 3-1 interlock collapsing alu's. *IEEE Transactions on Computers*, 43(3):257–268, March 1994.

[18] S. Vassiliadis, B. Blaner, and R. J. Eickemeyer. Scism: A scalable compound instruction set machine architecture. *IBM Journal of Research and Development*, 38(1):59–78, January 1994.

[19] S. Vassiliadis, J. Phillips, and B. Blanner. Interlock collapsing alu's. *IEEE Transactions on Computers*, 42(7):825–839, July 1993.

[20] D. W. Wall. Limits of instruction level parallelism. In *Proceedings of the 4th International Conference on Architectural Support for Programming Languages and Operating Systems*, pages 176–188, April 1991.

[21] S. Weiss and J. E. Smith. *Inside IBM Power and PowerPC.* Morgan Kaufmann Publishers Inc., San Mateo, CA, 1994.

Session 8

Heuristics for Register-constrained Software Pipelining *

Josep Llosa, Mateo Valero and Eduard Ayguadé

Departament d'Arquitectura de Computadors
Universitat Politècnica de Catalunya
Campus Nord, Mòdul D6, Gran Capità s/n
08071, Barcelona, SPAIN
{josepll,mateo,eduard}@ac.upc.es

Abstract

Software Pipelining is a loop scheduling technique that extracts parallelism from loops by overlapping the execution of several consecutive iterations. There has been a significant effort to produce throughput-optimal schedules under resource constraints, and more recently to produce throughput-optimal schedules with minimum register requirements. Unfortunately even a throughput-optimal schedule with minimum register requirements is useless if it requires more registers than those available in the target machine.

This paper evaluates several techniques for producing register-constrained modulo schedules: increasing the initiation interval (II) and adding spill code. We show that, in general, increasing the II performs poorly and might not converge for some loops. The paper also presents an iterative spilling mechanism that can be applied to any software pipelining technique and proposes several heuristics in order to speed-up the scheduling process.

1. Introduction

Software pipelining [10] is an instruction scheduling technique that exploits the ILP of loops by overlapping the execution of successive iterations of a loop. There are different approaches to generate a software pipelined schedule for a loop [1]. Modulo scheduling is a class of software pipelining algorithms that rely on generating a schedule for an iteration of the loop such that when this same schedule is repeated at regular intervals, no dependence is violated and no resource usage conflict arises. Modulo scheduling was proposed at the beginning of the 80s [25]. Since then, many research papers have appeared on the topic [19, 18, 17, 29, 27, 31, 22], and it has also been incorporated into some production compilers (e.g. [24, 12]).

Exploiting more ILP results in a significant increase in the register pressure [23, 21]. The register requirements of a schedule are of extreme importance for compilers since any valid schedule must fit in the available number of registers of the target machine. Some practical modulo scheduling approaches use heuristics to produce near-optimal schedules with reduced register requirements [17, 22]. Other approaches try to reduce the register requirements of the schedules by applying a post-pass process [13, 28]. However, even a throughput-optimal schedule with minimum register requirements is useless if it requires more registers than the target machine has. In addition, as shown in [21], loops with high register requirements represent a significant amount of the execution time of the programs. When there is a limited number of registers and the register allocator fails to find a solution with the number of registers available, some additional action must be taken. Different alternatives to fit the register requirements of a modulo scheduled loop in the available number of registers were outlined in [26].

One of the options, used by the Cydra 5 compiler [12], is to reschedule the loop with an increased *II*. If, after several trials, the compiler is unable to find a valid schedule requiring less registers than available, the compiler schedules the loop using local scheduling techniques, i.e. without performing modulo scheduling. Rescheduling the loop with a bigger initiation interval (see Figure 1a) usually leads to schedules with less iteration overlapping, and therefore with less register requirements. Unfortunately, the register reduction is at

*This work has been supported by the Ministry of Education of Spain under contract TIC 429/95, and by CEPBA (European Center for Parallelism of Barcelona).

1072-4451/96 $5.00 © 1996 IEEE

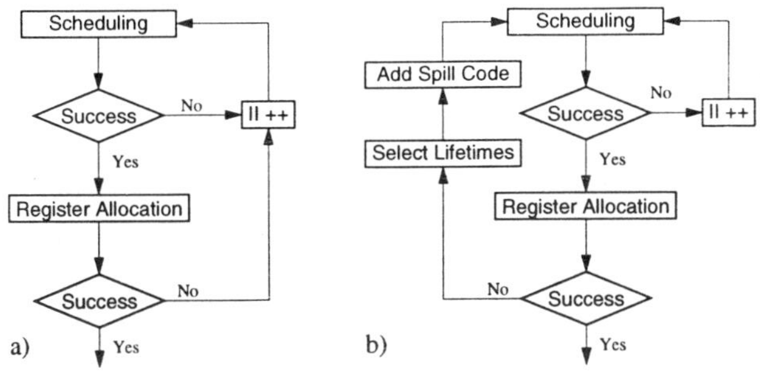

Figure 1. Flow diagram of the scheduling process with register reduction by: a) Increasing the II. b) Adding spill code.

the expense of a reduction in performance (less parallelism is exploited).

Another option is to spill some variables to memory, so that they don't waste registers for a certain number of cycles. For acyclic schedules, graph coloring [9] has been widely used to perform register allocation and adding spill code. Most subsequent research in the field of register allocation and spilling has mainly focused on improving heuristics for graph coloring [4, 6, 8, 7]. However, software pipelining has some constraints that hinder the use of traditional techniques for register allocation and spilling. For instance, lifetimes may cross the boundary of iterations and even can be longer than the II, interfering with themselves (in next iterations). Finally, modulo schedules are very compact —the goal is to saturate the most used resource— which complicates the addition of spill load/store operations without affecting the whole schedule.

Cyclic interval graphs [16] can deal with lifetimes that cross loop boundaries. Other register allocation heuristics have been proposed [26, 14], that deal with lifetimes larger than the II (in the presence of hardware support). However, none of these works deal with the addition of spill code (and its scheduling) for software pipelined loops. Software pipelining and spill code has been first considered (to the best of our knowledge) in [30], where spill load/store operations are added before scheduling the loop if, and only if, doing so does not increases the initiation interval.

In this paper, we treat the scheduling problem in a more general framework: generate modulo schedules with register constraints (as well as resource constraints). The above outlined alternatives (increasing the II and adding spill code) to schedule a loop with a limited number of registers are considered.

We show that increasing the II produces, in general, worse schedules (in terms of II) than adding spill code. In addition, we show that increasing the II might not converge to a solution (i.e. find a schedule requiring less than the available registers) for some loops. Also, it turns out that these loops represent a significant part of the execution time.

We propose an iterative algorithm for adding spill code to modulo schedules (see Figure 1b). If a loop requires more registers than available, we add spill code and reschedule the loop until a schedule requiring no more registers than available is found. Rescheduling is necessary, since the added load/stores might not fit in the schedule. The spilling method we propose, uses several heuristics in order to be a general method useful for any software pipelining mechanism (including methods that do not care about register requirements). In addition we also propose several heuristics to accelerate the iterative algorithm, so that the computational time required to produce the (register and resource constrained) schedules is small.

To evaluate the proposals of this paper, we use a register sensitive scheduling technique (HRMS [22]) as the core scheduler. In any case the techniques presented can also be used with other scheduling techniques. The evaluation has been performed using more than one thousand loops from the Perfect Club [5].

In Section 2 we make a brief overview of modulo scheduling, register allocation for modulo scheduling, and divide the lifetimes into two components that behave differently. Then we present the two approaches for register-constrained software pipelining: increase the II (Section 3) and add spill code (Section 4) introducing several heuristics for selecting the variables to spill, to schedule the spill operations and to accelerate the whole process. In Section 5 the different alternatives and heuristics are evaluated in terms of performance of the loops and scheduling time. Finally Section 6 states our conclusions.

2. Modulo Scheduling

2.1. Definitions

A loop is represented by a *dependence graph* $G = DG(V, E, \delta)$ where:

- V is the set of vertices of the graph G. A vertex (node) $v \in V$ represents an operation of the loop body.
- E is the dependence edge set. An edge $e = (u, v) \in E$ represents a dependence between two operations u, v.
- δ is a mapping $\delta : E \mapsto N$ that represents the *dependence distance* or *dependence weight*.

There is a dependence of distance δ_e associated to each edge $e = (u, v) \in E$ if the execution of operation v at iteration $i + \delta_e$ depends on the execution of operation u at iteration i.

The dependences can be of several types.

- *Control* dependences indicate that the target operation is executed (or not) depending on the outcome of the source operation.

- *Data dependences* between operations indicate accesses to the same storage location. For the purposes of this work, they have been further divided into *memory* ($MemE \subseteq E$) and *register* ($RegE \subseteq E$) data dependences. *Memory* data dependences are caused by accesses to the same memory location. *Register* data dependences are caused by accesses to the same registers. Since register allocation is performed after scheduling, only flow register data dependences are considered.

2.2. Overview of Modulo Scheduling

In a software pipelined loop, the schedule for an iteration is divided into stages so that the execution of consecutive iterations that are in distinct stages is overlapped. The number of stages in one iteration is termed **stage count**(*SC*). The number of cycles per stage is the initiation interval (*II*).

The execution of a loop can be divided into three phases: a ramp up phase that fills the software pipeline, a steady state phase where the software pipeline achieves maximum overlap of iterations, and a ramp down phase that drains the software pipeline. During the steady state phase of the execution, the same pattern of operations is executed in each stage. This is achieved by iterating on a piece of code, termed the **kernel**, that corresponds to one stage of the steady state phase.

The initiation interval *II* between two successive iterations is bounded either by loop-carried dependences in the graph (*RecMII*) or by resource constraints of the architecture (*ResMII*). This lower bound on the *II* is termed the **Minimum Initiation Interval** (*MII*= max (*RecMII*, *ResMII*)). The reader is referred to [12, 27] for an extensive dissertation on how to calculate *ResMII* and *RecMII*.

As an example consider the loop body of Figure 2a, whose optimized data dependence graph is shown in Figure 2b. For simplicity we assume (in this example) that all operations have a latency of two cycles, there are 4 general purpose functional units, and that each operation is fully pipelined and executes in one functional unit. Figure 2c shows a schedule for an iteration

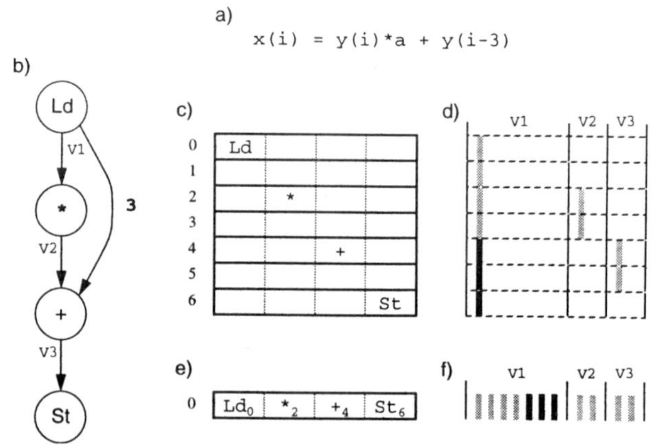

Figure 2. Example loop: a) Fortran code of the loop body. b) Optimized data dependence graph. c) Schedule of the loop. d) Lifetimes of one iteration. e) Kernel code. f) Register requirements (the shaded part is the scheduling component of the lifetimes).

with an initiation interval $II = 1$. In this case, the schedule is constrained only by resources (since it has no recurrences). We can initiate an iteration every cycle, since the loop requires 4 resources per iteration, and we have 4 available resources. Figure 2e shows the kernel code of the loop. In the kernel code, subindex of operations indicate the stage they belong to in the schedule of a single iteration of the original loop.

2.3. Register Requirements

Values used in a loop correspond either to loop-invariant variables or to loop-variant variables. Loop-invariants are repeatedly used but never defined during loop execution. Loop-invariants, have a single value for all the iterations of the loop and therefore they require one register each regardless of the scheduling and the machine configuration.

For loop-variants, a value is generated in each iteration of the loop and, therefore, there is a different value corresponding to each iteration. Because of the nature of software pipelining, lifetimes of values defined in an iteration can overlap with lifetimes of values defined in subsequent iterations. Figure 2d shows the lifetimes for the loop-variants corresponding to every iteration of the example loop. Lifetimes of loop-variants can be measured in different ways depending on the execution model of the machine. We assume (either in the examples and in the experiments) that a variable is alive from the beginning of the producer operation, until the start of the last consumer operation.

By overlapping the lifetimes of the different iterations, a pattern of length *II* cycles that is indefinitely repeated is obtained. This pattern (Figure 2f) indicates the number of values that are live at any given cycle (11 in this example).

As it is shown in [26], the maximum number of simultaneously live values (*MaxLive*) is an accurate approximation of the number of registers required by the schedule [1]. In all the examples of this paper, the register requirements of a given schedule are approximated by *MaxLive*, for simplicity. However, in Section 5 we measure the actual register requirements after register allocation.

Values with a lifetime greater than *II* pose an additional difficulty since new values are generated before previous ones are used. One approach to fix this problem is to provide some form of register renaming so that successive definitions of a value use distinct registers. Renaming can be performed at compile time by using modulo variable expansion (MVE) [20], i.e., unrolling the kernel and renaming at compile time the multiple definitions of each variable that exist in the unrolled kernel. A rotating register file can be used to solve this problem without replicating code by renaming different instantiations of a loop-variant at execution time [11]. In this paper we assume the presence of rotating register files.

2.4. Components of Lifetimes

Two components can be distinguished in the lifetime LT_u of a loop-variant u:

- A *scheduling component* $LTSch_u = t_v - t_u$ is caused by the scheduling distance in cycles between the producer u and the last consumer v.
- A *distance component* $LTDist_u = \delta_{(u,v)} \times II$ caused by the dependence distance $\delta_{(u,v)}$ between the producer u and the last consumer v. This component appears only in loop carried dependencess (i.e. when $\delta_{(u,v)} > 0$).

For instance in loop-variant V1 (Figure 2d) the shaded part corresponds to the scheduling component, $LTSch_{V1} = t_{+} - t_{Ld} = 4$, of the lifetime and the dark part corresponds to the distance component $LTDist_{V1} = \delta_{(Ld,+)} \times II = 3$. Notice that not all the parts must be present in the lifetime, for instance, the lifetime of loop-variants V2 and V3 has only the scheduling component. These two components will have different effects when reducing the register requirements of loops.

[1] For an extensive discussion on the problem of allocating registers for software-pipelined loops refer to [26]. The strategies presented in that paper almost always achieve the *MaxLive* lower bound. In particular, the wands-only strategy using end-fit with adjacency ordering almost never required more than *MaxLive* +1 registers.

3. Increasing the Initiation Interval

One of the approaches considered in this paper, is to reschedule the loop with an increased *II*. Register pressure is, to some extent, proportional to the number of concurrently executed iterations. Increasing the *II*, in general, reduces the number of stages in which the schedule is divided, and therefore, the number of simultaneously overlapping iterations. In addition, the scheduling component of the lifetimes can be shorter because a larger *II* imposes less resource constraints than a smaller one. Unfortunately, increasing the *II* reduces the register requirements at the expense of reducing the throughput of the schedule.

As an example, consider the loop of Figure 2 that, when scheduled with $II = 1$, required 11 registers for loop-variants. Figure 3a shows the same loop scheduled (for the same architecture) with $II = 2$. Notice that the scheduling components of the lifetimes (Figure 3b) have the same length in cycles as in the schedule of Figure 2 but due to the smaller number of overlapping iterations (4 instead of 7) these components require less registers. Unlike the scheduling component, the distance component of the lifetimes increases with the *II* since it is proportional to it. For instance $LTDist_{V1}$ has increased from 3 cycles to 6 cycles. Figure 3d shows the register requirements of the schedule with $II = 2$. The new schedule requires 7 registers instead of 11. Notice that only the scheduling component of the lifetimes has reduced the register requirements, while the distance component requires the same number of registers.

3.1. Behavior of Loops when Increasing the Initiation Interval

Increasing the *II* might produce an extremely inefficient code, especially if the loops require many more registers than available, since the register requirements are reduced at the expense of increasing the number of cycles per iteration. Figure 4a shows the register requirements of a loop from the Perfect Club when the *II* is increased. This loop requires 54 registers when scheduled with an optimal *II* of 7 cycles. To schedule the loop with 32 registers the *II* must be increased from 7 to 13 cycles, and performance is reduced to 53% of the original loop. If the loop is scheduled with 16 registers the initiation interval has to be increased up to

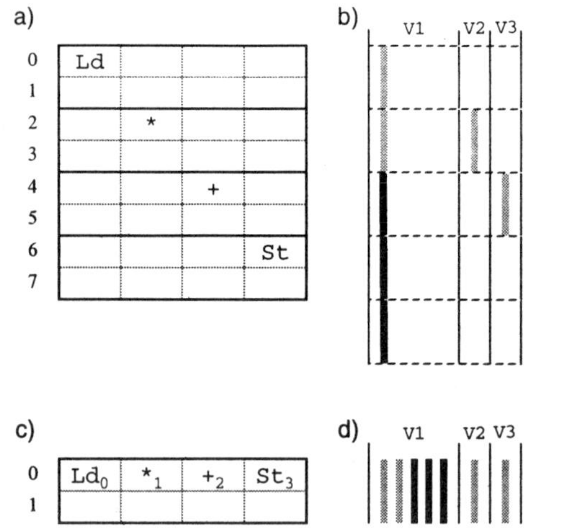

Figure 3. Example loop of Figure 2a scheduled with $II = 2$ to reduce register pressure: a) Schedule of the loop. b) Lifetimes of one iteration. c) Kernel code. d) Register requirements.

31 cycles, reducing performance to 22% of the original loop.

An additional problem with this technique is that, for some loops, it might not converge to the available number of registers. Figure 4b shows the behavior of a loop that, even though requiring only 55 registers (one more than the previous loop), it can not be scheduled with 32 registers. The loop achieves a permanent situation requiring 41 registers.

There are several reasons, mainly related with the "topology" of the DG, why a loop might not decrease the register requirements when the initiation interval is increased:

- The distance component of the loop-variants, since their lifetime increases with the initiation interval and the registers required never decrease however much the II is increased. For instance in loop 50 of APSI the distance component of loop variants acounts for 22 registers.
- The lifetime of loop-invariants is always II cycles. Therefore, they require one register each, independently of the schedule.
- The dependence graph might require more registers than available even using acyclic scheduling techniques (i.e. without overlapping iterations).

[2]The first loop of subroutine CPADE of the program APSI (ADM).

[3]The second loop of subroutine PADEC of the program APSI (ADM).

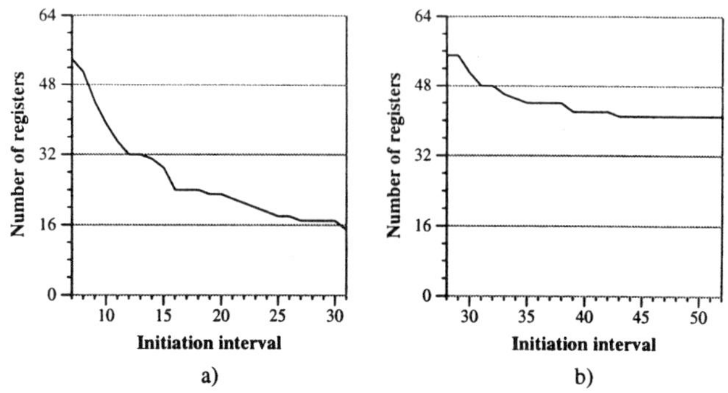

Figure 4. Behavior of the register requirements of two real loops when increasing the II: a) A loop that converges (loop 47 [2] of APSI). b) A loop that does not converge (loop 50 [3] of APSI).

4. Adding Spill Code

The other approach considered in this paper consists of spilling some lifetimes to reduce the register requirements. Due to some characteristics of software pipelining, traditional spilling techniques are difficult to apply. For instance, interference graphs cannot be used if the lifetimes are larger than the II (unless MVE is performed). Also, the addition of the spill code is difficult, since the schedules are very compact, requiring a heavy rescheduling of the loop. The option we investigated consists of the following steps:

- Select the appropriate lifetimes to spill.
- Add the required spill code for them.
- Perform modulo scheduling again.
- Repeat the register allocation.

Figure 1b shows the flow diagram of the scheduling process, adding spill code to reduce register pressure when required.

Rescheduling is necessary because the addition of loads and stores produces a different dependence graph requiring a different schedule. Unfortunately, it is possible in the new schedule that a different set of lifetimes might need to be spilled than those that have already been spilled.

4.1. Selecting Lifetimes to Spill

We have investigated two heuristics for selecting the lifetimes to be spilled.

Spill the longest lifetime regardless of the cost (in terms of additional operations required to add the associated spill code). The intuition is that large lifetimes free more registers. This criterion for selecting lifetimes is dubbed $Max(LT)$. In general, the largest lifetime will be larger than the II, so spilling the largest lifetime will free several registers at every cycle including the cycle with maximum register pressure.

Spill the largest Lifetime/Cost is similar to the previous one, but with the improvement that the cost (in terms of load and store instructions) of adding spill code is contemplated when selecting the lifetime to be spilled out. The value selected is the one with the highest relation $\frac{Lifetime}{Cost}$ where $Cost$ is determined by the number of additional memory operations. This criterion for selecting lifetimes is dubbed $Max(LT/Traf)$.

The number of additional memory operations depends on the number of consumers the value has, on whether the value is a loop-variant or a loop-invariant, and if some of the additional memory operations are redundant and can be removed from the dependence graph.

4.2. Adding Instructions for Spilling Lifetimes

Once a lifetime has been selected for being spilled, it is required to add the appropriate load and store instructions in the dependence graph, so that the selected lifetime is stored in memory after being produced, and reloaded before being consumed.

For each lifetime being spilled the following actions are performed:

- The set of edges $\subseteq RegE$ akin to the spilled lifetime is removed.
- One store is added just after the producing operations and a new edge $e \in RegE$ is added from the producer to the new store.
- One load is added just before each use of the spilled result and a new edge $e \in RegE$ is added between each one of the loads and the related consumer.
- A new edge $\in MemE$ is added between the store and each of the loads.
- The weights δ_e of each of the edges $e \in RegE$ added between the producer operation or between the loads and their respective consumer operations are set to zero. Likewise, the weights of the added edges from the store to the loads is set to the original weights that had the associated removed edges.

As an example, Figure 5b shows the resulting graph when spilling out value V1. Notice that the original edges have been removed. A new store, 'Ss', spills the value to memory and two new loads, 'Ls1' and 'Ls2', reload the value when required. Observe that by assigning the distance of the original edge (Ld,+) to the new memory edge (Ss,Ls2) the new values V11, V12, and V13 do not have a distance component in their lifetimes.

Up to now we have outlined the general process of adding spill operations, but there are cases where it is not required to add all the operations. Several particular cases have been taken into account:

- If the producer operation is a load (as in the example of Figure 5), adding spill code in the former way yields to suboptimal code with redundant operations. It is not necessary to store the result of the load since the corresponding value is already in a memory location and it can be loaded when required. In our example the resulting graph is depicted in Figure 5c.
- If at least one of the successors of the producer is a store, it is not necessary to add a new store to spill out the result.
- Finally, loop-invariants can also be selected for being spilled. In this case it is assumed that the store to spill out the value is executed before entering the loop.

4.3. Scheduling Spill Operations

Once the spill code has been added (including optimizations) the loop has to be re-scheduled. The objective of the spill code is to decrease the register requirements regardless of the scheduling method.

A situation that must be resolved is the likelihood of deadlocks. For instance, consider the Figure 5c. In a register insensitive scheduler, loop-variant V13 might have the largest lifetime and be selected for being spilled out. Notice that if spill code is added for this loop-variant, and the graph is optimized it results in a graph equivalent to the one of Figure 5c, which still requires spill code, leading to a deadlock situation.

To avoid this kind of deadlocks, the new loop-variants that appear because of spill operations are marked as *non-spillable*. For instance loop-variants V12 and V13 in the example of Figure 5c will be *non-spillable*. Therefore if the register requirements must be further reduced, a different lifetime must be selected.

Another situation that can appear is that, for a particular scheduling method, the register requirements

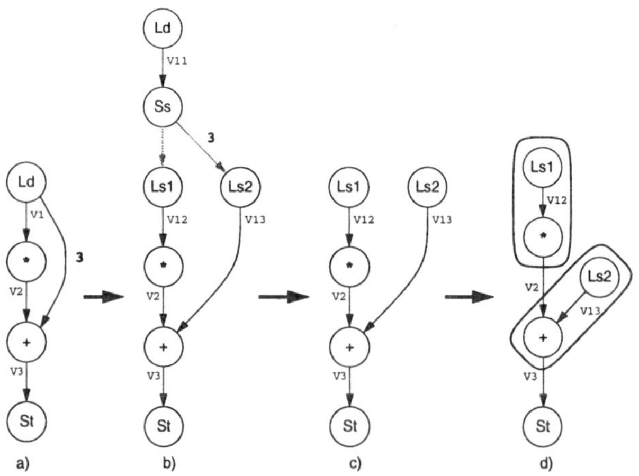

Figure 5. Adding spill code to the example loop of Figure 2a to reduce register pressure: a) DG of the original loop. b) DG after spilling lifetime V1. c) DG after optimizing redundant loads and stores. d) Operations scheduled closely to guarantee convergence.

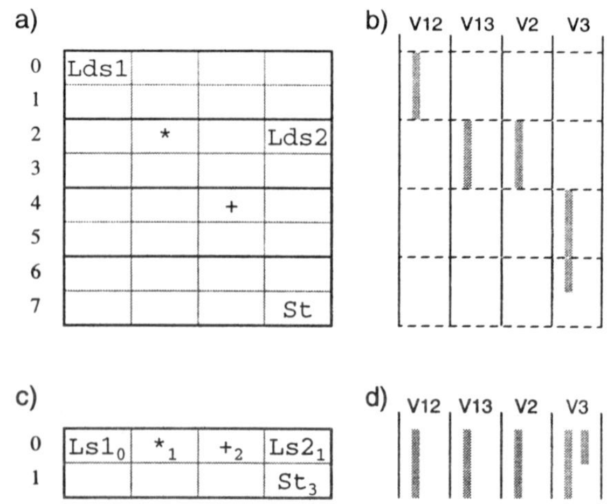

Figure 6. Schedule of loop of Figure 2a after adding spill code (Figure 5d): a) Schedule of the loop. b) Lifetimes of one iteration. c) Kernel code. d) Register requirements.

are not decreased, but increased. For instance, in the resulting graph of Figure 5c the scheduling step can schedule nodes 'Ls1' and 'Ls2' too far away from their respective successors, increasing the lifetime of loop-variants V12 and V13. This situation can result in a combined register pressure of loop-variants V12 and V13 bigger than the original loop-variant V1.

To prevent this case, operations connected by a *non-spillable* edge are forced to be simultaneously scheduled as a single "complex operation". Figure 5d shows the operations that must be scheduled as a "complex operation". According to this, operation $*$ must be scheduled exactly 2 cycles after operation 'Ls1' and operation '+' 2 cycles after operation 'Ls2'.

Figure 6a shows the resulting schedule. Notice that, even though operation 'Ls2' alone can be scheduled at cycle 0, operation '+' cannot be scheduled at cycle 2 —where it is forced to be scheduled if operation 'Ls2' is scheduled at cycle 0. An analogous situation occurs if 'Ls2' is scheduled at cycle 1. Consequently, 'Ls2' is forced to be scheduled at cycle 2 because operation '+' cannot be scheduled before cycle 4.

Figure 6b shows the lifetimes of loop-variants and Figure 6d shows the register requirements of this schedule. Notice that only 5 registers are required in contrast to 7 registers required if the *II* is increased by one. The lower register requirements are mainly due to the fact that the spill code has eliminated the distance component of the lifetime of loop-variant V1. It is also remarkable that the additional operations provoke an increase of the initiation interval (in this example the *II* of the spilled loop is also 2 cycles), which is a supplementary contribution to the reduction of the register requirements.

4.4. Behavior of Loops when Spilling Values

The addition of spill code to a dependence graph along with a reduction of the register requirements has the following negative effects:

- The memory traffic grows due to the additional memory operations.
- The *MII* can also augment if memory busses are saturated —or roughly saturated.
- Even for an optimal technique, it is difficult —and sometimes impossible— that the initiation interval reaches *MII*. The way in which spill operations are scheduled —i.e. like complex operations— prevents the scheduler from obtaining better schedules.

Figure 7 shows the evolution of the register requirements, *II*, *MII* and % of memory traffic as loop-variants are spilled, for the loops APSI 47 and APSI 50. For this example lifetimes have been selected using the $Max(LT)$ criterion.

For instance, notice in Figure 7a, that to schedule the loop APSI 47 with 32 registers, four lifetimes must be spilled out, and the *II* increases up to 14 cycles.

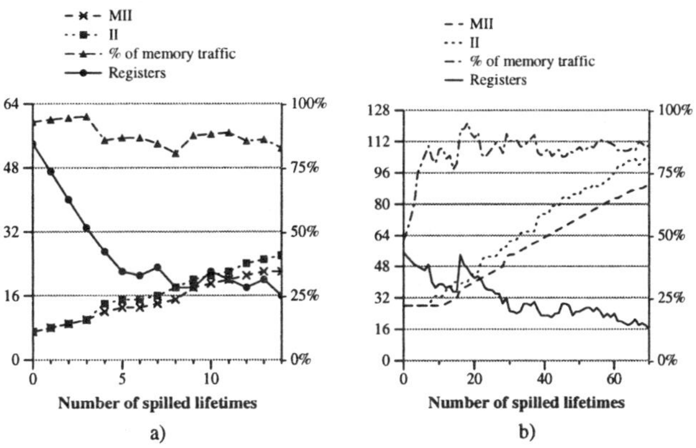

Figure 7. Behavior of the register requirements, *MII*, *II* and memory traffic of real loops when adding spill code: a) Loop 47 of APSI. b) Loop 50 of APSI.

Notice that, in this case, merely increasing the *II* allows this loop to be scheduled with 32 registers and an *II* of 13 cycles. Despite that in some particular cases increasing the *II* can be as good, or even better, as adding spill code, in general, adding spill code produces better schedules. For instance, by adding spill code, the loop APSI 47 can be scheduled with 16 registers and $II = 26$ cycles. In contrast, merely increasing the *II*, requires 31 cycles to schedule the loop with the same number of registers. Moreover, spill allows the loop APSI 50 to be scheduled with 32 and even 16 registers, while the technique of increasing the *II* failed to obtain a schedule even with 32 registers.

There are some results that need an additional comment. For instance, notice that the busses are never used 100%, and that in some cases spilling additional lifetimes decreases the bus usage. This is because, due to the "complex operations" added, the *II* increases faster than the *MII*, leaving some free bus slots. Another effect is that in some cases spilling additional lifetimes increases the register requirements. This is because the resulting graph is scheduled in a way that it requires slightly more registers. In addition in some cases the new graph might be scheduled with an smaller *II* (as in Figure 7b with 16 lifetimes spilled) leading to a noticeable increase in the register requirements (and also in memory traffic).

4.5. Increasing Efficiency

The main disadvantage of our approach to add spill code is that, for each variable spilled, the loop has to be rescheduled. This results in very low scheduling performance (i.e. the time to produce the schedules). In this section, we propose some simple techniques for boosting the performance of the scheduler to add spill code.

Spilling several lifetimes at once

The most obvious shortcut is to spill several lifetimes before rescheduling the loop. For this purpose, the decrease in register requirements of the new dependence graph must be estimated in order not to add an excessive amount of spill.

The register requirements are estimated by subtracting the lifetime selected from the schedule-dependent lower bound (*MaxLive*). Lifetimes will be selected until the lower bound is below the available number of registers.

Notice that this is an optimistic estimation since a lower bound is used instead of the actual register requirements. Furthermore, the decrease in register requirements caused by spilling a variable is not proportional to its lifetime because new —shorter— lifetimes are added to communicate the results to/from the added loads and stores.

Being so optimistic ensures that spill code is not added in excess. Loops with high register requirements will need several iterations to achieve the desired register requirements. Nevertheless, the number of times loops will be re-scheduled is extremely low compared with re-scheduling for each variable spilled out. For instance, if 32 registers are available, loops 47 and 50 from APSI are re-scheduled only once.

Pruning the search

Another area for performance improvement appears from the observation of the behavior of the *MII* and *II* in Figures 7a and 7b. Notice that when several variables have been spilled the *II* tends to be higher than the *MII*. This effect is caused by the *complex* operations that appear when spill code is added. So, in practice, for each time the loop is rescheduled, several schedules are tried with *II*'s ranging from *MII* to the final *II*.

It can also be observed that most of the time the *MII* is smaller than the *II* for which a valid schedule has been found in the previous re-scheduling iteration. It is also interesting to notice that the *II* almost never decreases from one iteration to the following.

Most time spent on unsuccessful scheduling attempts can be saved if, instead of exploring all the initiation intervals from *MII*, we explore from the maximum of the current *MII* and the previous *II*.

5. Experimental Evaluation

The effectiveness of the mechanisms to decrease the register requirements —in order to obtain valid schedules with a fixed number of registers— has been evaluated using HRMS [22] as the base scheduling technique. HRMS has been used because it is a fast, register-sensitive, software pipelining method. Nevertheless the techniques and heuristics proposed in this paper can be applied to any software pipelining method.

The techniques have been evaluated for a benchmark suite composed of a large number of innermost DO loops from the Perfect Club [5]. We have selected all loops composed of a single basic block. Loops with conditionals in their body have been previously converted to single basic block loops using IF-conversion [2]. We have not included loops with subroutine calls or with conditional exits. The dependence graphs have been obtained using the experimental ICTINEO compiler [3]. A total of 1258 loops, which account for 78% of the total execution time[4] of the Perfect Club, have been used.

We have used three functional unit configurations in order to provide a wider evaluation of the distinct techniques to reduce register pressure.

- Configuration P1L4 has 1 load/store unit, 1 Div/Sqrt unit, 1 adder and 1 multiplier. The adder and the multiplier have a latency of 4 cycles.
- Configuration P2L4 has 2 functional units of each kind with exactly the same latencies as P1L4.
- Finally, configuration P2L6 is like P2L4, but the adders and the multipliers have a latency of 6 cycles.

All configurations have in common a unit latency for store instructions, a latency of 2 for loads, a latency of 17 for divisions and a latency of 30 for square roots. For all configurations, all units are fully pipelined except the Div/Sqrt units which are not pipelined at all.

Functional unit configurations have been tested with 32 and 64 register files. This results in a set of experiments that ranges from moderate architectures (in terms of exploitable functional unit parallelism) with a large register supply to very aggressive architectures with a relatively limited register supply.

In Section 3 we have seen that increasing the *II* until a valid schedule (requiring no more than the available number of registers) is found, might not converge for some loops. Table 1 shows for all three configurations, how many loops never converge to 32 and to 64 registers. We have observed that the loops are the same (except in one case), independently of the configuration. In [21], using a register insensitive scheduler, the same loops (in fact one more loop) never converged to the desired number of registers for configuration P2L4. This behavior shows that, as suggested in Section 3, the main factor that determines the convergence of a loop is its topology.

Config.	Number of loops		% of dynamic cycles	
	64 regs.	32 regs.	64 regs.	32 regs.
P1L4	4	29	22%	35%
P2L4	4	30	20%	31%
P2L6	4	30	19%	29%

Table 1. Loops that never converge to a given number of registers, and % of cycles they represent.

Notice that only a few loops never converge to a solution. Unfortunately, the loops that cannot be scheduled with 64 and 32 registers represent about 20% and 30%, respectively, of the cycles of all 1258 loops when executed for the corresponding configurations assuming an infinite number of registers. From these results we conclude that increasing the *II* cannot be considered as a general purpose technique for register-constrained software pipelining.

The alternative technique we investigated is to add spill code. In Section 4 we have introduced two heuristics for selecting the lifetimes to spill. Figure 8a shows the overall performance of all the Perfect loops when using the two proposed spilling heuristics: $Max(LT)$ and $Max(LT/Traf)$. The heuristic that takes into account the cost of adding the spill code leads to schedules that have (for all configurations) better performance.

Notice that, when 64 registers are available there is almost no performance degradation due to the addition of spill code (even for the most aggressive configuration). Nevertheless, for all the 64-register configurations, the $Max(LT/Traf)$ heuristic produces schedules that (as expected) generate noticeable less memory traffic. Figure 8b shows the total memory traffic required by the loops when executed.

In Section 4 we also proposed two techniques for speeding-up the scheduling process (i.e. to reduce the compilation time). Figure 8c shows the time required to construct all the schedules. The scheduling time depends mainly on the quantity of spill to add (which is bigger for small register files). This is because for each variable to spill the loop is rescheduled. For the configurations with 64 registers, the scheduling time is about 15 minutes. Unfortunately, when only 32 registers are available (as in many of the existing microprocessors)

[4]Executed on an HP 9000/735 workstation.

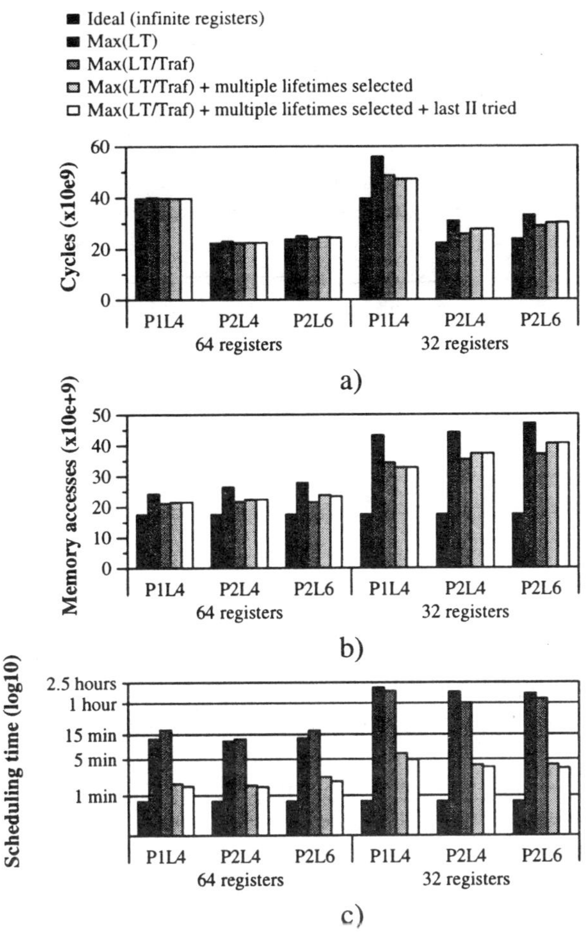

Figure 8. Evaluation of the spilling heuristics for several machine configurations: a) Cycles required to execute all the loops (in units of 10^9 cycles) b) Number of dynamic memory references (in units of 10^9) c) Time to schedule all the loops ($\log_{10}$ scale)

the scheduling time grows to more than 1 hour (1:40 for the worst case evaluated).

A technique for reducing the scheduling time is to spill several variables before re-scheduling the loop. As can be seen in Figure 8 the "$Max(LT/Traf)$+ multiple lifetimes selected" bar shows a small performance degradation (both in terms of execution time and memory traffic) in most of the cases. Nevertheless, for configuration P1L4 the heuristic produces a performance improvement. The small difference in performance is because a different set of variables is spilled if they are selected all together, or in separate steps (the loop has been rescheduled and the length of lifetimes varies). Since the selection is based on simple heuristics, selecting a slightly different set of variables can produce

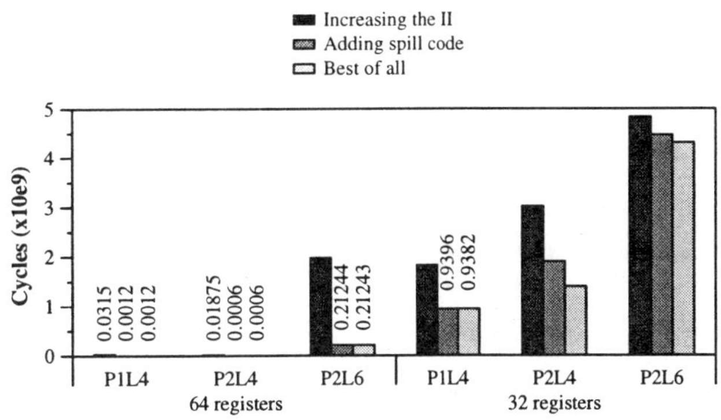

Figure 9. Increasing the II versus adding spill code: total execution time (in units of 10^9 cycles) of the loops that (1) require a reduction of the register requirements to fit in the available number of registers, and (2) converge to a solution by increasing the II.

either slightly better results or slightly worse results. Notice that this improvement reduces the scheduling time of the loops (for the configurations with 32 registers) from more than 1 hour to about 5 minutes.

In Figure 7 it can be observed that the II of loops with a high amount of spill code can be several cycles bigger than the MII because of the scheduling complexity introduced by the "complex" operations generated. As a consequence, the scheduler has to explore several schedules (from MII to the final II) before producing a valid schedule. If the loop must be rescheduled (with additional spills) and the new MII is lower than the previous II some time can be saved by skipping the exploration of the schedules from the current MII to the previous II. It can be noted that this optimization (bar "$Max(LT/Traf)$+ multiple lifetimes selected + last II tried" in Figure 8) reduces the scheduling time without any noticeable performance degradation. We consider that this combination of heuristics has the best behavior in terms of both execution time of the loops and compilation time.

Since increasing the II does not converge for some loops it is difficult to compare the spilling heuristics versus increasing the II. Therefore we performed a limited comparison using only the subset of loops that require more registers than available and that converges to a solution when the II is increased. Figure 9 compares the execution time of this subset of loops for the best set of heuristics ("$Max(LT/Traf)$+ multiple lifetimes selected + last II tried" bar in Figure 8) versus increasing the II. It must be said that the subset of loops compared varies depending on the machine configuration. Notice that, in all configurations, spilling produces schedules that, on average, have better performance than increasing the *II*. Even for some configurations (P2L6 with 64 registers) the advantage of spilling over increasing the *II* is astonishing.

Despite of this fact, we have observed that for a few loops spilling performs worse than increasing the *II*. Figure 9 also shows the performance of a combination of both techniques. The bar labeled "best of all" shows the total execution time of the loops when each loop is scheduled using the best technique for it. Notice that in some cases it produces a small reduction on the execution time of the loops. We have not implemented this improvement, but it would require a minor computational cost, if implemented as follows:

- If the loop requires additional registers, schedule it by adding spill code until a valid schedule is found.
- Once a valid schedule is found, schedule the loop with the same *II* but without the added spill code. If the schedule is valid for the available number of registers, then a better or equal schedule can be found by increasing the *II*
- Instead of exploring all the possible *II* configurations from *MII* until a valid schedule is found we can perform a binary search of the schedules between *MII* (lower bound) and the *II* obtained by adding spill code (upper bound).

With this implementation we only require to perform an additional schedule for the loops that require spill code. In addition this schedule will be performed fast, since it will be performed with a bigger *II* than required, having more available slots for the operations. Some loops will require additional scheduling steps, but we have observed that in most of the configurations this situation only arises for less than 10 loops (out of 1258). The worst case appears for configuration P2L6 with 32 registers, where 30 loops have better performance increasing the *II* than adding spill code.

6. Conclusions

In this paper, we have investigated several options to perform software pipelining with register constraints. Two options have been investigated in order to decrease register requirements when required: increasing the initiation interval (*II*), and adding spill code.

We have demonstrated that merely increasing the *II* does not converge to a solution for all loops. Even though it happens for a few loops, we have observed that they represent a significant amount of the execution time. For instance, if only 32 registers are available, the loops that never converge represent about 30% of the execution time.

When adding spill code, we have introduced heuristics to guarantee convergence independently of the scheduling technique: scheduling the spill loads/stores grouped with the predecessor/successor as a single "complex" operation and marking all variables whose producers/consumers are a spill load/store. We have also studied two heuristics for selecting the appropriate lifetimes: Selecting the largest lifetime and selecting the largest lifetime divided by the number of additional memory operations required. The last option proved to be more effective both, in terms of memory traffic and execution time (in cycles) of the resulting schedules.

We proposed two complementary heuristics to speed up the spill process. These heuristics caused a small performance degradation, but dramatically reduced the time required to produce a valid schedule with register constraints (from more than 1 hour to less than 5 minutes for the 1258 loops we used).

Finally, for the loops that achieve a valid schedule by increasing the *II*, we have compared the performance of these schedules with the schedules obtained by adding spill code. Adding spill code has proven, in general, to be more effective. Nevertheless, for a few loops, a better schedule was obtained by increasing the *II*. From this results we proposed a combination of both techniques that can be implemented without a noticeable increase in the compilation time. We have shown that this combination can produce better schedules than any of the techniques alone.

As future work, it remains to be studied other heuristics to select the variables to be spilled. For instance, if no hardware support (rotating register files) is provided for lifetimes larger than the *II*, cyclic interval graphs [16] can be used to perform the register allocation and to select the lifetimes to be spilled. Also in [14], even though they didn't dealt with the addition of spill code, there where heuristics proposed to select the variables to spill. Another possibility is to spill uses instead of variables, in any case, we do not expect a significant improvement, since most of the variables are used only once [15].

References

[1] V. Allan, R. Jones, R. Lee, and S. Allan. Software pipelining. *ACM Computing Surveys*, 27(3):367–432, September 1995.

[2] J. Allen, K. Kennedy, and J. Warren. Conversion of control dependence to data dependence. In *Proc. 10th annual Symposium on Principles of Programming Languages*, January 1983.

[3] E. Ayguadé, C. Barrado, J. Labarta, D. López, S. Moreno, D. Padua, and M. Valero. A uniform representation for high-level and instruction-level transformations. Technical Report UPC-CEPBA 95-01, Universitat Politècnica de Catalunya, January 1995.

[4] D. Bernstein, D. Goldin, M. Golumbic, H. Krawczyk, Y. Mansour, I. Nahshon, and R. Pinter. Spill code minimization techniques for optimizing compilers. In *Proc. of the ACM SIGPLAN'89 Conf. on Programming Languages Design and Implementation*, pages 258–263, July 1989.

[5] M. Berry, D. Chen, P. Koss, and D. Kuck. The Perfect Club benchmarks: Effective performance evaluation of supercomputers. Technical Report 827, Center for Supercomputing Research and Development, November 1988.

[6] P. Briggs, K. Cooper, K. Kennedy, and L. Torczon. Coloring heuristics for register allocation. In *Proc. of the ACM SIGPLAN'89 Conf. on Programming Language Design and Implementation*, pages 275–284, June 1989.

[7] P. Briggs, K. Cooper, and L. Torczon. Improvements to graph coloring register allocation. *ACM Transactions on Programming Languages and Systems*, 16(3):428–455, May 1994.

[8] D. Callahan and B. Koblenz. Register allocation via hierarchical graph coloring. In *Proc. of the ACM SIGPLAN'91 Conf. on Programming Language Design and Implementation*, pages 192–203, June 1991.

[9] G. Chaitin. Register allocation and spilling via graph coloring. In *Proc., ACM SIGPLAN Symp. on Compiler Construction*, pages 98–105, June 1982.

[10] A. Charlesworth. An approach to scientific array processing: The architectural design of the AP120B/FPS-164 family. *Computer*, 14(9):18–27, 1981.

[11] J. Dehnert, P. Hsu, and J. Bratt. Overlapped loop support in the Cydra 5. In *Proc. of the 3rd Int. Conf. Architectural Support for Programming Languages and Operating Systems (ASPLOS-III)*, pages 26–38, April 1989.

[12] J. Dehnert and R. Towle. Compiling for the Cydra 5. *The Journal of Supercomputing*, 7(1/2):181–228, May 1993.

[13] A. Eichenberger and E. Davidson. Stage scheduling: A technique to reduce the register requirements of a modulo schedule. In *Proc. of the 28th Annual Int. Symp. on Microarchitecture (MICRO-28)*, pages 338–349, November 1995.

[14] C. Eisenbeis, S. Lelait, and B. Marmol. The meeting graph: a new model for loop cyclic register allocation. In *Proc., Fifth Workshop on Compilers for Parallel Computers (CPC95)*, pages 503–516, June 1995.

[15] M. Franklin and G. Sohi. Register traffic analysis for streamlining inter-operation communication in fine-grain parallel processors. In *Proc., 25th Annual Internat. Symp. on Microarchitecture (MICRO-25)*, pages 236–245, December 1992.

[16] L. Hendren, G. Gao, E. Altman, and C. Mukerji. Register allocation using cyclic interval graphs: A new approach to an old problem. ACAPS Tech. Memo 33, Advanced Computer Architecture and Program Structures Group, McGill University, 1992.

[17] R. Huff. Lifetime-sensitive modulo scheduling. In *6th Conference on Programming Language, Design and Implementation*, pages 258–267, 1993.

[18] S. Jain. Circular scheduling: A new technique to perform software pipelining. In *Proceedings of the ACM SIGPLAN '91 Conference on Programming Language Design and Implementation*, pages 219–228, June 1991.

[19] M. Lam. Software pipelining: An effective scheduling technique for VLIW machines. In *Proceedings of the SIGPLAN'88 Conference on Programming Language Design and Implementation*, pages 318–328, June 1988.

[20] M. Lam. *A Systolic Array Optimizing Compiler*. Kluwer Academic Publishers, 1989.

[21] J. Llosa. *Reducing the Impact of Register Pressure on Software Pipelining*. PhD thesis, UPC. Universitat Politècnica de Catalunya, January 1996.

[22] J. LLosa, M. Valero, E. Ayguadé, and A. Gonzalez. Hipernode reduction modulo scheduling. In *Proc. of the 28th Annual Int. Symp. on Microarchitecture (MICRO-28)*, pages 350–360, November 1995.

[23] W. Mangione-Smith, S. Abraham, and E. Davidson. Register requirements of pipelined processors. In *Int. Conference on Supercomputing*, pages 260–246, July 1992.

[24] S. Ramakrishnan. Software pipelining in PA-RISC compilers. *Hewlett-Packard Journal*, pages 39–45, July 1992.

[25] B. Rau and C. Glaeser. Some scheduling techniques and an easily schedulable horizontal architecture for high performance scientific computing. In *Proceedings of the 14th Annual Microprogramming Workshop*, pages 183–197, October 1981.

[26] B. Rau, M. Lee, P. Tirumalai, and P. Schlansker. Register allocation for software pipelined loops. In *Proceedings of the ACM SIGPLAN'92 Conference on Programming Language Design and Implementation*, pages 283–299, June 1992.

[27] B. R. Rau. Iterative modulo scheduling: An algorithm for software pipelining loops. In *Proceedings of the 27th Annual International Symposium on Microarchitecture*, pages 63–74, November 1994.

[28] F. Sánchez. *Loop Pipelining with Resource and Timing Constraints*. PhD thesis, UPC Universitat Politecnica de Catalunya, October 1995.

[29] P. Tirumalai, M. Lee, and M. Schlansker. Parallelisation of loops with exits on pipelined architectures. In *Proc., Supercomputing '90*, pages 200–212, November 1990.

[30] J. Wang, A. Krall, M. A. Ertl, and C. Eisenbeis. Software pipelining with register allocation and spilling. In *Proc. of the 27th Annual Int. Symp. on Microarchitecture*, pages 95–99, November 1994.

[31] N. Warter and N. Partamian. Modulo scheduling with multiple initiation intervals. In *Proc. of the 28th Internat. Symp. on Microarchitecture*, pages 111–118, November 1995.

Software Pipelining Loops with Conditional Branches

Mark G. Stoodley and Corinna G. Lee
Dept. of Electrical and Computer Engineering, University of Toronto, Toronto, Ontario, Canada
{stoodla,corinna}@eecg.utoronto.ca

Abstract

Software pipelining is an aggressive scheduling technique that generates efficient code for loops and is particularly effective for VLIW architectures. Few software pipelining algorithms, however, are able to efficiently schedule loops that contain conditional branches. We have developed an algorithm we call All Paths Pipelining (APP) *that addresses this shortcoming of software pipelining. APP is designed to achieve optimal or near-optimal performance for any run of iterations while providing efficient code for transitioning between runs. A run is the execution of consecutive iterations that all execute the same path through a loop. APP accomplishes this by using techniques from modulo scheduling and kernel recognition algorithms, the two main approaches for software pipelining loops. We have implemented the APP algorithm in our research compiler and have evaluated its performance by executing its generated code on a VLIW instruction-set simulator. For a processor with five heterogeneous functional units, APP is able to add another 1% to 23% increase in performance over basic software pipelining by effectively pipelining loops with conditional branches.*

1. Introduction

During the past two to three years, renewed interest in VLIW architectures has grown, particularly in the microprocessor community which continues to search for techniques to exploit increasing amounts of instruction-level parallelism. To successfully exploit the parallelism in a VLIW architecture, a compiler must use aggressive scheduling algorithms especially for loops where it is expected that much of the execution time is spent. An effective technique for scheduling loops is software pipelining [3][16].

Software pipelining (SP) improves performance by overlapping the execution of different iterations of a loop. During the execution of a non-pipelined loop, the first iteration is started and executed to its completion. The second iteration is then initiated, executed until completion, and so on. In contrast, for a pipelined loop, the second iteration is allowed to begin before the first iteration has completed. The third iteration can start before the second or the first iteration has completed, and so on. The interval at which iterations are started is called the *initiation interval*, abbreviated II. The goal of the SP optimization is to find a schedule that overlaps iterations and uses the shortest possible initiation interval.

Finding the shortest possible initiation interval starts with a lower bound, called the *minimum initiation interval* (MII), which is the maximum of two hardware-based constraints [16]. Thus the effectiveness of software pipelining relies heavily on knowledge of the hardware that is being targeted. The first constraint is based on the resource usage in the loop and resource availability in the hardware. Since no processor resource can be over-committed, the resource requirements of all the operations in the loop determine a resource constraint, *ResMII*, on the II as follows:

$$ResMII = \underset{i \in \text{FU types}}{MAX} \left(\frac{\text{\#cycles requiring FU type } i}{\text{\#units of type } i \text{ in processor}}\right) \quad (1)$$

The second constraint is determined by the length of dependence cycles caused by recurrences and the number of iterations that the dependence cycle spans. The length of a dependence cycle is a function of the operational latencies of the target hardware. Since every edge in the data dependence graph (DDG) must be obeyed and there may be edges representing dependences between operations from different iterations, cycles can exist in the DDG which limit the II. The number of iterations spanned by the dependence cycle is called the *iteration distance*. For instance, if the dependence cycle is formed between operations from three consecutive iterations, then the iteration distance is two. The length of the longest cycle divided by that cycle's iteration distance is referred to as the recurrence constraint, *RecMII*:

$$RecMII = \underset{\text{all dependence cycles}}{MAX} \frac{(\text{length of cycle})}{(\text{iteration distance})} \quad (2)$$

Many algorithms have been developed that effectively software pipeline loops that consist of a single basic block and hence do not contain conditional branches [9][11][19][23][28]. These algorithms are able to find an overlapping schedule with an II equal to or nearly equal to the MII of a single basic-block loop. Conditional branches which result in arbitrary control flow, however, complicate the construction of an overlapping schedule. This is because different basic blocks could be executed for successive iterations of a loop resulting in different resource usage and cyclic data dependences for each iteration. This, in turn, results in potentially different initiation intervals for the different paths through the loop. It is the non-uniform initiation intervals that complicate the construction of an overlapping schedule.

Figure 1 illustrates this for a loop containing one conditional branch. Shown is the control flow graph for the loop and a possible dynamic execution sequence. Each assembly instruction is labelled Op*n* with those that are executed only on the False path in italics and those executed only on the True path in bold. We call a particular path through a loop an *iteration path*. The example loop contains two iteration paths and, in general, a loop with B conditional branches could contain up to 2^B iteration paths. In the execution sequence shown, the first iteration of the loop follows the True iteration path and consists of the basic blocks ACD, while the second iteration follows the False iteration path and consists of the blocks ABD, and so on.

Consider the execution of this loop on a small VLIW architecture consisting of an integer (INT) unit, a floating-point (FP) unit, and a branch (BR) unit. For simplicity, we assume that all opera-

1072-4451/96 $5.00 © 1996 IEEE

C Code

```c
for (i=0;i < N;i++) {
  if (x < threshold)
    z = (x + 1.0) * (2*x + 1.0);
  else
    z = threshold;
  sum += z;
  x = x * x;
 }
```

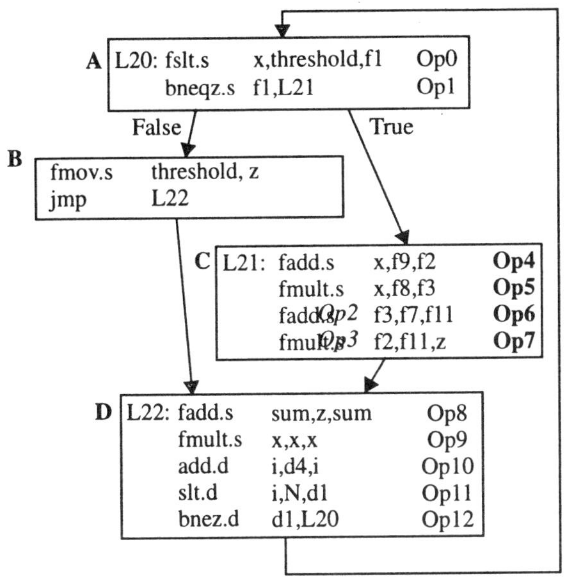

Possible Execution Sequence: T,F,F,F,F,T,T,T,F,T,T,T,T,T

Figure 1: Example Loop with One Conditional Branch and Two Iteration Paths

F Path=(A,B,D): Op0-Op1, *Op2-Op3*, Op8-Op12
T Path=(A,C,D): Op0-Op1, **Op4-Op7**, Op8-Op12

tions have a latency of one clock period. Then the initiation interval for the False path would be at least 4 clock periods since the most heavily used resource, the FP unit, is used four times and the longest cyclic dependence is only 1 clock period. For similar reasons, the initiation interval for the True path would have to be at least 7 clock periods.

If the execution of the loop consisted of iterations executing only the False path, then an overlapping schedule with an II of 4 clock periods would be optimal since the FP unit would be used during each clock period (once steady state has been achieved). Alternatively, if all the iterations executed only the True path, then the best schedule would be one with an II of 7 clock periods. However, these are only two of the 2^N possible sequences that the loop could take when executing N iterations. Finding a schedule that can optimally execute all possible execution sequences is obviously non-trivial. The situation becomes even more complicated when a loop contains more than one conditional branch resulting in more than two iteration paths.

One way to view the execution of a loop is as a sequence of *runs*, where a *run* is the execution of successive iterations following the same iteration path and the length of a run is the number of successive iterations executed. For example, the execution sequence given in Figure 1 consists of runs of length 1, 4, 3, 1, and 5. Software pipelining a loop with conditional branches can then be considered as two inter-related problems: generating schedules to execute a run of each iteration path and generating code for transitioning from one run to another.

We have developed an algorithm we call *All Paths Pipelining* that generates a near-optimal schedule for *all* iteration paths so that a run of any path will be executed with near-optimal performance. By generating efficient code to transition between runs, All Paths Pipelining (APP) can provide good performance for any loop execution that consists mainly of runs of reasonable length.

This is in contrast to profile-based algorithms, such as Modulo Scheduling with Multiple Initiation Intervals [27], that rely on branch probabilities to generate near-optimal code for the most frequently executed path at the expense of poor performance for the other paths. While excellent performance is possible when branch probabilities are heavily skewed and loop execution is dominated by one iteration path, poor performance will result with more balanced branch probabilities which cause execution to be distributed among several iteration paths. With more balanced branch probabilities, there can be a significant number of long runs of paths other than the most frequently executed one. However, a profile-based algorithm would not generate a schedule that could exploit these other runs.

For example, suppose the loop in Figure 1 follows the True path for 90% of the iterations in a profiled execution. Then the possible execution sequences will consist of mostly long runs of the True path interspersed with short runs of the False path and the occasional short True run. A profiled-based algorithm will optimally schedule for runs of the True path and ignore the opportunity to exploit the runs of the False path. Despite the non-optimal schedule for the False path, excellent performance is still possible because of the predominant long True runs.

Suppose instead that the branch probability is 60%. There are now many more possible execution sequences. Some consist of long runs of the True path and long runs of the False path while other execution sequences consist of a mixture of long and short runs of both paths. A profile-based algorithm exploits only the True runs. All Paths Pipelining, on the other hand, exploits both the True and False runs thus providing better performance as long as the transition code is efficient.

To determine what occurs in actual loop executions, we used our benchmark programs (described later in the Evaluation section) to gather the path frequencies of loops containing conditional branches. For the nine loops that were identified, Table 1 lists the number of iterations executed, the number of iteration paths in each loop, and the percentage of iterations that executed each path (only percentages for executed paths are given). Iteration paths are identified by the direction taken for each conditional branch in the path.

For six of the loops, execution is dominated by one iteration path. APP will do as well as previously developed algorithms for this type of loop. On the other hand, for the other three loops, execution is spread over two paths. Of particular interest are loops 6 and 7 which contain 7 and 5 conditional branches, respectively. The probabilities for most of the branches are heavily skewed towards one path with the exception of one or two. As a result, of

Table 1: Branch Characteristics of Benchmark Loops

Loop	Number of Iterations	Number of Iteration Paths	Iteration Path Frequencies
1 (ADPCM)	1536	2	F: 66%, T: 34%
2 (ED)	16384	4	FF: 2%, TF: 3%, TT: 95%
3 (LPC)	63	2	T: 100%
4 (SE)	64	2	F: 100%
5 (TRELLIS)	62	2	F: 100%
6 (G721c)	2407	128	FTFTTTT: 50%, TTTTTTT: 50%
7 (G721d)	2407	24	TTFTT: 50%, TTTTT: 50%
8 (V32c)	1924	2	T: 100%
9 (V32d)	15392	2	T: 100%

Table 2: Distribution of Run Lengths

Loop 1 (ADPCM)			Loop 2 (ED)			Loops 6&7 (G721c & G721d)		
Run Length	# of Runs	% of Iters	Run Length	# of Runs	% of Iters	Run Length	# of Runs	% of Iters
1	294	19.1	1	251	1.5%	1	32	1.3%
2	125	16.3%	2	125	1.5%	2	61	5.1%
3	55	10.7%	124	124	93.8%	3	145	18.1%
4	30	7.8%	125	1	0.8%	4	169	28.1%
5	7	2.3%	126	1	0.8%	5	76	15.8%
6	35	13.7%	127	1	0.8%	6	47	11.7%
12	1	0.8%	129	1	0.8%	7	29	8.4%
114	1	7.4%				8	16	5.3%
336	1	21.9%				9	12	4.5%
						10	3	1.2%
						11	1	0.5%

Figure 2: Distribution of Run Lengths

the possible 128 paths for loop 6 and 24 paths for loop 7, only two are executed. Nonetheless, because the two paths are executed with equal frequency, APP is expected to generate more efficient code than a profile-based algorithm.

In order to do well, however, APP relies on the presence of runs of reasonable length. It is possible, although unlikely, that the execution sequence for, say, loop 7 is the pathological one of successive iterations executing alternating paths. Intuitively, we expect most loop executions to contain runs of modest length assuming a reasonable distribution of execution sequences. This is because, of the 2^N possible sequences that could be executed for a loop with one conditional branch executing N iterations, only two have the worst-case characteristic of having all runs being of length one. All other execution sequences contain runs of length two or more.

To corroborate our intuitive explanation, we measured the lengths of the runs in the nine loops. Figure 2 shows the distribution of run lengths of the four loops that executed more than one iteration path. The distributions for the other five loops are uninteresting since each loop execution consists of only one run whose length is the number of iterations executed. Figure 2 also lists the percentage of iterations executed for a particular run length. For example, for the first loop, nearly 14% of the iterations, or 210 out of 1536 iterations, were part of a run of length 6.

Figure 2 shows that runs of lengths varying from 1 to 336 are executed in the four loops. Because loops 6 and 7 have identical distributions, the columns for those two loops have been combined in Figure 2. As indicated by its heavily skewed path frequencies, loop 2 is dominated by the execution of long runs: 97% of the iterations are part of a run of at least length 124. In contrast, iterations in the other three loops are likely to be in runs of length 11 or less. This was expected because these three loops have fairly balanced path frequencies. Although there is a significant number of short runs, the pathological case of alternating single runs (i.e., 100% of iterations are part of a run of length 1) does not appear. More importantly, despite the presence of many single runs, approximately half of the iterations are part of runs of length 5 or more.

The significant presence of short runs implies that transition code between runs must be efficient. This is to prevent the performance degradation due to transitions from cancelling out the benefit of optimizing runs. Ideally, we would like to execute transitions and runs with equal and high efficiency. We will show that the APP algorithm can achieve this goal in some cases, but in general we expect runs to be executed more efficiently than transitions.

In this paper, we describe in detail the All Paths Pipelining algorithm. We begin with a description of the algorithm. The algorithm does not rely on special hardware, such as predicated operations[5][27] or rotating register files[17][18], nor does it use profiling information. We then discuss other algorithms that software pipeline loops with conditional branches and contrast the various approaches with that taken by APP. The APP algorithm has been incorporated into our research compiler and we have evaluated its performance by executing its generated code on an instruction-set simulator. In the final section before concluding, we present the results of our evaluation.

2. The All Paths Pipelining (APP) Algorithm

The All Paths Pipelining algorithm consists of three steps: extract the iteration paths, software pipelining each path in isolation using a modulo scheduling algorithm [19], and finally insert code that is executed from one schedule to another when a subsequent iteration executes a different path. The first two steps will be discussed only briefly. The third step, called the *combine* algorithm, will be discussed in more detail since it is the major contribution of All Paths Pipelining.

In the first step of the algorithm, a traversal of the control flow graph for the loop identifies the iteration paths. The operations along each iteration path are extracted into a *trace*. This trace is similar to the one used in trace scheduling [8] except we restrict the extraction to a loop body rather than extract a trace for an entire program. Unconditional branch operations are not included in a trace because control can only flow in one direction from an unconditional branch.

Dependence edges that have both head and tail operations in the trace are included in the dependence graph for the trace. In addition, some dependence edges are added to each trace to disallow global and speculative code motions; for every branch *b* in the trace, a dependence is added to *b* from all operations that precede *b* in an iteration, and a dependence is added from *b* to every operation that follows *b* in an iteration. The third step of the algorithm is made easier by the presence of these dependence edges because they make each branch a synchronization point across all traces that contain that branch. Although some performance degradation may result from their inclusion, we believe that much of the potential benefit will still be achieved. In Section 4.1, we evaluate the performance impact of these additional edges.

In the second step, any SP algorithm for single basic-block loops can be used to create a pipelined kernel schedule[1] which can be pipelined for every trace individually. Note that the recurrence constraint used to calculate the MII for each trace includes the effects of the extra dependence edges added in the first step of APP. For this step, we augmented the modulo scheduling algorithm to handle strongly-connected components more effectively. Operations contained in strongly-connected components are given priority over all other operations when scheduling since it is these operations that limit the initiation interval. This algorithm is similar to the algorithms of Hsu [9] and Llosa *et al.* [13].

The third and last step of APP combines the kernel schedules for all the iteration paths into a single loop schedule that can execute any path that the original loop could support. To generate the loop schedule, the combine algorithm regenerates the kernel schedules while creating instructions for the transition code in a breadth-first order. In other words, VLIW instructions from different kernel schedules and VLIW instructions for transitions are created in an interleaved manner.

The kernel schedules are regenerated to simplify the creation of the transition code. As instructions from different kernels are created in a breadth-first order, transition code is also created whenever a branch operation is encountered in a kernel instruction. When an instruction for either a kernel or transition is being created, the combine algorithm checks to see if an equivalent instruction has been created already. If one has, the about-to-be-created instruction is replaced with a branch to the equivalent instruction.

To generate a loop schedule, the combine algorithm must address several issues. A VLIW instruction in the loop schedule may contain a (non-loop-back) branch operation. Another complication is that a VLIW loop instruction will most likely be executing operations from different iterations. A final difficulty is the actual creation of the kernel schedules and generation of transition code that is efficient. We discuss each of these difficulties in turn and then describe the combine algorithm.

1. We refer to the schedule of an individual iteration path as a *kernel schedule* while the schedule for the entire loop is called a *loop schedule*. Because APP creates multiple kernel schedules, the purpose of the third step is to generate a loop schedule that combines the kernel schedules.

2.1. Difficulties Pipelining Loops with IFs

The first difficulty arises because of a branch operation in a VLIW instruction. The branch operation will direct control flow either to stay in the current kernel or to begin executing operations on a different iteration path, in which case transition code must be generated for subsequent instructions. The schedule for the other iteration path may be quite different from the current kernel schedule, in particular the order in which operations are executed may be different. Moreover, execution for the other path may begin in the *middle* of that schedule since a branch operation is not always the first operation to be executed for an iteration.

When generating the code to branch out of the middle of one kernel schedule to enter into the middle of another kernel schedule, the combine algorithm must know what operations from the new kernel were scheduled to execute before the point at which the transition code is entering and make sure that the transition code reflects this. To make this easier to accomplish, we use the extra dependence edges added in APP's first step to guarantee that all pre-branch operations regardless of which iteration path is being followed will be scheduled to execute before the branch executes. For similar reasons, we use extra dependence edges to prevent all post-branch operations from being scheduled to execute before the branch. Thus when transitioning out of one kernel and into another, the combine algorithm needs to be concerned only about the operations *after* the branch.

The second difficulty involves creating a VLIW instruction that contains operations from different iterations. Complications arise because different iterations could be following iterations paths which have different kernel schedules. This corresponds to the situation where the VLIW instruction being created is part of some code transitioning out of one kernel and into another. In creating an instruction, the combine algorithm must handle conflicts in resource usage from the different iterations and must decide whether operations from a new iteration should be included.

To explain how the combine algorithm handles these issues, we describe how an instruction for the loop schedule is generated. Each created VLIW instruction keeps track of each iteration's progress in its kernel schedule by recording the elapsed time since initiation and using the elapsed time to index into the kernel schedule. We say that an iteration *contributes* to the loop schedule the instruction indexed by the iteration's elapsed time in its kernel schedule. In addition, if, for the *youngest* iteration in the instruction, the elapsed time is equal to the initiation interval of its kernel schedule S, then the combine algorithm starts a new iteration which uses the same kernel schedule S. The combine algorithm attempts to merge together the instructions contributed by all iterations, including any new iterations that were started, to create one loop instruction free of resource conflicts.

For the simpler case where the different iterations are following the same path (i.e., the instruction is part of a kernel), the merging of all contributed instructions will proceed smoothly. This is because a kernel schedule with an initiation interval of II has been designed to execute iterations that are initiated every II cycles in an overlapped manner without any resource conflicts.

The more complicated case is when different paths are being followed. The different kernel schedules were not designed to execute together in an overlapped manner and thus overlapping iterations in this case may result in resource conflicts. To avoid such conflicts, the iterations are processed one-by-one, with older iterations given priority, and each is allowed to advance in time only if the instruction it contributes does not result in a processor resource being overcommitted. If all iterations contributed their instructions, even though they were not designed to overlap, then all is well, and only one loop instruction is required. If not, then the next loop instruction will be created from only those iterations that did not contribute their instructions to the previously generated loop instruction. Note that new iterations can still be started in this situation as long as the appropriate amount of time has elapsed for the youngest iteration.

The third and final difficulty that the combine algorithm deals with is the creation of the kernel for each iteration path and the generation of efficient transition code. To accomplish both tasks, we build upon techniques from kernel-recognition algorithms. We identify *equivalent execution states*, a concept similar to that of functional equivalence used in Perfect Pipelining. An *execution state* is a point of execution between two instructions. Two execution states are equivalent if they satisfy four criteria. For the sake of brevity, we state only the criteria; an explanation for why each is needed is provided elsewhere [20].

The first two criteria are that both states must have the same number of active iterations and the epilog flag must be the same in both states. Any state that resulted from following the false direction from any loop-back branch is part of the epilog and thus has this flag set. This is significant because new iterations should not be initiated in the epilog. If one state is from the epilog and a second state is not, then the two states cannot possibly be equivalent if correct code is to be generated.

The third criteria is that the *live operations* of both execution states must be identical. A live operation is an operation that is yet to be executed at a given point in an iteration. The live operations for a loop with conditional branches can be computed at any point by merging the live operations along any possible future iteration path. It is important to note that the live operations are not local to a single iteration path but are computed from all paths.

The concept of live operations can be easily used to model simple resources. To deal with complex resources, the live operation comparison would need to take into account the types of resources required by each operation as well as the time at which each of those resources is required. This would be a simple extension to the live operations concept, but would obviously increase the overhead of comparing two execution states for equivalence.

The fourth and final criteria is that live registers in *corresponding* active iterations in two execution states cannot be live simultaneously in either execution state. For example, suppose a register R1 is live in the ith active iteration of an execution state E1 and another register R2 is live in the ith active iteration of another execution state E2. Then for E1 and E2 to be considered equivalent, R1 cannot also be live in E2 and R2 cannot be live in E1.

For a more detailed explanation, consider a hypothetical SP schedule for a loop with three operations Op1, Op2, and Op3. Assume that the SP schedule has Op1 scheduled in the first instruction, Op2 in the second instruction, and Op3 in the third instruction, and has an initiation interval of one cycle. Although this example involves a loop that contains no branches, the technique for identifying register conflicts is equally applicable to loops with any number of iteration paths. Suppose Op1 writes a register R that is read by Op3. To break write-after-read, inter-iteration dependence edges, R is privatized and temporarily promoted to a vector register[1], a technique also known as modulo-variable expansion [11]. In Figure 3, five copies of this hypothetical SP schedule have been overlapped and the lifetime of each element in R[] is indicated by a gray-shaded vertical line. Each row represents a VLIW instruction, labelled on the left. The instructions have been placed so that operations from the same iteration are vertically aligned.

Observe that instructions I2, I3, I4, *etc.* execute the same operations, suggesting that these instructions are equivalent and that I2 should form the kernel. To check this, we check for register conflicts in the execution states before instruction I2 and before I3. In the execution state before I2, R[0] is live and yet to be read by Op3 of the first iteration. In the execution state before I3, R[1] is live and yet to be read by Op3 of the second iteration. In addition, the first *active* iteration in the execution state before I2 is the first iteration, while the first active iteration in the execution state before I3 is the second iteration. Thus, R[0] and R[1] are live registers in the corresponding first active iterations of the two execution states suggesting that the states may be equivalent.

If these two execution states were equivalent, then the same instruction is to be used for both states and, moreover, registers R[0] and R[1] would be demoted to the same scalar register since they correspond to the value being read by Op3. However, R[0] and R[1] are also live simultaneously in the execution state before I2 and thus must be demoted to different scalar registers for correct execution. Since assigning R[0] and R[1] to the same register as well as different registers is contradictory, these two execution states cannot be considered equivalent even though they have equivalent live operations. Thus instructions I2 and I3 must both be generated.

Note that instructions I2 and I4 also execute the same operations. Again we check for equivalence by considering the execution states before I2 and before I4. The live registers in corresponding active iterations are R[0] and R[2] (both are yet to be read by the first active iteration in each state) as well as R[1] and R[3] (both will be read by the second active iteration in each state). R[0] and R[2] are not live simultaneously in either execution state and neither is R[1] and R[3]. Hence as long as the other three criteria for equivalency are satisfied, these two states are equivalent and one instruction can be generated for I2 and I4. Furthermore, R[0] and R[2] are to be demoted to the same scalar register, say r11, and R[1] and R[3] are to be demoted to another scalar register, say r12. Also, because the instruction to execute after I3 is equivalent to I2, a branch operation is inserted into I3 to cause control to go to I2.

By checking for register conflicts, a kernel can be automatically unrolled until conflicts no longer exist. In the example above, we explained why instruction I2 could not by itself form the kernel because of register conflicts. By including I3, a kernel

1. A vector register, in this case, is only a notational convenience used by the compiler to identify private registers. No physical vector registers are assumed to exist, and every vector register is demoted to a scalar register before code is emitted.

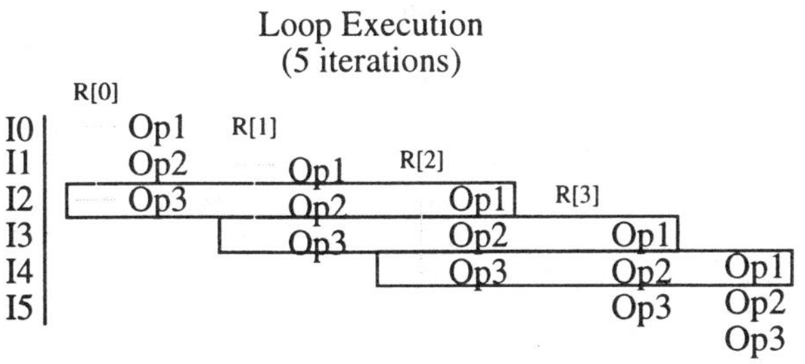

Figure 3: Detecting the Kernel for a hypothetical SP schedule

could be formed free of conflicts. A special rotating register file could be used in lieu of unrolling the kernel to avoid register conflicts and still achieve near-optimal II [17][18].

If two execution states pass the four criteria described above, then they are equivalent. Neither the elapsed time nor the kernel schedule followed by each iteration is used to determine the equivalence of execution states. Only the live operations, live vector registers, number of active iterations, and the epilog flag are used. Using the live operations results in a more general condition of equivalence because it allows iterations that are following different kernel schedules to be found equivalent. Of course, if non-unit operational latencies are allowed, the live operations condition would need to be augmented to take into account operations that have been issued but not yet completed.

The overhead required to compare two execution states for equivalence is kept to a minimum by evaluating the four criteria in increasing order of complexity. Comparing the number of active iterations and the epilog flags for both states can be done in O(1) time. These conditions are evaluated first. Next, the live operations of the two states are compared, requiring O(# live operations) time. Lastly, the live registers are examined for conflicts in O(# live registers) time. The first of these conditions that fails will end the equivalence comparison. Only closely matching execution states will need to evaluate the latter conditions, and in many cases, determining that a pair of execution states are not equivalent will only take O(1) or O(# live operations) time.

Identifying equivalent states automatically creates kernels as well as generates efficient transition code. Equivalent states could represent different aspects of a loop's schedule. They could be the end of a kernel and beginning of a kernel. A kernel is then created by simply replacing the execution state at the kernel's end with a loop-back branch to the kernel's beginning. Equivalent states could also represent a point of execution in some transition code that is in fact equivalent to some already existing execution state in the kernel being transitioned to. By identifying equivalent states we can determine as quickly as possible after leaving one kernel when we can enter another. A third possibility is that an instruction common to two kernels has been found. An example of this will be shown in the next section.

2.2. The Combine Algorithm

We are now ready to describe the details of the combine algorithm. Figure 4 lists the steps in the algorithm. Among the information kept for an execution state is information about the iterations that are active in the execution state. Recorded for each active iteration are the set of possible paths that an iteration could be following, the actual path that is being followed, and a time index into the kernel schedule of the active path. The time index indicates how much of the kernel schedule has already been incorporated into the loop schedule.

The algorithm keeps a queue of execution states that have yet to be added to the loop schedule. The queue initially contains one execution state that corresponds to the entry point of the loop with one active iteration at time zero. An execution state is taken off the queue and a new iteration is initiated and added to the execution state if the correct amount of time has elapsed since the youngest iteration in the execution state was started. The path followed by the new iteration is the same as the one followed by the youngest iteration.

The execution state is then compared to the execution states that have already been added to the loop schedule. The naive approach of sequentially comparing the state against all previously processed states would be prohibitively expensive, especially for large loops. To reduce the number of comparisons needed, each processed execution state is stored in a bucket that is accessed through a a hash table. States are stored in the same bucket if they are almost equivalent. Indexing into the hash table is based on state characteristics that affect equivalency. To determine if the current execution state has already been created, the bucket into which it would be stored is computed. Only the execution states in this bucket need to be compared against the current state.

If an equivalent execution state is found, then control is redirected to that state's position in the loop schedule rather than to the current execution state and we are done processing the execution state.

Otherwise no matching execution state was found. In this case, the current state is added to the hash table and a loop instruction and successor states are created.

First, all iterations are marked as either unrestrained or restrained. If there were some iterations that did not contribute an instruction when processing the state's predecessor, then those will be marked as unrestrained now and those that did contribute will be marked as restrained. In this way, previously non-contributing iterations will eventually contribute their instructions to some execution state while contributing iterations are restrained from advancing until all iterations have contributed their instruction.

Iterations can also be marked restrained if a cross-trace dependence is detected. Cross-trace dependences are dependences between operations that originate from different paths in the loop. For instance, an operation from the False path may set register R1 and an operation from the True path may read register R1 in a subsequent iteration. If any cross-trace dependence edge will be violated by allowing an iteration to contribute an instruction, then that iteration is marked as restrained so that the dependence is not violated.

Once iterations have been marked appropriately, the fall-through successor is created by making a copy of the current execution state.

Each unrestrained iteration is then examined, oldest iteration first, to determine whether it can contribute its instruction to the loop instruction being created. If an iteration's instruction can be contributed, then the elapsed time for that iteration's schedule is

```
Until queue is empty:
  get execution state from queue
  start a new iteration if appropriate
  if execution state is equivalent to an
                                  execution state in loop
    redirect flow of execution to equivalent
                                          execution state
  else
    add execution state to hash table
    create loop instruction and successor states:
      mark all iterations as restrained or
                                             unrestrained
      construct a fall-through successor
      for each unrestrained iteration:
        if contributed instruction fits then
          add to loop-schedule instruction
          advance time for this iteration's
                                   schedule in successors
          demote vector registers used in
                                  contributed instruction
          if branch scheduled, create duplicate
                                                successor
    record register conflicts
    put all successors on queue
  endif
```

Figure 4: The Combine Algorithm

advanced by one time step in all the successor states, and vector register demotions are done. If a branch operation is contributed as part of an iteration's instruction, then a new successor execution state is created by duplicating the existing successor and indicating that a new path is being followed in the new successor.

After the loop instruction and successor states have been created, the register conflicts are recorded based on which registers are simultaneously live in different active iterations. Any successors that were created as the state was processed are then added to the queue, resulting in a breadth-first creation of the loop schedule.

To demonstrate the APP algorithm, we have applied it to the loop from Figure 1. The control flow graph for the example loop is reproduced in Figure 5a and the loop schedule generated by APP is shown in Figure 5b. Operations that execute only on the False iteration path are presented in italics while the operations that execute only on the True iteration path are presented in bold. The unit in which an operation is executed is listed by each operation in Figure 5a, while each VLIW instruction is labelled on the left for easy reference in Figure 5b. Primed operations are from the iteration following the iteration of unprimed operations. Due to space limitations, we describe only the generated loop schedule; a full description of how APP generates the loop schedule is provided elsewhere [20].

Recall that the F path has a minimum initiation interval of four cycles while the T path supports a minimum initiation interval of seven cycles. Note that the F kernel (I4, I6, I8, I10) is exactly four cycles long, and the T kernel (I5, I7, I9, I12, I6, I8, I11) is seven cycles long. Runs of iterations that follow the F or T iteration path will, thus, achieve the minimum possible execution time.

Moreover, switching execution from the F path to the T path or vice-versa incurs no additional processor cycles. The instruction (I8) that contains the branch operation (Op1) is common to the kernels for both iteration paths; hence whichever instruction is executed next will be part of a kernel schedule and no additional transition code is needed to drain one pipeline schedule and fill the other. Although it is not always the case that the instruction containing the branch is common to several iteration paths, it is still possible to transition from one kernel schedule directly into another.

Regardless of which direction the Op1 branch operation takes in any iteration, the floating-point unit will be saturated for all iterations once one of the kernel schedules is entered. Neglecting the time spent in the prolog and epilog, the schedule in Figure 5b provides optimal execution throughput for the example loop. This loop could not execute any faster on this processor. Of course, in general for different loops or different processor configurations, optimal execution of transitions between iteration paths is not always possible resulting in transition instructions that contain operations from more than one path. On the other hand, executions of runs of iteration paths are near optimal.

3. Related Work

Because dealing with multiple IIs for a single loop schedule is rather complex, much of the earlier work on software pipelining loops with conditionals used a single fixed II for the entire loop schedule [5][10][11][24][21][27]. A single kernel schedule would be produced that contained all possible paths through a loop. By using predicated operations with if-conversion [4][5][10][19][27], the kernel's II could be shortened. However, execution of successive iterations of the same path could be sub-optimal because operations from other paths must be included in the single kernel's schedule.

Only a few algorithms have been developed that can generate multiple kernel schedules with different IIs for different iteration paths. Most have focussed on generating code that seamlessly transitions from one kernel schedule to the next rather than producing near-optimal kernels for all iteration paths. By using sub-optimal kernels for some iteration paths, a transition from one path to another is typically handled by the sub-optimal kernel itself and no additional transition code is needed.

Enhanced Pipeline-Percolation Scheduling (EPPS) [6][7] was one of the first such algorithms. It uses extremely aggressive speculative scheduling combined with register renaming to pull up as many future computations as possible. This is allowed in a more limited sense over the loop-back branch as well, resulting in pipeline schedules. It has been shown, however, that EPPS does not deal effectively with complex resource patterns [3], and due to the greedy scheduling of operations may not generate kernels that are as efficient as possible.

Perfect Pipelining[1][2] is a kernel-recognition technique that generates VLIW instructions one at a time. When an instruction is created, it is compared to all previously created instructions for functional equivalence. Two instructions are functionally equivalent if all future computations from both instructions are identical. If the current instruction is found functionally equivalent to another, it can be replaced by a branch to the equivalent instruction. In this way, the kernels of a loop are identified, and code expansion is also reduced. The primary drawbacks of this

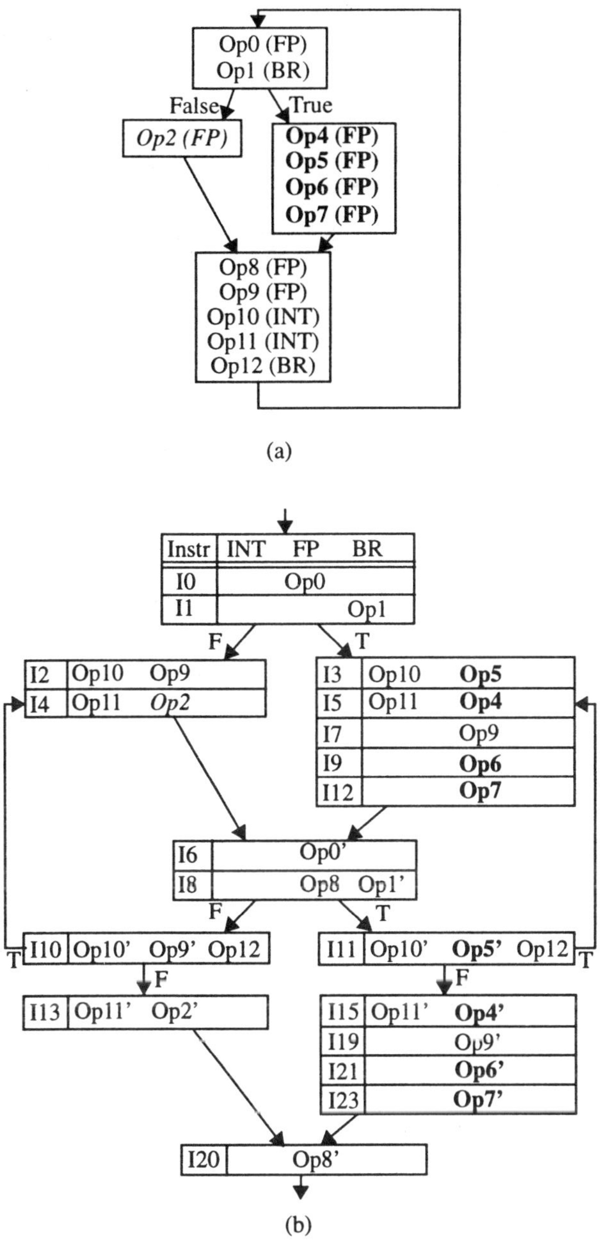

Figure 5: Demonstrating APP

Figure 5a: Control flow graph of loop from Figure 1
Figure 5b: Pipelined loop schedule produced by APP

approach are that the emergence of short kernels is not guaranteed due to its greedy approach, and that efficient kernel recognition can be prevented if different parts of the loop can iterate at different rates due to dependence cycles.

A more recent technique called Modulo Scheduling with Multiple Initiation Intervals (MSMII) [26] creates a loop kernel with several predicated loop-back branches (potentially one per iteration path). Unlike the two previous techniques, MSMII is based on modulo scheduling [15], whereby operations are placed into VLIW instructions. Path priorities are assigned based upon dynamic profiling of the loop, and operations are then placed in the kernel so that the highest-priority paths use an initiation interval close to the MII for that path. Predicated operations are used to execute the correct operations and loop-back branch based upon which path is actually executed dynamically. There are two main drawbacks of this approach. First, both hardware support and dynamic information about the program's execution are required for the algorithm to be effective. Second, the resource usage of different iteration paths must share functional units which may unnecessarily increase the initiation interval of all paths, especially if these paths have equal priority.

Lastly, the Global UnRoll-Pipeline-Reroll (GURPR) [22] approach attempts to produce near-optimal schedules for individual iteration paths and then add code for transitioning between the kernel schedules. The GURPR algorithm consists of three steps similar in nature to those used in APP. The first two steps are virtually identical except that GURPR uses a kernel-recognition algorithm called URPR [23] for the second step. For the third step, GURPR uses a simplistic approach to merge the pipeline schedules. Unfortunately, the generated transition code was found to be so inefficient that loop execution time was often dominated by the time to execute the transitions between the pipelined schedules. Because of this result, the successors to GURPR, GURPR* [21] and GPMB [24], abandoned the first two steps and used a single initiation interval for all iteration paths.

All Paths Pipelining draws upon the advantages of the two approaches to software pipelining: modulo scheduling and kernel recognition [3]. Modulo scheduling is used in the second step while the combine algorithm in the third step uses kernel-recognition techniques similar to those developed for Perfect Pipelining.

All Paths Pipelining improves upon the above-mentioned work in several ways. By using a modulo scheduling algorithm in the second step, APP benefits from many of the advantages of this approach. For example, the initiation intervals for individual paths are always optimal or near-optimal [11][15]. Moreover, a modulo scheduling algorithm can deal effectively with complex resource patterns [15], and by using a modulo scheduling algorithm, the recognition of the kernels when generating the final loop schedule is much simpler than in Perfect Pipelining. The code generated by APP executes transitions between pipeline schedules much more efficiently than the GURPR approach. APP also seamlessly deals with the kernel unrolling that is often required for modulo-expanded variables [11]. Moreover, APP does not rely on either profiling information or special hardware such as predicated operations to achieve good performance. Finally, APP has been implemented in our research compiler while a perusal of the literature indicates that most software pipelining algorithms using multiple II's have not yet been incorporated into a compiler.

4. Evaluation of APP

We have implemented the APP algorithm in our compiler that we are developing as part of research on architectures and compilers for signal processing applications. Although we have implemented and evaluated APP in this context, its use is not limited to architectures for signal processing. APP does not rely on program structures that are specific to this application domain nor does it use hardware features specific to signal processing architectures.

The VLIW architectural model we used to evaluate the APP algorithm is shown in Figure 6. This model has five functional units: one addressing unit (AU0), one integer unit (INT0), one floating-point unit (FP0), one memory unit(MU0), and one program control unit (PCU). Three register files (address, integer, and floating-point) support these functional units. Each register file contains 32 32-bit registers. The architecture uses a four-stage pipeline: fetch, decode, execute and writeback. All pipeline stages have unit latency. Branches are predicted not-taken and a one-cycle stall results for taken branches.

The compiler system consists of three parts: a front-end compiler, a post optimizer, and an architectural simulator. The front-end compiler is a port of the GNU gcc compiler that generates a sequential stream of operations targeted for the architecture. The post optimizer performs optimizations specific to the new architecture, including the APP implementation where the sequential operations are compacted into the VLIW instructions required by the simulator. The simulator performs a cycle-by-cycle simulation of the execution of a program on the architecture described above and includes support for I/O operations and statistics generation.

We first present the performance results of the code generated by APP, and then address the issues of code expansion and compilation time.

4.1. Performance Results

Table 2 shows the advantage of isolating each iteration path in the loops from Table 1. We show the initiation intervals achieved by local scheduling, the minimum initiation intervals achievable by a single-II technique based upon predicated execution, and the minimum initiation intervals achievable by isolating each iteration path. In five of the nine loops, pipelining the iteration paths individually provides a performance advantage. In the other four loops, performance is identical to that of the single-II technique. Note that these initiation intervals are not necessarily achievable by a particular pipelining technique due to interactions between dependence cycles.

To evaluate the dynamic performance of APP-scheduled code, we report results for three scheduling options. The baseline scheduling option (Local) uses list scheduling [12] for all code. The second scheduling option (SP) applies the APP algorithm to loops that have no conditional branches. All other code, including loops with conditional branches, is scheduled using list scheduling. The third scheduling option (APP) uses the full APP algorithm on all loops with any number of iteration paths. Again, all other code is list-scheduled.

We also present two performance limits to provide an indication of 1) how close APP's performance is to the maximal achievable performance, and 2) where the performance is being lost. The first limit (Max) represents the least amount of time that the processor could execute each loop and compute the correct result. This limit is similar to the MACS bound [14], but is extended to deal with loops with at least one conditional branch. The Max limit is calculated by assuming that every iteration can execute in the amount of time dictated by the MII of the iteration path that the iteration uses dynamically. Recall that the MII is simply the maximum of the resource constraint ResMII (Eq. 1) and the recurrence constraint RecMII (Eq. 2). The recurrence constraint does not include the effects of the dependence edges added in the first step of the APP algorithm. For every target loop, the number of iterations that use each iteration path is collected during a simulation of each program. If the maximum of ResMII and RecMII for an iteration path k is MII(k), then the minimum execution time for each loop is then calculated as:

$$LoopTime = \sum_{iter\ path\ k} MII(k) \times (\#\text{iters using path } k) \qquad (3)$$

The execution time used for the Max limit is then the execution time of all code not in inner loops plus *LoopTime*.

The second performance limit, MaxAPP, is identical to the Max limit, except that the additional edges from the first step of the APP algorithm are included. This limit identifies where the most performance is lost. The difference between Max and MaxAPP indicates the performance lost due to the additional edges used by the APP algorithm. The difference between MaxAPP and APP indicates the performance lost due to inefficiencies in the transition, prolog, and epilog code generated by APP.

The benchmark suite used to validate and evaluate the APP algorithm consists of typical DSP applications from signal and image processing. All the applications in this suite contain at least one loop with conditional branches. Table 3 gives a brief description of each of the application programs. Table 3 also shows the performance for the different scheduling options and limits for each benchmark. Performance is given as the percentage improvement in performance over the execution time on a scalar architecture.

Table 3 confirms previous results showing that software pipelining alone provides significant improvement in performance over local scheduling. Augmenting SP with the APP algorithm

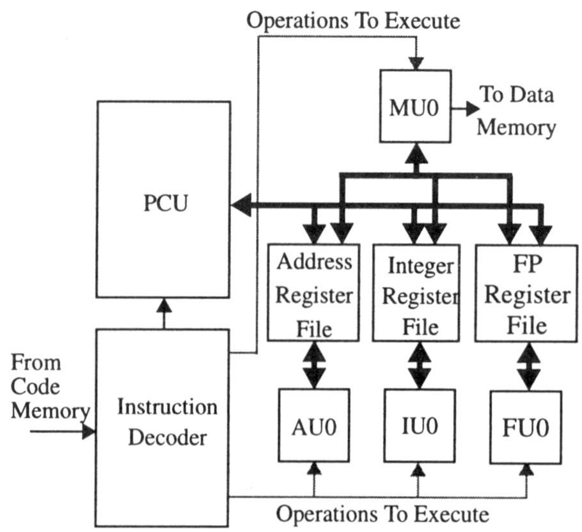

Figure 6: The UTDSP architecture

Solid lines are data buses and dotted lines are the buses passing control information for the operations.

Table 3: Minimum Initiation Intervals

Loop	Local II	Single II	Per-Path II	Best
1	7/7	5	4/4	per-path
2	12/12/12/12	9	7/7/7/7	per-path
3	6/5	4	4/4	either
4	10/11	8	8/8	either
5	9/10	10	6/5	per-path
6	33/32	29	27/26	per-path
7	26/26	18	17/17	per-path
8	8/4	4	4	either
9	19/18	18	18	either

further improves performance for every program albeit by differing amounts. The percentage increase in performance that APP provides over SP ranges from 1% to 23%.

APP provides 11% and 23% more performance gain than SP for G721c and G721d, respectively, demonstrating that APP is able to exploit additional parallelism in the loops with conditional branches. Note that extremely long runs were not necessary to produce these performance gains. The loops in these two applications contain runs of length 11 or less.

For ADPCM and TRELLIS, APP provides 4–5% more performance gain than SP. The performance improvement provided by APP for ADPCM is comparable to the maximum possible (Max), indicating there is little room for further improvement. For TRELLIS, APP's performance improvement is comparable to MaxAPP but there is a slight gap between APP's performance and the Max performance, indicating that the extra dependence edges are preventing APP from achieving better performance.

The lower improvements can be attributed to one of three causes. For ED and LPC, software pipelining already achieves comparable performance to the Max performance, indicating that only a small fraction of the program's total execution time is spent executing the loops that contain conditional branches. For SE and V32d, there is a gap between the performance increase based on the MaxAPP limit and APP's performance improvement, indicating APP loses about a 5% performance improvement due to executing code for transitions, prolog and epilog. V32d also loses an additional 9% improvement due to the additional dependence edges as indicated by the gap between MaxAPP and Max. The extra edges are also the reason for why APP is unable to improve the performance of V32c significantly.

By comparing APP's performance increase to those of the performance limits, we can determine the impact on performance of the transition code and the dependence edges added in the first step of APP. APP's performance for ED, ADPCM, and TRELLIS is comparable to that of Max, indicating, for these programs, that efficient transition code is generated and that the additional dependence edges do not adversely affect performance significantly.

Efficient transition code is also generated for V32c, V32d, and G721c. However, the performances of these three applications are adversely affected by the extra dependence edges, as indicated by the 4%, 9%, and 17% differences, respectively, between the Max-APP limit and the Max limit. Recall that G721c executes a loop with 128 iteration paths and the large number of extra dependence edges obviously affects the attainable performance improvement.

4.2. Code Expansion

Table 4 shows the expansion in code size over locally compacted code and the number of overlapped iterations in each kernel schedule that is executed for the nine loops from Table 1. Code size for each loop is measured in instructions.

For five of the loops, the code expansion was less than a factor of two. In fact, the code size for loop 4 decreased due to the limited global code motion APP can per form. Operations were pulled from below the conditional construct into both conditional paths. No overlap of iterations was possible due to dependence cycles, but the movement of operations reduced the time to execute a single iteration, while also reducing the size of the code. Code size for loop 9 did not increase because the software pipelining algorithm was unable to perform better than the local scheduler.

Three different characteristics of the remaining four loops result in their excessive code expansion. Loop 6, recall, contains 128 iteration paths which produce 2.5 times more code than a local scheduler. However, given the large number of iteration paths, a factor of 2.5 is surprisingly small indicating that APP was able to find many equivalent states among the iteration paths. A large number of conditional branches which result in many iteration paths does not necessarily imply overly excessive code expansion.

Table 4: Percentage Performance Improvements Over Scalar Architecture

Application	Description	Local	SP	APP	Max APP	Max
G721d	Decoder from G721 protocol	0.17	0.17	0.40	0.49	0.52
G721c	Coder from G721 protocol	0.17	0.17	0.28	0.32	0.49
TRELLIS	Trellis decoder	0.38	0.51	0.56	0.57	0.59
ADPCM	Adaptive Pulse Code Modulation	0.32	0.34	0.38	0.39	0.39
ED	Edge Detection	0.42	0.50	0.51	0.51	0.51
LPC	Linear Predictive Coder	0.43	0.54	0.54	0.55	0.55
SE	Spectral Estimation	0.45	0.46	0.46	0.52	0.52
V32d	Decoder from V32 Modem protocol	0.32	0.33	0.33	0.37	0.46
V32c	Coder from V32 Modem protocol	0.38	0.38	0.40	0.42	0.46

For loops 1 and 7, the code expansion is due to the unrolling of kernels to satisfy register constraints.

The code expansion for loop 5 is the result of two kernel schedules supporting a different number of active iterations. The kernel schedule for one path in loop 5 executes 3 iterations at once, while the other kernel schedule executes 4 (indicated in third column of Table 4). Transitioning between such kernels is complex and requires many instructions to perform efficiently, as entire iterations must be drained or filled in the pipeline. Although not evident from Table 4, Loop 7 also has kernel schedules with a different number of active iterations, accounting for much of its code expansion. These kernel schedules are for iteration paths that are not executed for the loop and hence do not appear in Table 4.

Clearly the code expansion for loops 5 and 7 is unacceptable. Much of the expansion is due to the different number of active iterations. One possible technique to reduce the expansion is to use local scheduling for one of the paths so that the active number of iterations for that schedule is only one. This would be similar to the loop schedules generated by APP for loops 3 and 8. Although there are still a different number of active iterations, one of the kernels schedules is now a simple locally compacted schedule. The combine algorithm could then create more regular transition code with the penalty that performance on the locally scheduled path would be poor. This can be minimized by using profiling to identify a rarely used path. For example, the code expansion for loop 5 could be significantly reduced if only the False path were pipelined and the True path was locally scheduled.

Another technique for reducing code expansion is to use predication with APP. Such a technique could be applied to loop 7 as well as loop 6. For both of these loops, most of the branches are easily predicted as indicated by Table 1. Predicating the operations dependent on heavily biased branches could be applied before APP, leaving only the balanced branches to be scheduled by APP. Although some performance may be lost due to the use of the single-II approach, we believe this would reduce the code growth tremendously for these types of loops.

4.3. Compilation Time

We conclude our evaluation of APP by addressing its large time complexity. Since the second step of the algorithm involves software pipelining each iteration path individually, APP is at least $O(2^B)$ where B is the number of branches in the target loop. The combine algorithm itself, being similar to Perfect Pipelining, also has exponential time complexity for certain loops [2]. While this is of theoretical concern, our APP implementation scheduled each program in the benchmark suite except for G721c in less than ten seconds (wall-clock time) on a Sun Sparc5 workstation. The G721c benchmark, with its loop having 128 iteration paths, was scheduled in just under two minutes. We consider this reasonable, as APP is not an optimization that would likely be used during the development cycle when compilation time is of critical importance.

Table 5: Code Expansion and Number of Overlapped Iterations

Loop	Code Expansion	Number of Overlapped Iterations
1	4.75	4/4
2	2.0	2/2/2/2
3	1.67	1/2
4	0.92	1/1
5	12.5	3/4
6	2.5	2/2
7	11.87	2/2
8	1.88	2/1
9	1.0	1/1

5. Summary and Conclusions

The All Paths Pipelining algorithm enhances existing modulo schedulers with techniques used in kernel-recognition schedulers to effectively software pipeline loops containing conditional branches. APP is designed to exploit the execution of successive iterations that take the same path through a loop while providing efficient code for iterations that change paths. Because modulo scheduling requires runs of only modest length (probably around 6 or 8 iterations) to provide excellent performance, APP does not require extremely long runs to significantly improve performance.

The basic approach used by APP is to schedule each iteration path individually using a traditional single-basic-block modulo scheduling algorithm. APP then uses kernel-recognition techniques in the *combine* algorithm to merge the kernel schedules into a single loop schedule that contains both multiple kernels with possibly different initiation intervals as well as code for transitioning between the kernels. By using modulo scheduling for individual iteration paths, APP is able to obtain near-optimal execution for a run of *any* iteration path. Moreover, by using the concept of *equivalent execution states*, the combine algorithm efficiently recognizes kernels as they are being generated, produces efficient transition code for switching execution between the kernels, and aggressively reduces code expansion in many cases.

The APP algorithm was implemented in our research DSP compiler, and then evaluated using a suite of typical DSP applications targeting a VLIW architectural configuration with five functional units. Simulation results show that APP is able to add another 1% to 23% increase in performance to basic software pipelining. Efficient transition code was generated for six out of nine applications, concretely demonstrating the effectiveness of APP's approach in minimizing transition code.

Lastly, it must be emphasized that, although the APP algorithm has been evaluated using DSP applications, there are no features of the algorithm that rely on program structures that are specific to DSP applications or hardware features that are specific to DSP processors. Although cache effects due to code expansion and serializing on branches may degrade performance, the APP algorithm could be successfully applied to general-purpose codes where loops with conditional branches are believed to be more common and to represent larger fractions of program execution time.

References

[1] Aiken, A., and Nicolau, A. A realistic resource-constrained software pipelining algorithm. In *Advances in Languages and Compilers for Parallel Processing* (A. Nicolau, D. Gelernter, T. Gross, and D. Padua, eds.), Pitman/MIT Press, London. pp. 274-290. 1991.

[2] Aiken, A., and Nicolau, A. Perfect pipelining: A new loop optimization technique. In *Proc. of the 1988 European Symposium on Programming, Springer Verlag Lecture Notes in Computer Science*, #300. pp. 221-235. 1988.

[3] Allan, V.H., Jones, R.B., Lee, R.M., and Allan, S.J. Software pipelining. *ACM Computing Surveys*, Vol. 27, No. 3, pp. 367-432, September 1995.

[4] Allen, J.R., Kennedy, K., Porterfield, C., and Warren, J. Conversion of control dependence to data dependence. In *Proc. of the Tenth Annual ACM Symposium on Principles of Programming Languages*. pp. 177-189. 1983.

[5] Dehnert, J.C. and Towle, R.A. Compiling for the Cydra 5. *The Journal of Supercomputing*, 7, pp. 181-228. 1993.

[6] Ebcioglu, K., and Nakatani, T., A new compilation technique for parallelizing loops with unpredictable branches on a VLIW architecture. In *Languages and Compilers for Parallel Computing*, D. Gelernter, Ed., MIT Press, Cambridge, MA. pp. 213-229. 1993.

[7] Ebcioglu, K. A compilation technique for software pipelining of loops with conditional jumps. In *Proc. of the 20th Microprogramming Workshop*. pp. 69-79. 1987.

[8] Fisher, J.A. Trace scheduling: A technique for global microcode compaction. In *IEEE Transactions on Computers*, C-30 7. pp. 478-490. 1981.

[9] Hsu P.Y.-T. *Highly concurrent scalar processing*. Ph.D. thesis. University of Illinois, Urbana-Champaign, Illinois. 1986.

[10] Huff, R.A. Lifetime-sensitive modulo scheduling. In *Proc. of the SIGPLAN '93 Conference on Programming Language Design and Implementation*. pp. 258-267. 1993.

[11] Lam, M. Software Pipelining: An effective scheduling technique for VLIW machines. In *Proc. of the ACM SIGPLAN '88 Conference on Programming Language Design and Implementation*, pp.318-327, 1988.

[12] Landskov, D., Davidson, S., Shriver, B.D., and Mallett, P.W. Local microcode compaction techniques. In *ACM Computing Surveys* vol. 12. pp. 261-294. 1980.

[13] Llosa, J., Valero, M., Ayguade, E., and Gonzalez, A. Hypernode reduction modulo scheduling. In *Proc. of the 28th Annual International Symposium on Microarchitecture*. pp. 350-360. 1995.

[14] Mangione-Smith, W.H., Shih, T.-P., Abraham, S.G., and Davidson, E.S. Approaching a machine-application bound in delivered performance on scientific code. In *Proc. of the IEEE*, Vol. 81, No. 8. pp. 1166-1178. 1993.

[15] Rau, B.R. Iterative modulo scheduling: An algorithm for software pipelining loops. In *Proc. of the 27th Annual International Symposium on Microarchitecture*. pp. 63-74. 1994.

[16] Rau, B. R. and Fisher, J.A. Instruction-level parallel processing: history, overview, and perspective. *The Journal of Supercomputing*, 7, pp. 9-50, 1993.

[17] Rau, B.R., Lee, M., Tirumalai, P.P., and Schlansker, M.S. Register allocation for modulo scheduled loops: strategies, algorithms, and heuristics. In *Proc. of the ACM SIGPLAN 1992 Conference on Programming Language Design and Implementation*, pp. 283-299. 1992.

[18] Rau, B.R. Yen, D.W.L., Yen, W., and Towle, R.A. The Cydra 5 departmental supercomputer: design philosophies, decisions, and trade-offs. In *IEEE Computer*. pp. 12-25. Jan, 1989.

[19] Rau, B.R. and Glaeser, C.D. Some scheduling techniques and an easily schedulable horizontal architecture for high performance scientific computing. In *Proc. of the Fourteenth Annual Workshop on Microprogramming*. pp. 183-198, 1981.

[20] Stoodley, M.G. *Scheduling Loops with Conditional Branches*. M.A.Sc. thesis. University of Toronto. 1995.

[21] Su. B. and Wang, J. GURPR*: A new global software pipelining algorithm. In *Proc. of the 24th Annual International Symposium on Microprogramming*. pp. 175-180. 1991.

[22] Su. B., Ding, S., Wang, J., and Xia, J. GURPR--A method for global software pipelining. In *Proc of the 20th Annual Microprogramming Workshop*. pp. 88-95. 1987.

[23] Su, B., Ding, S., and Xia, J. URPR--An extension of URCR for software pipelining. In *Proc. of the 19th Annual Workshop on Microprogramming*. pp. 104-108. 1986.

[24] Tang, Z., Chen, G., Zhang, C., Zhang, Y., Su, B., and Habib, S. GPMB--Software Pipelining Branch-Intensive Loops. In *Proc. of the 26th Annual International Symposium on Microprogramming*. pp. 21-29. 1993.

[25] Tirumalai, P., Lee, M., and Schlansker, M.S. Parallelization of loops with exits on pipelined architectures. In *Proc of Supercomputing '90*. pp. 200-212. 1990.

[26] Warter-Perez, N.J. and Partamian, N. Modulo scheduling with multiple initiation intervals. In *Proc. of the 28th Annual International Symposium on Microarchitecture*. pp. 111-118. 1995.

[27] Warter, N.J., Bockhaus, J.W., Haab, G.E., and Subramanian, K. Enhanced modulo scheduling for loops with conditional branches. In *Proc. of the 25th Annual International Symposium on Microarchitecture*. pp. 170-179. 1992.

[28] Vegdahl, S.R. A dynamic-programming technique for compacting loops. In *Proc. of the 25th Annual International Symposium on Microarchitecture*. pp. 180-188, 1992.

Combining Loop Transformations Considering Caches and Scheduling

Michael E. Wolf, Dror E. Maydan and Ding-Kai Chen
Silicon Graphics, Mounain View, CA

Abstract

The performance of modern microprocessors is greatly affected by cache behavior, instruction scheduling, register allocation and loop overhead. High level loop transformations such as fission, fusion, tiling, interchanging and outer loop unrolling (e.g., unroll and jam) are well known to be capable of improving all these aspects of performance. Difficulties arise because these machine characteristics and these optimizations are highly interdependent. Interchanging two loops might, for example, improve cache behavior but make it impossible to allocate registers in the inner loop. Similarly, unrolling or interchanging a loop might individually hurt performance but doing both simultaneously might help performance.

Little work has been published on how to combine these transformations into an efficient and effective compiler algorithm. In this paper, we present a model that estimates total machine cycle time taking into account cache misses, software pipelining, register pressure and loop overhead. We then develop an algorithm to intelligently search through the various possible transformations, using our machine model to select the set of transformations leading to the best overall performance. We have implemented this algorithm as part of the MIPSPro commercial compiler system. We give experimental results showing that our approach is both effective and efficient in optimizing numerical programs.

***Keywords**: cache tiling, outer loop unrolling, loop interchange, fission, fusion, instruction scheduling.*

1.0 Introduction

High level loop transformations such as fission, fusion, tiling, interchanging and outer loop unrolling are individually well known to improve cache utilization, instruction scheduling and register allocation.[1] Difficulties arise because the interactions between these optimizations and between these machine characteristics are complicated and highly machine dependent.

Consider optimizing the following loop nest for a superscalar processor such as the MIPS R10000 having a 32KB on-chip cache with a 32B line size.

```
subroutine nest(a, b, c)
real*8 a(1000)
real*8 b(1000,1000),c(1000)
DO j = 1, 1000
    DO i = 1, 1000
        a(j) = a(j) + b(j, i) * c(j)
    END DO
END DO
end
```

Let's start by considering only the interchange transformation. The decision of whether to interchange or not cannot be made without intimate knowledge of both the cache system and the processor details. If we do not interchange, we expect a cache miss each iteration because the *b* reference is not stride one. If we interchange, each reference is stride one, so we expect only one miss for *b* every four iterations.

But the cache performance is only part of the story. Without interchange, each iteration requires only one multiply-add and one load. Assuming that we can reassociate reductions and ignoring cache misses this will take one cycle per iteration on the MIPS R10000. If we interchange, we have to do two extra loads and one extra store per iteration. Since the R10000 has only one load/store unit, the interchanged loop will take four cycles per iteration, ignoring cache misses.

Depending on the cache miss penalty, interchange might help or might hurt performance. Adding other transformations into the mix further complicates matters. We can both interchange and outer loop unroll our example as follows.

1. We use the term *outer loop unrolling* instead of *unroll-and-jam* because when loop bounds are not constant, the specific transformation applied is not an *unroll* followed by a *jam*, but a more complicated transformation that has the equivalent effect on scheduling. Likewise, we use the term *tiling* rather than *strip-mine and interchange* for the same reason.

1072-4451/96 $5.00 © 1996 IEEE

```
DO i = 1, 1000,4
   DO j = 1, 1000
      a(j) = a(j) + b(j,i)*c(j)
      a(j) = a(j) + b(j,i+1)*c(j)
      a(j) = a(j) + b(j,i+2)*c(j)
      a(j) = a(j) + b(j,i+3)*c(j)
   END DO
END DO
```

The references are still all stride one. In each iteration, we need to do one store and six loads. Ignoring cache misses, each iteration takes seven cycles or 1.75 cycles per original iteration. So, we can retain the cache benefits of interchange, while getting a schedule that is almost as good as the non-interchanged case. On the other hand, more registers are required. For this loop, we probably have sufficient registers, but on bigger loops unrolling might lead to register spilling.

From our example, we have seen that we can not make optimal choices about transformations individually. We have also seen that we need to model the entire system in order to select the best overall transformations. We have designed and implemented a compiler algorithm for loop permutation, outer unrolling, tiling, fission and fusion that takes into account all these factors. Essentially, we enumerate the search space of possible transformations, selecting the set of transformations that we estimate will give us the best possible overall performance. By intelligently pruning the search space, we show that we can be both effective and efficient. There is much discussion in the literature on combining transformations to improve cache reuse. For example, Wolf discusses an algorithm combining unimodular transformation (e.g. interchange and skewing) and tiling to quickly determine a good blocking for the cache [W91]. Carr, McKinley, Tseng and Coleman study the order of loops within a tile and methods for choosing block sizes to avoid cache interference [CMT94][CM95]. These works and others provide searching heuristics and models that can be helpful in cache optimization, but they do not consider other aspects of performance. Carr, Kennedy and Guan optimize for cache and instruction scheduling, much as we do [CK94][C96][G95]. However, their work only applies to outer unrolling. The main contribution of this paper is that we combine a wide set of optimizations considering the effects of both caches and instruction scheduling.

In the next section, we briefly discuss the mechanics of our algorithm. Section 3 and 4 are the heart of our paper. Section 3 describes how we estimate the performance of a potential transformation. In Section 4, we discuss how we efficiently search the transformation space to find an effective set of transformations to apply. In Section 5 we compare our results to earlier SGI compilers that used preprocessors from KAI and to Carr and Guan [C96][G95].

2.0 Mechanics of the Transformations

Our algorithm is based on the concept of Singly Nested Loop Nests (SNLNs). A Singly Nested Loop Nest is a perfectly nested loop nest, or an imperfect one where the imperfect code does not contain any loops or other complex control flow. Only *CALLs*, *IFs* and simple statements are allowed in the imperfect code. Consider the example below:

```
DO i = 1, N
   DO j = 1, N
      DO k = 1, N
         IF () ...
         DO l = 1, N
            S1
         END DO
      END DO
      DO m = 1, N
         S2
      END DO
   END DO
END DO
```

This loop contains three SNLNs. One is the nest containing the *i* and *j* loops, one is the nest containing the *k* and *l* loops, and the third is the *m* loop. According to the definition, we could have said that there are five SNLNs: *i*, *j*, *k*, *l* and *m*. We can define *maximal* SNLNs, which result from an SNLN partitioning such that no two SNLNs can be combined to form a single (larger) SNLN. The maximal SNLN partitioning is unique, in this case the one with the three SNLNs.

This definition of maximal SNLN is useful because it is the most general shape of loop nest that we know how to tile, outer unroll and permute. For the purposes of this paper, we do not consider non-inner SNLNs, i.e. maximal SNLNs containing other SNLNs inside. So in the above example, we would not transform the *i* and *j* loops. Our approach can easily be extended to outer SNLNs as well. In fact, since transforming the outer SNLNs does not really affect instruction scheduling, we can treat outer SNLNs separately and only consider how transforming them affects cache behavior.

Let us begin by discussing perfect loop nests. It is a result of standard dependence analysis that if the loops within the nest can be arbitrarily interchanged, then arbitrary tiling and arbitrary outer loop unrollings are also legal, as are arbitrary combinations of these transformations. We call such loops *fully permutable*. A Transformable Loop Nest (TLN) is a fully permutable SNLN. To be fully permutable, all dependence arcs from and to array references within the nest must either be carried outside the outermost loop of the nest, or all components of the dependence vectors corresponding to loops within the nest must be non-negative.

Imperfect nests can be reduced to perfect nests in two ways. First, imperfect code might be fissionable, perhaps after application of scalar expansion. Second, we can move the imperfect code into the body of the TLN. For example:

```
DO i = 1, N
   S1
   DO j = i+1, N
      S2
   END DO
END DO
```

can, at least conceptually, be rewritten as

```
DO i = 1, N
   DO j = i+1, N
      IF (j == i+1) S1
      S2
   END DO
END DO
```

Given this rewriting, we can apply dependence analysis to test for legality. Note this rewriting is only legal if we are guaranteed that whenever an iteration of the DO *i* loop executes, then an iteration of the DO *j* loop also executes. We use an integer linear equation solver to prove this legality [MHL91].

The details of transforming non-perfectly nested loops and loops with non-rectangular bounds are beyond the scope of this paper, but it should be known that our system is quite aggressive. We are able to permute any perfectly nested or distributable TLN. We do not interchange other imperfect nests because interchanging them would introduce IFs into the innermost loop. We can tile any TLN, generating efficient IF code (outside the innermost loop) to protect the imperfect computations; we can outer unroll any perfect or distributable nest with invariant bounds, or any TLN of depth 2.

The concept of TLNs leads to a three phase algorithm. In phase 1, we use loop fission and fusion to create deep SNLNs and to collect all maximal SNLNs. Phase 2 transforms the SNLNs and phase 3 reduces register pressure in the innermost loop, if necessary.

Phase 1: Consider the following example,

```
DO i
   DO j1
      DO k1
      END DO
   END DO
   DO j2
      DO k2
      END DO
   END DO
END DO
```

We have the choice of creating one 3-deep SNLN by fusing loop *(j1,k1)* and *(j2,k2)* or creating two 3-deep SNLNs by fissioning loop *i* into two loop nests, *(i1,j1,k1)* and *(i2,j2,k2)*. In the current implementation, we prefer fusion over fission largely because fusion improves cache reuse and causes less loop overhead. Additionally, we have another chance to fission large loops in phase 3 of our algorithm. This is not always the correct decision. If one of the original loops has "bad" dependences, fusing the two loops can inhibit later transformations on the entire nest. If, instead we had chosen fission, we might still have been able to later transform one of the two resultant loops. This situation can be avoided if phase 1 and 2 are more tightly coupled or if we have a back-tracking mechanism. Both are considered as possible future enhancements.

We use a recursive algorithm for phase 1. Given an outer loop, we recursively build maximal SNLNs for all the children of the loop. We then try to use fusion or fission to combine the children SNLNs with the parent loop.

Phase 2: Given the SNLNs built in phase 1, the core of our algorithm searches for the best loop permutation, the best unrolling factors and the best tile sizes. These will be described in detail in Sections 3 and 4.

Phase 3: We mentioned earlier that certain inner loops might not be register allocatable. For each innermost loop that requires spilling, according to the register model described in Section 3.1, we fission the loop into smaller register allocatable loops. The algorithm starts out by building a statement dependence graph in which each node is a statement and the edges indicate scalar or array data dependences among statements. Some of the scalar edges can be removed when scalar expansion is considered. Next we identify the maximal *Strongly Connected Components*, SCCs, in the dependence graph. All statements belonging to the same SCC have to stay in the same loop after fission to preserve data dependences. An SCC dependence graph is then built as a result of an acyclic condensation of the statement dependence graph.

We could fission the loops so that each SCC is in its own loop, but that would be excessive. Our goal is to combine multiple SCCs such that

- as many loops are register allocatable as possible; and
- the number of loops is as small as possible.

We put SCCs without dependence predecessors in a free list. We pick a seed SCC from the free list and then add to the free list those SCCs dependent only on the seed SCC. We select the seed that will result in the most new SCCs being added to the free list. Then we heuristically rank SCCs in the free list. An SCC with more variables in common with the seed SCC will have a higher ranking. Similarly, an SCC containing new variables not in the seed SCC will have a lower ranking. We visit the free list in priority order, and merge into the seed the highest ranking SCC that will not result in register spilling according to the model. This process is repeated until no spill-free merging is possible. Then, a new seed SCC is chosen and the merging process resumes. Finally, we fission the loop and scalar expand those variables with defs and uses in different resultant loops.

Note that our three phase algorithm is not guaranteed to produce the best transformations. It is possible, for example, that in a loop with register allocation problems, it is better to first fission the nest and then try to unroll it. So while we search through the best unrollings, tilings and permutations, we do not do so for each possible fissioning of the loops. We have chosen what we believe is a good compromise that allows us to chose among many interrelated transformations while retaining compile time efficiencies.

3.0 Modeling

Our transformation algorithm depends upon having an evaluation function that can estimate how many cycles a given (possibly transformed) loop nest will take to run on our target. We actually combine the results from two different models. First, the processor model models scheduling and register pressure. Second, the cache model models the cycles lost due to cache misses, and also cycles lost to start-up time of the inner loop, so that the costs of tiling, which often shortens the inner loop, can be accurately computed.

Actually, the models compute cycles per iteration, where in this context "iteration" means a single iteration of the source loop, before transformation. Thus outer-loop unrolling by a factor of two does not approximately double the cycles per iteration, but rather, often decreases it.

3.1 Processor Model

Our goal in this subsection is to estimate how well the code generator will schedule an inner loop given a set of loop optimizations and ignoring cache effects. Without actually scheduling the loop, it is impossible to exactly predict how well a loop will be scheduled. Since we are going to be exploring a large set of potential transformations (potentially hundreds of combinations), we can not generate code, register allocate and schedule each combination. Instead, we use a high level model to estimate bounds on scheduling. Given uncertainty, we bias our model to limit unrolling.

We model three types of constraints: computational resources, latencies and registers.

3.1.1 Computational Resource Modeling

Our machine has a finite amount of resources; FP adders, ALUs, load/store units, etc. We first find a bound on the schedule considering only these resources. We ignore dependences and latencies. We divide the resources into four categories: floating point, memory, integer and issue.

Our instruction scheduler is table driven. Each machine instruction has entries for the resources it will require in different cycles. We use the same table to compute floating point resource limits. We walk the inner loop. For each floating point instruction, we map the instruction into the corresponding machine instruction. For many instructions, this mapping is trivial. A double precision add in the intermediate representation (IR) maps directly into a machine level double precision add. Other instructions are a bit more complicated. For example, a complex add in the IR maps into two floating point adds in the machine level. As another example, a multiply feeding an add in the IR maps into the single "madd" machine instruction. We keep a count for each machine resource. Given a machine instruction, we use the scheduling table to increment the count of each resource used by that instruction. If our machine has multiple units of certain resources, we divide the count appropriately. After walking the code, we find the maximum count over all the resources and use that as our estimate of the floating point resource requirements. Note that this estimate ignores floating point common sub-expressions, or CSEs (common floating point expressions, not common memory references). Since our algorithm runs before the scalar optimizer, we do not know what expressions will be CSE'd. Underestimating the number of CSEs is a conservative error in that it leads to less unrolling.

There is much more commonality among floating point memory references than among floating point operations.

In fact, one of the main reasons we unroll a loop is to expose memory reference CSEs. Therefore, we can not simply walk the code and count the number of references to get an estimate of memory resources. Instead, we walk the code and gather all array references. Scalars need not be loaded or stored inside the loop. Similarly, inner loop invariant array references need not be considered. We put all the variant array references into equivalence classes. Two references are in the same equivalence class if they reference the same location within a small number of iterations, 6,of the inner loop. For example, the two array references a[i] and a[i+1] will be put in the same equivalence class. When referencing a[i+1], our software pipeliner will save the value in a register and will use that value rather than referencing a[i] in the next iteration. If an equivalence class contains both a load and a store to the same location, and the first load comes lexically before the first store, that class requires two memory references. For example, given the statement "a[i] = a[i] ...", we must load the old value of a[i] and store the new value. Otherwise, each equivalence class requires one memory reference. We divide the number of estimated references by the number of memory units to get a memory resource bound.

Numerical codes tend not to have much integer computation. Integer computations are also difficult to estimate at loop nest optimization time. Before scalar optimizations, it is difficult to know how memory addresses will be strength reduced and CSE'd, so we do not know how much arithmetic will be required to compute addresses. We therefore take the conservative approach and assume that every inner loop requires three ALU operations; one branch, one increment to a base register for addressing the array references and one increment for counting loop iterations. We therefore divide three by the number of ALUs. In most loop nests dominated by floating point and memory operations, the number of integer operations do not make a difference. In code well balanced between floating point and memory operations, considering integer operations leads us to unroll loops slightly more than we would have otherwise. Hopefully this exposes more memory CSEs and leads to better schedules.

We consider issue resources separately because they are limited by the combination of other resources. On the R10000, for example, we have resources for two floating point operations, two ALU operations and one memory reference per cycle, but we can only issue four total instructions per cycle. For the issue resource, we add together the number of ALU and memory instructions as computed above. To this sum, we add the number of floating point instructions. The number of floating point instructions is distinct from the floating point resource requirement since, for example, a floating point divide may take up many cycles of resources, but it need only be issued once. Given the sum, we divide by the number of issue units.

Finally, our resource cycle estimate is the maximum of the floating point limit, the memory limit, the integer limit and the issue limit.

3.1.2 Latency Modeling

The cycle time of a loop might also be limited by the latency of dependent operations, in other words the length of a recurrence. Since we are software pipelining inner loops, we do not need to worry about intra-iteration memory dependences. Only inter-iteration dependences affect the latency of a software pipelined schedule. Our algorithm for estimating latencies comes from the software pipelining literature [L88][RGSL96].

We build a dependence graph for the loop. We add a vertex for each floating point load and each floating point store. Each edge in the graph is marked with a latency and a distance. We add an edge to every store from every load in the same statement. These edges will have a latency equal to the sum of the latencies of the operations going from the load up to the store. So for example, given the statement a[i] = (b[i] + c[i]) / d[i], there will be an edge with the latency of a floating point division from the load of d[i] to the store. Similarly, there will be an edge from the load of b[i] and another from the load of c[i] to the store with the latency of a floating point add plus the latency of a floating point division. The reference, d[i], can be loaded immediately before the division while b[i] and c[i] must be loaded before the add, and the add must complete before the division can begin. All the edges will have a distance '0' signifying that the memory references and floating point operations are occurring in the same iteration. Given a flow memory dependence, we add an edge to the graph from the store to the load with latency '0' and the distance in iterations of the dependence. So given, for example

a[i] = ...
... = a[i-2]

we add an edge from the store to the load with latency '0' and distance '2'. This represents the fact that the load in a particular iteration must wait for the store from two iterations earlier to complete.

From the literature, the latency limit of the loop is the maximum over all cycles in the graph of the sum of the latencies in the cycle divided by the sum of the distances in the cycle. We use the algorithm from our software pipeliner to compute this limit.

3.1.3 Modeling Floating Point Registers

Loop transformations can increase register pressure. After some transformations, it can become impossible to schedule a loop without spilling registers.

When modeling register pressure, we consider three effects: pipeline filling, invariant memory references and memory CSEs. Previous approaches have looked at expression trees rather than pipeline filling [CK94][ASU86]. Our approach comes from the belief that on modern superscalar machines, pipeline filling is much more important. Take for example the MIPS R8000 microprocessor. It can perform two floating point multiply-adds, or madds, per cycle, but the latency to load a value, perform a madd and then store the result is five cycles. Therefore, in order to run the machine at peak performance, we need to perform 10 madds in parallel. Each madd must write to a unique result register; otherwise the pipeline will stall. In addition, we need several floating point register as input registers (some of the input registers can be reused before the first madd completes). We define the pipeline filling requirements of a microprocessor to be the number of floating point registers required to keep the pipeline running at full speed. On the R8000, the requirement is 18 floating point registers. On the R10000, which has shorter latencies, the number is 14 registers.

Added to the number of pipeline filling registers are the floating point registers needed to hold the results of memory references. If an array load is invariant, we do not need to load it every iteration, but the price of avoiding a load is one register to hold its value. Similarly, given the two array loads a[i] and a[i-2], the software pipeliner will hold the value a[i] in a register for two iterations in order to avoid the second load. So, we group all the variant memory references in equivalence classes as we did when computing the memory resource requirements. The span of an equivalence class is the distance in iterations between the first and last reference in the equivalence class. The number of registers required to hold all the CSEs is the sum of the spans of all the equivalence classes. We add this number to the number of invariant registers and the number of pipeline filling registers to get the total floating point register requirement.

If the register requirement is less than the number of registers in the microprocessor, then there is no cost to the use of the registers. Otherwise, we can compute the cost as follows. We divide the total number of memory references by the number of registers required to hold the CSEs and invariants. Let's call this ratio *r*. We assume that we can trade off a register by instead performing *r* memory references. In other words, rather than keeping an invariant in a register, we can load it from memory, potentially multiple times per iteration. While register spilling can sometimes lead to disastrous results, on codes not limited by memory references we can sometimes spill for free. We add to the number of memory references required *r* times the number of excess registers required.

We tend to be conservative about unrolling. We never unroll a loop that we estimate will require register spilling, even if we believe that the spilling can be tolerated.

3.2 Cache Model

In our regime, the cache model has two tasks. First, in our algorithm the tile sizes are not known when the model is called, so the cache model must select a good tile size. Second, given that tiling, it determines an estimate for the "cache overhead" and also the "loop overhead"[1].

Suppose, for example, that the compiler needs to model the following matrix multiply loop without permutation and with the *i* and *j* loops each outer unrolled by a factor of two. Further suppose that the nest is to be tiled so that a tile of BjxBk is innermost. (The model will be asked to try to evaluate other tilings during other model invocations.)

```
DO i = 1, N
   DO j = 1, N
      c(i,j) = 0
      DO k = 1, N
         c(i,j) = c(i,j) +a(i,k)*b(k,j)
      END DO
   END DO
END DO
```

After the transformations, assuming for simplicity that *N* and *Bj* are multiples of two, the example looks as follows.[2]

1. By decreasing the number of iterations in the inner loop, tiling increases loop overhead. In particular, it increases the wind-up and wind-down costs of software pipelining.

2. The compiler does not transform the code until it has determined the transformation to apply. Instead, the model sees the original nest, a description of the current transformation of interest and a description of which variables will need to be scalar expanded.

```
DO j = 1, N
  DO i = 1,N
    c(i,j) = 0
  END DO
END DO
DO jj = 1, N, Bj
  DO kk = 1, N, Bk
    DO i = 1, N, 2
      DO j = jj, MIN(jj+Bj-1,N), 2
        DO k = kk, MIN(kk+Bk-1,N)
          c(i,j) = c(i,j) + a(i,k)*b(k,j)
          c(i+1,j) = c(i+1,j) + a(i+1,k)*b(k,j)
          c(i,j+1) = c(i,j+1) + a(i,k)*b(k,j+1)
          c(i+1,j+1) = c(i+1,j+1) + a(i+1,k)*b(k,j+1)
        END DO
      END DO
    END DO
  END DO
END DO
```

The model's tasks are to select a good Bj and Bk and to return a cache and loop overhead cost estimate for the selected Bj and Bk.

In order to achieve its two tasks, the cache model computes a formula for the cost (in cycles per iteration) of this transformation as a function of the unknown tile sizes. It then attempts to select a tile size that minimizes this function.

The model first computes a *footprint*, the number of bytes of the cache used by a reference or set of references within a loop nest. Consider the following example.

```
DO i = 1, N
  DO j = 1, M
    a(i), b(j), c(i,j), c(i+1,j)
  END DO
END DO
```

If each array element is eight bytes, and a cache line is 32 bytes, then our best estimate for the footprint sizes of the arrays are *a*: *(N+3) * 8* bytes, *b*: *(M+3) * 8* bytes and *c*: *M*(N+4) * 8* bytes. The *a* and *b* arrays are each expected to use three extra words because of the long cache lines. The *c* matrix is trickier. The *c* matrix has *M* columns, each of which is just like the *a* array, except that because of the *i* and *i+1*, it is as if there were *N+1* iterations. Note, though, that this estimate is incorrect if *c* is declared *c(N+1,*)*. In that case, there are no wasted cache lines except possibly for the first and last references in the nest. That is, the correct formula for *c* is smaller: *(M*(N+1)+3) * 8*. The exact method we use to compute a footprint is involved and beyond the scope of this paper.

We sort references into uniformly generated sets [GJG88], which are sets of references to the same array whose index expressions differ by at most constants in each dimension. We then compute one footprint for each uniformly generated set. That means that we compute a single footprint for the references *a(i,j)*, *a(i,j+1)* and *a(i+1,j)*. To compute the entire footprint for many references, we simply add the footprint for each uniformly generated set. This is logical, since there is likely to be very little reuse between uniformly generated sets. Thus, we add the footprints for *a(i)* and *b(i)*, and even for *a(i)* and *a(j)*.

We compute a total footprint for each subnest. In our matrix multiplication example above, we only need to evaluate footprints for the following nest:

```
DO i = 1, N, 2
  DO j = jj, MIN(jj+Bj-1,N), 2
    DO k = kk, MIN(kk+Bk-1,N)
```

There is no reuse across the *jj* and the *kk* loops as we chose the block sizes to be sufficiently large so that the inner tiles use up all of the effective cache. We compute a footprint for the *k* loop (the *Bk* iterations of *k*), a footprint for the *j* loop (the *Bj*Bk* iterations of the nest rooted at *j*), and a footprint for the *i* loop (the *N/2*Bj*Bk* iterations of the nest rooted at *i*). At this point, *Bj* and *Bk* are unknown; we develop a formula in which *Bj* and *Bk* are variables.

We say that loop *i* overflows the cache if the sum of the footprints for that loop exceed the cache size. Since most caches are not highly associative, we don't use the actual cache size, but instead the *effective cache size*. Since we do not attempt to model actual cache line interference[1], we must estimate how much of the cache we can use. For example, one study [LRW91] showed that using blocks that used only from 5% to 15% of the cache was optimal when we did not use more precise information about cache mappings. If we have more highly associative caches, smaller caches or shorter cache lines, the optimal percentage is larger. For each cache in the memory hierarchy, we choose a value based upon its characteristics and call that the effective cache size.

If the entire three-deep loop nest without tiling (i.e., with *Bj=Bj=N)* does not overflow the cache, then tiling only adds loop overhead and is harmful, so we do not tile.

In our example nest, *N* is unknown. Therefore, we assume that the *i* loop does overflow the cache, and we probably

1. Our model has a special provision for the case when array dimensions are near powers of two, since cache interference is a particular risk at that point, but that's beyond the scope of this paper. Cache line interference can be modelled more aggressively using techniques from [CM95].

want to tile, assuming we find sufficient reuse in the i and j loops to justify the overhead in the k loop. Ignoring edge effects to simplify the presentation, for this loop, the footprint for the i loop given that j is blocked by Bj and k by Bk is approximately $Fi = 8*(N*Bk + Bj*Bk + N*Bj)$ and likewise $Fj = 8*(Bk + Bj*Bk + Bj)$ and $Fk = 8*(Bk + Bk + 1)$. For simplicity of presentation, we will discuss the simplest version of the model in which Fk does not play a role, and we will ignore the fact that read misses and write misses might affect performance differently.

Our model assumes that in the first iteration of i, Fj bytes are brought in. Thus, on each subsequent iteration of i, roughly $(Fi-Fj)/(N-1)$ bytes are brought in. At this point, we guess that $N=100$; the exact value does not greatly effect the model.

Let d be the number of iterations of i across which data must live for all reuse to be taken advantage of. For example, we have $c(i,j)$, so to use the cache line maximally, data must survive in the cache through two iterations of i, since the cache line size is four, but we are stepping by two. The amount of the cache required to take advantage of all the reuse, the *requirements*, is approximately $Fj + (d-1)*(Fi-Fj)/(N-1)$. Assuming no cache interference, which in our model means that the requirements are much smaller than the effective cache size, the total number of misses will equal the *requirements* $* N/d$. When the requirements are close to the effective cache size, the interference is pretty small but not non-existent. We model the percent of the footprint that are misses because of cache interference to be proportional to *requirements/effective_cache_size*. Once we exceed the effective cache size, we add in another similar but much larger term proportional to *(requirements-effective cache size) /effective cache size*.

To convert the number of misses into a cycles per iteration penalty is not a matter of simply multiplying the miss rate by the miss penalty. Depending on cache characteristics (multiple outstanding references, prefetching, etc.), some of the cache miss cycles may be hidable by the processor cycles. So the cache model is passed the estimate of the processor cycles from the Processor Model (see Section 3.1) and uses this number to estimate how many of the cache miss cycles will actually stall the machine. The details are beyond the scope of this paper.

We add in our estimate of loop overhead, which is roughly $(((o/N) + o)/Bj + o)/Bk$ per iteration, where o is a constant appropriate for this processor and loop nest. This term will cause the compiler to prefer rectangular blocks when choosing Bj and Bk, with the inner loop executing more iterations, as is appropriate. Finally, we add in a term for the TLB, which is like small cache with a huge cache line.

In Section 4, we describe how we use our formula to find the ideal block sizes.

4.0 Searching for the Best Transformation

FIGURE 1. High-level description of TLN transformation algorithm

```
best_cost = infinity
best_trans = none
FOR each possible innermost loop DO
   unroll_trans = compute best outer
         unrolls for this inner loop
   unroll_cost = compute cost for this unrolling
   tile_trans = compute best outer permutation
         and tiling given unroll_trans
   tile_cost = compute cache and loop overhead
         cost given unroll_trans and tile_trans
   IF (tile_cost + unroll_cost < best_cost)
         best_cost = tile_cost +unroll_cost
         best_trans = unroll_trans and tile_trans
   END IF
END FOR
```

In this section, we show how we search through the possible transformations to find the set of transformations that lead to the best performance according to the models developed in the previous section. The number of possible different permutations, tilings and outer unrolls, and the distributions and scalar expansions that enable them is too large to search exhaustively. We prune the search by recognizing that there are different combinations of transformations that should have very similar performance and by evaluating combinations that might reasonably differ from each other in expected performance. Figure 1 contains a high-level description of our TLN optimization algorithm. This algorithm involves a major pruning of the search space, since decisions about outer unrolling are made independently from any tiling or permutation of non-innermost loops decisions. We can understand why this approach is effective by understanding how the different transformations alter scheduling, cache overhead and loop overhead, individually and in combination.

For scheduling, only the choice of innermost loop and the choice of outer unrolling factors matter. For cache blocking, the dominant factors are which loops are tiled innermost and, to a lesser but still important extent, the order of the loops within the tile. Outer unrolling does affect cache performance, but tiling is more effective than outer unrolling for cache optimization since it allows for larger tile sizes. Thus, only the choice of innermost loop is important to both, and our algorithm simply enumerates all possible innermost loops. Given each innermost loop, we can select the transformations to improve scheduling and the transformation to improve the cache relatively independently. Since outer unrolling affects the cache more than cache transformations affect the schedule, we choose the unrolling first and feed that into the cache model.

4.1 Selecting the Scheduling Transformation Given a Potential Innermost Loop

FIGURE 2. Choosing Outer Unrolling Factors

```
MAXPROD = 16 ; MAXUNROLLS = 16

algorithm select_driver(num_loops, inner_loop,
                        best_unrolls, best_cost) {
   Unrolls = Best_Unrolls = {1, 1, ...}
        Best_Cost = infinite
   Found_Ideal = FALSE

   if (num_loops >= 2) {
        can_reg_allocate = TRUE
        call select(1, 0, num_loops, inner_loop,
                        &can_reg_allocate)
   }
}
procedure select(curprod, curloop, num_loops,
                 inner_loop,can_reg_allocate) {
   BOOL can_allocate = TRUE;
   for u = 1 to MAXUNROLLS {
        if (u*curprod > MAXPROD || Found_Ideal ||
                 ! can_allocate) break
        Unrolls[curloop] = u;
        if (curloop < num_loops-1) {
          select(curprod*u, curloop+1, num_loops,
                 inner_loop, &can_allocate)
          if (u == 1 && can_allocate)
            *can_reg_allocate = FALSE;
        } else {
          this_cost = evaluate(Unrolls, inner_loop,
                               &can_allocate)
          if (this_cost < best_cost) {
            Best_Cost = this_cost
            Best_Unrolls = Unrolls
          }
        }
        if (curloop == inner_loop) break; // we do not
                        //unroll the inner loop
   }
}
```

Given a potential inner loop, we use the algorithm in Figure 2 along with the processor model in Section 3.1 to decide how much to unroll each outer loop. Essentially we enumerate all possible combinations of unrolling factors for all the outer loops. In contrast, Carr and Kennedy chose unrolling factors by solving an optimization problem in terms of the original operations, references and data dependences[CCK88] . This allows them to potentially be more efficient but at a small loss of accuracy. By enumerating the possible unrolling factors, we can potentially be completely accurate.

We limit ourselves to combinations where the product of all the unrolling factors is no larger than 16. We have not found a case in practice where larger factors can help. To improve compiler efficiency, we stop evaluating combinations whenever we find an "ideal" schedule. An "ideal" schedule is one limited by floating point resources. Unrolling further can not improve the floating point resource bound. We also do not evaluate combinations that we know we will not be able to register allocate. Consider for example a three deep nest. If we discover that the combination (3,1,1) (unrolling the outer loop by three) is unallocatable, we will not try the combination (4,1,1) nor the combination (3,2,1) since they are guaranteed to be unallocatable. We will, however, try the combination (2,2,1), since it may be allocatable.

We do not generate code for each combination we try; that would be much too inefficient. We do not perform any transformations to the code until we decide on which combination is best. Instead, we designed our evaluation algorithm to come up with a schedule estimate in terms of the original code and a potential transformation. Let us consider the various components of the estimate. The floating point resource bound is not affected by unrolling. The number of cycles required for the transformed source increases with the unrolling product, but since we compute an estimate per original iteration, i.e., normalized by the unrolling product, the floating point resource estimate is constant. Therefore, we only compute it once for a given loop nest. The memory resource bound is affected by unrolling. So, we must compute it for each possible combination. But, we do not unroll the code in order to compute it. Instead, we unroll a compact data structure describing all the array references. We then compute CSEs and invariants directly on this data structure. From Callahan, Cocke and Kennedy [CCK88], the latency limit per original iteration goes down directly in proportion to the unrolling product. So, we only compute the latency limit once per choice of potential inner loop. The pipeline filling register requirement is a constant for a given target architecture. The register requirements for invariant references and CSEs need to be evaluated once per unrolling combination. Once again, we unroll our data structure rather than the code.

We limit our transformations to nests of depth eight or less. If a nest is more deeply nested, we do not transform the outermost loops. Assuming a depth of eight, in the worst case there are 3,425 unrolling combinations for each potential inner loop. As we show in Section 5, in practice we are very efficient.

4.2 Selecting the Cache Transformation

FIGURE 3. Algorithm for Choosing Tiling for a Single Cache

```
tile_cost = infinite
tile_trans = null
Select locality_loops as follows:
   only select loops with some reuse.
   if more than three have some reuse, pick three with
         most reuse (loops with most reuse are precom-
         puted once for the nest)
FOR loops in POWER_SET(locality_loops)
   FOR each possible permutation of loops
         this_tile_trans = compute best tile sizes for this
            tiling/unrolling
         this_tile_cost = compute cache and loop
            overhead cost for this tiling/unrolling
         IF (this_tile_cost < tile_cost)
           tile_cost = this_tile_cost
           tile_trans = this_tile_trans
         END IF
   END FOR
END FOR
```

Figure 3 shows our algorithm for selecting a permutation and tiling for a cache. It begins by selecting all the non-innermost loops that have reuse. If there are more than three, then only the three with the most reuse are selected[1]. We do this pruning to keep the algorithm fast. Since it will not help cache performance to include a loop that has no reuse in the tiling, this pruning only may hurt when more than three loops, not including the innermost loop, have reuse. This case is very rare and, since we still tile the heuristically best loops, not at all catastrophic when it occurs.

We exhaustively select for tiling none, some or all of the (pruned) loops that have locality. We look at all possible orderings of those loops. For example, suppose we have the following nest

```
DO i = 1,N
   DO j = 1,N
      DO k = 1,N
```

and we are exploring loop k innermost, and both i and j have reuse. Then we will explore the following possibilities:

```
loops = {} -> (1) DO i = 1,N
                     DO j = 1,N
                     DO k = 1,N
loops = {i} -> (2) DO j = 1,N
                     DO kk = 1,N,Bk
                      DO i = 1,N
                       DO k = kk, MIN(N,kk+Bk-1)
loops = {j} -> (3) DO i = 1,N
                     DO kk = 1,N,Bk
                      DO j = 1,N
                       DO k = kk, MIN(N,kk+Bk-1)
loops = {i,j} -> (4) DO jj = 1,N,Bj
                      DO kk = 1,N,Bk
                       DO i = 1,N
                        DO j = jj, MIN(N,jj+Bj-1)
                        DO k = kk, MIN(N,kk+Bk-1)
                 (5) DO ii = 1,N,Bi
                      DO kk = 1,N,Bk
                       DO j = 1,N
                        DO i = ii, MIN(N,ii+Bi-1)
                         DO k = kk, MIN(N,kk+Bk-1)
```

Notice that the permutation determines the order of the inner loops. We tile all those loops except the outermost of them, and move those outer tiles outside the untiled loop. There are of course other ways to tile. For example, when loops = {j} above, we could instead have generated

```
DO i = 1,N
   DO jj = 1, N, Bj
      DO kk = 1, N, Bk
         DO j = jj, MIN(N,jj+Bj-1)
          DO k = kk, MIN(N,kk+Bk-1)
```

However, there is typically no advantage to this code over version (3) for a uniprocessor with a one-level cache. If $Bj = N$, then we take advantage of reuse in Bk iterations of k and N iterations of j. If $Bj < N$, then we lose some reuse in the j loop. Can we use a larger Bk to make up for it? No, because we could then have used the same Bk in (3) without ill effect. But with a small Bj, might we avoid overflowing the cache, thereby getting reuse in loop kk? When there's a great deal of reuse in k and very little reuse in j (but not so little that we don't want a few iterations in the tile), this can happen. So the pruning we have done by not

1. For each loop, we compute the footprint per iteration assuming that loop to be innermost, a technique inspired by [CMT94].

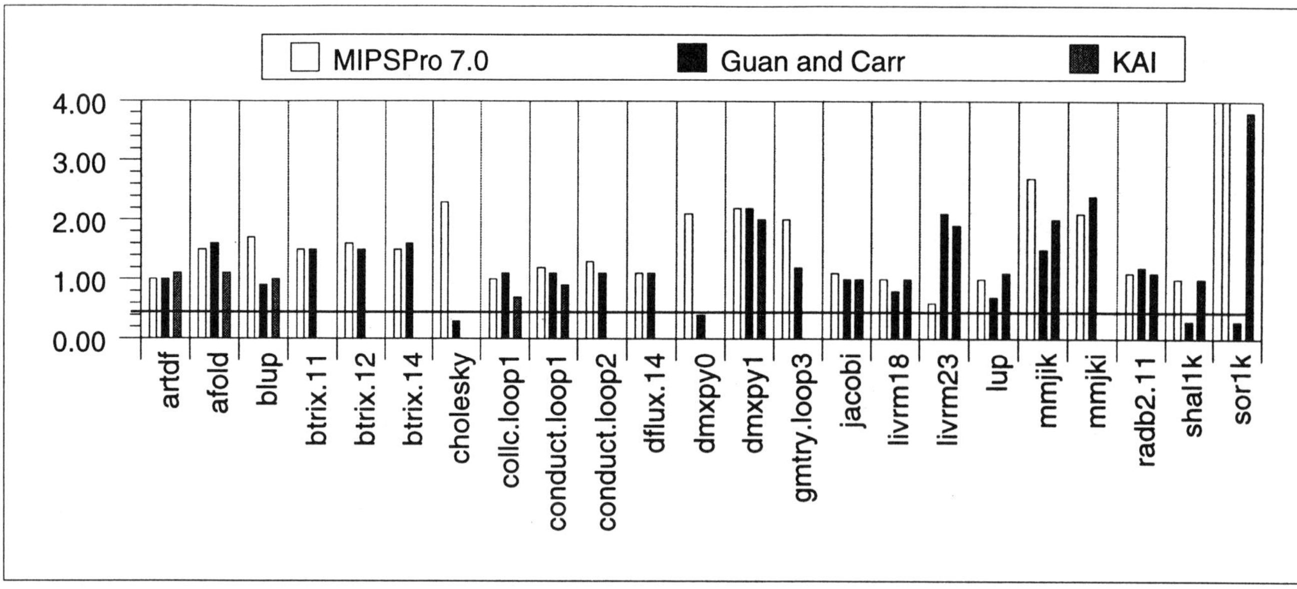

Figure 4: Outer Loop Unrolling for the R8000

considering this case can on very rare occasions be suboptimal.

Given the choice of which loops to tile, we need to choose the appropriate tile sizes. All we know about the tile sizes Bi is that they are positive, integral (multiples of the corresponding unrolling factors) and may be bounded (if we know the loop bounds). We pass these constraints to a solver. It does a (recursive) binary search for the best values. This works perfectly so long as the formula has only one minimum. Otherwise it might come up with some local minimum. The formulas we develop in fact produce very good answers in practice. The solver produces tile sizes and a cycles per iteration estimate. The run time of this search is $O((logN)^n)$, where n is the number of unknowns and N is the loop bound size. If N is unknown, then we heuristically use 100,000 as a bound. This search is fast, although to make sure it remains fast for deep loop nests, we require that all tile size variables be the same except for the innermost tile size. So, if we tile *Bi*, *Bj* and *Bk*, with *Bk* innermost, we require that *Bi=Bj*.

With these restrictions, we have reduced the search space significantly. It is easy to show that the number of times the inner loop of our algorithm is executed is $\Sigma_{i=0,n}\binom{n}{i}\times i!$, which is exponential in n. However, we have bounded n at three, so that the inner loop may execute at most 16 times, and then only when three loops other than the innermost loop have locality. The inner loop itself is not a function of n. So the $n=3$ case (four loops in the TLN) takes 32 times as long as the $n=1$ case (two loops in the TLN), but the algorithm does not slow down after that.

Note that we could instead execute the innermost loop $n+1$ times (again bounding n by 3 if we wish) by permuting the outer loops to execute in memory order, and just tiling the innermost loop and up to n outer loops, a la [CMT94]. We have found this inadequate because, in practice, the one number computed in the memory order computation does not adequately describe the situation. If loop bounds are small on a loop with good locality, the added overhead may or may not be a problem, depending on the tile sizes of innermore loops. Also, the untiled loop gets many more iterations but also has a greater risk of having reused data being removed from the cache; we give the model the chance to trade off these factors, possibly choosing small tile sizes further in, if overhead permits, to try to gain more reuse outside. Because of these situations, we have rejected the memory order approach, in favor of a slower but more accurate algorithm.

5.0 Experimental Results

Our algorithm is implemented as part of the MIPSPro 7.0 compiler, the new production compiler for SGI machines. We tested our algorithm using a set of kernels supplied to us by Guan [G95] and Carr. These are kernels extracted by them from SPEC, Perfect and RICEPS. Guan and Carr use an algorithm similar to ours for outer loop unrolling, but they do not consider interchange, cache blocking, fission nor fusion. To compare ourselves to them, we turned off these optimizations in our compiler. Since we were trying to isolate the non-cache effects of unrolling, we used a MIPS R8000 system, a 300MFlops peak computer, with a large, 4MB primary cache. We adjusted the size of a few of the benchmarks to make sure they fit inside the cache.

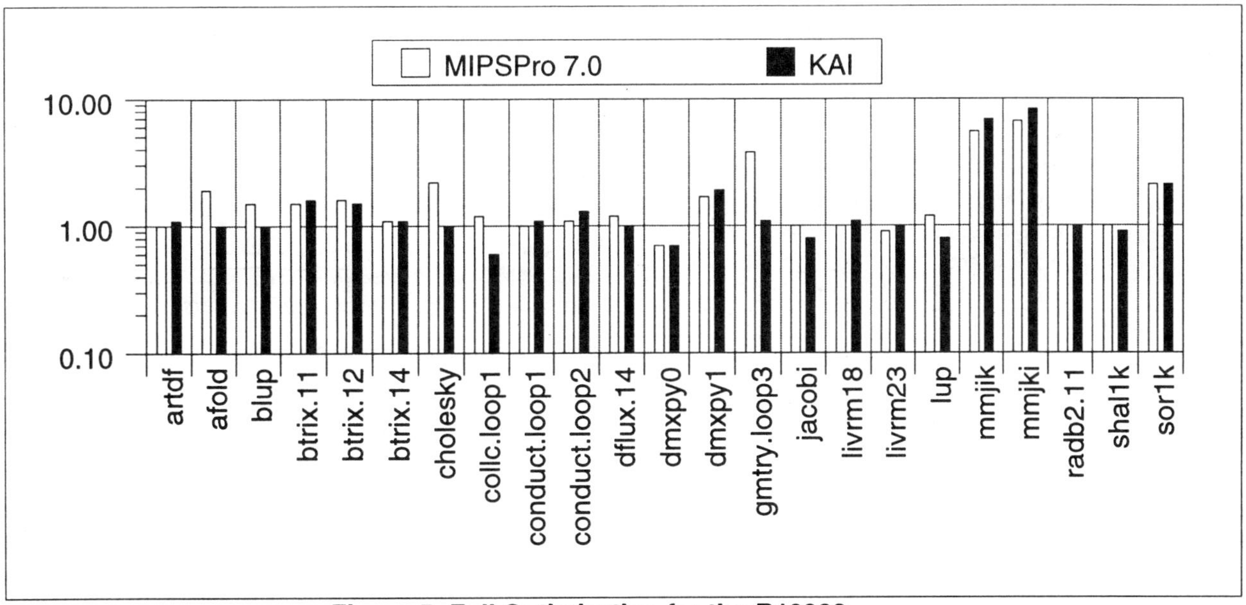

Figure 5: Full Optimization for the R10000

Figure 4 shows our results compared to Guan and Carr and compared to an earlier version of the MIPSPro compiler that used a preprocessor from Kuck and Associates. We normalized all results against a run with our compiler with outer loop unrolling turned off. Numbers larger than one indicate that unrolling improved performance. Since we were not able to turn off interchanging in the KAI preprocessor, we do not include numbers for KAI for those benchmarks that KAI decided to interchange. For all three systems, we used the same compiler back end from the new MIPSPro compiler. Thus our comparisons should only be affected by unrolling. A few of the kernels did not come with main programs. In one of the kernels, Guan and Carr unroll a timing loop. We do not include these kernels.

Our results look quite promising. Our only poor result is livrm23. In that case our unrolling confuses our software pipeliner due to a performance bug in the software pipeliner. By judiciously adding a set of parenthesis, we still unroll the same amount, but we eliminate the confusion and get good results. Guan and Carr do well on many kernels, but they do very poorly on a few. At the time we generated results, their algorithm was not well tuned for the R8000, and they overunrolled a few kernels, causing serious register problems. We believe that they would do better now. Our algorithm, though, has two advantages. Using the pipeline filling concept to estimate register pressure allows us to optimize for multiple machines without having to tune for each machine specifically. Second, because Guan and Carr use unrolling to improve cache behavior, they have a tendency to unroll more than we do. We use cache tiling, rather than unrolling to improve cache behavior. Cache tiling is more effective than unrolling in reducing cache misses, and it does not increase register pressure. In kernels suffering from large register requirements, if they model register pressure perfectly they will limit unrolling and therefore lose some of the cache benefits. If registers are not perfectly modeled, there is a larger probability that they will overunroll than that we will.

KAI is less successful than the other two algorithms on several kernels. On several kernels they either do not unroll or do not unroll sufficiently.

As a second comparison, we turned on all our optimizations and compared ourselves to KAI. To place more emphasis on cache effects, we ran on a newer machine, a MIPS R10000, with a smaller cache. In addition, we increased the data size of some of the kernels so that they would exceed the cache size of the R10000. Once again, we used the same back end for both our algorithm and KAI. The results are given in Figure 5.

Our optimizations improve performance on average (geometric mean) by 50%. KAI's improve performance by 30%. The only example that we do very poorly on is dmxpy0, a matrix-vector product. We perform an interchange that confuses our prefetching algorithm, so that we do not get any benefit from prefetching while the base algorithm gets a large benefit from prefetching. Part of the problem can be considered a performance bug in the prefetching algorithm, but part of the problem comes from the fact that we do not adequately integrate the prefetching algorithm into the rest of our decision algorithm.

Our algorithm may appear to be expensive. We are potentially enumerating a very large search space. We timed our compiler on an R10000 system compiling the SPECfp95 benchmarks. These are a set of fortran programs ranging from 200 to 7,000 lines. The total compilation times ranged from 2.9 to 74.2 seconds. The amount of time spent modeling both the processor and the cache ranged from 0.0 to 4.0 seconds. The amount of time spent both modeling and actually performing the optimizations mentioned in this paper ranged from 0.1 to 8.8 seconds. In the worst case, 22% of the compile time, or 1.2 out of 5.9 seconds, was spent modeling and performing the optimizations.

6.0 Conclusion

We have presented a compiler algorithm that applies fission, fusion, tiling, permutation and outer loop unrolling to optimize loop nests. This algorithm is based upon a model that estimates total machine cycle time taking into account cache misses, software pipelining, register pressure and loop overhead. The algorithm intelligently searches through the various possible transformations, using our model to select the set of transformations leading to the best overall performance. Our algorithm is part of a production compiler system. We have tested it and found it to generate, with a few exceptions, better code than two other systems. While our algorithm may appear to be inefficient, we have found its compile time to be very reasonable

ACKNOWLEDGEMENTS

We would like to thank Yiping Guan and Steve Carr for their generous help in providing us their benchmarks and the output of their compiler on the benchmarks.

Bibliography

[ASU86]Aho, A., Sethi, R., and Ullman, J. Compilers, Principles, Techniques, and Tools. Addison-Wesley, 1986.

[CCK88]Callahan, D., Cocke, J., and Kennedy, K. Estimating interlock and improving balance for pipelined machines. Journal of Parallel and Distributed Computing 5, 334-358, 1988

[C96]Carr, S.. "Combining Optimization for Cache and Instruction-Level Parallelism", In Proceedings of the 1996 Conference on Parallel Architectures and Compiler Techniques, Boston, MA, October 20-23, 1996.

[CK94]Carr, S. and Kennedy, K. Improving the Ratio of Memory Operations in Floating-Point Operations in Loops. ACM Transactions on Programming Languages and Systems 16(6) 1768-1810, Nov. 1994.

[CMT94]Carr, S., McKinley, K.S., and Tseng, C.. Compiler Optimizations for Improving Data Locality. Proceedings of the Sixth International Conference on Architectural Support for Programming Languages and Operating Systems, October 1994.

[CM95]Coleman, S. and McKinley, K.S., Tile Size Selection Using Cache Organization and Data Layout, In SIGPLAN'95: Conference on Programming Language Design and Implementation, June 1995.

[GJG88]Gannon, D., Jalby, W., and Gallivan, K. Strategies for cache and local memory management by global program transformation. Journal of Parallel and Distributed Computing, 5:587-616, 1988.

[G95]Guan, Y.. Unroll-And-Jam Guided by A Linear-Algebra-Based Data-Reuse Model. Masters Thesis, Computer Science Department, Michigan Technological University, 1995

[L88]Lam, M. Software pipelining: An effective scheduling technique for VLIW machines. In Proceedings of the '88 SIGPLAN Conference on Programming Language Design and Implementation, June 1988.

[LRW91] Lam, M., Rothberg, E., and Wolf, M.E. The Cache Performance and Optimizations of Blocked Algorithms. In Proceedings of the Fourth International Conference on Architectural Support for Programming Languages and Operating Systems, April 1991.

[MHL91]Maydan, D., Hennessy, J, and Lam, M., Efficient and Exact Data Dependence Analysis, In SIGPLAN'91: Conference on Programming Language Design and Implementation, June 1991

[RGSL96]Ruttenberg, J., Gao, G.R., Stoutchinin, A., and Lichtenstein, W., Software Pipelining Showdown: Optimal vs. Heuristic Methods in a Production Compiler, In SIGPLAN'96: Conference on Programming Language Design and Implementation, June 1996

[W91]Wolf, M.E., A Loop Transformation Theory and Improving Locality and Parallelism in Nested Loops, Ph.D. thesis, Stanford University, August 1992.

Session 9

Instruction Scheduling and Executable Editing

by Eric Schnarr and James R. Larus

Computer Sciences Department
University of Wisconsin–Madison
1210 West Dayton Street
Madison, WI 53706 USA
(608) 262-9519
{schnarr,larus}@cs.wisc.edu

Abstract

Modern microprocessors offer more instruction-level parallelism than most programs and compilers can currently exploit. The resulting disparity between a machine's peak and actual performance, while frustrating for computer architects and chip manufacturers, opens the exciting possibility of low-cost instrumentation for measurement, simulation, or emulation. Instrumentation code that executes in previously unused processor cycles is effectively hidden. On two superscalar SPARC processors, a simple, local scheduler hid an average of 13% of the overhead cost of profiling instrumentation in the SPECINT benchmarks and an average of 33% of the profiling cost in the SPECFP benchmarks.

1. Introduction

Modern microprocessors offer more instruction-level parallelism than most programs and compilers can currently exploit. For example, the most recent generation of RISC chips—the Digital Alpha 21164, IBM/Motorola Power PC 620, SGI R10000, and Sun UltraSPARC—are 4-way superscalar processors that execute up to four independent instructions in a single cycle. Even recent high-end x86 processors—the Intel Pentium Pro and AMD K5—are 3-way superscalars. Unfortunately, exploited instruction-level parallelism lags far behind the hardware capacity. Cvetanovic and Bhandarkar found that programs running on a 2-way superscalar Digital Alpha 21064 could dual issue only 20–50% of their instructions, which means that in 67–90% of cycles, only one instruction executed [3]. Similarly, Diep et al. found that on a 4-way superscalar Power PC 620, four integer SPEC benchmarks completed an average of 1.05–1.25 instructions per cycle and three floating-point SPEC benchmarks completed an average of 1.0–1.9 instructions per cycle [4].

This large disparity between a machine's peak and actual performance, while frustrating for computer architects and chip manufacturers, opens the exciting possibility of low-cost or even no-cost instrumentation for measurement, simulation, or emulation. Scheduling reduces instrumentation's perceived cost by putting instrumentation instructions in previously unused processor cycles. Instrumentation code that executes in unused cycles is effectively hidden.

Program instrumentation has been used for many purposes, including performance measurement, computer architecture simulations, and software fault isolation and error detection [1]. Although direct instrumentation typically incurs lower cost than alternative approaches, the increased program running time caused by instrumentation is occasionally a limiting factor and is always an annoyance. At one extreme, in parallel or real-time systems, instrumentation overhead can perturb system behavior by introducing time dilation. Even for less demanding applications, the cost of program profiling or error detection is currently too high for production codes. Previous instrumentation systems expended considerable effort to formulate efficient instrumentation code sequences [11], place them parsimoniously [2], and insert instrumentation without affecting a program's behavior [9]. However, few systems attempted to exploit instruction-level parallelism by scheduling the instrumentation code into a program.

This paper describes a simple instruction scheduler that we added to the EEL executable editing library [10]. We applied the scheduler to a common program instrumentation, which profiles basic block execution frequencies using a four-instruction sequence inserted into almost every basic block. On the 3-way superscalar

1072-4451/96 $5.00 © 1996 IEEE

SuperSPARC processor, scheduling hides an average of 11% of the SPECINT overhead and an average of 44% of the SPECFP overhead. On the 4-way UltraSPARC scheduling hides an average of 15% of overhead for the SPECINT benchmarks, but only 17% of overhead for the SPECFP benchmarks. This is the because EEL produces a worse schedule than was originally found in these highly optimized programs. Factoring out the differences in scheduling algorithms, we find that the integer benchmarks remain about the same (13%), while scheduling profile instrumentation in the SPECFP benchmarks hides 27%. In the future, these results may improve, and scheduling become even more attractive, with a more accurate and aggressive instrumentation scheduler and wider microarchitectures that offer further opportunities to hide instrumentation.

To implement instruction scheduling, we extended EEL with the specific details of a processor's microarchitecture. EEL records this and other architectural information using a concise, high-level specification describing the machine's instruction set architecture. A tool called Spawn [10] translates these specifications into executable C++ code, which becomes the part of EEL that decodes and interprets machine instructions. As part of this work, we extended the architecture specification language to capture salient features of a machine's microarchitecture and used this information to drive an instruction scheduler in EEL. This paper first describes this language extension and how EEL uses the information to schedule instructions. Then some timing measurements are given for scheduling instrumentation into the SPEC95 benchmarks.

The paper is organized as follows. Section 2 describes related work. Section 3 presents the extensions to Spawn and shows how they represent the information necessary for instruction scheduling. Section 4 describes our experiments on scheduling program instrumentation and presents the results. Finally, Section 5 concludes.

2. Related Work

This paper extends several areas of previous work. Patil and Fischer used a different form of parallelism to hide instrumentation overhead. On a multiprocessor, the ran on a second processor the code to check pointer and array accesses [12]. The additional processor reduced the perceived overhead of error checking by 2–55%. Our approach is more widely applicable since instruction-level parallel processors are, or soon will be, ubiquitous and because instruction-level parallelism permits a tighter coupling between program and instrumentation.

Proebsting and Fraser described an efficient algorithm for detecting structural hazards in single pipeline processors and a language for concisely describing these machines [13]. Our description language is more verbose, but it also captures the syntax and semantics of machine instructions and scheduling constraints for superscalar machines. Our algorithm is also more general, if less efficient, since it works for superscalar processors as well as single pipeline machines.

Gyllenhaal described the machine description language (HMDES) used in the Illinois IMPACT compiler [6]. This language, like Spawn's description language, describes instruction encoding and scheduling constraints. HMDES describes instructions from several perspectives, which together provide the basic information needed by instruction schedulers: instruction latencies and resource usage. Spawn represents this information more concisely as a single semantic expression for a group of instruction, which describes when these instruction acquire and release microarchitectural resources. Spawn descriptions also capture instruction semantics and binary instruction encodings.

Schuette detected processor errors using unused instruction slots on a VLIW processor [15]. His control-flow monitoring technique inserts check operations into unfilled VLIW instructions. This is similar to EEL's rescheduling of instrumentation, except that EEL also reschedules the original instructions and can handle many different forms of instrumentation. Because a VLIW has fixed size instructions, Schuette's instrumentation did not increase code size. Whereas on a superscalar machine, instrumentation code has a secondary effect of reducing performance by increasing instruction cache misses.

3. Spawn Extensions

Any executable editing tool depends on an accurate description of a machine's instruction set architecture. While most parts of EEL are machine independent, it still must disassemble, analyze, and modify binary machine instructions. Past experiences with executable editing tools demonstrated that the code that manipulates binary instructions is simple, but tedious and difficult to debug. For example, in the profiling and tracing tool qpt [9], over 2,000 lines of hand-written C code exist to manipulate binary instructions. Subtle errors in this code were difficult to detect by inspection and often lay undiscovered for months before a new input executable exercised them.

To remedy this problem and make EEL more easily portable across different processors, it uses a concise description of a machine's instruction set architecture written in a high-level architecture description language. These descriptions are short—the SPARC is 333 lines—and similar in form to the descriptions often found in architecture manuals, which makes them easier to validate. Errors overlooked in a code review are also more likely to arise during testing, since a single description of an instruction's encoding and semantics underlies many different EEL instruction manipulation functions and different instructions often share common code in the description file.

Spawn [10] is the tool that converts an architecture description into the C++ code used by EEL. Spawn analyzes descriptions written in SADL (Spawn Architecture Description Language) to detect errors and extract the syntactic and semantic information needed by EEL. Spawn then reads an annotated C/C++ file and replaces its annotations by appropriate code produced using information extracted from the description. The resulting C/C++ file is compiled and linked into EEL to provide efficient functions for manipulating binary instructions.

Instruction scheduling requires more detailed information than the architectural descriptions that sufficed previously for EEL. In particular, scheduling requires a model of a machine's microarchitecture, especially its execution pipeline. Since a microarchitecture is specific to each particular processor implementation, this level of detail entails writing many more descriptions, so each description should be concise and easy to modify. To support instruction scheduling, we extended SADL to include pipeline timing and resource utilization information. This new information can be combined with the instruction semantic description to provide a complete map of an instruction's actions as it moves through a processor's execution pipeline.

Ideally, one would like to separate a microarchitecture-specific description from a general architecture description. SADL only partially accomplishes this goal by supporting functions that can encapsulate some of the timing and resource usage characteristics. The coupling of architectural and resource allocation information is necessary to permit Spawn to determine not only which registers are read from and written to, but also when values are read and when result values become available. On the other hand, our experience modeling the hyperSPARC, SuperSPARC, and UltraSPARC processors showed that the architecture semantics are easily carried over into a description of different microarchitectures, despite large changes in the pipeline description.

A (micro)architecture description, written in SADL, describes several aspects of a machine's architecture: instruction encodings, instruction semantics, architectural registers, and pipeline resources. The first three aspects (encodings, semantics, and registers) are described elsewhere [10]. Section 3.1 describes how pipeline resources and timing operators are combined with instruction semantics to encode details of an execution pipeline. Section 3.2 describes how an instruction scheduler uses this information to predict pipeline behavior.

3.1. Describing an Execution Pipeline

The example in figure 2 shows how the architectural semantics and microarchitectural timing and resource usage might be described for three ALU instructions on a ROSS hyperSPARC processor [14]. It starts by defining all the pipeline resources needed to model the timing behavior of the instructions. Second, the architectural registers are defined, along with aliases used to restrict the register types and incorporate resource usage information. Finally, the

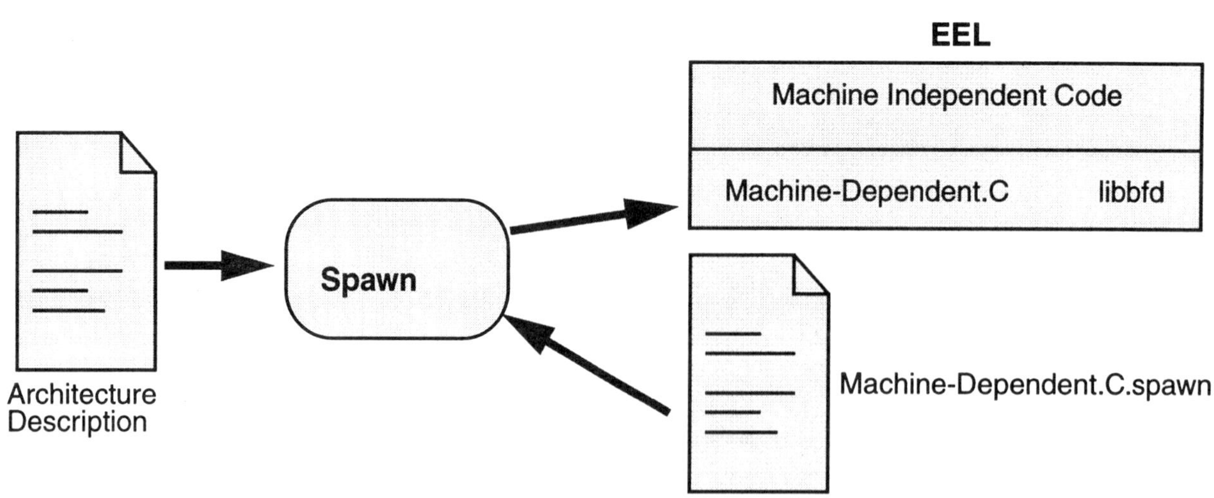

Figure 1: Spawn translates an architecture description written in SADL and an annotated C/C++ file into executable C++ code, which becomes the part of EEL that decodes and interprets machine instructions.

instruction semantics are defined along with their resource usage and timing characteristics.

Microarchitecture resources, such as register ports and ALUs, are described by a unit name and a value representing the number of copies of this resource in the processor. The ROSS hyperSPARC [14] described by this example is a dual-issue superscalar processor, with an ALU for arithmetic operations and an ALU for memory address calculations (LSU). The **ALUr** and **ALUw** units represent read and write ports to the register file for the arithmetic ALU. Similarly, the **LSUr** and **LSUw** units are ports used by the LSU. The values **multi** and **single** are used later to indicate if an instruction can be dual issued, or if it must execute by itself.

Architectural registers are described using the **register** declaration, and specifying the type and number of registers in the register file. This example declares a register file for the SPARC integer registers, where there are 32 registers each 32 bits wide. Aliases provide alternative ways to access the register file. They allow the registers to be accessed as an alternative type, and allow arbitrary SADL expressions to be combined with the register access. In this example, aliases are used to access the registers as 32 bit signed integers, and to specify the use of either an ALU read port or an ALU write port. The types are necessary later on in the description to disambiguate overloaded values and operators.

Description of the pipeline behavior of an instruction is combined with the instruction's semantic description. SADL commands **A**, **R**, **AR**, and **D** are used to describe when units are acquired and released and when the pipeline advances. The command **A** *<unit>* [*<num>*] acquires *<num>* copies of the unit, or stalls the pipeline if not enough copies of the unit are available. If *<num>* is omitted, it is assumed to be 1. **R** *<unit>* [*<num>*] releases *<num>* copies of a unit. The command **AR** *<unit>* [*<num>* [*<delay>*]] acts like the **A** command, but it also releases *<num>* copies of the same unit after the instruction executes for *<delay>* cycles. **AR** is handy for acquiring a resource for a fixed amount of time, without having to do explicit **R**'s later in the semantic expression. The command **D** [*<delay>*] advances the pipeline by *<delay>* cycles. In each cycle of an instruction's execution, Spawn applies all unit release events for the cycle first, followed by the all the unit acquire events. Extra delays are inserted if there are not enough free resources to accommodate all the unit acquire events.

An instruction scheduling algorithm must also know when registers are read from and written to. When an instruction reads a register, Spawn records in which cycle the read occurs. Writes are more difficult, since most pipelined implementations forward values between instructions [7]. When a value is computed, Spawn

```
// *** Define processor resources ***

// 2-way superscalar
unit Group 2

// flags for dual/single issue
val multi is AR Group, ()
val single is AR Group 2, ()

// ALU and LSU capacities
unit ALU 1, ALUr 2, ALUw 1
unit LSU 1, LSUr 2, LSUw 1


// *** Define registers ***

// general purpose registers (GPR)
register untyped{32} R[32]

// Alias for ALU read/write from GPR
alias signed{32} R4r[i]
   is AR ALUr, R[i]
alias signed{32} R4w[i]
   is AR ALUw, R[i]


// ** Define instructions ***

// Defining operators
val [ +         -
      &         |         ^       ]
 is (\op.\a.\b.
     A ALU, x:=op a b, D 1, R ALU, x)
  @ [ add32     sub32
      and32     or32      xor32 ]

// Defining shift operators
val [ <<        >>        >>      ]
 is (\op.\a.\b.
     A ALU, isShift, x:=op a b,
     D 1, R ALU, x)
  @ [ sll32     srl32     sra32 ]

// Get the second source operand
// or immediate value
val src2
 is iflag=1 ? #simm13 : R4r[rs2]

// Semantic description of the
// instructions add, sub, and sra
sem [ add       sub       sra     ]
 is (\op. multi,
     D 1, s1:=R4r[rs1], s2:=src2,
     R4w[rd]:=op s1 s2)
  @ [ +         -         >>      ]
```

Figure 2: Semantic description of the SPARC instructions add, sub, and sra. The resource usage and timing information are for the ROSS hyperSPARC microarchitecture.

remembers the cycle in which the computation finished. When this value is written back into a register, Spawn records the cycle in which the value was computed, not when the register assignment took place. Therefore in SADL, the computation of an instruction's result value must be computed in the cycle immediately preceding the cycle in which the value becomes available to the next instruction.

The example in figure 2 continues by describing the semantics and pipeline behavior of the instructions **add**, **sub**, and **sra**. This is accomplished using **val** declarations which act like macros, and **sem** declarations which bind semantic expressions to instruction mnemonics. The effect of the **sem** statement in this example is to bind the instructions **add**, **sub**, and **sra**, to their semantic expressions which: (1) restrict the pipeline to at most 2 simultaneous instructions and advance the pipeline by one cycle; (2) acquire one or two ALU read ports and read the register values; (3) acquire the ALU functional unit and compute the instruction's result value; (4) advance the pipeline by one cycle and release the ALU read ports and the ALU functional unit; (5) acquire an ALU write port and update the destination register; and (6) advance the pipeline by one cycle and release the ALU write port. From this description, Spawn infers that these instructions can be dual issued, execute in 3 cycles, read their operands in cycle 1, produce a value at the end of cycle 1 that subsequent instructions can use, and update the register file in cycle 2. Note that an extra cycle was put before reading the registers, since the **sethi** instruction produces a value which is available at the end of cycle 0, and can be used by another instruction issued in the same cycle.

Given a machine description written in SADL, Spawn analyzes the instruction encodings, semantics, and timing. Instructions with identical timing and resources allocation patterns are grouped together to save space in the generated C++ code. Each group records the number of cycles it takes for a member instruction to pass completely through the pipeline, the resources acquired in each cycle, and the resources released in each cycle. Spawn also associates a cycle number with every access to the integer or floating point register file, for both reads and writes. For reads, this number indicates the pipeline execution cycle when the read occurs. For writes, it indicates when the written value actually becomes available to subsequent instructions, not when the value is written to the register file.

3.2. Predicting Pipeline Behavior

The key metric used by EEL's instruction scheduler is the number of cycles that the next instruction must wait before entering the execution pipeline. SADL describes the resource usage and timing for individual instructions. This information can describe the execution behavior of many superscalar processors executing a straight-line sequence of instructions.

Spawn passes this information to an instruction scheduler by filling in annotations in the C++ function, **pipeline_stalls**, which given a sequence of instructions, computes when the next instruction can start execution (see Appendix A for an overview of this function). This function starts with a representation of the microarchitecture pipeline state generated by previous instructions in the instruction sequence. The pipeline state includes history information, such as the last cycle in

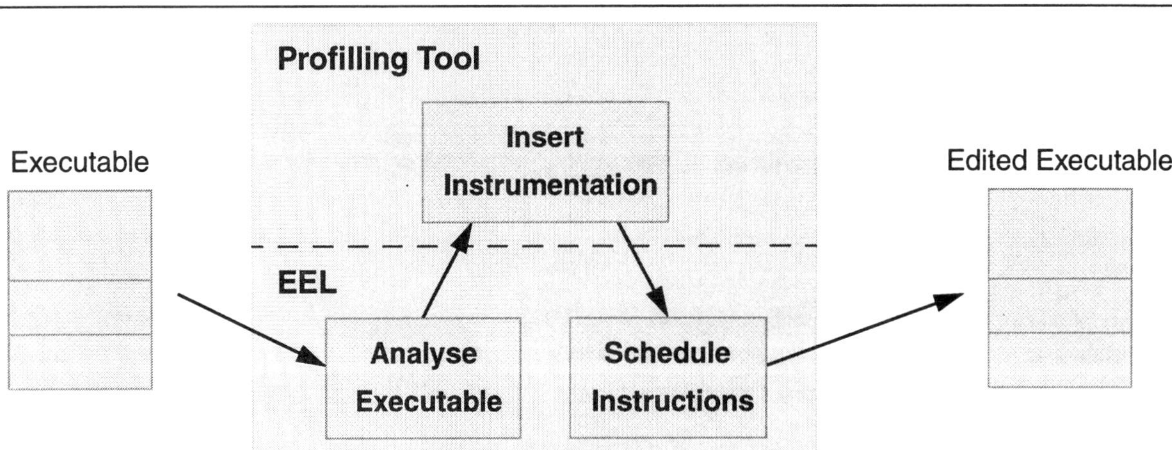

Figure 3: EEL schedules instrumentation by first analyzing the executable and allowing the application specific code (e.g., the program profiling tool) to select and place instrumentation. A new executable is then generated, which includes the instrumentation instructions. Scheduling is performed on each basic block as it is laid out in the new executable, causing the original and new instructions to be scheduled together.

which each register was read and written and which units are currently acquired by previous instructions. **pipeline_stalls** uses this state information as it simulates the pipeline execution of the new instruction and computes how many stall cycles are needed to satisfy the RAW, WAR, WAW dependencies and structural hazards.

The Spawn microarchitecture models can describe only a subset of all the factors affecting the integer and floating point pipelines. Our goal has been to describe actual machines rather than hypothetical systems, so for simplicity, the Spawn descriptions only model the execution pipelines themselves. The descriptions contain no information about a processor's memory interface to instruction prefetching, write buffering, or instruction and data cache behavior. **pipeline_stalls** does not compute stalls due to these mechanisms. On the other hand, few scheduling algorithms take these features into account since their behavior is data-dependent (c.f. [8]). In addition, SADL does not yet describe out-of-order execution, since it was not needed for the descriptions produced so far.

4. Scheduling Instrumentation

EEL schedules instructions in a basic block (local scheduling). The instructions in the block come either from the original program (for rescheduling) or a combination of the program and instrumentation code. If instrumentation contains branches, the scheduler only processes the regions of straight-line code. The scheduler uses a common two pass list scheduling algorithm [7]. The first pass starts at the end of the block and works backwards to compute the length (in cycles) of the dependence chain between every instruction and the end of the block. This computation only considers the stalls required between data dependent instructions.

The second pass starts at the beginning of the block and works forward, to order instructions with list scheduling. The instruction with the highest priority of any instruction that can be legally scheduled at this point is put next in the schedule. An instruction's priority is determined primarily by how few stalls it requires before it can start execution (as computed by **pipeline_stalls**). If two instructions require the same number of stalls, the instruction farthest from the end of the block, using the metric computed in the first pass, is scheduled first. If two instructions still have the same priority, the instruction listed earlier in the original code sequence is chosen under the assumption that the instructions were previously scheduled.

When computing data dependencies in both passes, the scheduler conservatively assumes that loads and stores from the original code access the same address. We also assume that loads and stores in instrumentation code access the same address, which differs from the address accessed by original instructions. This permits instrumentation loads and stores, which typically do not conflict with the original loads and stores, more freedom of movement. Since some instrumentation's memory references are more constrained, there are options to limit the movement of instrumentation code.

4.1. Limitations on Hiding Instrumentation

On aggressive superscalar machines, one could hope that all instrumentation code could be hidden in unused pipeline stall cycles. Unfortunately, processor limitations, such as memory latency (a load on the hyperSPARC has a one cycle latency) and resource usage (stores on the hyperSPARC use the LSU for 2 cycles and loads use it for 1 cycle), limit the cycles in which to hide instrumentation. A further problem is that in many programs, most basic blocks are short and so present few opportunity to hide instrumentation. Even when aggressively optimized, the SPEC95 integer benchmarks have average dynamic block size of 2.9 instructions.

Finally, scheduling instrumentation does not reduce instruction (or data) cache misses caused by instrumentation, since the additional instructions increase the code size regardless of how few stalls the program incurs. Lebeck and Wood proposed a model for the instruction cache effects of program instrumentation, which reasonably accurately predicted that instrumentation that increases a program's size by a factor of E, will increase cache misses by $E \times \sqrt{E}$ [11]. Profiling increases a program's text size by a factor of 2–3. Fortunately, many programs have low instruction cache miss rates, so the increase is not significant.

4.2. Scheduling Profiling Instrumentation

We scheduled QPT2's slow profiling instrumentation [2], which adds 4 instructions—set immediate, load, add, and store—into most basic blocks in a program. This code can execute in 4 cycles on both SuperSPARC and UltraSPARC processors. Blocks with a single instrumented single-exit predecessor or a single instrumented single-entry successor are not instrumented. The SuperSPARC experiments ran on dual processor Sun SPARCstation 20 equipped with 50Mhz SUN SuperSPARC [17] processors, running Solaris 2.4. The UltraSPARC experiments ran on an 12-slot Ultra Enterprise 4000/5000 with 167Mhz Sun UltraSPARC processors [16] running Solaris 2.5. The test programs were compiled with the Sun C and Fortran compilers (version 4.0), using the options "-fast -xO4 -xarch=v8 -xchip=super -xdepend -dn" and "-fast -xO4 -xarch=v8 -xchip=ultra -xdepend -dn" for the SuperSPARC and UltraSPARC respectively. We did not use the compiler

Benchmark	Avg. BB Size	Uninst. Time	Inst. Time	Sched. Time	% Hidden
099.go	2.9	739.2	1830.7 (2.48)	1582.4 (2.14)	22.7%
124.m88ksim	2.2	432.8	1208.2 (2.79)	1081.4 (2.50)	16.4%
126.gcc	2.2	305.9	833.4 (2.72)	798.7 (2.61)	6.6%
129.compress	3.0	278.9	523.8 (1.88)	482.6 (1.73)	16.8%
130.li	2.0	395.3	856.4 (2.17)	760.8 (1.92)	20.7%
132.ijpeg	6.2	438.0	678.7 (1.55)	646.8 (1.48)	13.3%
134.perl	2.4	428.3	1025.1 (2.39)	963.0 (2.25)	10.4%
147.vortex	2.1	538.9	1224.0 (2.27)	1136.3 (2.11)	12.8%
CINT95 Average	**2.9**		**2.28**	**2.09**	**14.8%**
101.tomcatv	13.8	310.1	360.9 (1.16)	354.1 (1.14)	13.4%
102.swim	49.0	447.4	471.5 (1.05)	532.8 (1.19)	-255.0%
103.su2cor	10.2	315.7	368.6 (1.17)	357.9 (1.13)	20.2%
104.hydro2d	4.7	608.8	805.3 (1.32)	724.8 (1.19)	41.0%
107.mgrid	32.4	582.7	643.7 (1.10)	579.2 (0.99)	105.8%
110.applu	12.5	471.8	566.6 (1.20)	541.5 (1.15)	26.5%
125.turb3d	6.1	655.5	917.6 (1.40)	907.3 (1.38)	3.9%
141.apsi	10.4	312.6	384.6 (1.23)	375.8 (1.20)	12.2%
145.fpppp	33.9	869.5	960.2 (1.10)	955.6 (1.10)	5.0%
146.wave5	10.9	362.4	375.9 (1.04)	376.3 (1.04)	-3.2%
CFP95 Average	**18.4**		**1.18**	**1.15**	**16.7%**

Table 1: Slow profiling instrumentation on the UltraSPARC. *Avg. BB Size* is the (dynamic) average basic block size (instructions). *Uninst. Time* is a program's un-instrumented execution time (seconds). *Inst. Time* is a program's instrumented, but unscheduled execution time. The number in parentheses is the ratio to the un-instrumented time. *Sched. Time* is the instrumented time after scheduling. Finally, *% Hidden* is the fraction of instrumentation overhead hidden by scheduling.

Benchmark	Avg. BB Size	Uninst. Time	Inst. Time	Sched. Time	% Hidden
099.go	2.9	741.1 (1.00)	1775.9 (2.40)	1582.4 (2.14)	18.7%
124.m88ksim	2.2	394.9 (0.91)	1185.6 (3.00)	1081.4 (2.74)	13.2%
126.gcc	2.2	306.6 (1.00)	824.7 (2.69)	798.7 (2.61)	5.0%
129.compress	3.0	273.2 (0.98)	522.8 (1.91)	482.6 (1.77)	16.1%
130.li	2.0	407.7 (1.03)	853.8 (2.09)	760.8 (1.87)	20.8%
132.ijpeg	6.2	449.9 (1.03)	687.9 (1.53)	646.8 (1.44)	17.3%
134.perl	2.4	431.6 (1.01)	1000.6 (2.32)	963.0 (2.23)	6.6%
147.vortex	2.1	532.5 (0.99)	1277.9 (2.40)	1136.3 (2.13)	26.6%
CINT95 Average	**2.9**		**2.29**	**2.12**	**13.2%**
101.tomcatv	13.8	321.0 (1.03)	363.2 (1.13)	354.1 (1.10)	21.5%
102.swim	49.0	510.6 (1.14)	543.8 (1.06)	532.8 (1.04)	33.0%
103.su2cor	10.2	310.5 (0.98)	370.5 (1.19)	357.9 (1.15)	21.1%
104.hydro2d	4.7	570.9 (0.94)	791.3 (1.39)	724.8 (1.27)	30.2%
107.mgrid	32.4	508.9 (0.87)	590.8 (1.16)	579.2 (1.14)	14.2%
110.applu	12.5	466.7 (0.99)	575.8 (1.23)	541.5 (1.16)	31.4%
125.turb3d	6.1	666.6 (1.02)	937.5 (1.41)	907.3 (1.36)	11.1%
141.apsi	10.4	319.5 (1.02)	401.1 (1.26)	375.8 (1.18)	31.0%
145.fpppp	33.9	885.6 (1.02)	1113.5 (1.26)	955.6 (1.08)	69.3%
146.wave5	10.9	352.8 (0.97)	376.4 (1.07)	376.3 (1.07)	0.0%
CFP95 Average	**18.4**		**1.22**	**1.16**	**27.3%**

Table 2: Slow profiling instrumentation on the UltraSPARC, with original instructions first rescheduled by EEL.

Benchmark	Avg. BB Size	Uninst. Time	Inst. Time	Sched. Time	% Hidden
099.go	2.8	1873.1	4695.1 (2.51)	4417.9 (2.36)	9.8%
124.m88ksim	2.3	1226.2	3003.2 (2.45)	2876.7 (2.35)	7.1%
126.gcc	2.2	863.4	2543.9 (2.95)	2466.8 (2.86)	4.6%
129.compress	3.0	1529.7	1751.3 (1.14)	1845.4 (1.21)	-42.5%
130.li	2.0	1066.3	2501.8 (2.35)	2101.6 (1.97)	27.9%
132.ijpeg	6.4	1153.8	1810.9 (1.57)	1716.7 (1.49)	14.3%
134.perl	2.3	1113.2	2187.8 (1.97)	2190.5 (1.97)	-0.3%
147.vortex	2.1	1721.7	4395.3 (2.55)	3900.4 (2.27)	18.5%
CINT95 Average	**2.9**		**2.19**	**2.06**	**10.9%**
101.tomcatv	11.4	1287.4	1420.2 (1.10)	1391.6 (1.08)	21.5%
102.swim	66.1	1280.0	2239.3 (1.03)	2214.7 (1.02)	41.5%
103.su2cor	10.1	1099.6	1385.3 (1.26)	1303.0 (1.18)	28.8%
104.hydro2d	4.4	2255.5	2760.5 (1.22)	2599.8 (1.15)	31.8%
107.mgrid	46.9	1481.2	1566.6 (1.06)	1628.5 (1.10)	-72.5%
110.applu	9.3	1661.3	2008.5 (1.21)	1853.6 (1.12)	44.6%
125.turb3d	5.7	1974.3	2858.9 (1.45)	2745.3 (1.39)	12.8%
141.apsi	11.8	911.2	1073.8 (1.18)	1020.7 (1.12)	32.6%
145.fpppp	28.2	2655.7	3916.2 (1.47)	3190.9 (1.20)	57.5%
146.wave5	13.3	1116.9	1466.4 (1.31)	1095.9 (0.98)	106.0%
CFP95 Average	**20.7**		**1.23**	**1.13**	**43.5%**

Table 3: Slow profiling instrumentation on the SuperSPARC.

options that generate UltraSPARC-specific code, since our instruction scheduler is currently configured for the SPARC version 8 instruction set. In all cases, we ran the programs using the scripts that come with the SPEC95 benchmarks, specifying the longest running ("ref") inputs.

Table 1 contains measurements for the UltraSPARC. Scheduling hides an average of 15% of slow profiling overhead for integer benchmarks, and 17% for floating point benchmarks. The integer programs execute many small basic blocks (average 2.9 instructions per block), so there is little opportunity to schedule added instrumentation among the original program instructions. This is compounded by the fact that for purely integer codes, the UltraSPARC can launch at most two instructions in parallel, instead of its maximum four instructions per cycle.

Neither of these problems should affect floating point programs, so it is at first surprising that they performed no better than the integer benchmarks. In fact, scheduling can hide a greater percentage of the instrumentation overhead for floating point programs, but performance is lost due to other factors. EEL's instruction scheduler is quite simple, as it only schedules within basic blocks using a simple heuristic algorithm. It does not perform as well as the optimizers in the SUN C and Fortran compilers that compiled the benchmarks. Since EEL schedules original program instructions as well as added instrumentation, it can produce a worse schedule for the original instructions while trying to hide the added overhead. Hence the benefit of hiding overhead is lost by de-scheduling in the floating point benchmarks, with their highly optimized, long basic blocks.

To factor out the effect of EEL's scheduler, we performed a variation of the previous experiment on the UltraSPARC. First EEL's scheduler reschedules the benchmarks, without adding any instrumentation. Then slow profiling instrumentation was added, but not scheduled among the original instructions. Finally both the added instrumentation and original instructions were scheduled together. Table 2 contains the results of this experiment. The results for integer benchmarks are the similar to before (average 13% hidden), but the results for floating point benchmarks are better. Scheduling now hides 27% of instrumentation overhead for the floating point benchmarks, with no significant outliers.

Table 3 contains measurements for benchmarks compiled for and run on the SuperSPARC, and the results are similar to those obtained for the UltraSPARC. Scheduling hides an average of 11% of profiling overhead for the integer benchmarks, and 44% of the overhead for floating point benchmarks.

5. Conclusion

This paper investigated the benefits of combining instruction scheduling with executable editing. Measurements on the SPEC95 benchmarks show that on a 3-way superscalar machine scheduling can hide an average of 11–44% of the overhead introduced by program profiling instrumentation. On a more modern, 4-way superscalar, the scheduler can hide an average of 16–17% of the profiling overhead. A sub-optimal scheduling algorithm limits the visible improvement from scheduling instrumentation, since it may reschedule original program instructions poorly.

Already, the benefits of scheduling program instrumentation are clear enough that existing and future instrumentation systems should adopt this simple technique to reduce instrumentation overhead. In addition, this approach promises to help reduce the cost of error checking, such as array bounds or null pointer tests, to a level at which it may routinely be included in production code.

Acknowledgments

Many thanks to Gurindar Sohi for the use of the UltraSPARC machine used to collect numbers for an early version of this paper, and to Bob Roessler for arranging the loan of the machine used in our initial UltraSPARC experiments. Mark Hill suggested that the scheduler model the L2 cache in the UltraSPARC. Vinod Grover and Kurt Goebel provided helpful comments on a draft of this paper.

This work is supported in part by Wright Laboratory Avionics Directorate, Air Force Material Command, USAF, under grant #F33615-94-1-1525 and ARPA order no. B550, an NSF NYI Award CCR-9357779, NSF Grants CCR-9101035 and MIP-9225097, DOE Grant DE-FG02-93ER25176, and donations from Digital Equipment Corporation and Sun Microsystems. The U.S. Government is authorized to reproduce and distribute reprints for Governmental purposes notwithstanding any copyright notation thereon. The views and conclusions contained herein are those of the authors and should not be interpreted as necessarily representing the official policies or endorsements, either expressed or implied, of the Wright Laboratory Avionics Directorate or the U.S. Government.

References

[1] Ali-Reza Adl-Tabatabai, Geoff Langdale, Steven Lucco, and Robert Wahbe, "Efficient and Language-Independent Mobile Programs," in *Proceedings of the SIGPLAN '96 Conference on Programming Language Design and Implementation (PLDI)*, pages 127-136, May 1996.

[2] Thomas Ball and James R. Larus, "Optimally Profiling and Tracing Programs," *ACM Transactions on Programming Languages and Systems (TOPLAS)*, vol. 16, no. 4, July 1994, pages 1319–1360.

[3] Zarka Cvetanovic and Dileep Bhandarkar. Characterization of the Alpha AXP Performance Using TP and SPEC Workloads. In *Proceedings of the 21st Annual International Symposium on Computer Architecture*, pages 60–70, April 1994.

[4] Trung A. Diep, Christopher Nelson, and John Paul Shen. Performance Evaluation of the PowerPC 620 Microarchitecture. In *Proceedings of the 22nd Annual International Symposium on Computer Architecture*, pages 163–174, June 1995.

[5] Linley Gwennap. Intel's P6 Uses Decoupled Superscalar Design. *Microprocessor Report*, 9(2):9–15, February 16 1995.

[6] John C. Gyllenhaal. A Machine Description Language for Compilation. Master's thesis, Department of Electrical Engineering, University of Illinois, Urbana IL, September 1994.

[7] John L. Hennessy and David A. Patterson. *Computer Architecture: A Quantitative Approach*. Morgan Kaufmann, 1990.

[8] Daniel R. Kerns and Susan J. Eggers. Balanced Scheduling: Instruction Scheduling When Memory Latency is Uncertain. In *Proceedings of the SIGPLAN '93 Conference on Programming Language Design and Implementation (PLDI)*, pages 278–289, June 1993.

[9] James R. Larus. Efficient Program Tracing. *IEEE Computer*, 26(5):52–61, May 1993.

[10] James R. Larus and Eric Schnarr. EEL: Machine-Independent Executable Editing. In *Proceedings of the SIGPLAN '95 Conference on Programming Language Design and Implementation (PLDI)*, pages 291–300, June 1995.

[11] Alvin R. Lebeck and David A. Wood. Active Memory: A New Abstraction for Memory-System Simulation. In *Proceedings of the 1995 ACM Sigmetrics Conference on Measurement and Modeling of Computer Systems*, pages 220–230, May 1995.

[12] Harish Patil and Charles Fischer. Efficient Run-time Monitoring Using Shadow Processing. In *2nd International Workshop on Automated and Algorithmic Debugging (AADEBUG '95)*, St. Malo, France, May 1995.

[13] Todd A. Proebsting and Christopher W. Fraser. Detecting Pipeline Structural Hazards Quickly. In *Conference Record of the Twenty-First Annual ACM Symposium on Principles of Programming Languages*, pages 280–286, Portland, Oregon, January 1994.

[14] ROSS Technology, Inc. *SPARC RISC User's Guide: hyperSPARC Edition*, September 1993.

[15] Michael A. Schuette. Exploitation of Instruction-Level Parallelism for Detection of Processor Execution Errors. Ph.D. thesis, Electrical and Computer Engineering, Carnegie Mellon University, Pittsburgh PA, January 1991.

[16] SUN Microsystems, Inc. *UltraSPARC-I User's Manual*, August 1995.

[17] Texas Instruments. *SuperSPARC User's Guide*, October 1993.

Appendix A: Function pipeline_stalls

```
unsigned long
pipeline_stalls(unsigned long cycle,   // cycle when mi starts executing
                UnitValues &state,     // current pipeline state
                const mach_inst* mi)   // next instruction
{
    unsigned long stalls = 0;

  {{INST mi CATEGORY any::
    // All Spawn annotations now refer to instruction mi.

    unsigned long gid = {{GROUP}};     // mi's timing group
    long ii;

    // Trace[] records the resources used by this instruction in the current cycle.
    unsigned long trace[{{UNITS COUNT}}];
    for(ii=0; ii<{{UNITS COUNT}}; ++ii) trace[ii] = 0;

    // Search for stalls
    unsigned long mi_cycle = 0;    // current cycle in mi's pipeline
    while(mi_cycle <= {{GRP gid CYCLES}}) {

        // Units[] records the number of unused resources in this cycle
        // after allocating resources for all previous instructions.
        unsigned long* units = state[cycle];
        bool advance = true;

        // Test for structural hazzards.
        if(advance)
            for(ii=0; ii<{{GRP gid ACQUIRE mi_cycle COUNT}}; ++ii) {
                unsigned long unit_val =
                    units[{{GRP gid ACQUIRE mi_cycle UNIT ii}}] -
                    trace[{{GRP gid ACQUIRE mi_cycle UNIT ii}}];
                if(unit_val < {{GRP gid ACQUIRE mi_cycle NUM ii}}) {
                    advance = false;
                    break;
                }
            }

        // Test for RAW hazzards.
        if(advance)
            for(ii=0; ii<{{R READ COUNT}}; ++ii)
                if({{R READ ii TIME}} == mi_cycle &&
                   cycle < state.write_cy[0][{{R READ ii}}]) {
                    advance = false;
                    break;
                }

        // Similar tests for WAR and WAW hazzards.
        ...

        ++cycle;  // Advance the execution pipeline for previously scheduled instructions.

        // Advance instruction pipeline or record the stall
        if(advance) {
            for(ii=0; ii<{{GRP gid ACQUIRE mi_cycle COUNT}}; ++ii)
                trace[{{GRP gid ACQUIRE mi_cycle UNIT ii}}]
                    += {{GRP gid ACQUIRE mi_cycle NUM ii}};
            ++mi_cycle;
            for(ii=0; ii<{{GRP gid RELEASE mi_cycle COUNT}}; ++ii)
                trace[{{GRP gid RELEASE mi_cycle UNIT ii}}]
                    -= {{GRP gid RELEASE mi_cycle NUM ii}};
        } else
            ++stalls;
    };;
  }}

    return stalls;
}
```

Instruction Scheduling for the HP PA-8000

David A Dunn and Wei-Chung Hsu
Hewlett-Packard Company
ddunn@cup.hp.com wei@cup.hp.com

Abstract

The PA-8000 is capable of reordering independent operations at run time, a task normally performed only by the instruction scheduler in the compiler. This paper presents some of the unique issues faced by an instruction scheduler for the PA-8000. Several features of the micro-architecture are presented along with the heuristics used in the production compiler to model that feature. These features include latency, resource constraints, instruction polarity, cache interfaces, and memory dependences. The performance results in the paper show that instruction scheduling remains an important compiler optimization, even for out of order machines.

1 Introduction

The HP PA-8000 is the first implementation of the PA-RISC 2.0 architecture [5]. This processor implements out-of-order execution, allowing the hardware to reorder operations at runtime. It is tempting to believe that this hardware feature subsumes the functionality of the instruction scheduler in the compiler. However, we have found that an instruction scheduler in the compiler is essential for achieving maximum performance on the PA-8000.

The heuristics used in a PA-8000 scheduler are substantially different than those used on previous PA-RISC implementations. This paper covers the micro-architecture of the PA-8000 and the scheduling methods used to maximize performance on that processor. All discussion is based on our experience in implementing the PA-8000 scheduler for the production HP compiler. When appropriate, results for the SPEC95 benchmark suite are presented.

Section 2 provides an overview of the PA-8000 micro-architecture, with special focus on features that impact scheduling. Section 3 discusses the balancing of scheduling for resource utilization versus scheduling for latency. Section 4 is dedicated to details of the micro-architecture that require special treatment by an instruction scheduler. And Section 5 discusses the impact of algorithms that perform instruction scheduling over extended program regions.

2 PA-8000 micro-architecture

The PA-8000 is an out-of-order superscalar processor. This processor can issue up to four operations per clock cycle and aggressively reschedules operations to maximize the use of its functional units. A block diagram of the overall micro-architecture is shown in Figure 1.

The PA-8000 is designed around a fifty-six entry Instruction Reorder Buffer (IRB) [3]. The IRB is divided into two independent queues, one for Arithmetic and Logic Unit (ALU) operations and one for memory operations. Instructions in the IRB can be executed out of order, increasing the available Instruction Level Parallelism (ILP) in the instruction stream. The retire block commits the results of operations to the externally visible machine state (memory and the architectural registers). To maintain the in-order semantics of the PA-RISC instruction set, this retirement is performed in source order.

Each instruction goes through several stages before being retired. The fetch unit retrieves four instructions each cycle forwarding them to the sort block for processing. The sort block takes each instruction quad and inserts the corresponding operations into the IRB. Most operations consume a single entry in the IRB. Branches and base modifying memory instructions occupy an entry in both queues. The sort block can insert up to eight operations in a single cycle, matching the bandwidth of the fetch unit. The PA-8000 allows two ALU and two memory operations to begin execution every cycle. This instruction launch can be performed out of order, maximizing the utilization of the functional units. After the instruction has been executed, it waits in the IRB for the retire unit to commit its results.

Every cycle, the retire unit can retire up to two operations from each of the queues; two from the ALU queue and two from the memory queue. Only one store can be retired per cycle. Although the retirement bundle has flexible boundaries, instructions must be retired in program order. This provides a definite limit on the PA-8000 execution bandwidth that is dependent upon the instruction schedule.

Given the fixed retirement bandwidth of the PA-8000, it seems logical for the instruction scheduler in the compiler

1072-4451/96 $5.00 © 1996 IEEE

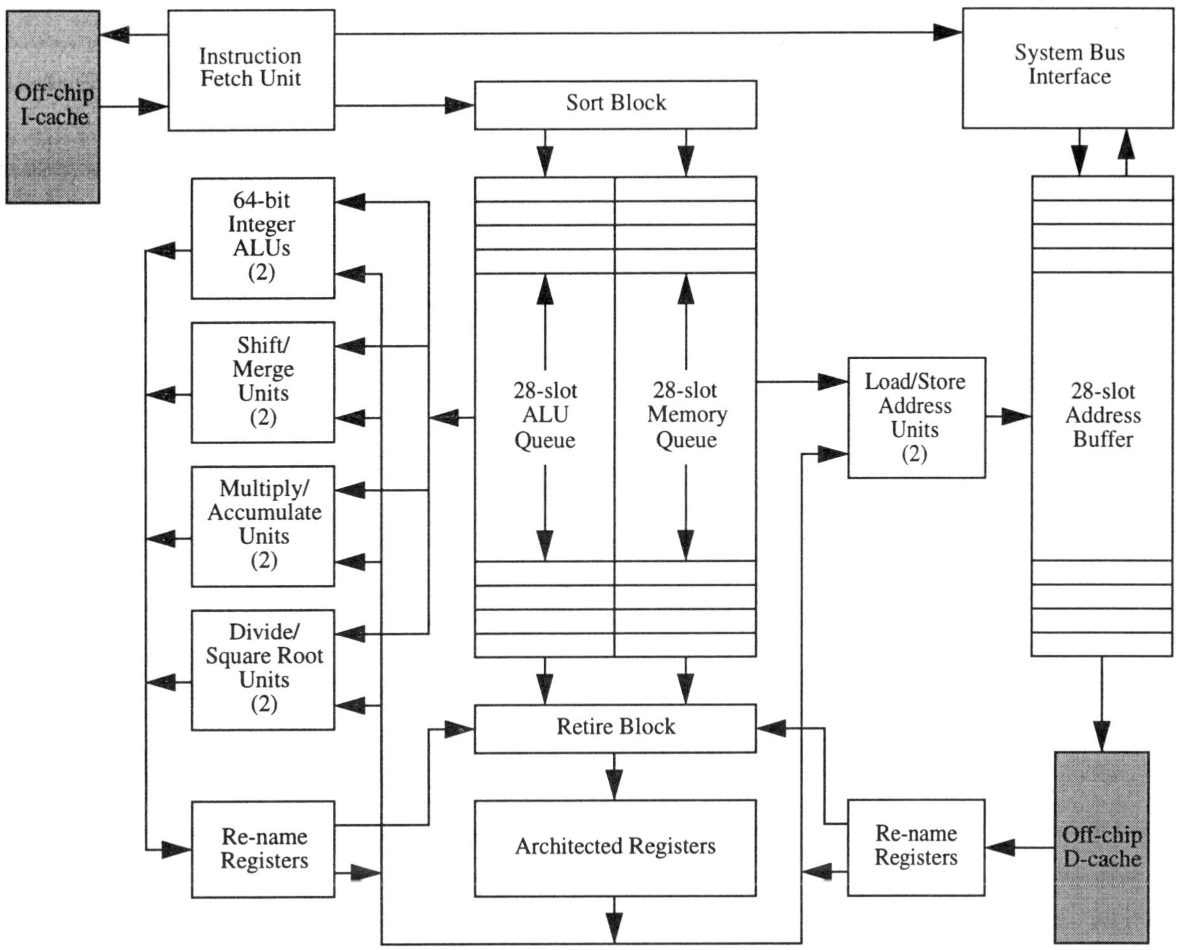

Figure 1: PA-8000 block diagram

to try to maximize the utilization of the retirement unit. The large retirement bandwidth, combined with the latency hiding of the PA-8000, make scheduling for the PA-8000 significantly different than scheduling for previous PA-RISC processors.

The IRB holds up to fifty-six operations which have been inserted but not yet retired. While in this buffer, the operations are launched and executed based on the availability of their inputs. Two operations from each queue may be launched every cycle. The selection of these operations is based on their insertion order in the respective queues. Operations which are inserted into an odd buffer slot are launched on the odd functional unit, and even polarity operations are launched on the even unit. Polarity related issues will be discussed in Section 4.

Arbitration logic in the IRB selects the oldest ready operation on each polarity for launch during the current cycle. Since this arbitration is performed based on source ordering, the instruction scheduler should present the critical operations early in the instruction stream. By bringing these operations into the buffer earlier, the instruction scheduler helps the PA-8000 launch critical operations soon after their inputs become available.

Integer ALU operations execute in a single cycle, enabling the launch of dependent operations one cycle later. Floating point operations typically take three cycles to execute on the dual Floating Multiply and Accumulate (FMAC) units. Memory accesses are also handled by dual functional units. A load which hits in cache will usually complete execution three cycles after the initial launch. Both the FMAC and memory units are fully pipelined.

Although the operations clearly have latencies, the IRB can hide this from the retire unit by completing operations before they reach the top of the reorder buffers. This out-of-order execution allows the instruction scheduler to not honor the latency between dependent operations without forcing a hardware stall. This freedom was not available on previous PA-RISC processors.

3 Resource Utilization vs. Instruction Latency

Given the PA-8000's ability to hide latency, the applicability of traditional latency driven scheduling techniques is questionable. This section explores some of the issues surrounding scheduling with regard to retirement bandwidth and instruction latency.

Since the retirement unit can only retire two ALU operations and two memory operations per cycle, it may be reasonable to completely disregard instruction latency and schedule strictly for retirement utilization. Consider the Directed Acyclic Graph (DAG) and schedules shown in Figure 2.

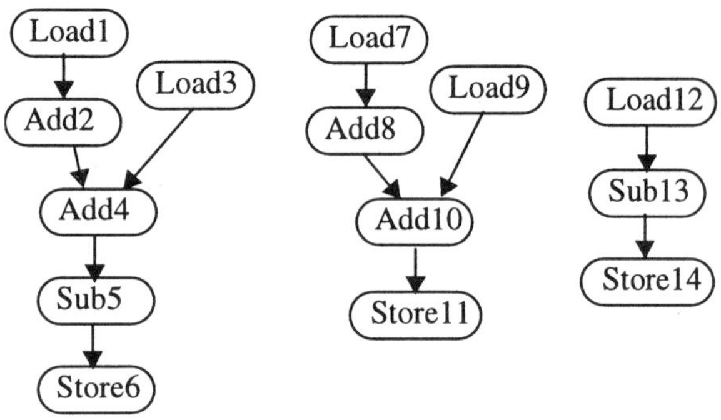

Latency Schedule
Load1 Load7
Load3 Load9
Load12 Add2 Add8
Add4 Add10 Store11
Sub5 Sub13 Store6
Store14

Retirement Schedule
Load1 Add2 Load3 Add4
Sub5 Store6 Load7 Add8
Load9 Add10 Store11
Load12 Sub13 Store14

Figure 2: DAG and Potential Schedules

Each ALU operation is assumed to be a simple integer operation. The schedule based on fulfilling latency is shown on the left. The scheduling algorithm expects all operations shown on a single line to retire in one cycle. A store may retire in the same cycle as the operation that computes the value being stored (due to early address calculation in the decoupled queues). The operations may actually retire faster due to completion of operations before they reach the top of the instruction queues. This would occur if an operation outside of the scheduler's scope stalls, allowing the hardware to launch operations earlier than the scheduler predicted. The best case retirement bundling is indicated by boxes around the instructions. Notice that it will take a minimum of six cycles to retire the instruction stream.

The schedule on the right is based strictly on maximizing the retirement bandwidth and places dependent operations in the same cycle without regard for latency. Notice that this schedule could retire in only four cycles, providing the potential for substantial speedup. Since these instructions easily fit inside the 56 entry reorder buffer, it is not unreasonable to assume that all operations will have completed execution when they reach the top of their respective queues. This schedule also has the advantage of minimizing register lifetimes; temporary values can be consumed by the very next instruction in the stream. This is a significant benefit for a four wide machine implementation of an architecture that contains only 31 general registers and 28 double precision floating point registers.[1]

We can see that ignoring latency when scheduling has the potential for improving performance on the PA-8000. However, the hardware must still execute dependent operations sequentially. The latency between operations still exists, it is simply hidden. Is it reasonable to assume that latencies will be hidden in the IRB? Consider the DAG shown in Figure 3. The latency free schedule is shown on the right. For this example, we will assume integer operations. Each load takes three cycles, and the other operations take a single cycle. The maximum path length in the DAG is eight cycles, but the instruction bundles can retire in only three cycles.

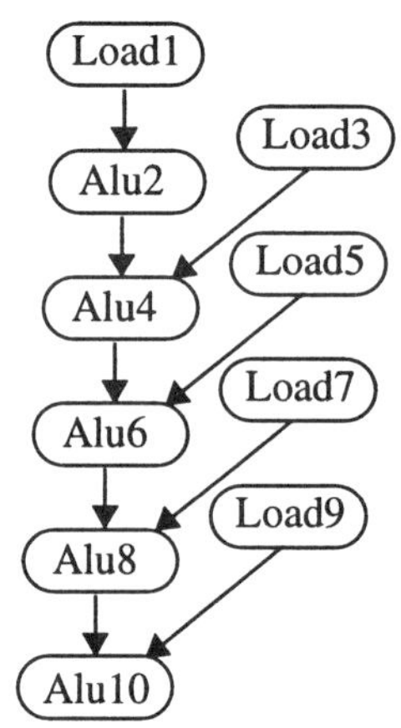

Retirement Schedule
Load1 Alu2 Load3 Alu4
Load5 Alu6 Load7 Alu8
Load9 Alu10

Figure 3: Long Dependence Chain and Schedule

A model of this instruction stream executing on the PA-8000 is given in Figure 4. For simplicity, we assume that the queue is completely full when the first quad is inserted in the reorder buffers. We also assume that four operations are retired from the queue each cycle. Launch arbitration is not modeled, so each operation will launch as soon as it could theoretically do so. At cycle 0, the first instruction quad has been inserted into the IRB. Load1 and Load3 have been launched for execution on the two load/store address units. At cycle 1, the next four instructions have been inserted and the loads have all progressed one stage in the memory access pipeline. Finally at cycle 3, the first two loads have obtained their data from the cache. This allows Alu2 to launch, enabling Alu4 on the next cycle. The final

1. One of the 32 architected general registers and one of the 32 architected floating point registers always contain a 0. Three other floating point registers are used for exception information.

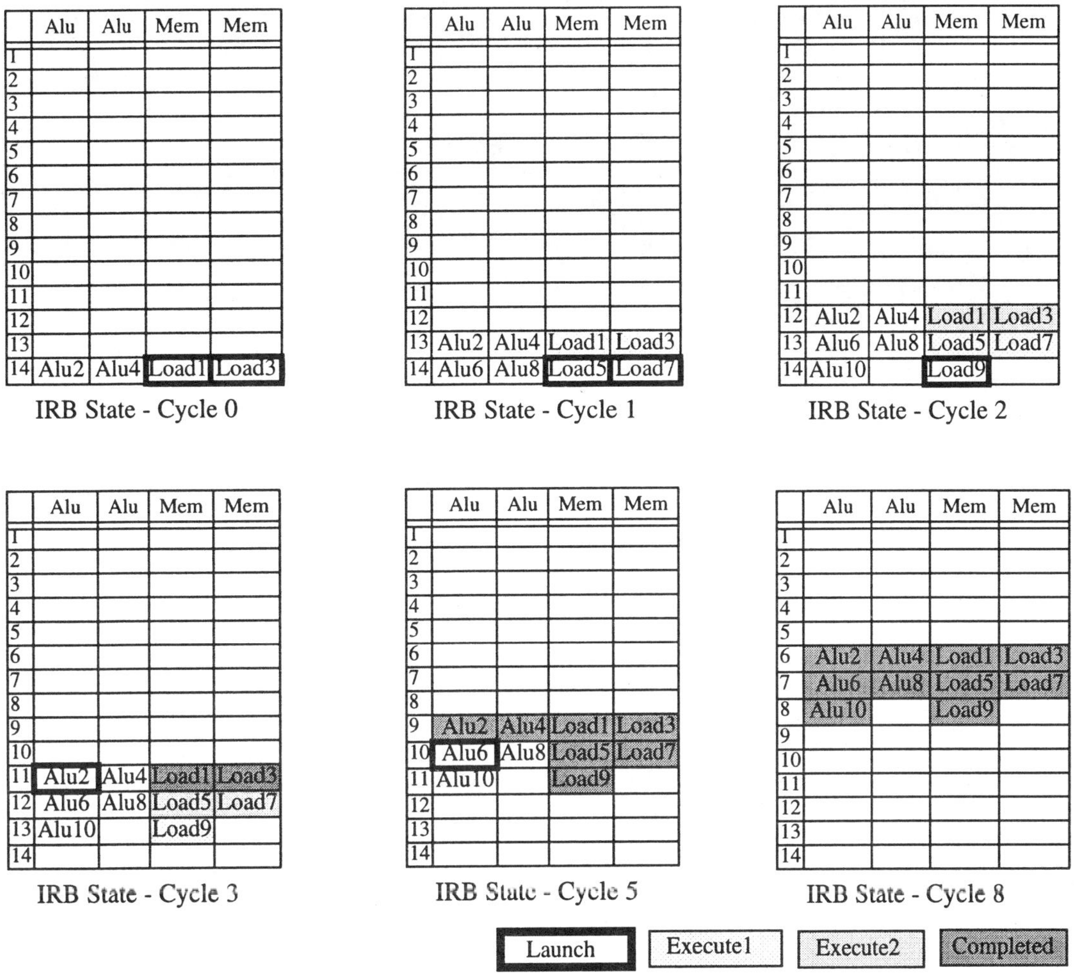

Figure 4: Model of PA-8000 Executing Integer

state shown, cycle 8, indicates all operations in our example have completed execution. This has happened six cycles before the first quad will reach the retirement unit. In addition, when the last quad completes execution, it is still eight cycles from retirement. This provides evidence that scheduling without regard for latency is reasonable for integer operations, even for integer loads.

Floating point ALU operations on the PA-8000 take substantially longer to execute than integer ALU operations. Because of this difference, it is not reasonable to assume that latency free scheduling will work for floating point code based on the previous example. Consider the same DAG and schedule, shown in Figure 3, for floating point operations. PA-8000 FMAC operations execute in three cycles, so the path length in the DAG is eighteen. However, the retirement utilization is still only three cycles. Figure 5 shows a model of the PA-8000 executing this floating point code. This model uses the same assumptions as the previous integer model.

The first state shown in the figure is the IRB at cycle 3. At this time all instructions have been inserted and the first two loads have returned their values from the cache. Alu2 will launch during this cycle and complete executing at cycle 6. Cycle 6 is not shown; during cycle 6 Alu4 begins execution. At cycle 9 we can see that all loads have completed, however we are just beginning the third ALU operation. At cycle 13, the first four operations have reached the top of the IRB. All of these operations have completed operation so the bundle retires smoothly at the end of the cycle. However, cycle 14 runs into a problem. Alu8 has reached the top of the queue but is still one cycle from completion. We cannot retire Alu8 during cycle 14 so only Load5, Alu6, and Load7 are retired. This wastes an ALU retirement slot which might have been useful for retiring another instruction. At cycle 15, the retire unit is able to retire both Alu8 and Load9. However, Alu10 has just begun execution and blocks the retirement of subsequent instructions. This wastes another retirement slot for both the ALU and memory buffers. Finally, at cycle 18, Alu10 completes and can retire. By this time, we have experienced several stalls in the retire unit. These stalls occur because operations must be retired in source order, but cer-

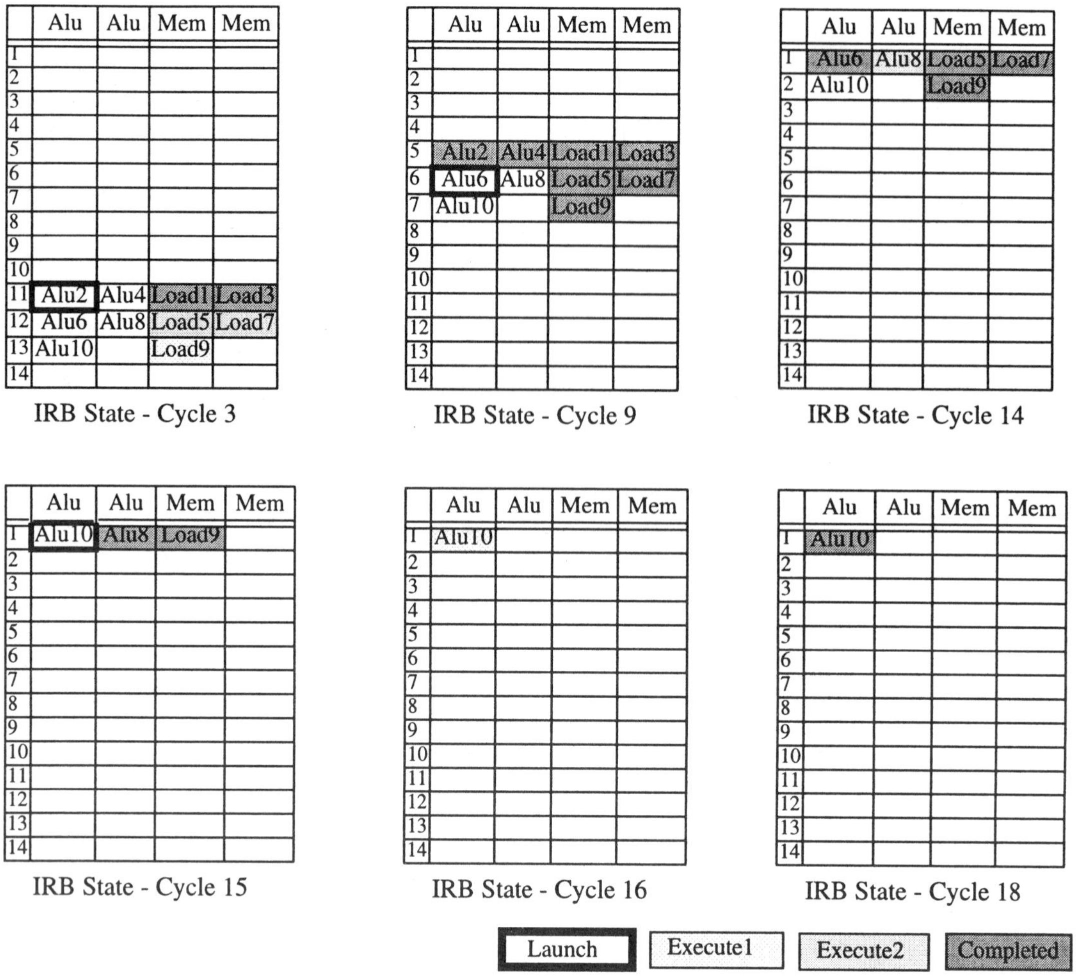

Figure 5: Model of PA-8000 Executing FP

tain operations are not complete when the instruction before them retires. Altogether, six ALU retirement slots and five memory retirement slots are wasted before retiring the last instruction. Clearly latency is an issue for floating point codes, even on an out-of-order machine.

The examples indicate that dependent integer operations may be scheduled in the same cycle, concentrating on retirement utilization rather than latency. For floating point operations, the instruction scheduler must interleave independent operations with the dependence chain. Since instruction selection does consider critical path, some interleaving will occur naturally. However, it may be necessary for the scheduler to force the early selection of less critical operations. This does not mean that we must enforce the full three cycles of latency between floating point operations. Rather, a partial latency model could be used to help reduce the retirement stalls without unnecessarily hurting retirement bundling. A new schedule for the example DAG is shown in Figure 6. This schedule does not allow two dependent floating point operations to be placed

Load1 Load3
Alu2 Load5 Load7
Alu4 Load9
Alu6
Alu8
Alu10

Figure 6: Partial Latency Schedule

in a single retirement cycle. We will assume the scheduler has filled the gaps in the schedule with other independent operations. If these gaps are not filled, retirement bandwidth is wasted. Since the retirement bundles are flexible, the hardware may actually pack the instructions into less cycles than predicted by the instruction scheduler. This flexibility helps reduce the amount of wasted bandwidth without resorting to trace scheduling or other speculative scheduling techniques.

By using the modified schedule, we hope to avoid the retirement stalls which we encountered in the previous example. In order to determine the efficacy of the modified

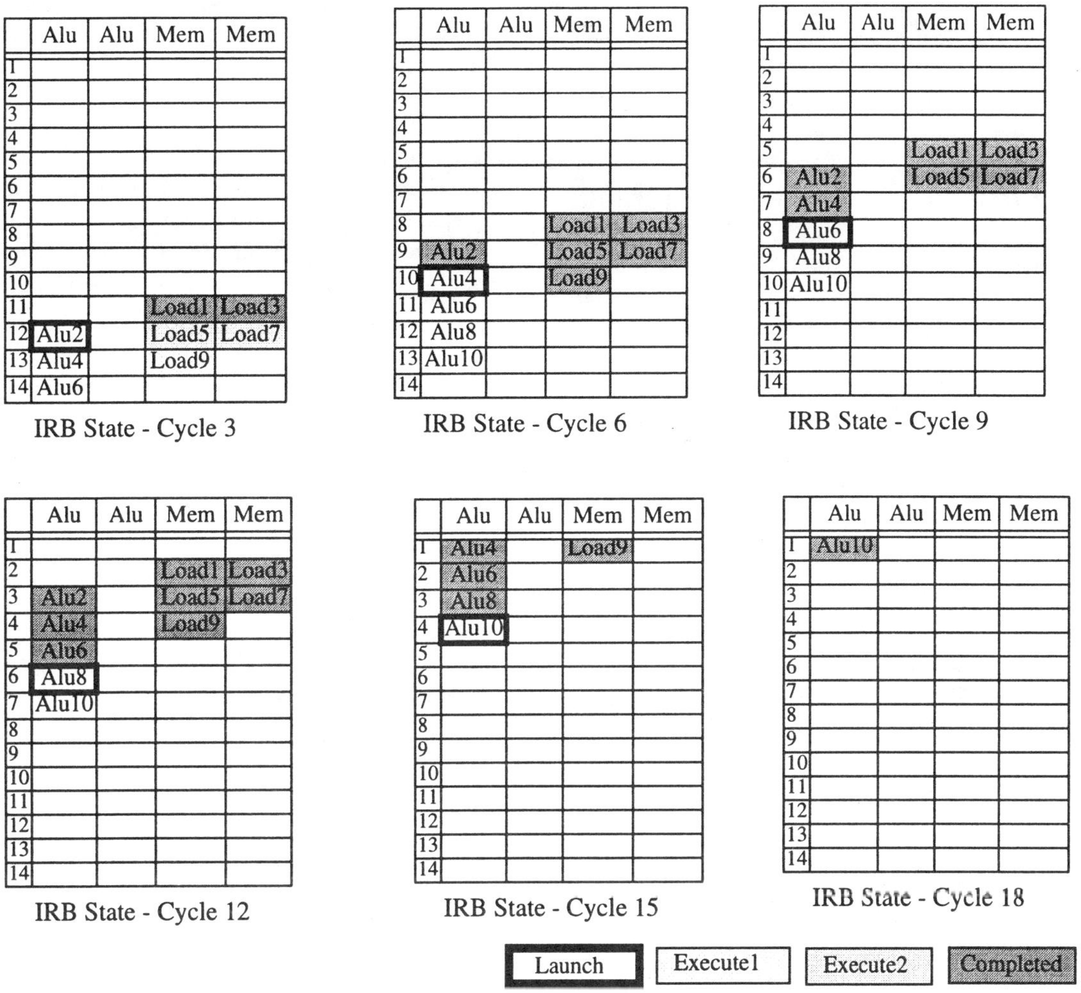

Figure 7: Execution Model for Partial FP

schedule, a model of its execution is shown in Figure 7. This model uses the same assumptions as the previous examples. Using this new schedule, we once again avoid wasting retirement bandwidth due to stalls. Even though the Floating Point Unit (FPU) operations need three cycles to execute, the instruction scheduler only needed to honor one cycle of latency to avoid forcing a stall. This observation is key in crafting an instruction scheduler for the PA-8000.

Although the previous example indicates no stalls, several characteristics are not being modeled. These characteristics could in fact result in a stall. The first factor is launch contention for the functional units. Prior instructions on the same polarity may be ready which would delay the launching of operations in our dependence chain. These delays could prevent subsequent operations from being ready to retire when they reach the top of the reorder buffers. This contention is very difficult to model in the instruction scheduler since it depends on dynamic behavior which may cross basic block boundaries.

Another significant characteristic is the existence of long latency operations. On the PA-8000, both the floating point divide and cache miss take substantially longer than it takes to retire the entire IRB. This long delay is likely to stall the processor with the long latency operation at the top of the IRB. Dependent operations are also going to be close to the top of the IRB. After completing the long latency operation, the dependent operations may force another stall while they execute. By scheduling unrelated operations between the long latency operations and the dependent operations, we can reduce the magnitude of these secondary stalls.

In order to determine the best scheduling model for the PA-8000, we have measured the performance of the SPEC95 suite using four different scheduling models. The Zero latency model uses latency free bundling, interleaving operations based only on critical path. Under this model dependent operations, both integer and floating point, may be scheduled in the same cycle. The One cycle latency model continues to use latency free bundling for integer operations (including loads) but will not place dependent floating point operations in a single cycle. The Two cycle latency model places two cycles between dependent FPU operations, but continues to ignore integer latency. And the final, Full latency, model respects all integer and FPU latencies. This full latency model corresponds to the traditional superscalar scheduling used for previous PA-RISC processors.

The experimental results are shown in Table 1. It is worth noting that both 132.ijpeg and 134.perl contain operations that are performed on the floating point unit (mostly integer multiply and divide). Hence they benefit more from the partial latency scheduling. All run times have been normalized to the two cycle latency model. This model seems to provide the best overall performance and is the model used in the production compiler. However, this result is closely tied to the specific features of the PA-8000 microarchitecture. It is likely that scheduling for a larger IRB would need to respect less latency. Similarly, scheduling for a smaller reorder buffer would need to respect more latency.

	Zero	One	Two	Full
099.go	0.98	1.00	1.00	1.00
124.m88ksim	0.99	0.99	1.00	1.01
126.gcc	1.01	1.01	1.00	1.00
129.compress	1.00	0.99	1.00	1.01
130.li	1.01	1.01	1.00	1.00
132.ijpeg	1.08	1.00	1.00	1.01
134.perl	1.05	1.00	1.00	1.02
147.vortex	1.01	1.01	1.00	1.01
101.tomcatv	1.07	1.01	1.00	1.01
102.swim	1.11	1.03	1.00	1.05
103.su2cor	1.06	1.02	1.00	1.01
104.hydro2d	1.06	1.00	1.00	1.00
107.mgrid	1.15	1.01	1.00	1.05
110.applu	1.20	0.99	1.00	1.01
125.turb3d	1.02	1.01	1.00	1.01
141.apsi	1.06	1.04	1.00	1.05
145.fpppp	1.02	1.00	1.00	0.99
146.wave5	1.06	1.01	1.00	1.04

Table 1: Latency Scheduling Results

These results show that instruction scheduling has significant performance impact even for processors that perform dynamic scheduling.

4 Scheduling for Special Cases

Some design decisions made in the implementation of the PA-8000 require special treatment from the instruction scheduler. This section discusses polarity scheduling, cache prefetch spreading and store-load dependence modeling.

4.1 Polarity Scheduling

As discussed in Section 2, instructions are launched to functional units according to their polarity in the reorder queue. For example, instructions in the even slots can only be launched to even functional units. This is to avoid the cost and complexity of a complete connection between instruction reorder queues and the functional units. However, this raises an issue about whether a special treatment such as polarity scheduling is needed from the instruction scheduler.

Two frequently asked questions are (a) if there is a mix of floating point and integer instructions, should we avoid scheduling all floating point instructions on one polarity (only using one FMAC unit), and (b) should we schedule a sequence of data dependent operations on the same polarity, since data dependent operations cannot make use of both units simultaneously anyway? For both questions, the answer is no: we do not need special polarity scheduling for pipelined operations.

For question (a), consider the fact that the ALU queue can launch two instructions per cycle. However, there are six functional units (two integer units, two FMAC units, and two fdiv/sqrt units) connected to it. Therefore, no schedule can make all functional units busy anyway. Scheduling operations (except for fdiv/sqrt operations) based on queue polarity would not improve functional unit utilization.

For question (b), consider the DAG and schedules shown in Figure 8. The first schedule looks better since

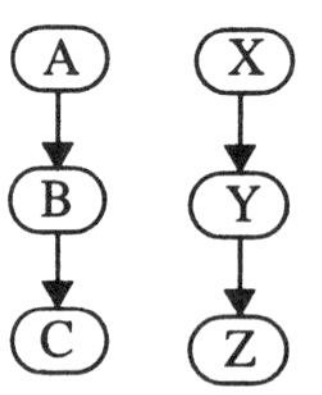

Schedule 1	Schedule 2
A	A
X	B
B	C
Y	X
C	Y
Z	Z

Figure 8: Alternative Schedules

instruction A and X are independent and are on different polarity so they may launch at the same time, and the next cycle, B and Y can be launched at the same cycle, and so on. However, the second schedule may work as efficiently as the first. The out-of-order execution logic still launches A and X at the same time if they are both in the IRB.

Even if A and X are on the same polarity, the schedule only requires one extra cycle to complete execution. During the launch of A, the queue can still launch an unrelated operation. These factors mitigate the need to consider polarity when scheduling pipelined operations.

Floating point divide (FDIV) and square root (SQRT)

instructions need polarity scheduling. This is because the FDIV/SQRT functional units are not pipelined, and they take many cycles (17 for single precision and 31 for double precision) to execute. If two independent FDIV/SQRT instructions are placed on the same polarity, the second one must wait until the first one is finished. For a FDIV/SQRT intensive loop, polarity scheduling has a potential to double the performance.

For a single basic block containing more than one FDIV/SQRT, the scheduler tracks ALU queue slots, and positions code so that successive independent FDIV/SQRT are of opposite polarity. Also, for a single basic block loop containing an odd number of FDIV/SQRT instructions, we have two approaches: (a) we pad a NOP in the loop so that the same instruction will flip polarity on each successive iteration, and (b) we request the loop unroller to unroll such loops an even number of times to get an even number of FDIV/SQRT operations to schedule. FDIV/SQRT polarity scheduling is performed during the final instruction scheduling phase to avoid polarity changes from instruction insertion and deletion in other optimizations. The performance of the above implementation is shown in Table 2. The first column is our polarity scheduling. The second column lets FDIV/SQRT instructions fall randomly. The last one deliberately places FDIV/SQRT on the wrong polarity. Several floating point codes show 1% to 3% gains in performance from polarity scheduling. More importantly, the last column shows that without polarity scheduling, the potential for performance loss is very significant.

	Polarity	Random	Pessimized
101.tomcatv	1.00	1.01	1.07
102.swim	1.00	1.02	1.04
103.su2cor	1.00	1.03	1.08
104.hydro2d	1.00	1.00	1.08
110.applu	1.00	1.01	1.02
141.apsi	1.00	1.02	1.13

Table 2: Polarity Scheduling Results

Readers may have an impression that FDIV/SQRT polarity scheduling is only meaningful for independent instructions. If two FDIV/SQRT instructions were data dependent, scheduling them on opposite polarity may be unnecessary. However, in the scheduler, we do schedule such data dependent FDIV/SQRT instructions on opposite polarity if there are no independent FDIVs to interleave with. For example, assume A and B are data dependent FDIVs. If we schedule A and B on the same odd polarity for the current block, and the next block has an independent FDIV C, it may also be on the odd polarity. In such a case, there will be no overlap in execution among the three FDIVs. Arranging A and B on opposite polarity avoids such pathological cases.

4.2 Prefetch Spreading

Cache misses are very expensive, especially for a wide superscalar implementation such as the PA-8000. When a memory operation that missed in the data cache reaches the top of the queue, it cannot retire until the data comes back from memory. Due to the long memory latency, the queue may fill up, stalling the instruction fetch unit. For loops with regular memory access patterns, the user can request the insertion of cache prefetch instructions (loads to general purpose register 0). Unlike regular memory operations, they can retire from the queue without waiting for data to come back when they miss. With cache prefetching, the optimizer can make the cache miss happen several iterations ahead (a prefetch instruction will fetch data to be used a few iterations later), effectively hiding memory latency. Readers are referred to [2] for a more detailed discussion on cache prefetching.

Prefetch instructions are scheduled like regular memory instructions. However, since prefetch instructions do not have consumers, they are usually scheduled last in a critical path driven scheduler. Hence, prefetches tend to be clustered at the end of a loop body. This approach works fine if most of the misses are clean. Dirty misses cause some performance problems. A dirty miss must write the data of the replaced line back to memory. This write-back makes the data path of the cache/memory interface busy for a few cycles. Therefore, a burst of dirty misses may block the launch of further cache misses. This is similar to structure hazards [6] that the compiler often models. However, this behavior is difficult to model in a deterministic way since the compiler does not know which memory operation may cause a dirty miss.

The above problem has several interesting characteristics: (a) For a loop with data prefetch instructions generated, cache misses usually occur on prefetch instructions. We should focus on prefetch instructions to minimize structure hazards caused by dirty misses; (b) The scheduling of prefetch instructions has no correctness issues, they may be scheduled anywhere in the loop body; (c) The structure hazard caused by dirty miss could be expensive, so the scheduler should provide as much room as possible between two possible misses; (d) Since the compiler does not know which prefetch is more likely to miss, all the prefetches should be treated equally.

Based on the above observations, we decided to spread prefetches evenly over the loop body. For instance, if a loop takes N cycles per iteration, and there are M prefetches, then we try to schedule a prefetch every N/M cycles. The performance impact of prefetch spreading on several SPEC95 programs with frequent cache misses is shown in Table 3.

	Speedup
101.tomcatv	1.03
102.swim	1.04
103.su2cor	1.00
104.hydro2d	1.01
107.mgrid	1.02
110.applu	1.09
146.wave5	1.03

Table 3: Prefetch Spreading Results

4.3 Store-Load Dependency Modeling

Memory operations can be launched out-of-order in PA-8000. The important issue here is maintaining correct data dependency when memory operations refer to the same memory location.

There is no danger in launching a store before a preceding load. The actual store of the data will not happen until its retirement time. Since instructions are retired in their program order, a preceding load will never get data from a subsequent store.

If a load is launched before a preceding store with the same address, the load could get stale data. Such cases are detected at retirement, causing a flush of the offending load and all subsequent instructions, forcing their re-execution.

If a load is launched after a preceding store with the same address, a store-load dependence will be detected. This launch of the load is aborted and a re-launch occurs when the preceding store is retired from the queue. Such a store-load dependency costs a few cycles. This is different from a typical operation latency in that the dependent instruction (i.e the load) can only launch when the producer is retired. Without sufficient padding between such store-load pairs, there will be unavoidable retirement stalls.

The optimizer minimizes the occurrence of such store-load pairs through register promotion and transformations that convert such stores to register copies. However, there are some common cases that the compiler cannot avoid. In the PA-RISC architecture, the move between general purpose registers and floating point registers must go through memory. Both integer to float conversion and integer multiply (using the floating point functional unit) introduce unavoidable store-load dependences.

The instruction scheduler explicitly models such dependences so that stores are scheduled a few cycles away from the corresponding load. This scheduling improves the performance of several programs by more than five percent.

5 Scheduling Over Extended Program Regions

In addition to scheduling inside a single basic block, compilers sometimes use scheduling over extended program regions to increase instruction level parallelism. The extended scheduling techniques include software pipelining [9][7] and trace scheduling [1]. The primary objective is to move independent operations from future basic blocks into the current block, increasing the utilization of resources in the current block. The PA-8000 has hardware that is designed to perform this same task. This section examines some of these scheduling techniques and discusses their applicability to the PA-8000.

5.1 Software Pipelining

For previous implementations of the PA-RISC architecture, the HP compiler has used software pipelining to improve performance on inner loops [8]. Software pipelining interleaves the instructions from multiple iterations of the loop to hide latency. Since these micro-architectures execute the instruction stream in the order presented, it is important for the compiler to expose the available parallelism. The PA-8000 does not completely rely on the compiler to expose parallelism. Rather, all instructions in the IRB are potential candidates for parallel execution.

Consider the loop given in Figure 9. This loop scales an array of doubles by a loop invariant scaling factor. On the surface, the current schedule looks very poor. However, the actual behavior on the PA-8000 is fairly good. Figure 9 also shows a conceptual view of how the register renamed loop looks in the IRB. Notice that multiple iterations of the loop coexist in the IRB. This allows the operations in different iterations of the loop to execute in parallel. In this example the multiply in the first iteration of the loop will not be able to launch until three cycles after the first load is launched. However, during this time the loads for the next

Small Assembly Loop

```
Label:
    Fload      0 (r1), fr4
    Fmpy       fr4, fr5, fr6
    Fstore     fr6, 0 (r1)
    Addib,<    1, r2, r2, Label
    Addi       8, r1, r1
```

IRB with Renaming

```
Fload 0(r1a), fr4a
Fmpy fr4a, fr5a, fr6a
Fstore fr6a, 0(r1a)
Addib 1, r2a, r2b
Addi 8, r1a, r1b
Fload 0(r1b), fr4b
Fmpy fr4b, fr5a, fr6b
Fstore fr6b, 0(r1b)
Addib 1, r2b, r2c
Addi 8, r1b, r1c
Fload 0(r1c), fr4c
Fmpy fr4c, fr5a, fr6c
Fstore fr6c, 0(r1c)
Addib 1, r2c, r2d
Addi 8, r1c, r1d
```

Figure 9: Execution of Small Loop

two iterations will have launched. The PA-8000 does not require the operations to be interleaved by the compiler, it can do the interleaving itself. The main bottleneck in this loop is not latency; the bottleneck is retirement bandwidth. Each iteration of the loop uses three ALU queue slots and three memory queue slots. Three of these slots are overhead associated with counting loop iterations and updating the address pointer. This overhead can be reduced by unrolling the loop [10].

Unrolling the loop, by a factor of four, reduces the retirement usage to nine memory slots (4 loads, 4 stores, and the branch) and six ALU slots (4 multiplies, the branch, and the add). This is a 25% reduction in the retirement cost of the loops. Like software pipelining, loop unrolling can reduce the stalls due to instruction latency. Unrolling places dependence chains from the different iterations in the same basic block, allowing the scheduler to interleave the chains. When executing the end of the unrolled loops, we rely on the IRB to interleave instructions from the next iteration. Because of the instruction retirement benefits, the PA-8000 compiler uses loop unrolling rather than software pipelining to improve the performance on inner loops.

One significant problem is encountered when scheduling unrolled loops: the top of the loop contains mostly loads and the bottom contains mostly stores. This uneven usage of the memory queue can lead to suboptimal performance. We conducted an investigation on using Circular Scheduling [4] to move the loads at the top of the loop into the under-utilized instruction bundles at the end of the loop. This requires that the scheduler either peel the loop or speculate trapping operations. Since neither of these fit well into the current optimizer framework, this optimization was not added.

5.2 Trace Scheduling

Trace scheduling is a common optimization technique to increase the available ILP. During trace scheduling, the scheduler moves instructions from the successor blocks that are likely to be executed into the current block. This technique has not been previously employed on PA-RISC. The operations which are most likely to be critical are loads. Since speculating loads can cause page violations that are not present in the original code, this optimization is unsafe without modifications to the instruction set architecture. The PA-8000 actually performs trace scheduling in hardware. As branches are fetched, the fetch unit predicts the destination of the branch and continues fetching from that destination. Since operations along the likely path are being inserted into the IRB, the critical operations in these blocks can be launched during the execution of instructions in the current block. This feature provides some benefit of trace scheduling without requiring architecture support.

6 Conclusion

We have found that instruction scheduling for the PA-8000 is a critical performance factor. This is true despite the ability of the hardware to reorder the execution of instructions. By scheduling for critical path and enforcing partial latencies, we are able to increase the utilization of the retirement bandwidth. Additionally, hardware details such as instruction polarity, dirty miss behavior, and store-load dependences impact the performance of different instruction schedules.

By considering the details of the PA-8000 micro-architecture, we designed an instruction scheduler that substantially improves performance. Rather than subsuming instruction scheduling, the out of order features on the PA-8000 change the scheduling heuristics that should be used. This combination of hardware and software scheduling provides excellent performance for PA-8000 based systems.

7 References

[1] Fisher, J. A., *Trace Scheduling: A Technique for Global Microcode Compaction,* IEEE Transaction on Computers, C-30(7), July, 1981.

[2] Gornish, Eddie, *Data Prefetching on the HP PA-8000*, HP Technical Report, 1996.

[3] Hunt, Doug, *Advanced Performance Features of the 64-bit PA-8000*, COMPCON 1995 Digest of Papers, pp. 123-128, March 1995.

[4] Jain, Suneel, *Circular Scheduling: A new Technique to Perform Software Pipelining*, Proceedings of the ACM SIGPLAN'91 Conference on Programming Language Design and Implementation (PLDI), pp. 219-227, June 1991.

[5] Kane, Gerry, *PA-RISC 2.0 Architecture*, ISBN 0-13-182734-0,Prentice-Hall, Englewood Cliffs, NJ, 1996.

[6] Kuck, David J., *The Structure of Computers and Computations, Vol. 1.*, John Wiley and sons, Inc., 1978.

[7] Lam, M., *Software Pipelining: an Effective Scheduling Technique for VLIW Machines*, Proc. *ACM SIGPLAN* '88, June 1988.

[8] Ramakrishnan, Sridhar, *Software Pipelining in PA-RISC Compilers*, Hewlett-Packard Journal, pp. 39-45, June 1992.

[9] Rau, B.R. and Glaeser, C.D., *Some Scheduling Techniques and an Easily Schedulable Horizontal Architecture for High-performance Scientific Computing*, MICRO-14, October, 1981.

[10]Shah, Lacky, *Intelligent Loop Unrolling*, HP Technical Report, 1996.

Meld Scheduling: Relaxing Scheduling Constraints across Region Boundaries

Santosh G. Abraham, Vinod Kathail
Hewlett-Packard Laboratories,
1501 Page Mill Road,
Palo Alto CA 94304
{abraham, kathail}@hpl.hp.com

Brian L. Deitrich
Center for Reliable and High
Performance Computing,
University of Illinois, Urbana, IL 61801
briand@crhc.uiuc.edu

Abstract

Meld scheduling melds the schedules of neighboring scheduling regions to respect latencies of operations issued in one region but completing after control transfers to the other. In contrast, conventional schedulers ignore latency constraints from other regions leading to potentially avoidable stalls in an interlocked (superscalar) machine or incorrect schedules for non-interlocked (VLIW) machines. Alternatively, schedulers that conservatively require all operations to complete before the branch takes effect produce inefficient schedules.

In this paper, we present general data structures for maintaining latency constraint information at region boundaries. We present a meld scheduling algorithm that generates latency constraints at the boundaries of scheduled regions and utilizes this information during the scheduling of other reigions. We present a range of design options and describe the reasons behind our particular choices. We cover certain pitfalls and discuss how to develop an algorithm that addresses these issues. We evaluate the performance of meld scheduling on a range of non-interlocked machine models on a set of SPEC 92 and Unix benchmarks. We also investigate the sensitivity of the performance improvements due to changes in issue width and instruction latencies.

Keywords: *instruction scheduling, global scheduling, latency constraint propagation, instruction-level parallel processors, compiler optimization*

1 Introduction

Scheduling algorithms are usually oblivious of constraints coming in from blocks or regions that are already scheduled and hence may make scheduling decisions that lead to poor schedules. In a non-interlocked machine, the processor does not interlock to ensure that the inputs are available before issuing an operation. For such machines, the compiler schedules code to guarantee that an operation completes before a dependent operation issues. Within a scheduling region, the scheduler delays the issue of a dependent operation to ensure that its inputs are available. Across scheduling regions, a scheduler must ensure that certain constraints are satisfied on entry or exit of a region. For instance, one convention is to assume that on entry all operations have their inputs available. In this case, the scheduler must guarantee that all operations complete before control is transferred to another region. In contrast, a meld scheduler generates latency constraints imposed by scheduled regions, propagates constraints to the boundaries of a region to be scheduled, and translates these constraints to edge constraints recognized by the local region scheduler.

The example in Figure 1 illustrates the benefits of meld scheduling. Assume that load and arithmetic operations take four and three cycles respectively. In Figure 1(a), the conventional scheduler delays the branch to issue in cycle `7`, in order to guarantee that the load operation `e` in block `B1` completes before the branch is taken. In this example, there is an immediate use of `r6` in cycle `0` of block `B3`, but the conventional scheduler is oblivious of the schedule in block `B3` and always delays the branch. As illustrated in Figure 1(b), meld scheduling relaxes the scheduling constraint on the branch and schedules it in cycle `5` of block `B1`. When scheduling `B3`, meld scheduling recognizes the incoming constraint from the load `e` to its use, and delays the issue of operation `1` to cycle `2`. In this example, meld scheduling is able to reduce the schedule length of block `B1` without increasing the schedule length of block `B3`. Eventually, the propagation of latency constraints to successor blocks does increase the schedule length of block `B5` by `2` cycles. But the savings in the schedule length in the more frequently executed blocks more than makes up for the loss in the less frequently executed blocks. The weights on the blocks represent the profiled or estimated execution frequency of the block. In this example, meld scheduling improves weighted schedule length, a measure of overall execution time, by approximately 10%.

The utility of meld scheduling for interlocked machines is less apparent. In an interlocked machine, the processor detects that inputs to an operation are not yet available using interlock hardware and delays the issue of the operation dynamically through stall cycles. For such machines, the scheduler assumes the inputs to be available at the entry and furthermore, considers branches for placement as soon as the operations generating live-out values are scheduled. Thus, the scheduler for an interlocked

1072-4451/96 $5.00 © 1996 IEEE

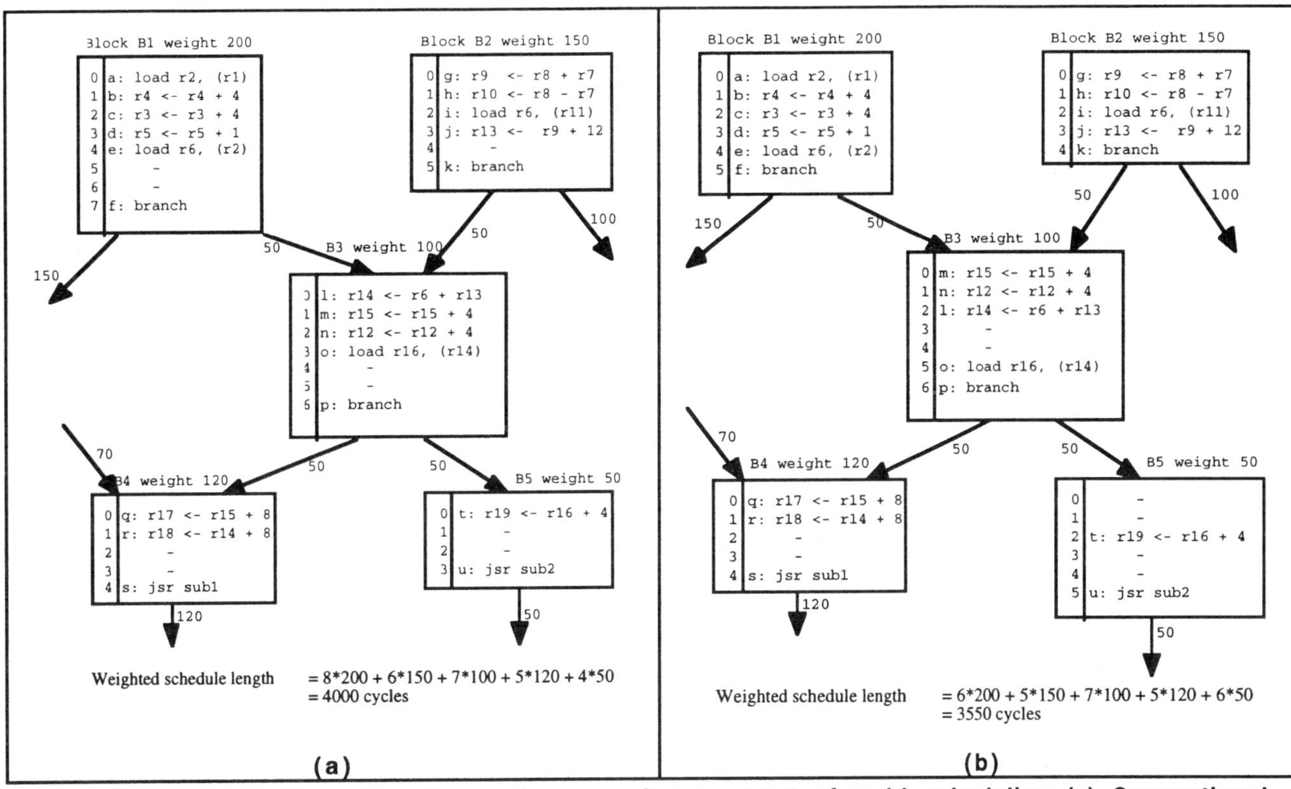

Figure 1. Example illustrating the performance improvement of meld scheduling (a) Conventional scheduler (b) Meld scheduler

machine can schedule branches in cycles 5 and 4 of blocks B1 and B2, optimistically assuming that there will not be immediate uses of live-out values in successor blocks. However, if there are immediate uses of the live-out values, the processor stalls till completion of the live-out generating operations. In the example in Figure 1, the use of r6 in cycle 0 of block B3 causes stalls of 2 and 1 cycles, when the predecessor block was B1 and B3 respectively. In contrast, with meld scheduling the branches are scheduled early, but the uses of live-outs from predecessor blocks B1 and B2 are delayed in block B3 to cycle 2. Thus, an interlocking machine does not stall on the meld-scheduled code in Figure 1b. Meld scheduling is not necessary for correctness in interlocked machines, but can lead to improved overall performance through reductions in stall cycles. In this particular example, meld scheduling increases weighted schedule length and reduces stall cycles by the same amount, so there is no net improvement. In general, meld scheduling as described in this paper may or may not improve execution time for an interlocked machine.

Scheduling techniques that schedule larger regions reduce the potential for performance improvement due to meld scheduling. For instance, superblocks are composed of a linear trace of basic blocks [1]. In contrast to conventional basic block scheduling which does not propagate latency constraints to its successor blocks, superblock scheduling automatically considers latency constraints imposed by operations scheduled so far in basic blocks that are part of the superblock. Thus, superblock scheduling can provide much of the same benefits as meld scheduling in conjunction with basic block scheduling. Other global scheduling techniques [2-7] are cognizant of latencies over larger regions. Since the number of dynamic scheduling boundaries that are crossed decreases when larger scheduling regions are employed, the additional performance improvement due to meld scheduling decreases as the scheduling regions get larger. As developed in this paper, meld scheduling can be applied in conjunction with almost any choice of scheduling region short of the entire function to provide additional performance improvements. Meld scheduling is complementary to schedulers that operate on individual regions, enabling higher performance for a given scheduling region or enabling the use of smaller scheduling regions for a desired level of performance.

The rest of this paper is organized as follows. The next section presents the architectural model. Section 3 describes the meld scheduling algorithm. Section 4 presents experimental evaluation of meld scheduling. Section 5 describes related work and the final section summarizes the results of this work.

2 Architecture models

As we have discussed earlier, meld scheduling can improve the performance of both VLIW and superscalar processors. For the rest of this paper, we use a family of non-interlocked VLIW machines based on the HPL

PlayDoh architecture [8]. Each machine has a set of integer, floating point, memory and branch units and is capable of issuing an instruction containing several operations in each cycle. Each instruction consists of a set of operations, where each machine operation is a RISC-style operation with source and destination operands.

We assume that functional units are fully-pipelined. Thus, operations compete for resources in the issue cycle only, and operations from different instructions (necessarily issued in distinct cycles) do not compete for resources. As a consequence, we need to maintain only latency constraints and do not need to consider resource usage constraints across region boundaries. This reduces the amount of inter-region information and simplifies constraint propagation during meld scheduling. The technique presented in this paper, however, can be extended to handle resource-usage constraints for machines which do not have flow-through pipelines.

In order to investigate the effects of varying issue width and latencies, we consider a range of machine models parameterized by width and latency. The four combinations of widths labeled W1 through W4 are presented in Table 1 and the four combinations of latencies labeled L1 through L4 are presented in Table 2. A particular machine model, W2L2, is a particular width choice (W2) and latency choice (L2) from this table, capable of issuing up to seven operations consisting of two integer, two floating-point, two load/store operations and one branch operation.

	Integer units	Floating point units	Memory units	Branch units
W1	1	1	1	1
W2	2	2	2	1
W3	4	2	2	1
W4	4	4	4	1

Table 1. Number of units in various machine models

	Int ALU	Float Add	Int/ Float Mpy	Int/ Float Divide	Load	Store	Branch
L1	1	1	1	4	1	1	1
L2	1	3	3	8	2	1	1
L3	2	4	4	12	3	1	1
L4	5	6	10/12	15/16	5	3	3

Table 2. Latencies of operations in various machine models

3 Meld scheduling algorithm

In this section, we first present the data structures used for representing inter-region constraints, then describe the overall algorithm followed by more detailed descriptions of various refinements. Figure 2 illustrates how block B3 in Figure 1 is meld scheduled and we will use Figure 2 as the running example in this section.

3.1 Data structures for inter-region constraints

When a region is picked up for scheduling, data structures for representing inter-region constraints are constructed. This data structure contains a distance map and a set of latency maps.

DEF: A *distance map* specifies the shortest distance in cycles from each entry to each exit of a scheduled region.

In Figure 2, the distance map for block B1 specifies the distance from entry a to exit f to be 6 cycles. Since a basic block has only one entry and one exit, its distance map contains only one value. In a single-entry region, the distance map provides the distance from the entry to each exit. In a superblock, the distance to each exit is its *exit time,* the sum of the schedule time of the exit (branch) operation and the branch latency.

DEF: A *latency map* is a table of operand and latency dangle pairs; when queried with a particular operand, it either returns the associated latency dangle (if present in the table) or returns a default value.

Entries can be created, modified, or removed from the map and the default value of a map may be modified. The latency dangle is one of two types.

DEF: A *required dangle* of an operand specifies the number of cycles after control leaves a region through an exit (or enters a region through an entry) that an operation defining/using the operand completes.

DEF: An *available dangle* of an operand specifies the number of cycles after control enters a region through an entry (or leaves a region through an exit) that an operation defines/uses the operand.

In order to ensure that the required dangles that a scheduled region exports through its exits are honored by its successors, each unscheduled region imports required dangle constraints through its entries. In Figure 2, Block B1 exports a required dangle of 2 on r6, indicating that r6 is written two cycles into a successor block, by the load operation in flight on exit from B1. The required dangle on r6 is a constraint that unscheduled successor blocks must satisfy when they are scheduled eventually. Block B3 imports a required dangle of 2 in order to enforce the constraint that r6 must not be referenced for the first two cycles of the schedule for B3. Similarly, in order to exploit the available dangles that a scheduled regions exports through its entries, each unscheduled region imports available dangles through its exits. In Figure 2, Block B4 exports an available dangle of 1 on r14, indicating there is no use of r14 till cycle 1 by operation r. The available dangles indicates the ability of a scheduled region such as B4 to absorb some of the latencies from its predecessors. Block B3 imports an available dangle of 1 on r14, permitting operations that define r14 to complete up to one cycle after control transfers out of block B3. The available dangles relaxes constraints on scheduling B3.

A particular latency map is characterized and named by three independent attributes: export/import, entry/exit, and def/use. Thus, Figure 2 shows the import entry def map, one of the latency maps for Block B3, at the top left-hand corner of Block B3. We describe these attributes next.

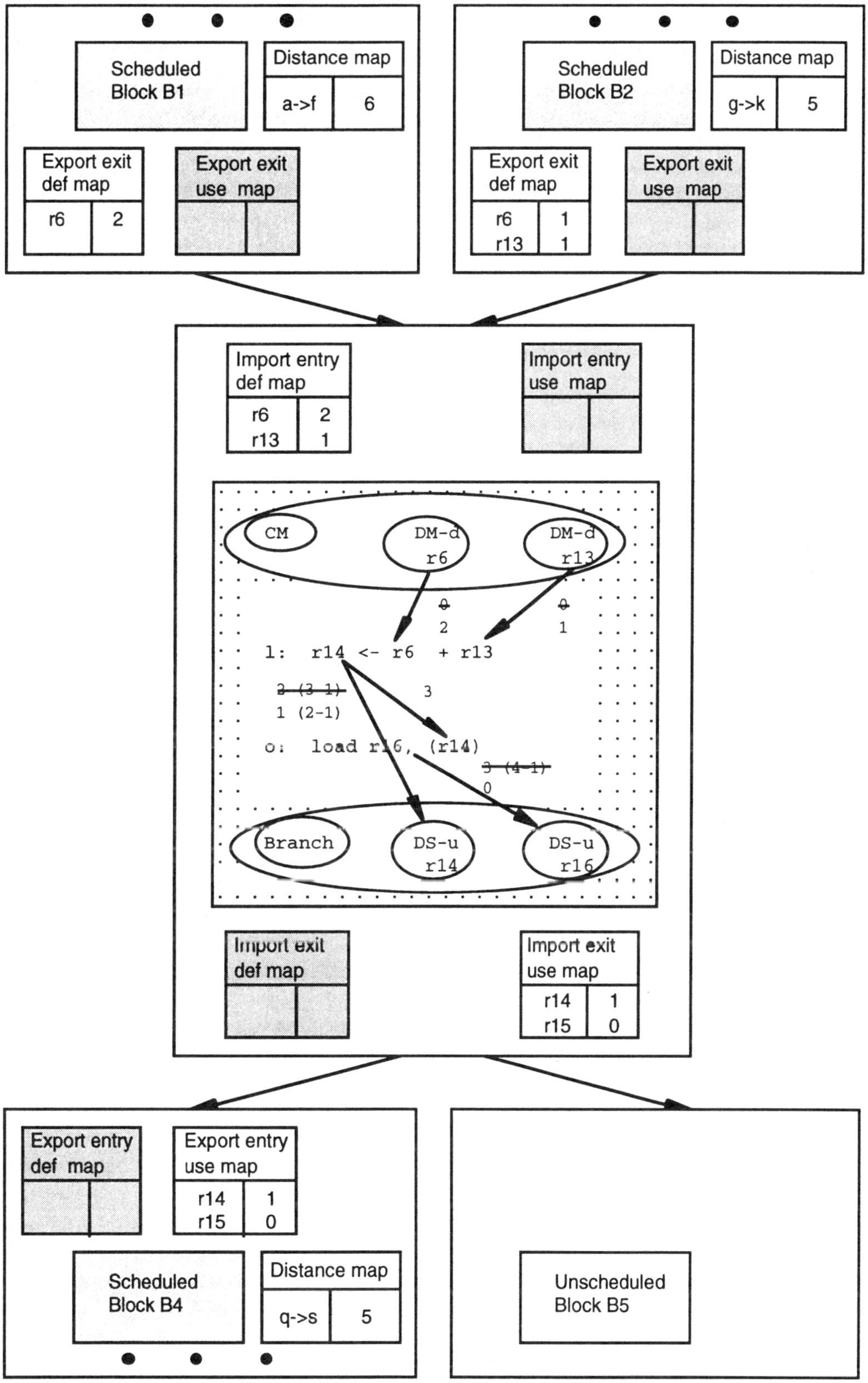

Figure 2. Propagation of latency constraints and conversion to edge constraints

DEF: An *export map* of a region contains constraints that this (necessarily) scheduled region imposes on other as yet unscheduled regions.

DEF: An *import map* of a region contains constraints that other neighboring scheduled regions impose on this (necessarily) unscheduled region.

DEF: An *entry* map is at the entry of a region.

DEF: An *exit* map is at the exit of a region.

DEF: A *def map* contains constraints due to definitions of variables/operands.

DEF: A *use map* contains constraints due to uses of variables/operands.

Export maps are created after a region is scheduled and are persistent throughout the scheduling process. Figure 2 shows the latency map structures just before `B3` is scheduled. Thus, blocks `B1`, `B2`, `B4`, which have been scheduled, have export maps at their entries and exits, even though only the export maps relevant to scheduling `B3` are shown. Import maps for a region are created just before a region is scheduled and are destroyed immediately after the region is scheduled. Thus, when `B3` is scheduled, only the import maps for `B3` are live. `B5` does not have any meld data structures because it is as yet unscheduled.

The export maps are formed by inspecting the schedules for a region. The required dangles from the export exit maps are propagated to the import entry maps. Thus, the export exit def maps of blocks `B1` and `B2` are used to form the import entry def map for `B3`. The available dangles from the export entry maps are propagated to the import exit maps. Thus, the export entry use map for `B4` is used to form the import exit use map for `B3`. The import map constraints are translated to edge constraints that are recognized by the local scheduler. We will discuss the edge constraints shown in Figure 2 later in Sections 3.6 and 3.7. Note that the def and use constraints are completely orthogonal; data flows from export def maps to import def maps and from export use maps to import use maps. Depending on the scheduling discipline and machine model, some maps may be unnecessary. For instance, in certain machine models latencies of anti- and output dependencies are always zero and consequently, required use dangles are always zero. For such machines, the shaded maps in Figure 2, such as the export exit use map, can be eliminated.

The default value of an entry export map specifies the maximum available dangle for all operands. For instance, if we do not allow latency dangles into `jsrs` and `returns` and require all operations to complete before a `jsr` or `return`, the default value of the export entry maps of block B4 is set to 4. The default value of an export exit map is always set to zero.

Drawing an analogy to data-flow problems, the export maps together with the distance maps specify the transfer function for a scheduled region. Just before a region is scheduled, the constraints at each exit (up-exposed constraints) are determined by examining the entry export maps and distance maps of scheduled successors. Similarly, the constraints at each entry (down-exposed constraints) are determined by examining the exit export maps and distance maps of scheduled predecessors. The latency maps themselves form the gen sets in the data-flow problems. The distance maps indirectly form the kill functions, reducing each operand-latency pair by the distance and killing any pairs whose latency drops to zero or less.

3.2 Overview of the algorithm

An overview of the meld scheduling algorithm is shown in Figure 3. The scheduling regions tile the entire function and we iterate over the scheduling regions in some priority order. Once a region is picked for scheduling, we create the meld data structures for this region. We propagate the export maps from neighboring predecessor scheduled regions and build the import entry maps. We transfer the required dangles in the import entry maps to edge constraints. We propagate the export maps from neighboring successor scheduled regions and build the import exit maps. We use the available dangles in the import exit maps to relax the edge constraints to the exits. Using these augmented edge constraints, we schedule the region. After scheduling, we construct export maps for each entry and exit. We calculate the minimum entry to exit distance for each pair of entry and exit nodes and construct the distance map for this region.

```
Iterate over scheduling regions in some priority order {
   • Propagate export exit maps from predecessors and
     build import entry maps
   • Transfer required dangles from import entry maps
     to edge constraints
   • Propagate export entry maps from successors and
     build import exit maps
   • Use available dangles from import exit maps to
     relax edge constraints
   • Schedule region
   • Inspect schedule and build export maps and
     distance maps for this region
}
```

Figure 3. Meld scheduling algorithm overview

3.3 Lazy versus eager propagation

We have been implicitly assuming lazy propagation of constraints; just before a region is scheduled, we propagate constraints to the region and construct its import maps. Lazy propagation collects constraints from other scheduled regions only when necessary. However, lazy propagation may visit a scheduled region many times, each time for constructing the import map for a different region. In contrast, eager propagation always keeps the import maps at the boundaries between scheduled and unscheduled regions up to date. Thus, when the meld scheduler picks a region for scheduling, it forms the region's import maps by locally combining the import maps of immediate predecessors/successors. However, after a region is scheduled, eager propagation must update the import maps of all scheduled regions reachable through other scheduled regions. Eager propagation may update a particular import map many times, each time after scheduling a different region. Thus neither lazy nor eager propagation is consistently better than the other. Lazy propagation has the advantage that the import maps are transient data structures. We believe that lazy propagation is easier to debug and maintain, because the validity of persistent data structures (export maps and distance maps) can be verified by locally examining a scheduled region. We use lazy propagation in our implementation and experiments.

3.4 Iteration order

In conventional scheduling, the order in which regions are scheduled does not affect the schedule lengths because the scheduler is oblivious of the schedules of other regions. In meld scheduling, a region scheduled earlier in the iteration order only needs to honor constraints from a few already scheduled regions. Therefore, in comparison to conventional scheduling, regions scheduled earlier have a relatively shorter schedule length and regions scheduled later have a longer schedule length. Therefore, we sort regions in decreasing profiled or estimated execution frequency order and schedule them in sorted order. In the example in Figure 1, Blocks B1 and B2 have the highest execution frequency, are scheduled earlier by the meld scheduler and have shorter schedule lengths than in the conventional schedule. In contrast, block B5 has a lower execution frequency, is scheduled last, and has a longer schedule length than with the conventional scheduler.

3.5 Propagating latency constraints to import maps

Recall that import entry maps summarize the constraints from the export exit maps of predecessor scheduled regions. The required dangle from a predecessor region's exit is reduced by the minimum distance from that exit to the entry of the region being meld scheduled. Similarly, the exit import maps summarize the constraints from export entry maps of successsor scheduled regions. The available dangle from a successor entry is increased by the minimum distance from the exit of the region being scheduled to that entry. We consider the propagation of export exit maps to compute import entry maps in more detail. A similar procedure is used to compute import exit maps.

We separate the computation of import entry maps into two steps: first, calculating the distance from the entry to exits of regions reachable through scheduled regions and second, composing the maps at these exits for forming the import entry maps. We calculate the distance using a modified version of Dijkstra's shortest path computation algorithm (see [9]). We form a unique region exit identifier by combining the region id with the exit operation id. In the distance table, we associate with each exit identifier two pieces of information; the current shortest path to this exit and whether this exit has been expanded. Initially, we enter the immediate predecessor exits of the entry of the region being scheduled into a distance table. In each subsequent step, we expand an unexpanded exit with the shortest distance from the distance table. We consider the immediate predecessor region's exits for inclusion in the distance table. An exit is included if its region has not been scheduled and the distance from the exit to the entry is less than `max_dangle`. The constant *`max_dangle`* is set to the maximum expected required dangle, typically the latency of the longest operation. If the distance table already contains the exit, the associated distance is set to the minimum of the current distance value and the computed distance through the expanded exit. The procedure terminates when all exits are expanded. The distance values in the distance table are the shortest distances from each of the exits to the entry of the region being scheduled.

The example in Figure 4 illustrates the distance calculation scheme. The left-hand side of Figure 4 shows the control flow graph, with scheduled regions shaded and marked with an S and unscheduled regions unshaded and marked with an U. The right hand side of Figure 4 shows the node that is expanded in each step and the updated distance table after each step. In Step 1, the entry of the region being scheduled is expanded and its immediate predecessor exits are entered in the table, viz. `E3` and `E6`, with distance of `0`. In Step 2, we choose the exit `E3` for expansion. We consider the immediate predecessor scheduled exits for inclusion in the table; in this case, `E2`. We use the available entry-exit distance map to calculate the distance of the minimum path from such exits to the entry through the exit being expanded. For exit `E2`, this distance is `14+0=14`. In this example, we assume that `max_dangle` is `10`. Since the distance from `E2` exceeds `10`, we know that no dangle through this exit can reach the entry and so we do not include `E2` in the table. After marking `E3` as expanded, in Step 3 the algorithm expands `E6`. The distance from `E1` to the entry through `E6` is `5` and we enter this information in the table. Exit `E5` is also an immediate predecessor exit of region `R5`. However, since `R4` is unscheduled, we ignore this exit and all reachable predecessor exits through `E5`, viz. `E4`. We do not need to consider required dangles through `E4` because region `R4` will eventually absorb those dangles. Once all the exits in the table are expanded, the algorithm terminates and the table contains the minimum distances to all relevant exits.

Once the distances are available, we iterate over all the exits in the distance table and compose the export exit maps at these exits using the distances from the distance table to form the import entry maps. The composition step is shown in Figure 5. We iterate over the constraints in an export exit map. For each such constraint, we look up the import map for a corresponding constraint and update it. We then calculate the distances from an exit to all relevant entries using a procedure similar to that illustrated in Figure 4 and compose the export entry maps to determine the import exit maps.

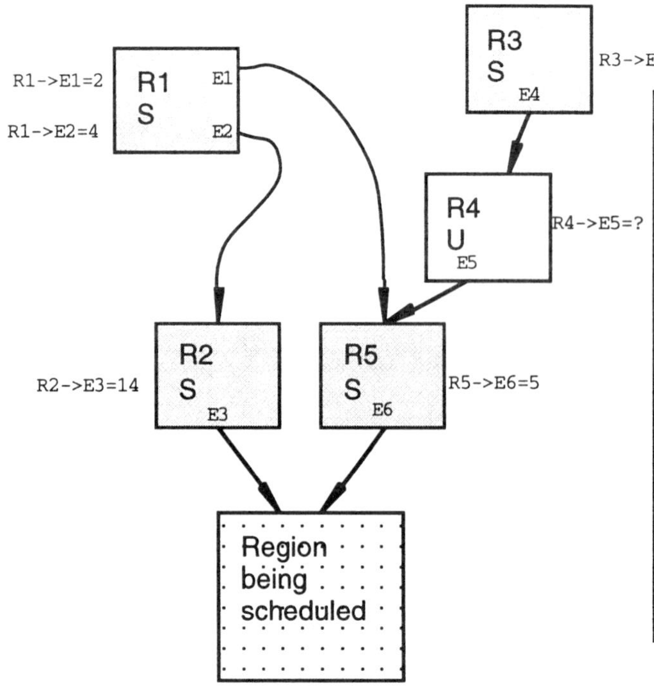

Step	Action		
	Map	Dist.	Expanded
Step1	Expand entry		
	R2E3	0	N
	R5E6	0	N
Step2	Expand R2E3		
	R2E3	0	Y
	R5E6	0	N
Step3	Expand R5E6		
	R2E3	0	Y
	R5E6	0	Y
	R1E1	5	N
Step4	Expand R1E1		
	R2E3	0	Y
	R5E6	0	Y
	R1E1	5	Y

Figure 4. Example illustrating distance calculation

```
procedure compose_import_entry_map (export_exit_map,
        distance, import_entry_map) {

    Iterate over pairs in export_exit_map {
      Set dangle_operand and required_dangle from pair;
      req_dangle_at_entry = required_dangle - distance;
      if (req_dangle_at_entry > 0 AND
          (dangle_operand is not in import_entry_map OR
           req_dangle_at_entry > current_dangle in
                                    import_entry_map)) {
         enter (dangle_operand, req_dangle_at_entry) in
             import_entry_map;
      }
    }
}
```

Figure 5. Computing import entry map from export exit maps

3.6 Latency map to dependence edge constraints

In this step, we transfer the constraints in the import maps into constraints that are recognized by the local scheduler. The entry import maps contain required dangles that place additional constraints on scheduling operations relative to the entry. Typically, these constraints are enforced by placing edges from the entry node to individual operations with latency markings indicating the minimum amount by which an operation should be delayed relative to the entry. The exit import maps relax constraints on scheduling operations relative to the exit. To begin with, each operation is constrained so that it completes before control leaves a scheduling region through an exit. If a particular operation's operands are not present in the import maps, then the constraint can be relaxed so as to merely guarantee that the operation is issued before control leaves the region. Otherwise, the constraint can be relaxed by the available dangle specified in the import maps.

For concreteness, we describe the details of transferring the import map constraints to edge constraints in the intermediate representation of our research compiler, Elcor. In Elcor, each entry has a start node called a Control-Merge pseudo-operation (shown as CM in the example in Figure 2). Each CM may have associated Data-Merge (DM) pseudo-operations that define (DM-d) or use (DM-u) operands. An exit or branch operation, may have Data-Switches (DU) that define (DS-d) or use (DS-u) operands. The Data-Merges and Data-Switches are scheduled implicitly with the associated CM or Branch operation.

For each pair in the import map at the entry, we ensure that there is a DM-d and a DM-u that define and use the associated operand respectively. In the example in Figure 2, the operands `r6` and `r13` appear in the import entry def map and therefore, we create DM-d operations that define the operands `r6` and `r13`. The DM-u operations are not shown but are created. Similarly, we create DS-u operations for `r14` and `r15`. In addition to dependence edges between real operations, we draw edges from DM operations and from/to the DS operations. Initially, the latencies on edges from the DM operations are set to zero and the latencies of edges to the DS operations are set to (latency of the operation - branch latency) to ensure that the operation completes before control leaves the region. For each constraint in the entry import maps, we set the latencies of the outgoing edges from the corresponding DM operations to the latency specified in the import maps. In the example in Figure 2, we set the latencies on edges originating from the DM associated with `r6` to `2`. For each constraint in the import exit maps, we reduce the latencies of the incoming edges to the corresponding DS operations by the latency in the import maps. In Figure 2, we reduce the latency on the edge from operation `l` to the DS-u by `1` (the value in the import exit map for `r14`) from `2` to `1`. There is no constraint in the import exit map for the operand `r16` and therefore, the outgoing edge latency on operation `o` is reduced to `0`.

3.7 Generating export maps from scheduled region

After scheduling a region, we generate the export maps for that region. The export maps describe the constraints imposed by this region on other, as yet unscheduled, regions and are formed by scanning the scheduled code for this region.

In our implementation, the export entry maps are formed incrementally by iterating over all operations in the superblock and scanning all operands of each operation. For each scanned operand, we compute the cycle at which it starts reading/writing. If the operand is not present in the export entry map, we create an entry associating the operand with the computed value; otherwise, we replace the current value with the computed value if it is lesser.

The export exit maps are computed as follows. In one forward scan through the superblock, we incrementally form a pseudo exit def map and pseudo exit use map to record the end times that an operation finishes reading or writing an operand. When we reach a branch, we record its exit time (branch schedule time + branch latency). When we have scanned all operations with schedule times less than the exit time, we generate the export exit def map and export exit use map for the exit by subtracting the exit time from the end times in the pseudo maps and discarding any entries whose required dangle drops to zero or less.

3.8 Refinements

In this section, we elaborate the details of the basic algorithm, and propose efficient ways of handling certain special cases.

3.8.1 Cycles in CFG

Cycles in the control flow graph (CFG) can potentially lead to incorrect schedules. Consider the example in Figure 6. Region `R2` has been scheduled and region `R3` is being scheduled. Consider the dependence carried through region `R2` from the load to its use in region `R3`. To this point, we have left unspecified whether the region being scheduled is treated as scheduled or unscheduled during the import map calculation. If region `R3` is treated as unscheduled, then it does not export constraints. The load may be scheduled in the last cycle of region `R3` and the use in cycle `0`. If the load latency is larger than the sum of the schedule length of region `R2` and the branch latency, the dependence between the load and its use may be violated. We address such dependencies carried through cycles consisting of scheduled regions. Thus, when a region is picked for scheduling, its export constraints (export maps and entry-exit distances) are set to conservative initial values.

One conservative setting is zero for all references in the entry and exit export maps and zero for all entry-exit distances. The zero setting for the entry maps indicate that no dangles from a region are allowed to dangle into the same region. The import maps are then calculated, during which these preliminary export constraint settings are used if the region is contained in a cycle in the CFG in which all other regions are scheduled. In the previous example, the use of the load appears in the preliminary export entry map of region `R3` and hence also appears in the import exit map with an allowed dangle equal to the entry-exit distance of region `R2`. Hence the load is constrained to complete before control enters region `R3` again through region `R2` and correctness is preserved.

In our implementation, we calculate less conservative preliminary export maps with the potential for better performance. After picking a superblock for scheduling, we calculate the depth of each operation in the superblock. The depth of an operation is the length of the longest path from the start node to this operation. Alternatively, it is the earliest schedule time of the operation that will obey all dependence constraints and hence is a lower bound on schedule time on a finite resource machine. This depth is used in determining a conservative estimate for available dangle for the operands of the operation. Similarly, we use the depth of the branch operation to calculate preliminary entry-exit distances.

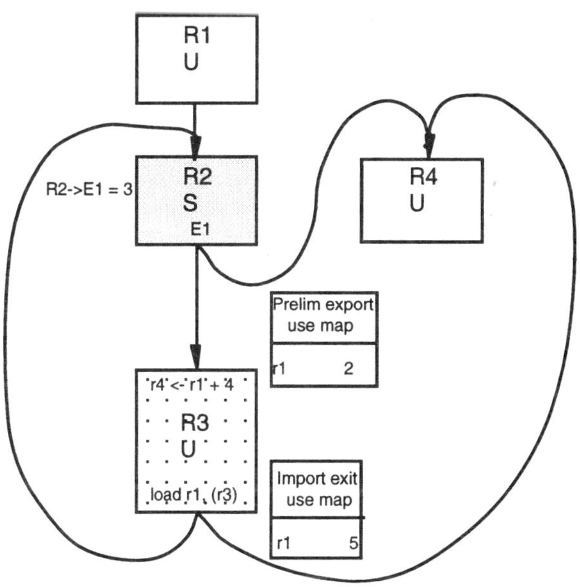

Figure 6. Handling cycles in control-flow graph

In the example in Figure 6, assume the use operation has a depth of 2. Using this value in the preliminary export map, we calculate an import exit use map constraint of 5 on r1. The load may be scheduled with an outgoing dangle of up to 5.

3.8.2 Pass-through dangles

In the example in Figure 7, both regions R1 and R3 are already scheduled and region R2 is picked up for scheduling. Note the dependence from the load in the last cycle of region R1 to the use in cycle 0 of region R3. If region R2 is scheduled in less than 4 cycles, the dependence is not satisfied. An incoming required dangle for which there is no internal reference but an upward available dangle is referred to as a pass-through dangle. The load constraint appears in the import entry def map of region R2 and the use constraint in the import exit use map. But the transfer of these import map constraints to edge constraints is unclear.

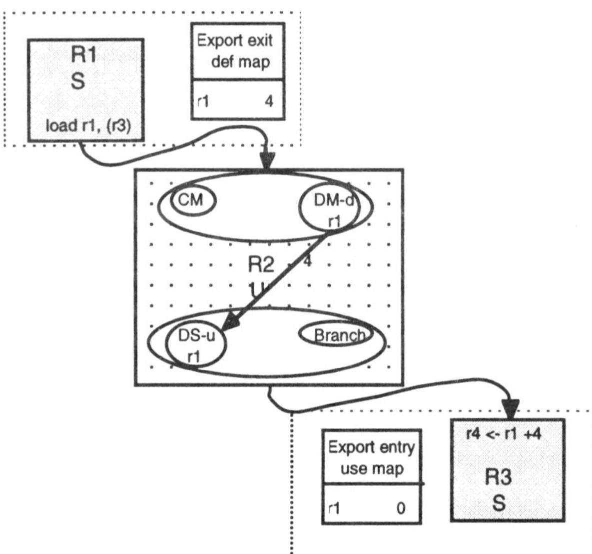

Figure 7. Handling of pass-through dangles

In our implementation, pass-through dangles are handled as follows. Data-Merges and Data-Switches are created for constraints in the entry and exit import maps. Subsequent edge-drawing connects the Data-Merge to the Data-Switch. The edge latency is set first from the entry import map; in this case to 3 (required dangle of 4 minus branch latency of 1). The edge latency is then reduced by the available dangle from the exit import map; in this case it remains at 3 because the available dangle is 0. Since the Data-Switch is implicitly scheduled with its branch, we ensure that the branch is scheduled in cycle 3 or later and the load to use dependence is satisfied in the above example.

3.8.3 Inter-region output and anti-dependences

In the example in Figure 8(a), there is a definition of r6 in the region being scheduled and an up-exposed available def dangle on r6 of 2 cycles. The meld scheduler, as described, insers a Data-Switch defining r6 associated with the branch and an edge from the definition of r6 to the Data-Switch with a latency of (divide latency (12) - branch latency (1) - available dangle (2) = 9). The insertion of this edge delays the exit branch. An alternative is to push the operation defining r6 below the exit branch. The branch is now not delayed, potentially improving performance. A similar situation occurs with anti-dependences. In the case of inter-region anti- and output-dependences, the operation can be scheduled either sufficiently above or below a branch but not within a window around the branch.

Though these constraints can be handled also as resource constraints, we model these constraints somewhat imperfectly as edge constraints. We compare the depth of the defining operation and the exit operation to determine whether it is better to constrain the defining operation below or above the branch. If the defining operation has a larger depth and it is currently above the branch, we move the defining operation and all its dependent operations below the branch in the sequential order. Figure 8(b) illustrates how we move the defining operation below the branch. On the other hand, if the defining operation is currently below the branch, we may choose to move it and

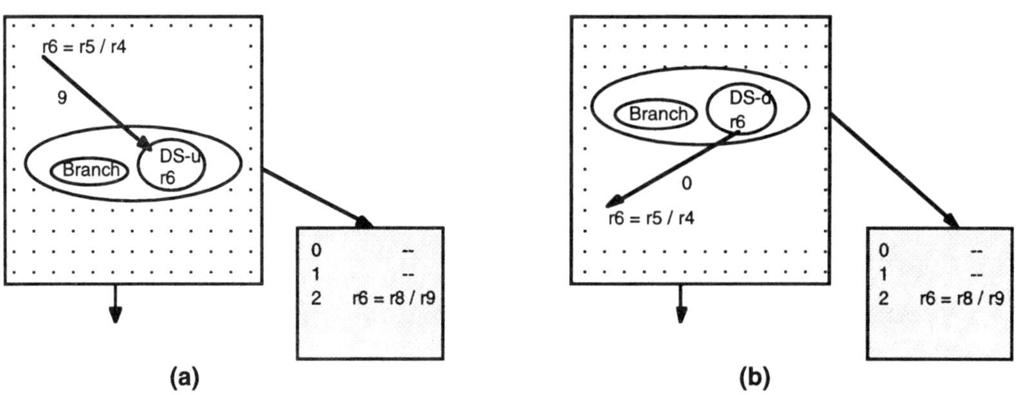

(a) (b)

Figure 8. Handling inter-region output dependences

the operations on which it is dependent above the branch. Finally, we draw an appropriate edge to satisfy the up-exposed def dangle. In Figure 8(b), we draw an edge from the branch to the definition of r6.

3.9 Complete algorithm

The complete algorithm for meld scheduling as implemented in the Elcor compiler is described in Figure 9. This algorithm accommodates all the refinements described earlier in this section. Careful consideration is given in the complete algorithm to reduce the number of times the dependence graph is constructed. Our dependence graph construction step is expensive, and we do not support incremental updates to the dependence graph. The dependence graph is required before certain steps in the meld scheduler such as depth-based heuristics and transferring of map constraints to edge constraints. On the other hand, certain steps in the meld scheduler, such as pushing operations below branches or inserting Data-Merge or Data-Switch nodes require reconstructing the dependence graph.

4 Experimental evaluation

In this section, we present experimental results obtained by our meld scheduling implementation. We use the IMPACT compiler from the University of Illinois IMPACT project to get input in aggressively-optimized superblock form [1]. The IMPACT compiler performs traditional global optimizations, unrolls loops eight times, forms superblocks and applies ILP optimizations to each superblock. The memory disambiguation information computed by the IMPACT compiler is part of the input. In addition, the input code contains profile information; each superblock is annotated with weights indicating how often each superblock is executed and how often each exit is taken. The Elcor compiler at HP Labs takes the input in superblock form, performs data-flow analyses, constructs dependence graphs and schedules each superblock. Although the Elcor compiler supports meld scheduling for both modulo scheduling and superblock/hyperblock scheduling, the experiments did not use modulo scheduling for loops.

To quantify the benefits of meld scheduling, we need a baseline model that does not propagate latency constraints. We considered two alternatives, both of which involve padding schedules with enough no-ops to ensure correct execution on non-interlocked machines. The first alternative simply allows no latency dangles from the region being scheduled. Thus, for each exit, the operations issued before the exit must also complete before the control transfers to the successor region. A problem with this approach is that it causes side-exits of a superblock to be delayed, and consequently, forces operations that are control-dependent on the branch to be also delayed. Thus, this approach increases the schedule length to other exits including the main exit from the superblock. The second alternative is to allow latency dangles through exits into successor regions but ensure that the dangles are absorbed by the *immediate* successors. This can be done as described below.

```
Iterate over scheduling regions in frequency order {
    • Create meld scheduling constraints data structures for region;
    • Build import entry map for the entry;
    • Construct dependence graph for the region;
    • Constrain latencies on entry edges using import entry maps;
    • Calculate depth for ops in region;
    • Set preliminary export entry map and entry-exit
      distances for the region;

    • redraw_edges = FALSE
    • Iterate over exits of region {
          - Calculate cutoff distance to limit the traversal for building import exit maps;
          - Build import exit map for this exit using the cutoff distance;
          - Handle problematic cases of inter-region anti and output dependences as follows:
                  Iterate over problematic operations {
                    Decide placement with respect to this exit using the heuristic;
                    if (operation is moved or constrained by up-exposed dangles) redraw_edges = TRUE;
      }
    • if (redraw_edges) {
          - Delete dependence edges and reconstruct dependence graph
          - Constrain entry edges using entry import maps
      }
    • Iterate over exits of region {
          - Relax latency constraints on edges to exit using import exit maps
      }
    • Schedule region
    • Sort operations in sequential order by schedule times
    • Scan and build export maps and distance maps for this region
}
```

Figure 9. The complete algorithm for meld scheduling

After scheduling is complete for the entire function, we inspect the immediate predecessors, calculate the maximum incoming dangle and insert a block of no-ops that absorbs this dangle. The second alternative gives better performance than the first, since no-ops are inserted once at the top of superblocks as opposed to once at each of the exits. In order to obtain a fair comparison between meld and no-meld, we use the second alternative as the baseline or *no-meld* model.

To quantify how much of the available performance improvement our technique is able to capture, we define an upper bound on the performance improvement. The upper bound is calculated by allowing regions to dangle into neighboring regions, but ignoring the dangle when calculating performance. This represents the best case in which all outgoing dangles can be exported without any attendant cost of absorbing incoming dangles. It is important to note, however, that this upper bound is unachievable in many cases on both non-interlocked and superscalar machines. We refer to the upper bound as the *ignore-dangles* model.

For each machine model, we schedule the code first using the no-meld model and then using the meld scheduler. The upper bound is computed while scheduling using the no-meld model by simply ignoring the dangles. The reported execution time improvements are based on weighted schedule lengths and not based on actual simulation. The execution time of a particular block is obtained by summing up the contributions of each of its exits. The contribution of a particular exit is the product of the number of times this exit was taken during profiling times the exit time of the exit. For a branch, the exit time is the sum of the branch's schedule time and the branch latency. This method is fairly accurate for a pure VLIW machine, because the run-time issuing of instructions tracks the compiler-generated schedule. However, it does not account for cache misses, branch mis-predictions, TLB misses, etc. These other factors are expected to be similar with or without meld scheduling and are not expected to affect significantly the accuracy of our evaluation of meld scheduling.

Figure 10 shows the performance improvement over no-meld for a set of Unix and SPEC92 benchmarks on the W2L2 and W2L3 machine models described earlier in Section 2. Note that the W2 model is capable of issuing up to seven operations per cycle, consisting of two integer, two float, two memory operations and one branch. Each bar in the figure has two components. The first gray component indicates the execution time improvement of meld scheduling over the no-meld case. The second black component indicates the additional execution time improvement under the ignore-dangles model. Thus, the two components together represent the upper bound discussed earlier. Meld scheduling improves execution time between 1 and 9% for the W2L2 model and between 1.7% and 9.8% for the W2L3 model. Note that the black component in the bar graphs are very small, especially for

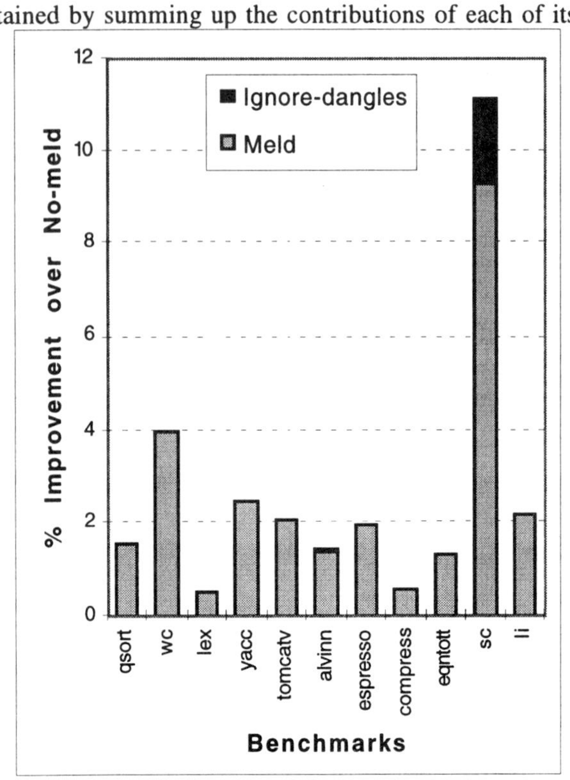

(a)

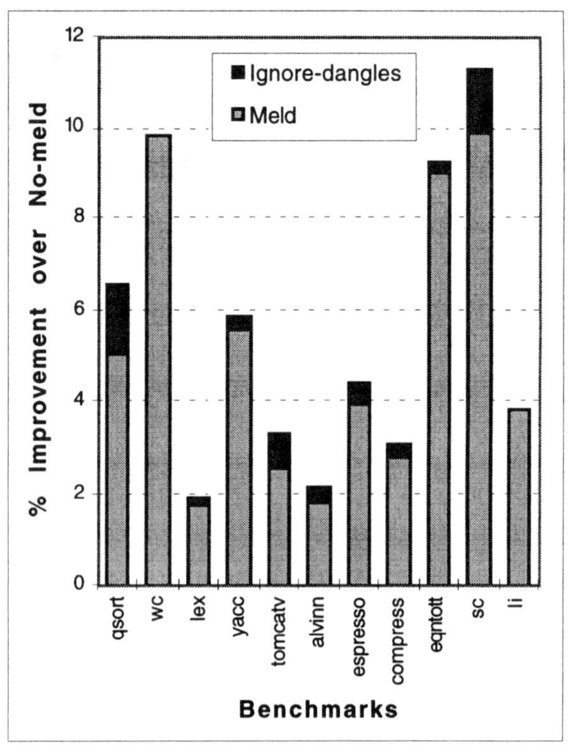

(b)

Figure 10. Performance improvement due to meld scheduling and the upper bound for various benchmarks. (a) Machine model W2L2 (b) Machine model W2L3

the W2L2 model, indicating that our meld scheduler absorbs almost all the inter-superblock latency dangles. With the longer latencies of the W2L3 model, meld scheduling gives higher execution time improvements but does not reach the (potentially unrealizable) upper bound on many of the benchmarks. For the W2L3 model, the difference between improvements due to meld scheduling and the upper bound varies from 0 to less than 1.5%.

It is interesting to compare the results for the integer benchmarks such as sc with the ones for the floating-point benchmarks such as alvinn. In both machine models, floating-point latency is higher than the integer latency. Thus, it may seem that meld scheduling should provide greater improvement on floating-point benchmarks as compared to integer benchmarks. However, floating-point benchmarks are highly loop-intensive and inter-region dangles are less of a problem, since most of the performance-critical dangles occur at the back edges. Modulo scheduling of loops [10-13] is capable of handling these dangles during scheduling. Loop unrolling provides similar benefits. In our experiments, loops were unrolled eight times reducing the impact of inter-region dangles on the overall performance. For example, the average size of the superblocks was 88 operations for alvinn and only 28 for sc. Moreover, superblocks in alvinn were executed from start to finish with a probability of 0.96, while the probability on sc was only 0.4. Thus, the dynamic number of operations executed before control transfers to another scheduling region is much larger for alvinn than for sc. Since opportunities for hiding inter-region dangles increases with the density of dynamic inter-region control transfers, meld scheduling shows better performance improvement for sc than for alvinn. Note that, for both alvinn and tomcatv, the meld scheduler absorbs almost all the inter-region latency dangles for W2L2 model and comes very close to the upper bound for W2L3 model.

Figure 11 shows detailed results for the yacc benchmark on all 16 machine models. We estimate the performance improvement of an in-order superscalar over the no-meld model as follows. We schedule using a conventional scheduler permitting dangles through superblock exits and ignoring dangles on superblock entries. For each control flow edge, we compute the number of stall cycles as follows. We determine the required dangles through the associated exit and the available dangles from the associated entry of the control flow edge and find the maximum difference between the required dangle and available dangle. We compute the product of the edge frequency and the stall cycles and sum over all control flow edges to obtain an estimate of stall cycles on an in-order superscalar machine. Note that this estimated performance is not based on actual simulation and does not consider the effect of overlapping stalls due to cache misses, TLB misses, branch mis-predictions and other dynamic factors. Each pair of bars in Figure 11 shows the performance improvements for a particular width and latency combination. The first bar of each pair is as in Figure 10; the lower portion shows the performance improvement due to meld over the no-meld model and the upper black portion shows the remaining gap to the ignore-dangles upper bound. The lower gray portion of the second bar shows the estimated performance improvement of a superscalar machine over the no meld model. The top

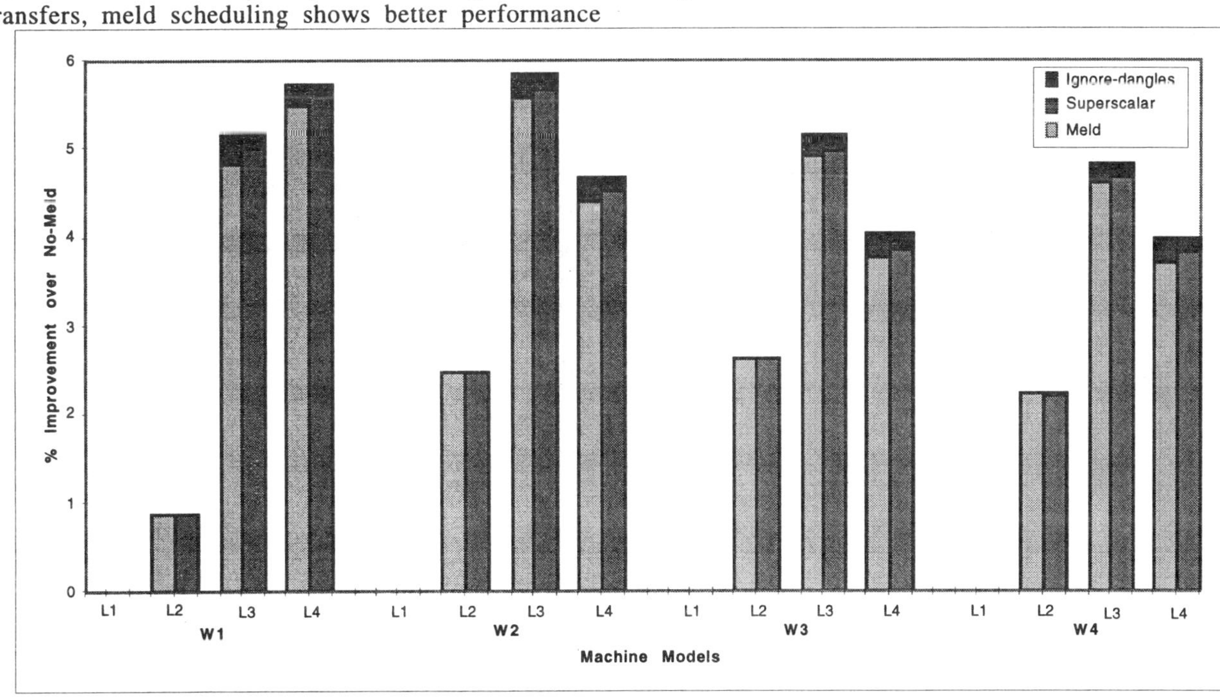

Figure 11. Estimated performance improvement due to in-order superscalar, meld scheduling and the upper bound on various machines for the benchmark yacc

black portion shows the the gap between the estimated superscalar performance and the ignore-dangles upper bound. As expected, when the latencies are unity as in the L1 machine models, there are no latency dangles and hence no improvement. For the L2 models, superscalar and meld scheduling achieves the upper bound. In the other two models, L3 and L4 the gap is around 0.2%. In all the cases, estimated superscalar performance is slightly better than meld scheduling on a VLIW machine model, but by no more than a fraction of a percent.

Overall, for small latency models, the possible improvement is limited by the outgoing dangles. For wider issue widths and larger latencies, the schedule length is dominated by the critical path and the dangles become smaller relative to the schedule length. Thus, the overall improvement (as a ratio) using meld scheduling is large when latencies are large and when the available parallelism matches the machine parallelism.

5 Related work

There is a substantial body of work in the area of instruction scheduling for instruction-level parallel (ILP) machines [2, 4-7, 14, 15, 1] . Most of the work, however, is directed at two related areas. The first area is the type of scheduling region, *e.g.*, trace, superblock, hyperblock, general dag, innermost loops. The motivation here is either to enlarge the scope of scheduling or to simplify compiler engineering. The second area is the actual scheduling algorithm and heuristics used within a region. Many of these scheduling technique are developed in the context of superscalar machines [5, 6, 1]. Thus, they accurately model resource-usage and latencies within a region in order to get the best performance. But they ignore the constraints at region boundaries in the hope that any required run-time stalls will not affect the performance significantly.

In contrast, both the Multiflow Trace machine and Cydra 5 relied on their respective compilers to manage all resources and latencies. (Cydra 5 did have a latency-stalling mechanism but only for memory operations.) Consequently, the Multiflow compiler [2, 3, 14] and the Cydra 5 compiler [15] used some form of meld scheduling to ensure correctness and to get good performance. However, there is no evaluation of the benefits provided by meld scheduling over simple-minded approaches such as padding. This paper generalizes the technique and quantifies the benefits of meld scheduling.

In the Multiflow compiler [3, 14], resource-usage and latency constraints at region boundaries are represented as *partial schedules*. After a trace has been scheduled, partial schedules for each entry and each exit are exported to the surrounding code. The scheduling of a trace honors some or all of the partial schedules coming from scheduled predecessors and successors. If the trace being scheduled has a scheduled predecessor at the main entry, then the predecessor's partial schedule is placed in the first few instructions of the schedule. Similarly, the partial schedule coming from a scheduled successor at the main exit is placed in the last few instructions of the schedule. After a trace has been scheduled, partial schedules at side entries are merged with the schedule. There is no special treatment given to cycles in the flow-graph. The main loop, *i.e.*, pick a trace, schedule it, export constraints, handles cycles naturally inserting appropriate compensation blocks to reconcile constraints if necessary.

In the Cydra 5 compiler [16, 15], acyclic scheduling is done at a basic-block level after a global instruction motion phase. In a basic block, instructions are scheduled from bottom to top. An unscheduled basic block honors all resource-usage and latency constraints coming from scheduled predecessors and successors. Constraints at an entry (exit) are computed by looking at all predecessors (successors), not just the immediate ones, that fall within a pre-defined number of cycles. Cycles in the flow-graph are handled as follows. The scheduler computes the constraints for the exit of the block, schedules the block except for the start node, computes constraints for the start node, and finally, places the start node in the schedule. Note that no compensation code is inserted during scheduling.

The technique presented in this paper builds on the one in the Cydra 5 compiler. In contrast to both the Cydra 5 compiler and the Multiflow compiler, the technique presented in this paper can accommodate general region topology and different scheduling paradigms. The constraint propagation part of the technique is capable of handling general multi-entry, multi-exit regions. The way constraints are computed and honored, by necessity, depend on the scheduler. Currently, we have implemented meld scheduling in the context of two different schedulers, modulo scheduler for loops and superblock/hyperblock scheduler for the rest of the code, and integrated them using the same framework. In contrast to the Multiflow compiler, our technique never introduces any blocks just to reconcile constraints, since a region honors all constraints coming from its scheduled predecessors and successors. We do, however, assume flow-through pipelines and don't handle resource usage constraints across region boundaries, which both the Multiflow and Cydra 5 compilers do. This assumption reduces the amount of information and simplifies constraint propagation. The technique presented in this paper, however, can be easily extended to handle resource-usage for machines which do not have flow-through pipelines.

6 Conclusions

Conventional scheduling algorithms operate without relevant information about the schedules of previously scheduled regions. In this paper, we develop general data structures consisting of export maps on a per entry and per exit basis and entry-exit distance maps. We develop general and efficient algorithms for propagating this information to the entries and exits of a region being scheduled. In contrast to previous work, our meld constraint representation and propagation schemes are independent of the underlying scheduling region and scheduler.

In the context of meld-scheduling in conjunction with superblock scheduling, we identify and address a few pitfalls and additional optimizations. Latency constraints may propagate through other scheduled regions back to the region being scheduled. In the presence of such cycles, we develop techniques to detect such cases as well as to relax constraints using depth information. Latency constraints may come in from the entry and exit on an operand that is not present within the region. In this case, the scheduling of the exit must be delayed sufficiently to satisfy the constraint. In our meld scheduler, such pass-through dangles are handled in a uniform manner similar to other constraints. Upward exposed def dangles impose constraints on inter-region output- and anti-dependencies in a strict VLIW machine. Our heuristics reorder operations, if necessary, to reduce the impact of such constraints. The complete algorithm is developed with attention to space- and time-efficiency.

We define a baseline no-meld schedule in which pads of no-ops are inserted at the entry of each scheduled region to absorb incoming dangles from immediate predecessor regions. In comparison to the no-meld scheduler, our meld scheduler improved weighted schedule length, a measure of execution time, between 1% and 10% on machine models with non-unit latencies. Our meld scheduler also came close to ignore-dangles, an (unrealizable) upper bound on any meld scheduling strategy, coming within 0.2% on most machine models on yacc and within 1.5% on W2L2 and W2L3 machine models on all benchmarks.

Though the main focus of this paper is on developing and evaluating a general meld scheduler, an interesting observation is that the schedule for in-order interlocked machines corresponds to the ignore-dangles schedule. Thus, the gap between ignore-dangles and meld is also an upper-bound on how much better these machines can do than a non-interlocking machine scheduled using the meld scheduler. On our benchmarks, the performance gap between the ignore-dangles upper bound and meld scheduling is small. Our detailed investigation of the yacc benchmark considered a broad range of machine models and also estimated the performance of an in-order interlocked machine. The estimated performance is only slightly better than the performance of a non-interlocking machine scheduled using our meld scheduler. The performance difference between interlocking and non-interlocking machines is a function of the machine model, the scheduling region used, the availability and use of profile information. Furthermore, note that the results in this paper do not account for dynamic effects such as cache misses and branch mis-predictions. We eventually hope to enhance meld scheduling for interlocked machines, employing heuristics that decide whether to enforce or ignore constraints coming in from different regions.

Acknowledgements

We thank Bob Rau for suggesting improvements in our cycle handling capability and in the presentation of our experimental results. We also thank all the members of Compiler and Architecture Research group at HP Labs.

7 Bibliography

1. W. W. Hwu, *et al.* The superblock: an effective technique for VLIW and superscalar compilation. *The Journal of Supercomputing* 7, 1/2 (1993), 229-248.
2. J. A. Fisher. Trace scheduling: A technique for global microcode compaction. *IEEE Transactions on Computers* C-30, 7 (1981), 478-490.
3. J. R. Ellis. *Bulldog: A Compiler for VLIW Architectures.* (The MIT Press, Cambridge, MA, 1985).
4. A. Nicolau. *Percolation scheduling: a parallel compilation technique.* Technical Report TR 85-678, Department of Computer Science, Cornell, 1985.
5. D. Bernstein and M. Rodeh. Global instruction scheduling for superscalar machines. *Proceedings of the SIGPLAN '91 Conference on Programming Language Design and Implementation* (1991), 241-255.
6. S. A. Mahlke, *et al.* Effective compiler support for predicated execution using the hyperblock. *Proceedings of the 25th Annual International Symposium on Microarchitecture* (1992), 45-54.
7. S.-M. Moon and K. Ebcioglu. An efficient resource-constrained global scheduling technique for superscalar and VLIW processors. *Proceedings of the 25th Annual International Symposium on Microarchitecture* (Portland, Oregon, 1992).
8. V. Kathail, M. S. Schlansker, and B. R. Rau. *HPL PlayDoh architecture specification: Version 1.0.* Technical Report HPL-93-80, Hewlett-Packard Laboratories, Palo Alto CA, 1993.
9. A. V. Aho, J. E. Hopcroft, and J. D. Ullman. *Data Structures and Algorithms.* (Addison-Wesley Publishing Company, Reading, MA, 1983).
10. B. R. Rau and C. D. Glaeser. Some scheduling techniques and an easily schedulable horizontal architecture for high performance scientific computing. *Proceedings of the Fourteenth Annual Workshop on Microprogramming* (1981), 183-198.
11. M. Lam. Software pipelining: an effective scheduling technique for VLIW machines. *Proceedings of the ACM SIGPLAN '88 Conference on Programming Language Design and Implementation* (1988), 318-327.
12. B. R. Rau. Iterative modulo scheduling: an algorithm for software pipelining loops. *Proceedings of the 27th Annual International Symposium on Microarchitecture* (San Jose, California, 1994), 63-74.
13. D. M. Lavery and W. W. Hwu. Unrolling-based optimizations for software pipelining. *Proceedings of the 28th Annual International Symposium on Microarchitecture* (Ann Arbor, Michigan, 1995).
14. G. Lowney, *et al.* The Multiflow Trace Scheduling Compiler. *The Journal of Supecomputing* 7, 1/2 (1993), 51-142.
15. J. C. Dehnert and R. A. Towle. Compiling for the Cydra 5. *The Journal of Supercomputing* 7, 1/2 (1993), 181-228.
16. S. Srivastava. Implementation of Global Scheduling. 1988, Cydrome Internal Document.

Session 10

Custom–Fit Processors: Letting Applications Define Architectures

Joseph A. Fisher, Paolo Faraboschi and Giuseppe Desoli

Hewlett-Packard Laboratories Cambridge
1 Main Street, Cambridge, MA 02142
{jfisher,frb,desoli}@hpl.hp.com

Abstract

In this paper we report on a system which automatically designs realistic VLIW architectures highly optimized for one given application (the input for this system), while running all other code correctly. The system uses a product-quality compiler that generates very aggressive VLIW code. We retarget the compiler until we have found a VLIW architecture idealized for the application on the basis of performance, a cost function and a hardware budget.

We show that we can automatically select architectures that achieve large speedups on color and image processing codes. Specialization is shown to be very valuable: The differences between architectural choices, even among reasonable-seeming architectures having similar costs, can be very great, often a factor of 5 (and sometimes much more). We show also that specialization is also very dangerous. A reasonable choice of architecture to fit one algorithm can be a very poor choice for another, even in the same domain. There is sometimes an architecture, near in cost and performance to the best, that does much better on a second algorithm.

1. Introduction: Custom-Fit Processors

Many people had the same reaction upon first becoming aware of VLSI microprocessors: can we somehow design these chips by merely writing a program that describes what they are to do? This is the "silicon compiling" problem in its full glory. Despite amazing progress in areas such as compiling control circuits using a "sea of gates" approach, and despite tremendous progress in the automation of many of the steps of design and production, we are very far from taking a functional description of a microprocessor and automatically producing a silicon layout.

Although silicon compiling is well beyond us, in this paper we consider an even more ambitious problem: rather than generating a microprocessor automatically from a high-level description, we would like to generate it from the applications it will run. In particular, given an embedded processor running on an "appliance" product, we call the general-purpose processor which is designed to scream on the embedded application a "Custom-Fit Processor". The process we use to derive this processor design falls into the general class of technologies referred to as Hardware/Software Codesign [18, 15, 16, 20].

Generating Custom-Fit Processors automatically is a superset of generating general-purpose processors, and is thus strictly harder still. When faced with such an overwhelmingly impossible task, there are two approaches generally taken:

- One can build a very small thing (e.g. synthesizing a 4-bit adder) and hope to learn while approaching reality from below.
- One can build a "toy", filled with unreality, and then try to make it successively more realistic, approaching reality from above.

Here we suggest a third approach, and our research program is dedicated to carrying this out:

- One can restrict the problem one is attacking, but then, within that restricted framework, do something that is completely realistic and is an end-to-end solution. From that base, move towards a less-restricted solution. In a sense, this starts out being realistic, but approaches greater generality "from the side".

The restriction we impose is the following: We design a VLIW [11] architecture in which virtually all characteristics can be changed: memory sizes and hierarchy, register sizes and ports, the "cluster" structure of the architecture, the kinds of functional units and their repertoires, the latencies of the functional units, and the connection and communication topologies of all of these. At the same time,

1072-4451/96 $5.00 © 1996 IEEE

the code transformations that are done as part of the hardware/software codesign process are applied. This adds to that mix the limitations of what the compiler is capable of. Any codesign system will have this latter restriction, almost always much more than we do. Unfortunately, this is almost never acknowledged in research results.

Within this framework our methodology is easy to describe, and similar to what has been described elsewhere (for example, in [14, 12, 13, 2, 8, 19, 3, 6, 7]). For example De Gloria and Faraboschi [8] carry out almost exactly this framework, but using tools which are much less mature.

This framework is particularly interesting right now, because it is now practical to put enough millions of transistors on an inexpensive die to make a very powerful and general VLIW – witness the media processors now appearing from several vendors [9, 21, 4, 10].

1.1. This Investigation

We believe the work described below is unique in the following sense:

- We are doing it with a productized, ambitious compiler that exposes and schedules a lot of ILP. Previous studies have been done in environments in which very small percentage differences have been available; at best they have found small factor speedups. Instead, we find very large factor speedups, even between relatively similar cost, reasonable-seeming architectures.

The experiments done here are a characterization of the effectiveness of tailoring ILP hardware to given applications. We are attempting to shed light on the following broad questions:

- What is the performance of custom hardware at a given cost, when compared to more general hardware at that same cost?
- How does the hardware you would build differ for different sections of code in similar application areas? How does it differ from hardware built for several routines at the same time?
- How effective are search methods aimed at finding the appropriate architecture?

2. Experimental Methodology and Infrastructure

2.1. The C Compiler

Our main tool in this investigation is the *Hewlett-Packard Laboratories Cambridge C Compiler*. It is a direct descendant of the Multiflow compiler, which has been reported upon in detail elsewhere, particularly in [17]. For our purposes, it has the following qualities:

- It is a productized, real-world, highly-optimizing compiler.
- It generates ILP code as aggressively as any compiler we have ever heard of; we think more than any other compiler ever built.
- It generates code from table-driven architectural descriptions in the following sense: if you have a description of an architecture for which you are generating good code, you can change most of the "normal" architectural parameters to produce a new model, and continue to generate good code.

We thus are able to use it to explore a design space of architectures to fit a processor to a given application.

2.2. Searching For A VLIW Architecture

Our basic experimental method involves the following loop:

- Using some search method, search for a new candidate architecture
- Measure the cost of the architecture
- Build a version of our compiler that generates good code for that architecture
- Generate the code
- Measure the goodness of the code
- Repeat until satisfied

In the past, many researchers have implemented similar loops. They have typically concentrated upon search techniques, or upon the selection of special-purpose functional units to match the functionality needed in a loop. Our philosophy here is different. Following the RISC/VLIW religion, we want to build simple hardware that does the basic, simple operations, but uses lots of ILP to get a speedup. So we try to match the *structures* and *sizes* of the architecture to the application, rather than specific opcodes.

Similarly, it is likely that search techniques to prune the space of architectures under consideration would be very successful. Here, instead, we searched exhaustively through a huge space: despite being real-world tools, our tools are fast enough and computers are now sufficiently fast enough to make this practical. We are confident that any good search technique could cut down significantly on our processing time (see Table 3) without greatly affecting the results reported upon here.

2.3. Benchmarks

We were interested in measuring how different an application-specific microprocessor would be when tailored for different tasks within a single application domain. These seem like relevant questions: right now people build chips to do specifically one subtask of an application, when a general-purpose processor is not sufficient (e.g. for MPEG video compression/decompression); additionally, we now have media processors, which are specialized for an application area, but not a single subtask. This makes intuitive sense, as the subtasks in a single application area often seem to have similar compute structures, as is the case in media processing.

Benchmark	Description
A	FIR symmetrical filter implemented using a 7x7 convolution kernel.
C	Inverse DCT transform with dequantization of the DCT coefficients. The algorithm used is the Arai, Agui and Nakjima algorithm for scaled FDCT/IDCT, with some improvements, as described in [1, 22].
D,E	Color conversion from the RGB to the YCbCr color space (and vice versa, as described in the JPEG standard)
F	Halftoning via standard Floyd-Steinberg error diffusion (no stochastic weights update). The benchmark produces triplets containing 1 bit halftoned pixels.
G	1D bilinear scaling by integral factors along columns.
H	3x3 median filter using the standard algorithms, not using a "smart" version of the median.

Table 1. The individual benchmarks.

We picked color output routines, which are quite easily available in the public domain, and are quite similar to those used in many media-processing applications. These routines often contain a large quantity of potential ILP. All the benchmarks except C have as input a row of a full color RGB image. We have converted all floating point to fixed, as is common in this kind of processing. Proper source code transformations have been applied to all benchmarks to expose ILP (loop transformations, if-conversion, etc.). These same transformations speed the code up on virtually all superscalar and VLIW architectures and implementations. Table 1 describes the benchmarks we used.

We wanted to know how architectures which were optimized for those individual routines would compare with architectures optimized for collections of the routines. Thus we also ran combinations of the above, jammed into single loops, avoiding the intermediate memory store/load otherwise needed. Table 2 shows a description of the "jammed" benchmarks.

Benchmark	Description
GF	1D bilinear scaling followed by Floyd-Steinberg halftoning.
GEF	1D bilinear scaling followed by E, a YUV→RGB color space conversion, followed by Floyd-Steinberg halftoning.
DH	RGB→YUV color space conversion followed by a 3x3 median filter.
DHEF	RGB→YUV color space conversion followed by a 3x3 median filter, followed by E, a YUV→RGB color space conversion, followed by Floyd-Steinberg halftoning.

Table 2. The jammed benchmarks.

For example, figure 1 shows the D (Floyd-Steinberg error diffusion) benchmark in C, implemented in the standard form found in image processing literature.

2.4. Running the Experiment

The experiment was set up in such a way that we were rebuilding a compiler for each architecture and then running the compilation for all benchmarks and for different unrolling factors. When the compiler started spilling register contents for a given unrolling, we stopped considering that unrolling factor and all larger ones.

The performance of clustered architectures (see Section 3.1) was not computed for all possible combinations, to avoid an exponential explosion of runtime and data. To account for clustering, we computed a "correction value" as a function of the number of clusters, by running a set of separate experiments for a few significant architecture data points in the defined space. In our experience, this approximation is enough to account for the effects of clustering.

For this experiment, we ran 5730 compilations of the benchmarks, on 191 architectures (plus their associated clustering values). The time to re-compile a customized compiler was relatively short (about 50 seconds), since only the machine model needed to be re-linked into the executable.

The time to run a single compilation benchmark varied significantly between a couple of seconds and a few minutes. On average, it took on the order of 28 seconds per benchmark, adding up to about 48 hours of running time for the whole experiment. The platform used for the experiment was a 9000/770 HP workstation, 100MHz clock, 256MB main memory.

```
FSDline ( ubyte * linein,
          ubyte * lineout,
          int plane_size )
{
  int i, color;
  int16 *ep, Err[3], errTemp[3];
  int16 errTempOff[3], oldErr[3];
  ubyte *dp, *op, out[3], bitmask;

  dp = linein;
  ep = errBuf + 3;
  op = lineout;
  Err[0] = Err[1] = Err[2] = 0;

  errTemp[0] = ep[-3 + 0];
  errTemp[1] = ep[-3 + 1];
  errTemp[2] = ep[-3 + 2];
  bitmask = 0x80;

  for (i = 0; i < plane_size; i++)
  {
    for (color = 0; color < 3; color++)
    {
      errTempOff[color] = errTemp[color];
      errTemp[color] = ep[color];
      oldErr[color] = Err[color];
      Err[color] =
         (errTemp[color] + ((Err[color]*7+8)>>4)+
         ((int) dp[color] << ((2*8)-13)));
      out[color] =
         ((Err[color] > (128 << ((2*8)-13)))
         ? out[color] | bitmask : out[color]);
      Err[color] =
         ((Err[color] > (128 << ((2*8)-13)))
         ? Err[color] - (255 << ((2*8)-13))
         : Err[color]);
      errTempOff[color] += ((Err[color]*3+8)>>4);
      errTemp[color] =
         ((Err[color] * 5 + oldErr[color]+8)>>4);
      ep[-3 + color] = errTempOff[color];
      op[color] = out[color];
    }
    dp += 3, ep += 3;
    if (bitmask == 0)
    {
      op = op + 3;
      out[0] = out[1] = out[2] = 0;
      bitmask = 0x80;
    }
    else
      bitmask = bitmask >> 1;
  }
}
```

Figure 1. The Floyd-Steinberg algorithm.

Table 3 shows the basic data concerning the computation time of the experiment.

3. Architecture Cost and Performance

Computing the cost and performance of an architecture from a set of high-level parameters (such as number of ALUs, multipliers, registers, ports, etc.) is a nontrivial task. Several implementation choices exist and the trade-off between choices varies widely depending upon available VLSI technology, target application, area and power requirements, design methodology and so on.

In this paper we have simplified the problem and only

# runs	5730
# architectures	191
runtime per architecture	897s (15 m)
compiler time per benchmark	28s
compiler compile time per arch.	50s
total time	171449s (48 h)

Table 3. Experiment computation time.

consider the cost of building the CPU datapath. Other factors, such as pinout requirements and cost of the memory system, are not considered in the cost equations. Considering these factors would affect the numbers we report, but probably would not materially affect our conclusions.

We estimate the cost of the datapath in terms of silicon real estate relative to a baseline configuration. The figures that we use are derived from an analysis of existing designs in current VLSI technology. They are certainly not close to exact figures, but we believe are representative enough to support the conclusions of this paper.

3.1. Clusters and Architectural Parameters

Our architecture template (Figure 2) is a multi-cluster machine, composed of (nearly) identical clusters containing functional units and local register banks. The communication between clusters happens across a set of global connections, and is explicitly scheduled by the compiler. The Multiflow Trace [5] follows exactly this structure. The reason for clusters, which are not independent, but rather share a single long instruction, is to avoid register banks with too many ports. Thus instead of a single register bank supporting, say, 8 ALUs, we might split it into 4 register banks, each supporting two ALUs. In order to use an ALU, the operands it requires must be in the associated register bank, or must be moved there with an explicit move in a prior instruction. The fact that the different clusters are (nearly) identical makes the chip easier to fabricate as well. The cluster differ in that the single branch unit resides on cluster #0 and is not duplicated in the others.

In addition to that, we consider a multi-level memory system composed of a *Level 1 Memory* and a *Level 2 Memory*. *Level 1* Memory is used to model the global memory of the system, and has a fixed throuput for all the experiments. *Level 2* Memory varies in terms of number of parallel accesses and latency.

Table 4 explains the parameters we take into account. Some of the settings we used were completely determined by our choice of the initial parameters. These include register file ports, communication paths and cycle speed. Table 5 shows a description of these derived parameters.

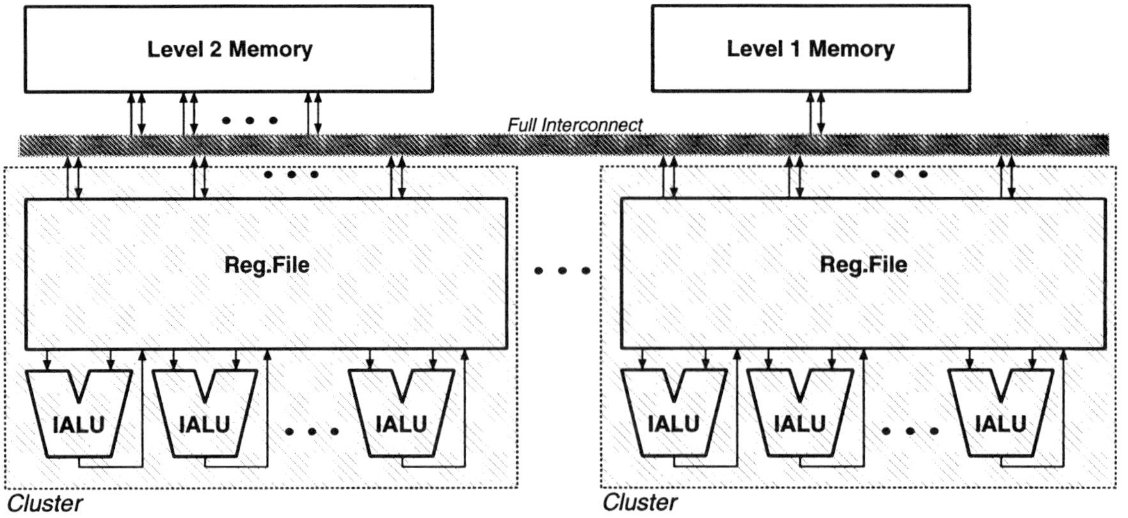

Figure 2. The architecture template

Parameter	Description
Clusters	Ranges between 1 and 16.
IALUs	Ranges between 1 and 16. All operations have latency of 1 cycle, except multiplications (2 cycles, pipelined).
ALU Repertoire	We eliminated floating point units by hand before we started. These routines do little floating point, and the cost function would have eliminated it in any case, so we saved the trouble. Among the integer units, the only choice presented in this experiment is whether or not a given ALU is capable of integer multiply. We allowed between 1/4 and 1/2 the ALUs to be IMULs, however at least 1 IMUL was always present. This methodology allows us to give any opcode choice to the compiler. We limited this experiment for expository reasons, and because our philosophy in general is to design an architecture from building blocks rather than synthesizing lower-level special- purpose hardware.
Register Sizes	We allowed between 64 and 512 registers total (for all clusters).
Memory System	We picked many different configurations for this experiment, but found that considering all of them muddied the insights available in this paper, but did not change the results. We thus decided to limit the exposition to only a few choices: always a single *Level 1 Memory* port and between 1 and 4 accesses to *Level 2 Memory*. The latency of an access to *Level 1 Memory* is always 3 cycles (non-pipelined), while the latency to *Level 2 Memory* varies from 2 to 8 cycles (non-pipelined).

Table 4. The architecture parameters.

Parameter	Description
Register Ports	We varied these with the requirements of the other functional units. In a full system, it is useful to consider this an independent variable, since it greatly affects the cost of the system.
Connectivity	As in the number of register ports, we varied the connectivity according to the needs of the functional units, but it could have been allowed to be a more general parameter (and in the production of a chip you will build, will be).
Cycle Speed	We used an approximation to quantify the effect of cycle speed of our architectural choices. This is how we believe it best to treat cycle speed in a system like this, though sometimes it may be considered an independent parameter, as in making silicon technology choices, or in area vs. speed tradeoffs in designing functional blocks.

Table 5. The derived parameter settings.

3.2. The "Baseline" System

We used as our baseline system one with 1 ALU, which could do IMUL, 1 reference to *Level 1* Memory and 1 to *Level 2* Memory (8 cycle latency), and 64 registers, all in 1 cluster. Our costs and performance models, explained in the following sections, are scaled to make this system cost 1 unit.

Note that this system is capable of a great deal of ILP, due to its multiple issue capability, and its pipelining.

3.3. Computing Architecture Cost

The cost function for an architecture is computed as follows:

$$COST = c \cdot X_{dp}(p) \cdot (Y_{reg}(r,p) + Y_{alu}(a) + Y_{mul}(m))$$

- c is the number of clusters
- a is the number of ALUs per cluster
- m is the number of ALUs per cluster able to do integer MULs
- r is the number of registers per cluster
- l is the number of memory accesses per cluster
- p is the number of ports of the register file in a cluster, computed as a function of the ALUs (a), and the memory ports (l): $p(a,l) = (3 \cdot a) + (2 \cdot l)$
- $X_{dp}(r,p)$ is the datapath width of a cluster, computed as: $X_{dp}(p) = k_1 \cdot p$
- $Y_{reg}(r,p)$ is the register file height for a cluster, computed as: $Y_{reg}(r,p) = r \cdot (k_2 \cdot p + k_3)$
- $Y_{alu}(a)$ is the height of the ALUs for a cluster, computed as: $Y_{alu}(a) = k_4 \cdot a$
- $Y_{mul}(m)$ is the height of the MULs for a cluster, computed as: $Y_{mul}(m) = k_5 \cdot m$
- $k_1 \cdots k_5$ in the above equations are fitting parameters computed from observation of existing designs.

The costs range from 1.0 (for the baseline) to about 100 for the most ambitious architectures (16 ALUs, 8 MULs, 512 registers, 4 memory ports, 1 cluster). For example, Table 6 shows the cost of some of the architectures that we have considered in our experiments.

These numbers are certainly approximate, but we believe they are realistic enough to allow one to generalize from the results of this study.

3.4. Cycle Speed

The complexity of an architecture impacts the cycle time, a factor we must take into account in any realistic evaluation. In this experiment, we have tried to come up with a reasonable derating factor (vs. the baseline architecture) that applies a cycle time increase as a function of the register file ports. The underlying assumption is that, as in most designs, the read stage of the pipeline is the limiting factor for cycle speed.

The function that we use assumes a quadratic relationship between cycle time and number of ports, and, for example, Table 7 gives the following values for some of the architectures we considered:

IALU	IMUL	L2MEM	REGS	Clusters	Cost
1	1	1	64	1	1.0
2	1	1	64	1	1.7
4	2	1	128	1	6.5
4	2	1	128	2	3.6
8	4	1	256	1	28.7
8	4	1	256	2	13.1
8	4	1	256	4	7.4
16	8	1	512	1	93.4
16	8	1	512	2	38.4
16	8	1	512	4	19.0
16	8	1	512	8	12.2

Table 6. Examples of the cost of some of the architectures considered in the experiments. Costs are expressed as relative ratios versus the cost of the baseline configuration (the first line of the table). L2MEM is the number of level2 memory ports.

IALU	L2MEM	Clusters	Cycle
1	1	1	1.0
2	1	1	1.1
4	1	1	1.5
4	1	2	1.1
8	1	1	2.7
8	1	2	1.4
8	1	4	1.1
16	1	1	7.3
16	1	2	2.7
16	1	4	1.5
16	1	8	1.1

Table 7. Examples of cycle speed derating factors for different architecture configurations. Again, values are relative to the baseline configuration (the first line of the table).

4. Results

The performance of the benchmarks ("*su*") and the cost ("*c*") of the architectures are displayed on Tables 8, 9, 10 and Figures 3, 4.

In our experiments, we describe architectures by means of a n-uple of 6 parameters:

$$(a, m, r, p_2, l_2, c)$$

where

- a is the total number of ALUs
- m is the total number of ALUs capable of executing an integer MUL
- r is the total number of registers
- p_2 is the total number of parallel accesses to *Level 2* Memory
- l_2 is the latency in cycles of accesses to *Level 2* Memory
- c is the number of clusters

So, for instance, the description *(4 2 256 1 4 4)* (first line of Table 8) identifies an architecture with 4 ALUs (1 per cluster), 2 of them capable of a MUL, 256 registers (64 per cluster), 1 port to *Level 2* memory with a 4-cycle access latency and 4 clusters.

The basic unit of measure for our experiments is called "Speedup", and it represents the factor performance improvement that the given architecture gets on the benchmark in question, compared to the running time of that benchmark on the baseline system. Note that this is *not* the speedup due to instruction-level parallelism. The baseline system already offers a significant amount of ILP. In this paper we wanted to avoid the "maxpar wars", and just concentrate on the relative evaluation of the choices we had.

4.1. Architectural Performance Vs. Cost

Figure 3 is a scatter diagram that shows the cost and speedup for each of the 191 architectures (after the best cluster arrangement had been selected) for each of the individual algorithm benchmarks (A, C, D, F, G, H), while Figure 4 shows the same for the jammed benchmarks. The line in each scatter diagram is drawn through all of the best cost/performance alternatives for each benchmark.

Note that most of the diagrams contain various performance levels in which several points are approximately in a straight horizontal line. In those cases, the apparent explanation is that the increasing costs as one goes to the right are due to the addition of features to the leftmost architecture that are not helping it achieve much better performance on the given benchmark. Sometimes a feature is very relevant to a benchmark, and then a new plateau is reached with several points in a higher performance level straight line as that feature is added.

4.2. Design For One Algorithm, Run Another

One of the things we most wanted to find out in this experiment was this: when you design for one application or algorithm and run on another, what happens? In particular, one might expect to run into these situations:

1. Perhaps specialization hardly matters at all. Architectures for a given application all perform pretty much the same, with small percentage differences among them, as long as one considers only "reasonable" architectures. Or,
2. Perhaps architectures differ a lot, but there is some independent measure of goodness for them that does not vary much with the benchmarks (except in the grossest of choices, such as whether to include floating point hardware). Architectures built for applications in a narrow domain are more-or-less "well ordered" That is, for any two architectures, the same one is virtually always better than the other across the applications. Or,
3. Perhaps the architectures optimized for different algorithms differ a lot, and how good they are heavily depends upon which algorithm was used to guide the choice.

To answer these questions in the context of the experiment done here, we decided to set up several situations in which a designer might choose an architecture. We allowed the following two degrees of freedom:

- An upper bound on the cost of the architecture. We arbitrarily chose costs of 5, 10, and 15 as constraints a designer might be working with. We call these low, medium, and high cost architectures, respectively.
- The degree to which the designer would be willing to select an architecture that was not the absolute best for the algorithms for which the architecture was optimized, in order to perform better on the other applications.

In particular, in Tables 8, 9, 10 we considered, for each algorithm, the architecture that would do best without exceeding the COST parameter.

When the RANGE parameter was 0, the architecture was chosen without considering the other applications at all, and the table (in this case the *(Range=0%)* portion of the Tables) shows, in the rows across, how well that architecture performed on each application. However, what if the hardware designer wanted to optimize for a given algorithm, but knew something about the domain and was willing to factor in, at least somewhat, other algorithms? In the middle portion of the Tables we show what happens when the designer does the following: For each algorithm, attempt to pick the best

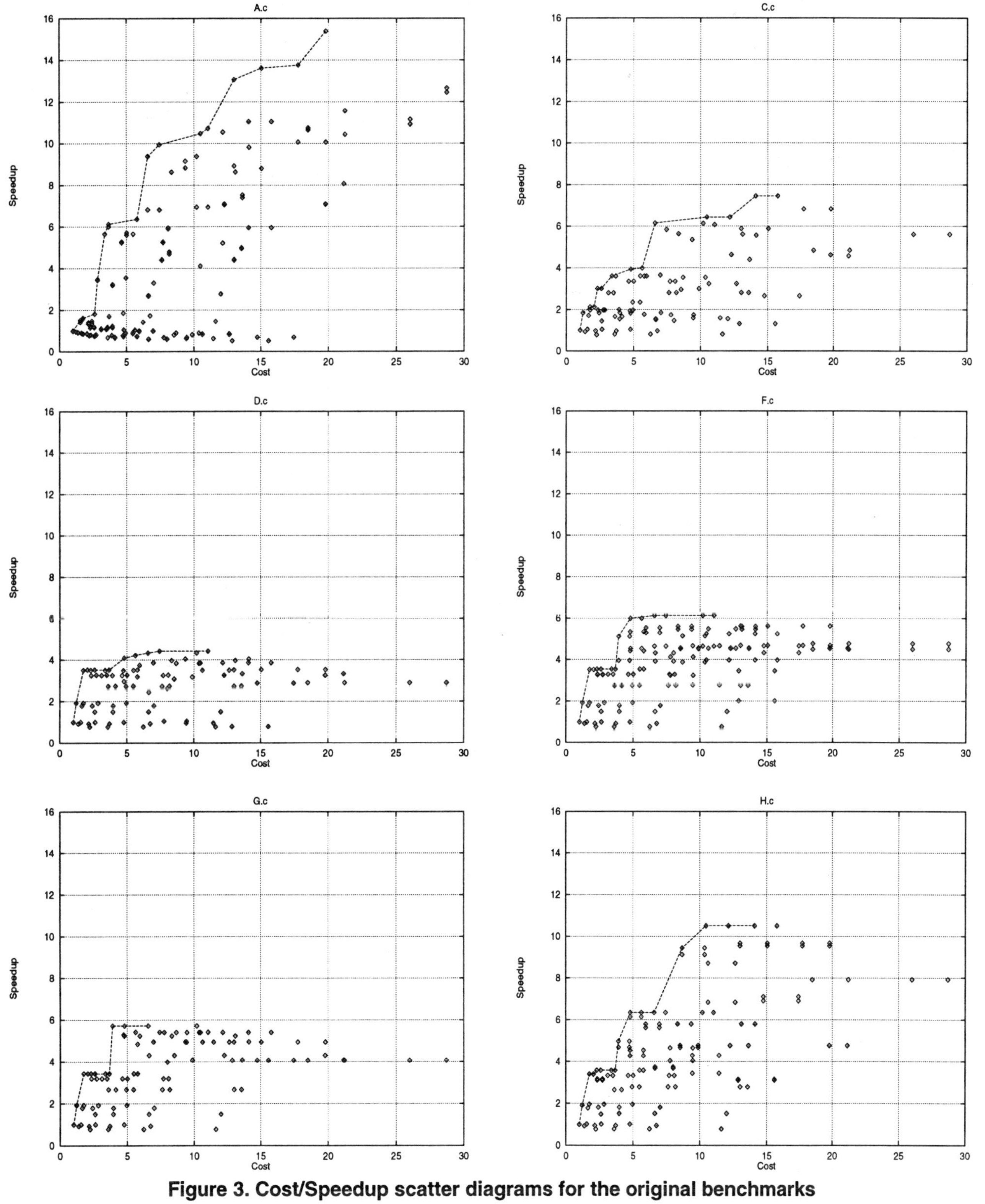

Figure 3. Cost/Speedup scatter diagrams for the original benchmarks

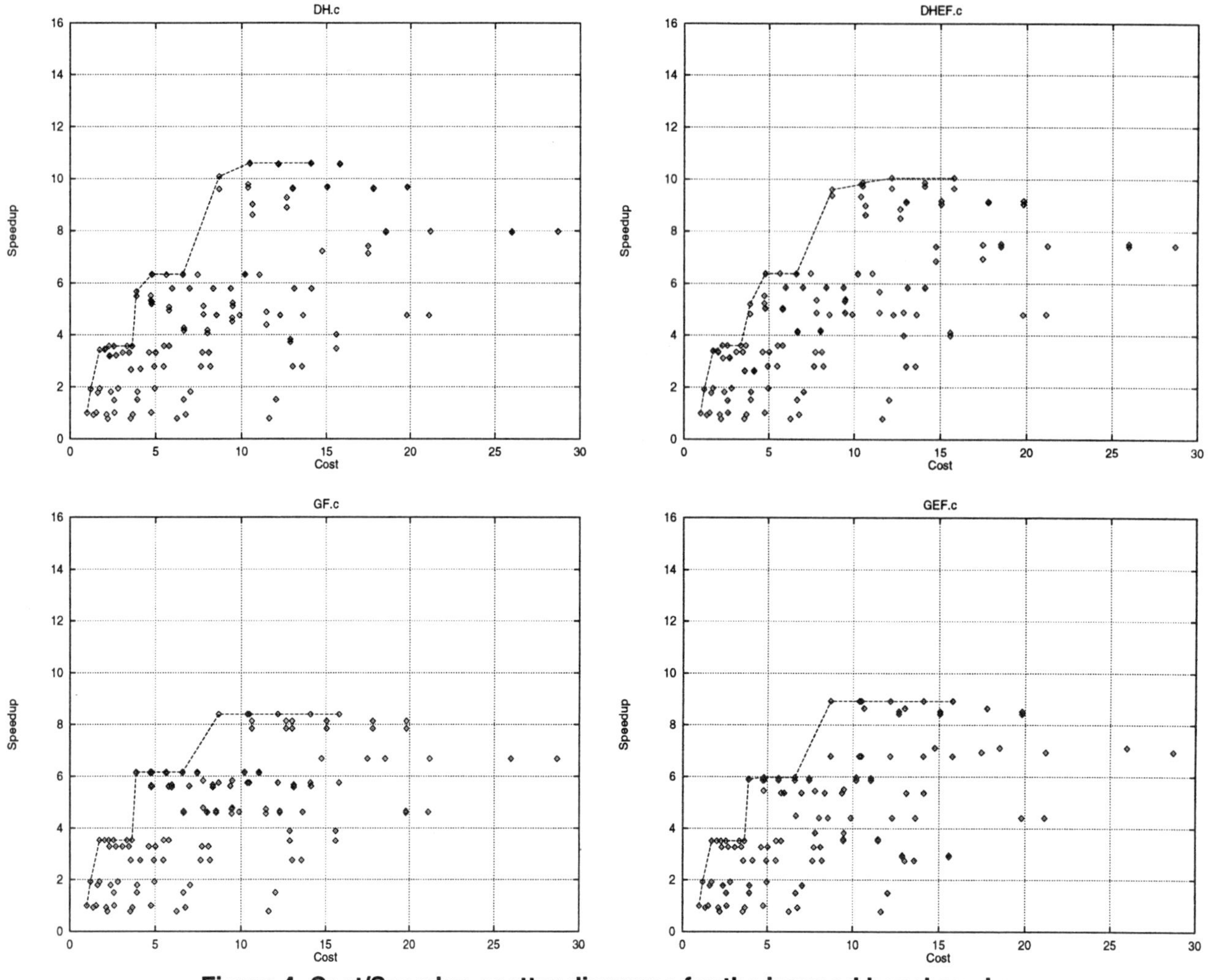

Figure 4. Cost/Speedup scatter diagrams for the jammed benchmarks

architecture, but be willing to back off by as much as 10% of performance (the RANGE parameter) in order to make the average of the other applications better. For the medium cost models, in fact, it is also instructive to see what happens when the designer is willing to give up as much as 50% of the performance to make the others better.

For example, in the medium cost tables, the architecture chosen as the best for algorithm GEF executed that application with a speedup over the baseline of 8.93. But when the RANGE is allowed to go to 50%, the selection mechanism decides to give up 8 of its ALUs, and with that budget buy back another 128 registers (and make some other small changes). This has the effect of lowering the GEF speedup over the baseline from 8.93 down to 5.97. However, in so doing, it makes the overall performance go from an average of 3.9 up to 5.8, and it makes A go from a pathological .89 speedup to 6.82. (Note that in the original model chosen for GEF, there were too many ALUs and too few registers for an algorithm like A. The compiler gets greedy and gets into trouble. This is a known problem, and one hard to avoid with schedulers of this nature. The revised architecture choice gets back to a more balanced system).

Finally, we looked at the question of which architecture minimized the total running time of all the applications at a given cost. Since we used the same mechanism as the above (but with the RANGE set to infinity), we reproduced the result as the same sort of table. However, in that case all the architectures make the same decision, so we only show a single line, at the bottom of each table, giving the performance of the architecture on the given application.

Again following the medium cost model picking an architecture for GEF, the picker gives back just a little more performance than it had at the 50% RANGE (by making changes that are "at the noise level") but improves the overall average from 5.8 to 6.1.

Cost=5.0 Range=0%											
Arch Desc	(su,c)	A.c	C.c	D.c	F.c	G.c	H.c	GF.c	GEF.c	DH.c	DHEF.c
A(4 2 256 1 4 4)	(3.7 3.6)	6.12	3.60	3.52	3.54	3.43	3.58	3.53	3.52	3.56	3.60
C(8 2 128 1 4 4)	(3.8 4.8)	1.05	3.93	4.09	6.00	5.72	6.35	6.16	5.86	6.33	6.38
D(8 2 128 1 4 4)	(3.8 4.8)	1.05	3.93	4.09	6.00	5.72	6.35	6.16	5.86	6.33	6.38
F(8 2 128 1 4 4)	(3.8 4.8)	1.05	3.93	4.09	6.00	5.72	6.35	6.16	5.86	6.33	6.38
G(8 2 128 1 4 4)	(3.8 4.8)	1.05	3.93	4.09	6.00	5.72	6.35	6.16	5.86	6.33	6.38
H(8 2 128 1 4 4)	(3.8 4.8)	1.05	3.93	4.09	6.00	5.72	6.35	6.16	5.86	6.33	6.38
GF(8 2 128 1 4 4)	(3.8 4.8)	1.05	3.93	4.09	6.00	5.72	6.35	6.16	5.86	6.33	6.38
GEF(8 2 128 1 8 4)	(3.8 4.8)	1.04	3.93	4.09	4.53	5.72	6.15	6.14	5.97	6.31	6.36
DH(8 2 128 1 4 4)	(3.8 4.8)	1.05	3.93	4.09	6.00	5.72	6.35	6.16	5.86	6.33	6.38
DHEF(8 2 128 1 4 4)	(3.8 4.8)	1.05	3.93	4.09	6.00	5.72	6.35	6.16	5.86	6.33	6.38

Cost=5.0 Range=10%											
Arch Desc	(su,c)	A.c	C.c	D.c	F.c	G.c	H.c	GF.c	GEF.c	DH.c	DHEF.c
A(4 2 256 1 4 4)	(3.7 3.6)	6.12	3.60	3.52	3.54	3.43	3.58	3.53	3.52	3.56	3.60
C(8 2 128 1 4 4)	(3.8 4.8)	1.05	3.93	4.09	6.00	5.72	6.35	6.16	5.86	6.33	6.38
D(8 2 128 1 4 4)	(3.8 4.8)	1.05	3.93	4.09	6.00	5.72	6.35	6.16	5.86	6.33	6.38
F(8 2 128 1 4 4)	(3.8 4.8)	1.05	3.93	4.09	6.00	5.72	6.35	6.16	5.86	6.33	6.38
G(8 2 128 1 4 4)	(3.8 4.8)	1.05	3.93	4.09	6.00	5.72	6.35	6.16	5.86	6.33	6.38
H(8 2 128 1 4 4)	(3.8 4.8)	1.05	3.93	4.09	6.00	5.72	6.35	6.16	5.86	6.33	6.38
GF(8 2 128 1 4 4)	(3.8 4.8)	1.05	3.93	4.09	6.00	5.72	6.35	6.16	5.86	6.33	6.38
GEF(8 2 128 1 4 4)	(3.8 4.8)	1.05	3.93	4.09	6.00	5.72	6.35	6.16	5.86	6.33	6.38
DH(8 2 128 1 4 4)	(3.8 4.8)	1.05	3.93	4.09	6.00	5.72	6.35	6.16	5.86	6.33	6.38
DHEF(8 2 128 1 4 4)	(3.8 4.8)	1.05	3.93	4.09	6.00	5.72	6.35	6.16	5.86	6.33	6.38

Cost=5.0 Range=∞(=490%)											
Arch Desc	(su,c)	A.c	C.c	D.c	F.c	G.c	H.c	GF.c	GEF.c	DH.c	DHEF.c
all(8 2 128 1 4 4)	(3.8 4.8)	1.05	3.93	4.09	6.00	5.72	6.35	6.16	5.86	6.33	6.38

Table 8. Speedup results for low cost ($<$ 5.0) architectures.

5. Conclusions

From the above examples, we can see that, when using a real-world compiler and code that contains a lot of ILP, the architecture choices we make are quite sensitive to the application being tailored to.

By allowing the designer a little freedom to pick less than the absolute best implementation for the target applications, we can often make dramatic improvements in how that implementation will process other applications. This certainly flies in the face of the concept of "Custom-Fit Processing", especially when we see dramatic losses in performance of the original target algorithm that are made to satisfy the overall picture. This can be seen most dramatically in the medium-cost models, in which several of the algorithms run at 60-70% of their performance on a more tailored architecture, and on the low-cost model, in which one application gets into pathologically bad trouble and runs at about 17% of its performance on the architecture made for it.

We believe that, given the maturity and real-world properties of the tools we are using, this is probably a realistic assessment of what designers will face in doing high-level synthesis. If and when the cost of individual chip design becomes very much lower than it is today, it will make a lot of sense to build chips for the narrowest of embedded applications. Today, that seems like a dangerous route to attempt without a very strong apriori knowledge of what will run on the chip.

References

[1] Y. Arai, T. Agui, and M. Nakajima. A fast DCT-SQ scheme for images. *Trans. of the IEICE*, 71(11):1095, Nov. 1988.

[2] M. Auguin, F. Boeri, and C. Carriere. Automatic exploration of VLIW processor architectures from a designer's experience based specification. In *3rd Int. Workshop on Hardware/Software Codesign*, pages 108–115, Sept. 22-23, Grenoble, September 1994.

[3] A. Capitanio, N. Dutt, and A. Nicolau. Partitioned register files for VLIWs: A preliminary analysis of tradeoffs. In *Proceedings of the 25th Annual International Symposium on Microarchitecture*, pages 292–300, Portland, Oregon, December 1–4, 1992. IEEE Computer Society TC-MICRO and ACM SIGMICRO. SIG MICRO Newsletter 23(1–2), December 1992.

[4] B. Case. First TriMedia chip boards PCI bus. *Microprocessor Report*, 9(15):22–28, November 1995.

[5] R. P. Colwell, R. P. Nix, J. J. O'Donnell, D. P. Papworth, and P. K. Rodman. A VLIW architecture for a trace scheduling compiler. In *Proceedings of the Second International*

Cost=10.0 Range=0%											
Arch Desc	(su,c)	A.c	C.c	D.c	F.c	G.c	H.c	GF.c	GEF.c	DH.c	DHEF.c
A(8 4 256 1 4 4)	(6.1 7.4)	9.94	5.84	4.42	6.13	5.42	6.35	6.16	5.86	6.31	6.38
C(8 2 256 1 4 4)	(6.1 6.6)	9.38	6.15	4.33	6.13	5.72	6.35	6.16	5.86	6.33	6.38
D(8 4 256 1 4 4)	(6.1 7.4)	9.94	5.84	4.42	6.13	5.42	6.35	6.16	5.86	6.31	6.38
F(8 2 256 1 4 4)	(6.1 6.6)	9.38	6.15	4.33	6.13	5.72	6.35	6.16	5.86	6.33	6.38
G(8 2 256 1 4 4)	(6.1 6.6)	9.38	6.15	4.33	6.13	5.72	6.35	6.16	5.86	6.33	6.38
H(16 4 128 1 4 8)	(3.9 8.7)	0.89	3.54	3.83	5.14	5.41	9.45	8.39	8.93	10.09	9.61
GF(16 4 128 1 4 8)	(3.9 8.7)	0.89	3.54	3.83	5.14	5.41	9.45	8.39	8.93	10.09	9.61
GEF(16 4 128 1 4 8)	(3.9 8.7)	0.89	3.54	3.83	5.14	5.41	9.45	8.39	8.93	10.09	9.61
DH(16 4 128 1 4 8)	(3.9 8.7)	0.89	3.54	3.83	5.14	5.41	9.45	8.39	8.93	10.09	9.61
DHEF(16 4 128 1 4 8)	(3.9 8.7)	0.89	3.54	3.83	5.14	5.41	9.45	8.39	8.93	10.09	9.61

Cost=10.0 Range=10%											
Arch Desc	(su,c)	A.c	C.c	D.c	F.c	G.c	H.c	GF.c	GEF.c	DH.c	DHEF.c
A(8 2 256 1 4 4)	(6.1 6.6)	9.38	6.15	4.33	6.13	5.72	6.35	6.16	5.86	6.33	6.38
C(8 2 256 1 4 4)	(6.1 6.6)	9.38	6.15	4.33	6.13	5.72	6.35	6.16	5.86	6.33	6.38
D(8 2 256 1 4 4)	(6.1 6.6)	9.38	6.15	4.33	6.13	5.72	6.35	6.16	5.86	6.33	6.38
F(8 2 256 1 4 4)	(6.1 6.6)	9.38	6.15	4.33	6.13	5.72	6.35	6.16	5.86	6.33	6.38
G(8 2 256 1 4 4)	(6.1 6.6)	9.38	6.15	4.33	6.13	5.72	6.35	6.16	5.86	6.33	6.38
H(16 4 128 1 4 8)	(3.9 8.7)	0.89	3.54	3.83	5.14	5.41	9.45	8.39	8.93	10.09	9.61
GF(16 4 128 1 4 8)	(3.9 8.7)	0.89	3.54	3.83	5.14	5.41	9.45	8.39	8.93	10.09	9.61
GEF(16 4 128 1 4 8)	(3.9 8.7)	0.89	3.54	3.83	5.14	5.41	9.45	8.39	8.93	10.09	9.61
DH(16 4 128 1 4 8)	(3.9 8.7)	0.89	3.54	3.83	5.14	5.41	9.45	8.39	8.93	10.09	9.61
DHEF(16 4 128 1 4 8)	(3.9 8.7)	0.89	3.54	3.83	5.14	5.41	9.45	8.39	8.93	10.09	9.61

Cost=10.0 Range=50%											
Arch Desc	(su,c)	A.c	C.c	D.c	F.c	G.c	H.c	GF.c	GEF.c	DH.c	DHEF.c
A(8 2 256 1 4 4)	(6.1 6.6)	9.38	6.15	4.33	6.13	5.72	6.35	6.16	5.86	6.33	6.38
C(8 2 256 1 4 4)	(6.1 6.6)	9.38	6.15	4.33	6.13	5.72	6.35	6.16	5.86	6.33	6.38
D(8 2 256 1 4 4)	(6.1 6.6)	9.38	6.15	4.33	6.13	5.72	6.35	6.16	5.86	6.33	6.38
F(8 2 256 1 4 4)	(6.1 6.6)	9.38	6.15	4.33	6.13	5.72	6.35	6.16	5.86	6.33	6.38
G(8 2 256 1 4 4)	(6.1 6.6)	9.38	6.15	4.33	6.13	5.72	6.35	6.16	5.86	6.33	6.38
H(8 2 256 1 4 4)	(6.1 6.6)	9.38	6.15	4.33	6.13	5.72	6.35	6.16	5.86	6.33	6.38
GF(8 2 256 1 4 4)	(6.1 6.6)	9.38	6.15	4.33	6.13	5.72	6.35	6.16	5.86	6.33	6.38
GEF(8 2 256 1 8 4)	(5.8 6.6)	6.82	6.15	4.33	4.64	5.72	6.35	6.14	5.97	6.31	6.36
DH(16 4 128 1 4 8)	(3.9 8.7)	0.89	3.54	3.83	5.14	5.41	9.45	8.39	8.93	10.09	9.61
DHEF(16 4 128 1 4 8)	(3.9 8.7)	0.89	3.54	3.83	5.14	5.41	9.45	8.39	8.93	10.09	9.61

Cost=10.0 Range=∞(=60%)											
Arch Desc	(su,c)	A.c	C.c	D.c	F.c	G.c	H.c	GF.c	GEF.c	DH.c	DHEF.c
all(8 2 256 1 4 4)	(6.1 6.6)	9.38	6.15	4.33	6.13	5.72	6.35	6.16	5.86	6.33	6.38

Table 9. Speedup results for medium cost (< 10.0) architectures.

Conference on Architectural Support for Programming Languages and Operating Systems, pages 180–192, Palo Alto, California, October 5–8, 1987. ACM SIGARCH, SIGPLAN, SIGOPS, and the IEEE Computer Society. *Computer Architecture News,* 15(5), October 1987; *Operating Systems Review,* 21(4), October 1987; *SIGPLAN Notices,* 22(10), October 1987.

[6] T. M. Conte and W. Mangione-Smith. Determining cost-effective multiple issue processor designs. In *Proc. 1993 Int'l. Conf. on Computer Design*, pages 94–101, Cambridge, MA, October 1993.

[7] T. M. Conte, K. N. P. Menezes, and S. W. Sathaye. A technique to determine power-efficient, high-performance superscalar processors. In *Proc. 28th Hawaii Int'l. Conf. on System Sciences*, volume 1, pages 324–333, Maui, HI, January 1995.

[8] A. De Gloria and P. Faraboschi. An evaluation system for application specific architectures. In *Proceedings of the 23th Annual International Workshop on Microarchitecture and Microprogramming*, pages 80–89, Orlando, Florida, November 27–29 1990. IEEE Computer Society TC-MICRO and ACM SIGMICRO.

[9] D. Epstein. Chromatic raises the multimedia bar. *Microprocessor Report*, 9(14):23–28, October 1995.

[10] D. Epstein. IBM extends DSP performance with Mfast. *Microprocessor Report*, 9(16):1,6–8, December 1995.

[11] J. A. Fisher. Very long instruction word architectures and the ELI-512. In *Proceedings of the 10th Annual International Symposium on Computer Architecture*, pages 140–150,

Cost=15.0 Range=0%											
Arch Desc	(su,c)	A.c	C.c	D.c	F.c	G.c	H.c	GF.c	GEF.c	DH.c	DHEF.c
A(16 4 256 2 4 8)	(6.8 13.0)	13.06	5.88	3.52	5.63	4.95	9.68	8.13	8.65	9.60	9.14
C(16 4 512 1 4 8)	(7.2 14.1)	11.04	7.46	3.86	5.25	5.41	10.50	8.39	8.93	10.61	9.88
D(8 4 512 1 4 4)	(6.1 11.0)	10.72	6.07	4.42	6.13	5.42	6.35	6.16	5.86	6.31	6.38
F(8 4 512 1 4 4)	(6.1 11.0)	10.72	6.07	4.42	6.13	5.42	6.35	6.16	5.86	6.31	6.38
G(8 2 256 1 4 4)	(6.1 6.6)	9.38	6.15	4.33	6.13	5.72	6.35	6.16	5.86	6.33	6.38
H(16 4 512 1 8 8)	(6.2 14.1)	5.95	7.46	3.86	3.98	5.41	10.52	5.75	6.79	10.58	9.74
GF(16 4 512 1 4 8)	(7.2 14.1)	11.04	7.46	3.86	5.25	5.41	10.50	8.39	8.93	10.61	9.88
GEF(16 4 512 1 4 8)	(7.2 14.1)	11.04	7.46	3.86	5.25	5.41	10.50	8.39	8.93	10.61	9.88
DH(16 4 512 1 4 8)	(7.2 14.1)	11.04	7.46	3.86	5.25	5.41	10.50	8.39	8.93	10.61	9.88
DHEF(16 8 256 1 4 8)	(7.1 12.2)	10.54	6.43	3.86	5.25	5.41	10.50	8.39	8.93	10.55	10.06

Cost=15.0 Range=10%											
Arch Desc	(su,c)	A.c	C.c	D.c	F.c	G.c	H.c	GF.c	GEF.c	DH.c	DHEF.c
A(16 4 256 2 4 8)	(6.8 13.0)	13.06	5.88	3.52	5.63	4.95	9.68	8.13	8.65	9.60	9.14
C(16 4 512 1 4 8)	(7.2 14.1)	11.04	7.46	3.86	5.25	5.41	10.50	8.39	8.93	10.61	9.88
D(8 4 512 1 4 4)	(6.1 11.0)	10.72	6.07	4.42	6.13	5.42	6.35	6.16	5.86	6.31	6.38
F(16 4 256 2 4 8)	(6.8 13.0)	13.06	5.88	3.52	5.63	4.95	9.68	8.13	8.65	9.60	9.14
G(16 4 512 1 4 8)	(7.2 14.1)	11.04	7.46	3.86	5.25	5.41	10.50	8.39	8.93	10.61	9.88
H(16 4 512 1 4 8)	(7.2 14.1)	11.04	7.46	3.86	5.25	5.41	10.50	8.39	8.93	10.61	9.88
GF(16 4 512 1 4 8)	(7.2 14.1)	11.04	7.46	3.86	5.25	5.41	10.50	8.39	8.93	10.61	9.88
GEF(16 4 512 1 4 8)	(7.2 14.1)	11.04	7.46	3.86	5.25	5.41	10.50	8.39	8.93	10.61	9.88
DH(16 4 512 1 4 8)	(7.2 14.1)	11.04	7.46	3.86	5.25	5.41	10.50	8.39	8.93	10.61	9.88
DHEF(16 4 512 1 4 8)	(7.2 14.1)	11.04	7.46	3.86	5.25	5.41	10.50	8.39	8.93	10.61	9.88

Cost=15.0 Range=∞(=19%)											
Arch Desc	(su,c)	A.c	C.c	D.c	F.c	G.c	H.c	GF.c	GEF.c	DH.c	DHEF.c
all(16 4 512 1 4 8)	(7.2 14.1)	11.04	7.46	3.86	5.25	5.41	10.50	8.39	8.93	10.61	9.88

Table 10. Speedup results for high cost (< 15.0) architectures.

Stockholm, Sweden, June 13–17, 1983. *Computer Architecture News,* 11(3), June 1983.

[12] M. Flynn and R. Winner. ASIC microprocessors. In *Proceedings of the 22th Annual International Workshop on Microarchitecture and Microprogramming*, pages 237–243, Dublin, Ireland, September 1989. IEEE Computer Society TC-MICRO and ACM SIGMICRO. SIG MICRO Newsletter 20(3), September 1989.

[13] B. Holmer and A. Despain. Viewing instruction set design as an optimization problem. In *Proceedings of the 24th Annual International Workshop on Microarchitecture and Microprogramming*, pages 153–162, Albuquerque, New Mexico, November 18–21 1991. IEEE Computer Society TC-MICRO and ACM SIGMICRO.

[14] I.-J. Huang and A. M. Despain. High level synthesis of pipelined instruction set processors and back-end compilers. In *Proceedings of the 29th ACM/IEEE Design Automation Conference*, pages 135–140. ACM Press, June 1992.

[15] A. Kalavade and E. A. Lee. A hardware/software codesign methodology for DSP applications. *IEEE Design and Test,* 10(3):16–28, September 1993.

[16] M. Langevin, J. Wilberg, P. Plöger, and H.-T. Vierhaus. A codesign methodology for high performance embedded systems. In V. Van Dongen, editor, *Proceedings of the High Performance Computing Symposium '95, Canada's Ninth Annual International High Performance Computing Conference and Exhibition*, pages 353–364, Montréal, Québec, July 10–12, 1995. Centre de Recherche Informatique de Montréal.

[17] J. Lowney, S. Freudenberger, T. Karzes, W. Lichtenstein, R. Nix, J. O'Donnel, and J. Ruttenberg. The Multiflow trace scheduling compiler. *The Journal of Supercomputing*, 7(1/2):51 142, May 1993.

[18] G. D. Micheli. Computer-aided hardware-software codesign. *IEEE Micro*, 14(4):10–16, August 1994.

[19] J. M. Mulder, R. J. Portier, A. Srivastava, and R. in 't Velt. An architecture framework for application-specific and scalable architectures. In *Proceedings of the 16th Annual International Symposium on Computer Architecture*, pages 362–369, Jerusalem, Israel, May 28–June 1, 1989. IEEE Computer Society TCCA and ACM SIGARCH. *Computer Architecture News,* 17(3), June 1989.

[20] S. Note, W. Geurts, F. Catthoor, and H. D. Man. Cathedral-III: Architecture-driven high-level synthesis for high throughput DSP applications. In *Proceedings of the 28th ACM/IEEE Design Automation Conference*, pages 597–602. ACM Press, June 1991.

[21] M. Slater. MicroUnity lifts veil on media processor. *Microprocessor Report*, 9(14):11–18, October 1995.

[22] G. Wallace. The JPEG still picture compression standard. *Commun. ACM*, 34(4):30–44, Apr. 1991.

Optimization for a Superscalar Out-of-Order Machine

Anne M. Holler
Hewlett-Packard Company
aholler@cup.hp.com

Abstract

Compiler optimization plays a key role in unlocking the performance of the PA-8000, an innovative dynamically-scheduled machine which is the first implementation of the 64-bit PA 2.0 member of the HP PA-RISC architecture family. This wide superscalar, long out-of-order machine provides significant execution bandwidth and automatically hides latency at runtime; however, despite its ample hardware resources, many of the optimizing transformations which proved effective for the PA-8000 served to augment its ability to exploit the available bandwidth and to hide latency. Further, machine-specific factors influenced all levels of optimization to a degree without precedent in the set of previous PA-RISC processors. While legacy codes benefit from the PA-8000's sophisticated hardware, recompilation of old binaries can be vital to realizing the full potential of the PA-8000, given the impact of new compilers in achieving peak performance for this machine.

1 Introduction

Superscalar RISC designs promise to break through the single cycle per instruction limit of RISC designs via exploiting instruction-level parallelism (ILP). Out-of-order execution exposes more ILP. Superscalar out-of-order designs' attributes of dynamic issue and dynamic scheduling are suited to maintaining upward compatibility with scalar in-order members of a processor family.

The PA-8000 [20,25] is the first implementation of the 64-bit PA-RISC 2.0 architecture [30]. The processor has a 56-entry reorder queue, organized as a 28-entry ALU queue and a 28-entry memory queue; this reorder queue is significantly longer than that of any other microprocessor currently available in the marketplace [34]. The PA-8000 is 4-issue superscalar, with 2 integer arithmetic/logic units, 2 shift/merge units, 2 load/store address units, 2 floating point multiply/accumulate units, and 2 floating point divide/square-root units. Given its lengthy reorder queue and wide issue, the PA-8000 might be expected to subsume certain functionality of the low level compiler optimizer, such as instruction scheduling. However, experience has demonstrated that the combination of innovative hardware and aggressive optimization, including compile-time scheduling, has made the PA-8000 the world's most powerful microprocessor at the time of its March 1996 announcement, with a peak SPECint95 ratio of 11.8 and a peak SPECfp95 ratio of 20.2. Software contributions to this performance are substantial; comparing the performance of legacy PA-7200 SPEC95 binaries run on the PA-8000 with binaries newly rebuilt for the PA-8000, SPECint95 is improved by more than 50% and SPECfp95 is improved by more than 120%.

All HP compilers for the PA-RISC share common optimizing components. The structure of HP compilers and the purpose of each optimizing component are shown in Figure 1 [24]. The user selects desired optimizing components with command-line options; for example, the low level optimizer may be invoked via -O and the high level optimizer is typically invoked via +O3 or +O4. The user may employ the profile-based optimization (PBO) framework to have data about a program gathered during instrumented runs on representative data sets and fed back into the optimization process. The optimizations described in this paper are incorporated in version 10.2 of the PA-RISC compilers.

The remainder of this paper is organized as follows. First, low level optimization for the PA-8000 is discussed with respect to procedure dependencies, true dependencies, and resource conflicts, which are three properties that have been identified as potentially limiting the performance of a superscalar processor [28]. Some recent general enhancements to the PA-RISC low level optimizer are covered as well. Next, aspects of high level optimization which were influenced by PA-8000-specific considerations are outlined. Performance measurements for the PA-8000 are then reported, along with observations on the process of tracking performance. Issues related to the execution of legacy code are noted. The paper concludes with lessons learned in optimizing for a superscalar out-of-order machine.

This paper discusses a number of optimization techniques known to compiler experts in academia and industry. References are provided, but some sources may have been unintentionally overlooked. All optimization techniques described were observed to yield measurable speedups for some important benchmark or application codes

1072-4451/96 $5.00 © 1996 IEEE

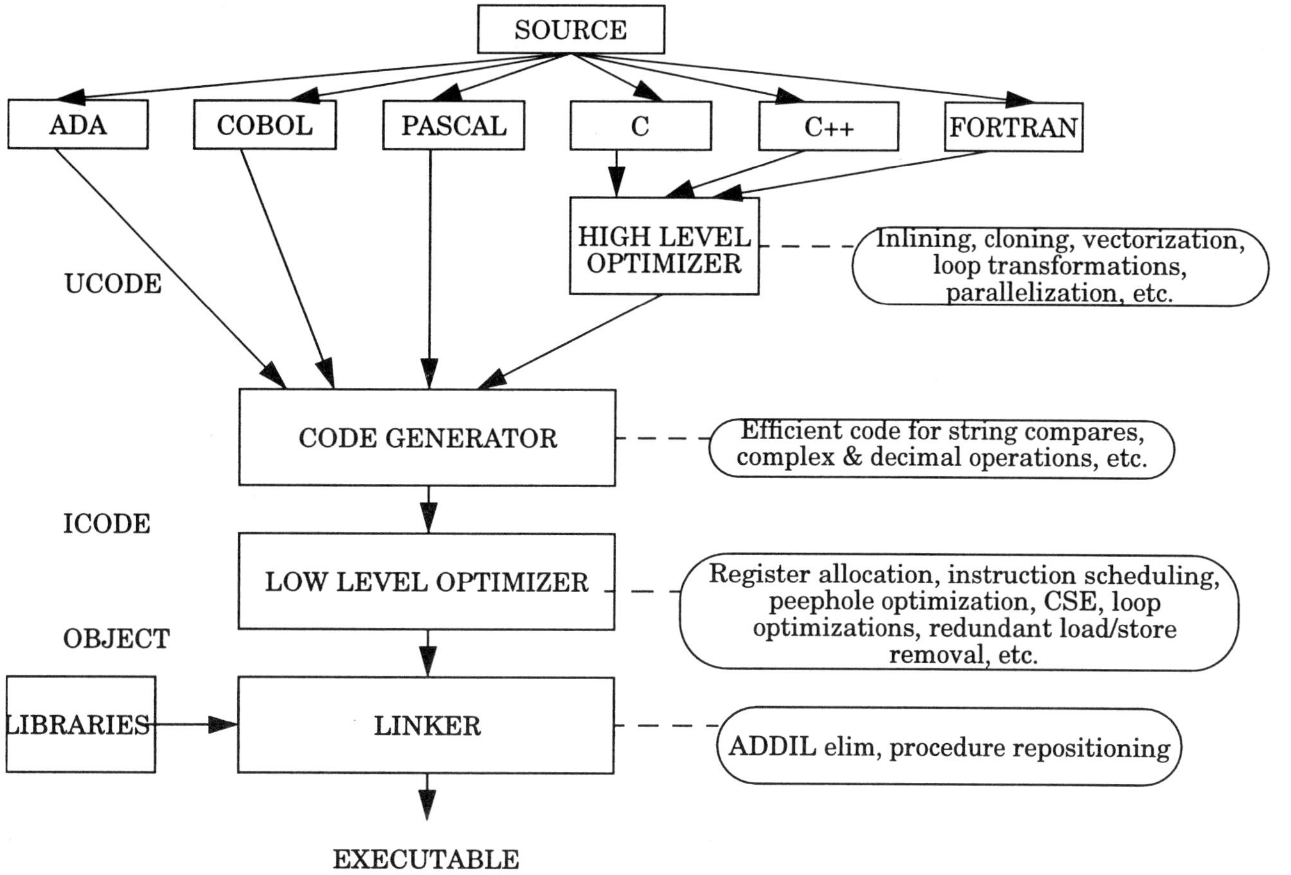

FIGURE 1: Structure of PA-RISC Optimizing Compilers

run on the PA-8000, but a detailed and meaningful study of the relative merits of each technique, taking into account the effects of compiler phase ordering, interactions between optimization techniques, machine implementation features and idiosyncrasies, input source code and data set selection, etc., is beyond the scope of this paper.

2 PA-8000 Low Level Optimization

The PA-RISC Low Level Optimizer (LLO) performs global optimizations within a procedure [29,21]. It consists of the following phases: basic block formation and optimization, interval construction and calculation of reaching dataflow information [27], global common subexpression elimination, calculation of need dataflow information, promotion of memory variables, loop optimizations, formation and optimization of definition/use webs, instruction scheduling, coloring register allocation, peephole optimization, branch optimization, branch reachability fixing, and (again) instruction scheduling. The LLO incorporates many aggressive low level techniques, including register reassociation [40], software pipelining [38], and region scheduling [MAHA94]. For processors in the PA-RISC family introduced prior to the PA-8000, the LLO handled virtually all machine-specific transformations.

2.1 Optimizing for Procedural Dependencies

As the amount of ILP being exploited grows, procedural dependencies rapidly become the limiting factor [23]. The PA-8000 supports both static and dynamic branch prediction, selectable on a per-page basis. Correctly predicted branches which hit in the branch target address cache incur no penalty, while mispredicted branches may have a relatively large penalty of around 6 cycles. Optimization strategies to reduce overhead for procedural dependencies involve decreasing the number of branches executed and/or increasing the accuracy of branch prediction.

Loop Unrolling

Loop unrolling [15], in which a loop body is replicated one or more times with appropriate adjustments to array indices and loop control code, reduces the iteration overhead associated with looping (i.e., increment/decrement, test, and branch). In addition, it exposes more cross-iteration ILP to the optimizer. While the PA-8000 hardware can automatically schedule instructions across iterations, loop unrolling and certain other optimizations it enables were found to be quite effective for this machine. Loop unrolling for the PA-8000 is discussed in detail in [41]; below is a brief description of loop unrolling in the PA-RISC LLO, with PA-8000 issues highlighted.

The fundamental heuristic related to loop unrolling is the selection of the unroll depth; several attributes of the PA-8000 are relevant to the selection criteria. One factor considered is the number of instructions in the loop. For this factor, unroll depth is chosen as a balance between the fact that the PA-8000 can handle substantial code size growth, by virtue of its large (1 megabyte) instruction cache, and the potential side-effects of code size growth, which may include increased register pressure leading to spilling or excessive compile time and space consumption. Another factor considered relates to data cache prefetching. If PA-8000 explicit data cache prefetch instructions (Section 2.2) will be inserted into the loop, and if the memory access stride is less than the cache line length in the original loop, it is desirable to limit the unroll depth so that the stride remains within the cache line length in the unrolled loop, to promote the efficacy of the prefetch overhead reduction algorithm. If recurrent scalar replacement (Section 2.4) has been performed, an unroll depth which matches the recurrence distance allows the removal of copies which carry values across iterations. Critical resource usage is also considered; in particular, the number of long latency floating point divide (FDIV) and square root (FSQRT) operations is counted, because an unroll factor which yields an even number of these operations in the loop body is preferable to aid FDIV/FSQRT polarity scheduling (Section 2.3). The expected trip count (which may be constant, based on profiling information, or derived from static heuristics) is also relevant; choosing an unroll depth which is a multiple of the expected trip count may tend to allow execution of the compensation loop[1] to be avoided. The user may suggest an unroll depth for the program's loops via a command line option. Finally, issues related to managing the unrolled loop are considered in selecting the unroll depth. An unroll depth which is a power of two allows the use of an inexpensive shift operation to determine how many times to execute the compensation loop; in this case, the compensation loop is executed prior to the unrolled loop, so that the index variable associated with the unrolled loop is not live on loop exit, improving the operation of register reassociation for the unrolled loop. An unroll depth which is not a power of two requires a more expensive operation to determine how many times to execute the compensation loop; in this case, the compensation loop is placed after the unrolled loop with its repetition factor determined by the remainder value of the unrolled loop's index variable, which is thus live on exit from the loop impacting register reassociation's efficacy.

1. The compensation loop is executed when there are too few iterations to be handled by the unrolled loop.

Perhaps surprisingly, application code may contain loops which iterate a constant number of times. This occurs, for example, when the code solves a problem which involves a fixed width in certain dimensions. Completely unrolling constant trip count loops and removing all loop overhead, even when the resulting code size growth is nontrivial, proved to be profitable on the PA-8000.

When a loop has a fairly small trip count, its iterate-or-exit branch can have a high misprediction rate. If control passes through this poorly predicted loop fairly often, performance may be impacted. In any such situation which does not lend itself to regular unrolling and for which the small trip count tends to usually have a particular value, the loop body can be replicated that number of times, with each copy retaining its own branch. This simple form of unrolling serves to split the loop's single branch point into several branch points, each of which is more predictable (i.e., each will likely fall through).

Superblock formation

Superblock formation [26] is an optimizing and an optimization-enabling transformation, which involves duplicating code so that certain incoming edges into a commonly executed path of the control flow graph can be removed. As a result, larger basic blocks are constructed and some control flow overhead is eliminated, reducing pressure on the PA-8000's branch prediction cache (BPC) and thereby improving its prediction accuracy. These changes can in turn be exploited in a number of ways. For example, after constructing superblocks, a common subexpression which was only valid on a certain path through the code could become available on a distinct path (thereby allowing a common subexpression elimination framework to effect a form of partial redundancy elimination). The PA-8000's tolerance for code size growth and its high branch misprediction penalty make this transformation attractive.

Superblock formation consists of identifying traces [18] which represent frequent paths through the code and then duplicating certain code along those traces, modifying or removing branches as appropriate. The LLO's algorithm is similar to that described in [9]. Using profile information collected via the PBO framework, traces are constructed by repeatedly picking the basic block with the highest execution frequency from a bucket of candidate basic blocks, initially filled with all basic blocks that meet a certain threshold execution level, and then forming an associated trace by selecting adjacent frequently-executed basic blocks. After traces are constructed, decisions concerning whether and how much tail duplication should be done are made. Tail duplication of blocks containing a large percentage of conditional branches is avoided, since introducing multiple copies of those branches can increase conflicts in the PA-8000's BPC. Superblocks are formed during the basic block construction phase, to allow subsequent phases to capitalize on the transformed code. However, some phase ordering issues are associated with this choice and are addressed by not creating superblocks which may interfere with loop optimizations or with if-conversion.

Assertion propagation

Assertion propagation is a technique which tracks the data relationships governing the execution of particular code paths, and which uses this information to eliminate redundant comparisons and associated branches [4,22]. These redundancies may have existed in the source code, or they may be an artifact of inlining or cloning. The technique improves code for all PA-RISC machines, but is particularly beneficial on the PA-8000, because of its high branch misprediction penalty.

Assertion propagation involves tracking relationships as dataflow information, and using arithmetic and logic rules to combine relationships at various control flow points. The technique can reveal redundancy which is directly manifest in the code stream or which may be exposed via path cloning. When a conditional branch is dominated by another conditional branch, and the outcome of the dominating conditional establishes the outcome of the dominated conditional (for example, both conditional branches involve identical comparisons or exact opposite comparisons), then the dominated conditional branch is directly unnecessary, and can either be removed or replaced by an unconditional branch. For example, for the code fragment:

```
$ww  COMIB,= 0,r5,$xx !If reg 5=0, branch to $xx
     ...
     B $zz           !Branch to label $zz
$xx  COMIB,= 0,r5,$yy !If reg 5=0, branch to $yy
```

if the only way to reach the conditional branch labeled $xx is through the conditional branch labeled $ww, then r5 is known to be equal to 0 at $xx, and the second conditional branch can be replaced by an unconditional branch:

```
$ww  COMIB,= 0,r5,$xx !If reg 5=0, branch to $xx
     ...
     B $zz           !Brnch to label $zz
$xx  B $yy           !Branch to label $yy
```

Code repositioning [37] may later preclude the need for the unconditional branch to $yy. When a conditional branch is the target of several other branches, each of which first sets up a value which is then tested by the conditional branch, then path cloning is performed: the preceding branches are modified to jump directly to the location to which the target conditional branch would jump, based on the value each source branch provides, and the target conditional branch is deleted. To illustrate this situation:

```
     COPY r0,r5      !Copy reg 0 (=0) to reg 5
$ww  B $xx           !Branch to label $xx
     ...
     LDI 1,r5        !Set register 5 to 1
$zz  B $xx           !Branch to label $xx
     ...
$xx  COMIB,= 0,r5,$yy !If reg 5=0, branch to $yy
```

if the only paths reaching the conditional branch labeled $xx are through the two unconditional branches at $ww and $zz, then the outcome of the comparison at $xx is determined by which of the two preceding branches was taken to reach $xx. Hence, the code can be converted to:

```
     COPY r0,r5      !Copy reg 0 (=0) to reg 5
$ww  B $yy           !Branch to label $yy
     ...
     LDI 1,r5        !Set register 5 to 1
$zz  B $xx           !Branch to label $xx
     ...
$xx  ...
```

If-conversion

On the PA-RISC architecture, all computational and branch instructions can nullify the execution of the following instruction. In the case of computational instructions, nullification is performed conditionally, based on the outcome of a test; this conditional nullification represents a simple form of predicated execution [14]. If-conversion is an optimization technique involving the conversion of conditional blocks of code to sequences of conditional simple statements; this technique can serve to transform control flow dependencies into data flow dependencies, by including the condition as an input to the operation [1]. The conditional simple statement semantics of if-conversion can be realized using nullification on a computational instruction, thereby avoiding branching. Surprisingly, although avoiding branching is quite desirable on the PA-8000, developing heuristics for deciding when to perform if-conversion was difficult.

The problem is that there are certain overheads associated with nullification on the PA-8000. Nullification engenders a latency; a non-branch conditionally nullified operation is not considered data-ready until its potentially nullifying instruction has launched for execution. Note that there would be no such latency if the instruction were simply located on a correctly-predicted branch path. More importantly, when an instruction is nullified, the dependencies which were established in the reorder queue are affected. In this regard, nullification is an anomaly for an out-of-order machine. The PA-8000 hardware accelerates the nullify-slot operation of certain instructions; these instructions are said to be in *select* convention.

A detailed description of if-conversion for the PA-8000 can be found in [3]. Factors governing its application include the amount of conditional code, the balance between the amount of then and else code for if-then-else constructs, and the execution frequency on alternative paths through the control flow graph. Producing candidate if-converted code sequences involves careful selection and efficient utilization of guarding conditionals, the use of unconditional code when appropriate, and the exploitation of select convention instructions. Estimated best-case processor cycles for the original and if-converted code are compared; computing these cycle counts was complicated by the difficulty in calculating cycles for an out-of-order machine, particularly with respect to expected misprediction costs [3]. If-conversion, judiciously applied, proved very effective for the PA-8000.

Static Branch Prediction Hinting

PA-RISC models introduced prior to the PA-8000 implemented static branch prediction, with the prediction implied by the direction of the branch: backwards taken, forwards not taken (BTFNT). The PA-8000 supports both dynamic and static branch prediction, with a method for explicitly specifying static branch prediction hints. A study which compares the two kinds of branch prediction on the PA-8000 found that static branch prediction performs better than dynamic in several cases: when a program's working set of branches does not fit in the PA-8000's 256-entry BPC, when important branches conflict in that direct-mapped untagged cache, and when there is little temporal locality in the use of branches [6]. A user can only request that an application be compiled for static branch prediction mode when that application is built using the PBO framework, because experimentation has shown that there is usually a large performance degradation associated with incorrectly hinted branches when static heuristics are used.

For static branch prediction mode, the LLO uses profiling information to rearrange code [37] and to provide appropriate PA 2.0 static branch prediction hints. The PA 2.0 conventions specify that unconditional pc-relative branches are predicted taken and that conditional pc-relative branches are predicted BTFNT, except for conditional pc-relative branches involving register-to-register comparisons, which are predicted BNTFT if the registers are specified with their numbers in descending order within the instruction. In practice, the backwards not taken hint has not proven useful, but the forwards taken hint has. To hint as taken any forward conditional pc-relative branches not involving register-to-register comparisons, various manipulations of the code are applied. Conditional branches containing comparisons against the constant value zero are mapped to register-to-register comparisons against general register zero (which is always zero) so that the register order convention can be employed. Conditional branches containing comparisons against non-zero constants are mapped to complementary conditionally-nullifying compare-and-clear instructions, with an unconditional pc-relative branch (which is predicted taken) to the target in the possibly-nullified slot. Similarly, forward branch-on-bit instructions to be predicted taken are mapped to appropriate extract instructions which possibly nullify an unconditional branch to the original target.

Hinting branching based on floating point comparisons presents additional challenges, because floating point compare instructions do not include conditional branching. Instead, they set a C-bit in the floating point status register, which is then tested by a conditionally-nullifying FTEST instruction, typically guarding an unconditional branch. This sequence has the effect that, in static branch prediction mode, all branches based on floating point comparisons would be predicted taken. Recall that backwards not taken hinting has not proven interesting; to hint forwards not taken, the unconditional branch following the FTEST is changed to a conditional branch comparing the immediate zero to register zero for equality; this branch is always taken, just like the original unconditional branch, but it is predicted not taken, since it falls into the default BTFNT convention.

Switch Statement Improvements

The code generated by PA-RISC compilers for a switch statement depends on heuristics involving a number of factors, including the number of alternative cases, the density with which those cases are packed across the range of the switch, and the expected frequency with which control will pass to each case. For the PA-8000, the evaluation of both a cascaded if-then-else strategy and a strategy of testing for certain specific cases peeled off of a jump table is influenced by the potentially high cost of branch misprediction. PA-8000 attributes are also reflected in the code to test that an item is within a range of case values. The PA-RISC sequence originally included a pair of conditional branch instructions which compared against the upper and lower bounds of the range; the sequence is now mapped (when possible) to code which first normalizes the value to be tested so that the lower bound can be treated as zero and then performs an unsigned comparison against the normalized upper bound of the range. The revised approach produces tighter code, in general: it creates fewer distinct basic blocks, and it can be more efficient when the original range bounds are too wide to fit in the conditional branch immediate field but the size of the range can be encoded within the field's width. On the PA-8000, however, the revised approach has additional benefits: reducing the number of branches diminishes pressure on the BPC in dynamic branch prediction mode and more importantly, saves retirement bandwidth,[1] since the revised code uses only one conditional branch instead of two.

When a jump table approach is used for a switch statement, the code sequence produced for machines introduced prior to the PA-8000 performed a register-indexed branch into a table of unconditional pc-relative branches to the target code. However, on the PA-8000 in dynamic branch prediction mode, the unconditional pc-relative branch can be mispredicted due to the vagaries of the BPC and in addition, that branch may also interfere with the history of other branches in the BPC. These potential problems are avoided by a code sequence in which the target address is loaded from an indexed table and then jumped to via a register-indirect branch. On the PA-8000, both the register-indexed branch in the original sequence and the register-indirect branch in the revised sequence are always mispredicted as not taken, because of the difficulty in having the hardware provide the register-dependent target address to the fetch unit if they were correctly predicted as taken. To avoid this misprediction for the most likely set of cases in the switch, a zero is placed in the jump table entries associated with that set, and then the register-indirect branch to

1. Conditional branches consume two slots in the reorder queue (one in the memory queue and one in the ALU queue) to serve as placeholders for recovery from mispredicted branches.

the address fetched from the table is placed in the possibly-nullified slot of an instruction comparing the entry fetched from the table against zero, with the code for the most likely case immediately following the register-indirect branch. When a case from this likely set is encountered, the register-indirect branch is simply skipped and control enters the code labeled for that case.

2.2 Optimizing for True Dependencies

The primary purpose of the PA-8000's reorder queue is to hide the latencies engendered by true dependencies. However, the queue's length represents a limitation on the machine's ability to do so. The optimizer can help by exposing ILP and avoiding long latency operations when possible.

Data Cache Prefetching

A cache miss on the PA-8000 has a latency which may be in excess of 50 cycles. To aid in hiding this latency, the PA-8000 supports the explicit data cache prefetch instructions defined by the PA 2.0 architecture. Encoded as integer loads to general register zero, these instructions (unlike normal loads) do not engender exceptions or traps and are not subject to retirement delays pending service from the cache.

Compiler-generated data cache prefetch [35] for the PA-8000 is discussed in detail in [19]; a brief overview is given here. The LLO will insert explicit data prefetch instructions into loops (including those with internal control flow) which contain regular data access patterns in terms of effective memory strides. Worst-case cache alignment of user data is taken into account, and runtime dimensioned arrays are supported. Given the expected cache miss latency, the number of loop iterations in advance of which to prefetch data is determined by the expected loop iteration latency, which depends on the composition of the loop and on PA-8000 scheduling information. The prefetch algorithm focuses on innermost loops, but prefetches for non-innermost loops as well, if they are expected to be executed relatively more often each time they are entered than loops nested within them. One interesting situation occurs when an enclosing loop is expected to be executed more often each time it is entered than a nested loop, and the two loops have conflicting stride directions. In this case, the LLO will reverse the direction of the prefetches in the nested loop, so that it will effectively be prefetching for future iterations engendered by the outer loop.

Data prefetch can increase performance on the PA-8000 dramatically. For several benchmarks, the speedups were between 50 and 100%. Unfortunately, data prefetch can also diminish performance. Prefetch instructions are added selectively to minimize their overhead without unduly compromising miss coverage by exploiting apparent group spatial and group temporal locality among references to different elements of the same array. Nevertheless, explicit data prefetch instructions consume retirement bandwidth and increase cache accesses, and these costs may not be offset by a corresponding decrease in data cache miss overhead, either because the prefetched data is already cache-resident (and in general, the compiler cannot determine this statically), or because the prefetched data displaces (or is displaced by) other needed cache data, or because the prefetched data is not actually used by the application. Due to the risk of performance loss, data prefetch is only performed at the user's request.

Instruction Scheduling for Dependent Chains

The instruction scheduling strategy for PA-RISC models introduced prior to the PA-8000 was focused on hiding latency; this strategy is not well-suited to the PA-8000. The latency-hiding approach tends to cluster load operations near the beginning of basic blocks, store operations near the end, and arithmetic operations in between. This layout wastes retirement bandwidth, since the PA-8000 can retire in program order a maximum of 2 memory operations and 2 arithmetic operations per cycle. To avoid the retirement bottleneck caused by temporal imbalance between the 2 queues, a latency-free critical path approach was developed, which assumed all latency could be hidden by the reorder queues. This approach proved to perform better than the latency-hiding approach, but had some difficulty with codes containing long dependence chains, particularly floating point codes since floating point operations have a 3 cycle latency which is not hidden by the queues for long sequences. Hence, a hybrid scheme was formulated, in which floating point latency was represented in such a way as to promote the scheduling of independent operations in the presence of long floating point dependence chains, while still providing a reasonable amount of temporal balance between the memory and ALU queues to allow efficient utilization of the retirement bandwidth. The scheme is discussed in detail in [16].

The instructions forming a long dependence chain may not be easily accessible to the optimizer. One example is when a long dependence chain occurs within the course of a millicode library routine's computation. However, a particular instance of this situation which is amenable to optimization is when a latency-bound library routine is repeatedly called with distinct arguments within a short time frame. In some cases, the LLO replaces a pair of calls to the same routine with a single call to a variant of the routine that returns two answers. The instructions in the microvectorized version of the routine are scheduled to overlap the dependence chains that would have been associated with different invocations of the original routine.

Strength Reduction

On the PA-8000, FDIV is a relatively long latency operation (17 cycles single precision, 31 cycles double precision). Hence, when a division is to be performed multiple times with the same divisor, it is preferable to compute the reciprocal and then to replace the division operations with multiplications. This strength reduction technique, termed FDIV weakening, is performed by the LLO in a variety of situations, involving both loops and straight-line code.

Note that the technique can affect floating point accuracy, and is only applied when the user has indicated that this type of optimization is acceptable.

The PA-RISC instruction set architecture does not include multiply or divide operations on operands in the integer registers. Several strength-reducing transformations are related to this design decision. Integer multiplication by a constant is replaced by a series of shift-add instructions. Integer division and remainder after division by a constant are computed using a floating point multiplication by the reciprocal, which is produced as a literal at compile time. Integer division and remainder after division by a variable are calculated using a floating point multiplication by the reciprocal, which is produced at run time.

Store Load Dependence Elimination

On the PA-8000, there is a multi-cycle delay between a store and a subsequent load from the same address. When such a store-load sequence occurs in close temporal proximity, the reorder queue may not effectively hide this latency, particularly in codes with dependence chains or other hazards. Optimized codes contain such sequences for a variety of reasons, including inadequate memory aliasing information, ambiguous dependency constraints, cross-procedure store and load of globals, parameter passing, register spill code, and transfer between the integer and floating point registers for conversion or use of the multiply operation on the floating point unit. The instruction scheduler models the same-address store-load latency, but has limited success at avoiding its effects. Even for intraprocedural sequences with adequate aliasing information, the scheduler may not be able to find sufficient ILP to cover the delay. Several optimizations were developed to reduce the impact of the store-load dependence latency. Store load dependence elimination is discussed in this section; tree height reduction is discussed in the following section.

Store load dependence elimination tracks stores and subsequent loads within a window of intervening instructions, the size of which is set based on the PA-8000's store-load latency and on its instruction width. This window is maintained across extended basic blocks, but is discontinued at a call site, since the overhead of the call will likely dwarf that of the store-load latency. If a matching (same address and width) store-load sequence is detected within the window, and if there are no ambiguous intervening stores and the register value being stored is still available at the load point, then the load is replaced by a copy or an extract, depending on how the width of the register value and the width of the memory operation compare. Note that the constraint concerning the register value being available at the load point implies that this transformation does not increase the number of instructions, and hence its direct effects seldom slow code down, unless the ALU queue was fully subscribed before the transformation.

2.3 Optimizing for Resource Conflicts

The PA-8000 has considerable hardware resources; however, there are some resource constraints that can have a significant impact on performance, if not finessed in some way. Some of these constraints stem from the need to simplify the hardware design, some are related to supporting features of the PA-RISC ISA which appear to be quirks with respect to an out-of-order machine, and some involve interactions with the memory hierarchy. New PA 2.0 instructions provided the opportunity to improve utilization of the machine's resources.

FDIV/FSQRT Polarity Scheduling

The PA-8000 has two FDIV/FSQRT units. However, to simplify the hardware, there is a constraint on both units being used simultaneously, which is that the two associated instructions must be of opposite polarity, i.e., one must have an even and the other an odd slot address in the reorder queue. Because the units are not pipelined and have a long latency (17 cycles for single precision, 31 cycles for double precision), a substantial performance benefit can be derived in some cases from laying out the code so that FDIVs and FSQRTs which are executed in close temporal proximity have opposite polarity.

The final instruction scheduling phase performs polarity scheduling in several situations. For a single basic block containing more than one FDIV or FSQRT, it tracks ALU queue slot addresses and positions code so that successive independent FDIVs or FSQRTs are of opposite polarity. For a single basic block loop containing an FDIV or FSQRT instruction without loop-carried dependence, it ensures that the loop has odd number of ALU instructions, by padding with a NOP if necessary, so that the same instruction will flip polarity on each successive iteration. If-conversion, loop unrolling, superblock formation, and assertion propagation, all discussed in Section 2.1, can aid polarity scheduling by transforming several basic blocks into a single basic block.

Nullified Delay Slot Scheduling

All PA-RISC branch instructions exhibit the delayed branch feature, meaning that the actual transfer of control occurs one instruction after execution of the branch. (This feature was useful in hiding branch latency for early PA-RISC implementations with single cycle branch delays, but is a relic with respect to the PA-8000, which has sophisticated branch prediction schemes to cope with potentially greater delays.) Execution of the delay slot instruction may be skipped by setting the nullify bit on the branch. When nullification is specified on a conditional branch instruction, the effect of the nullification depends on the direction of the branch: for a backward conditional branch, the delay slot instruction is nullified when the branch is not taken; for a forward conditional branch, the delay slot instruction is nullified when the branch is taken.

PA-8000 behavior related to the use of the nullify bit on computational instructions was discussed in Section 2.1 in association with if-conversion; behavior when the nullify bit is specified on conditional branch instructions is slightly different, because of the influence of branch prediction. Rather than waiting until the potentially nullifying instruction has been launched for execution, a possibly nullified delay slot instruction launches in accordance with the prediction for the branch. If branch prediction implies that the delay slot will not be nullified and it is not nullified, then the delay slot is launched early and filling it does not engender any penalty. Unfortunately, correct branch prediction does not always avoid penalties; if branch prediction implies that the delay slot will be nullified and it is nullified, then an instruction not in the select convention (see Section 2.1) may suffer a delay in launching. If branch prediction implies that the delay slot will not be nullified and it is nullified, then the delay slot instruction is relaunched with nullification and (again) the launch of an instruction not in the select convention may be delayed. Finally, if branch prediction implies that the delay slot will be nullified and it is not nullified, then the delay slot instruction is relaunched without nullification and suffers no more penalty than any other mispredicted instruction.

If the instruction scheduler can find a useful instruction to place in the delay slot, it does not employ nullification. Should the scheduler utilize nullification with the delay slot, an instruction in select convention is acceptable; a non-select convention instruction is rejected unless the potentially nullified slot is expected to be executed the majority of the time. Because of the risked impact of delaying a long latency operation, FDIV and FSQRT operations are not placed in a delay slot with nullification unless the slot is virtually always expected to be executed.

Prefetch Spreading

Prefetch spreading is a transformation that was found to improve utilization of the PA-8000's retirement and instruction queue bandwidth. Data prefetch instructions have no data dependent operations, so a critical path based instruction scheduling algorithm tends to cluster these instructions at the bottom of basic blocks. Unfortunately, this clustering can cause a bottleneck as follows. Ideally, data prefetch instructions engender the lion's share of data cache misses; some of those cache misses will involve lines which are dirty and hence must be written back to main memory before they can be reused. When a dirty miss occurs, the processing involved in the write-back busies the associated data path from the cache to the bus for several cycles, during which time no subsequent data cache misses may be serviced. Should a subsequent miss occur, independent instructions which follow the stalled operation may launch and complete execution, but they cannot retire, due to the machine's in-order retirement model. This bottleneck at the retirement stage can eventually result in the reorder queue becoming full, thereby forestalling latency-hiding for the operation.

Developing scheduling heuristics to address this situation was not straightforward, because the optimizer cannot, in general, precisely model when a dirty miss will occur or whether its latency would effectively be hidden. The worst-case approach of assuming all prefetch instructions cause dirty misses, introducing associated latency arcs, and having the critical path based instruction scheduler handle the reordering was found to yield too pessimistic a schedule, tending to cluster the prefetch instructions near the top of basic blocks, which is no better than the original scheme's tendency to cluster them at the bottom. Spreading data prefetch instructions equidistance apart, via moving independent instructions between them, was found to be a more effective way of hiding potential dirty miss latency. This is akin to the balanced scheduling approach, which exploits the ILP available in a program with respect to each load instruction to cope with variable delays [31].

Single-precision Floating Point False Dependence Avoidance

On the PA-RISC 1.1 and later architectures, there are 32 64-bit (double precision) floating point registers, which can also be used as 64 32-bit (single precision) floating point registers. To save hardware, the PA-8000 computes register dependencies with respect to double precision registers. Hence, if frX and frY are single precision registers which form the two halves of a double precision register, a false data dependence is recorded when frX is used within the same reorder window in which frY is defined. Because of this (false) dependence, the use instruction is not launched until the definition instruction completes execution. When the use instruction is launched, the fact that its established dependency is incorrect is detected before it can retire and the instruction is aborted, with its queue slot being marked for subsequent relaunching. Dependent instructions may be launched and aborted as well. Instructions which record false dependencies are aborted and relaunched approximately every 4 cycles until the source of the false dependence is retired, wasting bandwidth.

To address this problem, the coloring register allocator was revised to not assign both halves of a double precision register to two single precision items with overlapping lifetimes. While this "wasting" of registers might be expected to impact performance, the benefit of avoiding single precision false dependence outweighed any penalty from increased register pressure. The final instruction scheduling phase was also modified to not reorder instructions in a way which would introduce single precision false dependence.

Memory Access Coalescing

Due to the PA-8000's off-chip level-1 cache design, the minimum unit of transfer to the cache is a word (32 bits). A subword store is processed as the sequence: load word, merge subword data, write to cache store queue. Successive subword stores to the same word address are not automatically combined by the hardware, and there is multi-cycle latency between them. Furthermore, if they should launch out of order, then when the store which is first in program-sequential order retires, the reorder queue is flushed and instruction fetch is restarted at that instruction. The LLO coalesces memory accesses [13], i.e., it combines subword store sequences into word or even doubleword stores when it can determine that the associated data alignment is appropriate. Also, runtime library routines were coded to use as wide an access as possible.

Exploiting PA-8000 Instruction Set Extensions

PA 2.0 is the first 64-bit member of the PA-RISC family. Until the introduction of PA 2.0, 64-bit data items consumed two registers and operations on those items was handled via millicode calls. On PA 2.0, 64-bit data items can be kept in a single register and operations on those items can be performed inline.

PA-RISC integer load and store operations support 14-bit immediate offsets, but prior to PA 2.0, floating point load and store operations only provided 5-bit immediate offsets. The PA 2.0 instruction set extended the offsets on floating point memory operations to match those on integer memory operations. Use of the wider offsets results in tighter code sequences and, in particular, in improved register reassociation.

The shift amount register (sar) is a 6-bit control register which is used by the variable versions of the shift, extract, deposit, and branch-on-bit instructions. For members of the PA-RISC family introduced before PA 2.0, the following code sequence was produced for 32-bit signed integer "z = x << y":

```
SUBI      -1,y,temp  !1s cmplt for DEPW bitpos
MTSAR     temp       !Move temp to sar
DEPW,Z    x,sar,32,z !Bits #d most to least signf
```

and for "z = x >> y":

```
SUBI      -1,y,temp  !1s cmpl for EXTRW bitpos
MTSAR     temp       !Move temp to sar
EXTRW,S   x,sar,32,z !Bits #d most to least signft
```

The PA 2.0 ISA introduced MTSARCM (move ones complement to sar), which allows shorter idioms; for 32-bit signed integer "z = x << y", the PA 2.0 code is:

```
MTSARCM y
DEPW,Z    x,sar,32,z
```

and for "z = x >> y", the PA 2.0 code is:

```
MTSARCM y
EXTRW,S   x,sar,32,z
```

PA-RISC floating point comparisons set a compare bit (C-bit) in the floating point status register. Prior to the advent of PA 2.0, there was a single C-bit; PA 2.0 introduced multiple C-bits. The instruction scheduler utilizes multiple C-bits to hide latency, in sequences involving several independent code streams containing if-conversion.

FMPYFADD and FMPYNFADD are PA 2.0 instructions which implement floating point multiply and accumulate operations. These instructions take 4 operands, rb, ra, rd, and rc; FMPYFADD produces rc = rd + (rb * ra) and FMPYNFADD produces rc = rd - (rb * ra). On the PA-8000, each of the floating point instructions FMPYFADD, FMPYNFADD, FMPY, FADD, and FSUB takes the same number of cycles, so it is profitable to combine an FMPY-FADD or an FMPY-FSUB sequence into a single FMPYFADD or FMPYNFADD instruction. These instructions are synthesized for the PA-8000 target during the first instruction scheduling phase,[1] as explained in [5]. Several situations are considered. The most straightforward case is when the result of an FMPY is used only once, by an FADD or as the subtrahend of an FSUB; this substitution is essentially a peephole transformation. More complicated is the case when both operands of an FADD are distinct FMPYs; this involves a choice as to which of the two FMPYs should be included in the substitution. The PA-8000 instruction scheduler chooses to reduce the number of instructions on the code's critical path by selecting the FMPY with the longer path from the root nodes (the nodes near the start of the basic block). Another case is when a single FMPY feeds into two FADDs. Two FMPYFADDs are generated, unless the associated extension of the original FMPY's operands' live ranges engenders too much register pressure, in which case no transformation is performed. Finally, when a single FMPY feeds an FADD or FSUB eligible for synthesis, but there are other consumers of the FMPY result, the FMPY is duplicated and the FMPYFADD or FMPYNFADD is generated as appropriate; this shortens the path length to the result of the FMPY-FADD or FMPYNFADD, even though the total number of operations remains the same.

Two Target Operation Avoidance

Memory access instructions that specify base register modification produce two results. Thus, they occupy two slots in the reorder queue: one in the memory queue, to represent the memory reference itself, and the other in the ALU queue, to represent the base register modification operation. The retirement of these two parts of the original instruction must be coordinated to ensure exceptions are processed correctly. Hence, on the PA-8000, using two separate instructions to access memory and to perform address arithmetic consumes no more slots in the reorder queue than using a single base modification instruction (and may consume fewer slots if the address arithmetic operation can in turn be folded with another instruction). In addition, the former sequence allows more flexibility in retirement than the latter. Base modification memory access instructions are avoided for the PA-8000 target.

The FMPYADD instruction takes 5 operands, rm1, rm2, tm, ra, ta, and produces two (independent) results: 1) tm = rm1 * rm2, and 2) ta = ta + ra. FMPYSUB is similar, but computes ta = ta - ra. As was the case with the base-modifying memory access instructions, two slots in the reorder queue are used to handle the output of these two operations and the retirement of the two slots is coordinated. However, the insertion of these instructions into the reorder queue is more complicated than the insertion of base-modifying instructions. In each cycle, each queue is capable of

---

1. The generation of similar instructions (FMAs) is handled by the front-end of IBM's RS/6000 compiler, rather than by its optimizer. This approach allows FMAs to be produced even when optimization is not enabled, but may have difficulty recognizing certain situations in which FMAs can be employed and making trade-offs with respect to critical path when there is a choice concerning where to introduce an FMA.

accepting up to four instructions for insertion; depending on how many ALU operations there are in the instruction quad containing one or more FMPYADD or FMPYSUB operations, the complete quad may not be insertable in the same cycle. FMPYADD and FMPYSUB instructions are not generated for the PA-8000 target.

2.4 General Optimization Enhancements

The PA-RISC LLO is a mature component, including a wide range of global optimizations. The following general techniques were introduced in its 10.2 release.

Type-inferred aliasing

Type-inferred aliasing is an aggressive model of aliasing, in which a pointer is assumed to reference only objects of the type to which it is declared to point. The use of type-inferred aliasing, specified by an option, improves code by eliminating false dependencies, which can interfere with various optimizations including instruction scheduling and scalar replacement. The LLO aliaser [11] was extended to divide address-exposed objects into groups according to their type, and to assume that pointer dereferences alias only with address-exposed objects of the pointer's target type (and with dereferences of other pointers of its exact same type).[1] Not all codes are written in such a way that type-inferred aliasing can be applied; hence, several weaker models of aggressive aliasing are also supported. The user can indicate that type-inferred aliasing only applies to certain data types. He/she may request ANSI aliasing, which performs aliasing according to ANSI C rules, i.e., a "char *" pointer may point to any object that is the same size as or wider than a character, while any other kind of pointer only accesses objects of its specified type. Particular global variables can be declared as not address-exposed and particular pointers can be declared as unique (meaning that they do not alias with any other pointers); this information is difficult for the compiler to derive automatically. Type-inferred aliasing proved valuable in achieving peak performance on the PA-8000.

Scalar Replacement

Scalar replacement is a technique in which subscripted variables that are reused in innermost loops are assigned to scalar temporaries to facilitate their allocation to registers [7]. The PA-RISC LLO also applies the technique to loops with control flow [8] and to non-innermost loops. In addition, the LLO scalar-replaces non-subscripted variables, including structure field references and references through pointers, and uses the technique to provide a general framework for loop-duration promotion of scalar variables whose complete lifetimes do not warrant register promotion [17]. Conditional references are scalar-replaced, if the relevant address expression can be proven safe in its unconditional setting, subject to profitability. Scalar replacement is also applied to recurrent memory references, after which predictive commoning [36] is used to remove recurrent common subexpressions and to optionally perform recurrent FDIV weakening. Loop unrolling allows the associated copies in the loop body to be removed.

While performing scalar replacement, the LLO register-promotes the scalar temporary; register pressure heuristics are used to avoid over-allocation. Several transformations are applied in association with the register promotion. If an item with a loop invariant address is scalar-replaced and its reuse set within the loop begins with an unconditional store, then the scalar load which would usually be placed in the loop header is not materialized; similarly, if an item with a loop variant address is scalar-replaced and its reuse set within the loop begins with an unconditional store, then all associated loads located in the loop body are deleted. A loop variant reuse set is usually not scalar-replaced if the first load or last store is conditional; however, a reuse set containing a conditional first load is transformed if preceded by an unconditional store, and a reuse set containing a conditional last store is transformed if an unconditional store can safely and profitably be inserted at the end of the loop.

Note that scalar replacement can have beneficial effects on the PA-8000 which are somewhat indirectly associated with register promotion. If a load is launched out-of-order before a store to the same address then, when the store retires, entries in the reorder queue are purged and instructions following the store are refetched. (This scenario is only likely when the store is located in a potentially nullified slot and the following load is not.) Since the LLO's scalar replacement can register-promote in this situation, this expensive sequence is averted.

Shrink-Wrapping

The shrink-wrapping transformation migrates callee-saves registers' save and restore operations, which would normally be executed in a subprogram's prolog and epilog, respectively, to cheaper locations in the subprogram [10]. This transformation is intended to reduce the overhead associated with a subprogram call and is applied optionally, since it can interfere with register restoration during stack unwinding. In studying various codes, it was discovered that Chow's shrink-wrapping technique could not be applied for certain subroutines that might seem to contain "natural" shrink wrap opportunities, characterized by quick conditional exit paths. Analysis of the situation revealed that the control structure of many subroutines did not provide any pair of blocks surrounding a register's lifetime (other than the entry and exit blocks) with a suitable dominating, postdominating, control-equivalent relationship into which to migrate the prolog and epilog saves and restores. An original technique termed split-exit shrink-wrapping, which revises a subprogram's control structure by rewiring early exits to allow shrink wrapping to be applied, was devised.

1. A pointer of type "void *" needs to be type-cast into a pointer of a specific type before it can be dereferenced; type-inferred aliasing uses these type-cast operations to determine which objects may alias with each "void *" pointer.

3 PA-8000 High Level Optimization

The PA-RISC High Level Optimizer (HLO) handles transformations which depend on a high semantic level intermediate representation of the input code and/or on cross-procedure or cross-module processing. Such transformations include inlining, cloning, whole program analysis, parallelization, vectorization, loop interchange, and loop fusion. For the various implementations of the PA 1.0 and PA 1.1 architectures, the HLO was essentially machine-independent; however, for the PA-8000, the HLO's operation was influenced by machine-specific considerations.

3.1 Inlining

Inlining, in which a subprogram call is replaced by a copy of the callee's body with suitable substitutions for parameters and conflicting identifiers [12], improves performance on models across the PA-RISC family. However, it is particularly effective on the PA-8000, and heuristics governing its application were tuned accordingly. Not only does the PA-8000 have a large instruction cache, but also the subroutine return branch, which is indirect through a register, is not predicted on the PA-8000. Calls through pointers, which are also register indirect and not predicted, are potential bottlenecks as well. The HLO uses a combination of caller/callee site matching and profiling information to introduce a runtime test against the address of an indirect call's likely target, to choose between making the call and executing an inlined version of the recognized target. In addition, aggressive inlining yields benefits which compare favorably vis a vis interprocedural analysis in terms of facilitating other optimizations [39]; in some cases, significant speed ups were realized on the PA-8000 by flattening entire call trees.

3.2 Cache-Related Transformations

The HLO performs two categories of cache-related transformations: those intended to enhance locality and those intended to reduce various kinds of conflicts. Using the loop transformation framework described in [33], the HLO enhances locality by interchanging loops to place stride one accesses in the innermost loop. Loop fusion sometimes serves to improve locality as well. The PA-8000 uses a direct-mapped caching scheme, and cache conflicts between data items used in close temporal proximity occur in some codes. The HLO, under a user option, will attempt to reduce cache conflicts by inserting padding between items stored adjacently, so as to modify their addresses appropriately. In addition, the PA-8000's data cache is non-blocking; miss requests for up to ten distinct cache lines can be outstanding at a given time and cache misses which map to different banks are handled with less latency than those which map to the same bank. The HLO can also insert padding to reduce memory bank conflicts.

3.3 Latency-Related Loop Optimizations

Several HLO loop optimizations which consider latency were particularly important for PA-8000 performance. Vectorization of reduction loops increased the ILP available for exploitation by the PA-8000. A reduction is an operation that computes a scalar value from an array; a reduction loop is serialized with respect to accesses to that scalar value. However, if the operation is associative, it can be vectorized by computing separate scalar values for subpartitions of the array & then combining those values appropriately to compute the final scalar value [2]. HLO recognizes certain reduction loops and replaces them with calls to vectorized library routines.

Another key latency-related HLO loop transformation was loop interchange to make long latency operations loop invariant. For example, in the following code, the divisor varies in the inner loop.

```
      DO 10 J=1,N
            DO 10 I=1,M
10                X(I,J) = X(I,J) - (Z/Y(I))
```

However, if the loop were interchanged, then the divisor would become inner loop invariant, and the division could be moved out of the inner loop, reducing the number of long latency divisions done overall. Note that this motivation for loop interchange may conflict with that of enhancing spatial locality; in this example, interchanging will move stride one accesses out of the inner loop.

4 Performance

The authors chose to report performance with respect to the SPEC95 benchmarks, since these codes are widely available and familiar to many. The PA-8000 base optimization results for SPEC95 are given in the table below, along with key competitors' results. Note that as of third quarter 1996, the PA-8000 leads in both integer and floating point SPEC95 base performance. Optimization contributes strongly to the PA-8000's results; legacy binaries built for the PA-7200 achieve 7.8 SPECint95 and 9.0 SPECfp95 when run on the PA-8000.

SPEC95BASE	INT	FP
HP PA-8000 180MHz	10.8	18.3
Digital 21164A 400MHz	9.8	12.8
SGI R10000 200MHz	8.1	10.5
Sun Ultrasparc 200MHz	6.9	13.3

This paper has focused on the effect of compiler optimizations on performance, but many other factors contributed directly to the PA-8000's SPEC95 results, including the chip and system designs, the runtime library, the front-ends, the intermediate code generator, the linker, and the operating system. Indirect contributions are too numerous to enumerate, but one that deserves special mention is that of the performance simulator. The complexity of this machine made compile-time estimations of performance obsolete, and made accurate simulation crucial to determining the efficacy of optimizing transformations. Simulation measurements exposed critical tuning opportunities and brought to light counterintuitive attributes of code behavior. In addition, once prototype hardware was available, the on-chip performance monitoring functionality was very useful as well.

Note that legacy codes will suffer lost performance opportunity. Codes not recompiled with the 10.2 optimizer will not benefit from the optimizations introduced for that version, which include loop unrolling, superblock formation, assertion propagation, enhanced if-conversion, switch statement improvements, extended strength reduction, tree height reduction, memory coalescing, type-inferred aliasing, improved scalar replacement, shrink wrapping, and more. In addition, code not targeted for the PA-8000 may contain PA-8000 hazards, such as latency-based scheduling, store load dependence, FDIV/FSQRT polarity conflicts, nullified delay slot penalties, single precision floating point false dependence, and two target operations. More importantly, code not targeted for the PA-8000 will not exploit PA-8000 features, including extended static branch prediction hinting, data cache prefetching, FMPY-FADD/FMPYNFADD, multiple C bits, 64-bit integer support, long displacement floating point loads and stores, MTSARCM, etc.

5 Conclusion

The synergy between innovative hardware and aggressive optimization yields PA-8000's industry-leading performance. As has been suggested is the case for superscalar out-of-order machines [28], optimizing for procedural dependencies had a substantial impact on performance. Developing appropriate heuristics for such optimizations was challenging. Optimizing for true dependencies was more important than expected for this machine, given that it has a larger reorder queue than any other microprocessor in the marketplace. Optimizing for resource conflicts was important as well, despite the fact that the machine has a generous number of processing units and registers. High level optimization was influenced by machine-specific considerations.

6 Acknowledgments

Thanks to the anonymous reviewers for providing useful comments. The optimizations described in this paper (and more!) were implemented in the 10.2 release of the PA-RISC compilers by the low-level and high-level optimization teams. These teams were skillfully managed by Sridhar Ramakrishnan and Richard Schooler; the team members included Andy Ayers, Ricky Benitez, Bill Blume, Carl Burch, Dave Dunn, Eddie Gornish, Bob Gottlieb, Anne Holler, Wei-Chung Hsu, Jim Mattson, Adam Matusiak, Krishna Reddy, Lacky Shah, and others whose work we took credit for when they moved to other projects.

7 References

[1] Allen, J.R., Kennedy, K., Porterfield, C., and Warren, J., "Conversion of Control Dependence to Data Dependence", *POPL*, January 1983.

[2] Bacon, D., Graham, S., and Sharp, O., "Compiler Transformations for High-Performance Computing", *ACM Computing Surveys*, Vol. 26, No. 4, December 1994.

[3] Benitez, Manuel, "Exploiting Conditional Nullification on the PA-8000", *HP Technical Report*, 1996.

[4] Blume, W. and Eigenmann, R., "Symbolic Range Propagation", *Proceedings of the 9th International Parallel Processing Symposium*, April 1995.

[5] Blume, W., "Effective Floating Point Multiply Fused Add Code Generation", *HP Technical Report*, 1996.

[6] Burch, Carl, "PA-8000: A Case Study of Static and Dynamic Branch Prediction", *HP Technical Report*, 1996.

[7] Callahan, D. Carr, S., and Kennedy, K., "Improving Register Allocation for Subscripted Variables", *PLDI*, June 1990.

[8] Carr, S. and Kennedy, K., "Scalar Replacement in the Presence of Conditional Control Flow", *Software - Practice and Experience*, January 1994.

[9] Chang, P.P., Mahlke, S.A., and Hwu, W.-M., "Using Profile Information to Assist Classic Code Optimizations", *Software - Practice and Experience*, Vol. 21, December 1991.

[10] Chow, F.C., "Minimizing Register Usage Penalty at Procedure Calls", *PLDI*, June 1988.

[11] Coutant, D.S., "Retargetable High-Level Alias Analysis", *POPL*, January 1986.

[12] Davidson, J. and Holler, A., "Subprogram Inlining: A Study of its Effects on Program Execution Time", *IEEE Transactions on Software Engineering*, Vol. 18, No. 2, 1992.

[13] Davidson, J. and Jinturkar, S., "Memory Access Coalescing: A Technique for Eliminating Redundant Memory Accesses", *PLDI*, June 1994.

[14] Dehnert, J.C., Hsu, P.Y.-T., Bratt, J.P., "Overlapped Loop Support on the Cydra 5", *ASPLOS*, April 1989.

[15] Dongarra, J.J., and Hinds, A.R., "Unrolling Loops in FORTRAN", *Software - Practice and Experience*, Vol. 9, No. 3, 1979.

[16] Dunn, D.A. and Hsu, W.-C., "Instruction Scheduling for the HP PA-8000", *MICRO-29*, December 1996.

[17] Ebcioglu, K., Groves, R.D., Kim, K., Silberman, G.M., and Ziv, I., "VLIW Compilation Techniques in a Superscalar Environment", *PLDI*, June 1994.

[18] Fisher, J.A., "Trace Scheduling: A Technique for Global Microcode Compaction", *IEEE Transactions on Computers*, C-30, 7, July 1981.

[19] Gornish, E., "Data Prefetching on the HP PA-8000", *HP Technical Report*, 1996.

[20] Gwennap, Linley, "PA-8000 Combines Complexity and Speed", *Microprocessor Report*, November 14, 1994.

[21] Hanson, R., "New Optimizations for PA-RISC Compilers", *Hewlett-Packard Journal*, June 1992.

[22] Harrison, W., "Compiler Analysis of the Value Ranges for Variables", *IEEE Transactions on Software Engineering*, SE-3(3), May 1977.

[23] Hennessy, J. and Patterson, D., *Computer Architecture: A Quantitative Approach*, 2nd ed., Morgan Kaufmann Publishers, Inc., San Francisco, CA, 1996.

[24] *HP PA-RISC Compiler Optimization Technology White Paper*, HP Part No. 5963-7250E, March 1995.

[25] Hunt, Doug, "Advanced Performance Features of the 64-bit PA-8000", *COMPCON 1995 Digest of Papers*, March 1995.

[26] Hwu, W.W., et. al., "The Superblock: an Effective Technique

for VLIW and Superscalar Compilation", *The Journal of Supercomputing*, 7(1,2), 1993.

[27] Jain, Suneel and Thompson, Carol, "An Efficient Approach to Data Flow Analysis in a Multiple Pass Global Optimizer", *PLDI*, June 1988.

[28] Johnson, M., *Superscalar Microprocessor Design*, Prentice-Hall, Englewood Cliffs, NJ, 1991.

[29] Johnson, M.S. and Miller, T.C., "Effectiveness of a Machine-Level, Global Optimizer", *Symposium on Compiler Construction*, June 1986.

[30] Kane, Gerry, *PA-RISC 2.0 Architecture*, Prentice-Hall, Englewood Cliffs, NJ, 1996.

[31] Kerns, D.R. and Eggers, S.J., "Balanced Scheduling: Instruction Scheduling when Memory Latency is Uncertain", *PLDI*, June 1993.

[32] Kuck, D.J., *The Structure of Computers and Computations*, Wiley, New York, 1978.

[33] Li, W., "Compiling for NUMA Parallel Machines", *Ph.D. Thesis*, Cornell, 1993.

[34] "Chart Watch: RISC Processors", *Microprocessor Report*, January 22, 1996.

[35] Mowry, T.C., Lam, M.S., and Gupta, A., "Design and Evaluation of a Compiler Algorithm for Prefetching", *ASPLOS*, 1992.

[36] O'Brien, K., Hay, B., Minish, J., Schaffer, H., Schloss, B., Shepherd, A. Zaleski, M. "Advanced Compiler Technology for the RISC System/6000 Architecture", IBM, 1991.

[37] Pettis, Karl and Hansen, Robert, "Profile Guided Code Positioning", *PLDI*, June 1990.

[38] Ramakrishnan, Sridhar, "Software Pipelining in PA-RISC Compilers", *Hewlett-Packard Journal*, June 1992.

[39] Richardson, S. and Ganapathi, M., "Interprocedural Analysis vs. Procedure Integration", *Information Processing Letters*, Vol. 32, 1989.

[40] Santhanam, Vatsa, "Register Reassociation in PA-RISC Compilers", *Hewlett-Packard Journal*, June 1992.

[41] Shah, Lacky, "Intelligent Loop Unrolling", *HP Technical Report*, 1996.

Optimization of Machine Descriptions for Efficient Use

John C. Gyllenhaal Wen-mei W. Hwu
Center for Reliable and High-Performance Computing
University of Illinois, Urbana-Champaign, IL 61801
gyllen, hwu@crhc.uiuc.edu

B. Ramakrishna Rau
Hewlett Packard Laboratories
1501 Page Mill Road, Palo Alto, CA 94304
rau@hpl.hp.com

Abstract

A machine description facility allows compiler writers to specify machine execution constraints to the optimization and scheduling phases of an instruction-level parallelism (ILP) optimizing compiler. The machine description (MDES) facility should support quick development and easy maintenance of machine execution constraint descriptions by compiler writers. However, the facility should also allow compact representation and efficient usage of the MDES during compilation. This paper advocates a model that allows compiler writers to develop the MDES in a high-level language, which is then translated into a low-level representation for efficient use by the compiler. The discrepancy between the requirements of the high-level language and the low-level representation is reconciled with a collection of transformations that derive efficient low-level representations from the easy-to-understand high-level descriptions. In order to support these transformations, a novel approach to representing machine execution constraints has been developed. Detailed and precise descriptions of the execution constraints for the HP PA7100, Intel Pentium, Sun SuperSPARC, and AMD-K5 processors are analyzed to show the advantage of using this new representation. The results show that performing these transformations and utilizing the new representation allow easy-to-maintain detailed descriptions written in high-level languages to be efficiently used by ILP-optimizing compilers.

1. Introduction

Machine descriptions (MDES) have been used to specify execution constraints for several high-performance compilers [1][2]. These machine descriptions are primarily used to drive the instruction scheduler, which uses this information to avoid resource conflicts and data dependence interlocks. However, in future compilers more compiler modules will also need to use MDES information. As compilers push to increase the performance of processors by exploiting instruction-level parallelism (ILP), transformations such as predication and height reduction also need to use execution constraints to avoid over-subscription of processor resources[1]. Currently most compiler modules, including some schedulers, forgo the use of a machine description altogether and instead rely on heuristic "knobs" and algorithmic changes to tune for a specific processor. This is due, in part, to the difficulties involved in providing these modules with access to an accurate machine description, in a form they can efficiently use.

Since each scheduling decision, and potentially each optimization decision, for every operation involves checking execution constraints, the efficiency of such checks can significantly impact the compile time. As a result, compiler writers have faced the choice between two undesirable alternatives. One alternative is to sacrifice portability for accuracy. A compiler designed for a particular processor often uses an accurate, very low-level representation of the machine's description (commonly coded directly into the compiler), that must be tediously modified in order to be effective for subsequent processors. This approach is not desirable in the highly competitive microprocessor industry, where complex new processors are being rapidly designed and brought to the market. Timely development of effective compilers for these new processors is critical to the realization of their full performance potential.

The other alternative is to sacrifice accuracy in favor of portability. Compilers designed to support a wide range of processors, such as gcc, usually describe the machine to their instruction schedulers with easy-to-modify metrics, such as the function unit mix and operation latencies, but these metrics can only approximately model the complex execution constraints in today's superscalar processors. Inaccurate modeling of execution constraints during compilation makes it difficult for the compiler to properly address run-time issues such as resource conflicts and data dependence interlocks. As a result, unexpected execution cycles arise during run time. In processors that exploit high degrees of instruction-level parallelism (ILP), these extra execution cycles can have a significant effect on the overall performance. Accurate modeling of execution constraints is therefore necessary in order to properly utilize these complex processors.

The possibility of using a generic, high-quality scheduler and ILP optimizer driven by an MDES that can be quickly targeted to a new processor is attractive. This paper advocates a model which allows writers to develop an MDES in a high-level language, which is then translated into a low-level representation for efficient use by the compiler. The high-level language should be designed to allow the specification of detailed execution constraints in an easy-to-understand, maintainable, and retargetable manner. The low-level representation should be designed to allow the compiler to check execution constraints with high efficiency in both space and time. The discrepancy

[1] Although this paper will focus on modeling resource constraints, machine descriptions also contain other important information such as operation latencies, the modeling of bypassing and forwarding effects, and the mapping of this information to specific operations based on their opcode and the type of operands expected.

1072-4451/96 $5.00 © 1996 IEEE

between the requirements of the high-level language and the low-level representation should then be reconciled with a collection of transformations that derive efficient low-level representations from the easy-to-understand high-level descriptions.

The two-tier model is analogous to using high-level programming languages now that contemporary compiler technology has eliminated the benefits of using assembly language for general purpose programs. The user of a high-level machine description language is not required to be intimately familiar with modules using the machine description, and does not need to manually optimize the description for those modules. In fact, a few of the transformations described in this paper are adapted from the classical compiler techniques that helped make high-level programming languages so well accepted. There are, however, important transformations introduced in this paper that have no direct correspondence in the optimizing compiler domain. These transformations take advantage of the unique characteristics of an MDES to increase the efficiency of the resulting low-level representation.

In addition to describing and evaluating the transformations, a novel representation of resource constraints for complex processors is presented. This representation exposes critical information that can be profitably exploited by both these transformations and the compiler modules. This approach to representing machine execution constraints is based on the AND/OR-tree concept used in search algorithms. In order to show the effectiveness of the new representation and transformations, detailed and precise descriptions of the execution constraints for the HP PA7100, Intel Pentium, Sun SuperSPARC, and AMD-K5 processors are constructed in a high-level language. The low-level representation of these descriptions is then generated and used to drive a multi-platform list scheduler. Using a scheduler for the concrete evaluation of these transformations allows the rationale behind and the effect of each transformation to be clearly shown. Similar benefits should be seen by other compiler modules that can benefit from using an accurate machine description.

Although a specific high-level machine description language [3], low-level representation [4], multi-platform compiler [5], and multi-platform list scheduler [6] are being used to validate these techniques, the aim of this paper is to show the general applicability of these techniques, not to proselytize the specific components used. Concepts key to understanding the example and results will be briefly explained, but these explanations will only describe some of the above components' capabilities, and the interested reader is referred to the papers and reports that deal directly with these components.

A description and analysis of a common mechanism used to model resource constraints, which is used by this paper's machine descriptions, follows this section. A new representation of these resource constraints is introduced in Section 3, and is shown to be well suited for describing today's complex processors. An analysis of each MDES, before any transformations are performed, is presented in Section 4. In Section 5, the importance of adapting common-subexpression elimination, copy propagation, and dead-code removal to clean up machine descriptions is shown, as well as how the new representation facilitates these transformations. Section 6 provides a brief overview of the implications of using bit-vectors in the low-level

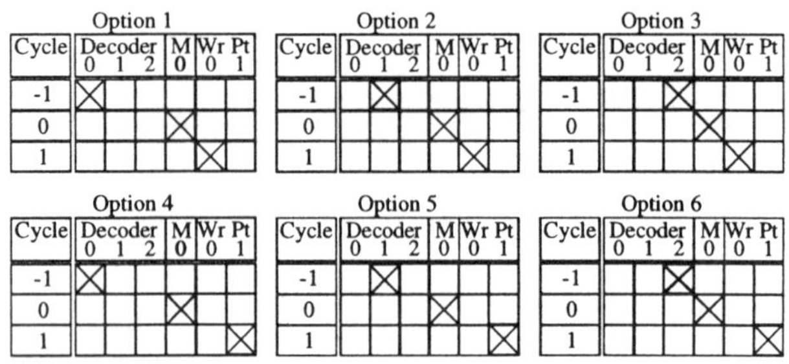

Figure 1: The six reservation tables that represent the resources used by the SuperSPARC's integer load operation.

representation of resource constraints in order to set the stage for the Section 7, which describes transformations that make the bit-vector representations more effective. Section 8 describes and analyzes a set of transformations which makes checking resource constraints more efficient. Section 9 summarizes the aggregate effect of all these transformations, with and without the new representation. In Section 10, a brief summary of related work is presented and is followed by some concluding remarks.

2. Modeling Resource Constraints

This paper's machine descriptions model the processor's resource constraints through the use of a set of *reservation tables* [7], an approach used by several high-performance MDES-driven compilers [1][2]. In particular, this paper's machine descriptions are based on the approach used by the Cydra 5 [1]. Each reservation table specifies a particular way an operation may use a processor's resources as that operation executes. For example, the resources used by the execution of a SuperSPARC's one-cycle integer load can be modeled with the six reservation tables (each called a *reservation table option*, or simply an *option*) that are shown in Figure 1. An integer load must use the SuperSPARC's only memory unit (M), but may use any of the three decoders (Decoder) and two register write ports (Wr Pt). The register read ports for the address generation unit are dedicated and do not need to be modeled. All option lists are prioritized (option 1 having highest priority), so for the order shown in this figure, the first available (lowest numbered) decoder and register write port will be used by the integer load. The "Cycle" column of these tables indicates the *usage time*, which indicates when each of these resources is used, relative to some chosen time point in the processor's pipeline. For all the examples and machine descriptions used in this paper, the point chosen to be time "zero" is the first stage of the execution pipeline. Therefore resources used during decoder stages have negative usage times, and resources used after execution completes, such as result buses and register write ports, have usage times around the operation's latency. A resource used at a particular usage time will be referred to as a *resource usage*. It should be noted that the resources modeled often do not represent actual processor resources, but are abstractions used to model the processor's scheduling rules. This approach was used in the construction of the machine descriptions used in this paper. These machine descriptions were designed to accurately

Number of Options	% of Scheduling Attempts	Operations Modeled
1	13.41%	Branches and serial ops
3	0.72%	Floating-point ops
6	14.37%	Load ops
12	4.92%	Store ops
24	9.24%	Shifts and cascaded IALU ops that use 1 read port
36	3.00%	Shifts and cascaded IALU ops that use 2 read ports
48	50.29%	IALU ops that use 1 read port
72	4.05%	IALU ops that use 2 read ports

Table 1: Option breakdown and scheduling characteristics for the SuperSPARC MDES.

and precisely model the processor's scheduling rules, and intuitive resource names were used solely to enhance the clarity of the machine descriptions.

Many of this paper's examples are drawn from the SuperSPARC MDES, so a brief and somewhat simplified overview of the SuperSPARC's execution constraints is necessary before continuing. The SuperSPARC [8] is an in-order superscalar processor that has three full decoders, four integer register read ports (RP), two integer register write ports, two integer ALU (IALU) units, one barrel shifter, one memory unit with a dedicated address generation unit, one branch unit, and support for one floating-point operation per cycle. The address generation unit and the floating-point function units have dedicated register ports which do not need to be modeled, but it is important to model the usage of the SuperSPARC's integer register read and write ports. All of the common integer operations have a one cycle latency, and the load operations also have a one cycle latency. However, load and store operations can cause address generation interlocks if they are not scheduled properly.

The SuperSPARC's design also allows the execution of two flow-dependent IALU operations in the same cycle. The second IALU operation, which utilizes this feature to execute a cycle early, is referred to as a *cascaded* IALU operation. The number of reservation table options required to model an IALU operation depends on the number of register source operands that the operation has. A non-cascaded IALU operation with one register source may use any one of the decoders, read ports, IALU units, and write ports, yielding $\binom{3}{1}\binom{4}{1}\binom{2}{1}\binom{2}{1}=48$ distinct combinations of these resource usages. The same non-cascaded IALU operation with two register sources, requiring two read ports, has $\binom{3}{1}\binom{4}{2}\binom{2}{1}\binom{2}{1}=72$ distinct combinations of resource usages. Each of these distinct combinations of resource usages is modeled by a reservation table option. There is only one IALU available to execute cascaded IALU operations, so cascaded IALU operations only have half the reservation table options of non-cascaded IALU operations. The appropriate set of reservation table options is chosen based on an operation's incoming dependence distances.

A breakdown of the number of reservation table options used to model the various operations in the SuperSPARC MDES is shown in Table 1. This first column specifies the number of scheduling options. The second column indicates the percentage of the time that a multi-platform list scheduler, driven by

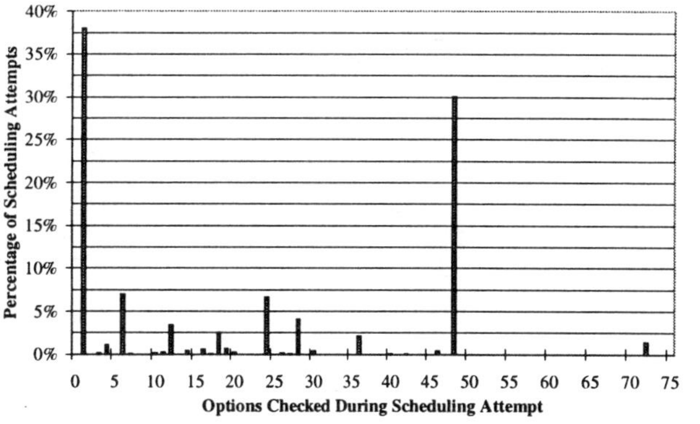

Figure 2: Distribution of options checked during each scheduling attempt using the SuperSPARC MDES.

this MDES and scheduling SuperSPARC SPEC CINT92 assembly code, attempted to schedule an operation with that many options during prepass scheduling. The last column gives a brief summary of the types of operation that have that many options. Note that for the SuperSPARC and the PA7100 MDES, branches are modeled as always using the last decoder in order to maximize scheduling freedom (since nothing may issue after a branch on these machines).

Although all of the reservation table options must be tested in order to determine that an operation cannot be scheduled, a variable number of the options need to be tested in order to determine that the operation can be scheduled. Figure 2 shows the distribution of options actually checked while scheduling for the SuperSPARC. On average, 2.05 scheduling attempts were required per operation, so roughly half of the time a scheduling attempt fails. The 30.05% peak at 48 options checked is primarily due to the fact that 58.50% of unsuccessful scheduling attempts were on operations with 48 options. Overall, 45.52% of the scheduling attempts required between 24 and 72 options to be checked. The 38.02% peak for one scheduling option checked is due mainly to scheduling attempts that succeed with the first option attempted. For successful scheduling attempts, 73.75% succeed with the first option tested, 8.23% tested between 2 and 16 options, 16.71% tested between 17 and 32 options, and 1.31% tested more than 33 options.

In the following sections, transformations will be presented that make testing each option nearly as efficient as possible. However, unless the number of options checked can be reduced, modeling complex machines exactly will remain expensive in terms of compile time. A new representation, presented in the next section, can dramatically reduce the number of options checked in complex machine descriptions.

3. A New Representation: AND/OR-Trees

The primary reason so many options need to be checked for complex processor descriptions is that the traditional representation for resource constraints hides useful information from the compiler. By exposing this useful information with the new representation presented below, the compiler can more efficiently check the resource constraints. This representation can also inherently reduce the MDES size (Section 4), facilitate size-reducing transformations (Section 5), and facilitate transformations to further optimize for resource conflict detection

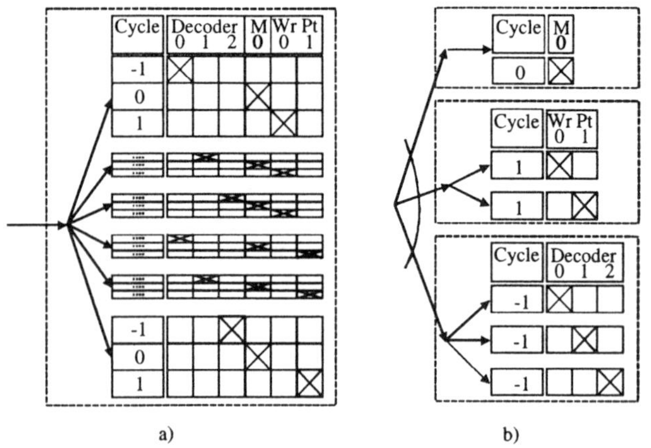

Figure 3: Two methods of modeling the resource constraints of a SuperSPARC integer load operation. a) The traditional OR-Tree representation. b) The proposed AND/OR-Tree representation.

(Section 8). Before describing this new representation, a brief review of the traditional representation is in order.

The traditional representation can be viewed as an OR-Tree, as shown in Figure 3a. This figure shows the six reservation table options for the SuperSPARC integer load (the same options that are shown in Figure 1). The options are in priority order (with the highest priority first), and if the resources for any of the options are available, the operation can be scheduled. The advantage of this representation is that for OR-trees with a small number of options, the OR-tree's resource constraints can be quickly and efficiently checked. For processors which have execution constraints that can be modeled with just a few reservation table options, it is difficult to improve upon the efficiency of this OR-tree representation.

The disadvantage of this OR-tree representation is that it does not allow an easy or efficient way of using information about why an option was not available. For example, if Option 1 (the top option) in Figure 3a is unavailable because write port 0 (Wr Pt 0) is unavailable, then Options 2 and 3 are also guaranteed to be unavailable. Although an inference engine could be programmed into the resource constraint check algorithm to eliminate these options, the overhead would more than negate the benefit.

The solution proposed in this paper is to use a new representation that is based on the AND/OR-tree concept used in search algorithms. This new representation is, in essence, an AND-tree of OR-trees, allowing multiple OR-trees to be used together in order to represent the resource constraints. An example of this new AND/OR-tree representation is shown in Figure 3b. The AND/OR-tree shown specifies the resource requirements for the SuperSPARC's integer load as requiring the memory unit(M), one of the two write ports (Wr Pt), and one of the three decoders. By utilizing the short-circuit properties of AND and OR, the resource constraint check algorithm can quickly determine which of the required resources are available (or if they are not available), without performing any unnecessary checks.

The algorithm overhead incurred by using this new representation is minimal, since it is built upon the OR-tree representation and does not require any new information from the OR-tree resource constraint checker (i.e. which option, if any, is available). In Figure 3, each of the OR-trees, which are enclosed in dotted boxes, can have the same internal representation and may have the same resource constraint checker algorithm applied to them. The compiler used for this paper's experiments does so and, for implementation efficiency, adds an outer loop around the OR-tree's algorithm that processes the array of OR-trees associated with an AND/OR-tree. Although some additional space is required to represent the AND-level of the tree, the use of AND/OR-trees can significantly reduce the size of the resource constraint description in the MDES, as shown in Section 4.

4. Original MDES Characteristics

In this paper, detailed and precise descriptions of the execution constraints for the HP PA7100, Intel Pentium, Sun SuperSPARC, and AMD-K5 are analyzed to show the rationale behind the transformations presented in the following sections and the advantages of using the AND/OR-tree representation. For this analysis, each of these machine descriptions is used to drive a multi-platform list scheduler, which is then used to schedule SPEC CINT92 assembly code for that platform. Each platform's assembly code (between 201011 and 282219 static operations) was generated using the level of profile-driven inlining, classical optimization, ILP optimization, and peephole optimization that had been found, through extensive tuning, to yield the highest possible execution-time performance for that platform[2]. The analysis also focused on prepass scheduling for the SuperSPARC and PA7100, and on postpass scheduling for the Pentium and K5. Prepass scheduling was not performed for the X86 processors due to the limited number of registers available. The SuperSPARC was described in Section 2, and the reservation table option breakdown of its machine description was shown in Table 1. A brief description of the other processors modeled, and their reservation table option breakdowns, is in order before analyzing the original characteristics of each MDES.

The PA7100 [9] is an in-order superscalar processor that has two decoders, and supports executing one floating-point operation in parallel to an integer or memory operation. The relative order of these two operations does not matter, so there are two options for most operations, as shown in Table 2. The Pentium [10] is an in-order superscalar X86 processor that has two execution pipelines. A detailed set of pairing rules is used to specify the operation combinations that may execute in parallel. Each operation has one or two reservation table options, as shown in Table 3. The K5 [11] is a four-issue, out-of-order, superscalar X86 processor that the MDES models as an in-order processor that can buffer operations between decode and execution. This processor converts X86 operations into one or more *Rops* (internal RISC operations), which may be dispatched in different cycles if the required resources are not available. Accurate modeling allows the scheduler to take advantage of this dynamic behavior, potentially increasing decoder and execution

[2] The relative performance level for each platform and benchmark varied, but each benchmark's performance was either close to, or better than, the published peak SPEC CINT92 numbers for that platform.

Number of Options	% of Scheduling Attempts	Operations Modeled
1	18.81%	Branch ops
2	81.19%	Ops that can use either decoder

Table 2: Option breakdown and scheduling characteristics of the PA7100 MDES.

Number of Options	% of Scheduling Attempts	Operations Modeled
1	45.42%	Ops that can execute in only 1 pipe
2	54.58%	Ops that can execute in either pipe

Table 3: Option breakdown and scheduling characteristics of the Pentium MDES.

Number of Options	% of Scheduling Attempts	Operations Modeled
16	14.72%	1 Rop ops with 1 unit choice
24	0.14%	2 Rop ops dispatched in 1 cycle (1 unit choice)
32	74.72%	1 Rop ops with 2 unit choices
48	5.91%	2 Rop bundled cmp+br dispatched in 1 cycle
64	2.56%	3 Rop bundled cmp+br dispatched in 1 cycle
96	0.19%	2 Rop ops dispatched in 1 cycle (2 unit choices)
128	0.66%	2 Rop bundled cmp+br dispatched over 2 cycles
192	0.15%	3 Rop ops dispatched over 2 cycles (subset of)
256	0.37%	2 Rop ops dispatched over 2 cycles (2 unit choices)
384	0.43%	3 Rop bundled cmp+br dispatched over 2 cycles
768	0.15%	3 Rop ops dispatched over 2 cycles (subset of)

Table 4: Option breakdown and scheduling characteristics of the K5 MDES.

utilization. The K5's design allows up to four X86 operations to be decoded each cycle and up to four Rops to be dispatched each cycle. It also has up to two execution units available for each type of Rop. As shown in Table 4, 89.44% of scheduling attempts are for one-Rop X86 operations that have 16 or 32 reservation table options. However, up to 768 reservation table options are required to accurately model a multi-Rop X86 operation, which can be dispatched over multiple cycles. Failure to model these operations correctly can impact performance in critical loops.

To clarify the notation in the tables, it should be noted that for both of the X86 processors, the compiler *bundles* each branch together with an appropriate condition-code-setting operation, in order to maximize scheduling freedom. The reservation tables for these bundled operations model the resources required by all the operations in the bundle. After scheduling, these bundled operations are converted back into individual operations.

Although it is not necessary for the high-level MDES language to support AND/OR-trees, AND/OR-trees provide a concise way of specifying complex resource usages. The machine descriptions used in this paper's experiments are written in a high-level MDES language that supports the specification of both OR-trees and AND/OR-trees. Every MDES, except the Pentium MDES, uses AND/OR trees extensively. (The Pentium's execution constraints do not have the flexibility that benefits from the use of AND/OR-trees.) In order to generate the OR-tree MDES representations for this paper's experiments,

MDES	Total Ops Sched.	Avg. Sched. Attempts Per Op	OR-Trees Avg. Options/ Attempt	OR-Trees Avg. Checks/ Attempt	AND/OR-Trees Avg. Options/ Attempt	AND/OR-Trees Avg. Checks/ Attempt	AND/OR-Trees Percent Checks Reduced
PA7100	201011	1.94	1.56	2.47	1.45	1.96	20.6%
Pentium	207341	1.47	1.49	3.99	1.49	3.99	0.0%
S-SPARC	282219	2.05	21.48	31.09	4.38	4.83	84.5%
K5	203094	1.62	19.59	35.49	5.20	5.73	83.9%

Table 5: Original scheduling characteristics of the machine descriptions for each target machine.

MDES	Number of Trees	OR-Trees Table Options	OR-Trees Size (bytes)	AND/OR-Trees Table Options	AND/OR-Trees Size (bytes)	AND/OR-Trees %Size Reduced
PA7100	15	40	2504	16	1384	44.7%
Pentium	37	34	14824	34	15416	-4.0%
SuperSPARC	24	333	17120	40	2624	84.7%
K5	33	4424	312640	64	4376	98.6%

Table 6: Original MDES memory requirements.

each MDES that uses AND/OR-trees was run through an MDES preprocessor that expanded out each AND/OR-tree specification into the corresponding OR-tree specification.

The scheduling characteristics for these machine descriptions, before any transformations are performed, are shown in Table 5. The second and third columns indicate how many operations were scheduled, and how many scheduling attempts were required, on average, before an operation was successfully scheduled. These two numbers will remain constant throughout all of the transformations (with either representation), and the exact same schedule is produced in each case, since all the execution constraints described in the machine descriptions are being preserved. It should be noted that the number of scheduling attempts required per operation can increase significantly with the use of more advanced scheduling techniques such as iterative modulo scheduling [12] and operation scheduling, and with the application of more ILP optimizations to the assembly code. However, the selected experimental setup closely models current compiler practices, and the benefit of this paper's AND/OR-tree representation and MDES transformations should only increase as more scheduling attempts are required, since they speed up detection of resource-constraint conflicts.

The fourth and sixth columns of Table 5 show the average number of reservation table options checked for each scheduling attempt, for the OR-tree and AND/OR-tree representations, respectively. The fifth and seventh columns show the average number of resource checks that were required for each scheduling attempts. The last column shows that for complex machine descriptions, before any transformations are performed, the use of the AND/OR-tree representation can reduce the number of resource checks per reservation table option by up to 84.5%.

The memory required to internally represent the resource constraints in the compiler used for this paper's evaluation is shown in Table 6. Although this internal representation has been extensively tuned to maximize the performance of the resource constraint checking algorithm, it also was designed to minimize memory requirements in ways that incur no performance penalty. To this end, the internal representation allows common information to be shared among AND/OR-trees and OR-trees, but in some cases a small amount of header informa-

MDES	Num. of Trees	OR-Tree Rep. Table Options	Size (bytes)	% Size Reduced	AND/OR-Tree Rep. Table Options	Size (bytes)	% Size Reduced
PA7100	13	24	1712	31.6%	14	1232	11.0%
Pentium	30	28	10816	27.0%	28	11296	26.7%
S-SPARC	19	277	14752	13.8%	30	1896	27.7%
K5	27	3704	266032	14.9%	55	3592	17.9%

Table 7: MDES memory requirements after eliminating redundant and unused information.

tion per item is duplicated to prevent performance degradation. Both the OR-tree and the AND/OR-tree internal representations have the same number of trees. However, the table shows that the AND/OR-tree representation, because it does not require the explicit enumeration of all the resource usage combinations (OR-tree options), can significantly reduce the memory required (a 98.6% reduction for the K5). Thus, before any MDES optimizations, the AND/OR-tree significantly reduces both the internal representation size and the number of checks required per attempt for complex resource constraint descriptions (i.e. the SuperSPARC and K5). This advantage will remain definitive after both representations are fully optimized.

The sizes shown in this paper for the AND/OR-tree representation reflect the extra memory required to store the AND level of the tree. In the Pentium MDES, the AND level always points to one OR-tree, so the AND/OR-tree representation will always be slightly larger. It should also be noted that the common information to be shared is entirely specified by the external MDES representation, in order to minimize the time required to load the MDES into memory. The number of trees and reservation table options shown in the table reflects only what the writer of the MDES specified as being shared. It is easy and natural to specify shared information in the high-level MDES language used, so most of the common information is shared in these machine descriptions. However, common information is often not shared in order to make the machine description more readable or easier to modify. In fact, some of the information in the MDES may not even be used. The transformations presented in the Section 5 will deal with these issues.

5. Eliminating Redundant or Unused MDES Information

Machine descriptions tend to evolve as a processor's execution constraints become more thoroughly understood, as the compiler's vocabulary of operations increases, and as these machine descriptions are ported to different or experimental processors in the family. As the machine descriptions evolve, the amount of redundant and unused information in the MDES tends to grow because, for an MDES writer, it is typically easier to just make a local copy of the information to be changed than to do the careful analysis required to safely modify or delete existing information. In fact, this was experienced both at Cydrome Inc., with creation and maintenance the Cydra 5 MDES, and by the authors of this paper's machine descriptions.

This redundant and unused information can be eliminated from the MDES by adapting the classical compiler optimizations (common sub-expression elimination, copy propagation, and dead-code removal [13]) to the MDES domain. In this paper's implementation, common sub-expression elimination and copy propagation were combined into one step that finds redundant MDES information and points all various references to that information to only one particular copy, and an adaptation of dead-code removal eliminates unreferenced information. These techniques greatly reduced the size required to represent all of the aspects of the MDES, such as resource constraints, operation latency, and operation format. Their effect on the resource-constraint description size in particular is shown in Table 7.

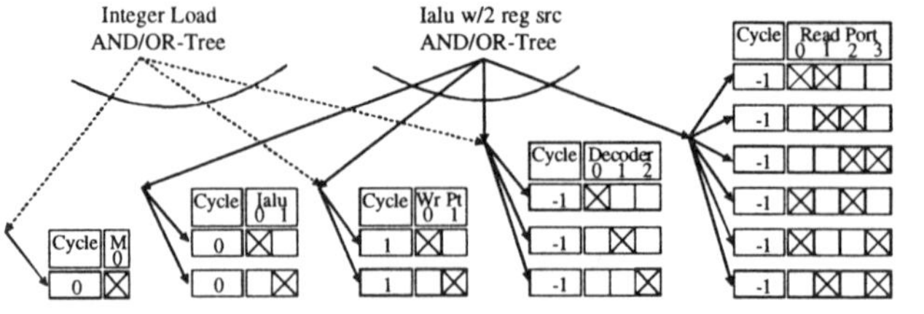

Figure 4: An example of how the AND/OR-tree representation can facilitate the sharing of OR-trees.

MDES	Total Ops Sched.	Avg. Sched. Attempts Per Op.	OR-Tree Avg. Options/ Attempt	Avg. Checks/ Attempt	AND/OR-Tree Average Options/ Attempt	Avg. Checks/ Attempt	Percent Checks Reduced
PA7100	201011	1.94	1.42	2.32	1.38	1.89	18.5%

Table 8: PA7100 scheduling characteristics after removing unnecessary options for memory operations.

It is interesting to note that the AND/OR-tree representation for the SuperSPARC and K5 machine descriptions benefited more from eliminating redundant information than the OR-tree representation. This is because the reservation table options in the AND/OR-tree representation typically specify the resource usages at a finer granularity (less usages per option) than the OR-tree options, allowing them to be shared more aggressively. In addition, the OR-trees in an AND/OR-tree tend to be more general-purpose, allowing entire OR-trees to be shared by several AND/OR-trees. An example of this second case is shown in Figure 4, where the OR-trees for decoder and register write port resource usages are shared by the SuperSPARC's integer load AND/OR-tree and the SuperSPARC's integer ALU (with two register sources) AND/OR-tree. In this way the AND/OR-tree representation facilitates further reduction of the MDES size.

The transformations for removing redundant information can also be adapted to more MDES specific circumstances, such as removing options from an OR-tree that can be determined to be impossible to satisfy. An option can be removed from an OR-tree if its resource usages are identical to, or a superset of, the resource usages for a higher-priority option, since the higher-priority option will always be selected if these resources are available. This case can arise when the use of preprocessor directives enumerates the various OR-tree options, and it can also arise as a machine description evolves, which is the case for the PA7100 MDES used in this paper. The PA7100 MDES was derived from the MDES for an earlier HP PA processor. During the retargeting, two of the reservation table options for the PA7100's memory operations became identical, but the MDES author never realized this since correct output was still generated. The effect this has on the PA7100's scheduling characteristics is shown in Table 8.

MDES	Memory Requirements (in bytes)					
	OR-Tree Rep.			AND/OR-Tree Rep.		
	Before	After	Diff.	Before	After	Diff.
PA7100	1712	1408	17.8%	1232	1128	8.4%
Pentium	10816	3224	70.2%	11296	3704	67.2%
SuperSPARC	14752	11152	24.4%	1896	1640	13.5%
K5	266032	183280	31.1%	3592	3136	12.7%

Table 9: MDES size characteristics before and after a bit-vector representation is used (one cycle/word).

MDES	Average Checks Per Scheduling Attempt					
	OR-Tree Rep.			AND/OR-Tree Rep.		
	Before	After	Diff.	Before	After	Diff.
PA7100	2.32	2.18	6.0%	1.89	1.76	6.9%
Pentium	3.99	2.31	42.1%	3.99	2.31	42.1%
SuperSPARC	31.09	26.69	14.2%	4.83	4.62	4.3%
K5	35.49	34.35	3.2%	5.73	5.30	7.5%

Table 10: Scheduling characteristics before and after a bit-vector representation is used (one cycle/word).

6. Utilizing Bit-Vector Representations

The results presented so far have not taken advantage of the fact that most resource-constraint checking algorithms, including the one used in this paper, use bit-vectors [14][15][16] to keep track of the resources used each cycle in what is referred to as a *resource usage map* (RU map). This design allows the RU map size to be minimized and efficiently initialized, and allows multiple resource usages to be checked (and reserved) with a single AND (OR) operation. In addition, using bits in the MDES to represent multiple resource usages can significantly decrease the MDES size. Although it is possible to pack more than one cycle's resource usages into a single memory word, it is not necessary to do so for the machine descriptions in this paper. The resource usage time transformation presented in the next section will reduce the number of checks to almost the minimum of one resource check per reservation table option.

The incremental effect of packing each cycle's resource usages into one memory word is shown in Tables 9 and 10. Before using bit-vectors, each resource usage was represented as a cycle/resource pair (one resource usage per check). After using bit-vectors, the resource usages were represented as a cycle/resource-vector pair (multiple resource usages per check possible, if the usages are in the same cycle). Although both representations require two words to represent each pair, the bit-vector representation typically requires less pairs per table. The Pentium MDES shows the most benefit, since modeling the Pentium's resource constraints required checking several resource usages in every cycle. The other machine descriptions didn't benefit as much, since their resource usage did not always fall within the same cycle. For example, the reservation table options shown in Figure 3a do not benefit from packing a cycle's resource usage into a single memory word, since there is only one usage per cycle. However, the resource usage time transformation presented in the next section will resolve this issue.

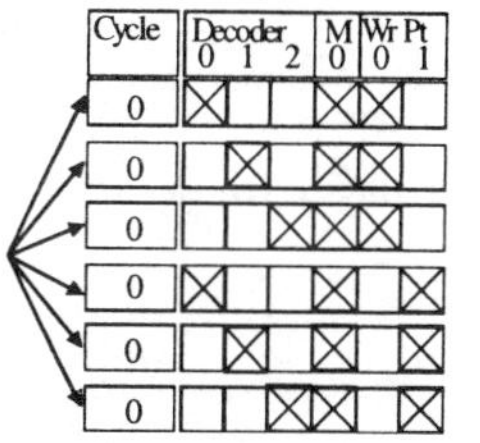

Figure 5: The OR-tree modeling the resource constraints for a SuperSPARC integer load operation, after transforming the resource usage times in order to better utilize the bit-vector representation.

7. Optimizing for Bit-Vector Representations

The use of the actual resource usage times, as in Figure 3a, can significantly reduce the effectiveness of using a bit-vector representation that packs one cycle's worth of resource usages into a single memory word. We address this problem by making use of the theory of pipelined, multi-function unit design [7][17]. For any ordered pair of reservation table options (A, B), t is a *forbidden latency* (i.e., an operation using reservation table option B cannot be initiated t cycles after an operation that uses reservation table option A) if and only if A and B have resource usages for some common resource at times i and j, respectively, such that i is greater than or equal to j and i-j = t. The set of all forbidden latencies between A and B is termed the *collision vector* for the ordered pair (A, B). A given schedule results in no resource conflicts if and only if, for every pair of operations, the difference in their scheduled times never violates the collision vector for the corresponding pair of reservation tables. Note that the actual reservation table options A and B are not directly important; only the collision vector for (A, B) is. Consequently, we could substitute any reservation table options A' and B' for A and B, respectively, as long as the collision vector for (A', B') is the same as that for (A, B). Further note that, in computing a forbidden latency, only the difference between the resource usage times i and j matters, not their actual values. In particular, we could add a common constant to both resource usage times without altering the forbidden latency.

With this in mind, the optimization that we use, for each resource, is to subtract a strategically selected constant from the originally specified resource usage times for that resource in every reservation table option, with a view to concentrating resource usages into as few time slots as possible. The constant may be different for each resource. This optimization is related to the one used by Eichenberger and Davidson [18]. Although minimization techniques can be used to find those constants that maximize the benefit, a simple heuristic was found to be highly effective for the forward-scheduling list scheduler and the processors considered in this paper. The heuristic is, for each resource, to pick the constant to be the earliest resource usage time for that resource (across all reservation table options). The result of this heuristic is to concentrate a far larger number of resource usages than before at time zero, thereby making the bit-vector approach more effective. For a backward-scheduling list scheduler, the constants should be chosen to make the latest usage time to be zero (or some constant). Applying this transformation to Figure 3a yields the OR-tree shown in Figure 5.

MDES	Memory Requirements (in bytes)					
	OR-Tree Rep.			AND/OR Tree Rep.		
	Before	After	Diff.	Before	After	Diff.
PA7100	1408	1168	17.0%	1128	1032	8.5%
Pentium	3224	3080	4.5%	3704	3560	3.9%
SuperSPARC	11152	7016	37.1%	1640	1584	3.4%
K5	183280	125488	31.5%	3136	3096	1.3%

Table 11: MDES memory requirements before and after transforming resource usage times (one cycle per word).

MDES	OR-Tree Rep.				AND/OR-Tree Rep.			
	Avg. Checks/Attempt			Checks/	Avg. Checks/Attempt			Checks/
	Before	After	Diff	Option	Before	After	Diff.	Option
PA7100	2.18	1.59	37.1%	1.12	1.76	1.55	11.9%	1.12
Pentium	2.31	1.57	32.0%	1.05	2.31	1.57	32.0%	1.05
S-SPARC	26.69	21.59	19.1%	1.01	4.62	4.49	2.8%	1.03
K5	34.35	19.87	42.2%	1.01	5.30	5.25	0.9%	1.01

Table 12: Scheduling characteristics before and after transforming resource usage times and sorting the resulting usages to check time zero first (one cycle per word).

In addition to making the bit-vector representation more effective, this transformation also has a subtle effect on the characteristics of the resource usage checks that can be taken advantage of. The resource usages that cause most of the resource conflicts now tend to be concentrated at time zero. The resource usages with times greater than zero are usually conflict free and are primarily there to delay the execution of later operations. For example, the non-zero-time divide-unit usages for a divide operation rarely prevent the operation from being scheduled (if the divide unit is available at time zero). However, while scheduling the next divide operation, the divide unit will not be available at time zero until the previous divide completes. Thus for a forward-scheduling list scheduler, the average number of checks before a conflict is detected is minimized by sorting the resulting usage checks so that time zero is checked first. In this manner, the same machine descriptions can be automatically tuned for other types of schedulers by adjusting the heuristic for picking the resource usage time shift constants and for the sorting of the resulting usage checks.

The MDES memory requirements after transforming the resource usage times are shown in Table 11. The size of the OR-tree representation is reduced up to 37.1% by using this transformation. There is less reduction for the AND/OR-tree representation since this representation tends to have fewer resource usages per option. The transformations presented in the next section do not change the MDES size, so these sizes are the final MDES sizes after full optimization.

The MDES scheduling characteristics after transforming the resource usage times and sorting the resulting usages to check time zero first are shown in Table 12. This transformation reduced the average number of resource checks per option to between 1.01 and 1.12, which is close to the ideal case of one check per option. As a result, the average number of options checked per attempt is what is truly dictating the number of checks required. Although the AND/OR-tree already has a clear advantage in this regard for the SuperSPARC and K5, the number of options checked is further reduced by the transformations in Section 8.

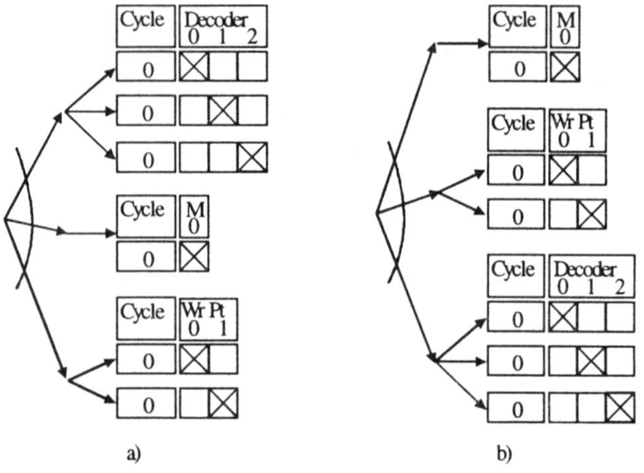

Figure 6: An example of optimizing the order of the OR-trees in an AND/OR-trees for resource conflict detection. a) Original order specified. b) After optimizing the order.

8. Optimizing AND/OR-Trees for Resource Conflict Detection

The structure of the AND/OR-tree representation allows additional transformations to be performed that can increase the chance of detecting resource conflicts early. The first transformation is to sort the sub OR-trees in the AND/OR-tree so that the OR-tree most likely to have a resource conflict (heuristically determined) is checked first. The following heuristic-based sort criteria were found to produce the most consistent results. The OR-trees are first sorted by the earliest usage time in each tree, since after the resource usage time transformation, most conflicts occur at usage time zero. For OR-trees with the same earliest usage time, sort by the number of options in each OR-tree, so that OR-tree with the fewest options is checked first. To break ties at this point, preference is given to the OR-trees that are shared by the most number of AND/OR-trees, since this gives an indication of which OR-trees have resources that are heavily used. Finally the original order specified is used to break any remaining ties. Figure 6a shows the OR-tree order originally specified in the MDES (and used for all previous analysis), and Figure 6b shows the order after sorting the OR-trees using the above criteria (only the second criterion applies).

A second transformation that can be applied is to remove resource usages that are common to all of the OR-tree options and place them in an OR-tree with just one option (creating one if necessary). This transformation works well when a resource common to all options is likely to cause a resource conflict. By pulling it out, this resource conflict can be detected earlier. This transformation can also be used to create some simple AND/OR-trees from OR-tree descriptions. Application of this transformation can actually increase the number of resource checks required, but the following application heuristics were found to yield good results. First, if there is already a one-option OR-tree that has a resource usage with the same usage time as the common usage, apply the transformation. (With bit-vectors, this transformation cannot hurt performance.) Also,

MDES	AND/OR-Tree Representation					
	Options Per Attempt			Checks Per Attempt		
	Before	After	Diff.	Before	After	Diff.
PA7100	1.38	1.38	0.0%	1.55	1.55	0.0%
Pentium	1.49	1.49	0.0%	1.57	1.57	0.0%
SuperSPARC	4.38	2.97	32.2%	4.49	3.08	31.4%
K5	5.20	4.32	16.9%	5.25	4.38	16.6%

Table 13: Scheduling characteristics before and after optimizing AND/OR-trees for resource conflict detection.

apply the transformation if the common usage is the only usage in the OR-tree with that usage time (each option in the OR-tree then has one less check, and in exchange only one check is added). Otherwise, the transformation should not be applied. In the machines descriptions used in this paper, all the applications of this transformation occurred due to the first application rule. After the usage time transformation the second case becomes rare or, for these descriptions, nonexistent.

The incremental effect of these transformations on the AND/OR-tree scheduling characteristics is shown in Table 13. Most of the AND/OR-trees in the SuperSPARC and K5 MDES are reordered, which significantly reduces the average number of options checked before a resource conflict is detected. The MDES sizes did not change due to these transformations.

9. Aggregate Effect of All Transformations

There are two important machine description aspects that are optimized by the transformations presented in this paper. The first one is the amount of memory needed by the compiler to represent the processor's resource constraints. Minimizing this size allows more MDES information to fit within the first-level cache during compilation and also reduces the overall memory requirements of the compiler. The aggregate effect on required memory of all the transformations presented in this paper is shown in Table 14. When applied to an OR-tree representation, these transformations reduce representations by as much as a factor of five. When these transformations are further combined with the AND/OR-trees, representations up to a hundred times smaller than the unoptimized OR-tree representation are produced[3]. For processors with flexible execution constraints (i.e. the SuperSPARC and K5), combining these transformations with the AND/OR-tree representation is especially effective.

The second aspect of the machine descriptions to be optimized is the number of resource checks per scheduling attempt. Minimizing this number reduces the time required to check resource constraints, making room in the compiler's time budget for more advanced scheduling or optimization techniques. The aggregate effect of all the transformations presented in this paper on the average number of resource checks required per scheduling attempt is shown in Table 15. As described in Section 4, these check-per-attempt statistics were generated using an MDES-driven multi-platform list scheduler to schedule SPEC CINT92 assembly code for each platform. When compared to the checks-per-attempt of the unoptimized OR-tree representation, these transformations reduced the number of checks required by the OR-tree representation by up to a factor

[3] As described in Section 4, the Pentium MDES does not take advantage of AND/OR-trees. The size increase is due to representation overhead.

MDES	Memory Requirements (in bytes)				
	Unoptimized	Fully Optimized With Bit-Vector Rep.			
	OR-Trees	OR-Trees	Reduction	AND/OR-Trees	Reduction
PA7100	2504	1168	53.4%	1032	58.8%
Pentium	14824	3080	79.2%	3560	76.0%
SuperSPARC	17120	7016	59.0%	1584	90.7%
K5	312640	125488	59.9%	3096	99.0%

Table 14: Aggregate effect of all transformations on MDES resource-constraint representation size.

MDES	Average Checks Per Scheduling Attempt				
	Unoptimized	Fully Optimized With Bit-Vector Rep.			
	OR-Trees	OR-Trees	Reduction	AND/OR-Trees	Reduction
PA7100	2.47	1.59	35.6%	1.55	37.2%
Pentium	3.99	1.57	60.7%	1.57	60.7%
SuperSPARC	31.09	21.59	30.6%	3.08	90.1%
K5	35.49	19.87	44.0%	4.38	87.7%

Table 15: Aggregate effect of all transformations on MDES scheduling characteristics.

of 2.6. When these transformations are combined with the AND/OR-trees, the number of checks were reduced by as much as a factor of ten. As was seen with the MDES-size aspect, combining these transformations with the AND/OR-tree representation is especially effective at reducing the number of checks required for processors with flexible execution constraints (i.e. the SuperSPARC and K5).

The trend that these tables show is that as the processors become more powerful and flexible, the AND/OR-tree representation, combined with the described transformations, becomes crucial for keeping under control both the MDES size and the number of checks per scheduling attempt. We expect the K5 MDES results to be representative of the latest generation of microprocessors, such as the Intel Pentium Pro and the HP PA8000.

10. Related Work

Eichenberger and Davidson [18] recently proposed a minimization algorithm which, for each reservation table option, generates an equivalent reservation table option with a minimum[4] number of resource usages. The total number of resources used to model the processor is also minimized, which facilitates packing multiple cycles of resource usages into a bit-vector. This algorithm, combined with a bit-vector representation, was shown to minimize both the memory required to represent each option and the number of resource checks per option. However, Eichenberger and Davidson do not address the problem of reducing the number of option checks per scheduling attempt.

The transformations presented in this paper reduce the number of resource checks and memory required per option to a level close to that obtained using the Eichenberger and Davidson algorithm, although a different approach is used. In addition, when combined with our proposed AND/OR-tree representation, our transformations simultaneously optimize the number of options checks per scheduling attempt, the number of

[4] This algorithm uses heuristics to avoid exhaustive searches. Although true minimums may not always be found, the results are near optimal.

resource checks per option, and the memory required to represent the processor's resource constraints.

Proebsting and Fraser [19], Müller [20], and Bala and Rubin [21] have proposed approaches that use finite-state automata, instead of resource reservation tables, to determine if an operation may be scheduled without a resource conflict. These techniques, when compared with the use of unoptimized reservation tables and representations, have shown significant reductions in the number of checks per scheduling attempt and in representation size. However, the combination of our transformations and AND/OR-tree representation appear to mitigate these advantages, even for complex resource constraints. In addition, as described in the literature, finite-state automata do not appear to support some advanced scheduling techniques, such as iterative modulo scheduling [12], which strategically unschedule operations in order to remove the resource conflicts that are preventing an operation from being scheduled. This requires the ability to identify and unschedule the operations that are causing the resource conflicts. This type of unscheduling is straightforward with reservation tables (implemented in [12]), but it is unclear how to do this type of unscheduling with finite-state automata.

11. Conclusions

This paper advocates a model which allows compiler writers to develop easy-to-understand, maintainable machine descriptions in a high-level language, which is then translated into a low-level representation for efficient use by the compiler. To reconcile the discrepancy between the requirements of the high-level language and the low-level representation, a collection of transformations was presented that derives efficient low-level representations from descriptions written in a high-level MDES language. In addition, a new resource constraint representation, AND/OR-trees, was introduced that facilitates the efficient description of complex execution constraints. Experiments showed that this AND/OR-tree representation, combined with the proposed transformations, produces small and efficient low-level representations requiring less than 3.5k bytes of compiler memory. This combination was also shown to greatly reduce, by up to a factor of ten, the number of resource checks per scheduling attempt required to model complex execution constraints. These results strongly support the assertion that precise and accurate machine descriptions, designed to be easy-to-maintain and written in a high-level language, can be translated into a low-level representation that can be efficiently used by an ILP compiler.

Acknowledgments

The authors would like to thank Rick Hank for the use of the HP-PA codegenerator and PA7100 machine description, Sabrina Hwu for the use of the Sparc codegenerator and the SuperSPARC machine description, Dan Lavery, Dave Gallagher, and Andrew Hsieh for the use of the X86 codegenerator and machine descriptions, Roger Bringmann for the use of the multiplatform list scheduler, the anonymous reviewers for the detailed reviews, and the IMPACT compiler team in general. The authors would also like to thank Mike Schlansker, Vinod Kathail, and the rest of the CAR group at HP Labs for valuable insight and discussion concerning countless machine description issues.

This research has been supported by the National Science Foundation (NSF) under grant MIP-9308013, Intel Corporation, Advanced Micro Devices, Hewlett-Packard, SUN Microsystems, NCR, and the National Aeronautics and Space Administration (NASA) under Contract NASA NAG 1-613 in cooperation with the Illinois Computer Laboratory for Aerospace Systems and Software (ICLASS).

References

[1] J. C. Dehnert and R. A. Towle, "Compiling for the Cydra 5," *The Journal of Supercomputing*, vol. 7, pp. 181-227, January 1993.

[2] G. P. Lowney et al., "The Multiflow trace scheduling compiler," The Journal of Supercomputing, vol. 7, pp. 51-142, January 1993.

[3] J. C. Gyllenhaal, B. R. Rau, and W. W. Hwu, "Hmdes Version 2.0 Specification," Technical Report IMPACT-96-3, The IMPACT Research Group, University of Illinois, Urbana, IL, 1996, *http://www.crhc.uiuc.edu/Impact/*.

[4] J. C. Gyllenhaal, *A machine description language for compilation*, Master's thesis, Department of Electrical and Computer Engineering, University of Illinois, Urbana, IL, 1994.

[5] P. P. Chang, S. A. Mahlke, W. Y. Chen, N. J. Warter, and W. W. Hwu, "IMPACT: An architectural framework for multiple-instruction-issue processors," Proc. 18th Ann. Int'l Symp. Computer Architecture, (Toronto, Canada), pp. 266-275, Jun 1991.

[6] R. A. Bringmann, *Compiler-Controlled Speculation*, Ph.D. thesis, Dept. of Computer Science, University of Illinois, Urbana, IL, 1995.

[7] E. S. Davidson, L. E. Shar, A. T. Thomas, and J. H. Patel, "Effective control for pipelined computers," Spring COMPCON'75 digests of papers, pp. 181-184, Feb. 1975

[8] G. Blanck and S. Krueger, "The SuperSPARC microprocessor," COMPCON Spring 1992, pp. 136-141.

[9] T. Asprey et al., "Performance features of the PA7100 microprocessor", IEEE Micro, pp. 22-35, June 1993.

[10] Intel, *The Pentium Microprocessor*. Santa Clara, CA, 1993.

[11] Dave Christie, "Developing the AMD-K5 architecture", IEEE Micro, pp. 16-26, April 1996.

[12] B. R. Rau, "Iterative Modulo Scheduling: An algorithm for software pipelining loops," Proceedings of the 27th Annual International Symposium on Microarchitecture, pp. 63-74, Nov. 1994.

[13] A. Aho, R. Sethi, and J. Ullman, *Compilers: Principles, Techniques, and Tools*. Reading, MA: Addison-Wesley, 1986.

[14] R. L. Kleir, "A representation for the analysis of microprogram operation," Proceedings of the 7th Annual Workshop on Microprogramming, Sept. 1974.

[15] D. J. DeWitt, "A control-word model for detecting conflicts between microprograms," Proceedings of the 8th Annual Workshop on Microprogramming, Sept. 1975.

[16] J. A. Fisher, *The Optimization of Horizontal MicroCode Within and Beyond Basic Blocks; An Application of Processor Scheduling with Resources*. Ph.D. thesis, New York University, 1979.

[17] P. M. Kogge, *The Architecture of Pipelined Computers*. McGraw-Hill, New York, 1991.

[18] A. E. Eichenberger and E. S. Davidson, "A reduced multipipeline machine description that preserves scheduling constraints," Proceedings of the Conference on Programming Language Design and Implementation, pp. 12-20, May 1996.

[19] T. A. Proebsting and C. W. Fraser, "Detecting pipeline structural hazards quickly," The 21st Annual ACM SIGPLAN-SIGACT Symposium on Principles of Programming Languages, pp. 280-286, Jan. 1994.

[20] T. Müller, "Employing finite automata for resource scheduling," Proceedings of the 26th Annual International Symposium on Microarchitecture, pp. 12-20, Dec. 1993.

[21] V. Bala and N. Rubin, "Efficient instruction scheduling using finite state automata," Proceedings of the 28th Annual International Symposium on Microarchitecture, pp. 46-56, Nov. 1995.

Author Index

Notes

Notes

Notes

Notes

IEEE COMPUTER SOCIETY
50 YEARS OF SERVICE • 1946-1996

http://www.computer.org

Press Activities Board

Vice President:
Joseph Boykin
CLARiiON Advanced Storage Solutions
Coslin Drive
Southborough, MA 01772
(508) 480-7286
FAX (508) 480-7908
j.boykin@computer.org

Jon T. Butler, Naval Postgraduate School
James J. Farrell III, Motorola
Mohamed E. Fayad, University of Nevada
I. Mark Haas, Tandem Computers, Inc.
Ronald G. Hoelzeman, University of Pittsburgh
Gene F. Hoffnagle, IBM Corporation
John R. Nicol, GTE Laboratories
Yale N. Patt, University of Michigan
Benjamin W. Wah, University of Illinois
Ronald D. Williams, University of Virginia

Editor-in-Chief
Advances in Computer Science and Engineering Board
Jon T. Butler
Naval Postgraduate School
Dept. of Electrical and Computer Engineering
833 Dyer Road #437, Code EC/BU
Monterey, CA 93943-5121
Phone: 408-656-3299 FAX: 408-656-2760
butler@cs.nps.navy.mil

Editor-in-Chief
Practices for Computer Science and Engineering Board
Mohamed E. Fayad
Computer Science, MS/171
Bldg. LME, Room 308
University of Nevada
Reno, NV 89557
Phone: 702-784-4356 FAX: 702-784-1833
fayad@cs.unr.edu

IEEE Computer Society Executive Staff
T. Michael Elliott, Executive Director
Matthew S. Loeb, Publisher

IEEE Computer Society Press Publications

The world-renowned Computer Society Press publishes, promotes, and distributes a wide variety of authoritative computer science and engineering texts. These books are available in two formats: 100 percent original material by authors preeminent in their field who focus on relevant topics and cutting-edge research, and reprint collections consisting of carefully selected groups of previously published papers with accompanying original introductory and explanatory text.

Submission of proposals: For guidelines and information on CS Press books, send e-mail to cs.books@computer.org or write to the Acquisitions Editor, IEEE Computer Society Press, P.O. Box 3014, 10662 Los Vaqueros Circle, Los Alamitos, CA 90720-1314. Telephone +1 714-821-8380. FAX +1 714-761-1784.

IEEE Computer Society Press Proceedings

The Computer Society Press also produces and actively promotes the proceedings of more than 130 acclaimed international conferences each year in multimedia formats that include hard and softcover books, CD-ROMs, videos, and on-line publications.

For information on CS Press proceedings, send e-mail to cs.books@computer.org or write to Proceedings, IEEE Computer Society Press, P.O. Box 3014, 10662 Los Vaqueros Circle, Los Alamitos, CA 90720-1314. Telephone +1 714-821-8380. FAX +1 714-761-1784.

Additional information regarding the Computer Society, conferences and proceedings, CD-ROMs, videos, and books can also be accessed from our web site at www.computer.org.

9/20/96